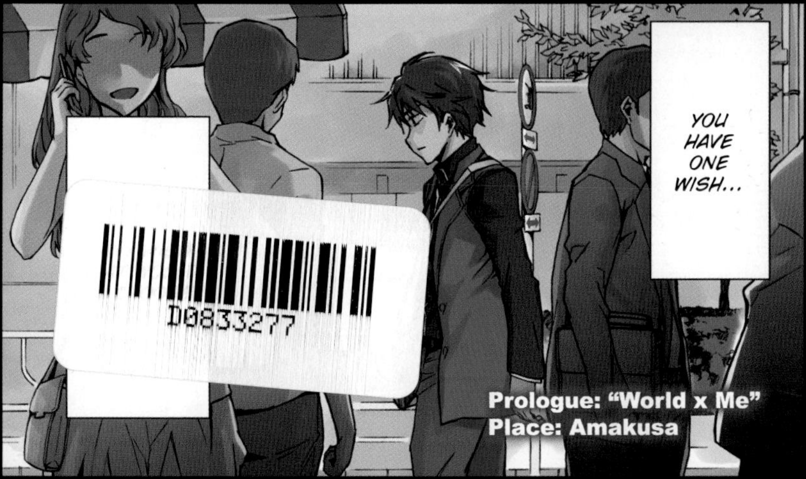
YOU HAVE ONE WISH...
Prologue: "World x Me"
Place: Amakusa


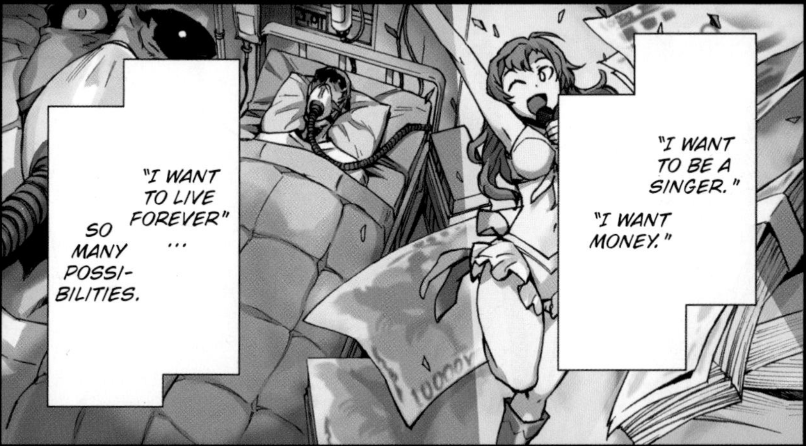
"I WANT TO BE A SINGER."
"I WANT MONEY."
"I WANT TO LIVE FOREVER"...
SO MANY POSSI-BILITIES.

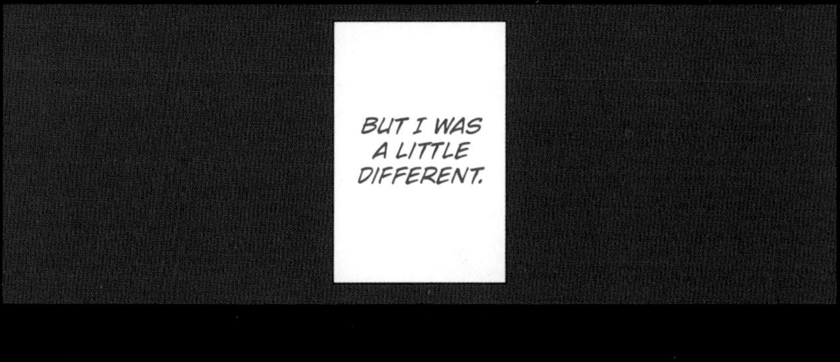
BUT I WAS A LITTLE DIFFERENT.

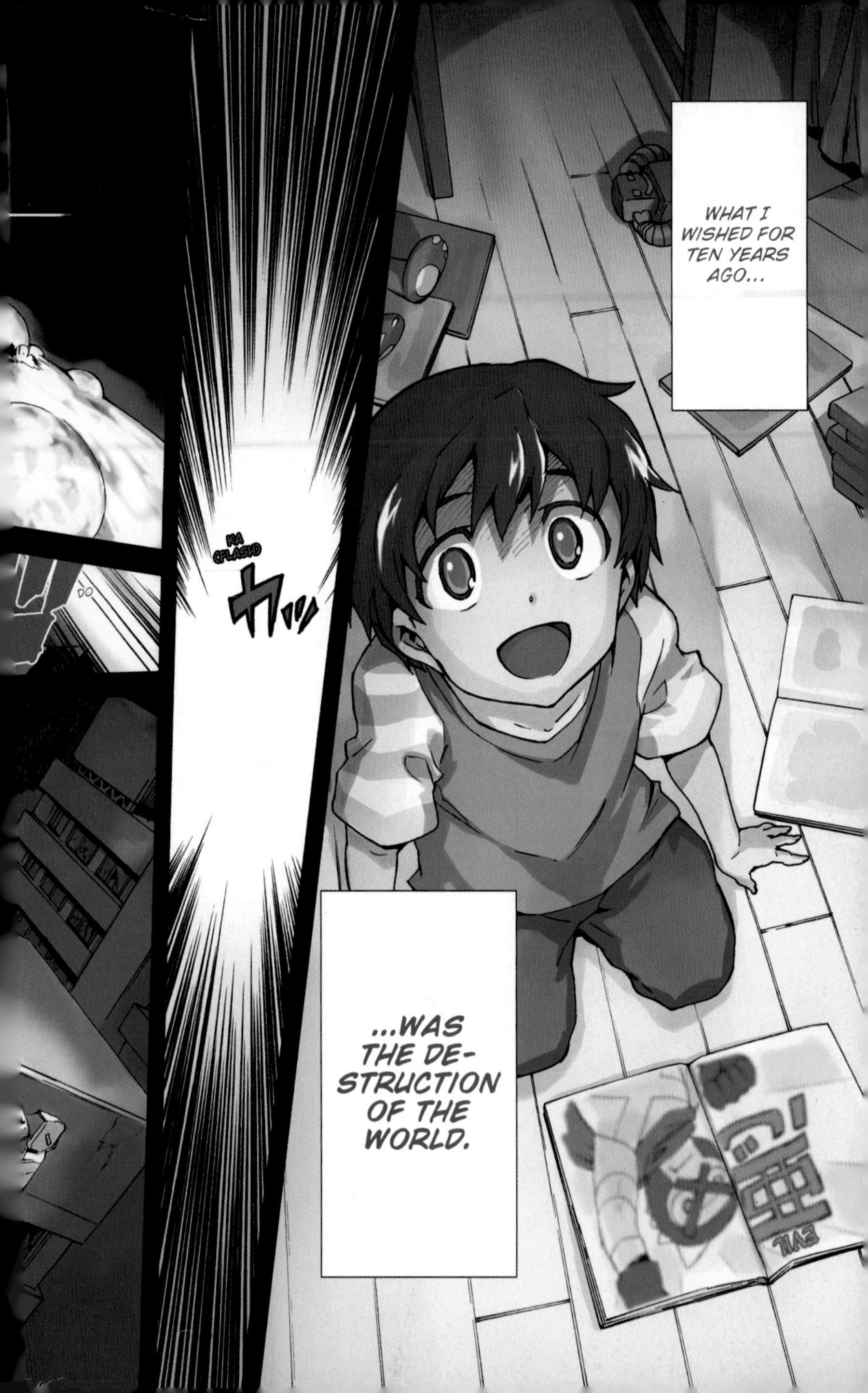
WHAT I WISHED FOR TEN YEARS AGO...
KA (FLASH)
カッ
DO
...WAS THE DE-STRUCTION OF THE WORLD.
EVIL

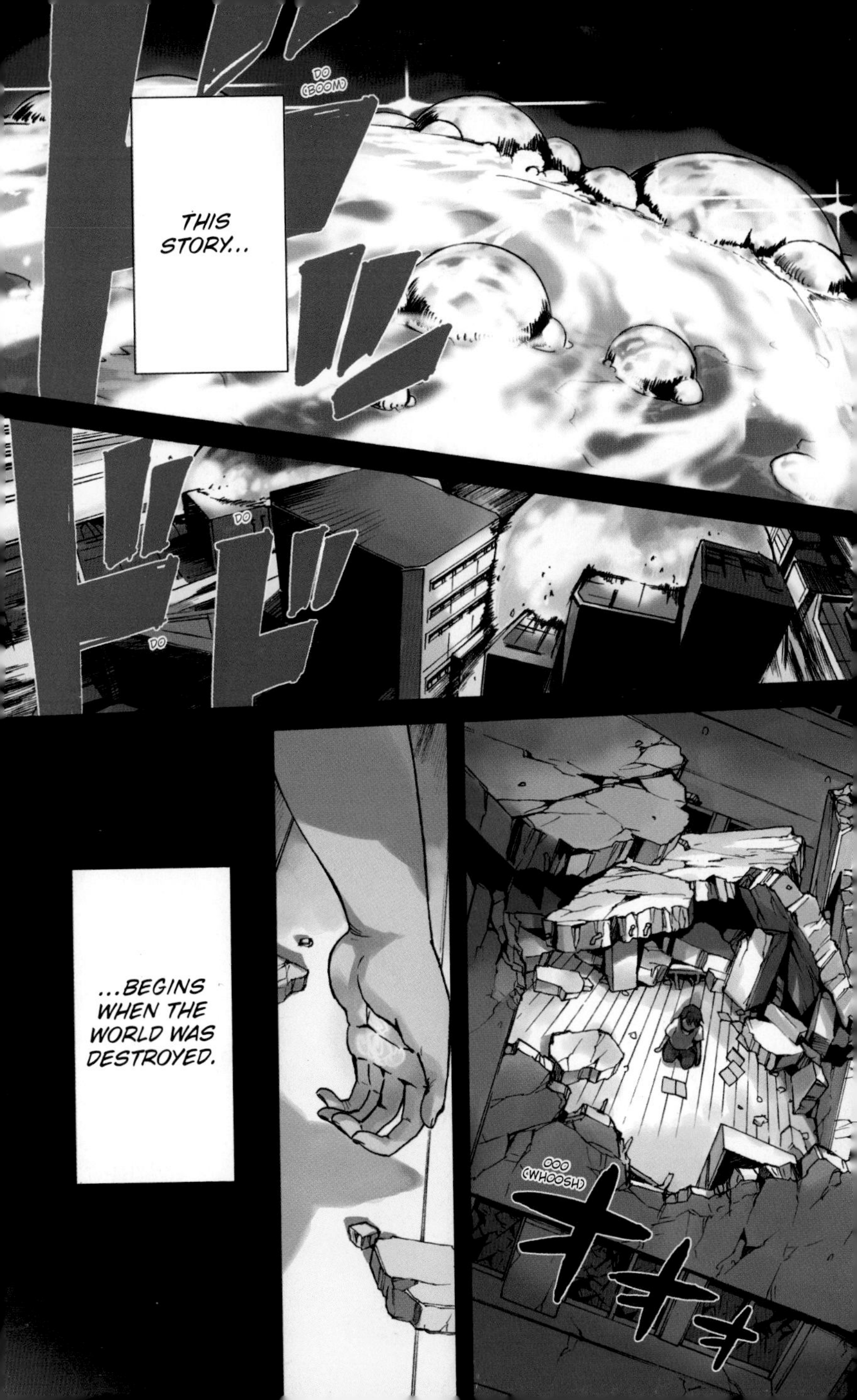
DO (BOOM)
THIS STORY...
DO
DO
OOO (WHOOSH)
...BEGINS WHEN THE WORLD WAS DESTROYED.

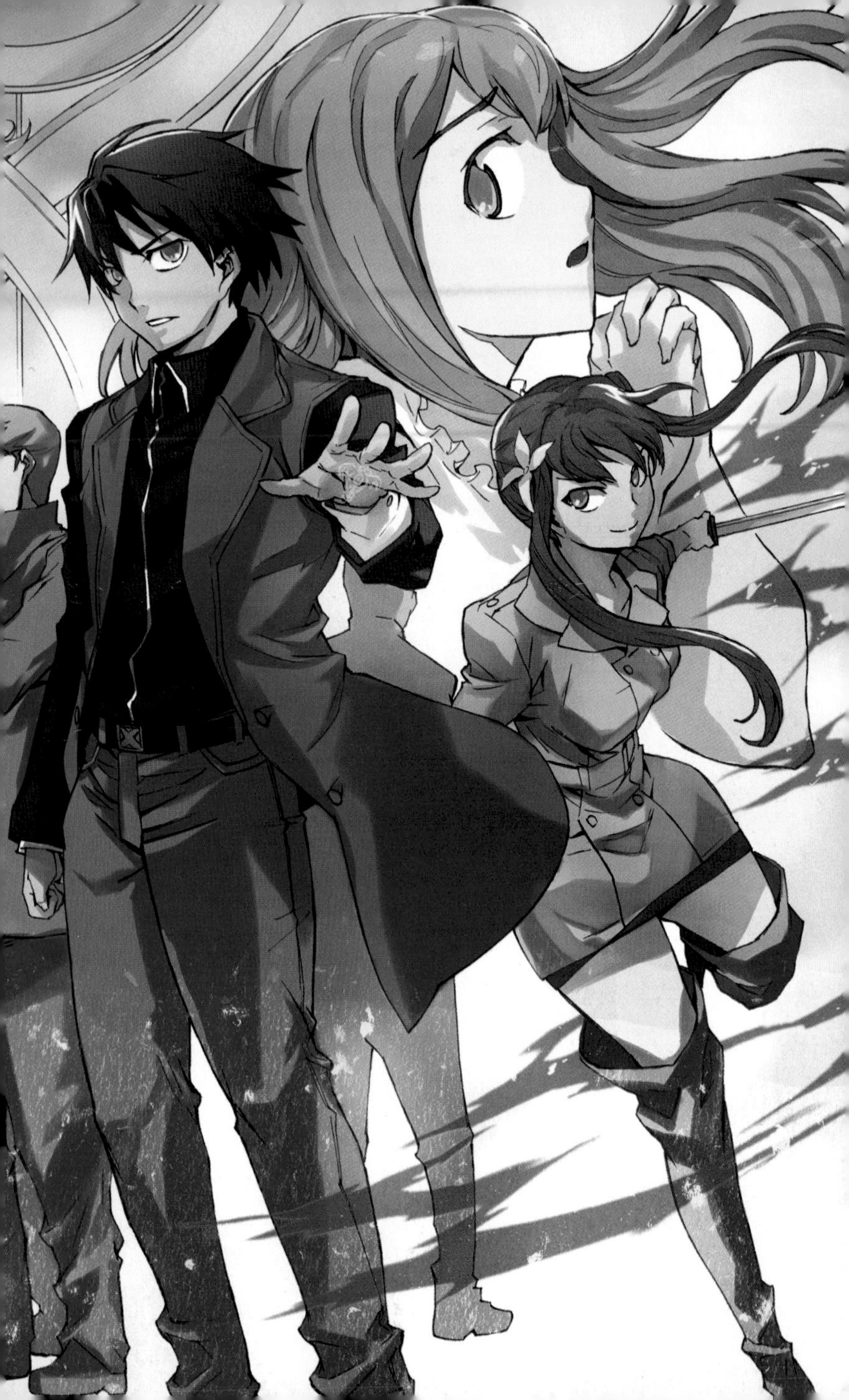

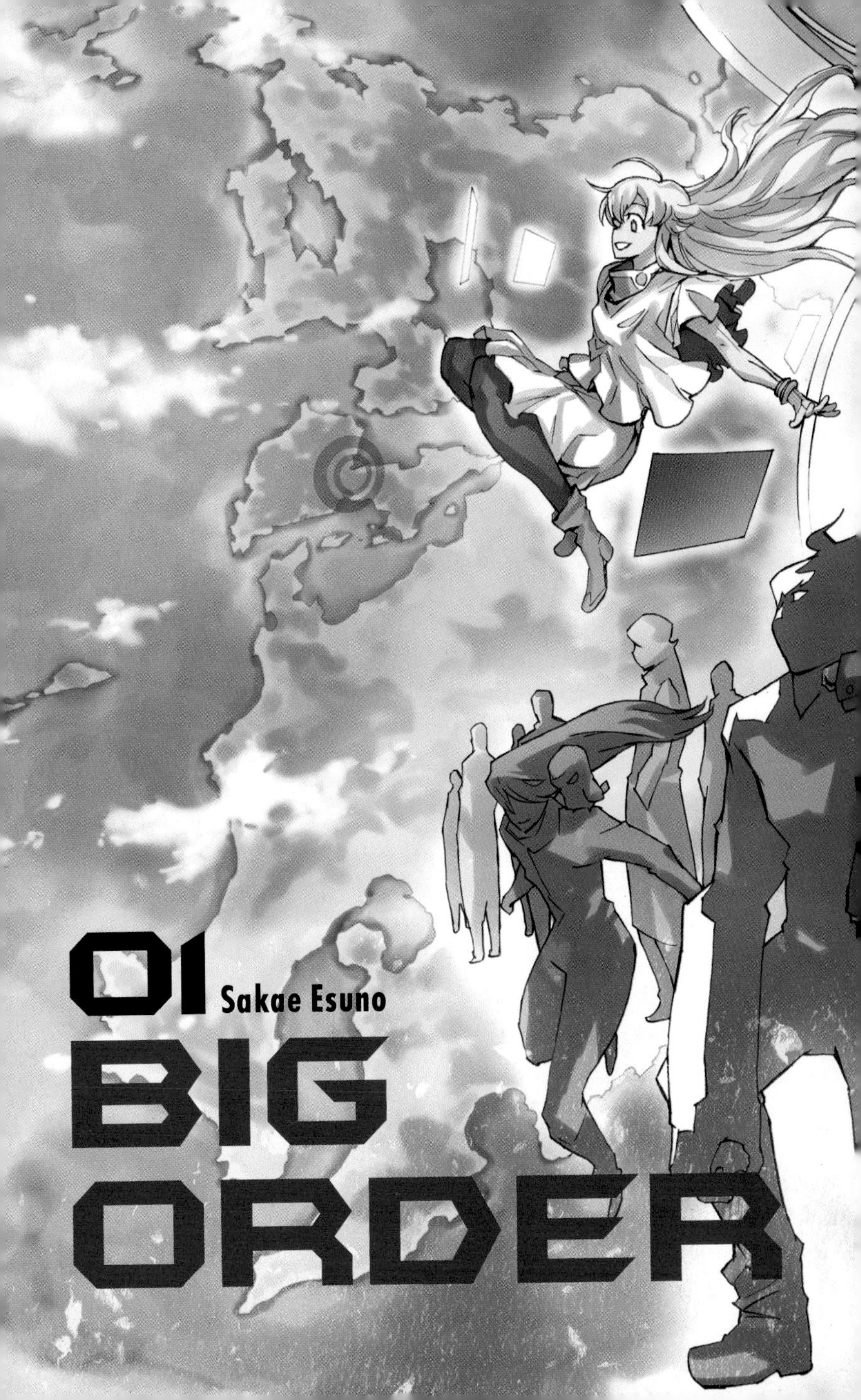
01
Sakae Esuno
BIG
ORDER

# BIG ORDER
TABLE OF CONTENTS



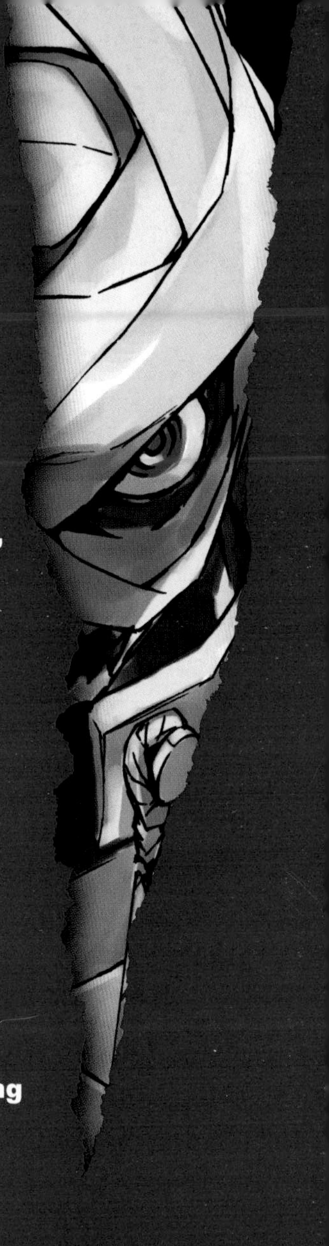

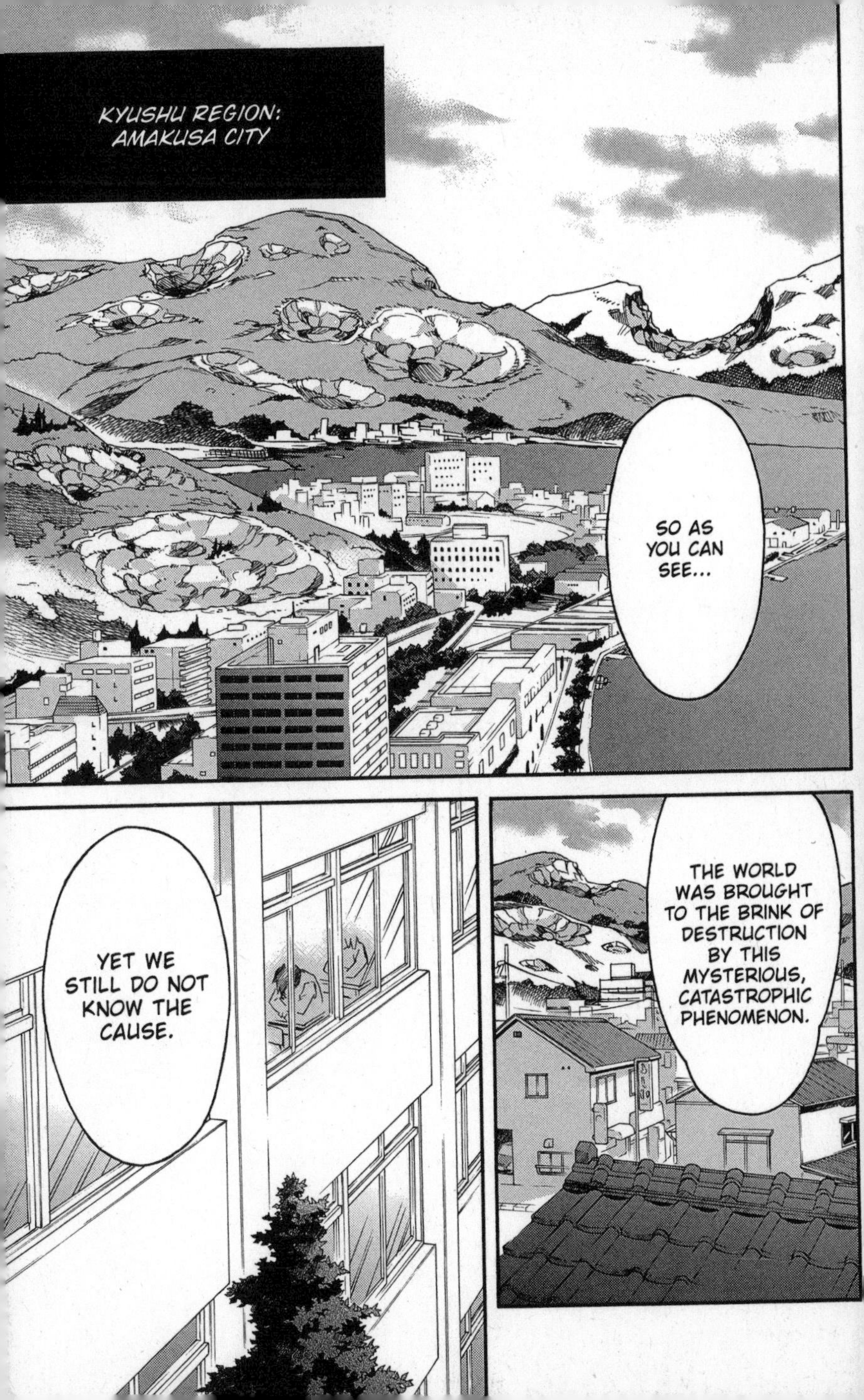
KYUSHU REGION: AMAKUSA CITY
SO AS YOU CAN SEE...
THE WORLD WAS BROUGHT TO THE BRINK OF DESTRUCTION BY THIS MYSTERIOUS, CATASTROPHIC PHENOMENON.
YET WE STILL DO NOT KNOW THE CAUSE.

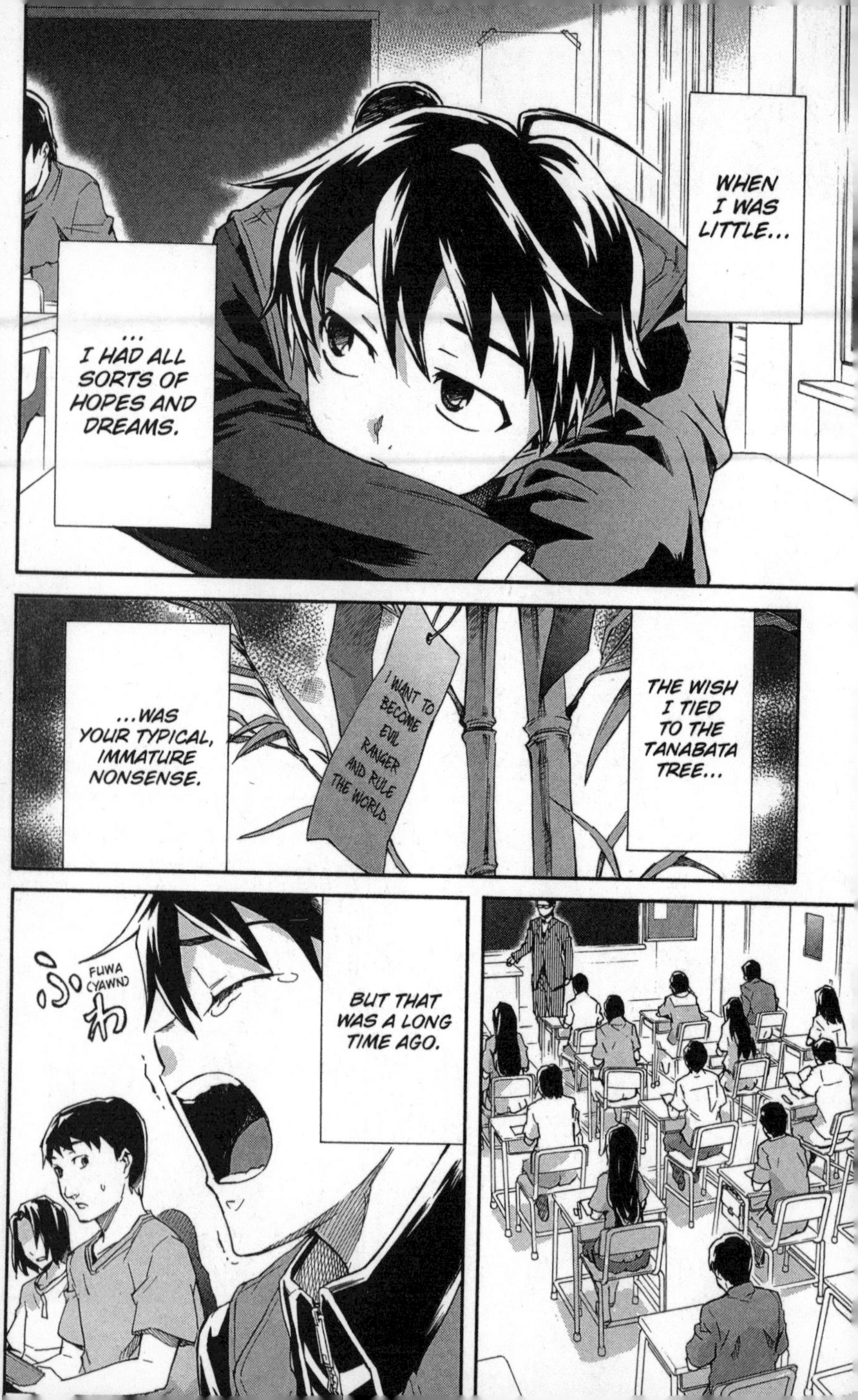
WHEN I WAS LITTLE...
...I HAD ALL SORTS OF HOPES AND DREAMS.
THE WISH I TIED TO THE TANABATA TREE...
I WANT TO BECOME EVIL RANGER AND RULE THE WORLD.
...WAS YOUR TYPICAL, IMMATURE NONSENSE.
BUT THAT WAS A LONG TIME AGO.
ふわ
FUWA (YAWN)

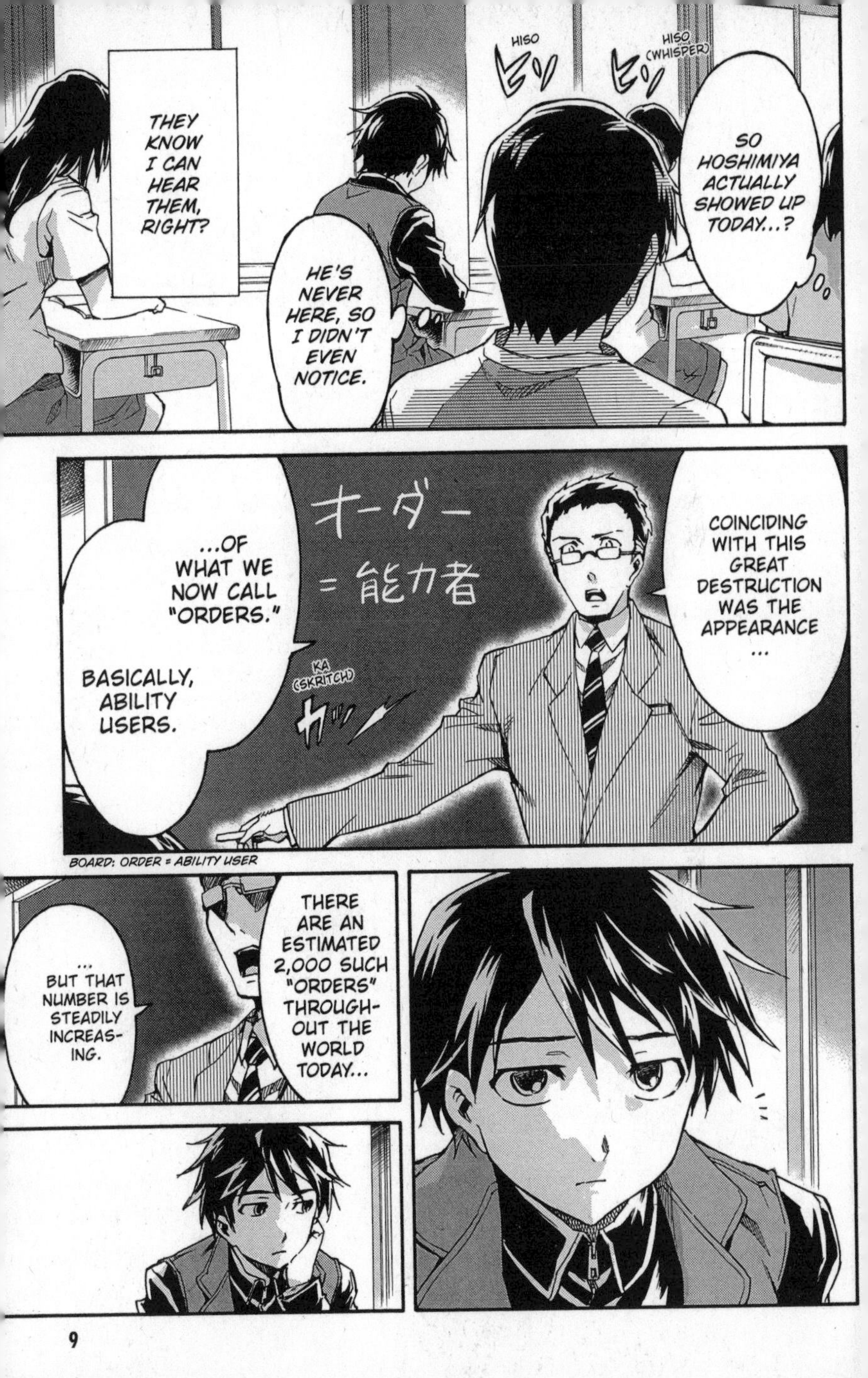
HISO
HISO (WHISPER)
SO HOSHIMIYA ACTUALLY SHOWED UP TODAY...?
HE'S NEVER HERE, SO I DIDN'T EVEN NOTICE.
THEY KNOW I CAN HEAR THEM, RIGHT?
COINCIDING WITH THIS GREAT DESTRUCTION WAS THE APPEARANCE...
オーダー
= 能力者
KA (SKRITCH)
...OF WHAT WE NOW CALL "ORDERS."
BASICALLY, ABILITY USERS.
BOARD: ORDER = ABILITY USER
THERE ARE AN ESTIMATED 2,000 SUCH "ORDERS" THROUGH-OUT THE WORLD TODAY...
...BUT THAT NUMBER IS STEADILY INCREAS-ING.

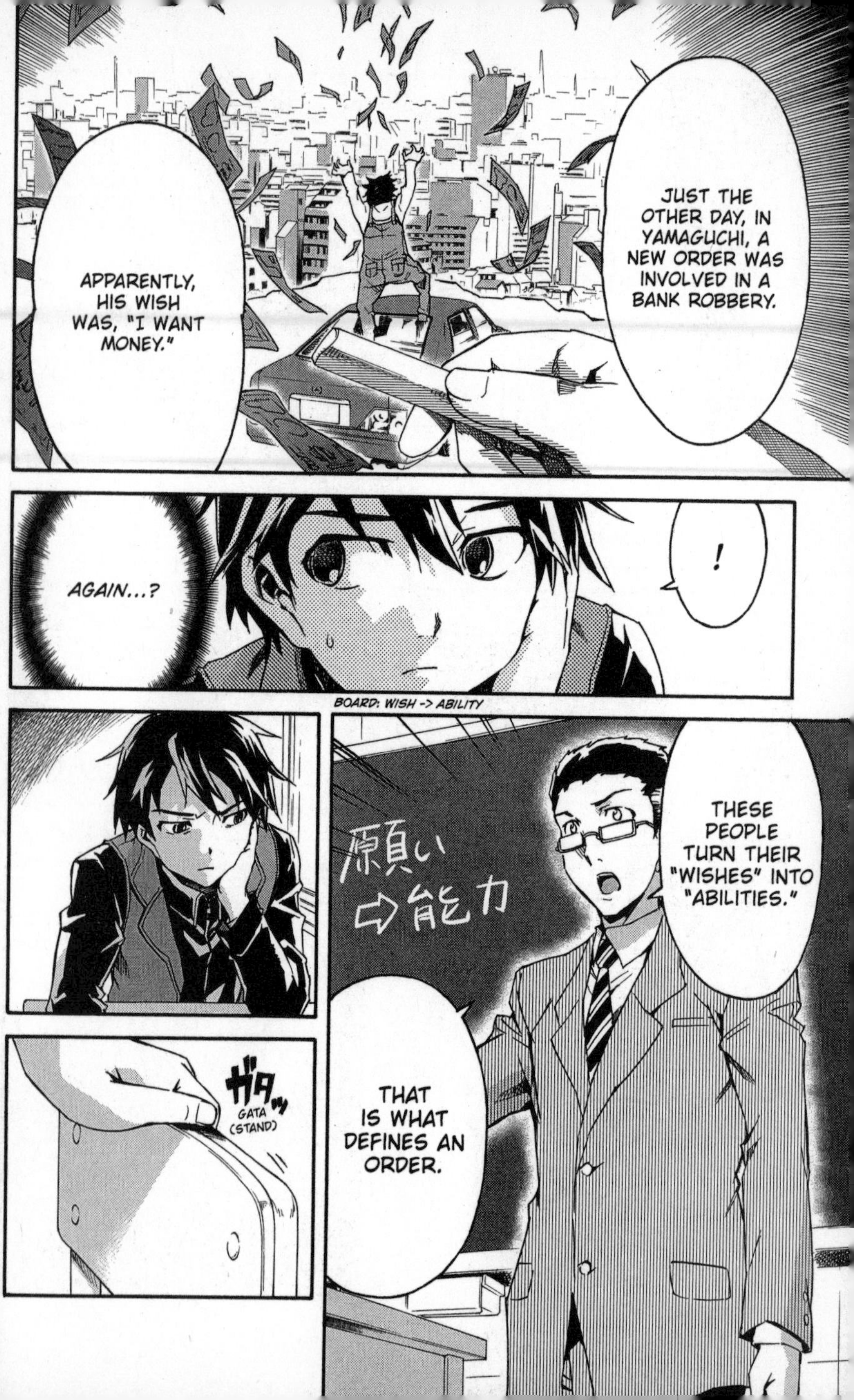
JUST THE OTHER DAY, IN YAMAGUCHI, A NEW ORDER WAS INVOLVED IN A BANK ROBBERY.
APPARENTLY, HIS WISH WAS, "I WANT MONEY."
!
AGAIN...?
BOARD: WISH -> ABILITY
THESE PEOPLE TURN THEIR "WISHES" INTO "ABILITIES."
願い ⇨ 能力
THAT IS WHAT DEFINES AN ORDER.
ガタッ
GATA (STAND)

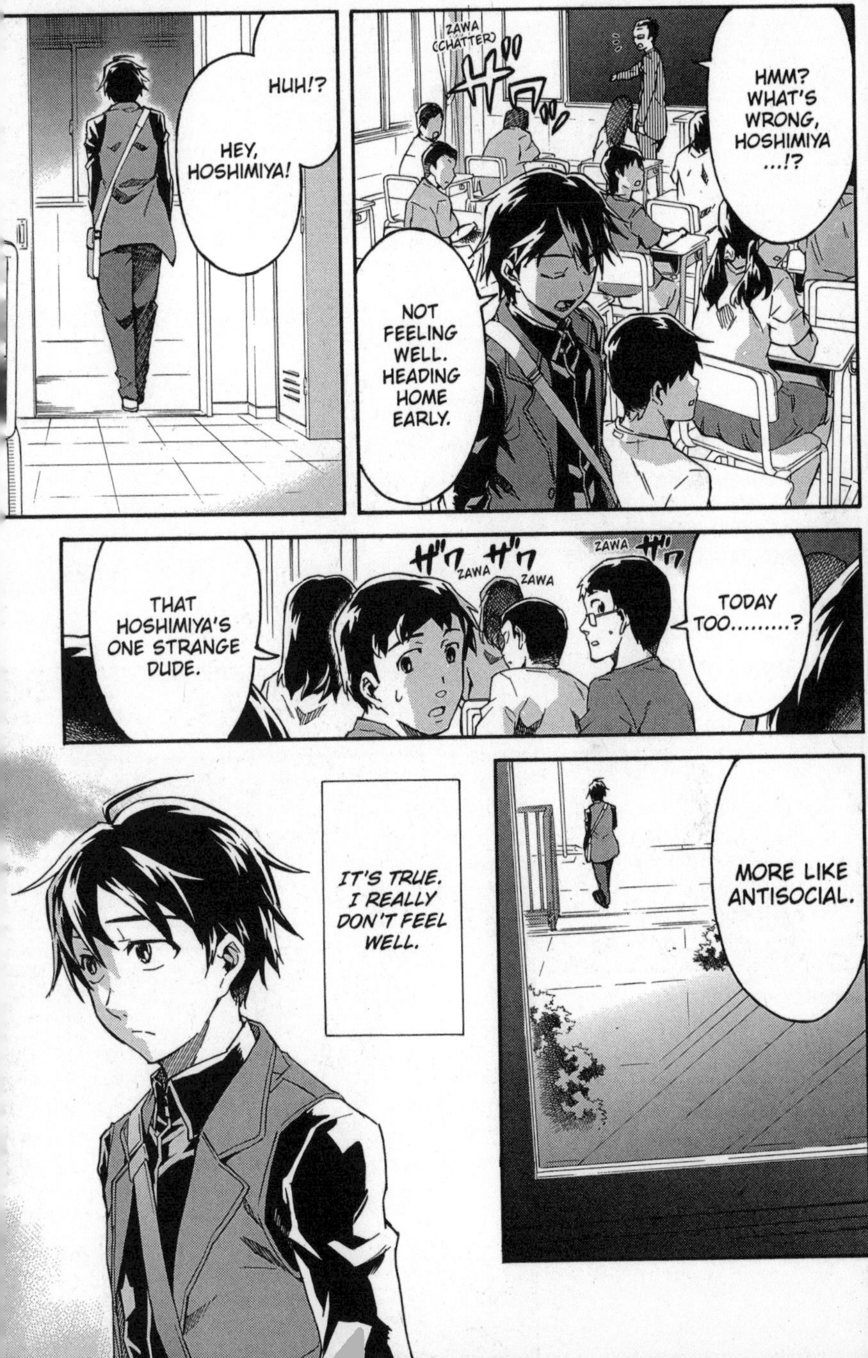
ZAWA (CHATTER)
HMM? WHAT'S WRONG, HOSHIMIYA ...!?
NOT FEELING WELL. HEADING HOME EARLY.
HUH!?
HEY, HOSHIMIYA!
ZAWA
TODAY TOO.........?
ZAWA
ZAWA
THAT HOSHIMIYA'S ONE STRANGE DUDE.
MORE LIKE ANTISOCIAL.
IT'S TRUE. I REALLY DON'T FEEL WELL.

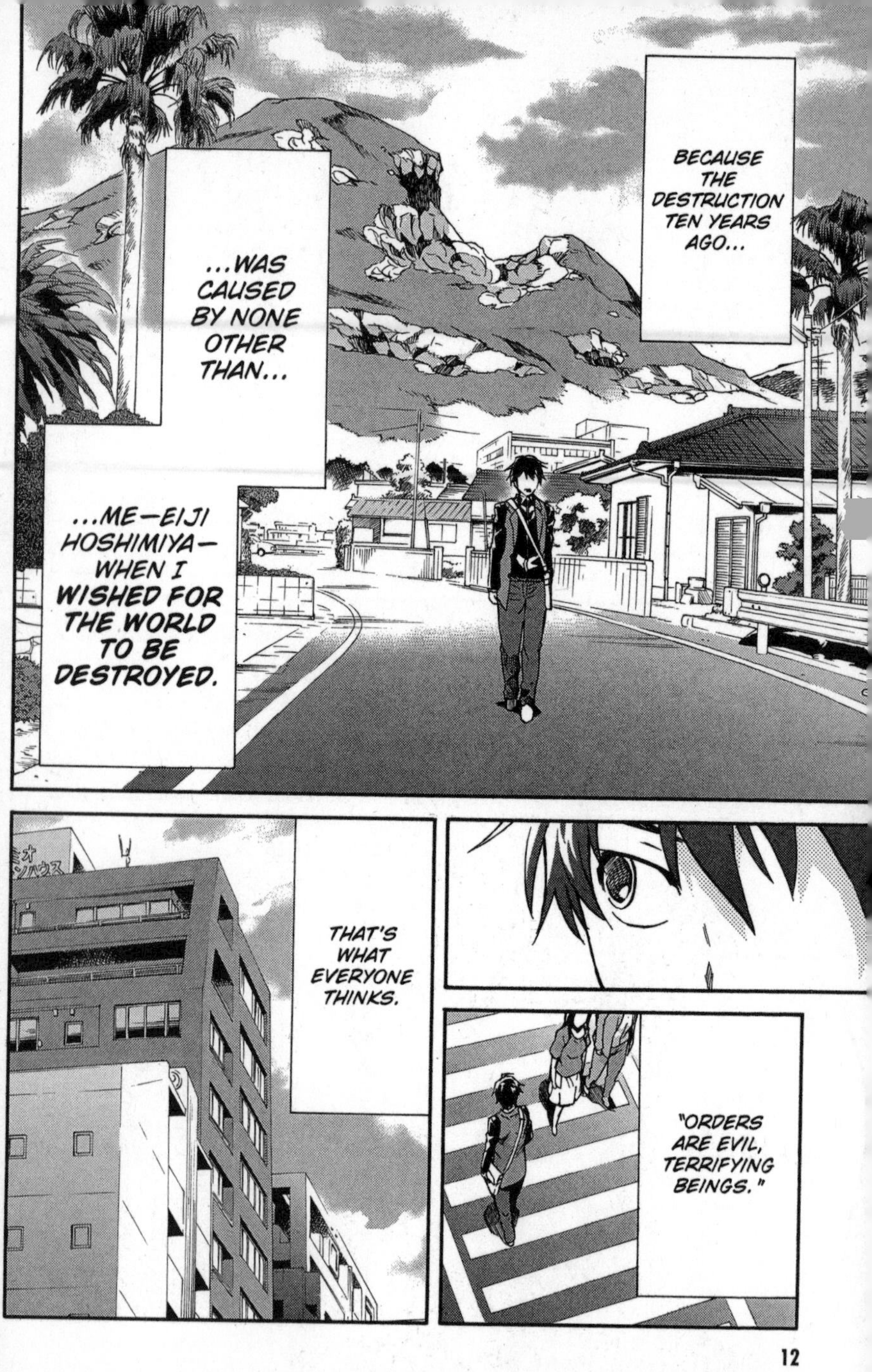
BECAUSE THE DESTRUCTION TEN YEARS AGO...
...WAS CAUSED BY NONE OTHER THAN...
...ME—EIJI HOSHIMIYA—WHEN I WISHED FOR THE WORLD TO BE DESTROYED.
"ORDERS ARE EVIL, TERRIFYING BEINGS."
THAT'S WHAT EVERYONE THINKS.

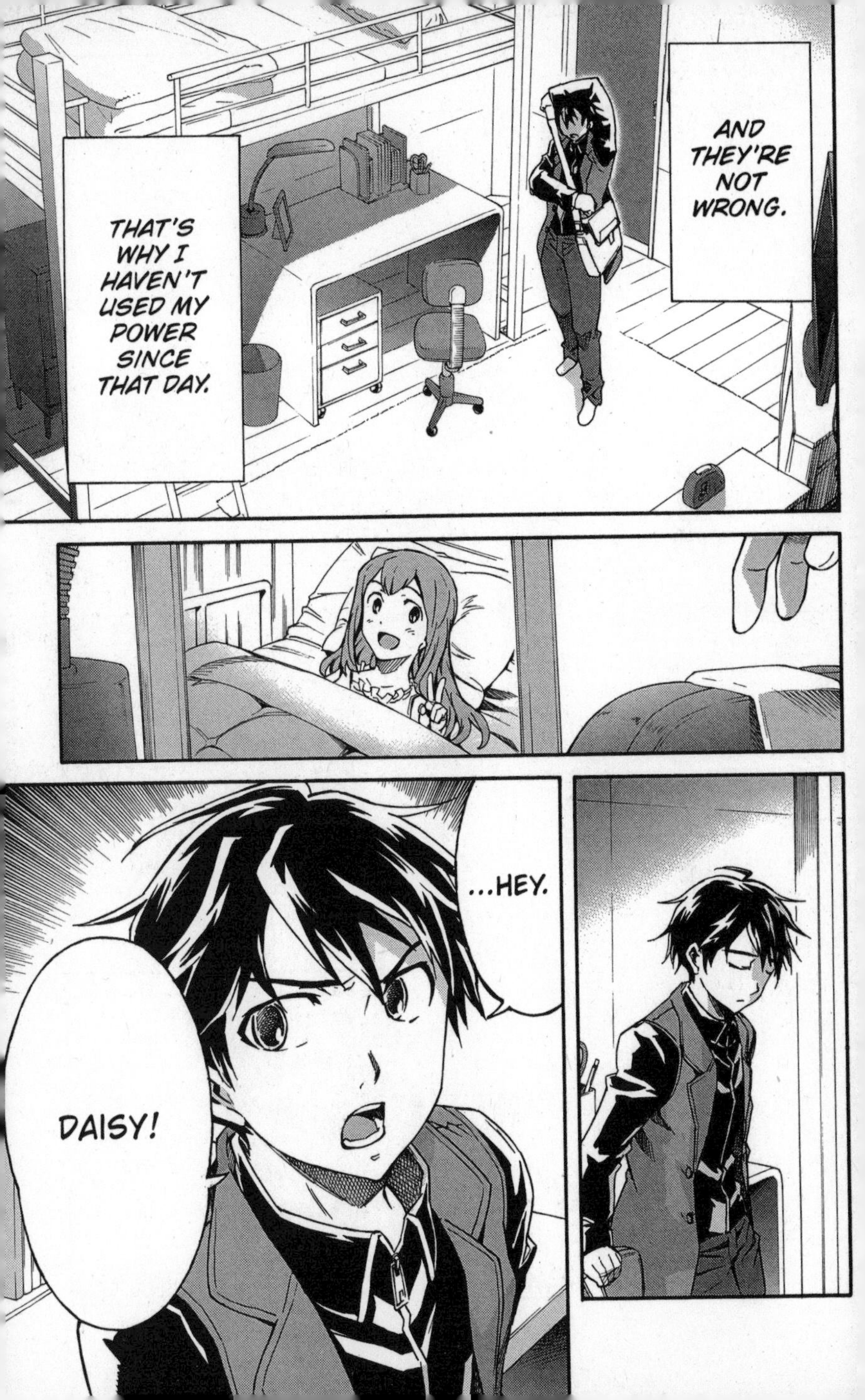
AND THEY'RE NOT WRONG.
THAT'S WHY I HAVEN'T USED MY POWER SINCE THAT DAY.
...HEY.
DAISY!

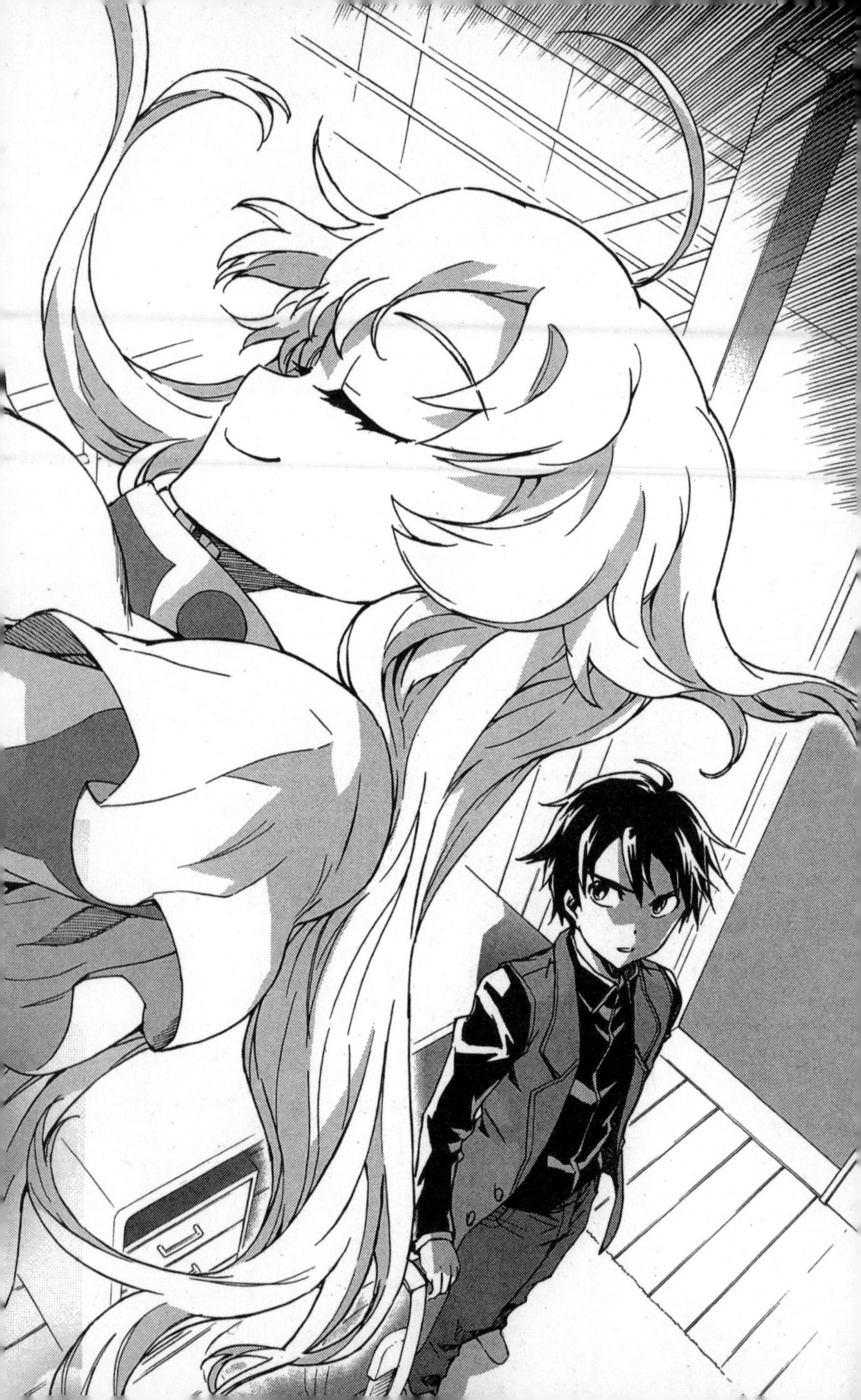

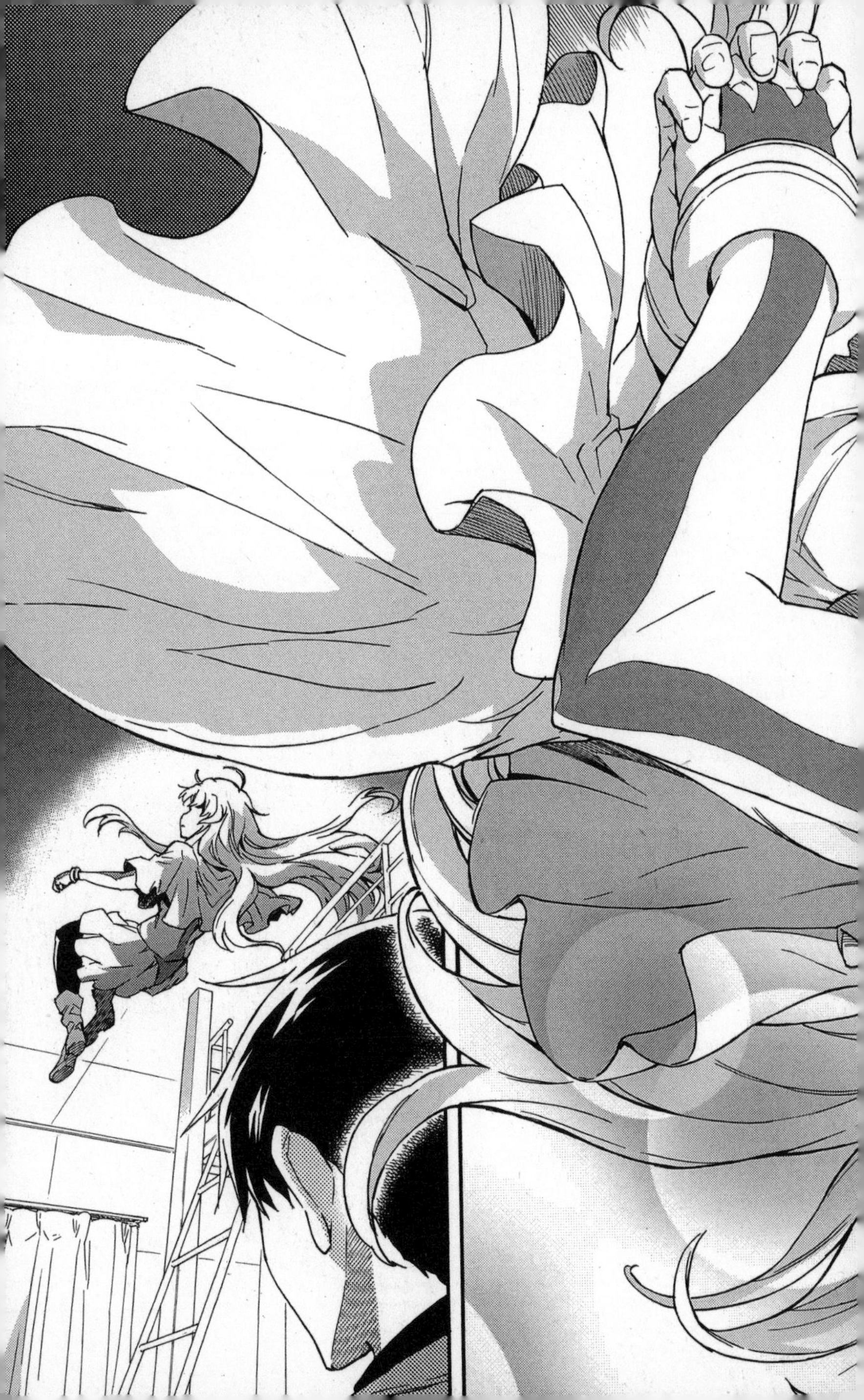

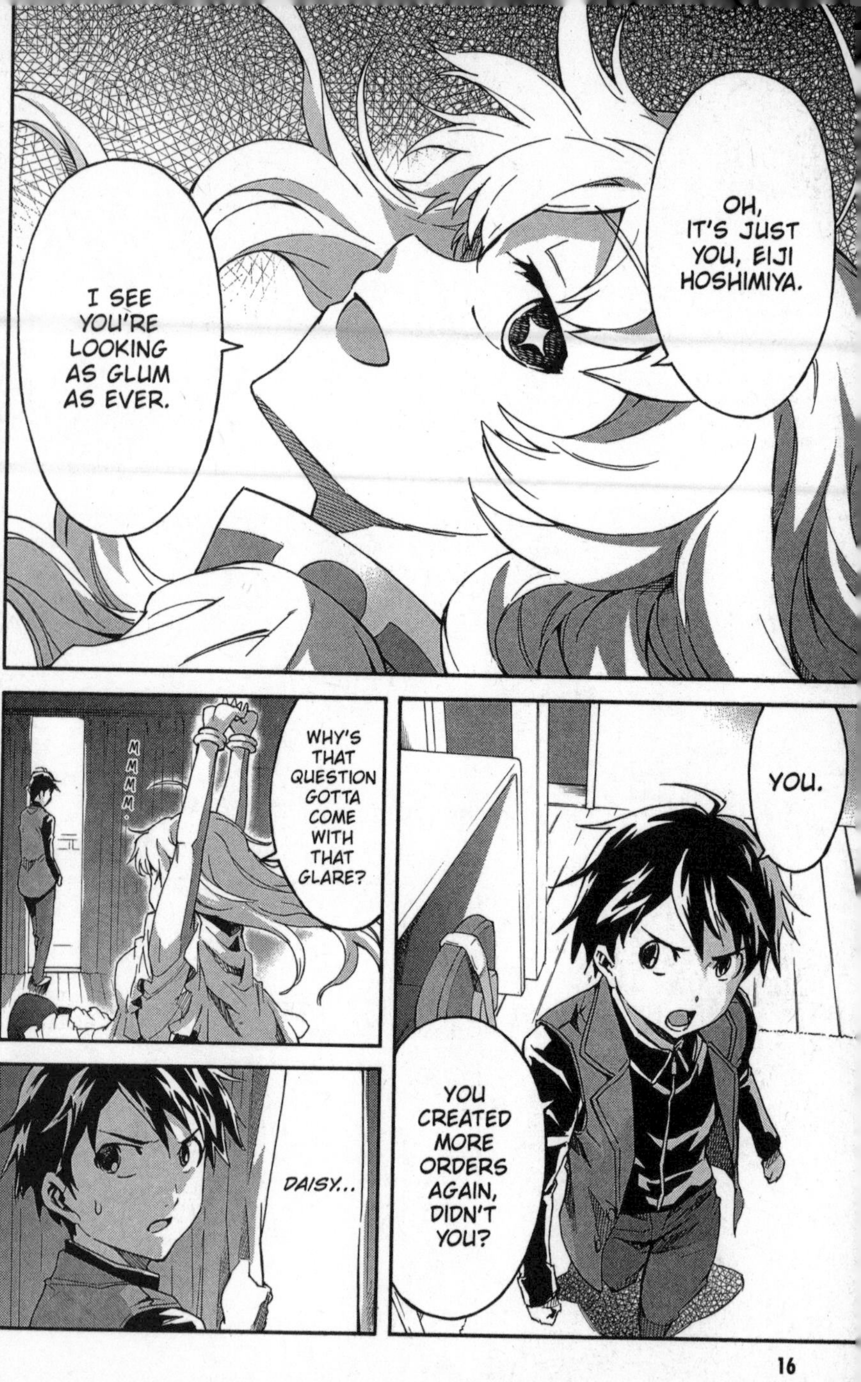
OH, IT'S JUST YOU, EIJI HOSHIMIYA.
I SEE YOU'RE LOOKING AS GLUM AS EVER.
YOU.
YOU CREATED MORE ORDERS AGAIN, DIDN'T YOU?
WHY'S THAT QUESTION GOTTA COME WITH THAT GLARE?
MMMM.
DAISY...

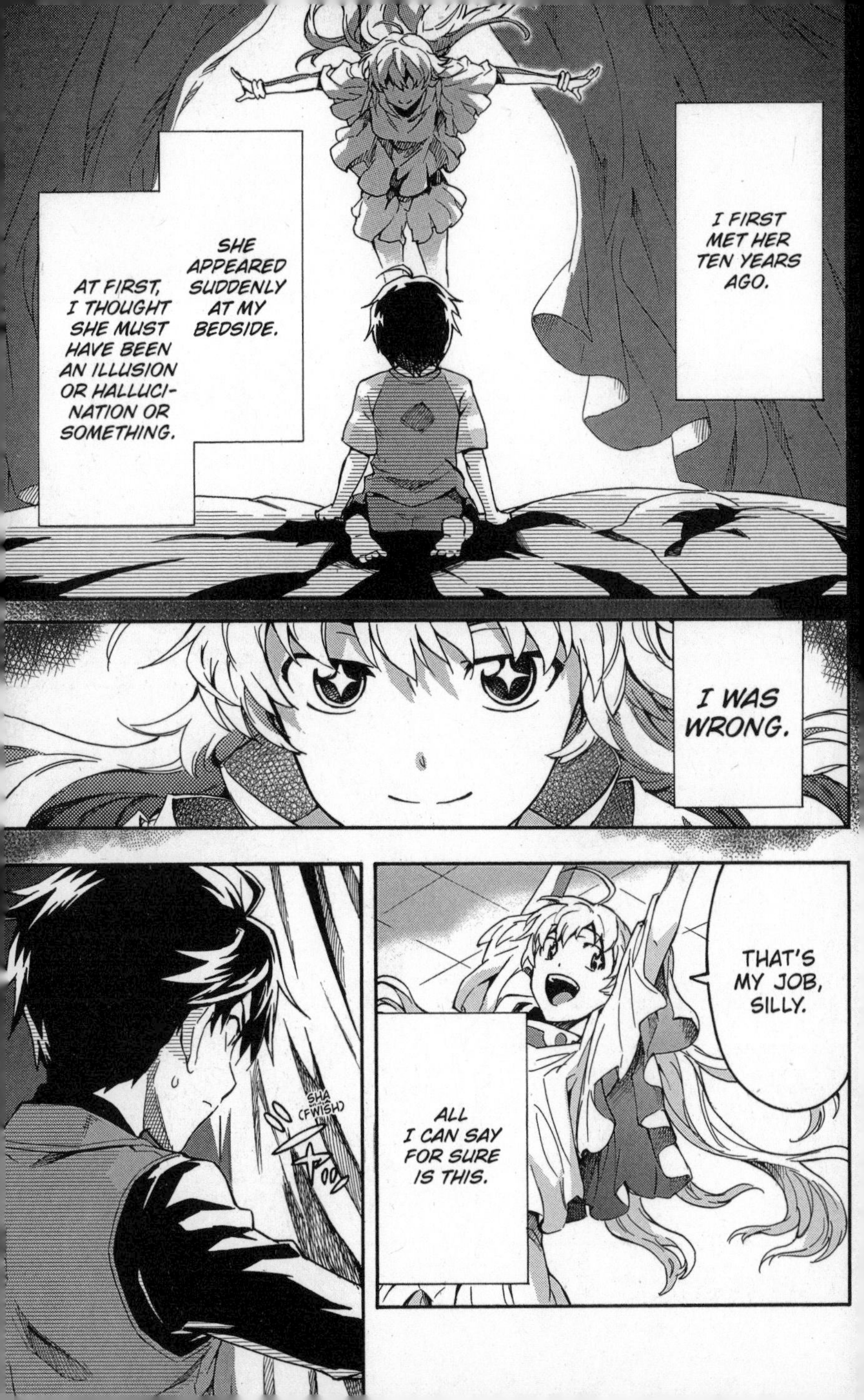
I FIRST MET HER TEN YEARS AGO.
SHE APPEARED SUDDENLY AT MY BEDSIDE.
AT FIRST, I THOUGHT SHE MUST HAVE BEEN AN ILLUSION OR HALLUCINATION OR SOMETHING.
I WAS WRONG.
THAT'S MY JOB, SILLY.
ALL I CAN SAY FOR SURE IS THIS.
SHA (FWISH)

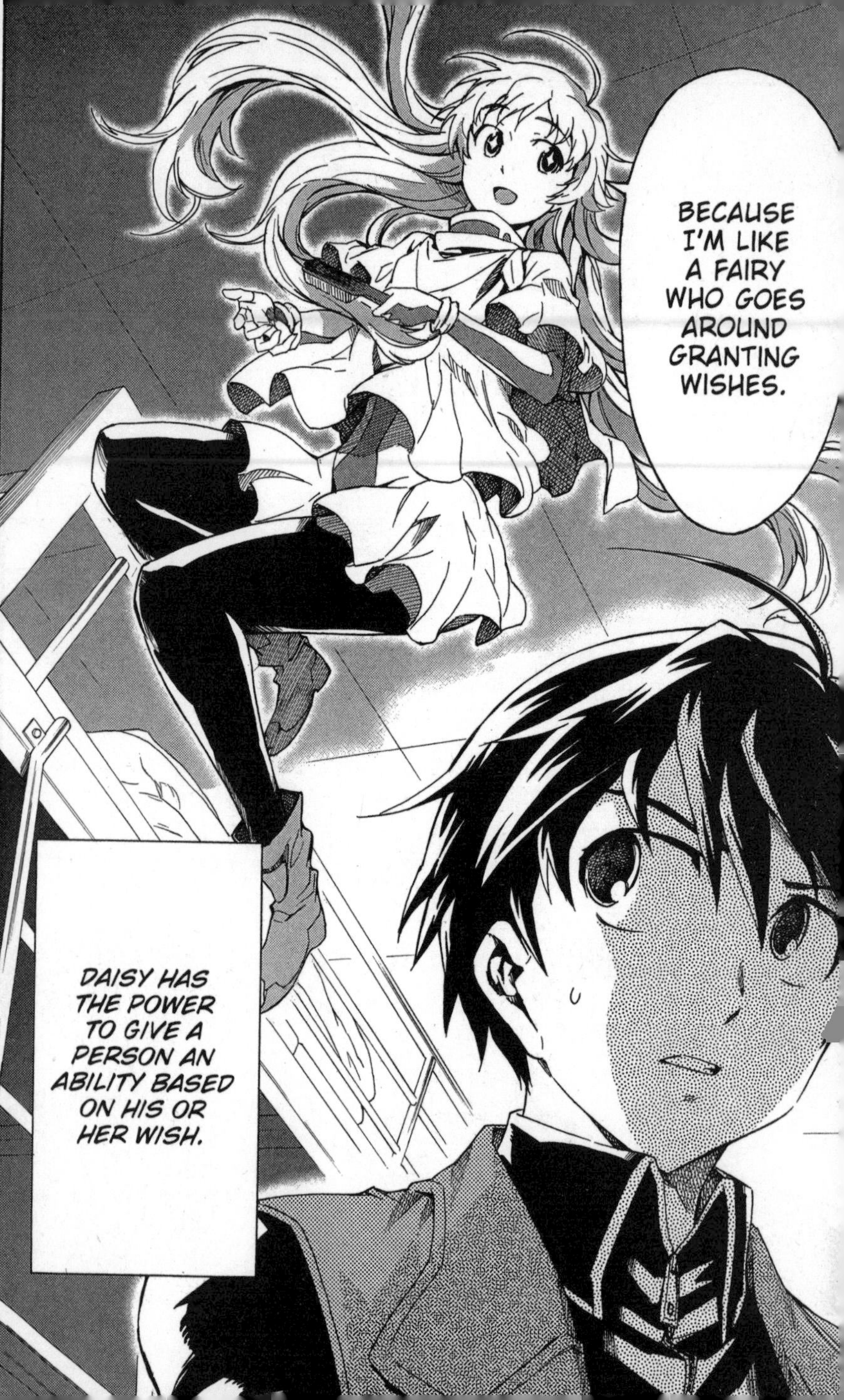
BECAUSE I'M LIKE A FAIRY WHO GOES AROUND GRANTING WISHES.
DAISY HAS THE POWER TO GIVE A PERSON AN ABILITY BASED ON HIS OR HER WISH.

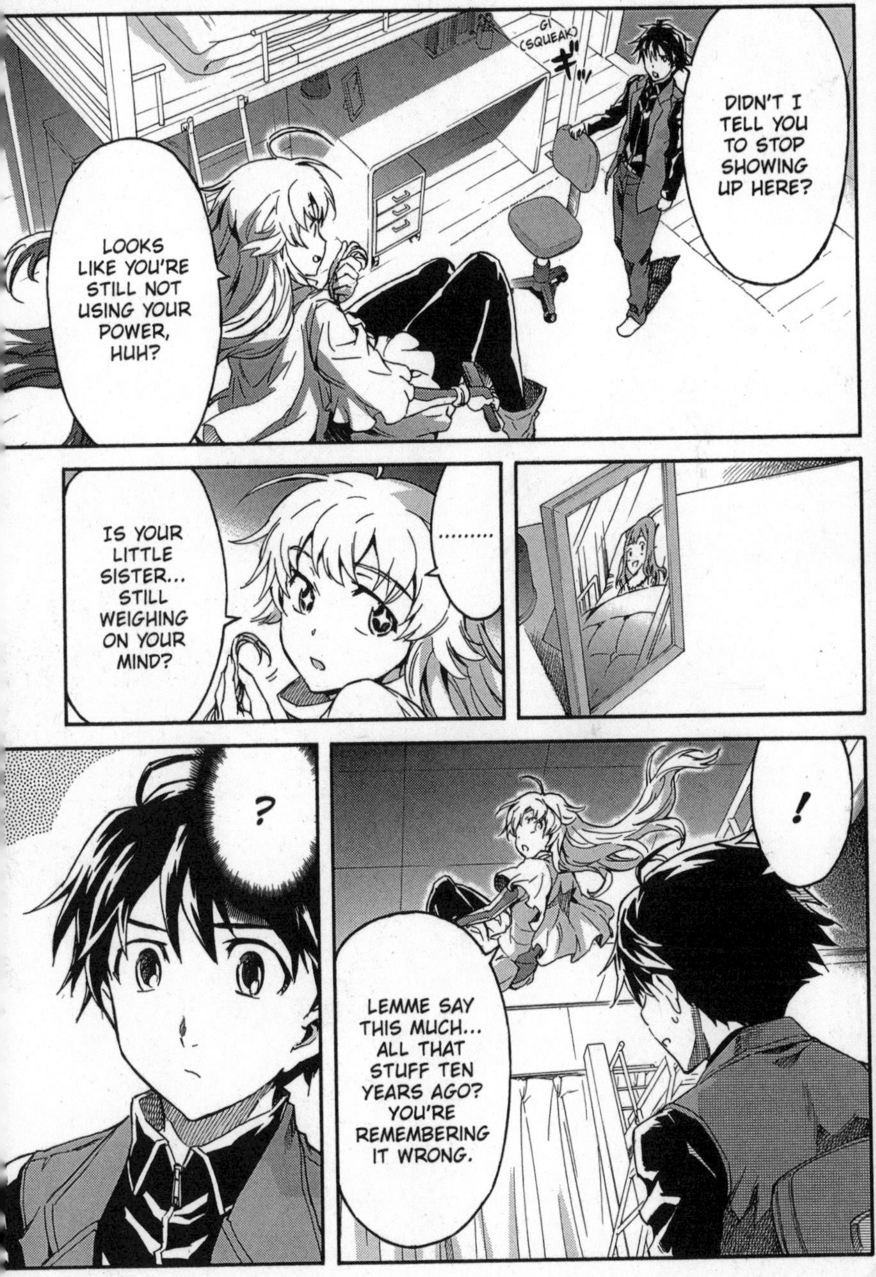
GI (SQUEAK)
DIDN'T I TELL YOU TO STOP SHOWING UP HERE?
LOOKS LIKE YOU'RE STILL NOT USING YOUR POWER, HUH?
..........
IS YOUR LITTLE SISTER... STILL WEIGHING ON YOUR MIND?
!
LEMME SAY THIS MUCH... ALL THAT STUFF TEN YEARS AGO? YOU'RE REMEMBERING IT WRONG.
?

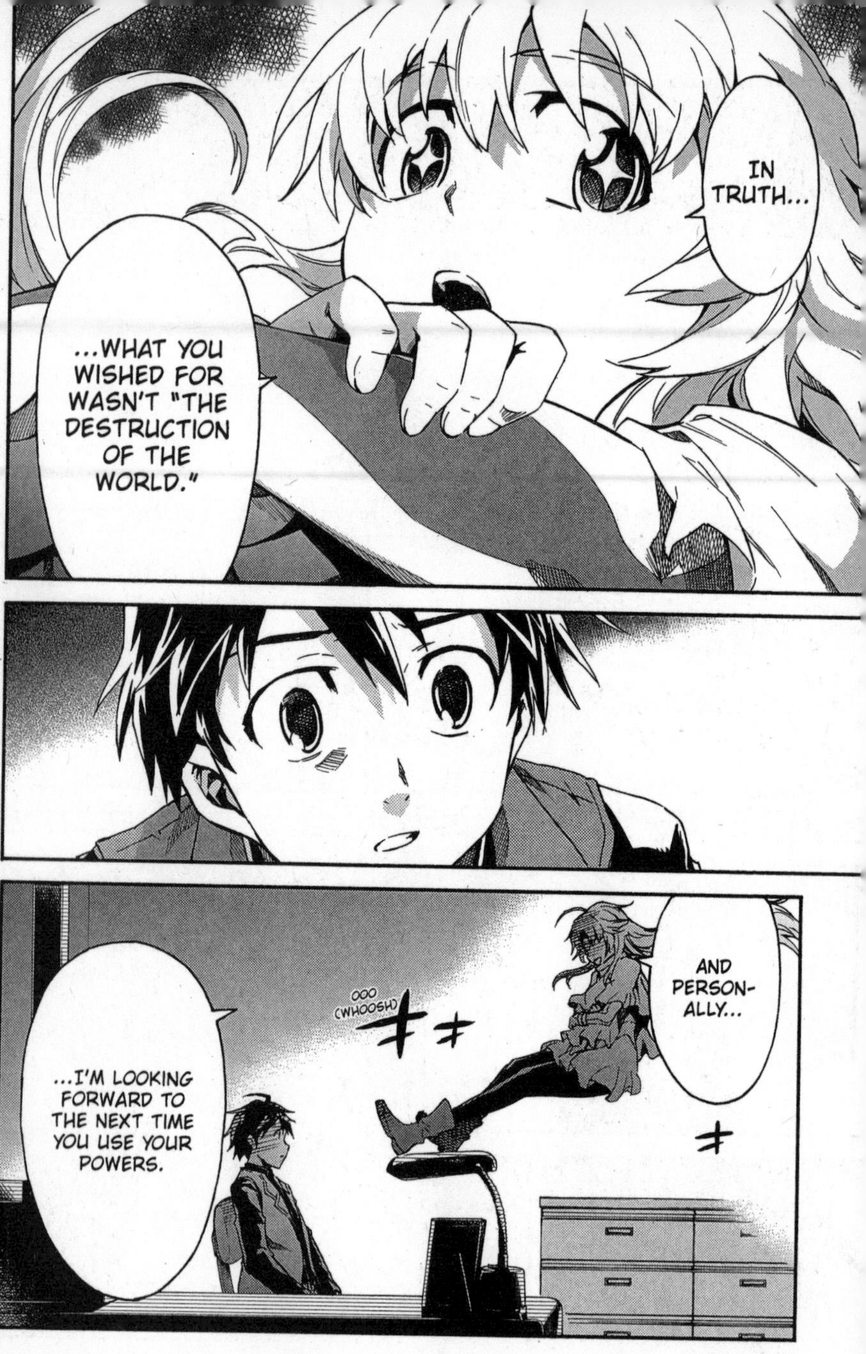
IN TRUTH...
...WHAT YOU WISHED FOR WASN'T "THE DESTRUCTION OF THE WORLD."
AND PERSON-ALLY...
OOO (WHOOSH)
...I'M LOOKING FORWARD TO THE NEXT TIME YOU USE YOUR POWERS.

## Subject 1: "Me x World"
## Place: Amakusa

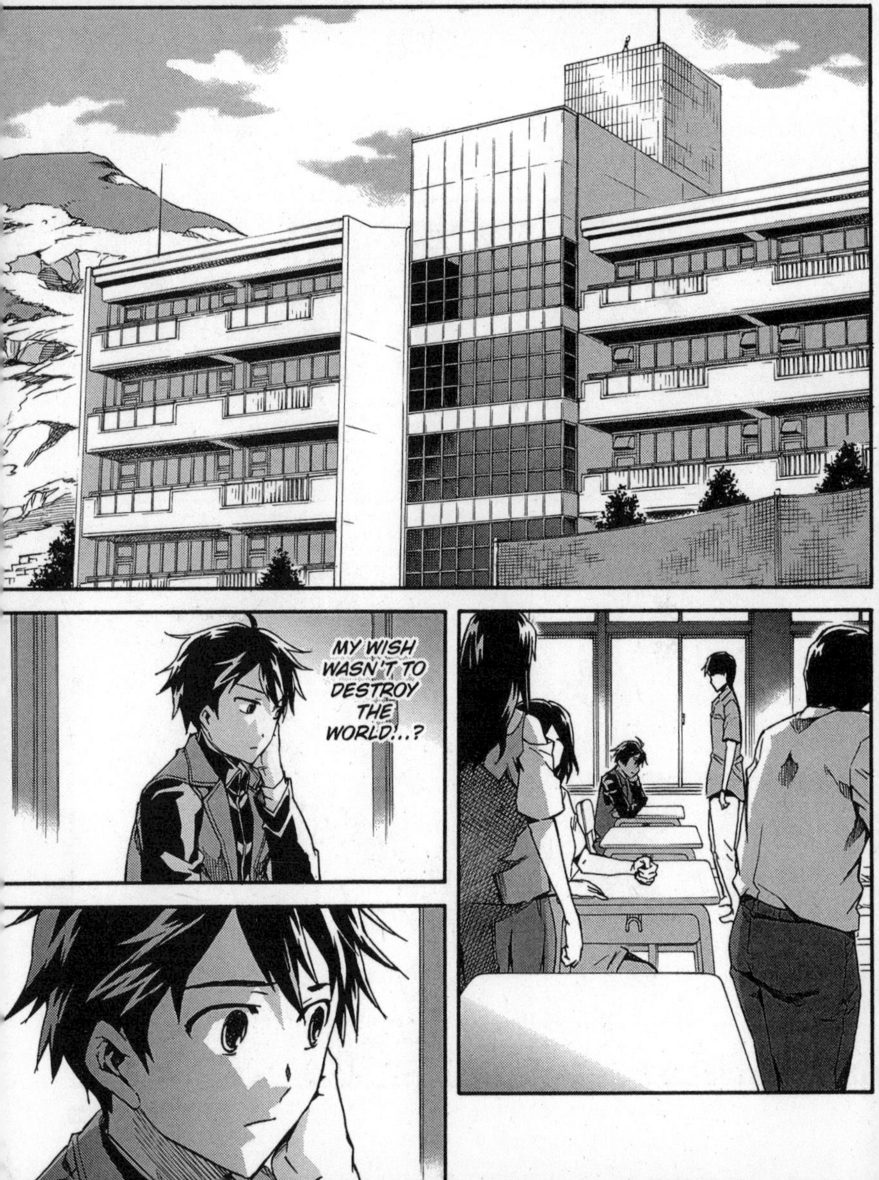
MY WISH WASN'T TO DESTROY THE WORLD...?

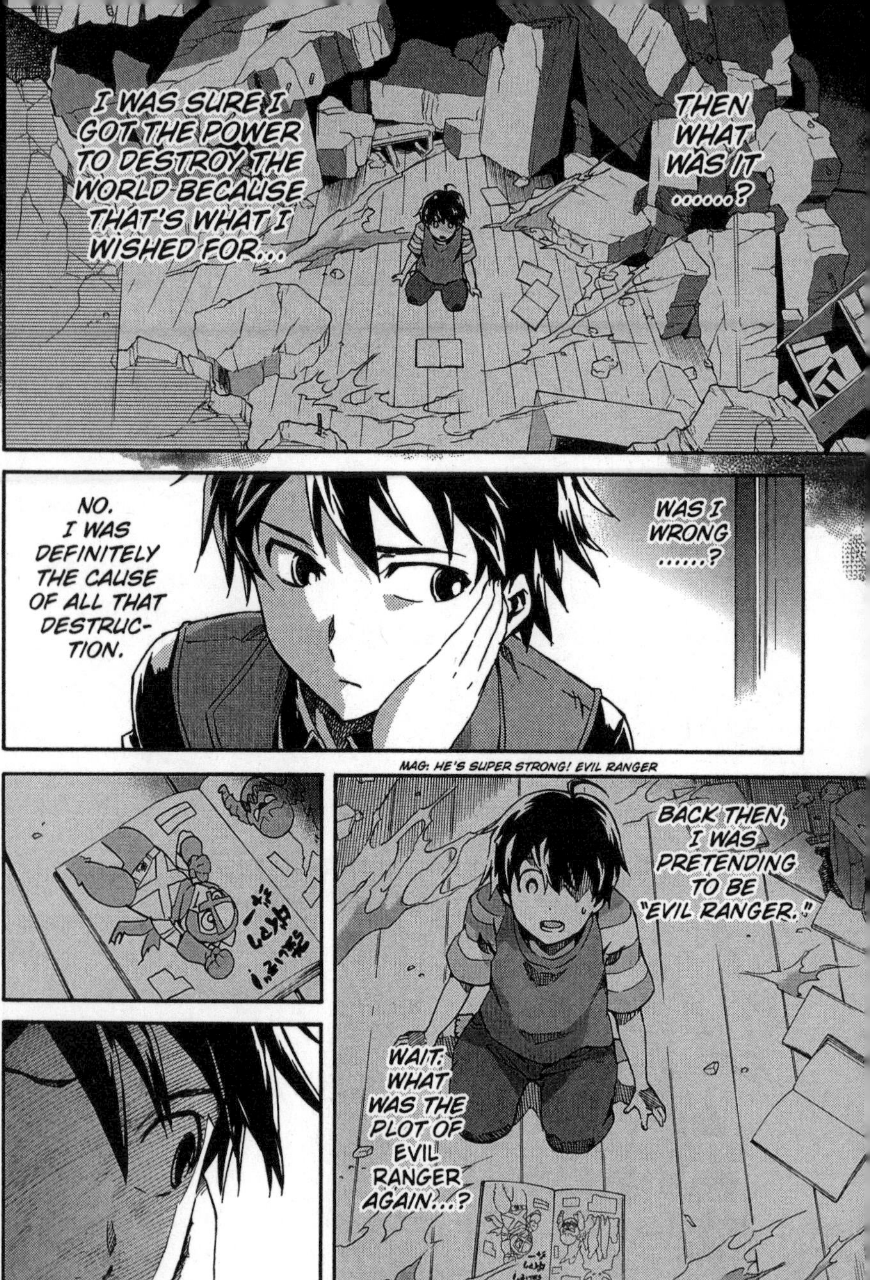
THEN WHAT WAS IT ......?
I WAS SURE I GOT THE POWER TO DESTROY THE WORLD BECAUSE THAT'S WHAT I WISHED FOR...
WAS I WRONG ......?
NO. I WAS DEFINITELY THE CAUSE OF ALL THAT DESTRUC-TION.
BACK THEN, I WAS PRETENDING TO BE "EVIL RANGER."
WAIT. WHAT WAS THE PLOT OF EVIL RANGER AGAIN...?
MAG: HE'S SUPER STRONG! EVIL RANGER

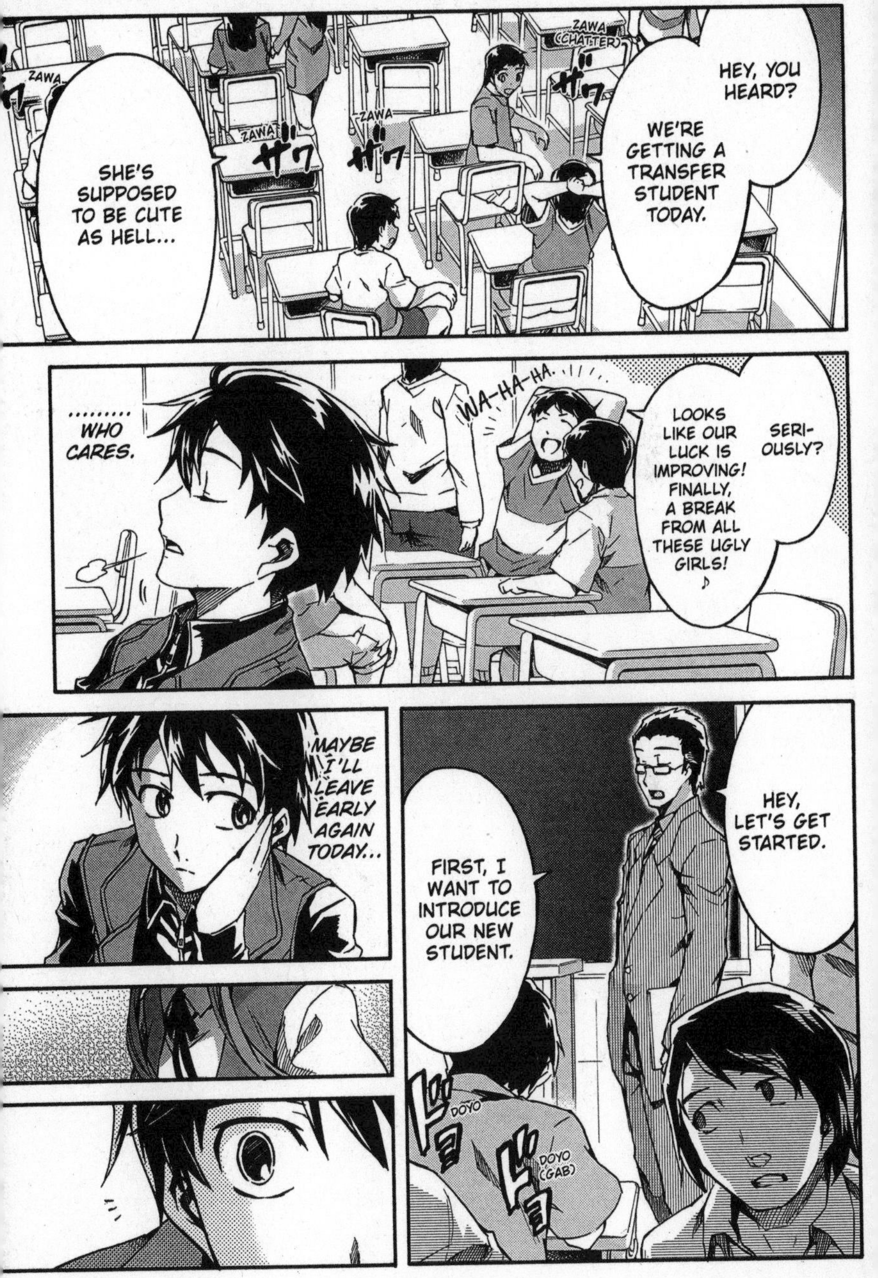
HEY, YOU HEARD?
WE'RE GETTING A TRANSFER STUDENT TODAY.
ZAWA (CHATTER)
ZAWA
ZAWA
ZAWA
SHE'S SUPPOSED TO BE CUTE AS HELL...
SERI-OUSLY?
LOOKS LIKE OUR LUCK IS IMPROVING! FINALLY, A BREAK FROM ALL THESE UGLY GIRLS! ♪
WA-HA-HA.
......... WHO CARES.
HEY, LET'S GET STARTED.
FIRST, I WANT TO INTRODUCE OUR NEW STUDENT.
DOYO
DOYO (GAB)
MAYBE I'LL LEAVE EARLY AGAIN TODAY...

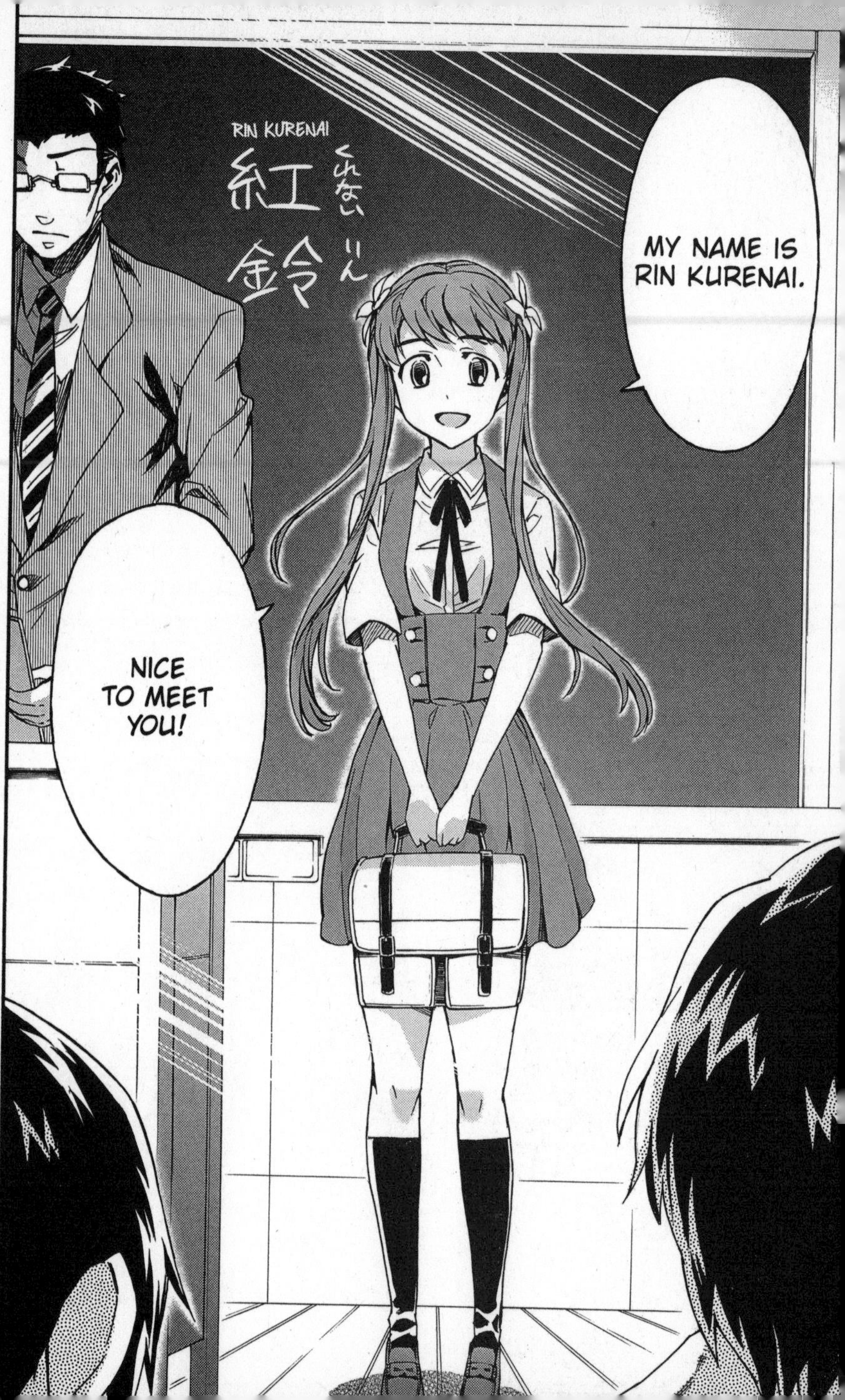
MY NAME IS RIN KURENAI.
RIN KURENAI
紅 くれない
鈴 りん
NICE TO MEET YOU!

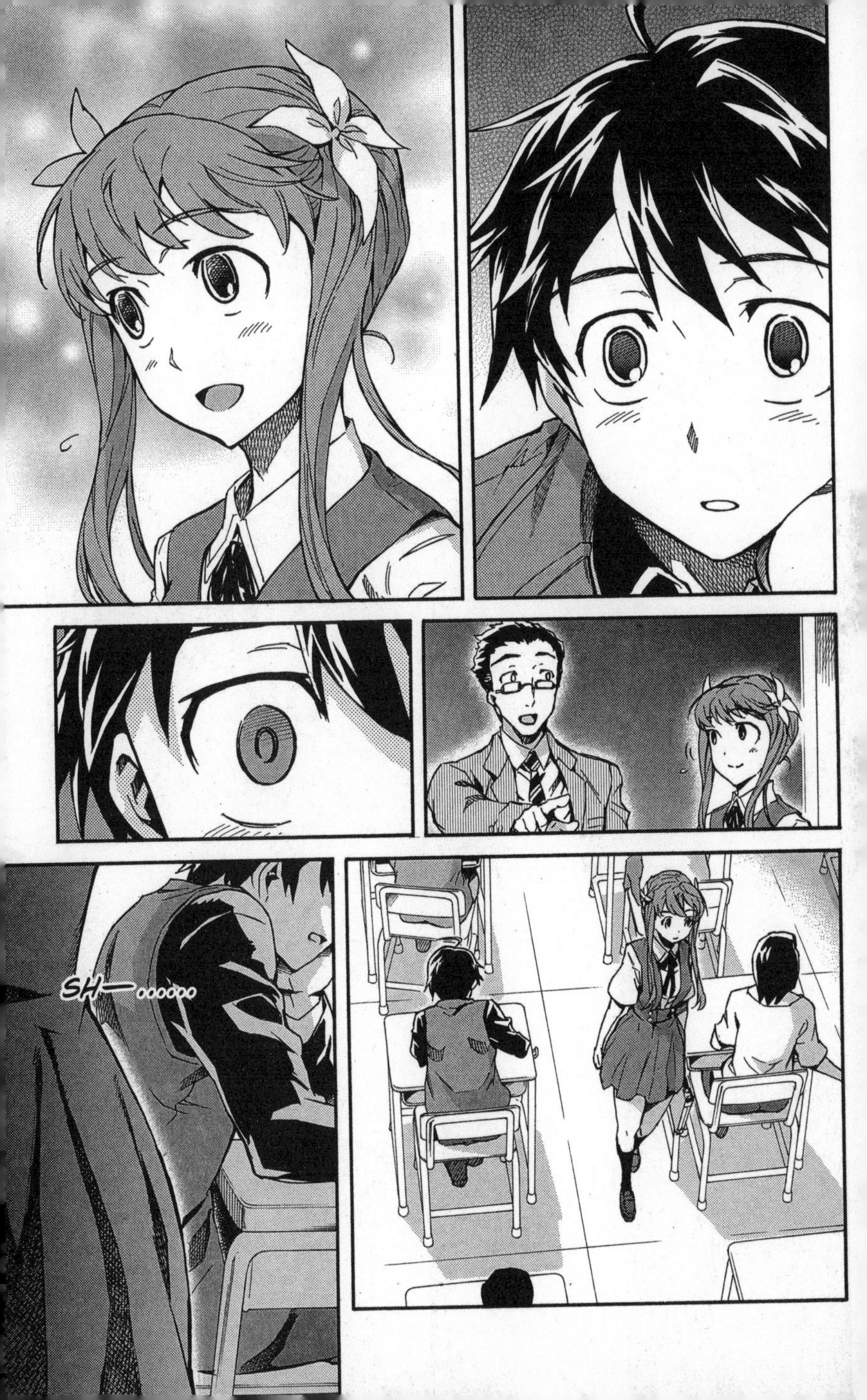
SH—oooooo

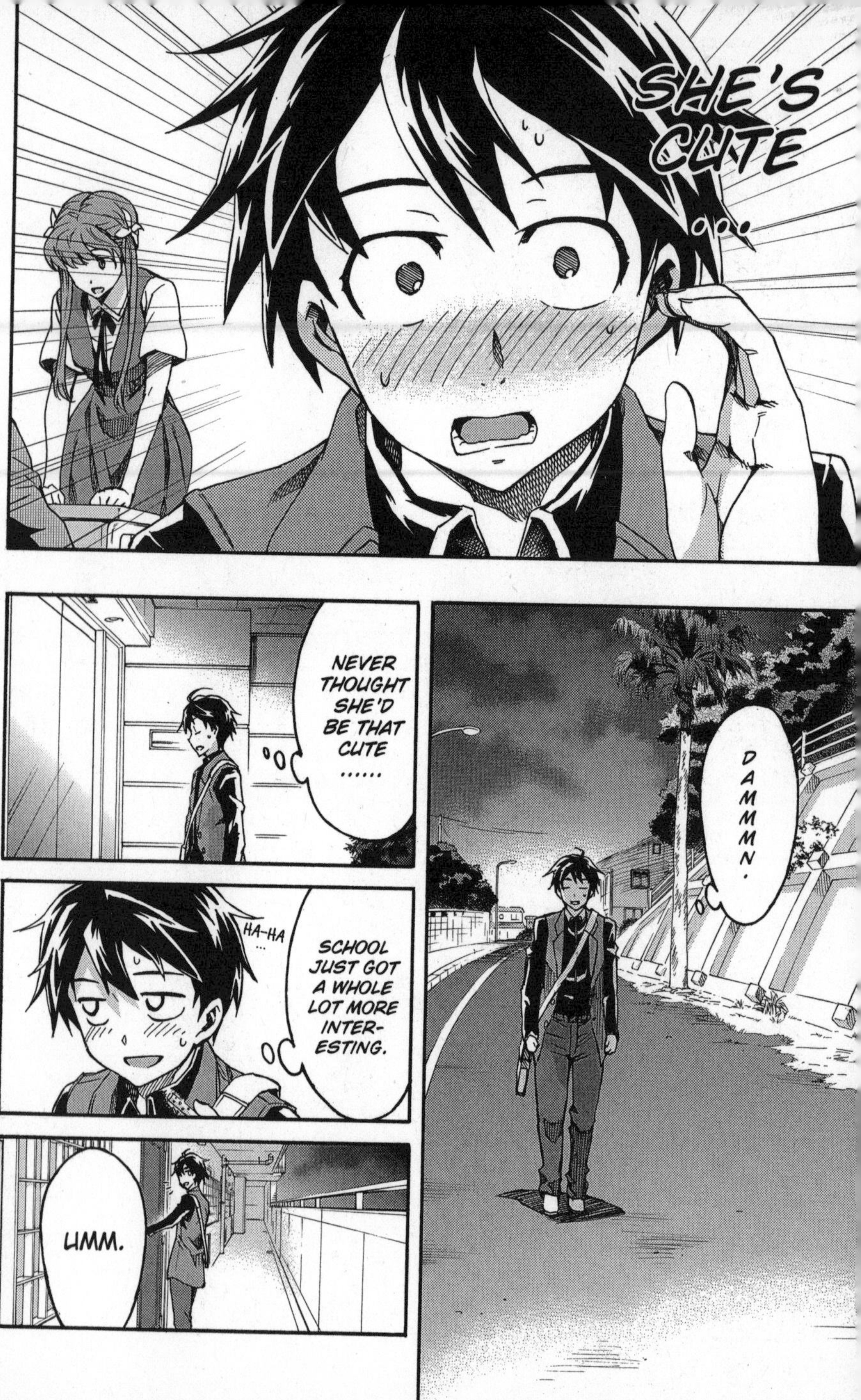
SHE'S CUTE...
DAMMMN.
NEVER THOUGHT SHE'D BE THAT CUTE......
HA-HA...
SCHOOL JUST GOT A WHOLE LOT MORE INTER-ESTING.
UMM.

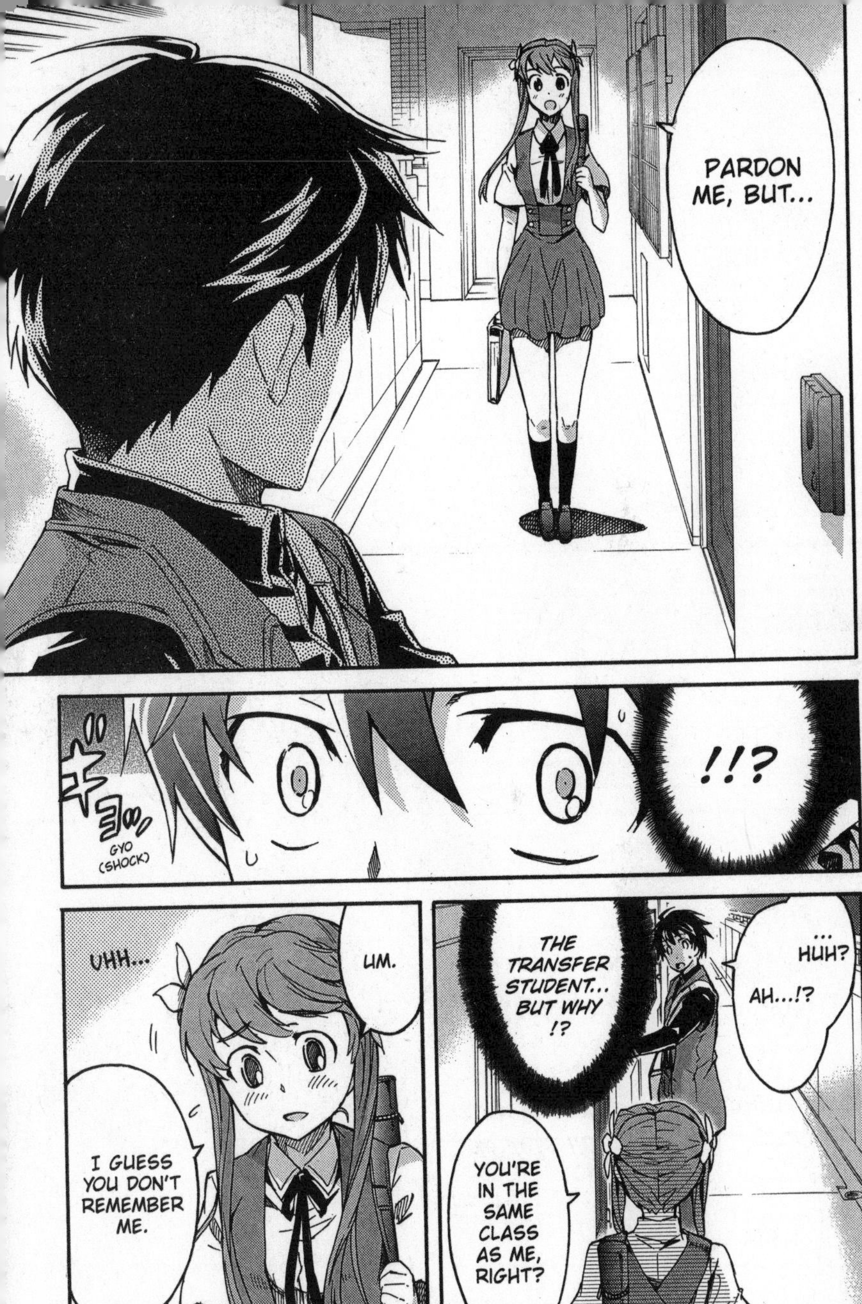
PARDON ME, BUT...
!!?
GYO (SHOCK)
... HUH?
AH...!?
THE TRANSFER STUDENT... BUT WHY !?
YOU'RE IN THE SAME CLASS AS ME, RIGHT?
UM.
UHH...
I GUESS YOU DON'T REMEMBER ME.

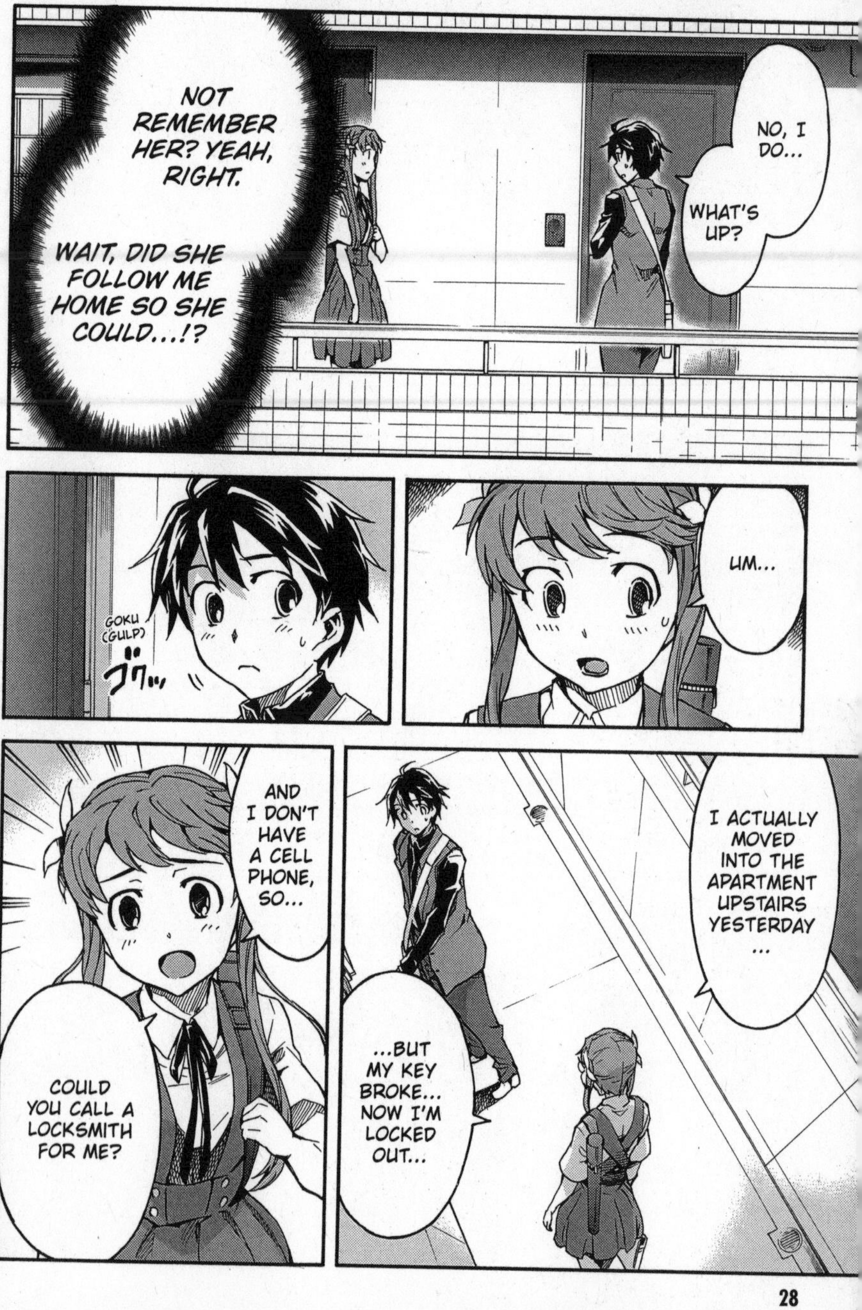

NO, I DO...
WHAT'S UP?
NOT REMEMBER HER? YEAH, RIGHT.
WAIT, DID SHE FOLLOW ME HOME SO SHE COULD...!?
UM...
GOKU (GULP)
ゴクッ
I ACTUALLY MOVED INTO THE APARTMENT UPSTAIRS YESTERDAY ...
...BUT MY KEY BROKE... NOW I'M LOCKED OUT...
AND I DON'T HAVE A CELL PHONE, SO...
COULD YOU CALL A LOCKSMITH FOR ME?

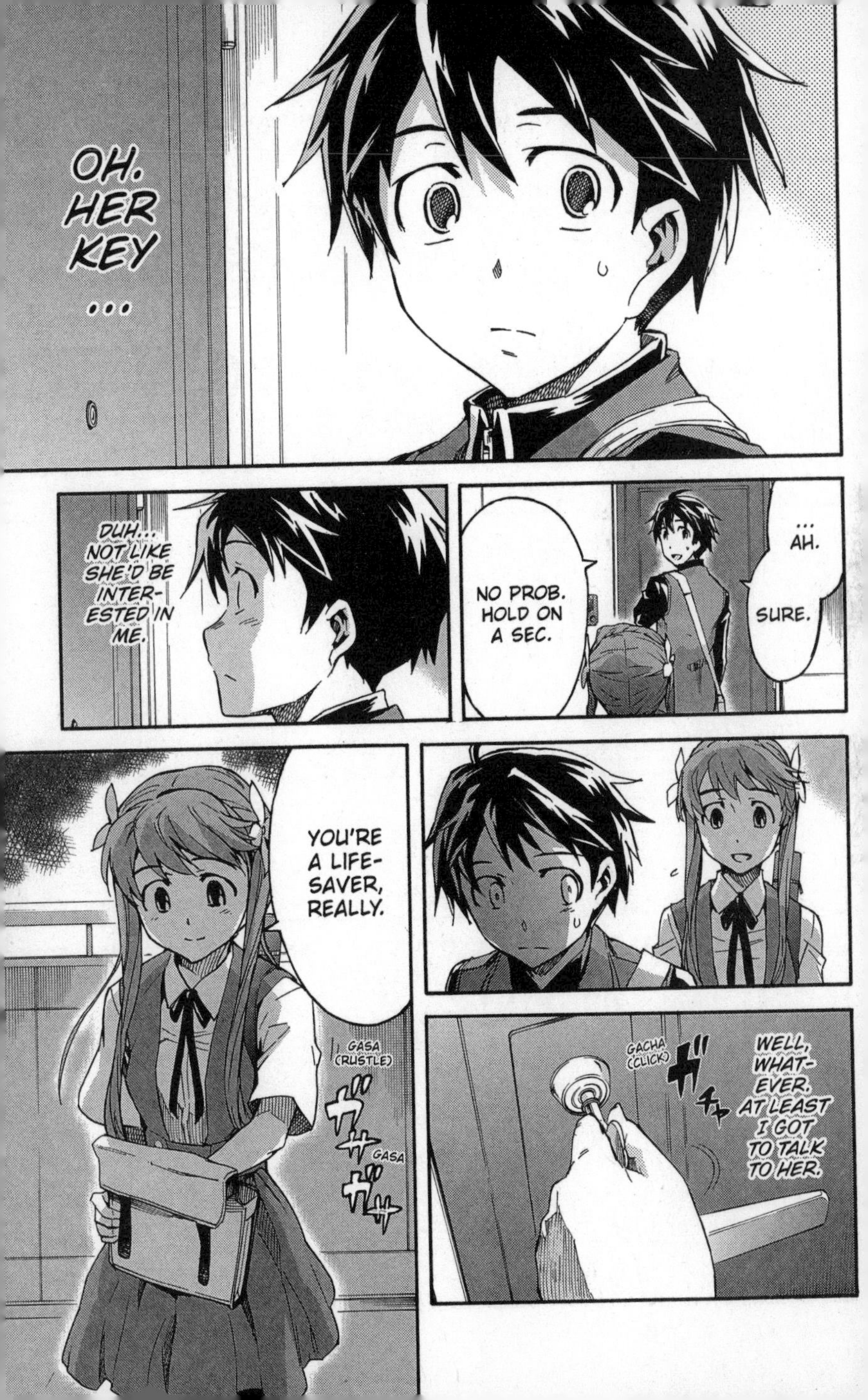
OH. HER KEY ...
... AH.
SURE.
NO PROB. HOLD ON A SEC.
DUH... NOT LIKE SHE'D BE INTER-ESTED IN ME.
YOU'RE A LIFE-SAVER, REALLY.
GASA (RUSTLE)
GASA
GACHA (CLICK)
WELL, WHAT-EVER. AT LEAST I GOT TO TALK TO HER.

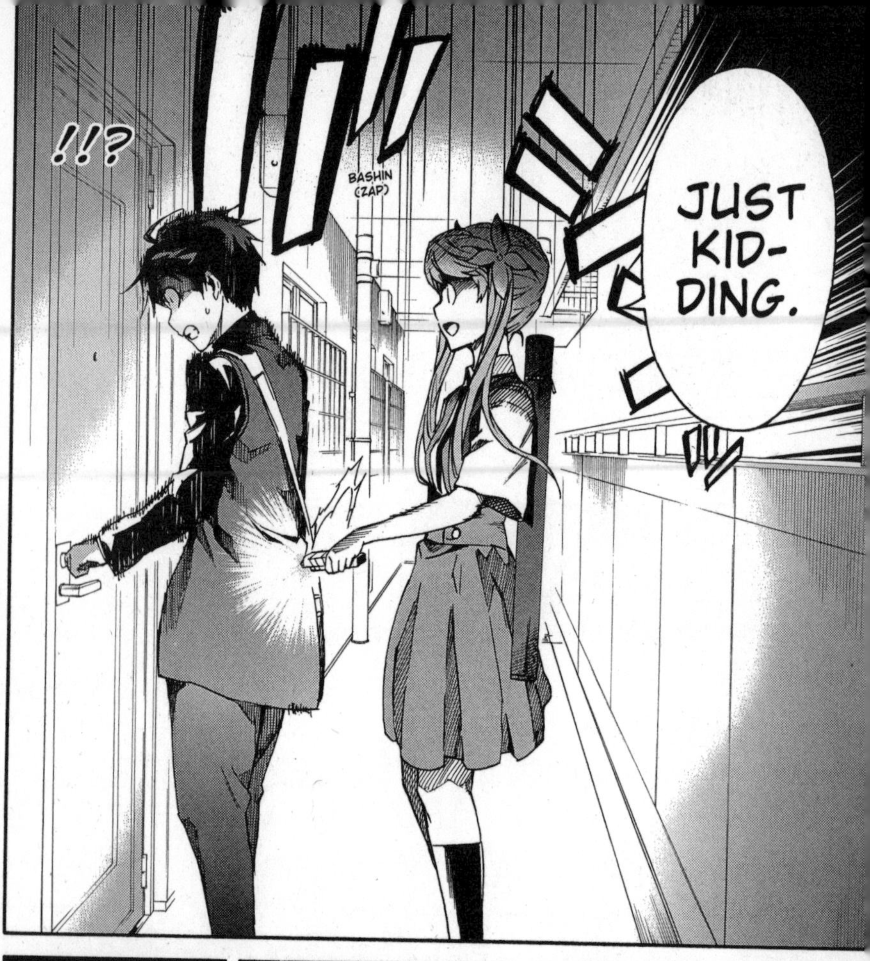
JUST KID-DING.
BASHIN (ZAP)
!!?

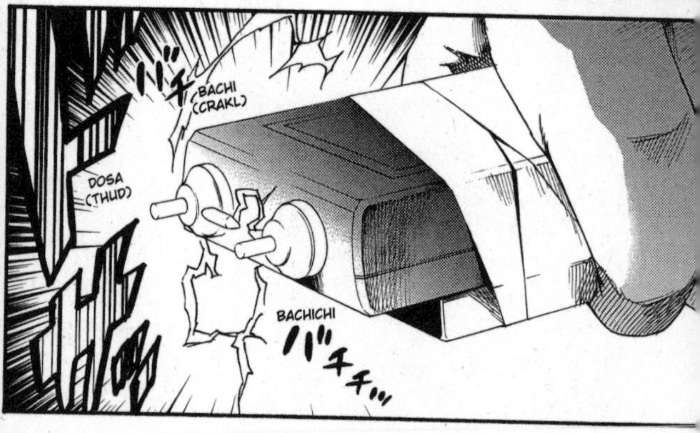
バチ
BACHI (CRAKL)
DOSA (THUD)
BACHICHI
バチチッ

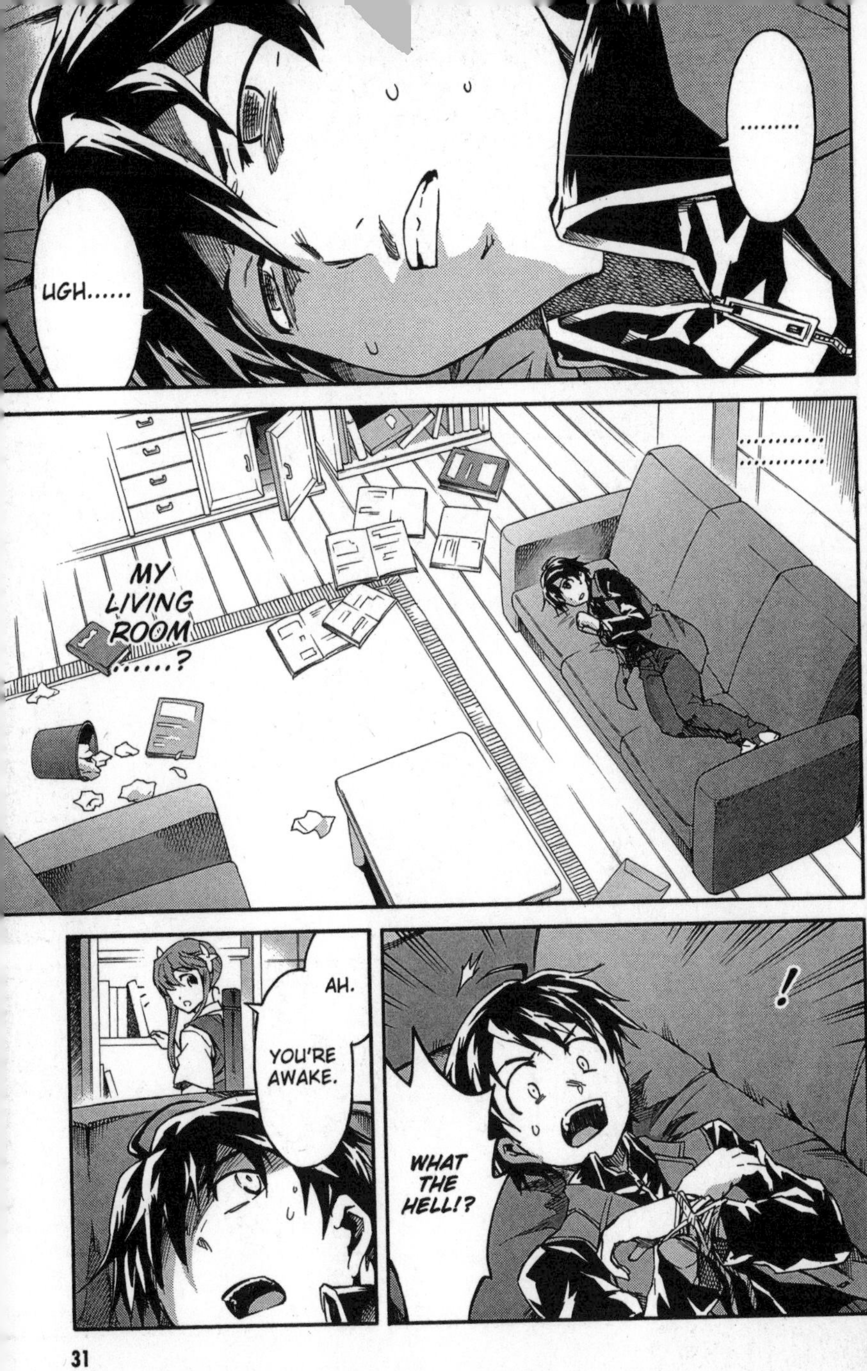
........
UGH......
..........
MY LIVING ROOM......?
!
WHAT THE HELL!?
AH. YOU'RE AWAKE.

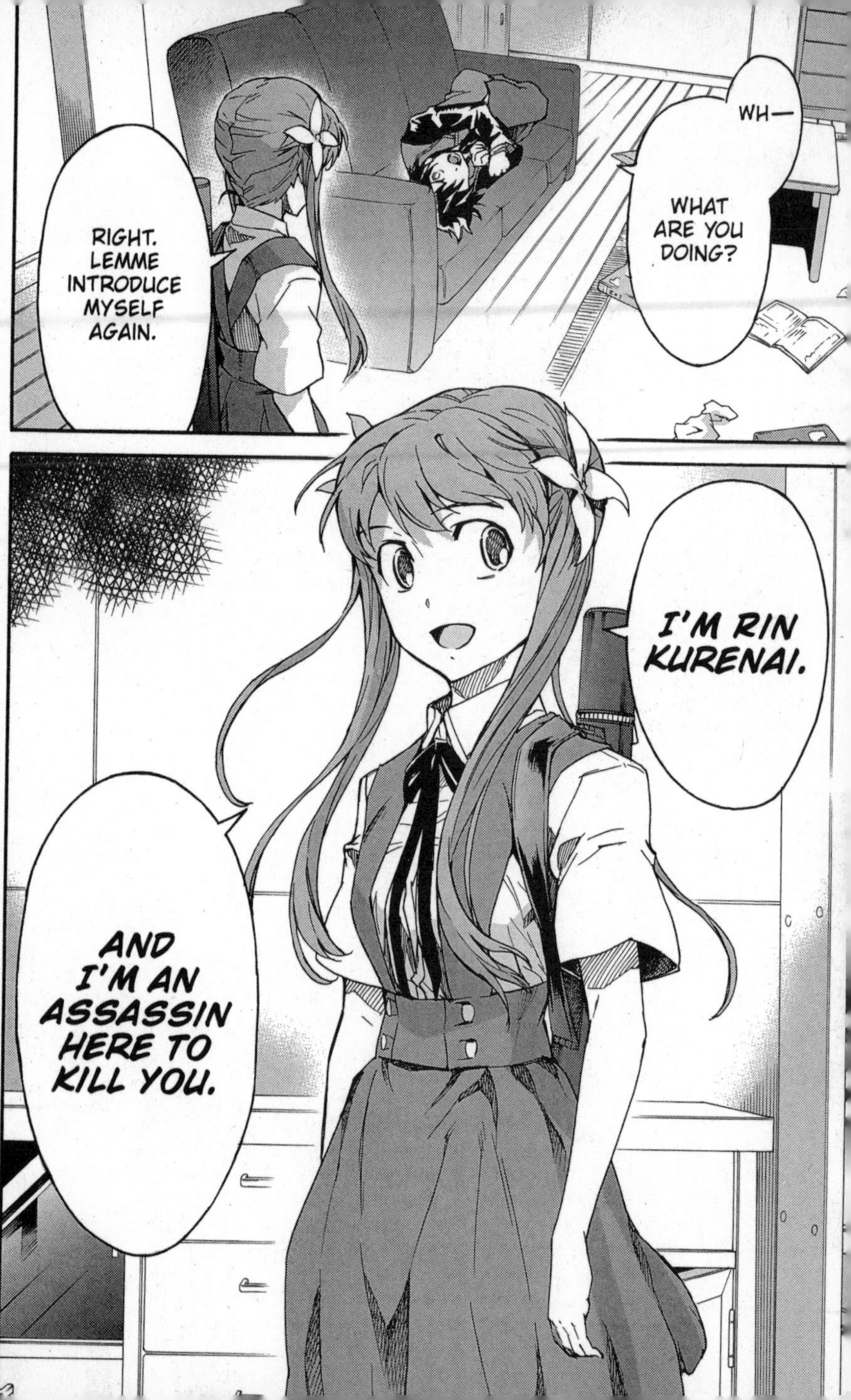
WH—
WHAT ARE YOU DOING?
RIGHT. LEMME INTRODUCE MYSELF AGAIN.
I'M RIN KURENAI.
AND I'M AN ASSASSIN HERE TO KILL YOU.

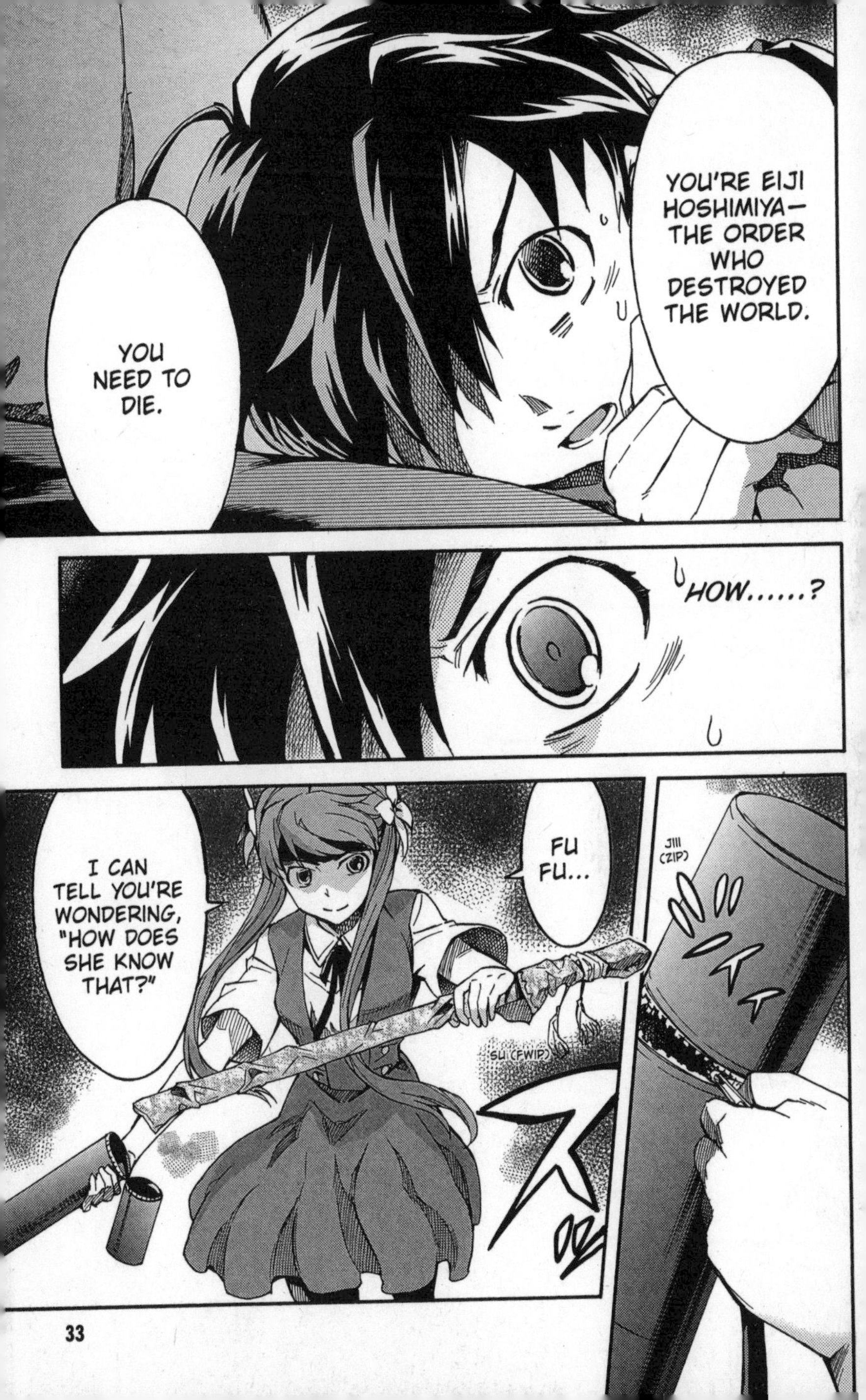
YOU'RE EIJI HOSHIMIYA—THE ORDER WHO DESTROYED THE WORLD.
YOU NEED TO DIE.
HOW......?
JIII (ZIP)
FU FU...
I CAN TELL YOU'RE WONDERING, "HOW DOES SHE KNOW THAT?"
SU (FWIP)

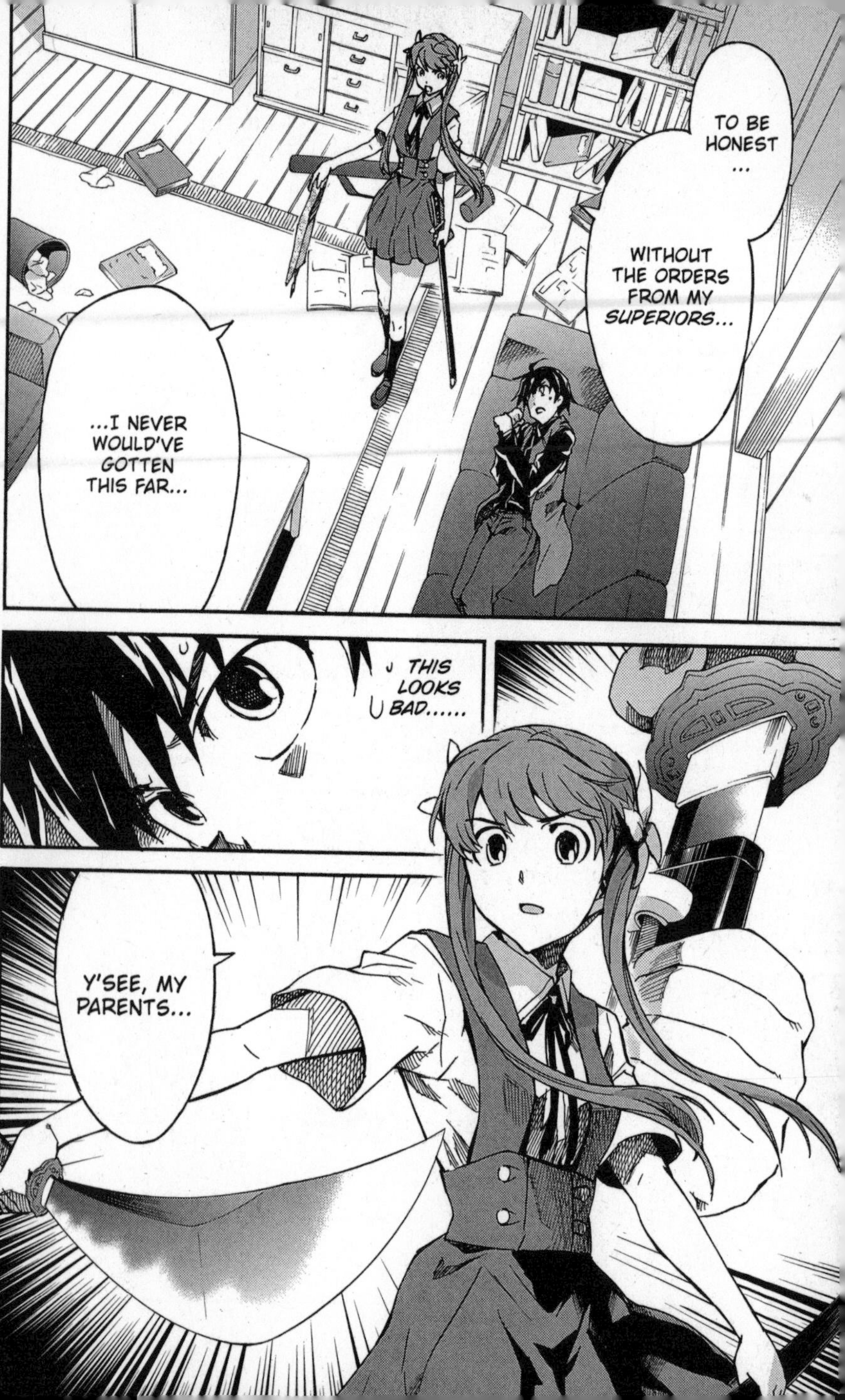
TO BE HONEST ...
WITHOUT THE ORDERS FROM MY SUPERIORS...
...I NEVER WOULD'VE GOTTEN THIS FAR...
THIS LOOKS BAD......
Y'SEE, MY PARENTS...

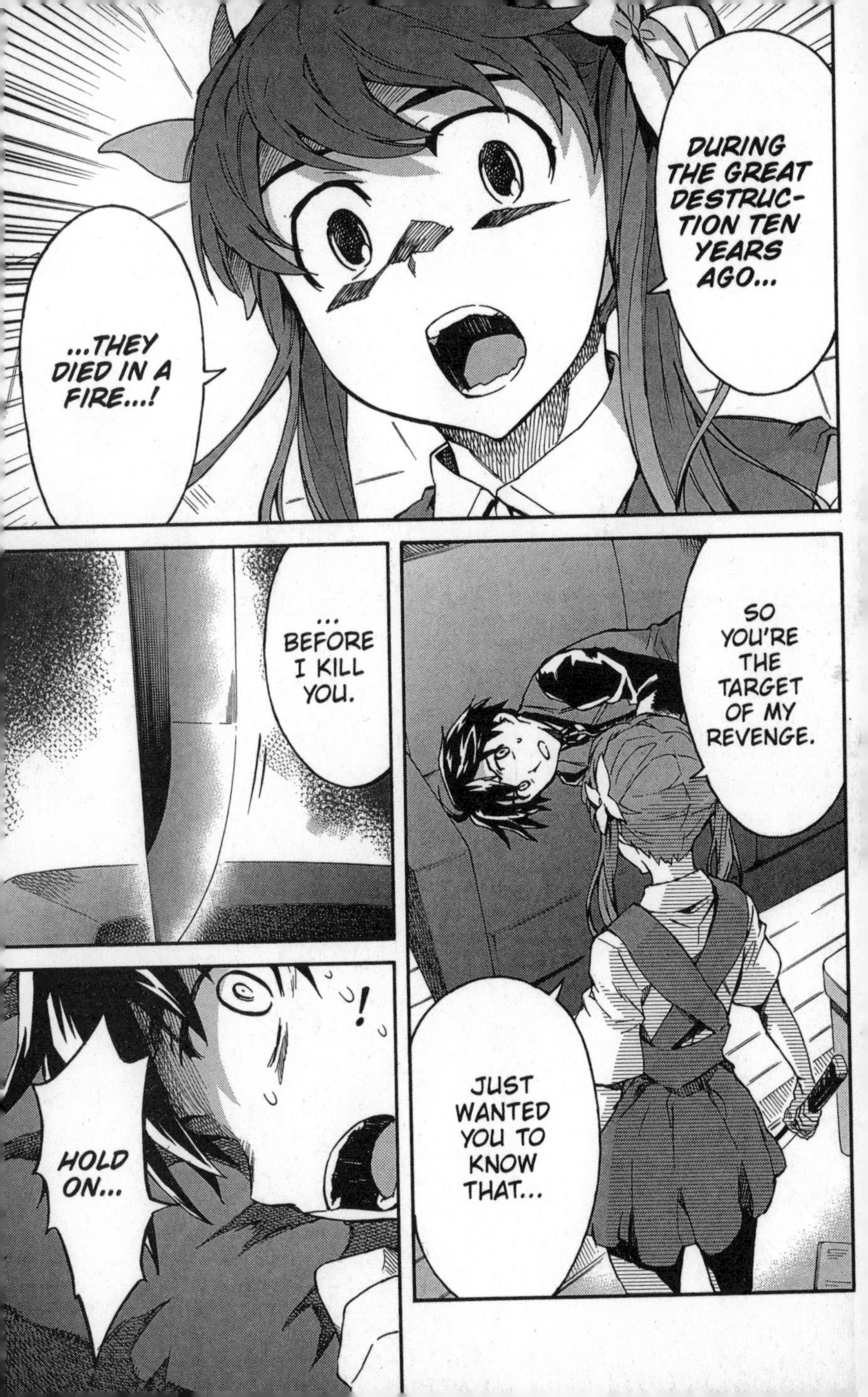
DURING THE GREAT DESTRUCTION TEN YEARS AGO...
...THEY DIED IN A FIRE...!
SO YOU'RE THE TARGET OF MY REVENGE.
JUST WANTED YOU TO KNOW THAT...
... BEFORE I KILL YOU.
!
HOLD ON...

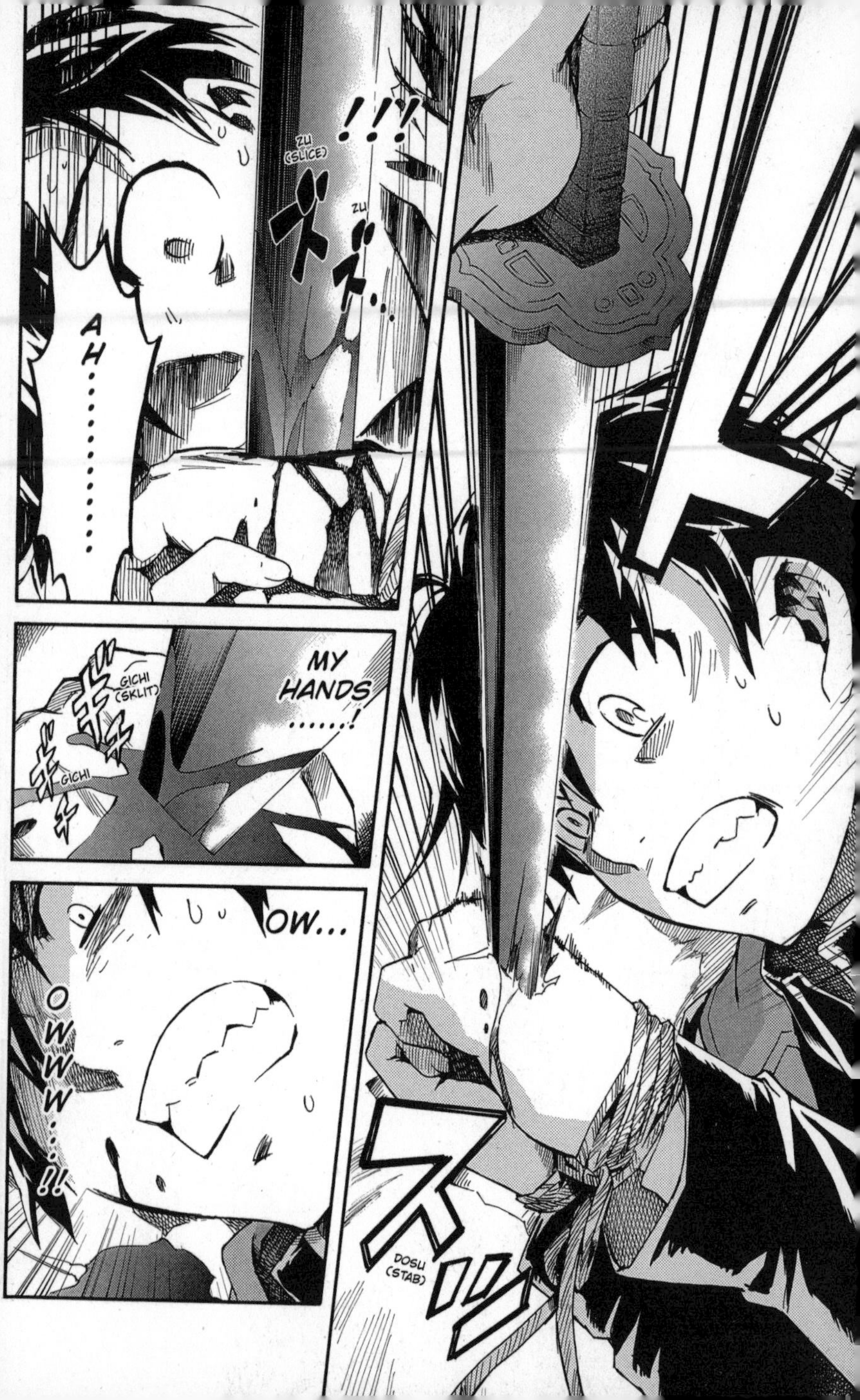
DOSU
(STAB)
!!!
ZU
(SLICE)
ZU
AH.........
MY HANDS
.......!
GICHI
(SKLIT)
GICHI
OW...
OWWW.....!!

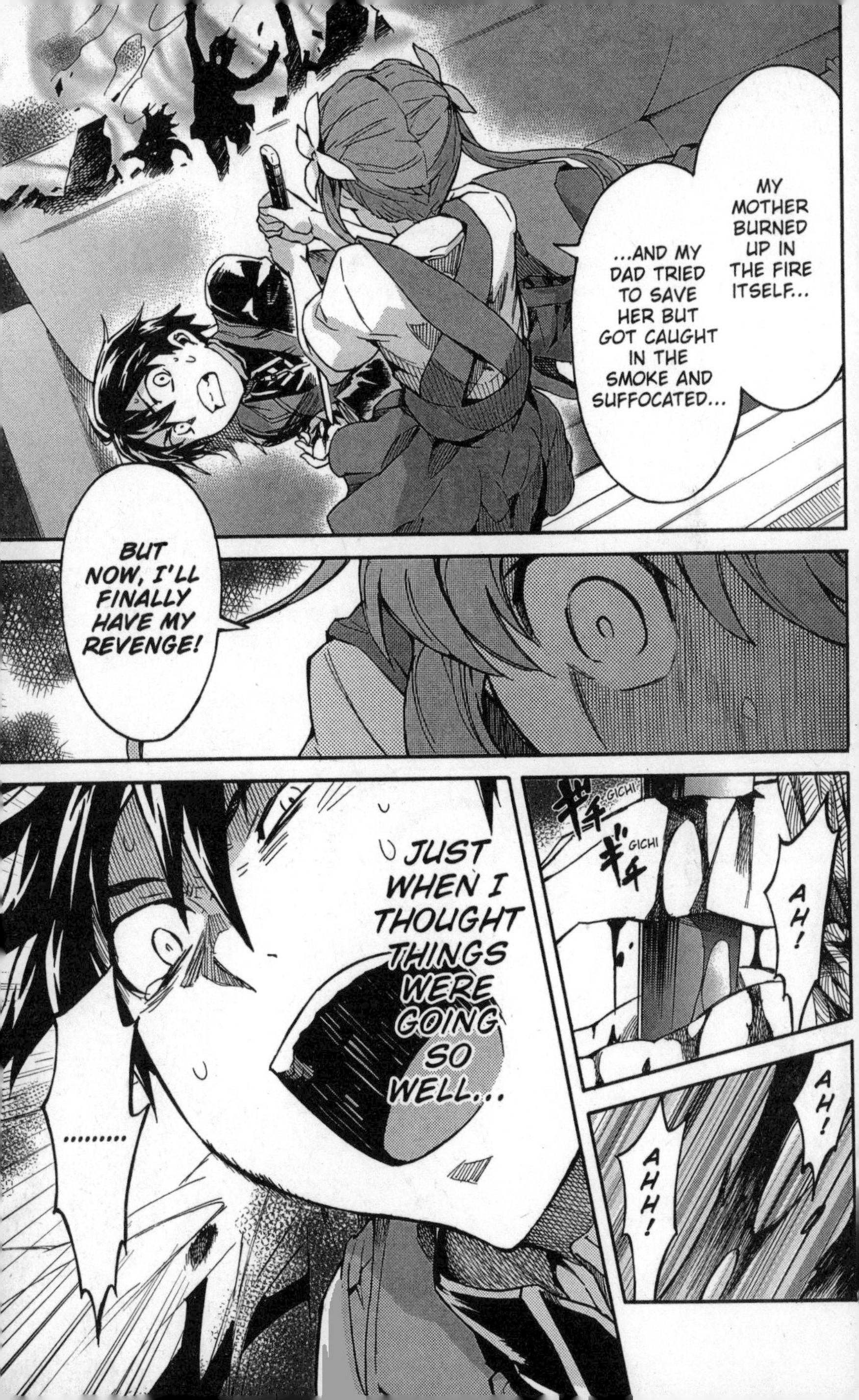
MY MOTHER BURNED UP IN THE FIRE ITSELF...
...AND MY DAD TRIED TO SAVE HER BUT GOT CAUGHT IN THE SMOKE AND SUFFOCATED...
BUT NOW, I'LL FINALLY HAVE MY REVENGE!
GICHI
GICHI
AH!
AH!
AHH!
JUST WHEN I THOUGHT THINGS WERE GOING SO WELL...
.........

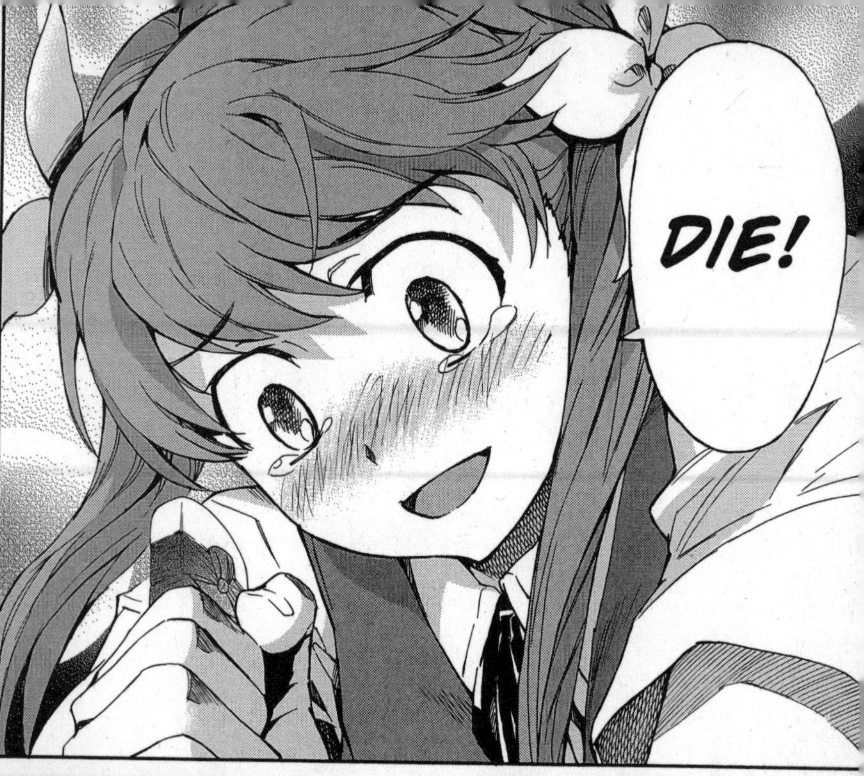
DIE!
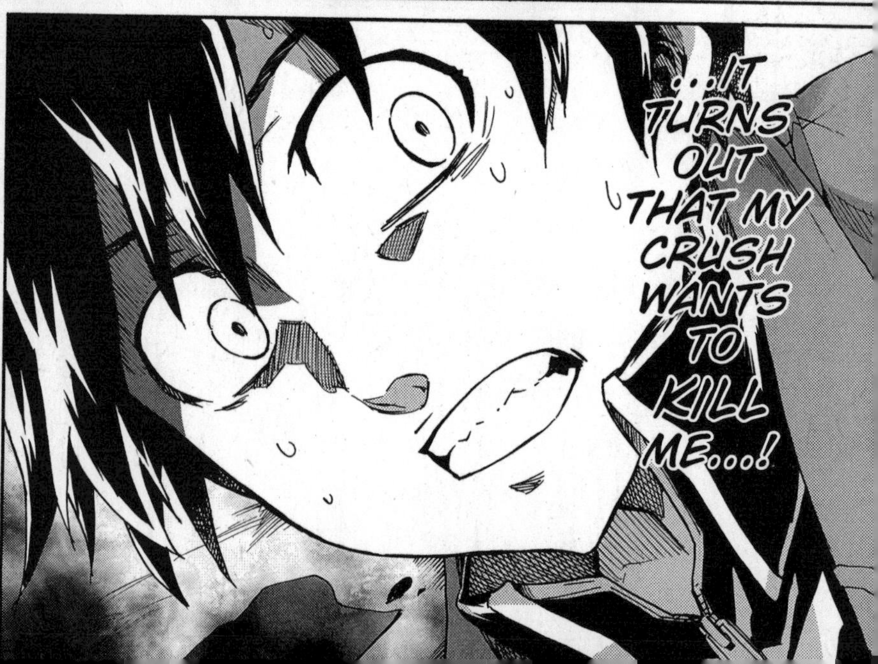
...IT TURNS OUT THAT MY CRUSH WANTS TO KILL ME...!

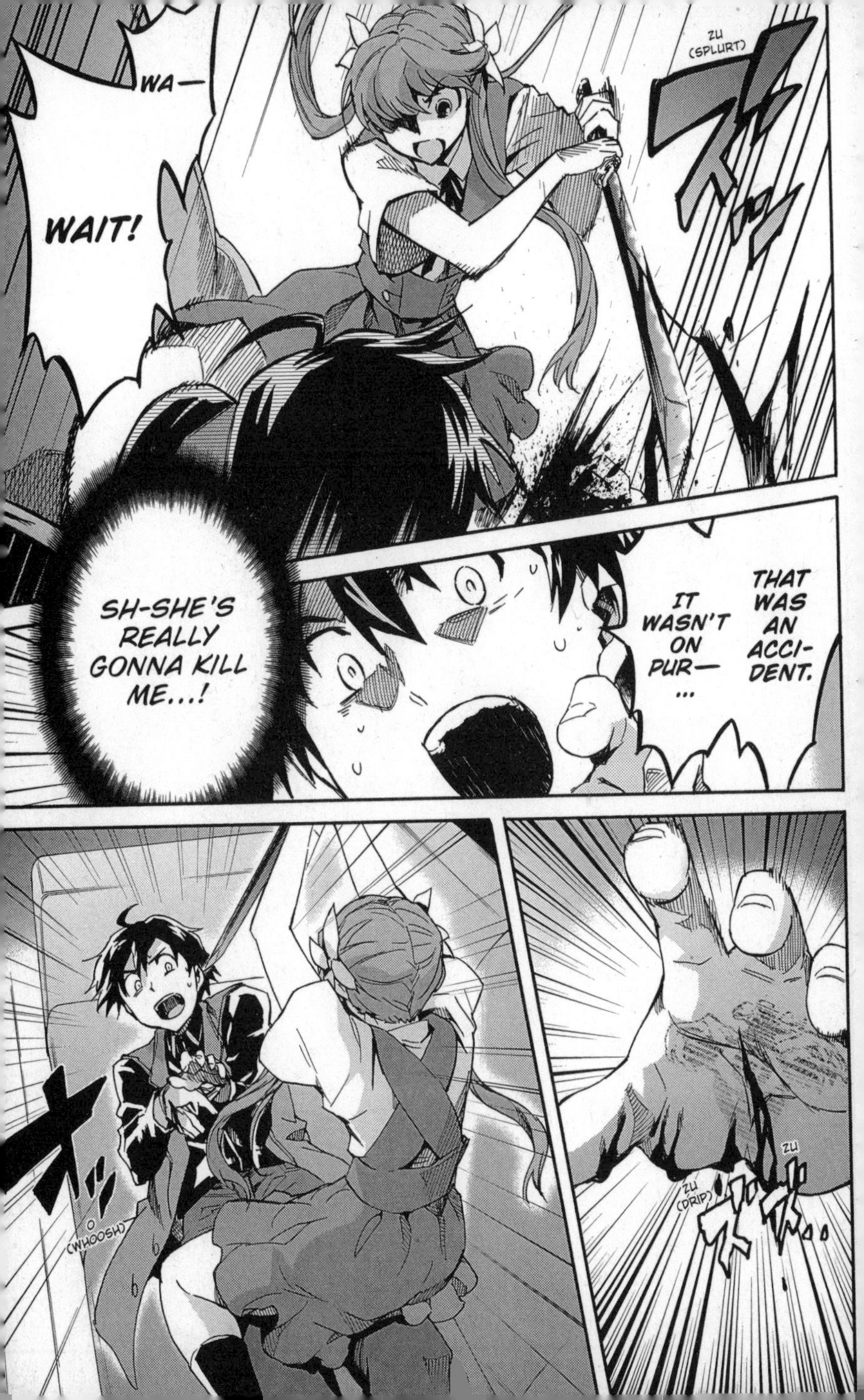
ZU (SPLURT)
WA—
WAIT!
THAT WAS AN ACCIDENT.
IT WASN'T ON PUR—...
SH-SHE'S REALLY GONNA KILL ME...!
ZU
ZU (DRIP)
O (WHOOSH)

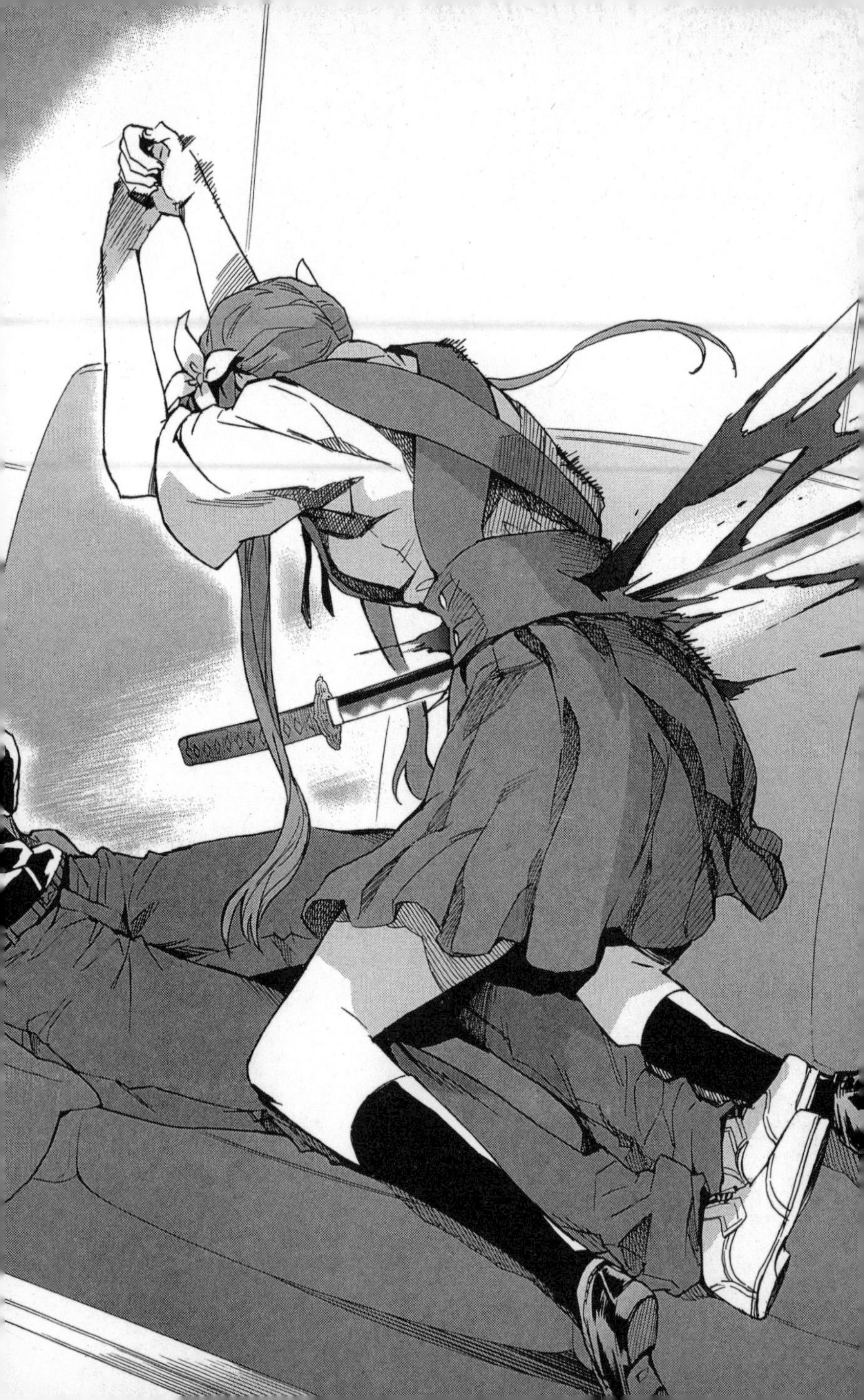

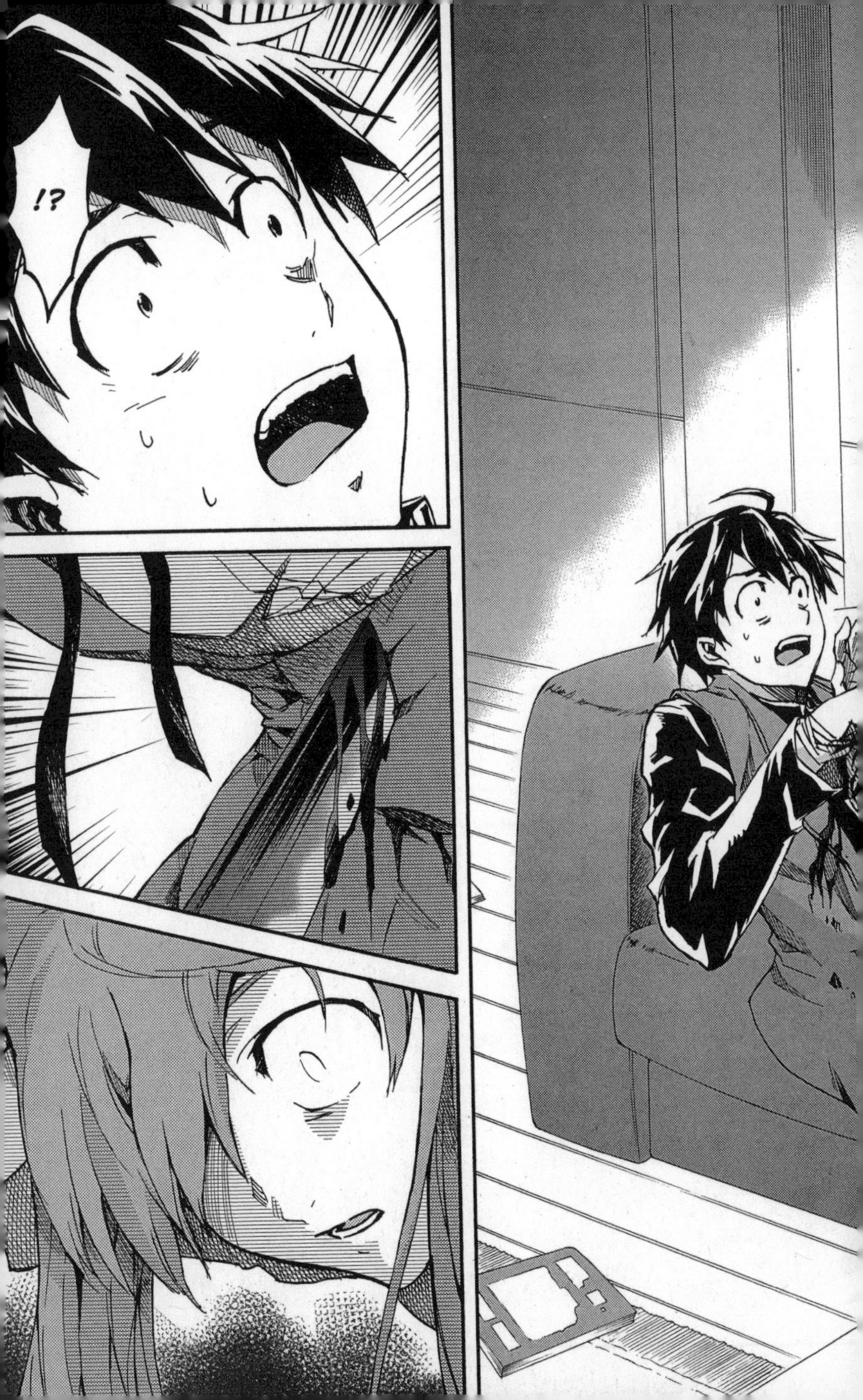
!?

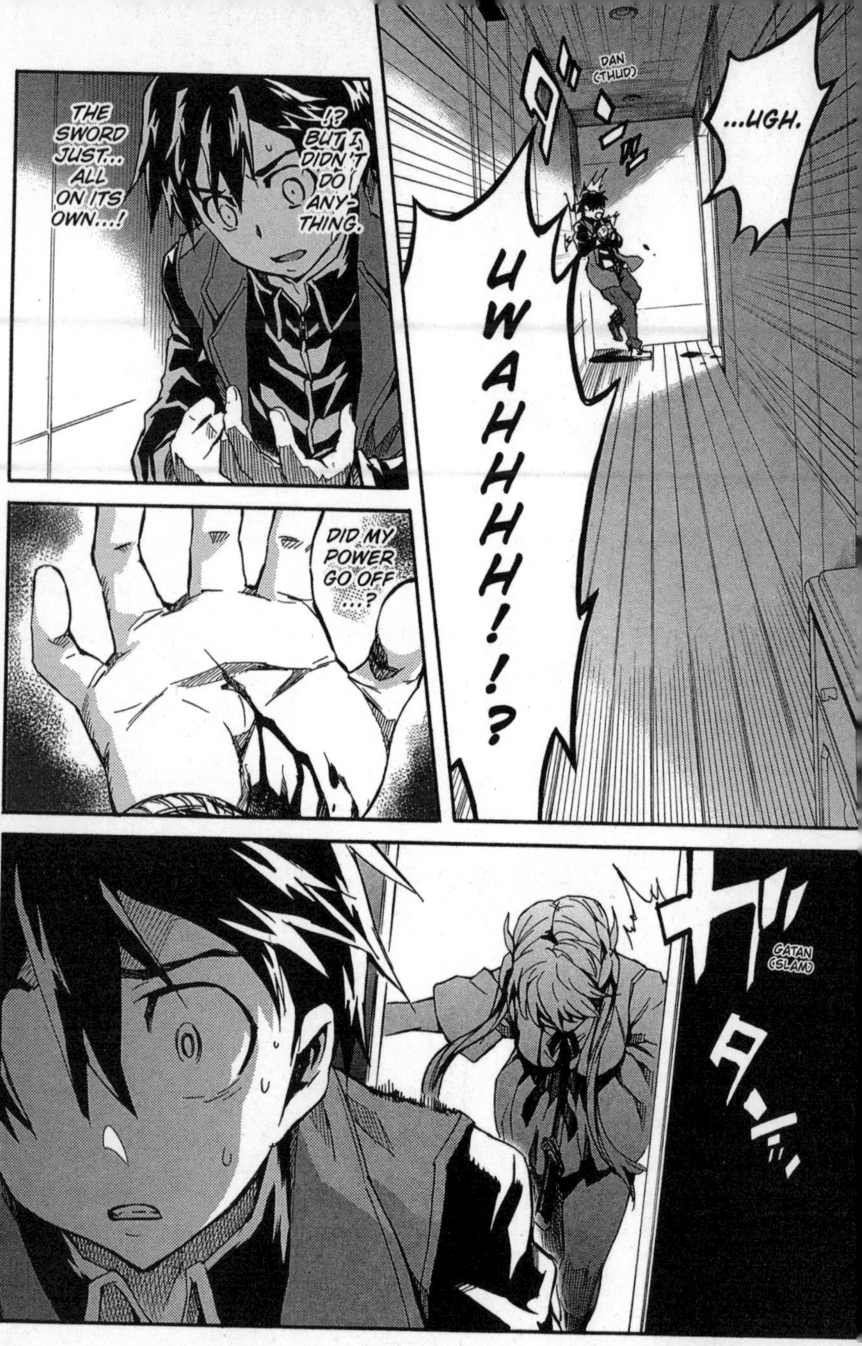
DAN (THUD)
...UGH.
UWAHHHHH!!!?
!? BUT I DIDN'T DO ANYTHING.
THE SWORD JUST... ALL ON ITS OWN...!
DID MY POWER GO OFF...?
GATAN (SLAM)

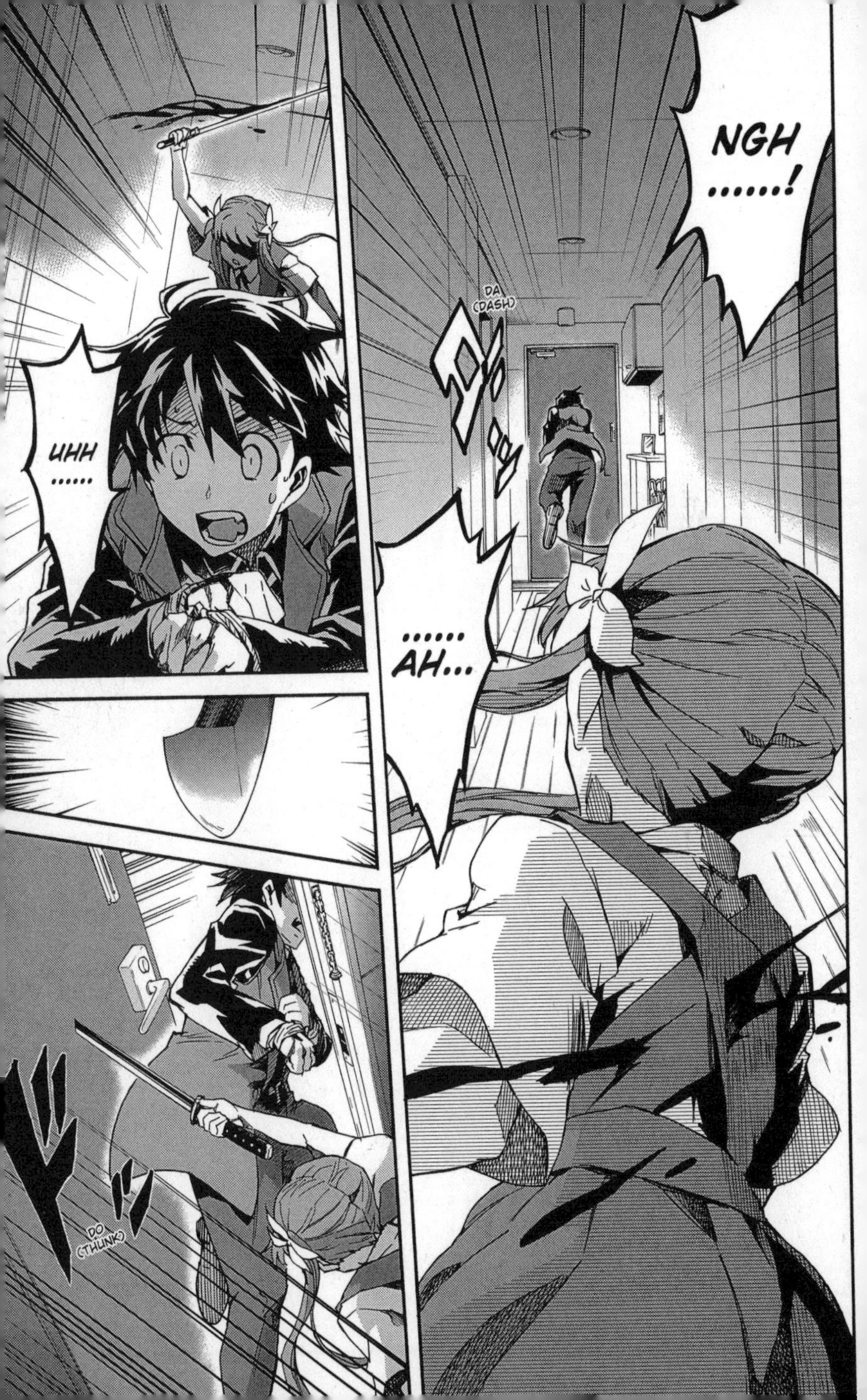
NGH ……!
DA (DASH)
…… AH…
UHH ……
DO (THUNK)

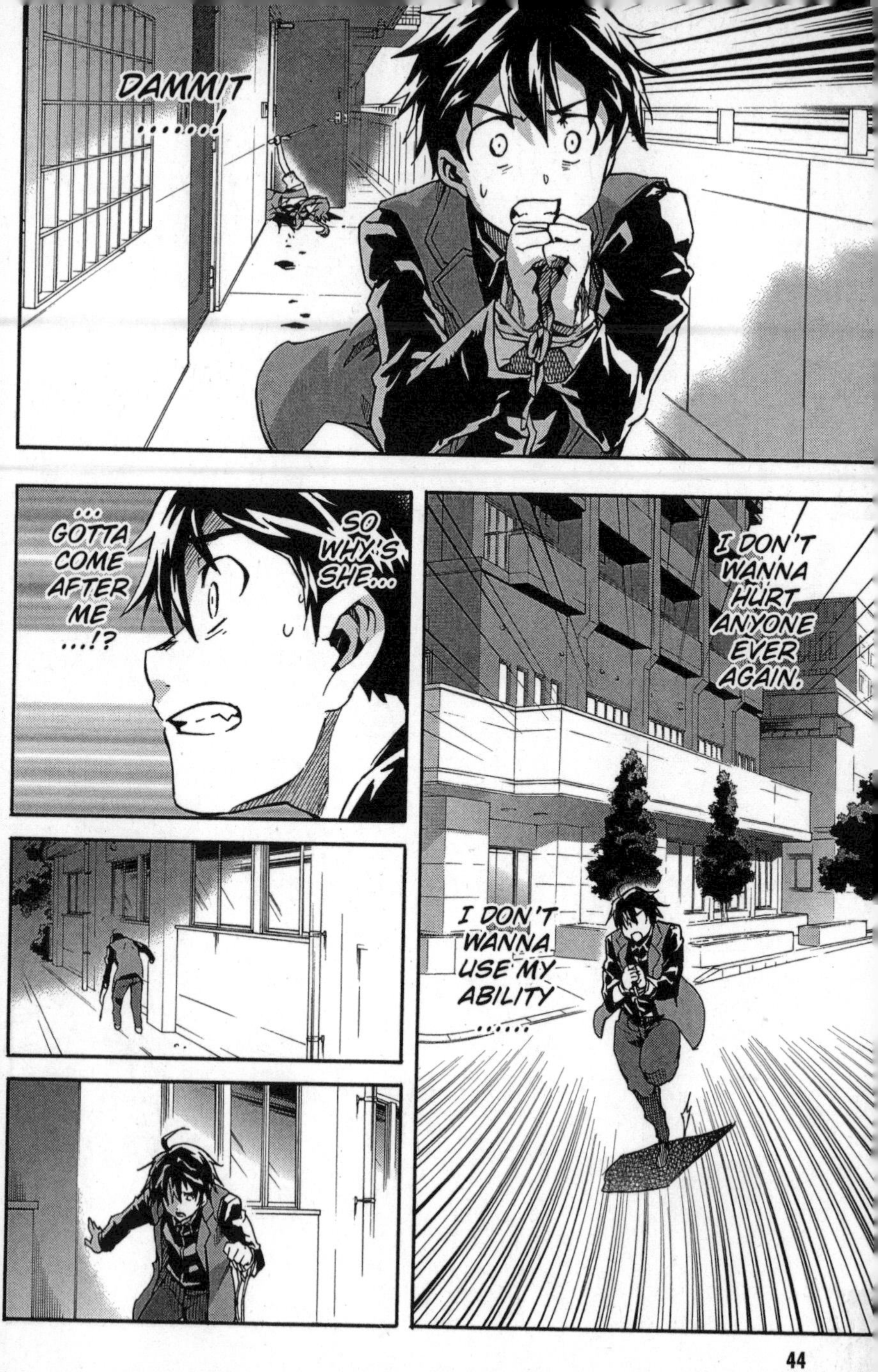
DAMMIT ......!
I DON'T WANNA HURT ANYONE EVER AGAIN.
I DON'T WANNA USE MY ABILITY ......
SO WHY'S SHE...
...GOTTA COME AFTER ME ...!?

I...
ENDED UP
HURTING
SOMEONE
AGAIN...

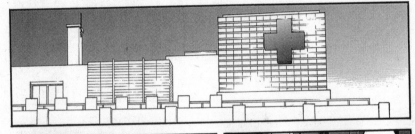

WHAT'S
GOING
ON?

HELLO
...

AH.

BIG
BROTHER
?

I THINK
UNCLE IS
STILL
ATTENDING
TO THE
OTHER
PATIENTS...

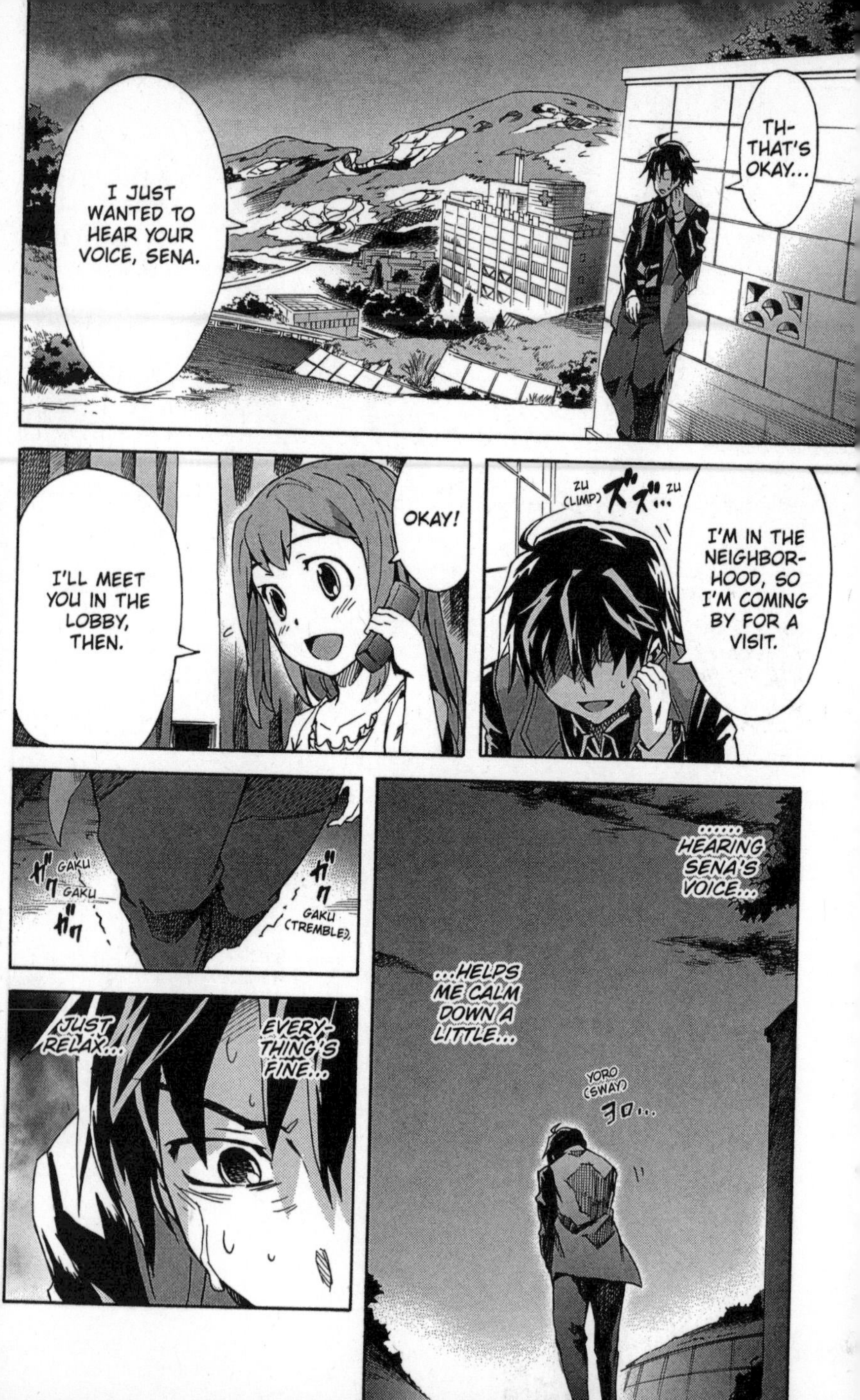
TH-THAT'S OKAY...
I JUST WANTED TO HEAR YOUR VOICE, SENA.
ZU (LIMP) ズズ... ZU
I'M IN THE NEIGHBOR-HOOD, SO I'M COMING BY FOR A VISIT.
OKAY!
I'LL MEET YOU IN THE LOBBY, THEN.
...... HEARING SENA'S VOICE...
...HELPS ME CALM DOWN A LITTLE...
YORO (SWAY) ヨロ...
ガク GAKU (TREMBLE)
ガク GAKU
ガク GAKU
ガク
EVERY-THING'S FINE...
JUST RELAX...

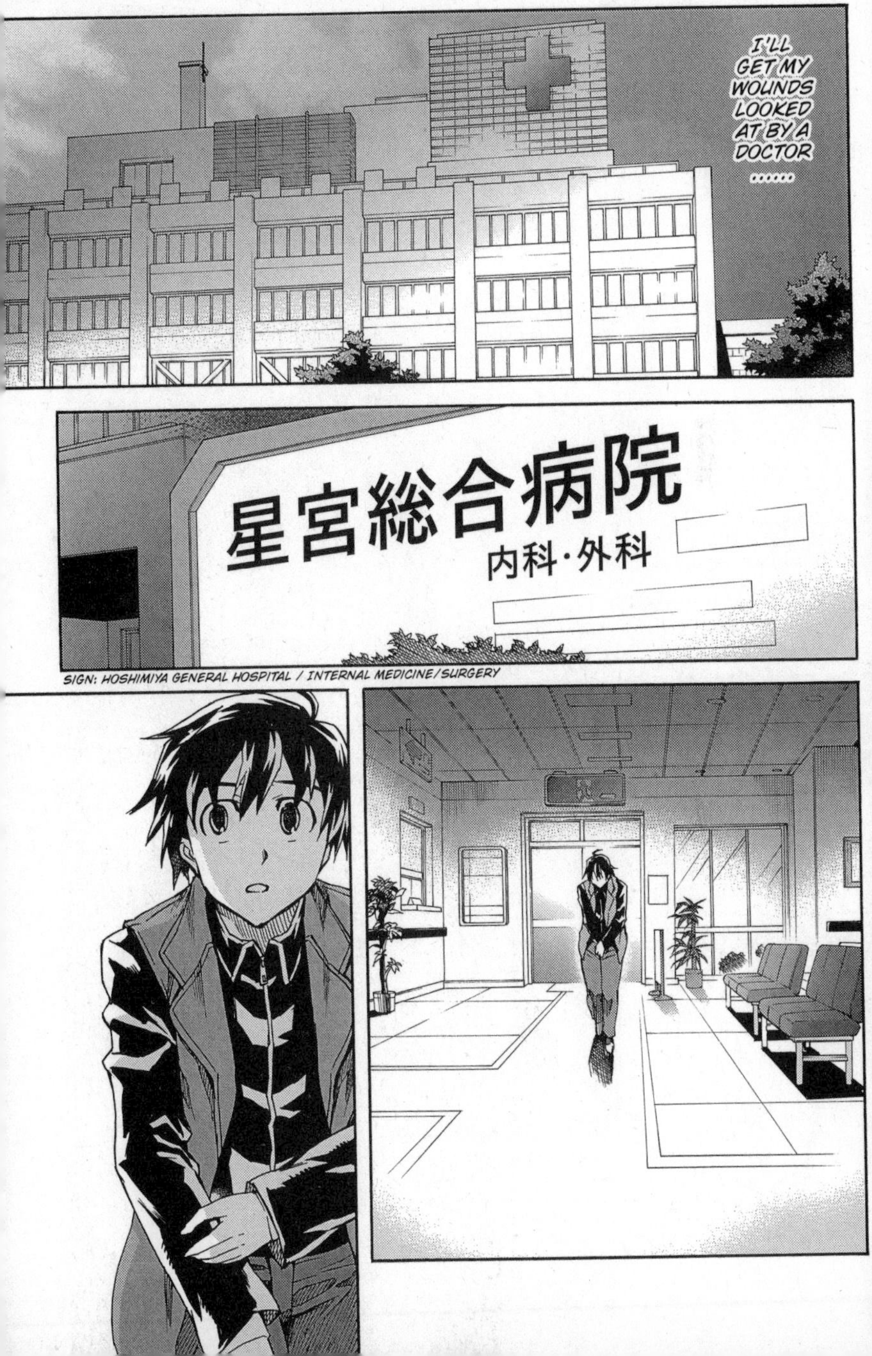
I'LL GET MY WOUNDS LOOKED AT BY A DOCTOR ......
星宮総合病院
内科·外科
SIGN: HOSHIMIYA GENERAL HOSPITAL / INTERNAL MEDICINE/SURGERY

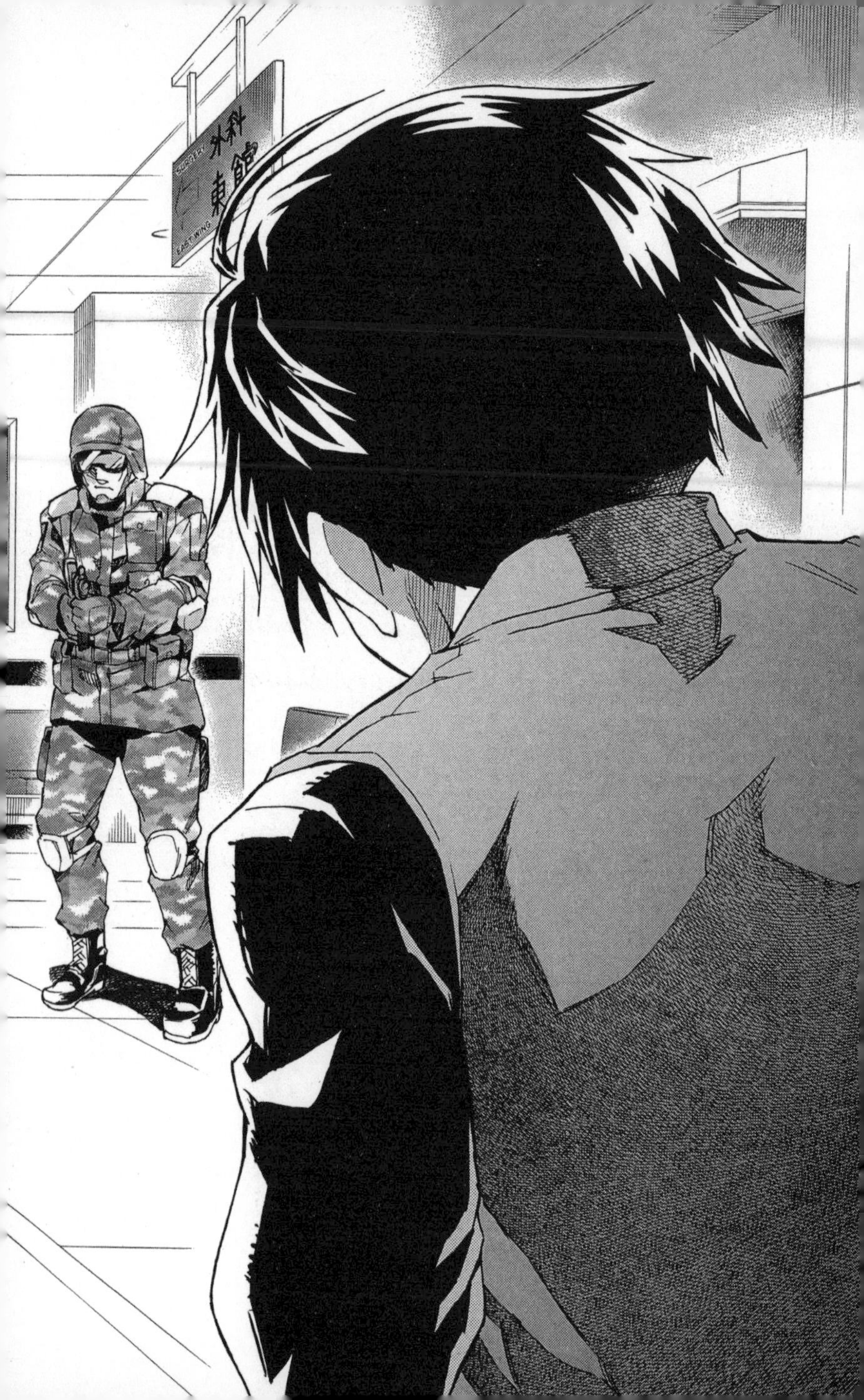
外科
SURGERY
東館
EAST WING

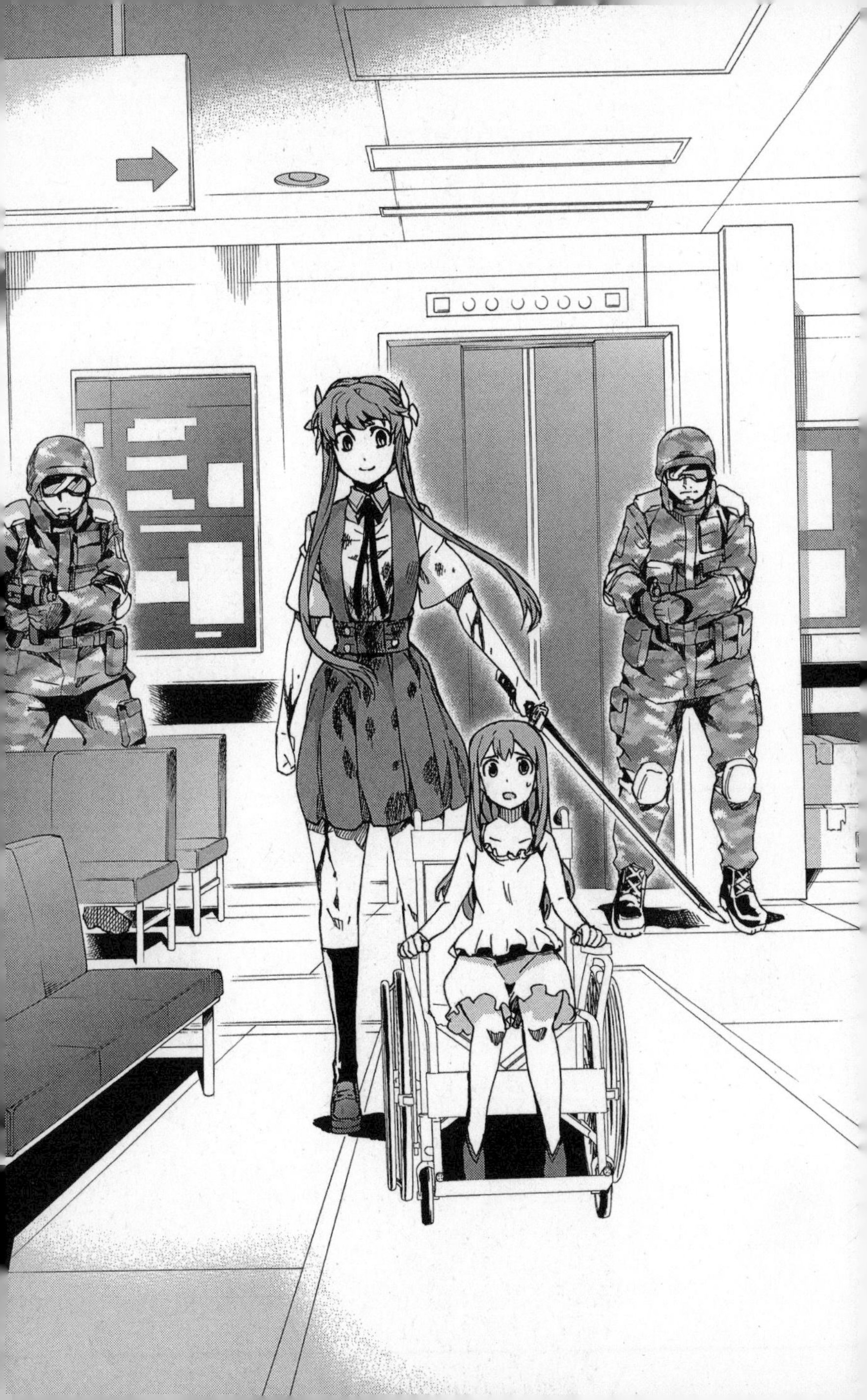

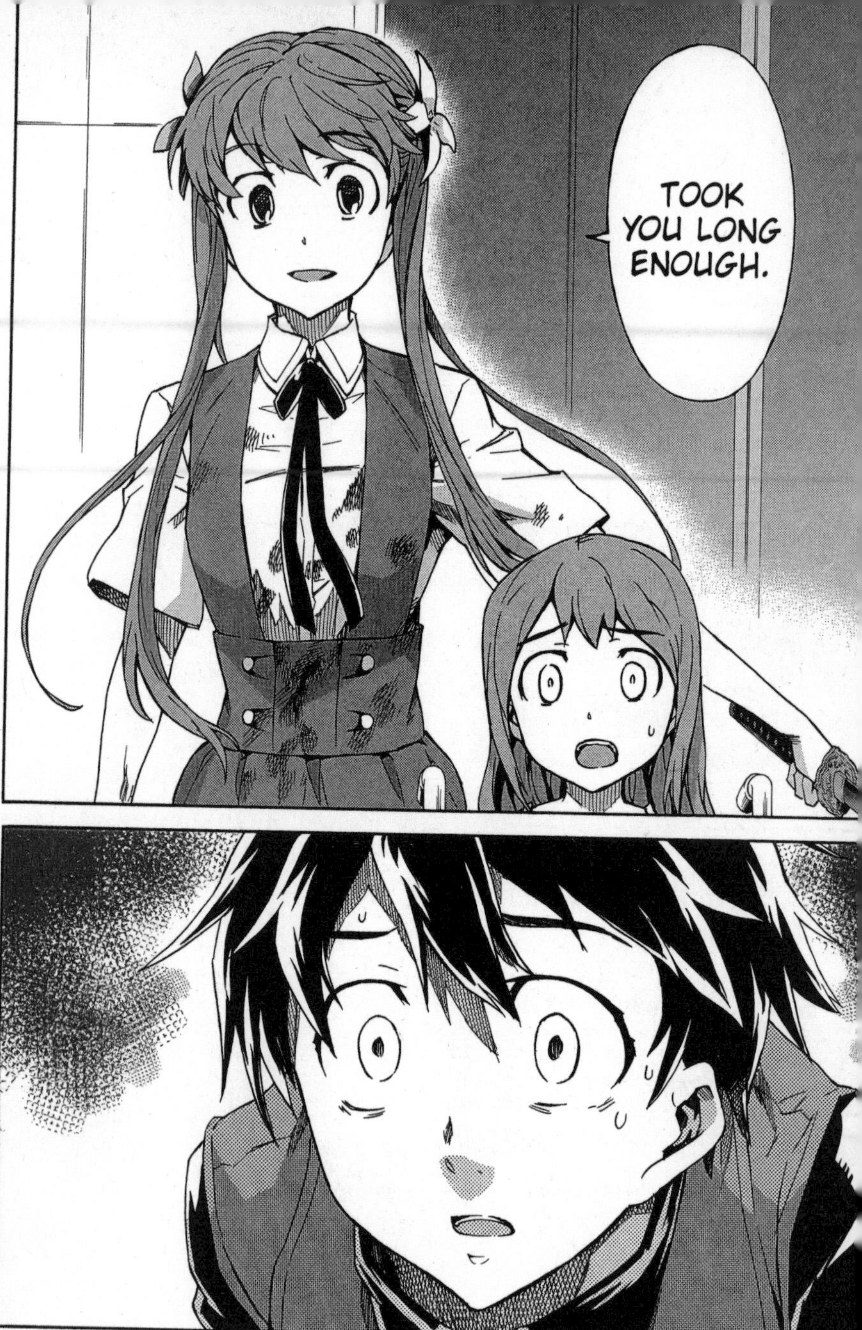
TOOK YOU LONG ENOUGH.

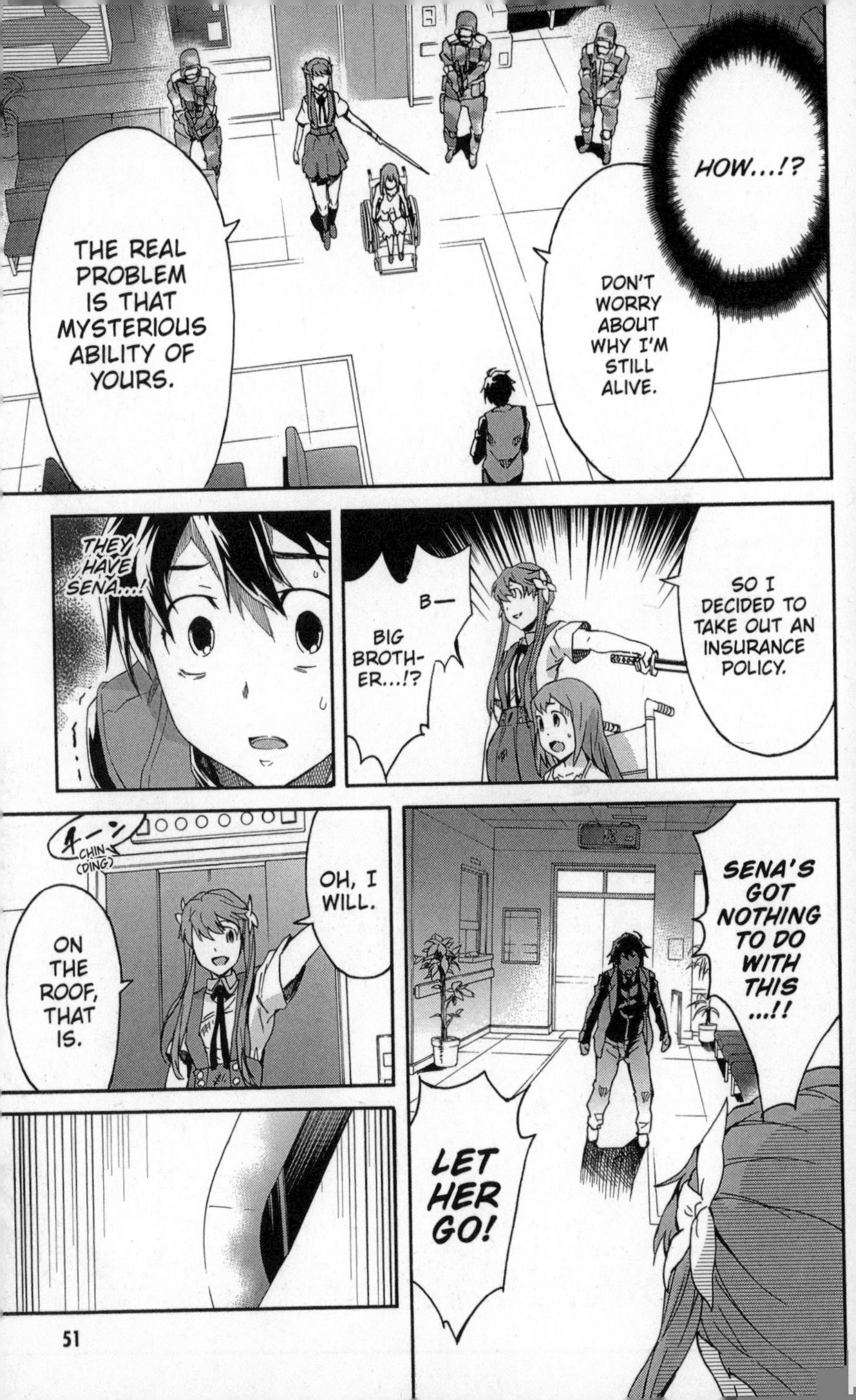
HOW...!?
DON'T WORRY ABOUT WHY I'M STILL ALIVE.
THE REAL PROBLEM IS THAT MYSTERIOUS ABILITY OF YOURS.
SO I DECIDED TO TAKE OUT AN INSURANCE POLICY.
B— BIG BROTH-ER...!?
THEY HAVE SENA...!
SENA'S GOT NOTHING TO DO WITH THIS ...!!
LET HER GO!
OH, I WILL.
チーン
CHIN (DING)
ON THE ROOF, THAT IS.

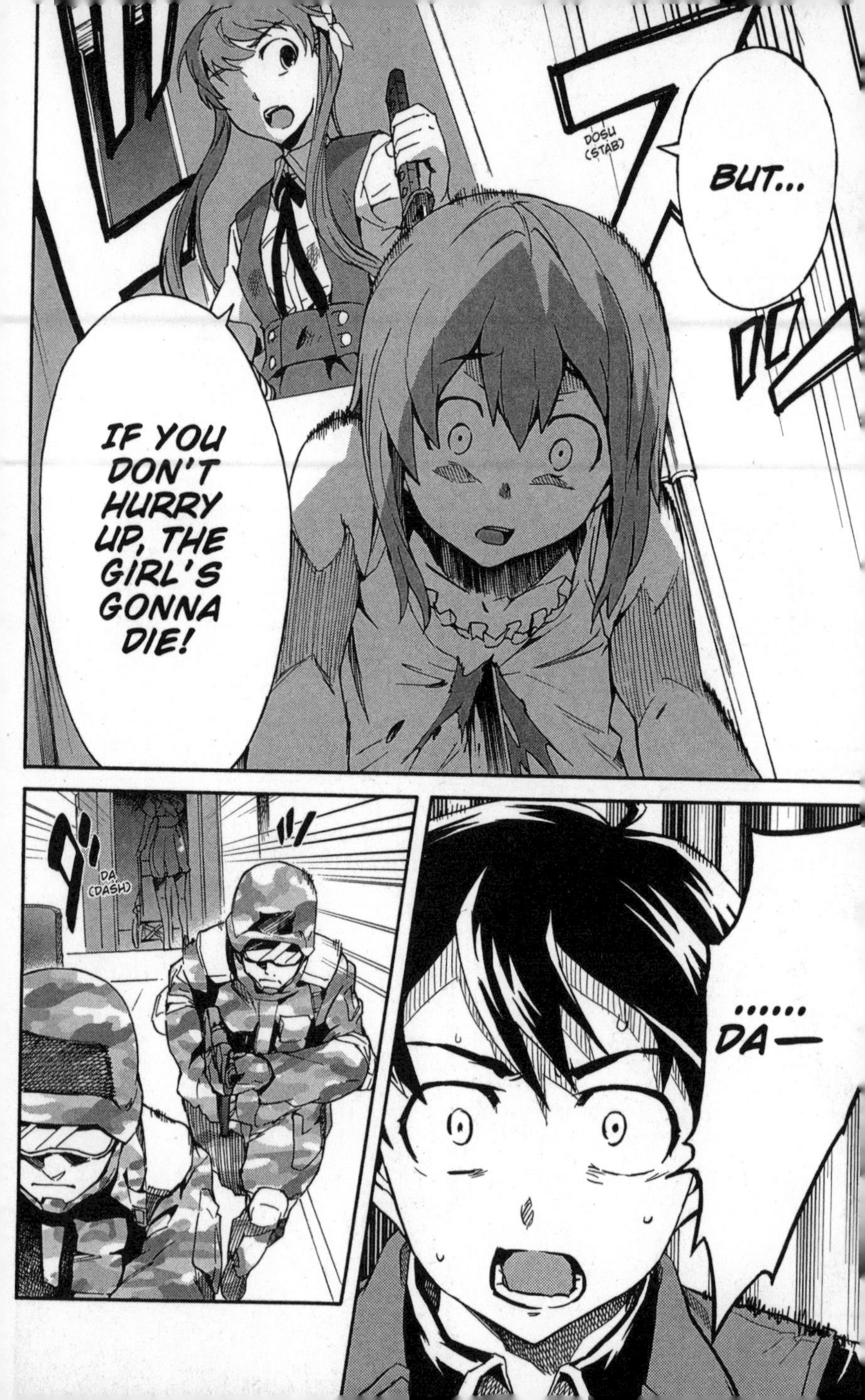
BUT...
DOSU (STAB)
IF YOU DON'T HURRY UP, THE GIRL'S GONNA DIE!
......DA—
DA (DASH)

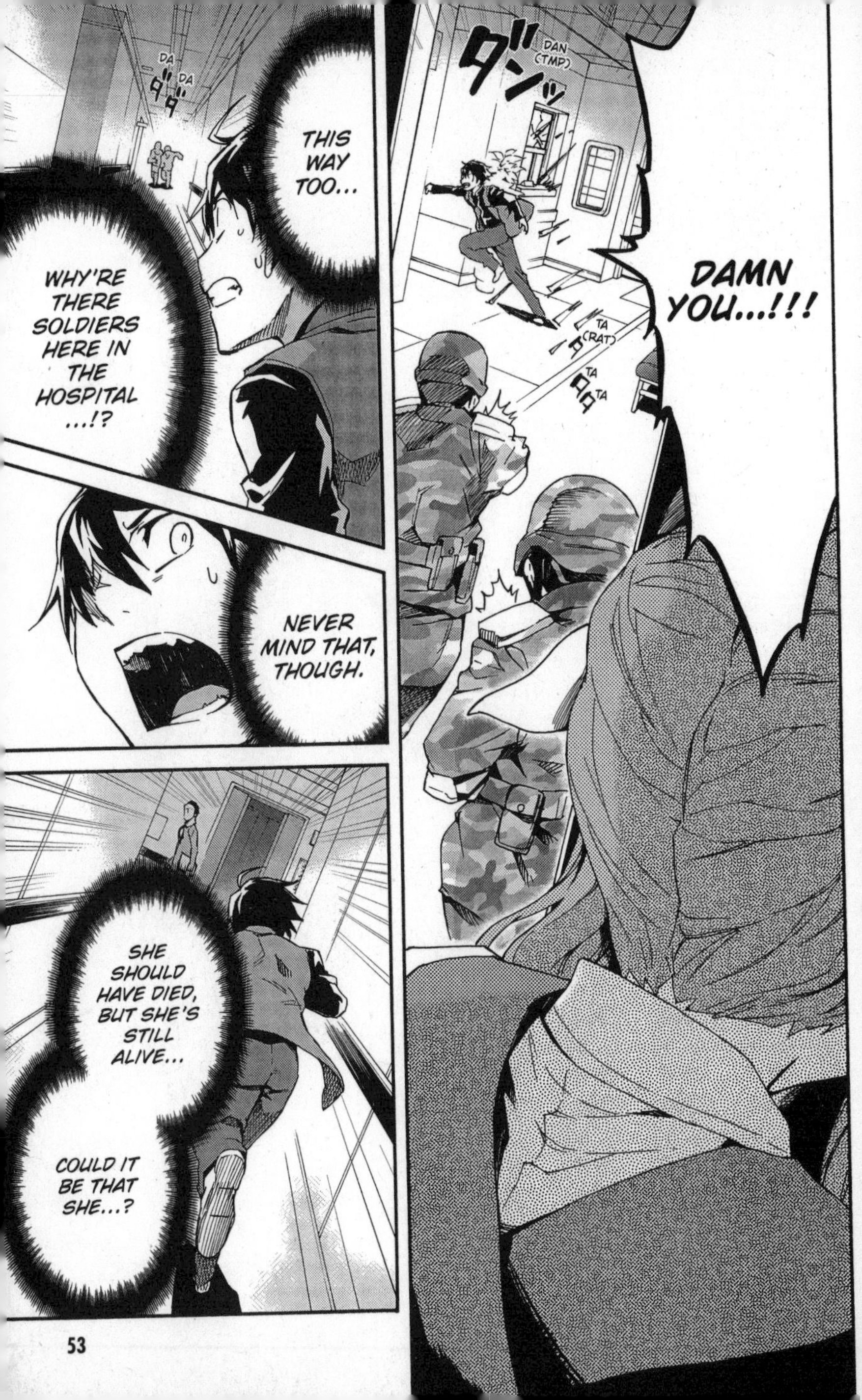
ダンッ
DAN (TMP)
DAMN YOU...!!!
TA (RAT)
TA
TA
ダダ
DA
DA
THIS WAY TOO...
WHY'RE THERE SOLDIERS HERE IN THE HOSPITAL ...!?
NEVER MIND THAT, THOUGH.
SHE SHOULD HAVE DIED, BUT SHE'S STILL ALIVE...
COULD IT BE THAT SHE...?

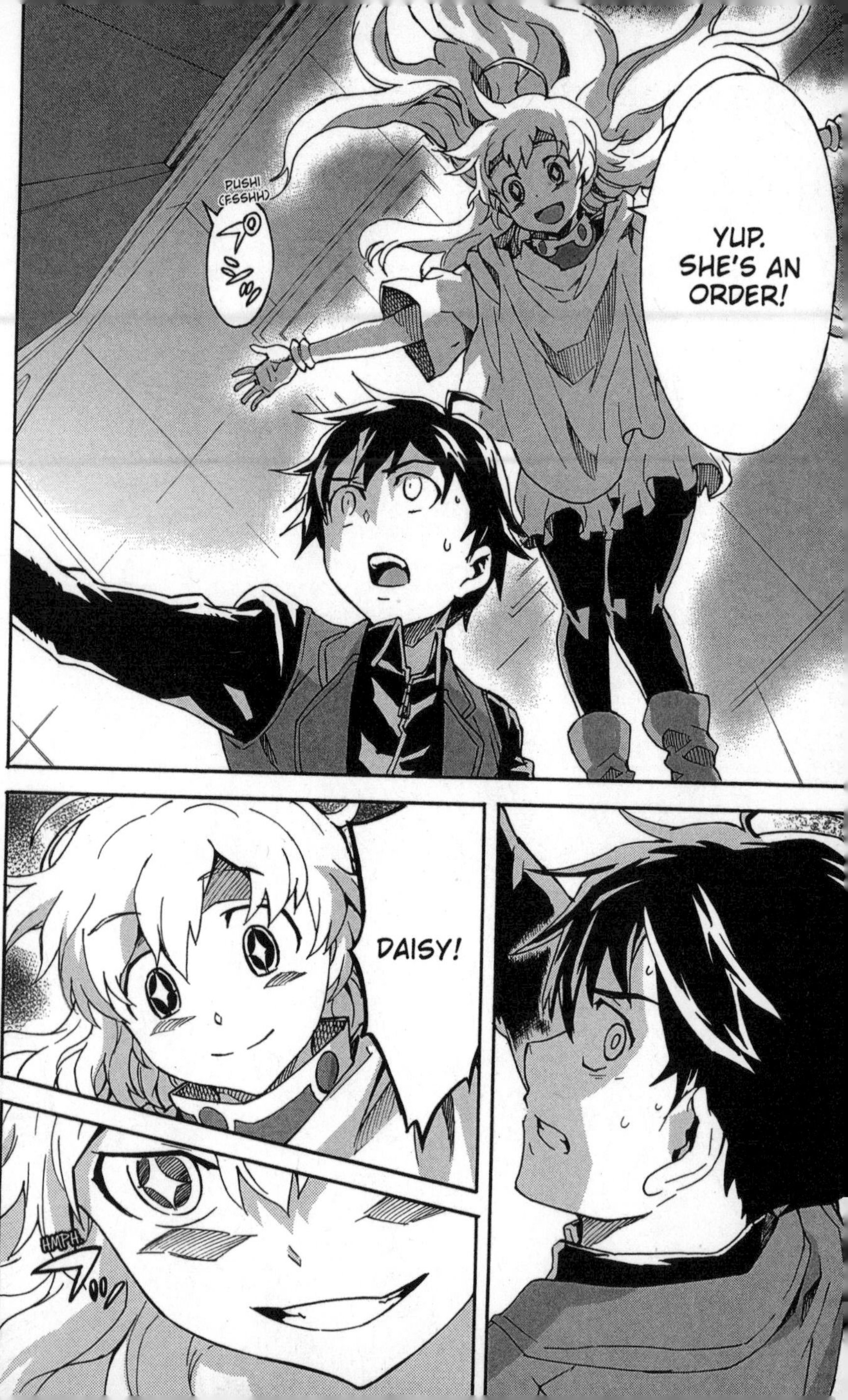
YUP. SHE'S AN ORDER!
PUSHI (FSSHH)
DAISY!
HMPH.

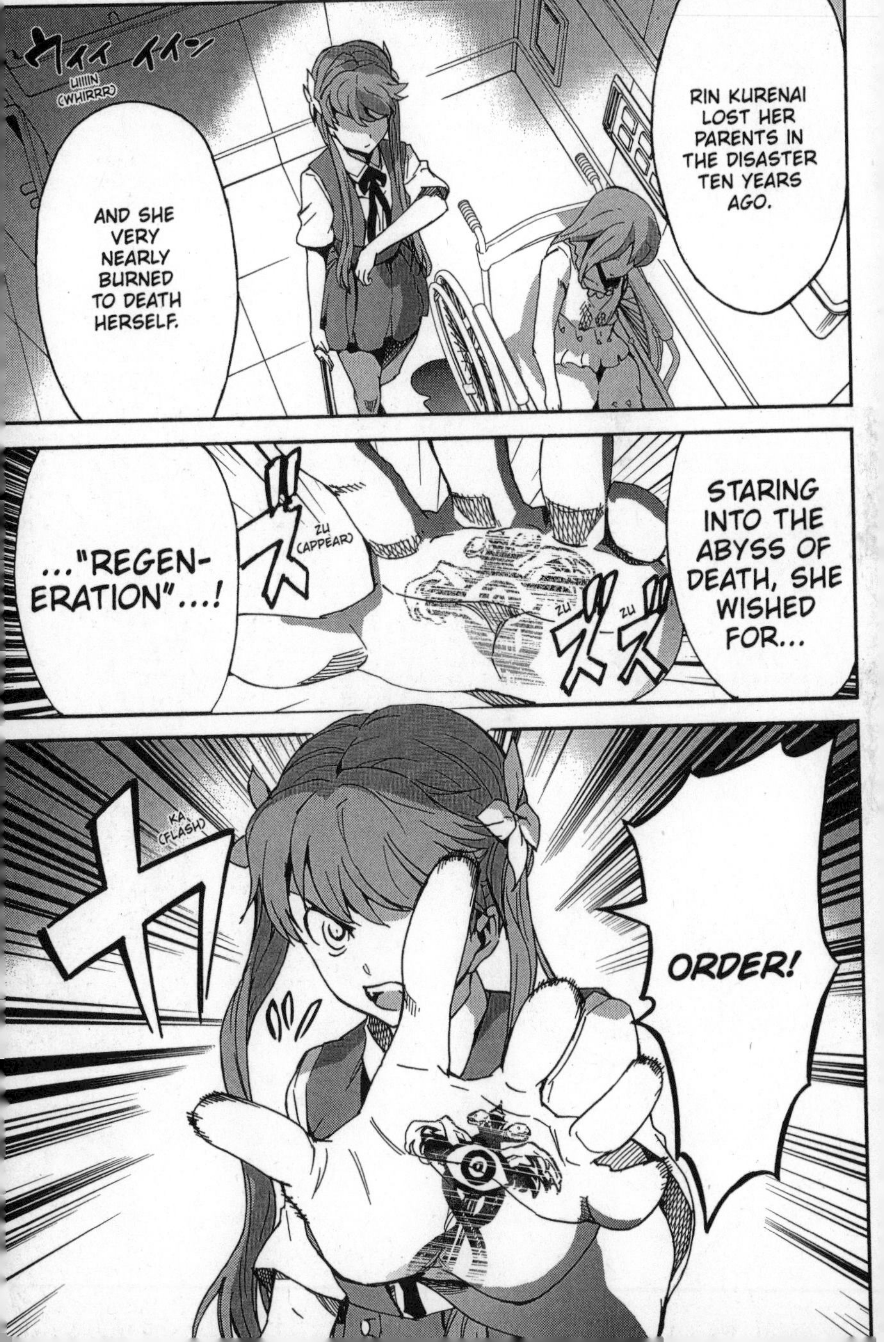
RIN KURENAI LOST HER PARENTS IN THE DISASTER TEN YEARS AGO.
ウィイ イイン
UIIIIN (WHIRRR)
AND SHE VERY NEARLY BURNED TO DEATH HERSELF.
STARING INTO THE ABYSS OF DEATH, SHE WISHED FOR...
ズズ
ZU ZU
ズ
ZU (APPEAR)
..."REGEN-ERATION"...!
ORDER!
カ
KA (FLASH)

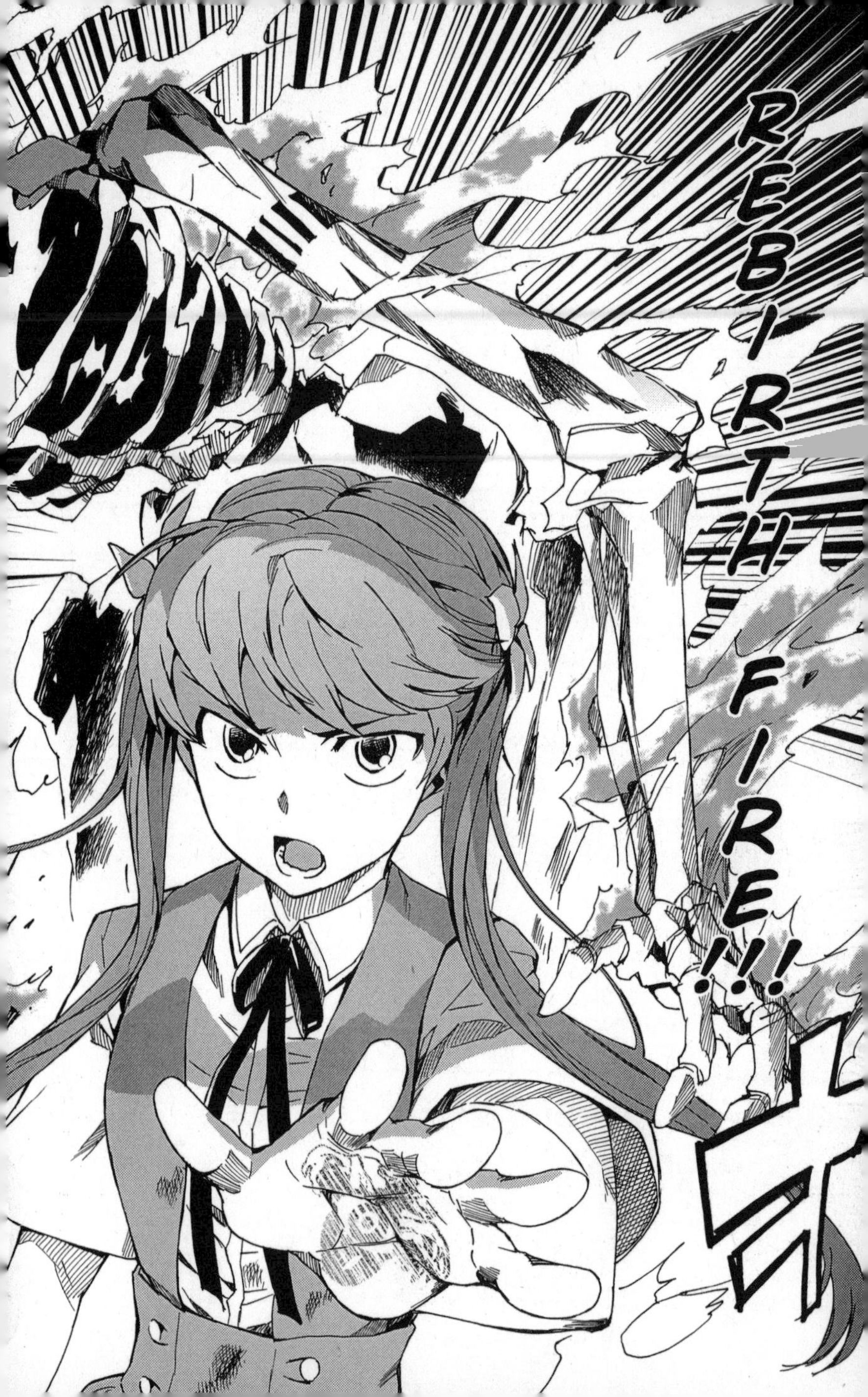
REBIRTH FIRE!!!

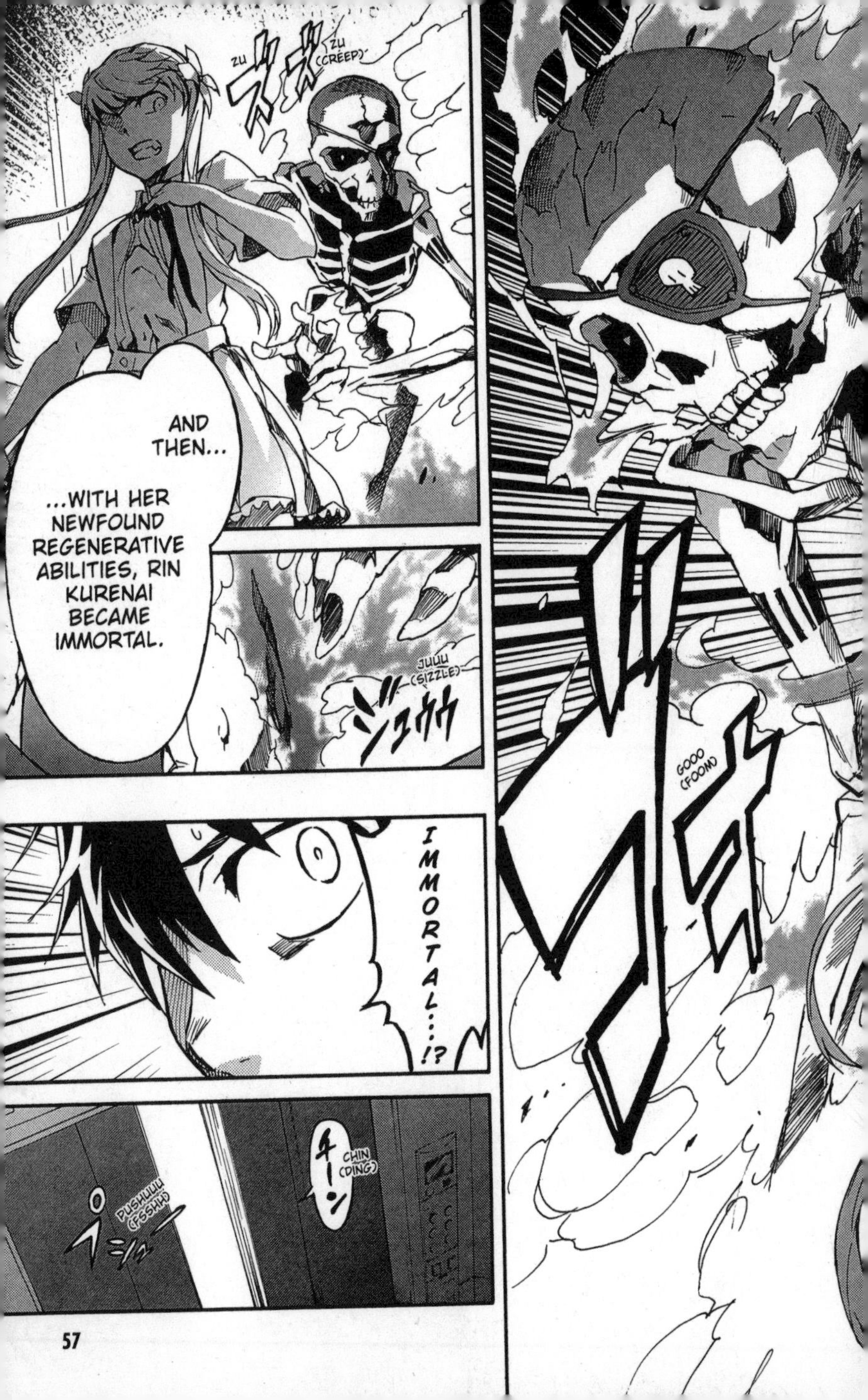
GOOO (FOOM)
ZU ZU (CREEP)
AND THEN...
...WITH HER NEWFOUND REGENERATIVE ABILITIES, RIN KURENAI BECAME IMMORTAL.
JUUU (SIZZLE)
IMMORTAL...!?
CHIN (DING)
PUSHUUU (FSSHH)

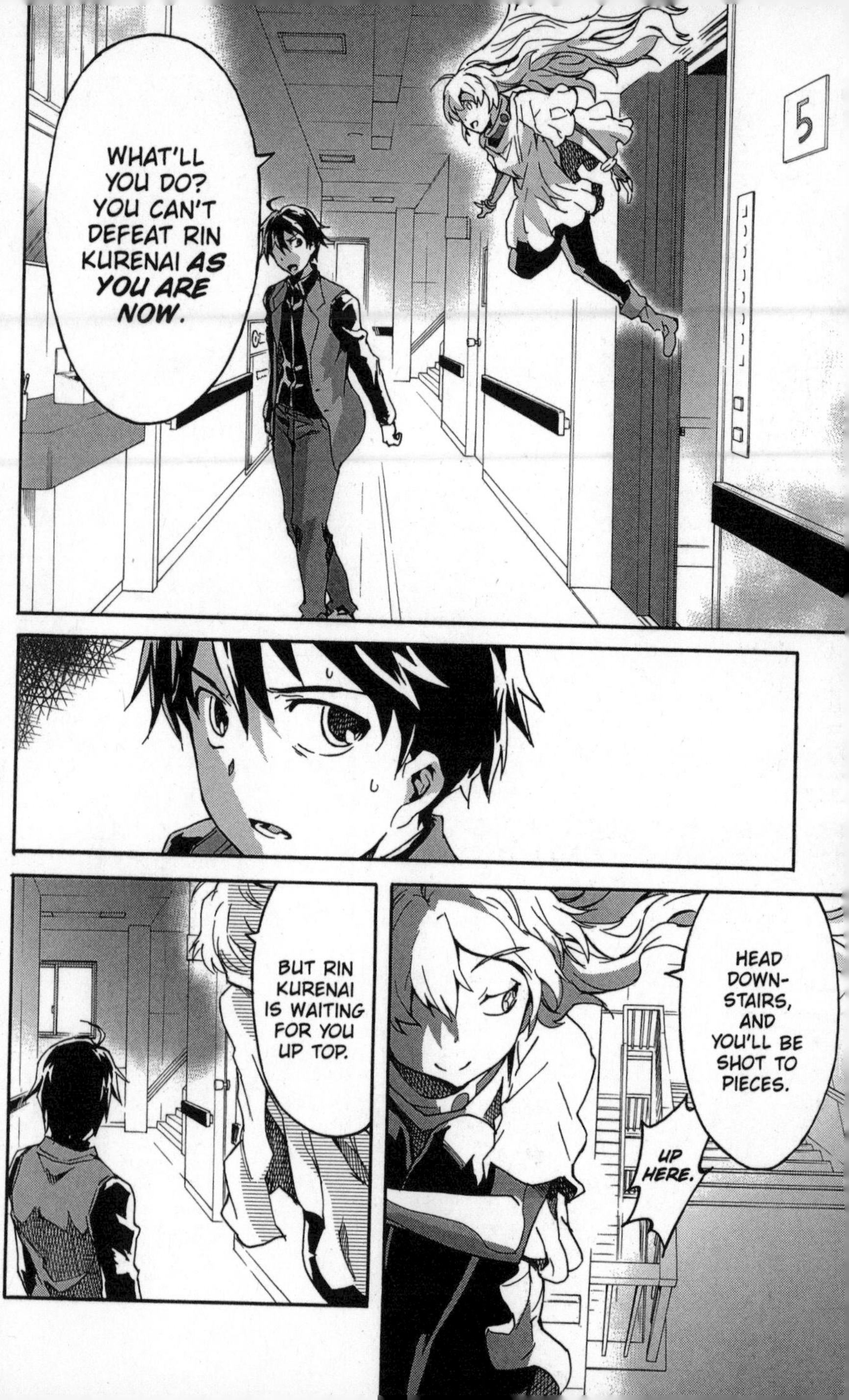
WHAT'LL YOU DO? YOU CAN'T DEFEAT RIN KURENAI AS YOU ARE NOW.
HEAD DOWN-STAIRS, AND YOU'LL BE SHOT TO PIECES.
UP HERE.
BUT RIN KURENAI IS WAITING FOR YOU UP TOP.

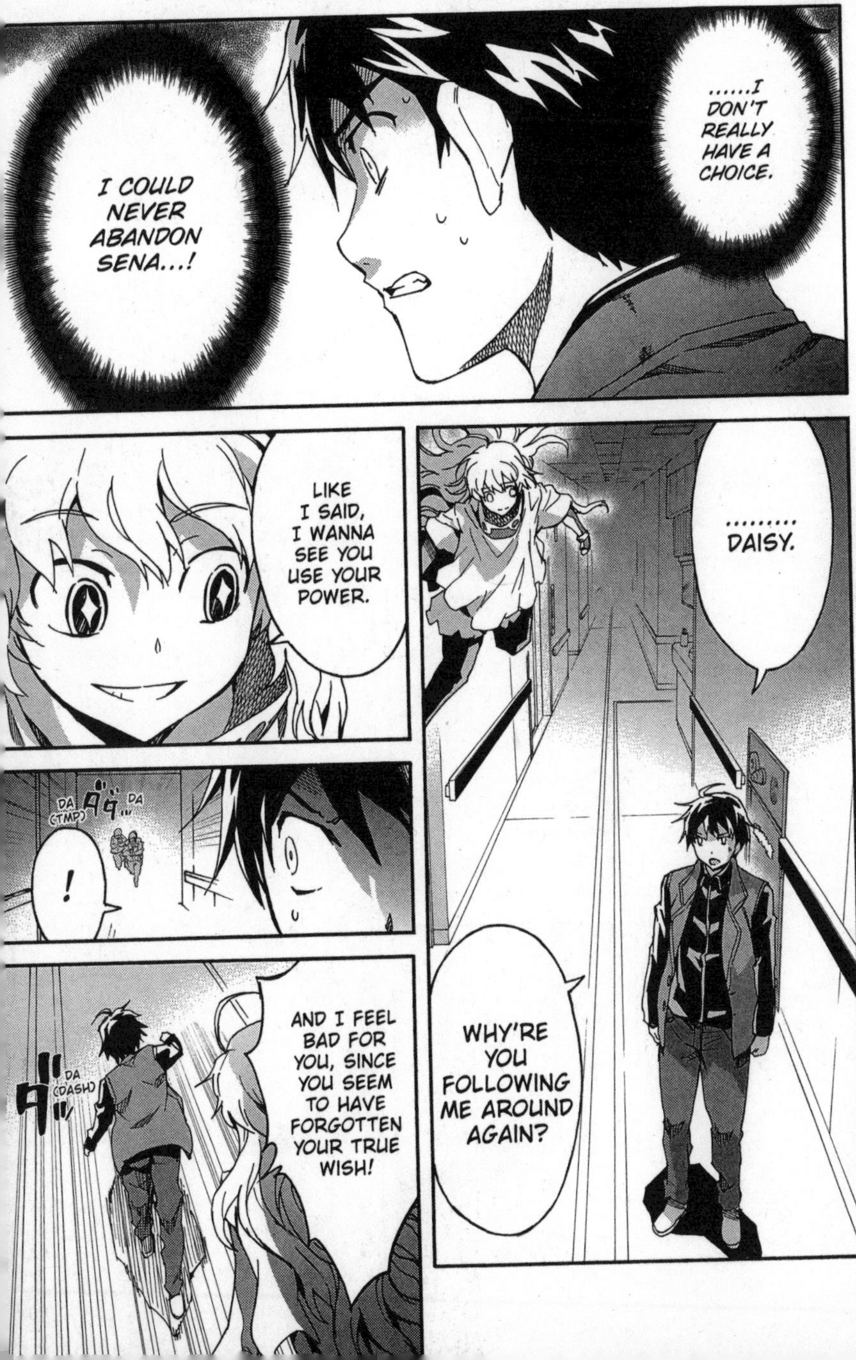

......I DON'T REALLY HAVE A CHOICE.
I COULD NEVER ABANDON SENA...!
.........DAISY.
WHY'RE YOU FOLLOWING ME AROUND AGAIN?
LIKE I SAID, I WANNA SEE YOU USE YOUR POWER.
DA (TMP) DA
!
AND I FEEL BAD FOR YOU, SINCE YOU SEEM TO HAVE FORGOTTEN YOUR TRUE WISH!
DA (DASH)

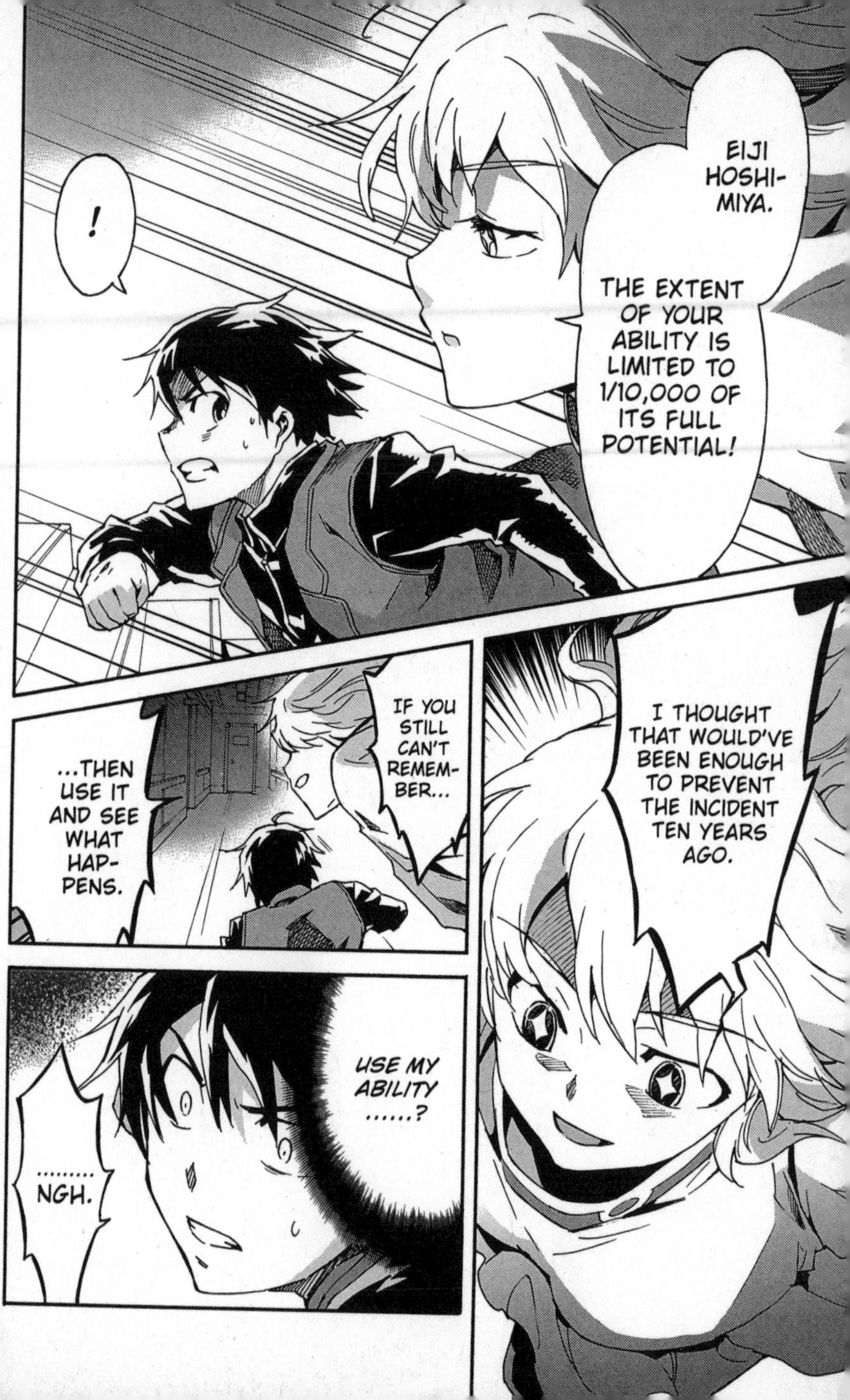
EIJI HOSHI-MIYA.
THE EXTENT OF YOUR ABILITY IS LIMITED TO 1/10,000 OF ITS FULL POTENTIAL!
!
I THOUGHT THAT WOULD'VE BEEN ENOUGH TO PREVENT THE INCIDENT TEN YEARS AGO.
IF YOU STILL CAN'T REMEMBER...
...THEN USE IT AND SEE WHAT HAPPENS.
USE MY ABILITY ......?
......... NGH.

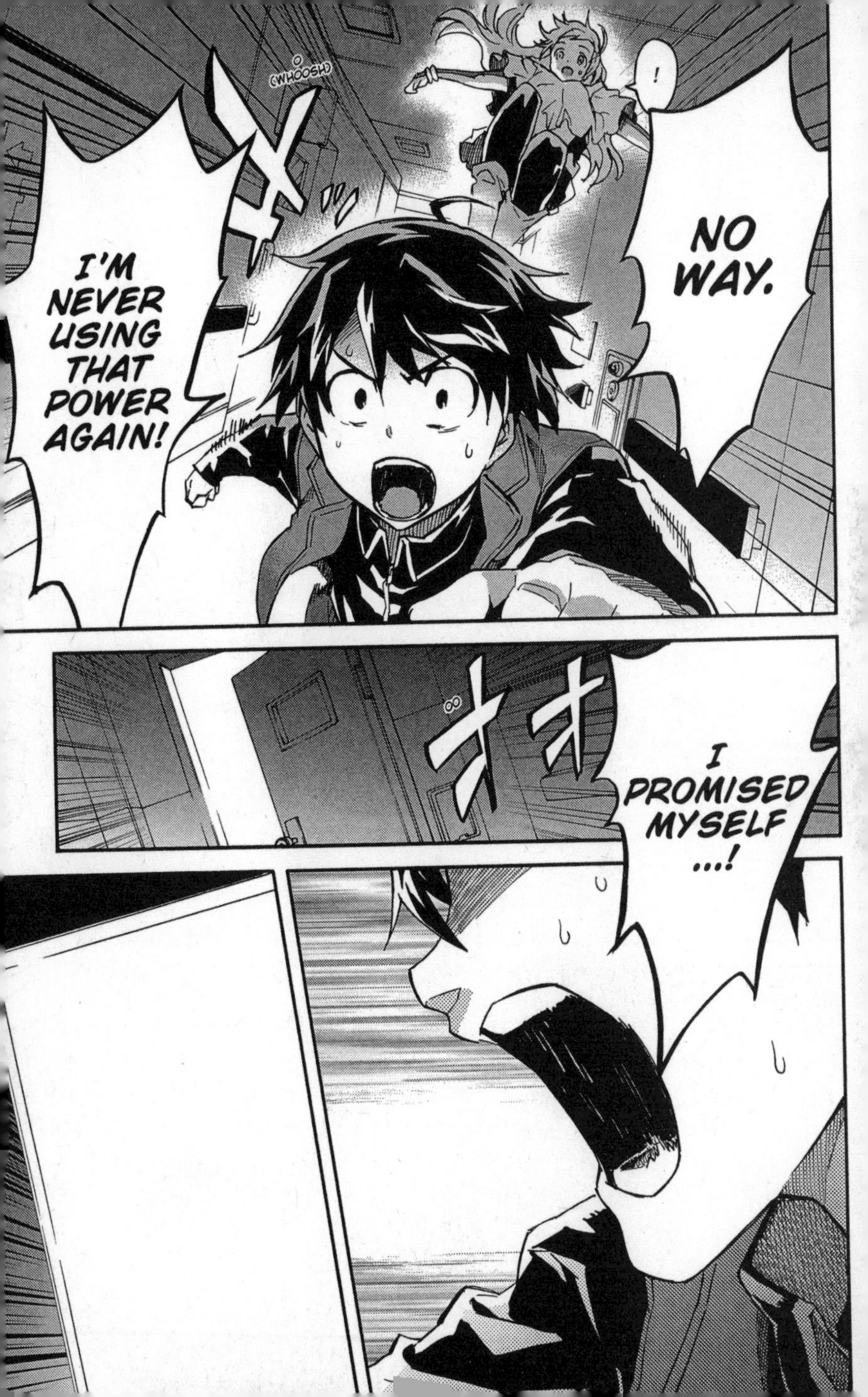
!
(WHOOSH)
NO WAY.
I'M NEVER USING THAT POWER AGAIN!
I PROMISED MYSELF ...!

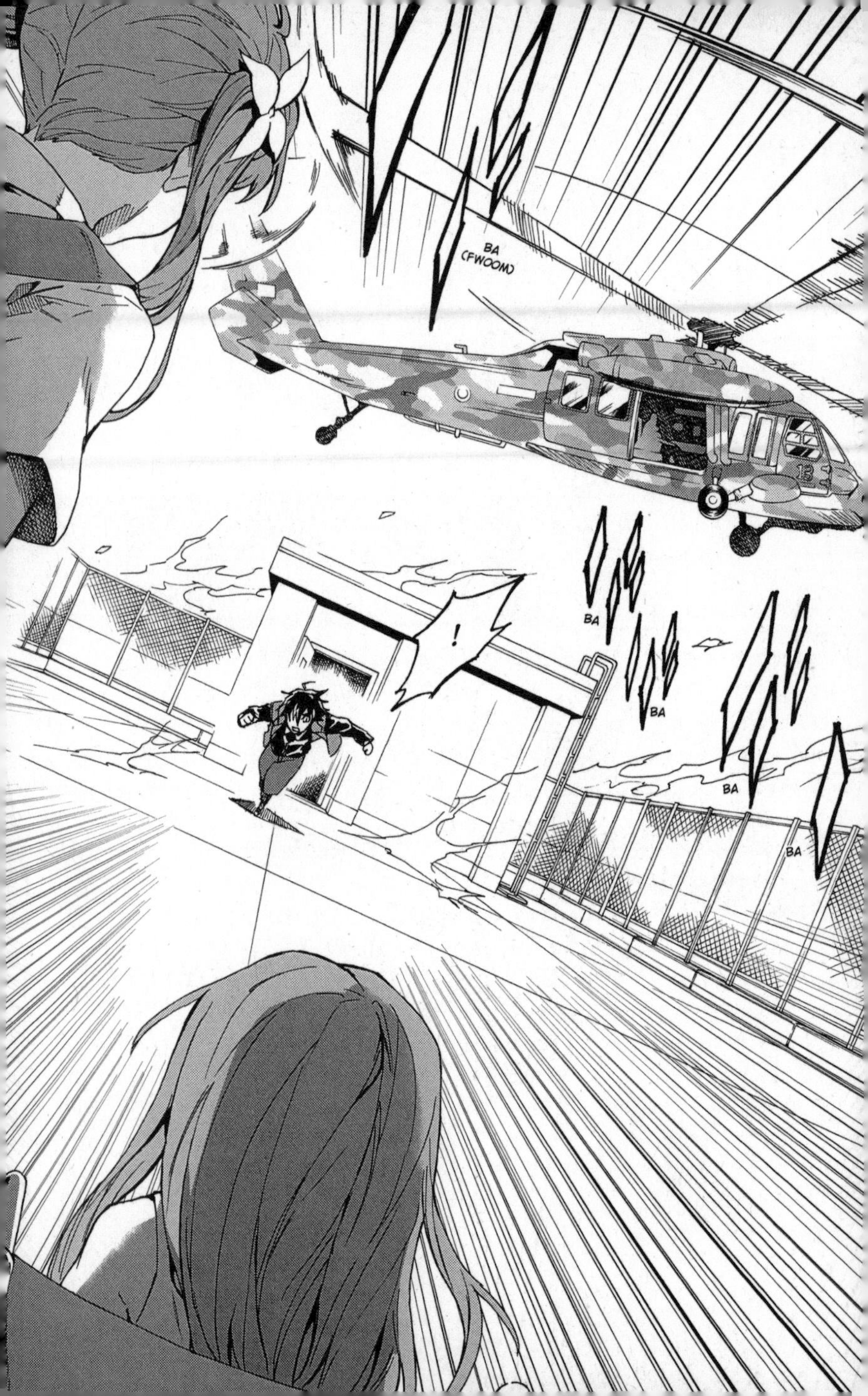
BA
(FWOOM)
BA
BA
BA
BA
!

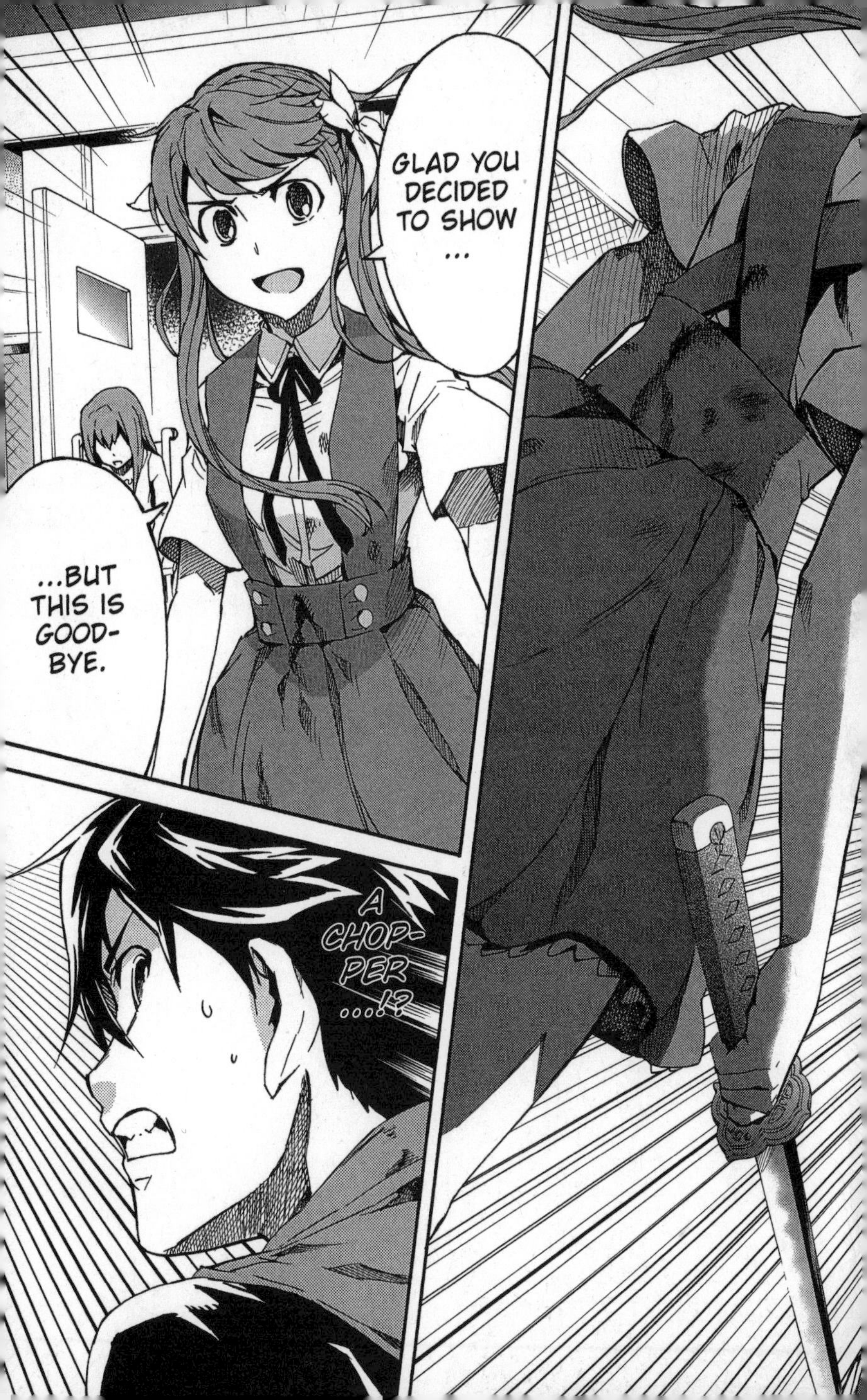
GLAD YOU DECIDED TO SHOW ...
...BUT THIS IS GOOD-BYE.
A CHOP-PER ...!?

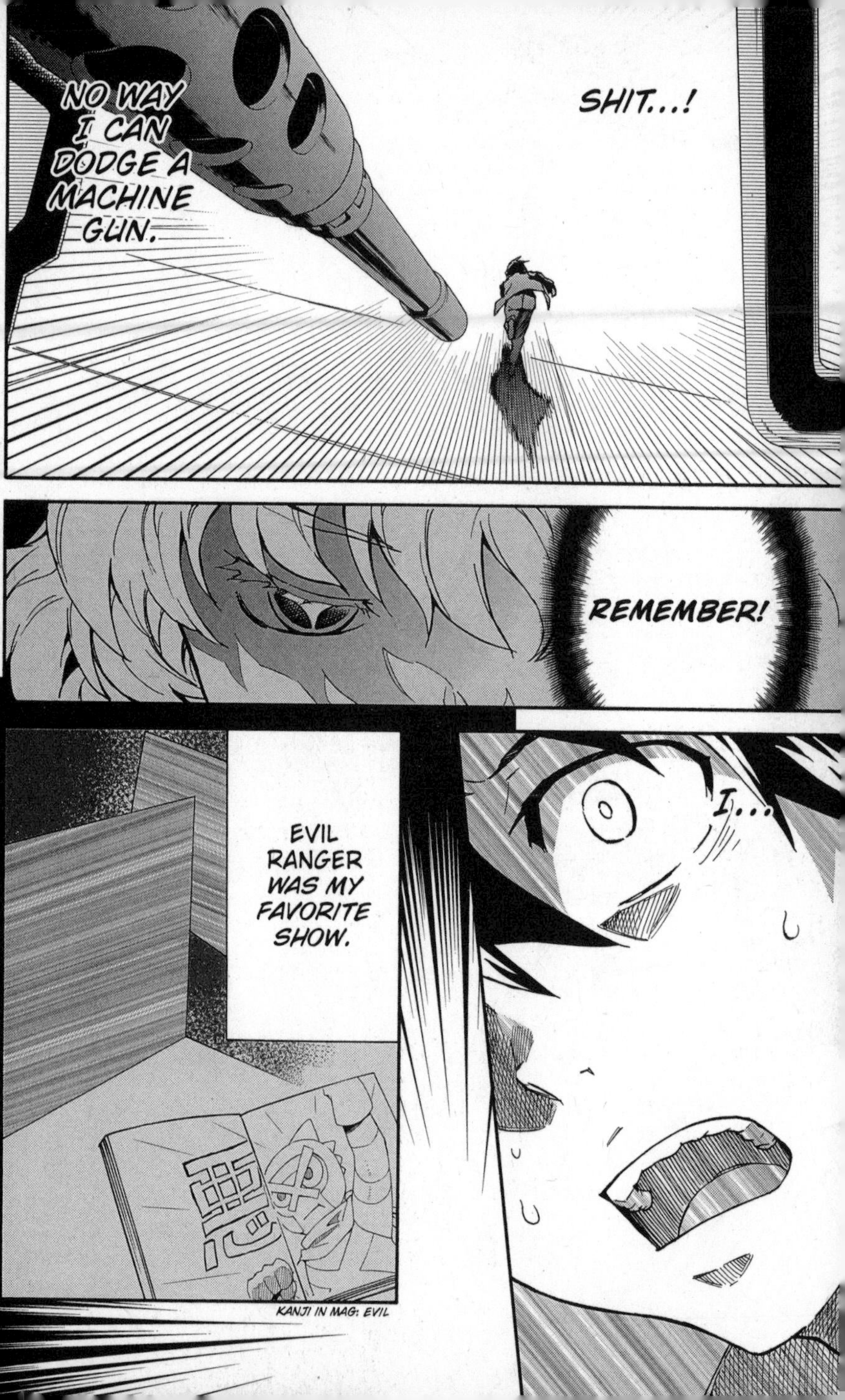
SHIT...!
NO WAY I CAN DODGE A MACHINE GUN.
REMEMBER!
I...
EVIL RANGER WAS MY FAVORITE SHOW.
KANJI IN MAG: EVIL

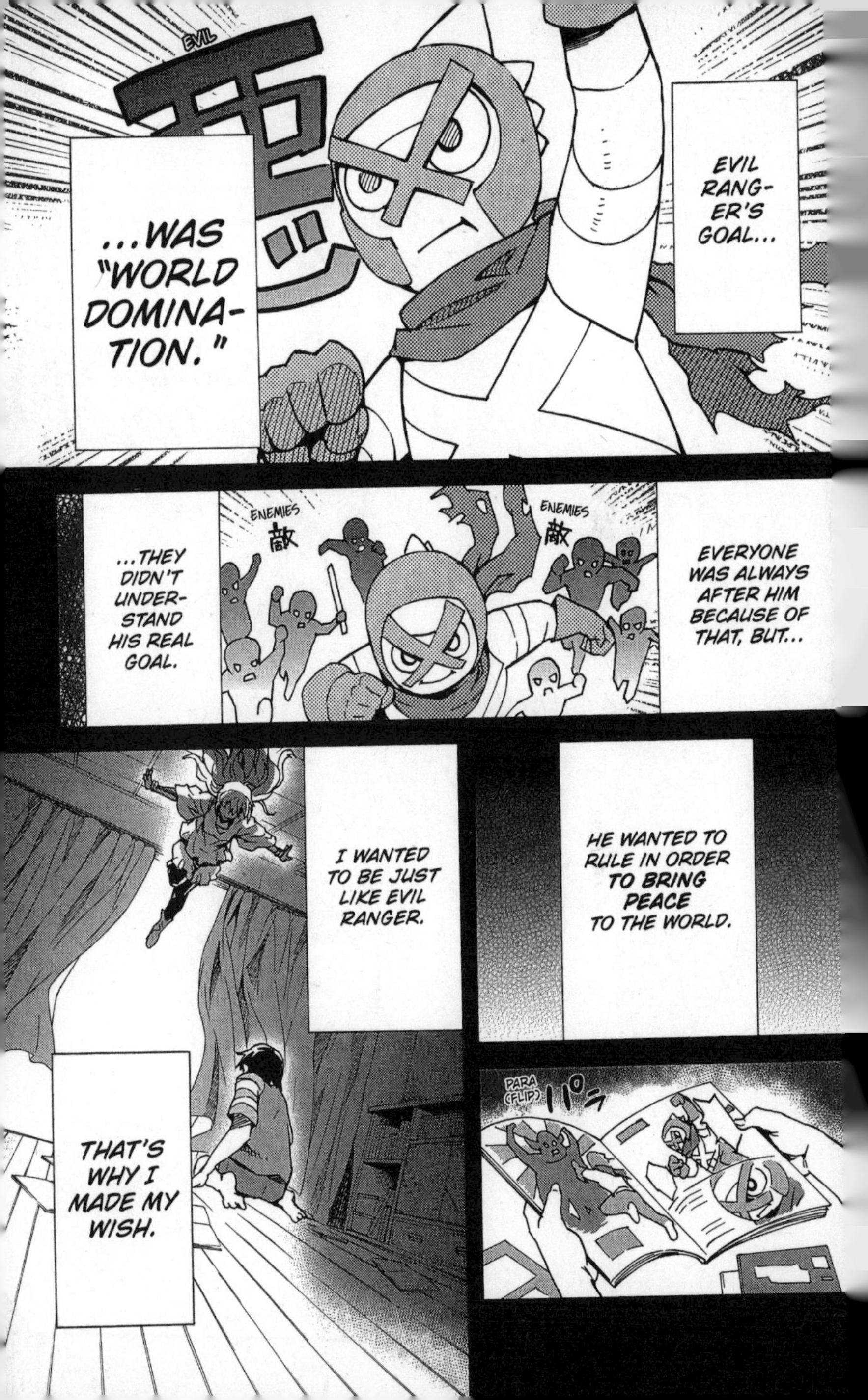
EVIL RANGER'S GOAL...
EVIL
...WAS "WORLD DOMINATION."
EVERYONE WAS ALWAYS AFTER HIM BECAUSE OF THAT, BUT...
ENEMIES
ENEMIES
...THEY DIDN'T UNDERSTAND HIS REAL GOAL.
HE WANTED TO RULE IN ORDER TO BRING PEACE TO THE WORLD.
PARA (FLIP)
I WANTED TO BE JUST LIKE EVIL RANGER.
THAT'S WHY I MADE MY WISH.

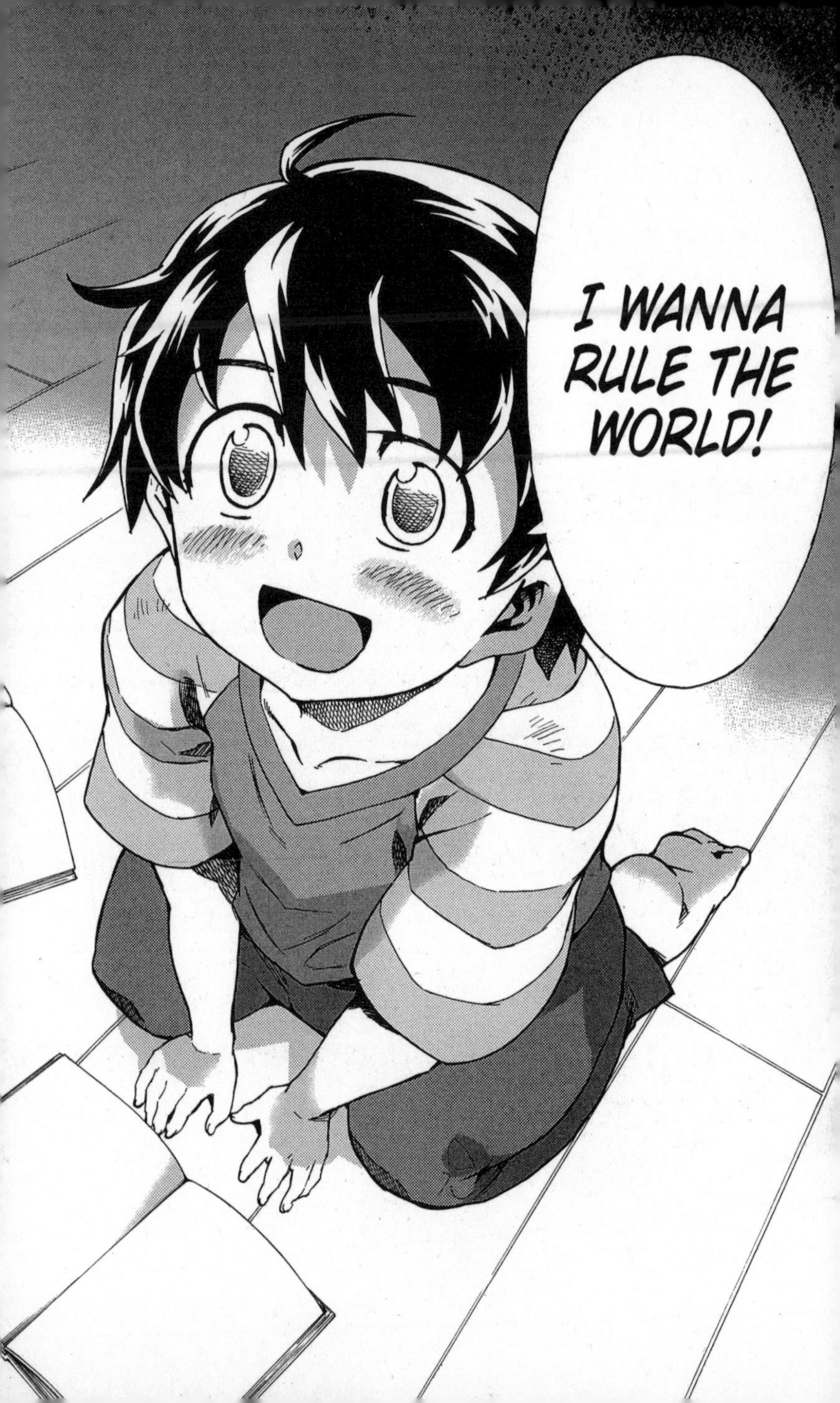
I WANNA RULE THE WORLD!

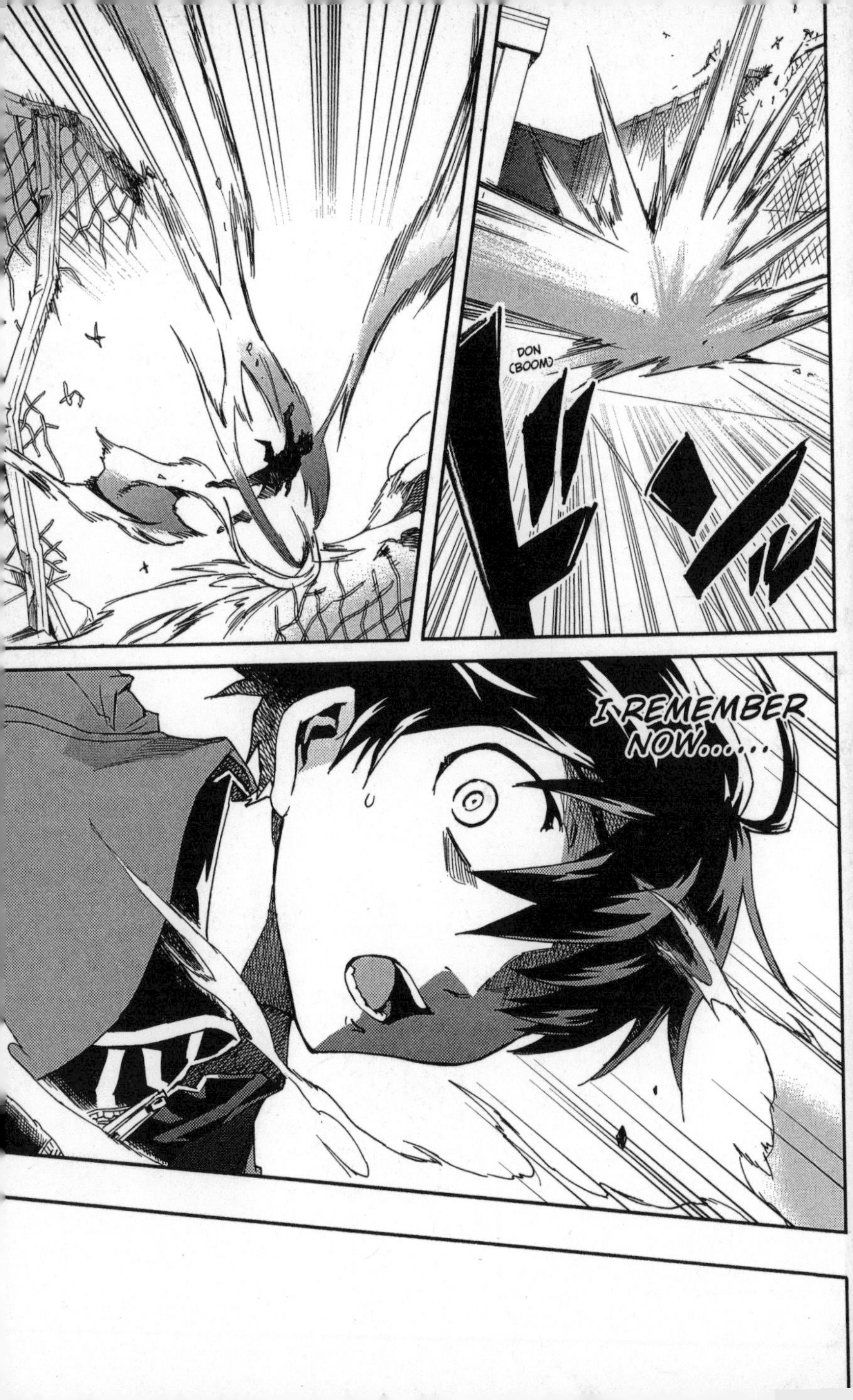
DON (BOOM)
I REMEMBER NOW......

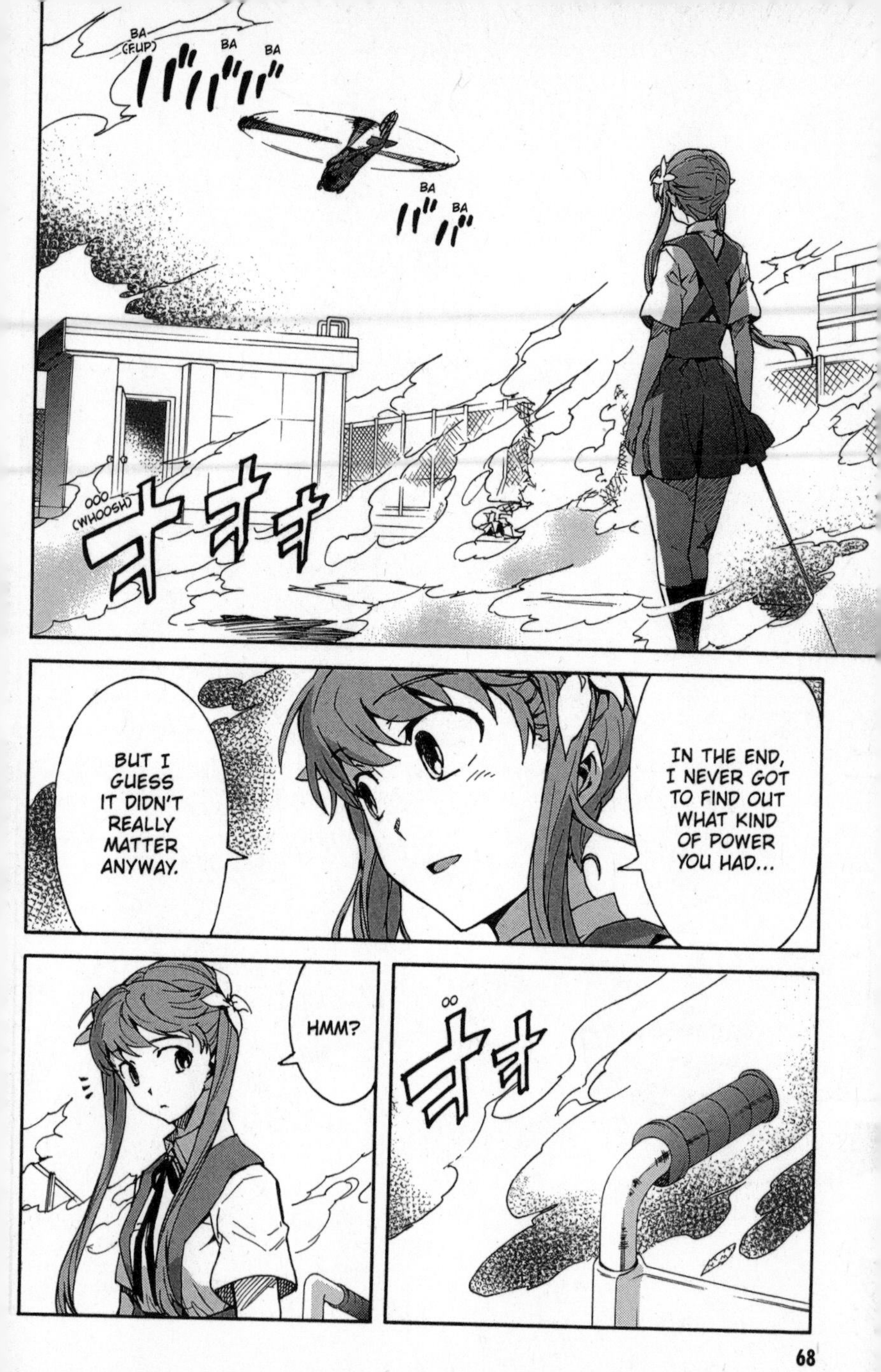
BA (FLIP) BA BA
BA BA
OOO (WHOOSH)
IN THE END, I NEVER GOT TO FIND OUT WHAT KIND OF POWER YOU HAD...
BUT I GUESS IT DIDN'T REALLY MATTER ANYWAY.
OO
HMM?

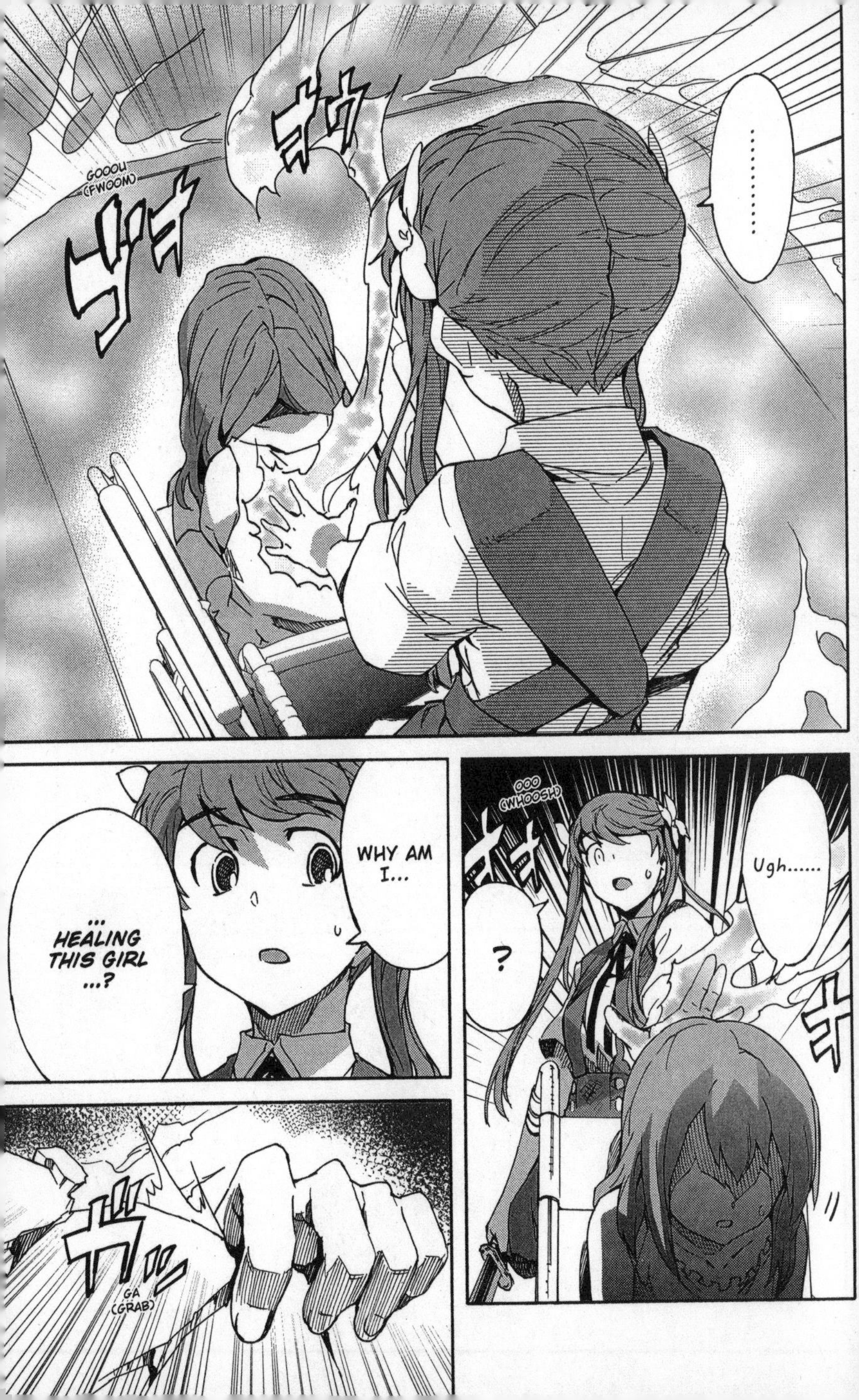
GOOOU (FWOOM)
......
OOO (WHOOSH)
Ugh......
?
WHY AM I...
... HEALING THIS GIRL ...?
GA (GRAB)

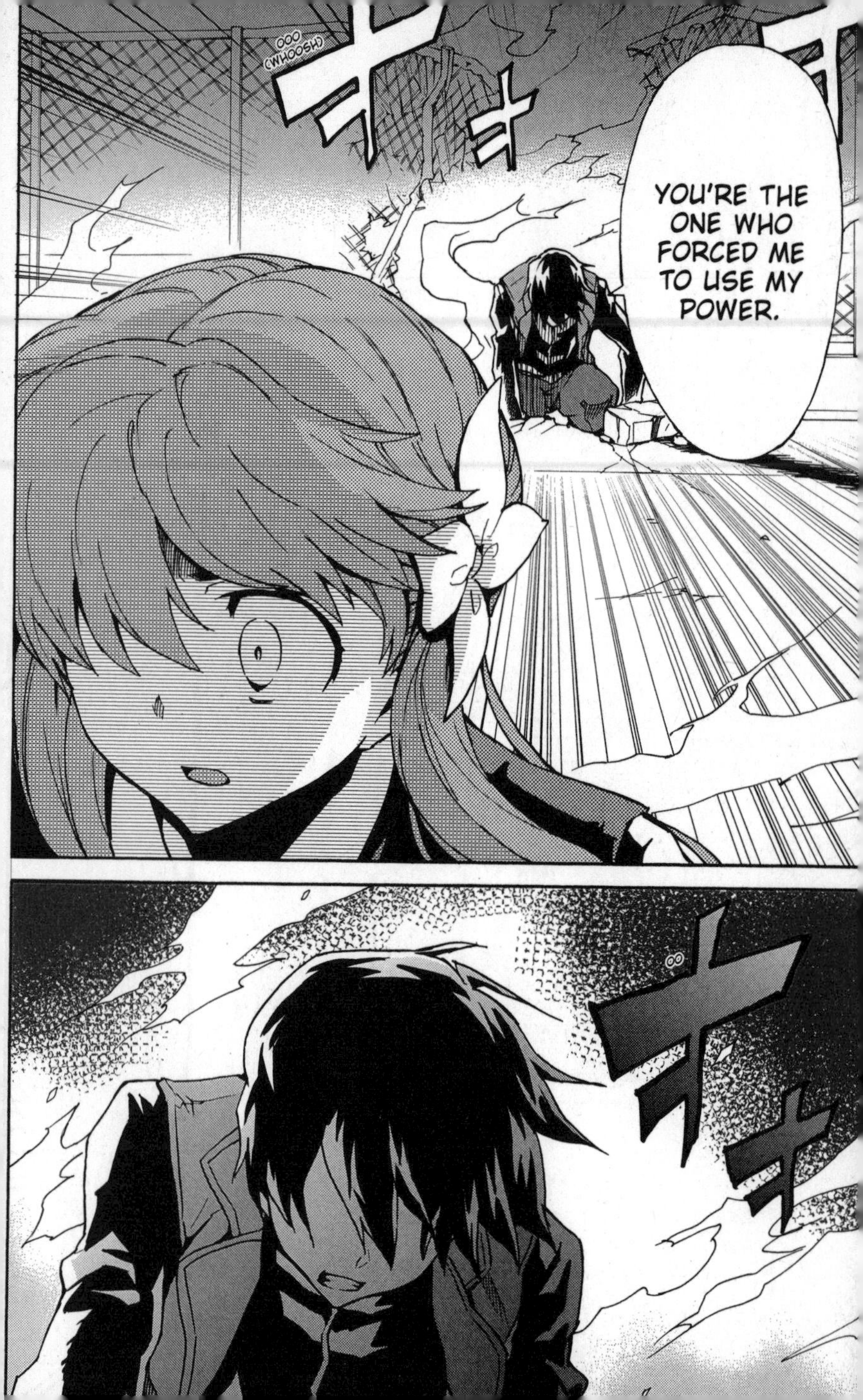
YOU'RE THE ONE WHO FORCED ME TO USE MY POWER.
OOO (WHOOSH)
OO

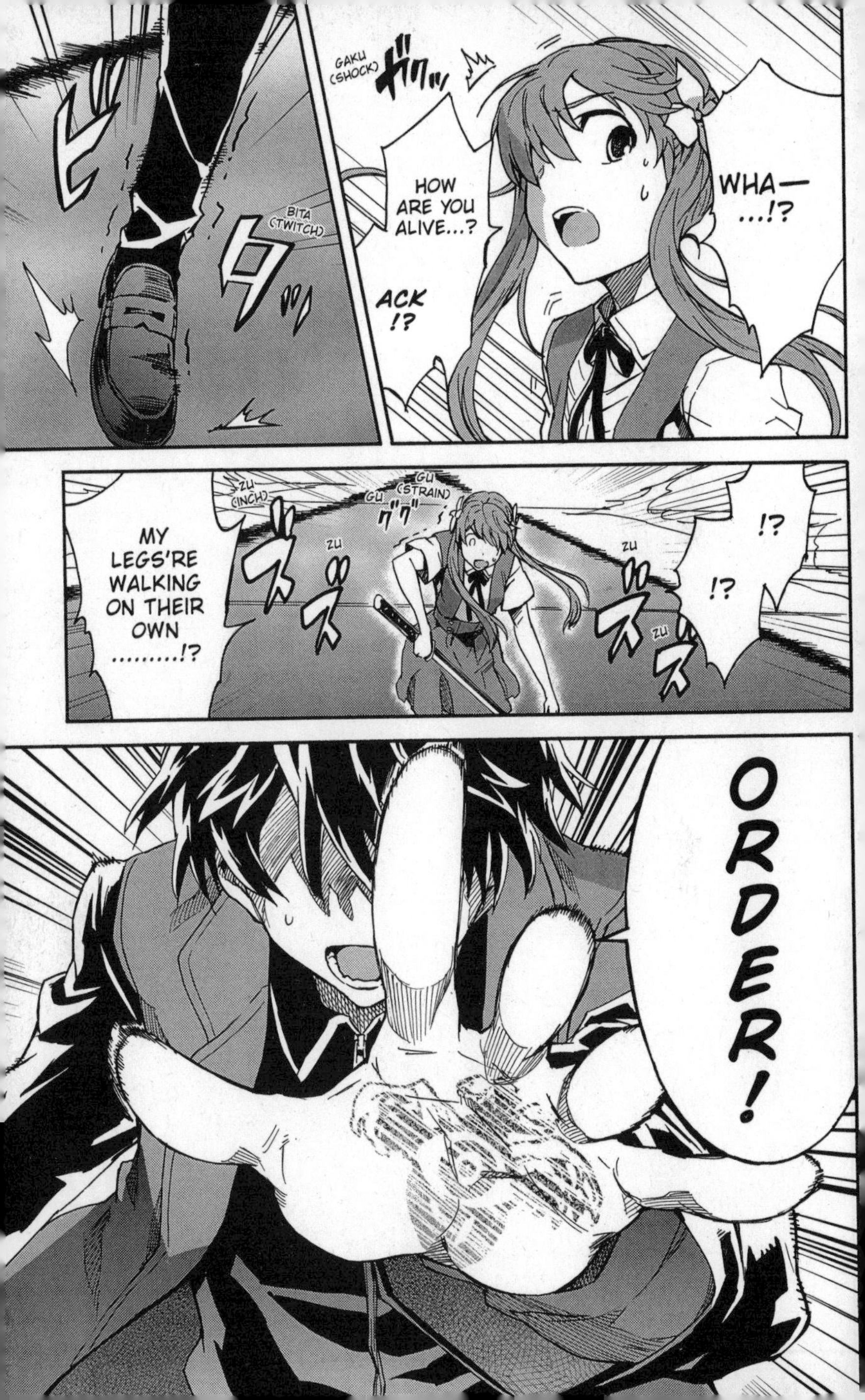

GAKU (SHOCK)
WHA— ...!?
HOW ARE YOU ALIVE...?
ACK !?
BITA (TWITCH)
!?
!?
ZU
ZU
GU GU (STRAIN)
ZU ZU (INCH)
MY LEGS'RE WALKING ON THEIR OWN ..........!?
ORDER!

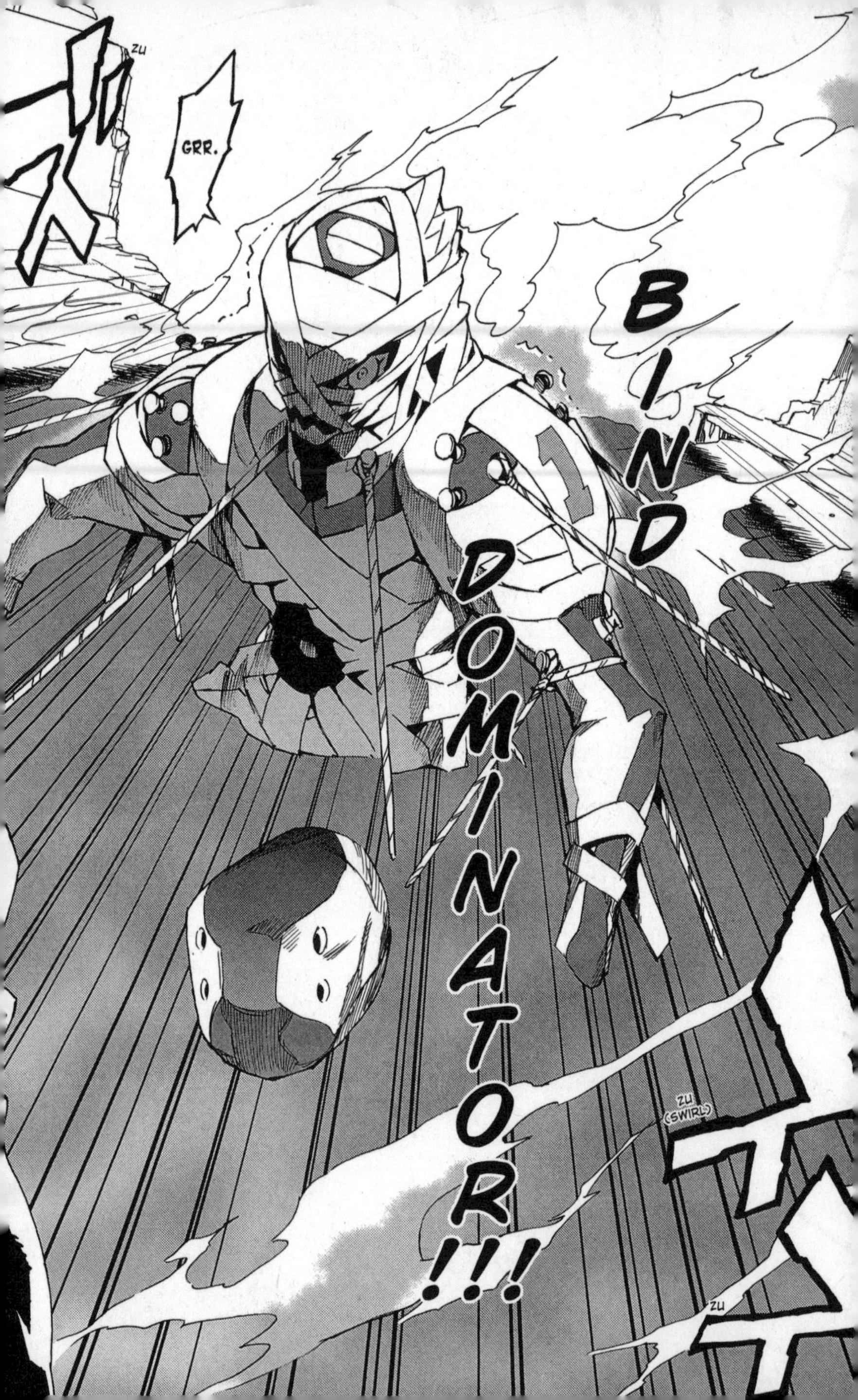
BIND DOMINATOR!!!
ZU
GRR.
ZU (SWIRL)
ZU

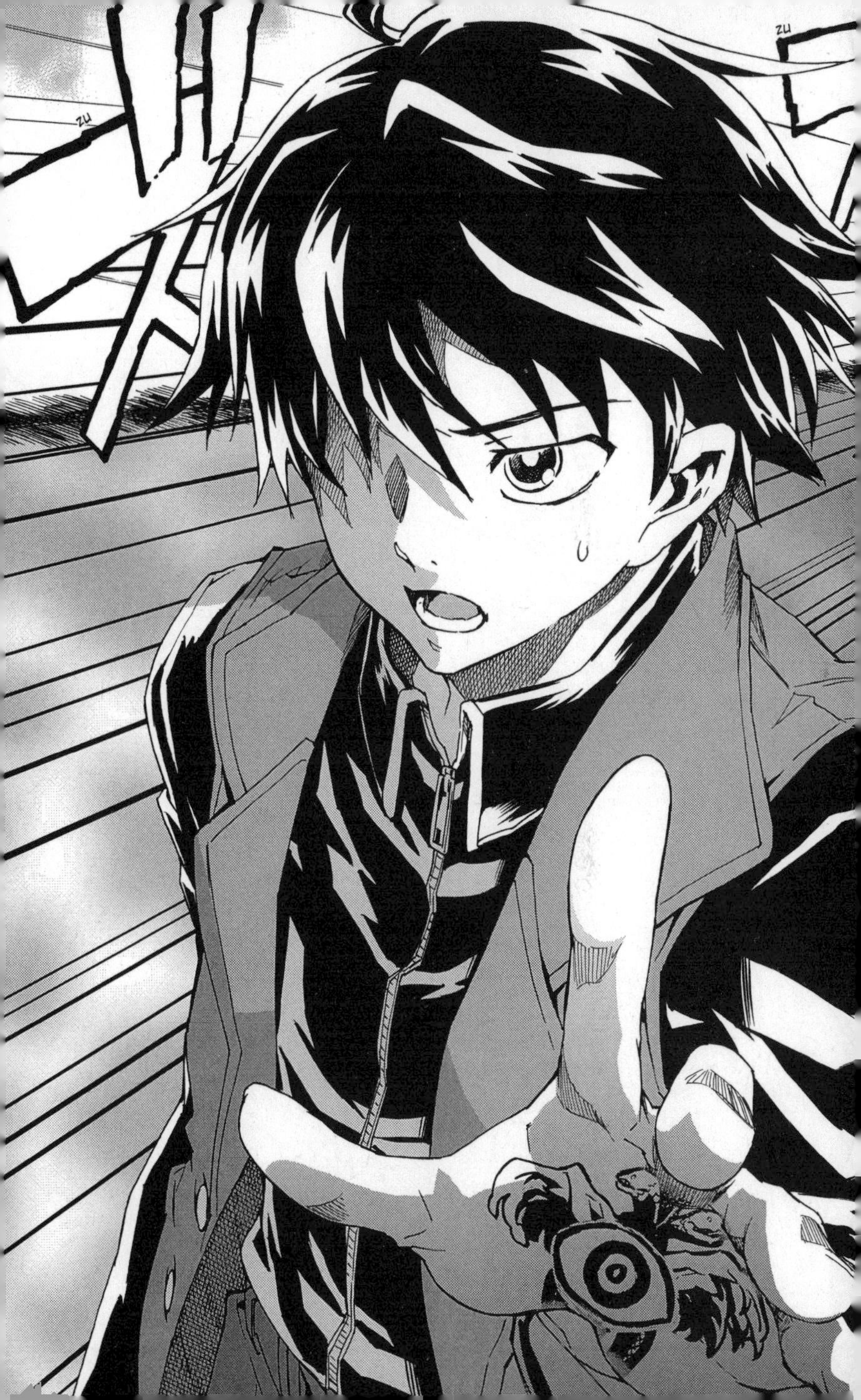
zu
zu

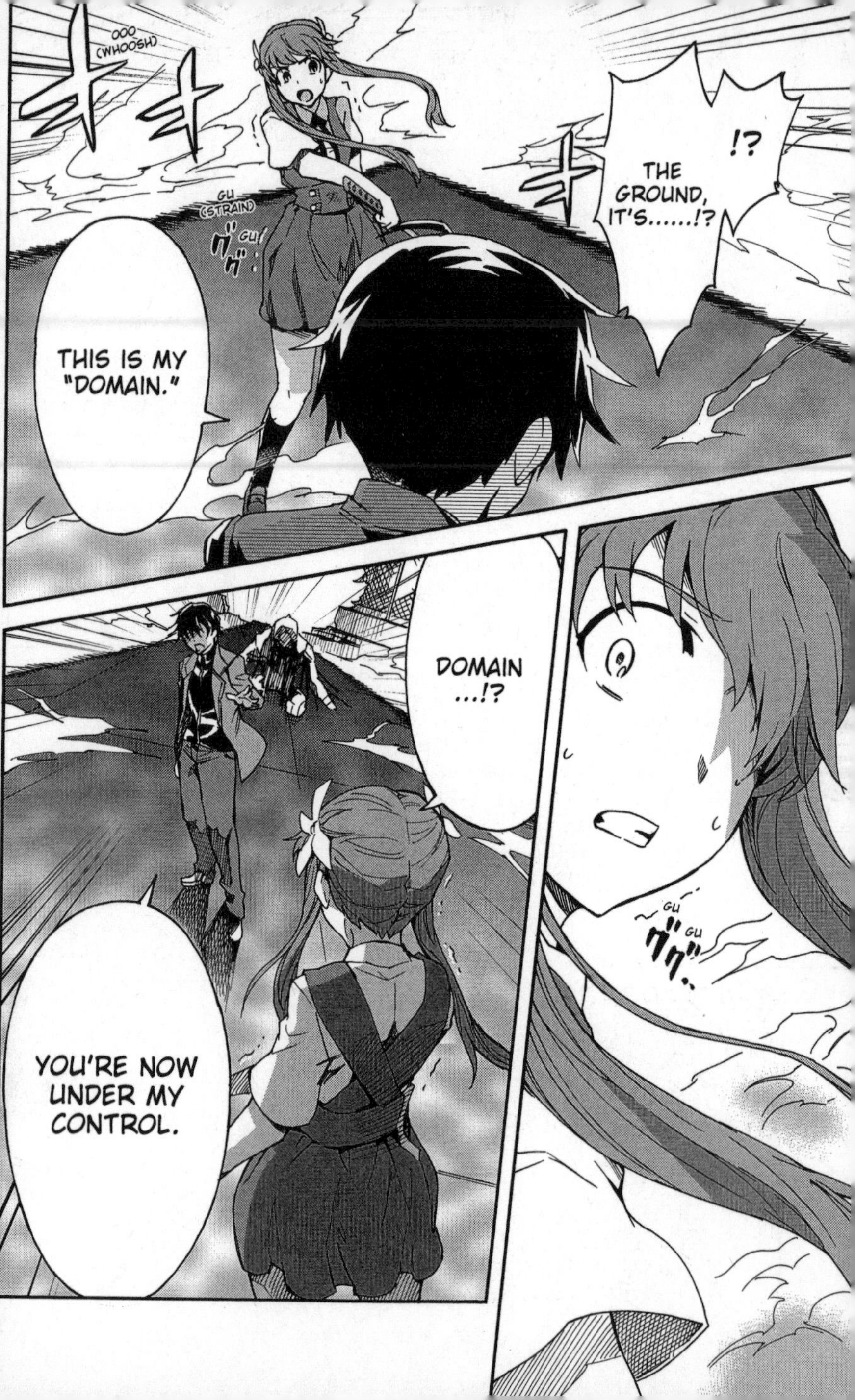
!?
THE GROUND, IT'S......!?
OOO (WHOOSH)
GU (STRAIN) GU!
THIS IS MY "DOMAIN."
DOMAIN ...!?
GU GU
YOU'RE NOW UNDER MY CONTROL.

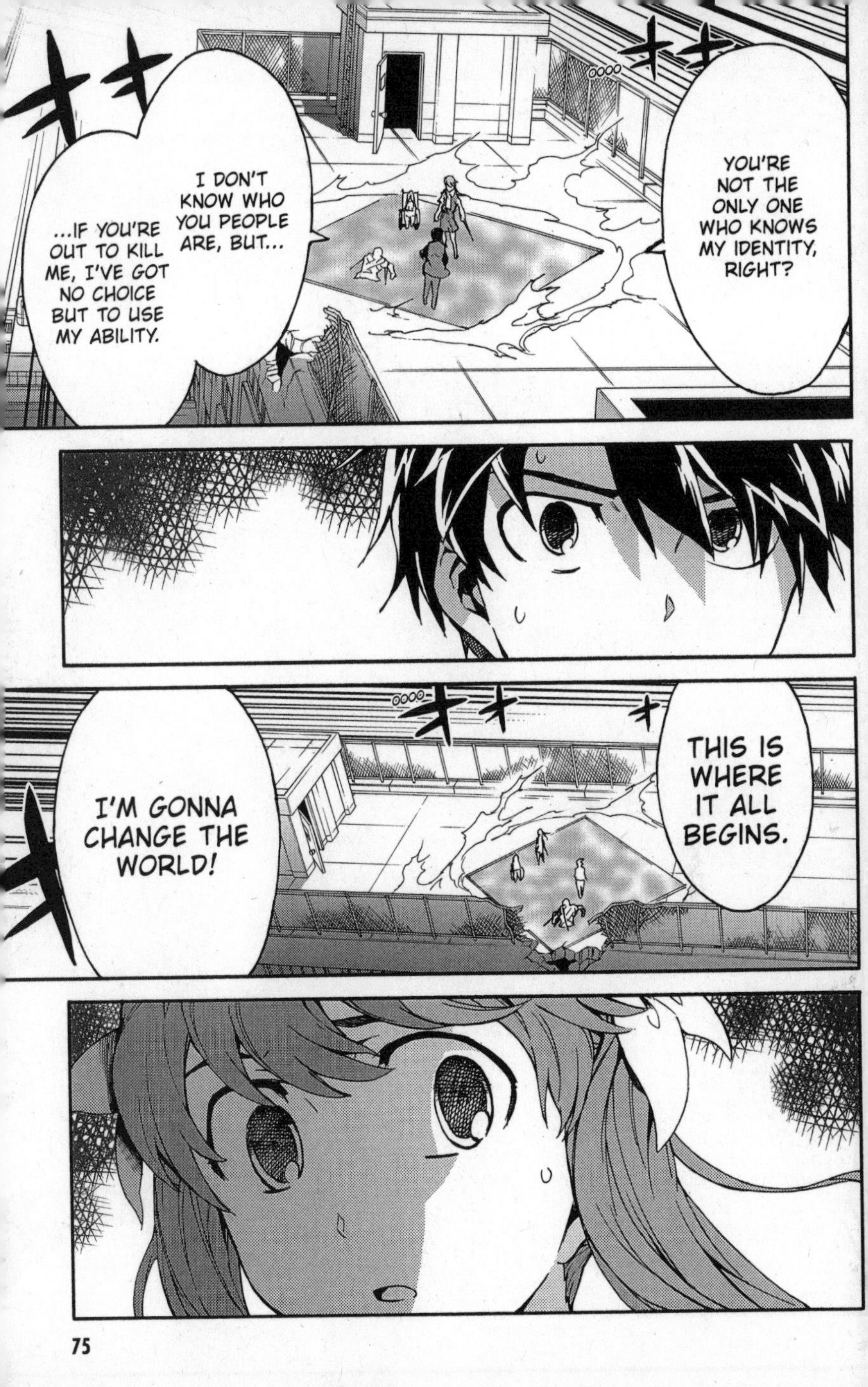
YOU'RE NOT THE ONLY ONE WHO KNOWS MY IDENTITY, RIGHT?
I DON'T KNOW WHO YOU PEOPLE ARE, BUT...
...IF YOU'RE OUT TO KILL ME, I'VE GOT NO CHOICE BUT TO USE MY ABILITY.
THIS IS WHERE IT ALL BEGINS.
I'M GONNA CHANGE THE WORLD!

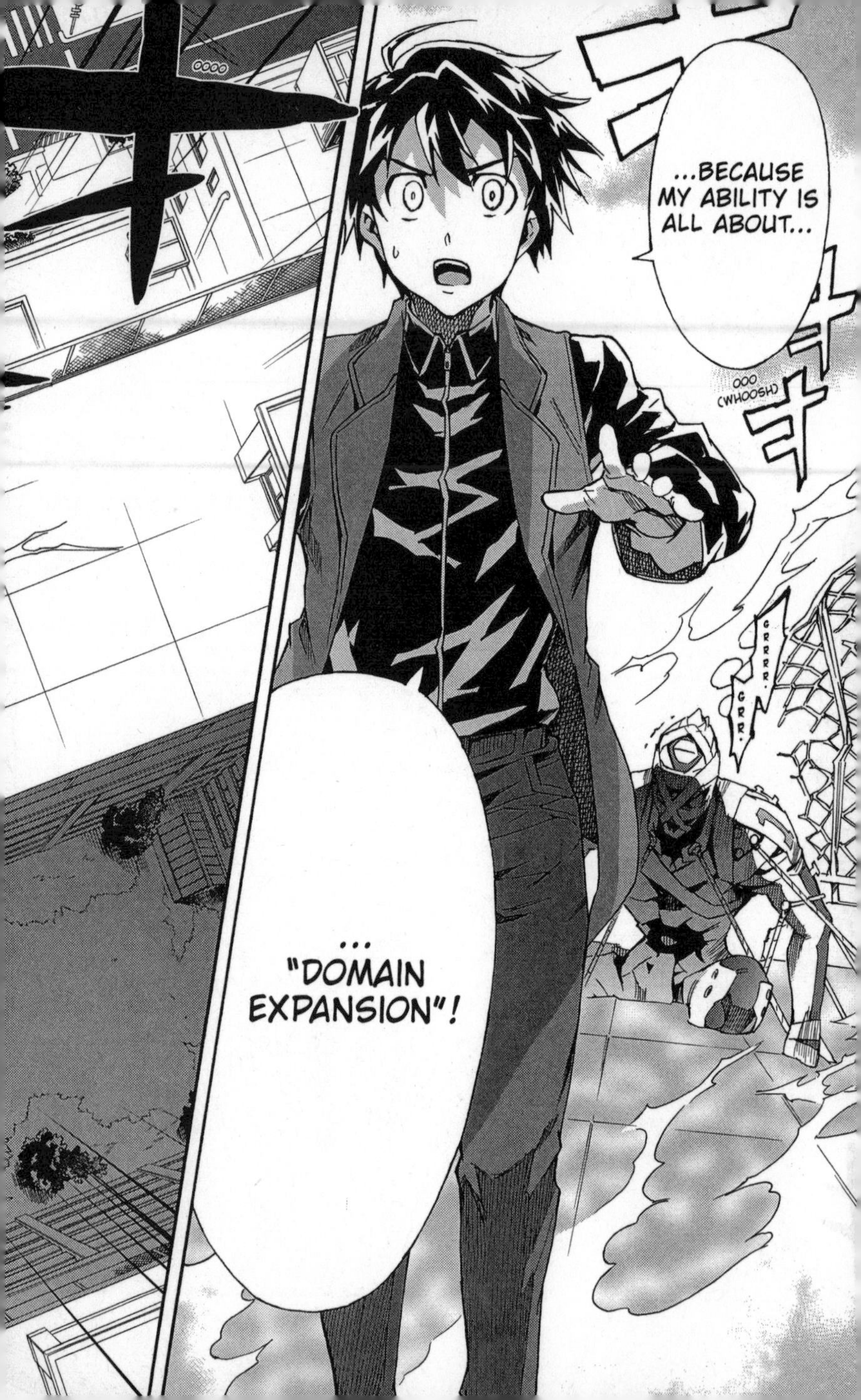
...BECAUSE MY ABILITY IS ALL ABOUT...
OOO (WHOOSH)
GRRRR. GRR.
... "DOMAIN EXPANSION"!

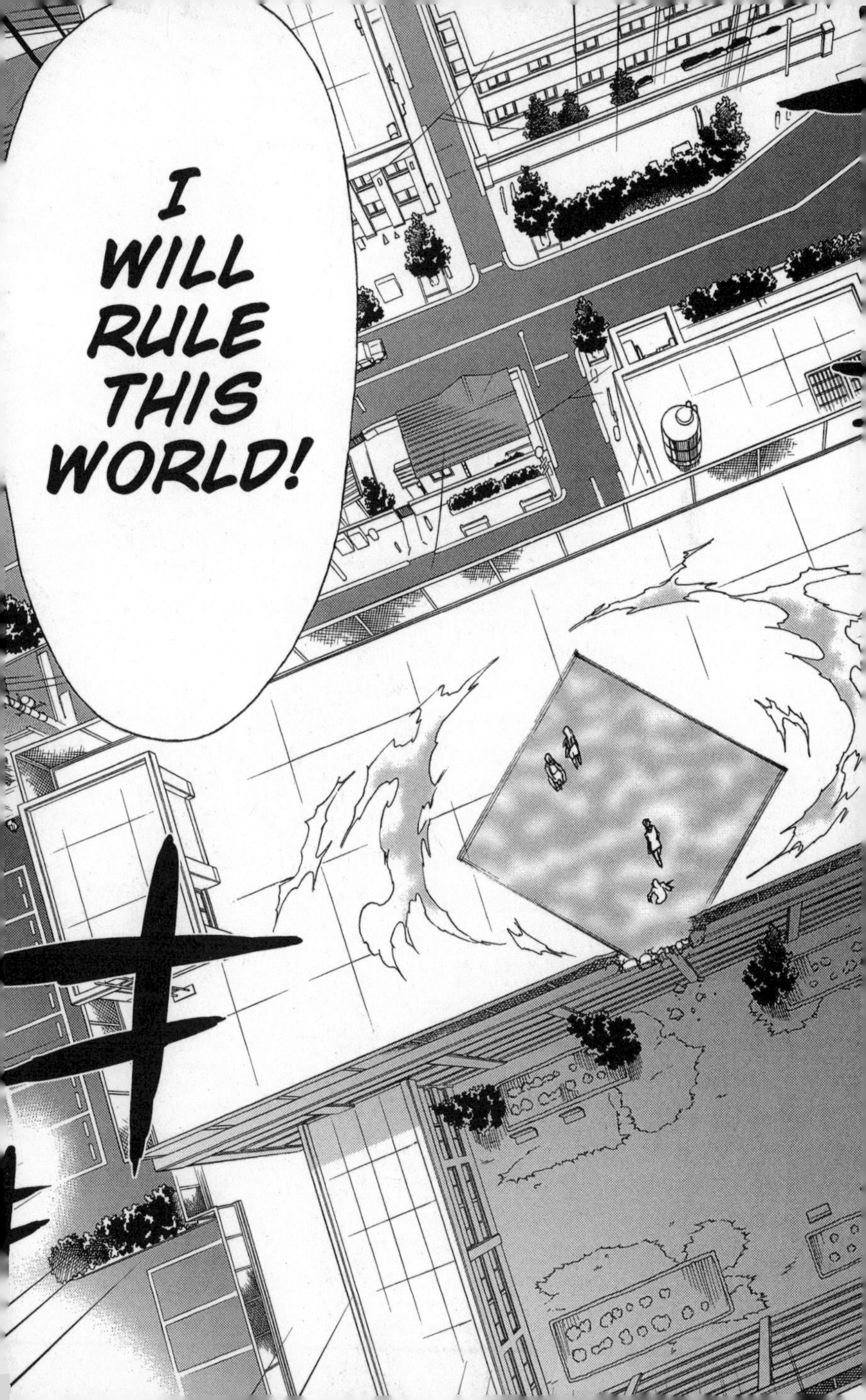
I WILL RULE THIS WORLD!

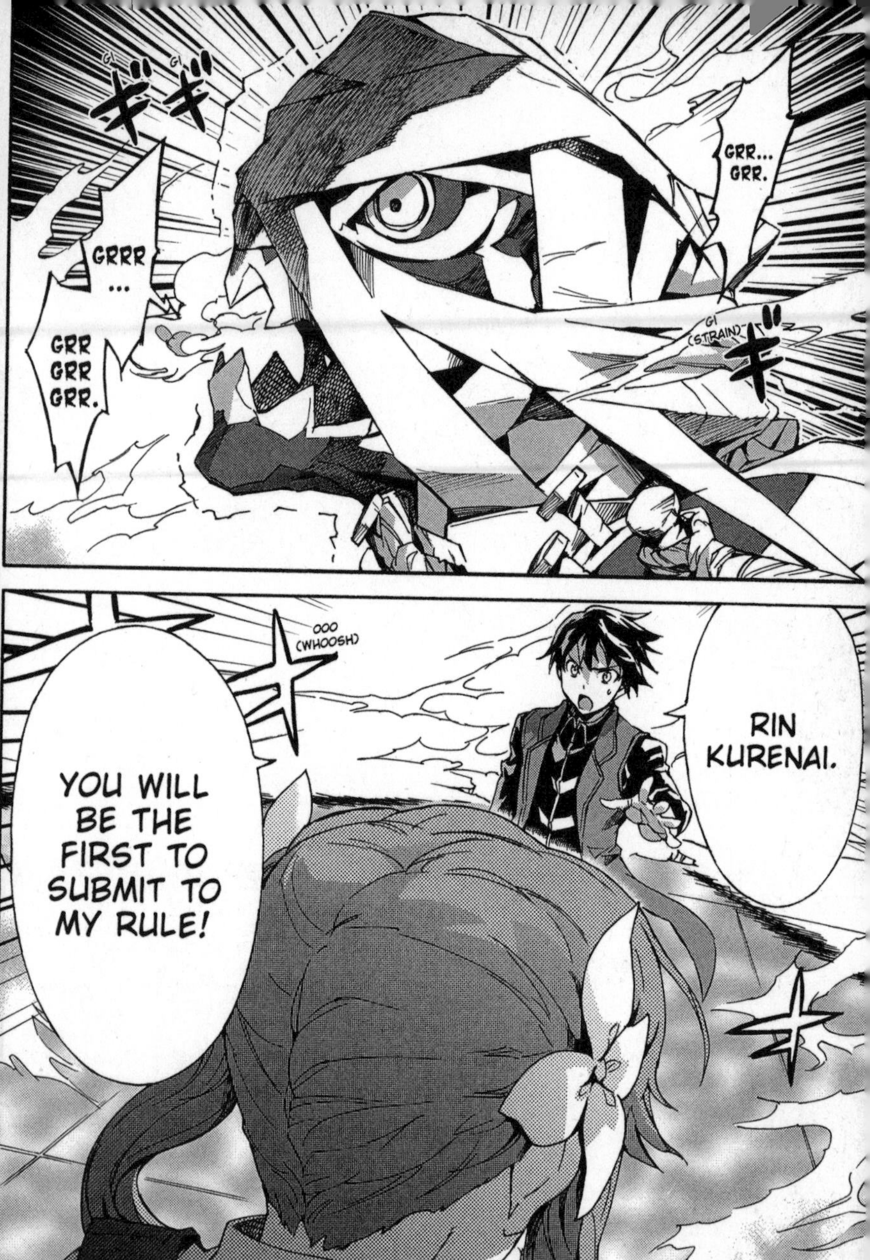
GRR... GRR.
GI (STRAIN)
ギ
GI GI
ギギ
GRRR ...
GRR GRR GRR.
RIN KURENAI.
OOO (WHOOSH)
YOU WILL BE THE FIRST TO SUBMIT TO MY RULE!

Subject 1: END

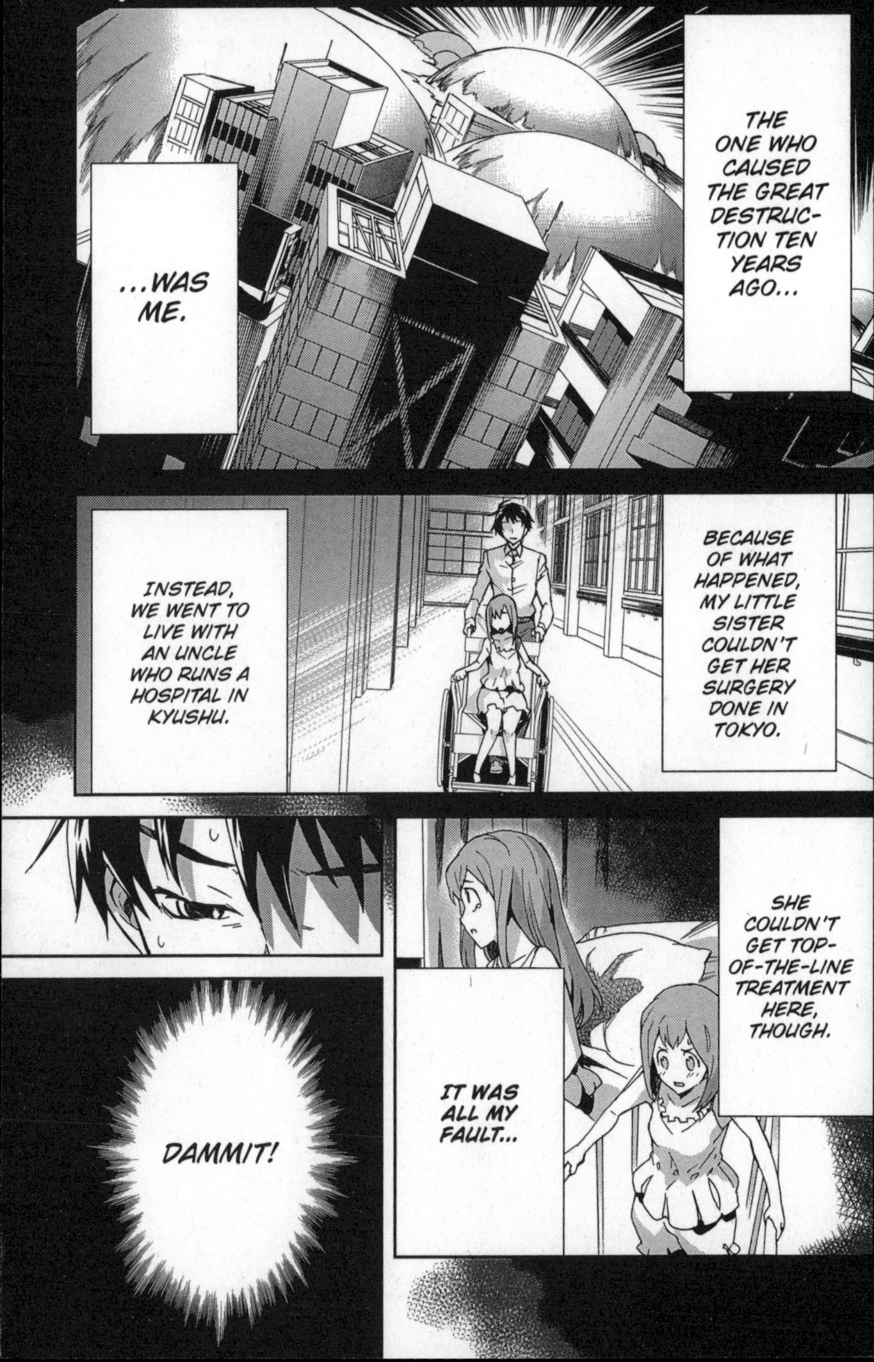
THE ONE WHO CAUSED THE GREAT DESTRUC-TION TEN YEARS AGO...
...WAS ME.
BECAUSE OF WHAT HAPPENED, MY LITTLE SISTER COULDN'T GET HER SURGERY DONE IN TOKYO.
INSTEAD, WE WENT TO LIVE WITH AN UNCLE WHO RUNS A HOSPITAL IN KYUSHU.
SHE COULDN'T GET TOP-OF-THE-LINE TREATMENT HERE, THOUGH.
IT WAS ALL MY FAULT...
DAMMIT!

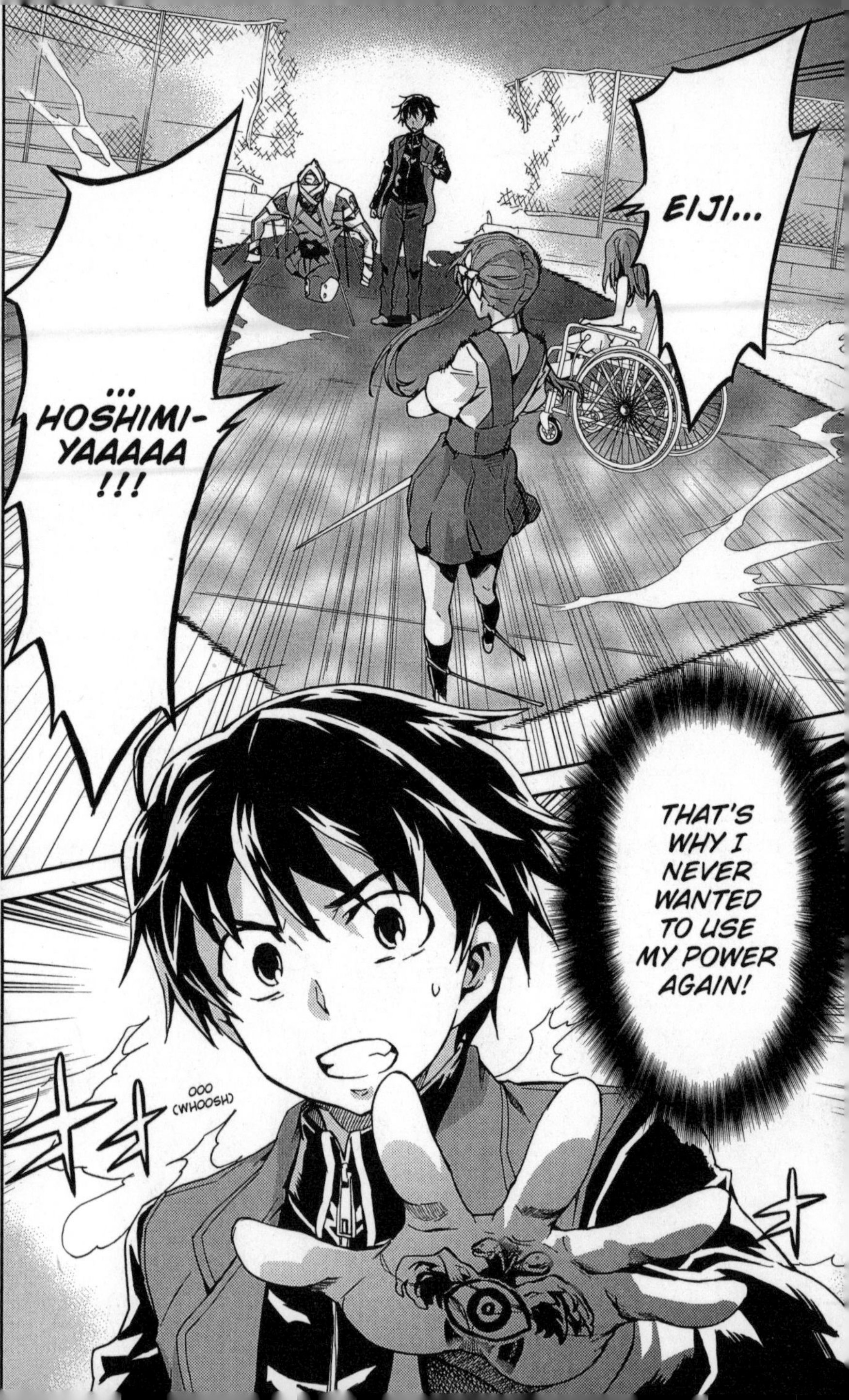
EIJI...
...HOSHIMI-YAAAAA!!!
THAT'S WHY I NEVER WANTED TO USE MY POWER AGAIN!
OOO (WHOOSH)

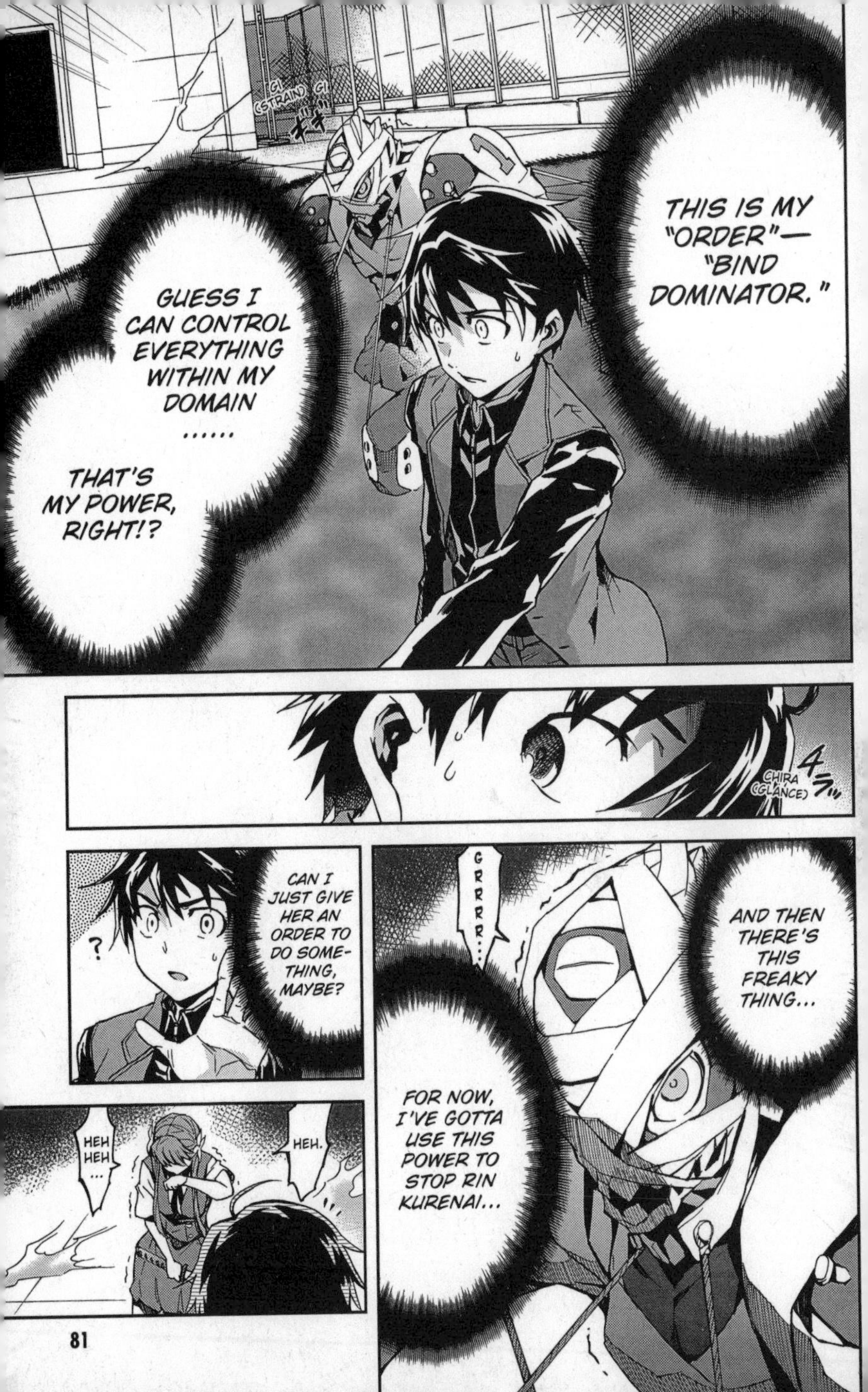
GI (STRAIN) GI
THIS IS MY "ORDER"— "BIND DOMINATOR."
GUESS I CAN CONTROL EVERYTHING WITHIN MY DOMAIN ......
THAT'S MY POWER, RIGHT!?
CHIRA (GLANCE)
GRRRR...
AND THEN THERE'S THIS FREAKY THING...
FOR NOW, I'VE GOTTA USE THIS POWER TO STOP RIN KURENAI...
CAN I JUST GIVE HER AN ORDER TO DO SOME-THING, MAYBE?
?
HEH.
HEH HEH ...

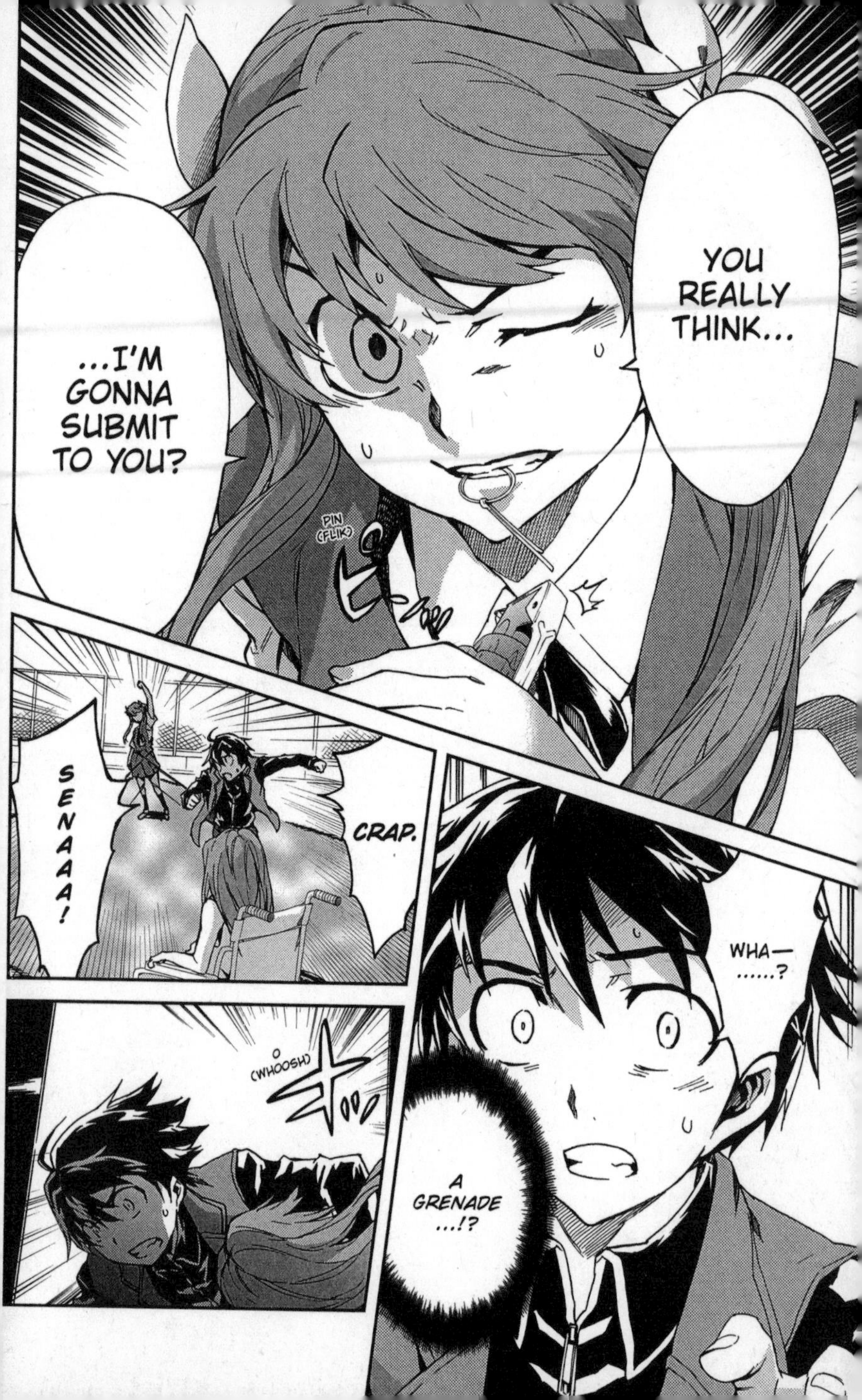
YOU REALLY THINK...
...I'M GONNA SUBMIT TO YOU?
PIN (FLIK)
WHA— ......?
A GRENADE ...!?
CRAP.
SENAAAA!
O (WHOOSH)

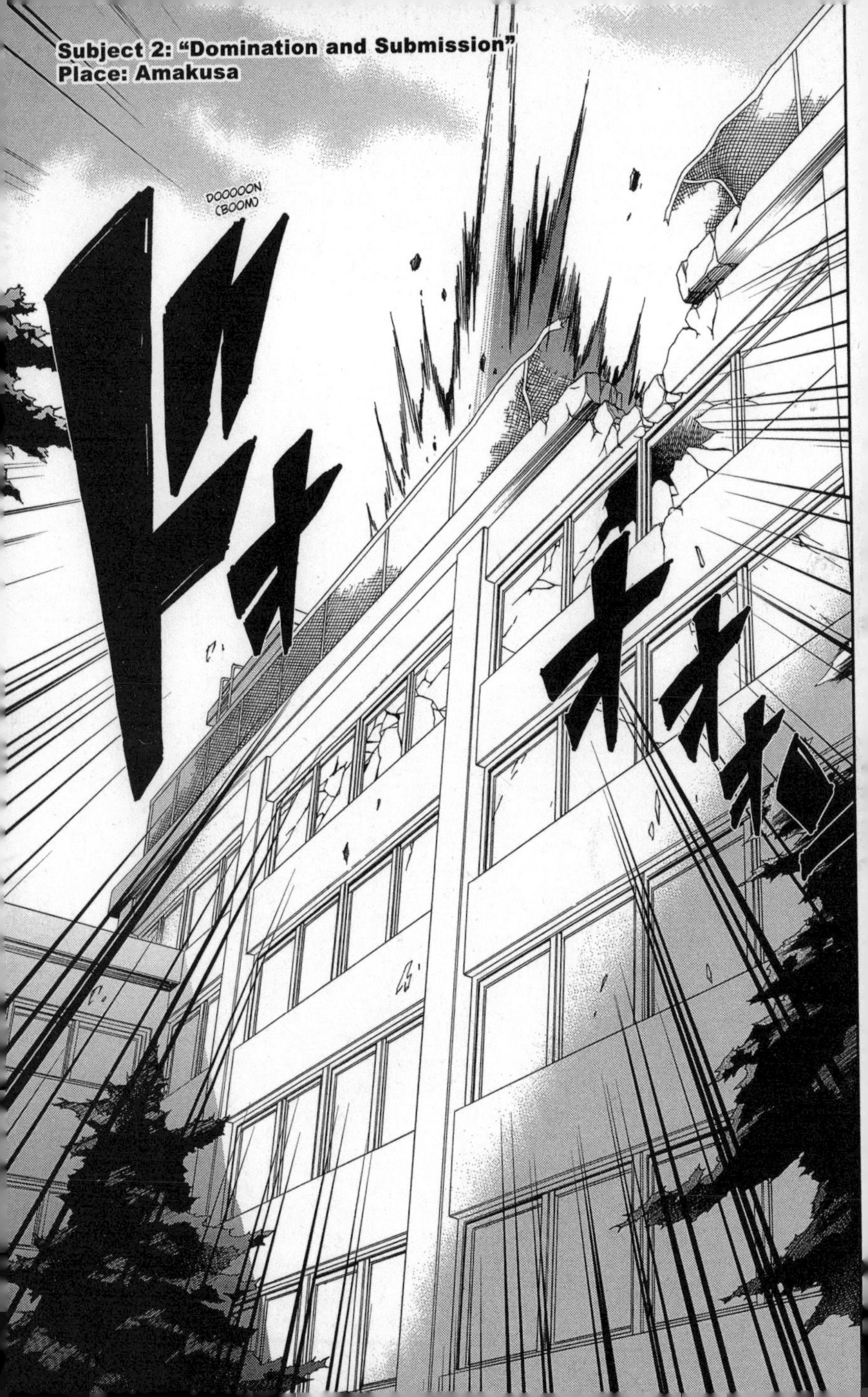
Subject 2: "Domination and Submission"
Place: Amakusa
DOOOOON
(BOOM)

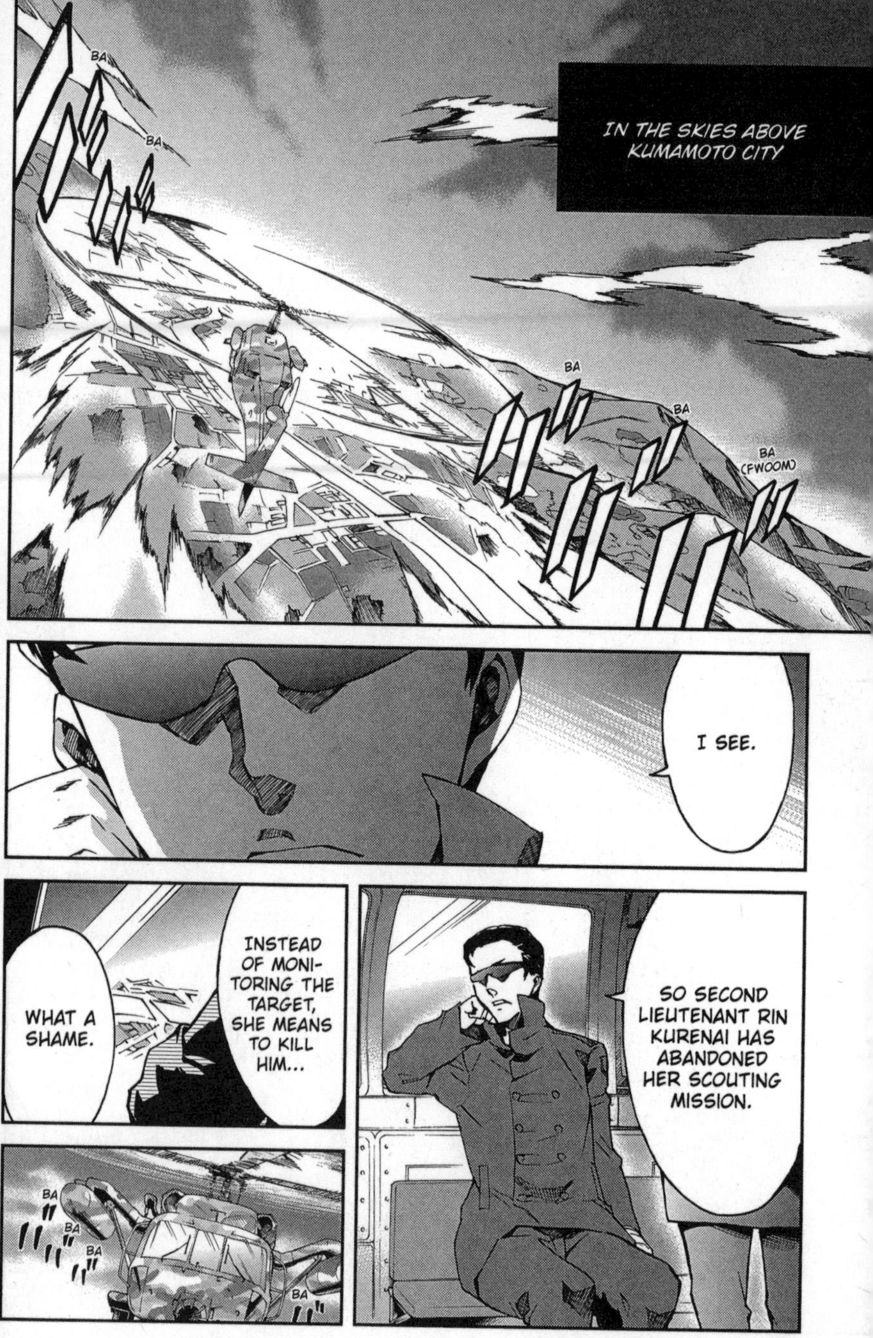
IN THE SKIES ABOVE KUMAMOTO CITY
BA
BA
BA
BA
BA (FWOOM)
I SEE.
SO SECOND LIEUTENANT RIN KURENAI HAS ABANDONED HER SCOUTING MISSION.
INSTEAD OF MONI-TORING THE TARGET, SHE MEANS TO KILL HIM...
WHAT A SHAME.
BA
BA
BA
BA

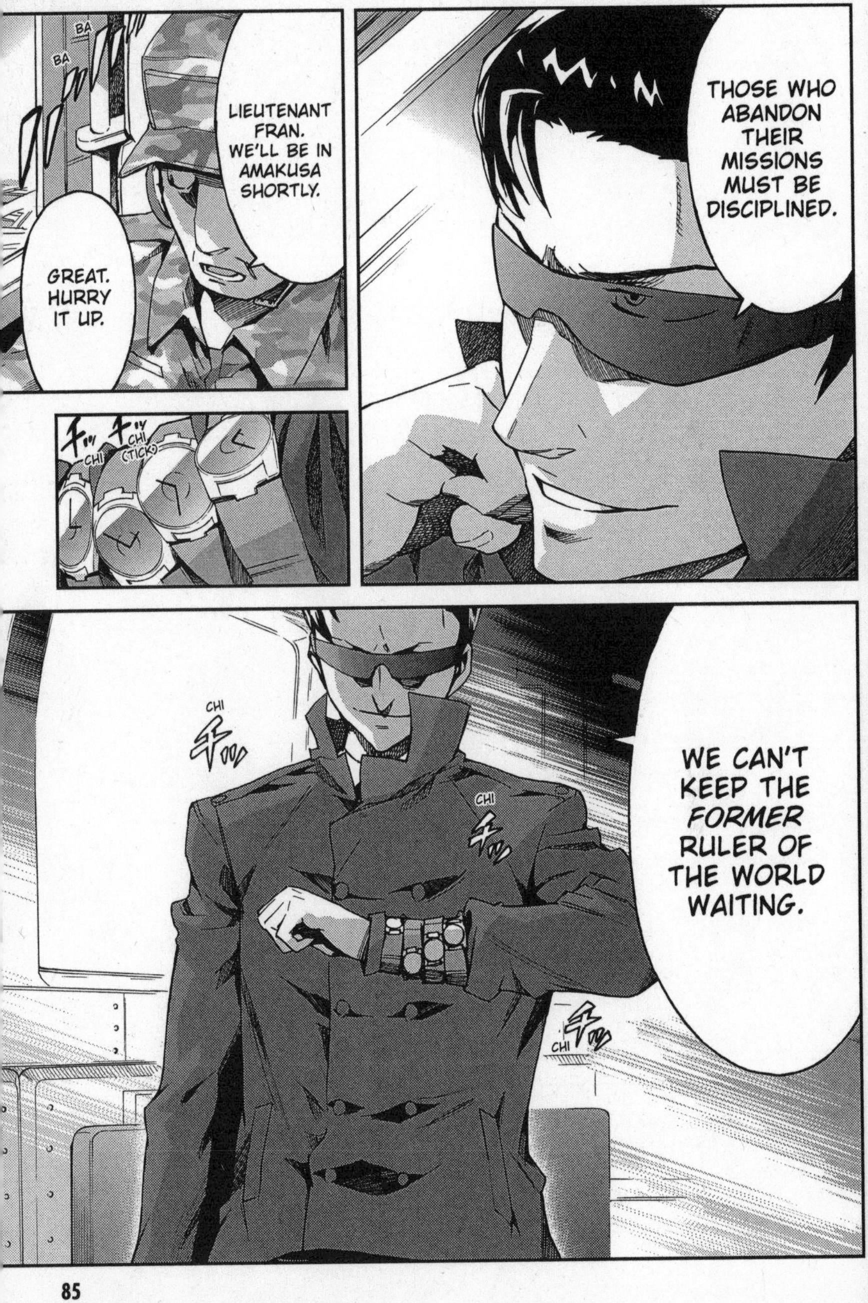
THOSE WHO ABANDON THEIR MISSIONS MUST BE DISCIPLINED.
LIEUTENANT FRAN. WE'LL BE IN AMAKUSA SHORTLY.
BA
BA
GREAT. HURRY IT UP.
CHI
CHI (TICK)
WE CAN'T KEEP THE *FORMER* RULER OF THE WORLD WAITING.
CHI
CHI
CHI

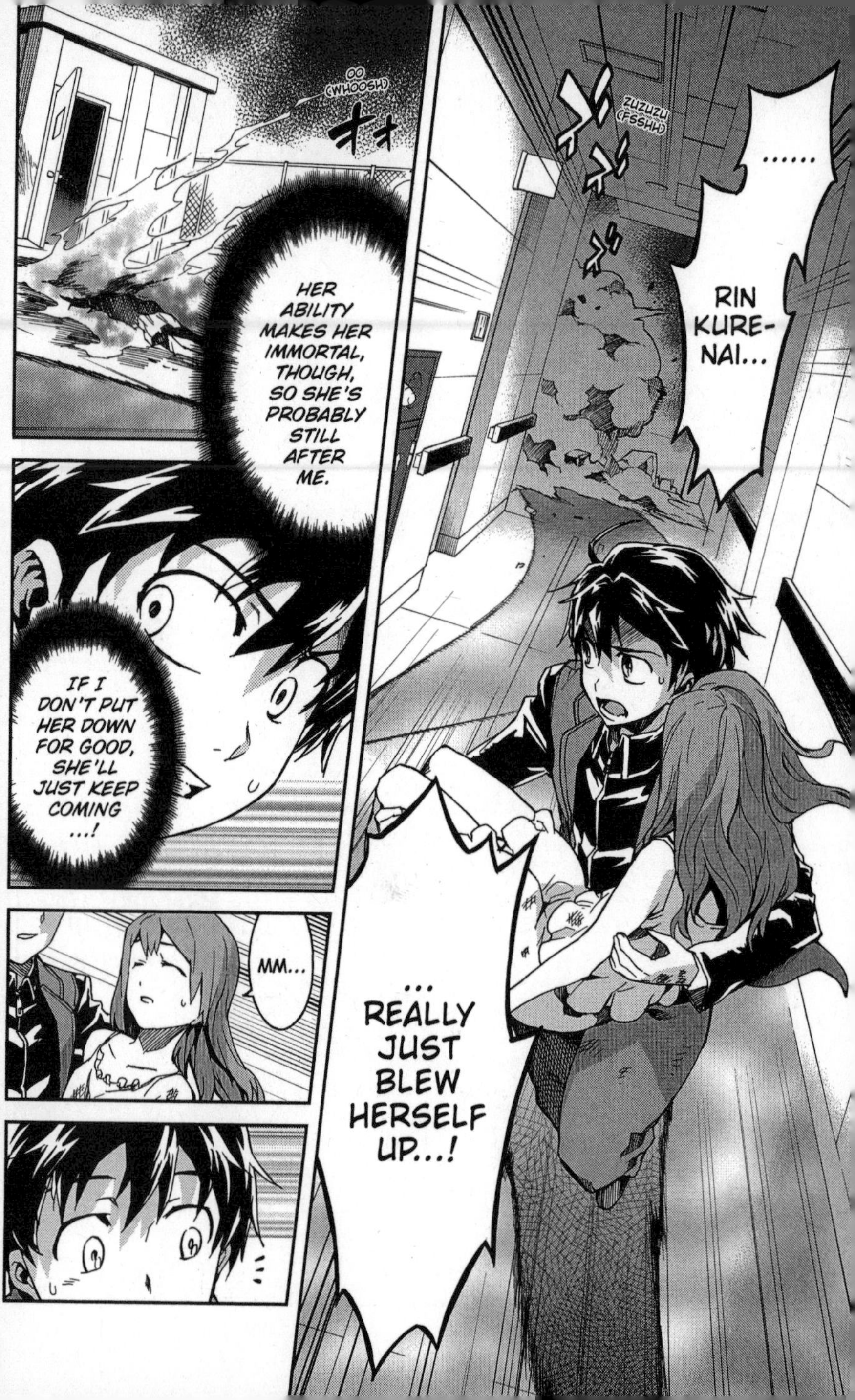
......
ZUZUZU (FSSHH)
RIN KURE-NAI...
...REALLY JUST BLEW HERSELF UP...!
OO (WHOOSH)
HER ABILITY MAKES HER IMMORTAL, THOUGH, SO SHE'S PROBABLY STILL AFTER ME.
IF I DON'T PUT HER DOWN FOR GOOD, SHE'LL JUST KEEP COMING...!
MM...

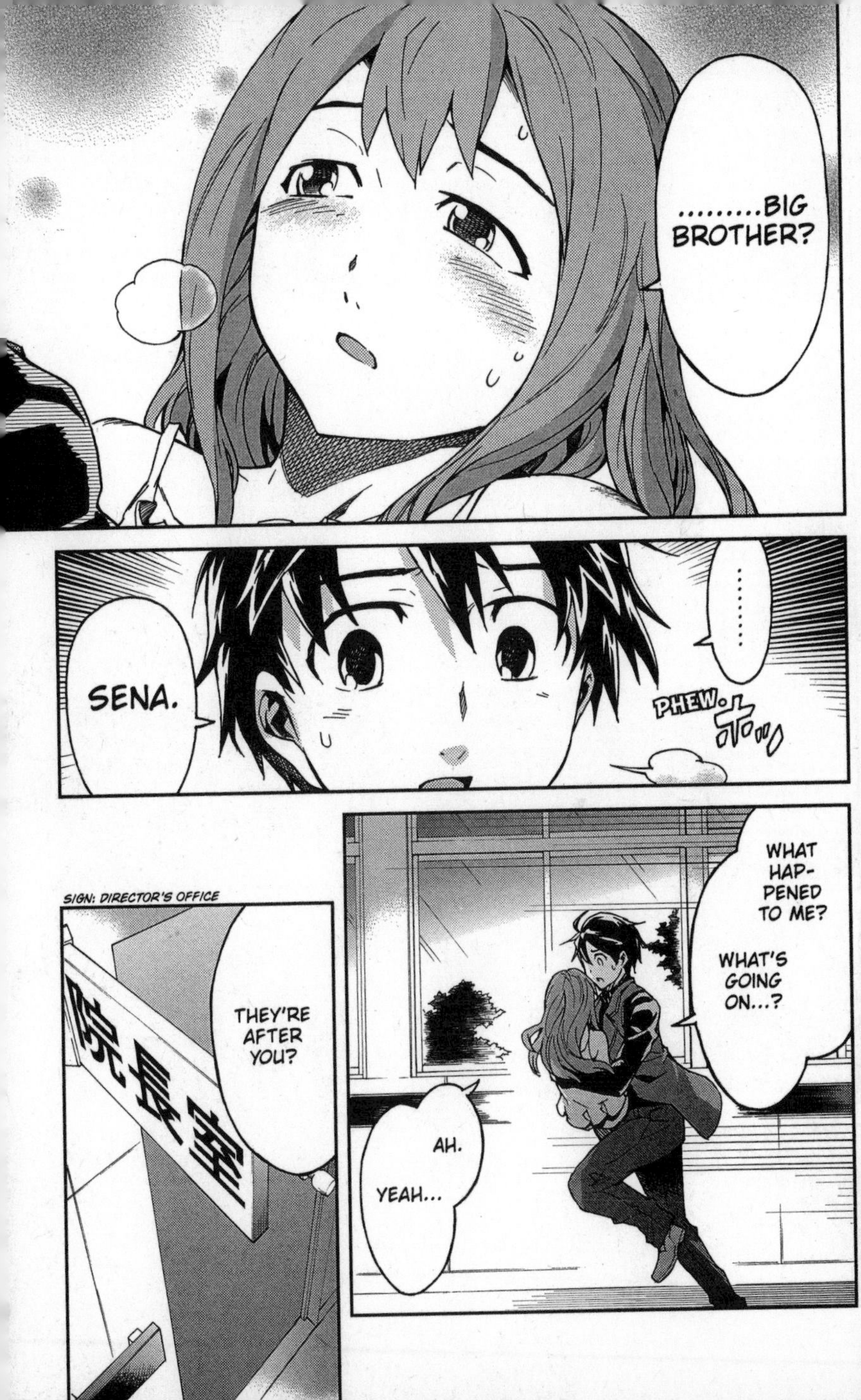
.........BIG BROTHER?
......
SENA.
PHEW
ホッ
WHAT HAP-PENED TO ME?
WHAT'S GOING ON...?
AH.
YEAH...
SIGN: DIRECTOR'S OFFICE
院長室
THEY'RE AFTER YOU?

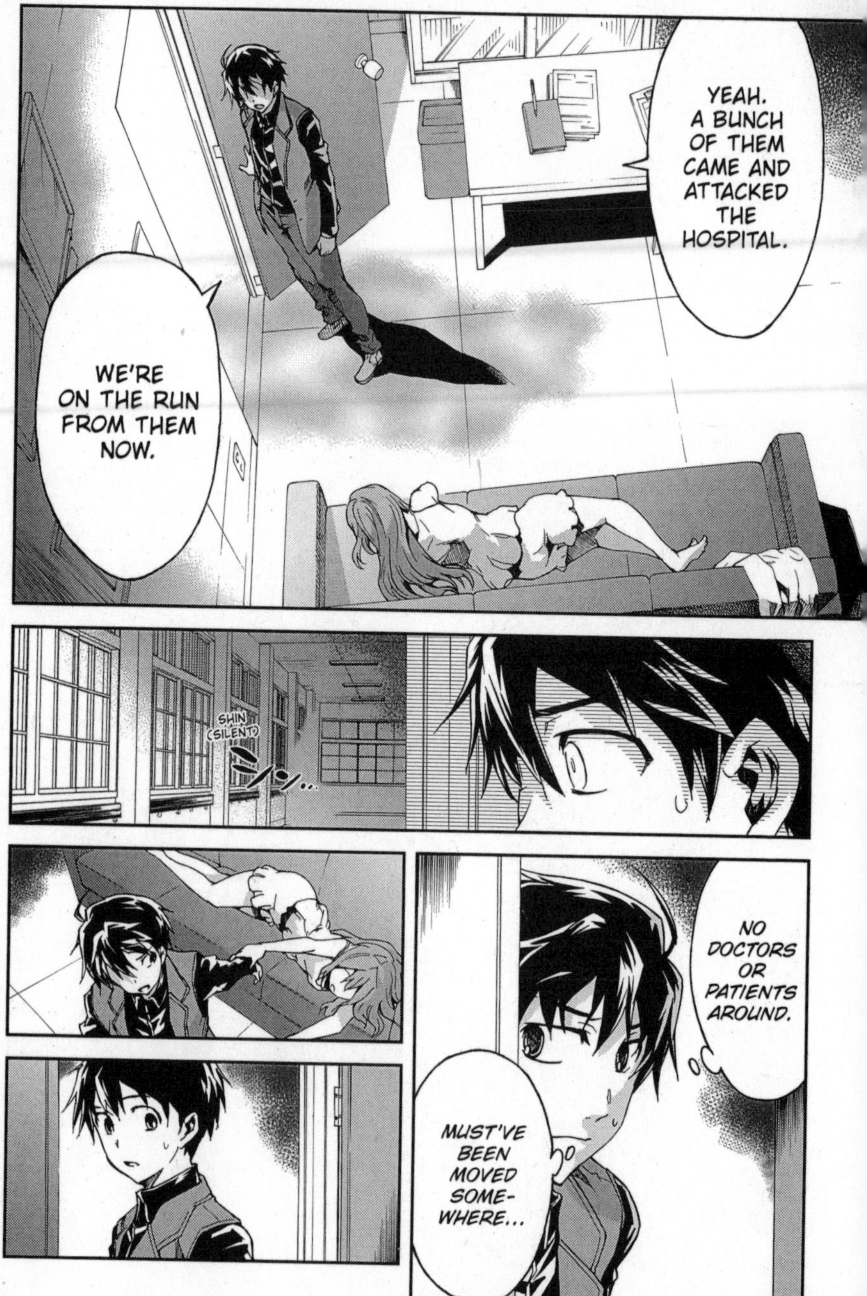
YEAH. A BUNCH OF THEM CAME AND ATTACKED THE HOSPITAL.
WE'RE ON THE RUN FROM THEM NOW.
SHIN (SILENT)
NO DOCTORS OR PATIENTS AROUND.
MUST'VE BEEN MOVED SOME-WHERE...

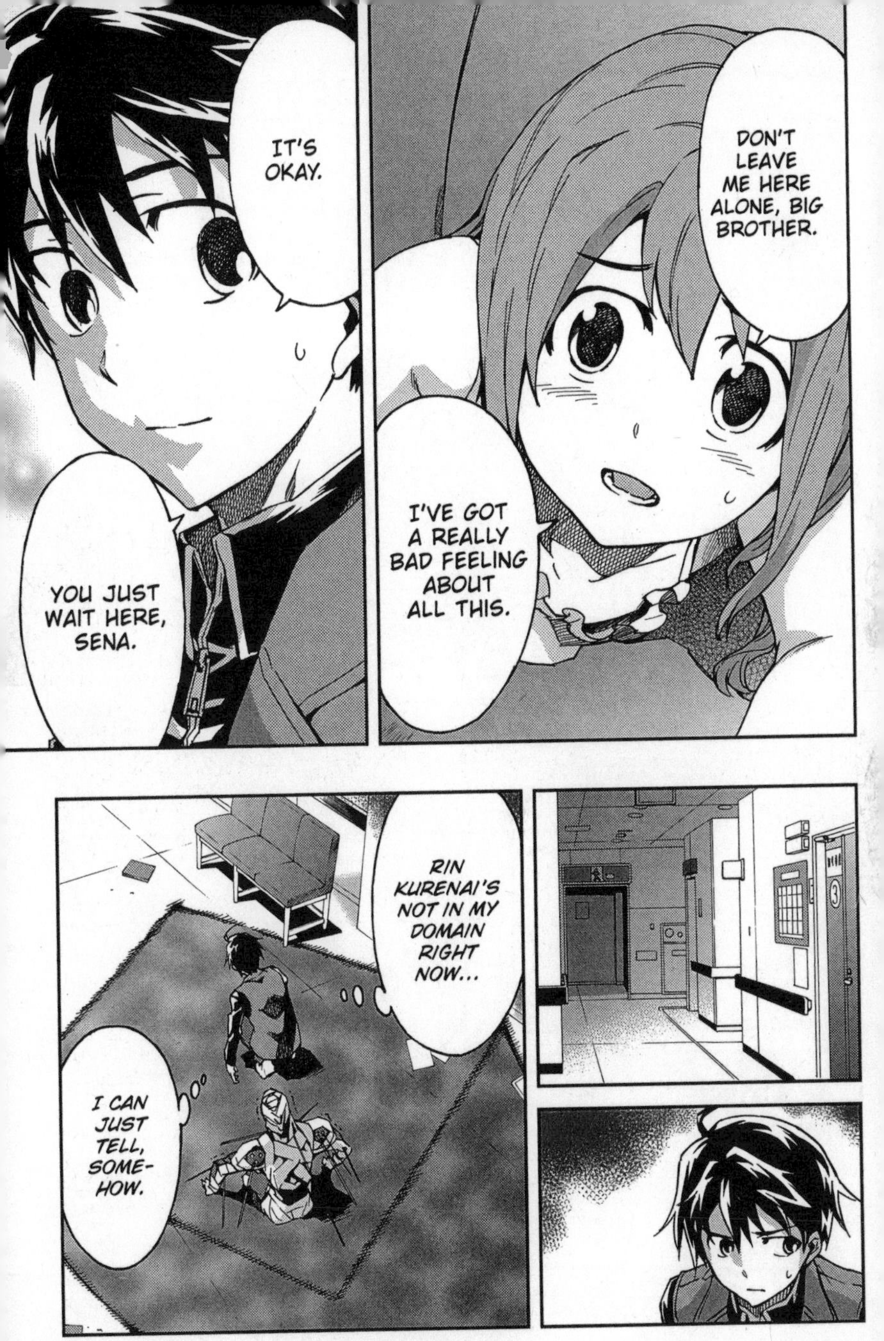
DON'T LEAVE ME HERE ALONE, BIG BROTHER.
I'VE GOT A REALLY BAD FEELING ABOUT ALL THIS.
IT'S OKAY.
YOU JUST WAIT HERE, SENA.
RIN KURENAI'S NOT IN MY DOMAIN RIGHT NOW...
I CAN JUST TELL, SOME-HOW.

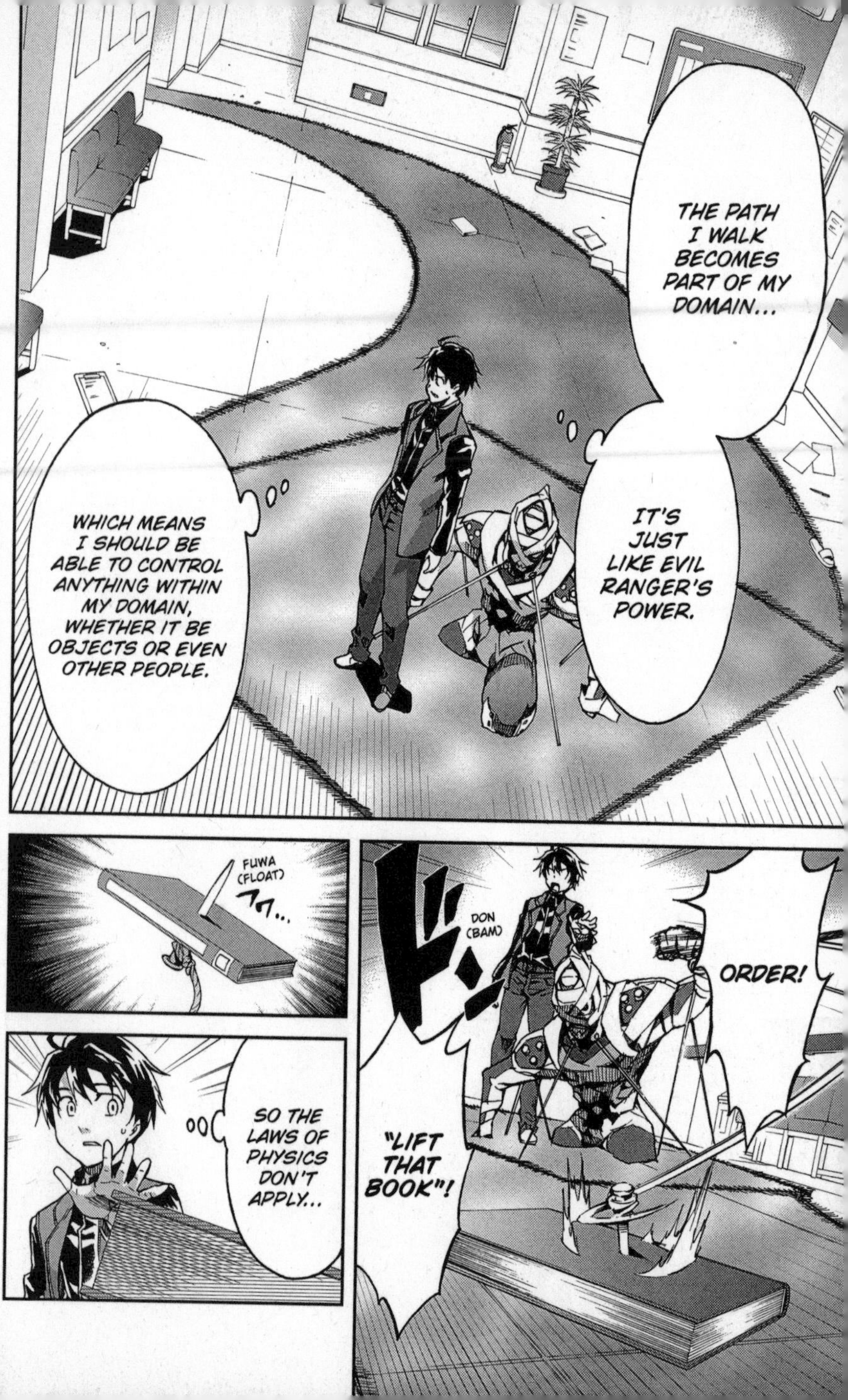
THE PATH I WALK BECOMES PART OF MY DOMAIN...
IT'S JUST LIKE EVIL RANGER'S POWER.
WHICH MEANS I SHOULD BE ABLE TO CONTROL ANYTHING WITHIN MY DOMAIN, WHETHER IT BE OBJECTS OR EVEN OTHER PEOPLE.
ORDER!
DON (BAM)
"LIFT THAT BOOK"!
FUWA (FLOAT)
SO THE LAWS OF PHYSICS DON'T APPLY...

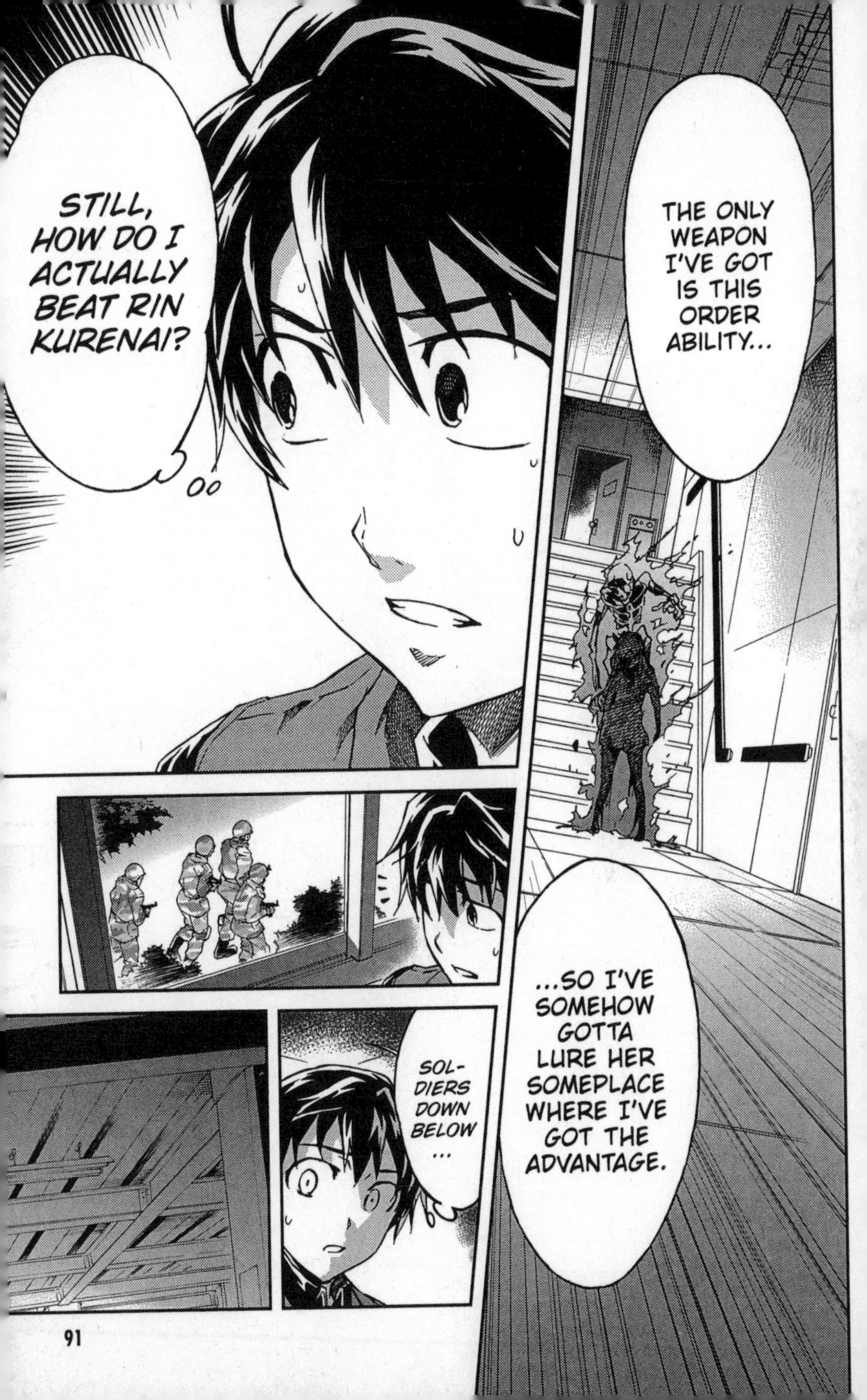
THE ONLY WEAPON I'VE GOT IS THIS ORDER ABILITY...
...SO I'VE SOMEHOW GOTTA LURE HER SOMEPLACE WHERE I'VE GOT THE ADVANTAGE.
STILL, HOW DO I ACTUALLY BEAT RIN KURENAI?
SOL-DIERS DOWN BELOW...

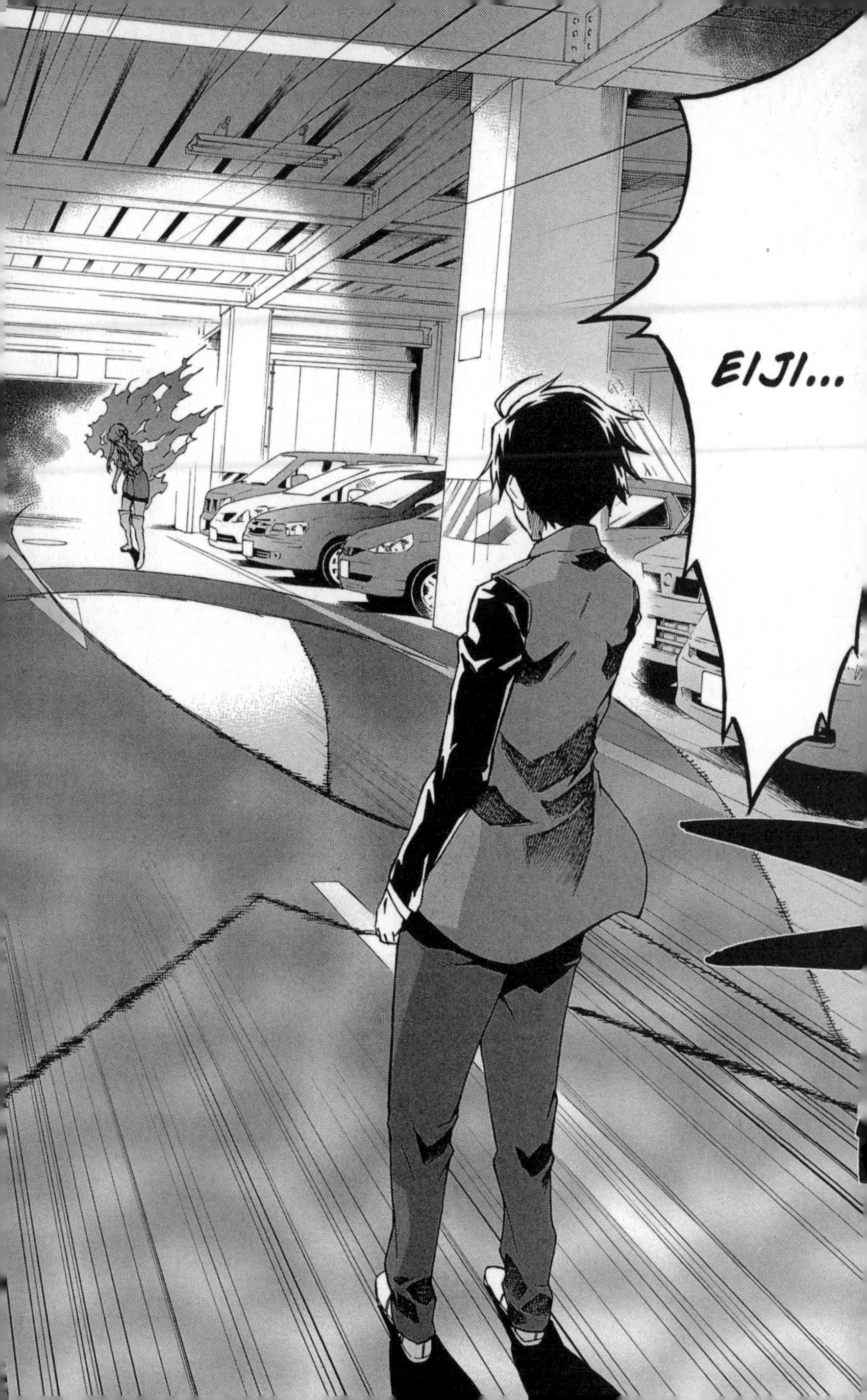
EIJI...

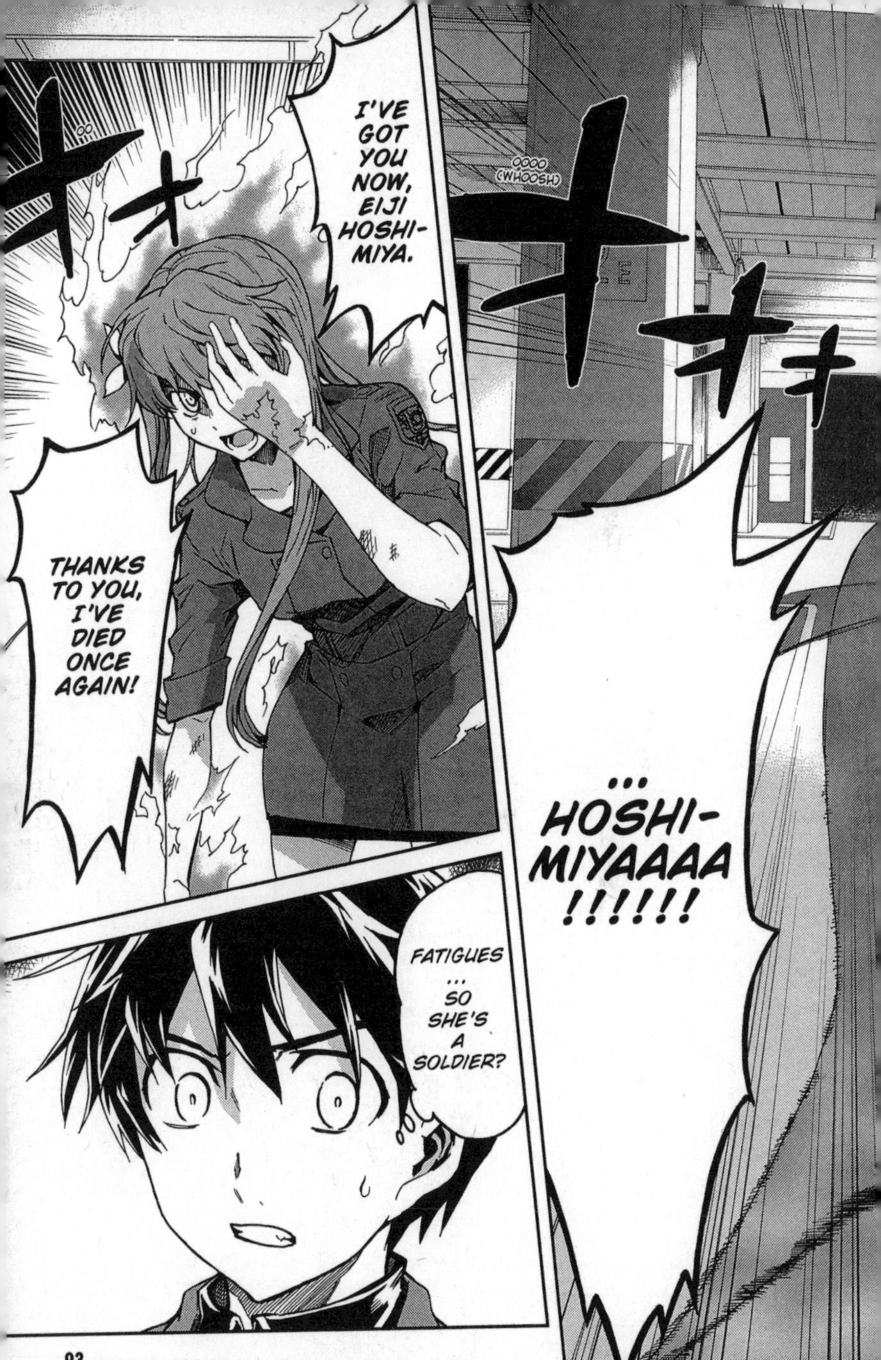
OOOO (WHOOSH)
...HOSHI-MIYAAAA!!!!!!
I'VE GOT YOU NOW, EIJI HOSHI-MIYA.
THANKS TO YOU, I'VE DIED ONCE AGAIN!
FATIGUES ... SO SHE'S A SOLDIER?

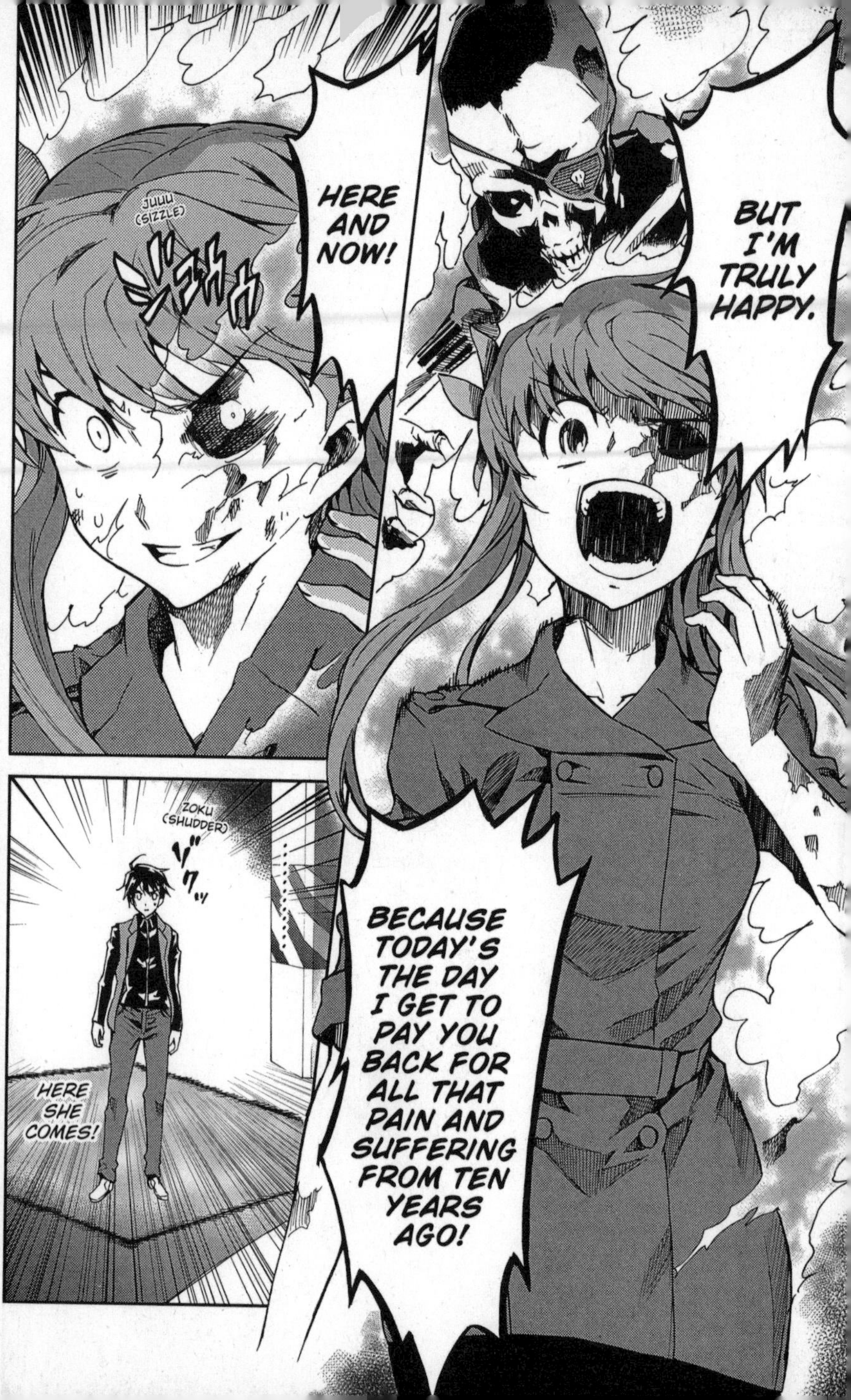
BUT I'M TRULY HAPPY.
BECAUSE TODAY'S THE DAY I GET TO PAY YOU BACK FOR ALL THAT PAIN AND SUFFERING FROM TEN YEARS AGO!
HERE AND NOW!
JUUU (SIZZLE)
ZOKU (SHUDDER)
HERE SHE COMES!

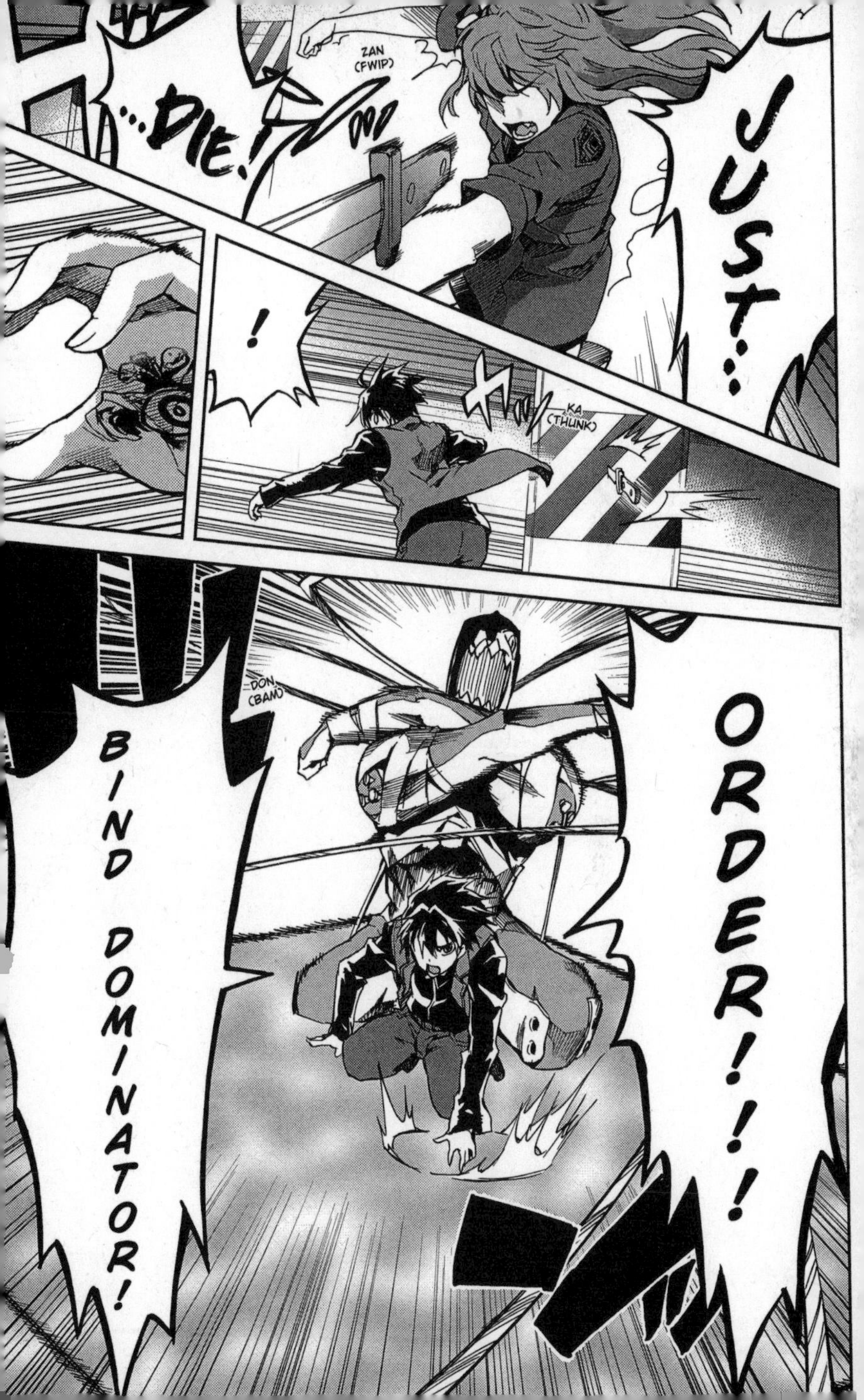
JUST...
...DIE.
ZAN (FWIP)
!
KA (THUNK)
ORDER!!!
DON (BAM)
BIND DOMINATOR!

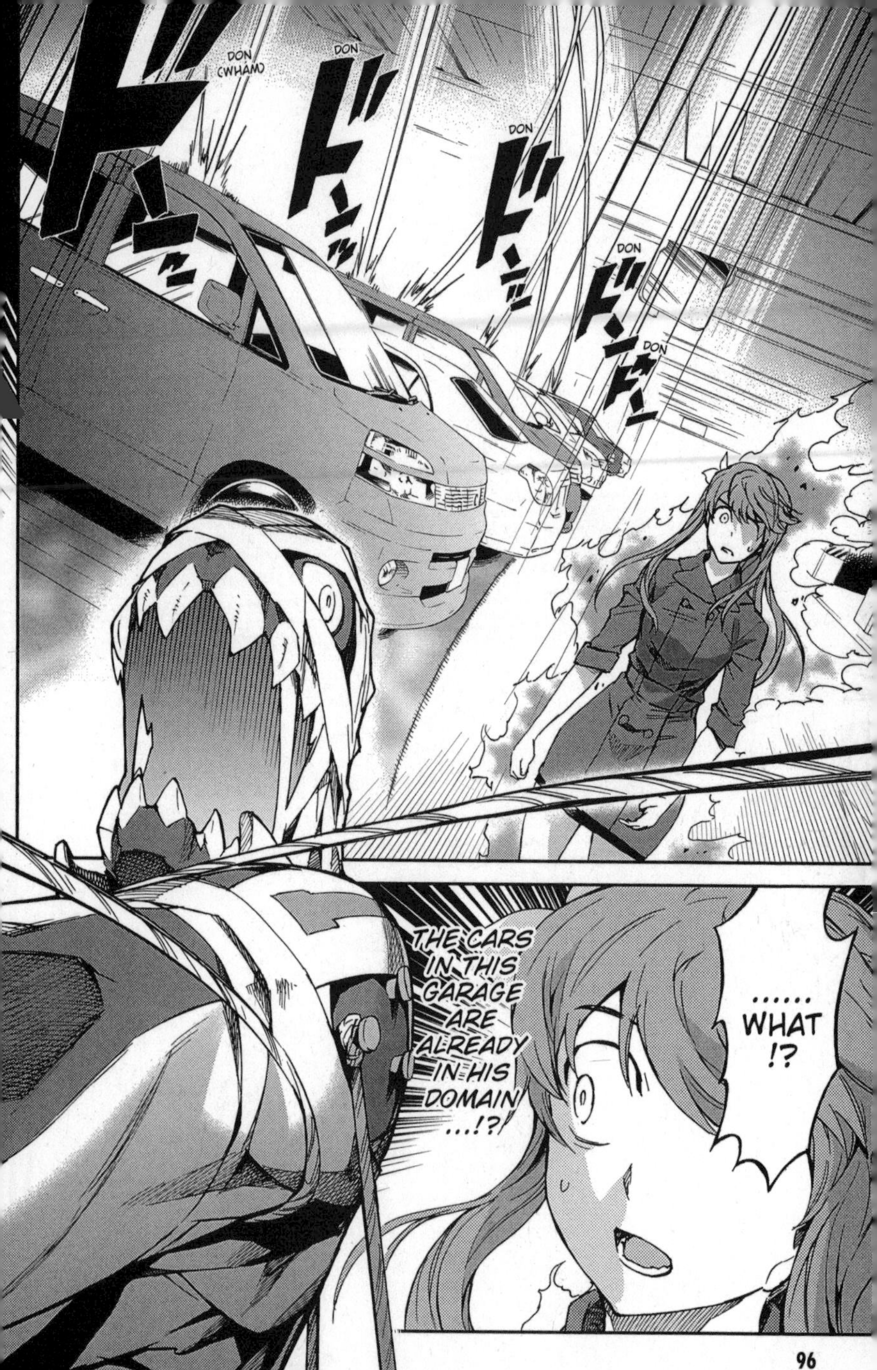
DON
DON
DON
DON
DON (WHAM)
......WHAT!?
THE CARS IN THIS GARAGE ARE ALREADY IN HIS DOMAIN...!?

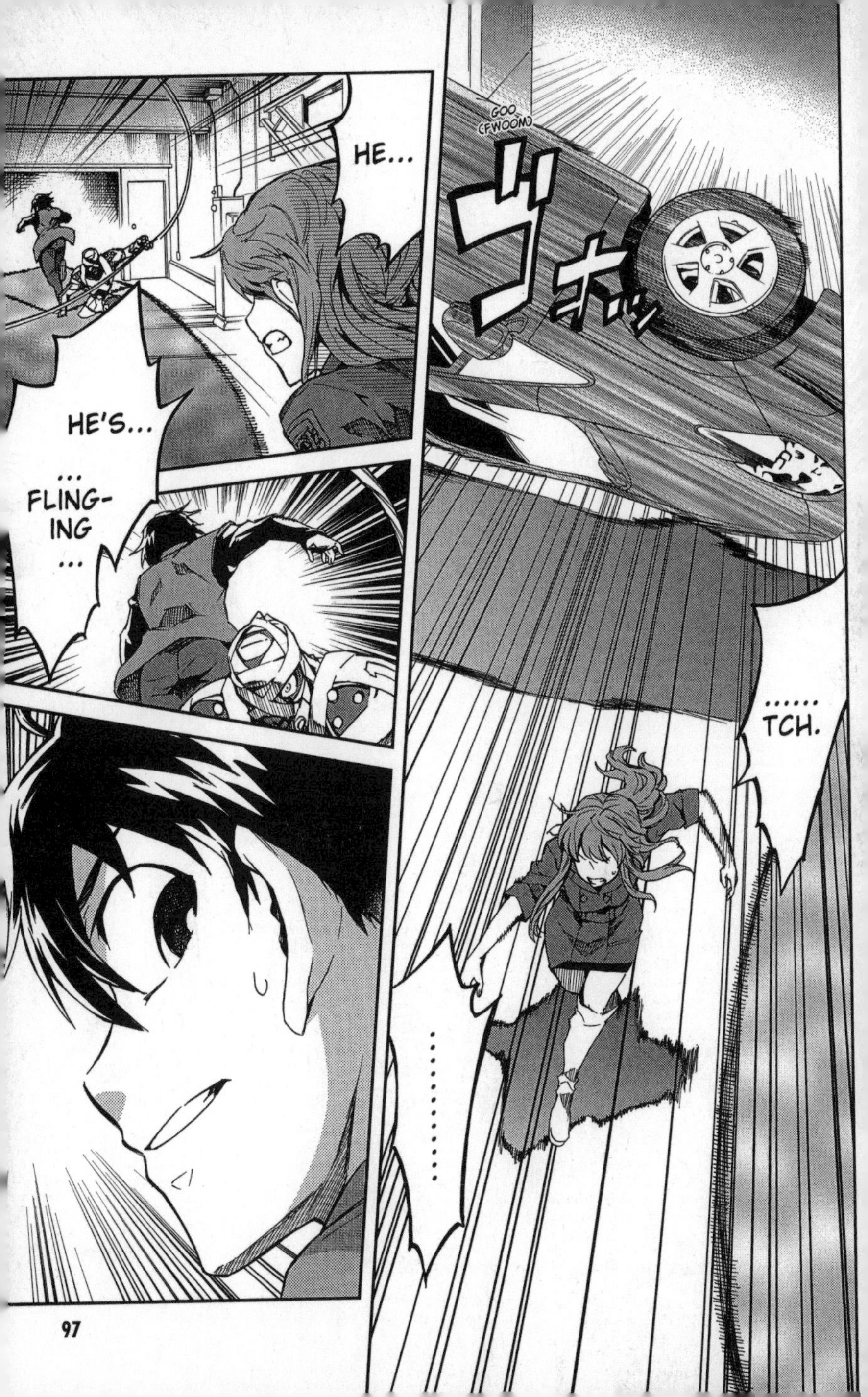
GOO (FWOOM)
……TCH.
HE…
HE'S…
…FLING-ING…
……

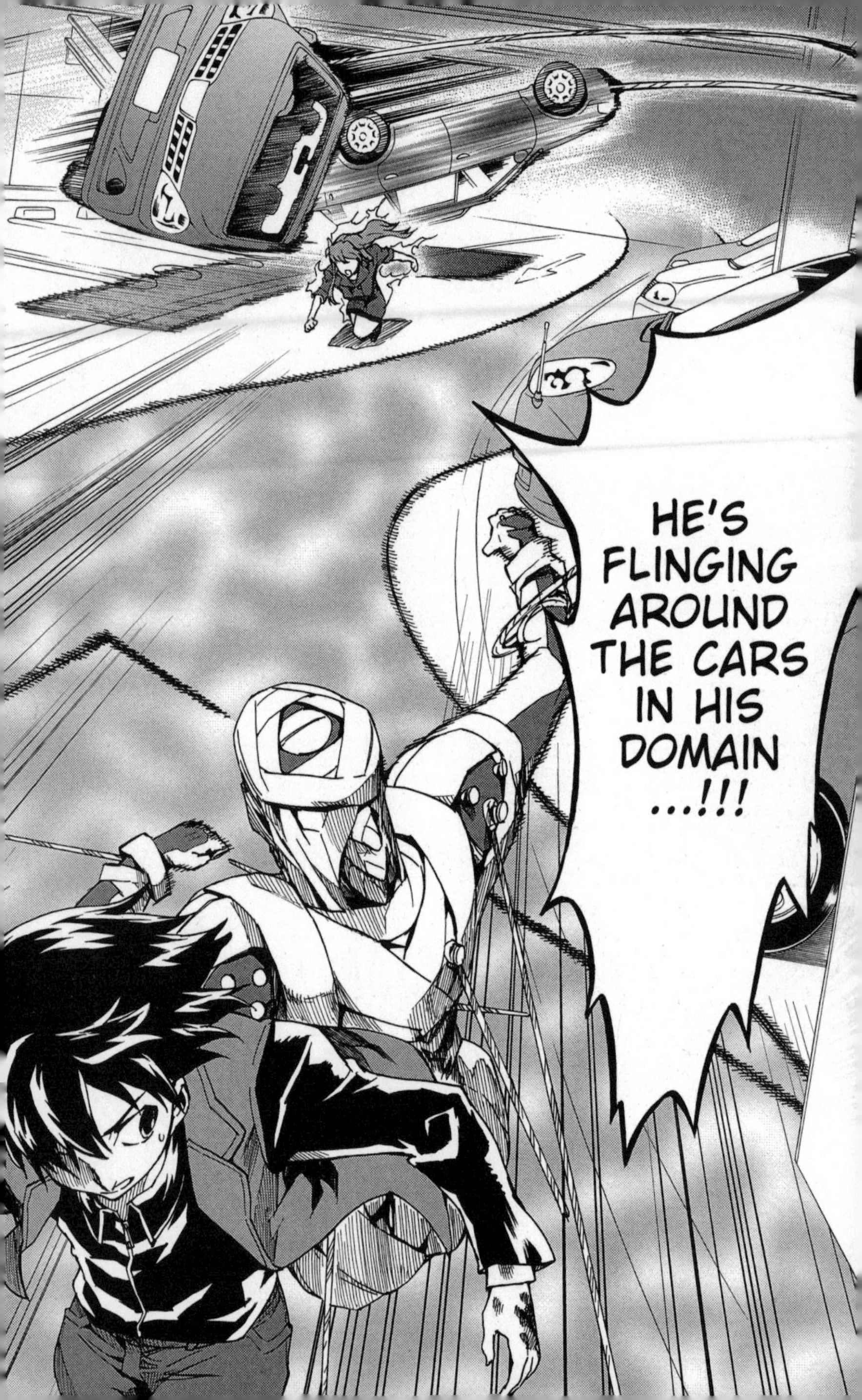
HE'S FLINGING AROUND THE CARS IN HIS DOMAIN ...!!!

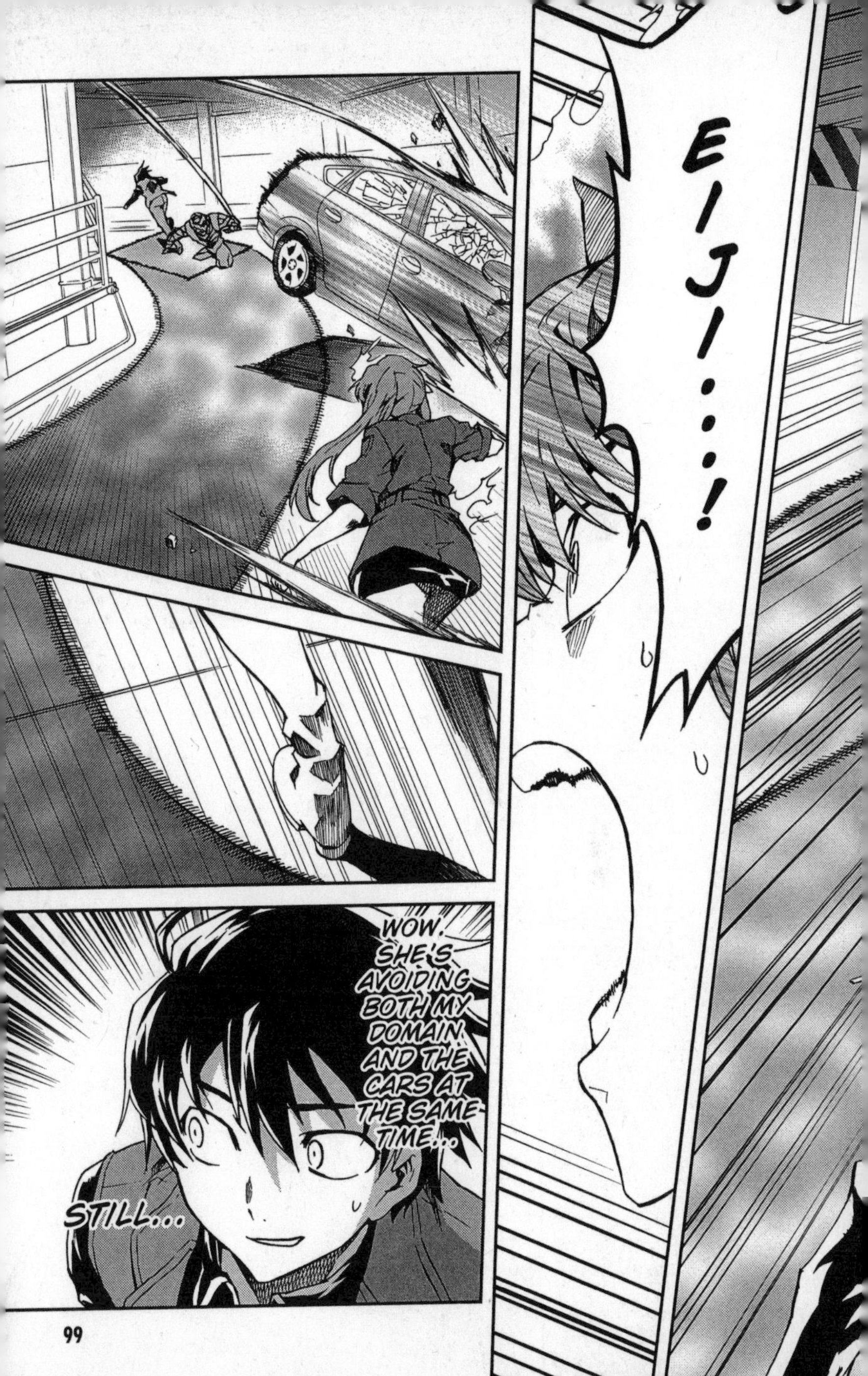
EIJI...!
WOW. SHE'S AVOIDING BOTH MY DOMAIN AND THE CARS AT THE SAME TIME...
STILL...

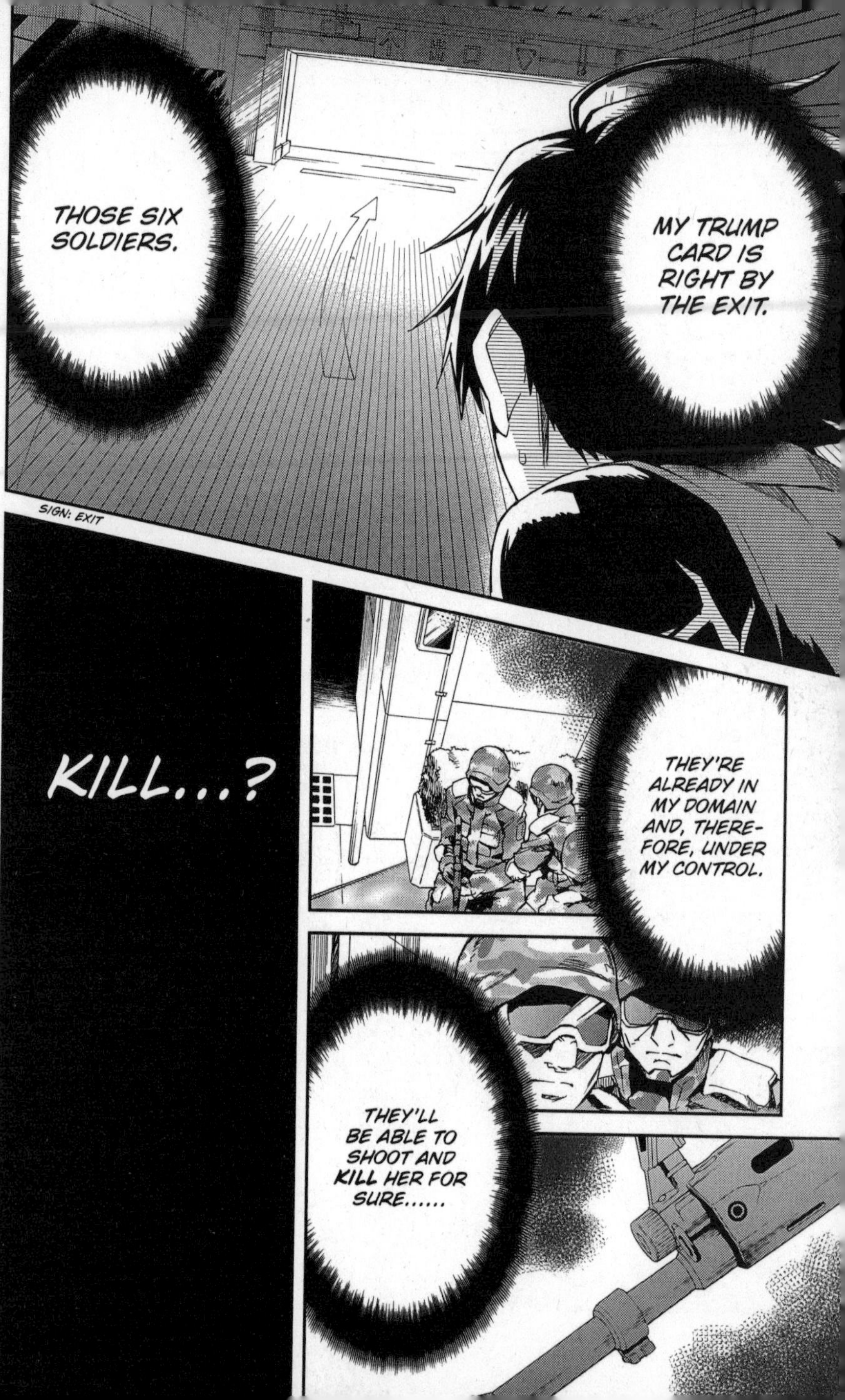
MY TRUMP CARD IS RIGHT BY THE EXIT.
THOSE SIX SOLDIERS.
SIGN: EXIT
THEY'RE ALREADY IN MY DOMAIN AND, THEREFORE, UNDER MY CONTROL.
THEY'LL BE ABLE TO SHOOT AND KILL HER FOR SURE......
KILL...?

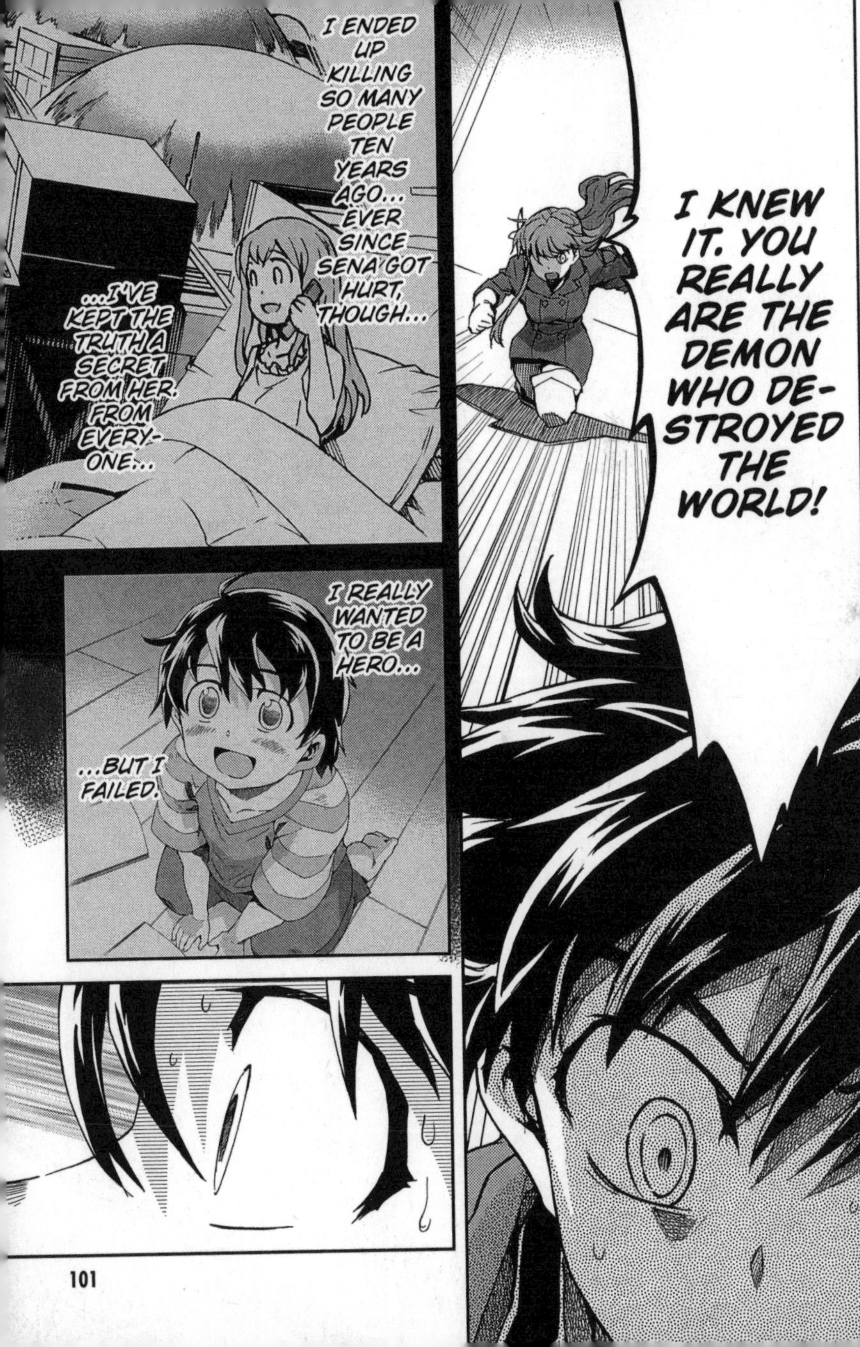
I KNEW IT. YOU REALLY ARE THE DEMON WHO DE-STROYED THE WORLD!
I ENDED UP KILLING SO MANY PEOPLE TEN YEARS AGO... EVER SINCE SENA GOT HURT, THOUGH...
...I'VE KEPT THE TRUTH A SECRET FROM HER. FROM EVERY-ONE...
I REALLY WANTED TO BE A HERO...
...BUT I FAILED.

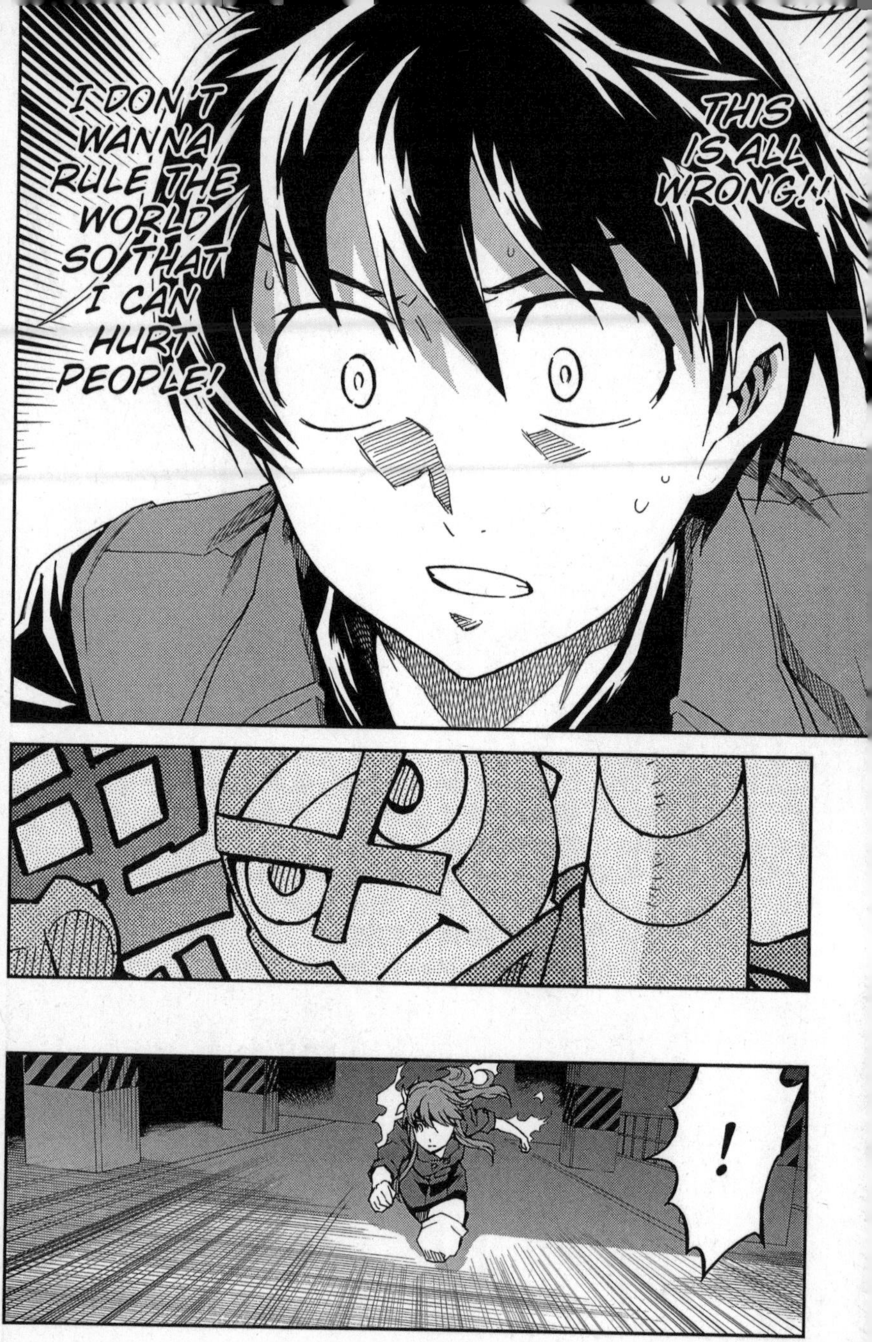
THIS IS ALL WRONG!!
I DON'T WANNA RULE THE WORLD SO THAT I CAN HURT PEOPLE!
!

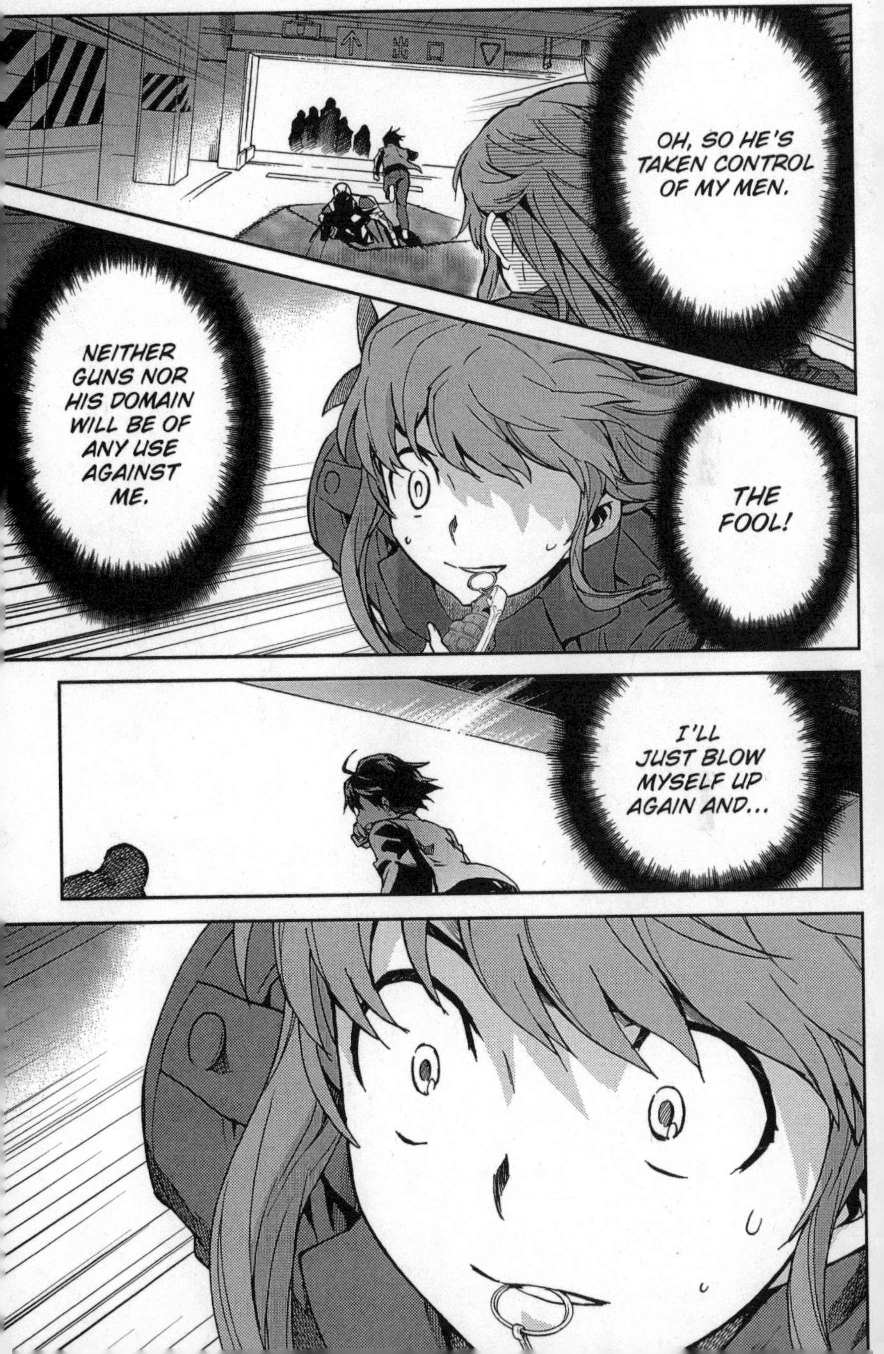
OH, SO HE'S TAKEN CONTROL OF MY MEN.
NEITHER GUNS NOR HIS DOMAIN WILL BE OF ANY USE AGAINST ME.
THE FOOL!
I'LL JUST BLOW MYSELF UP AGAIN AND...

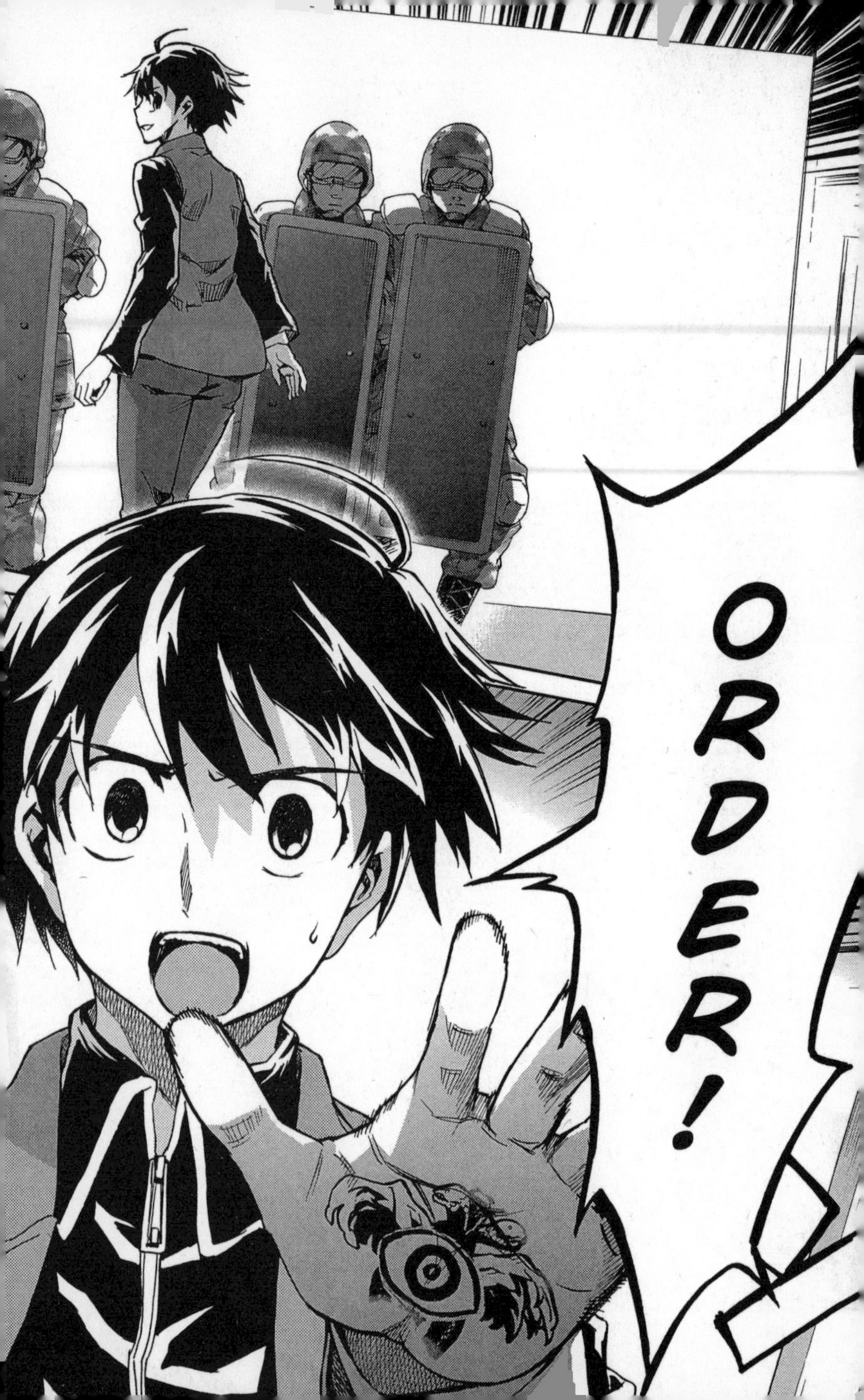
ORDER!

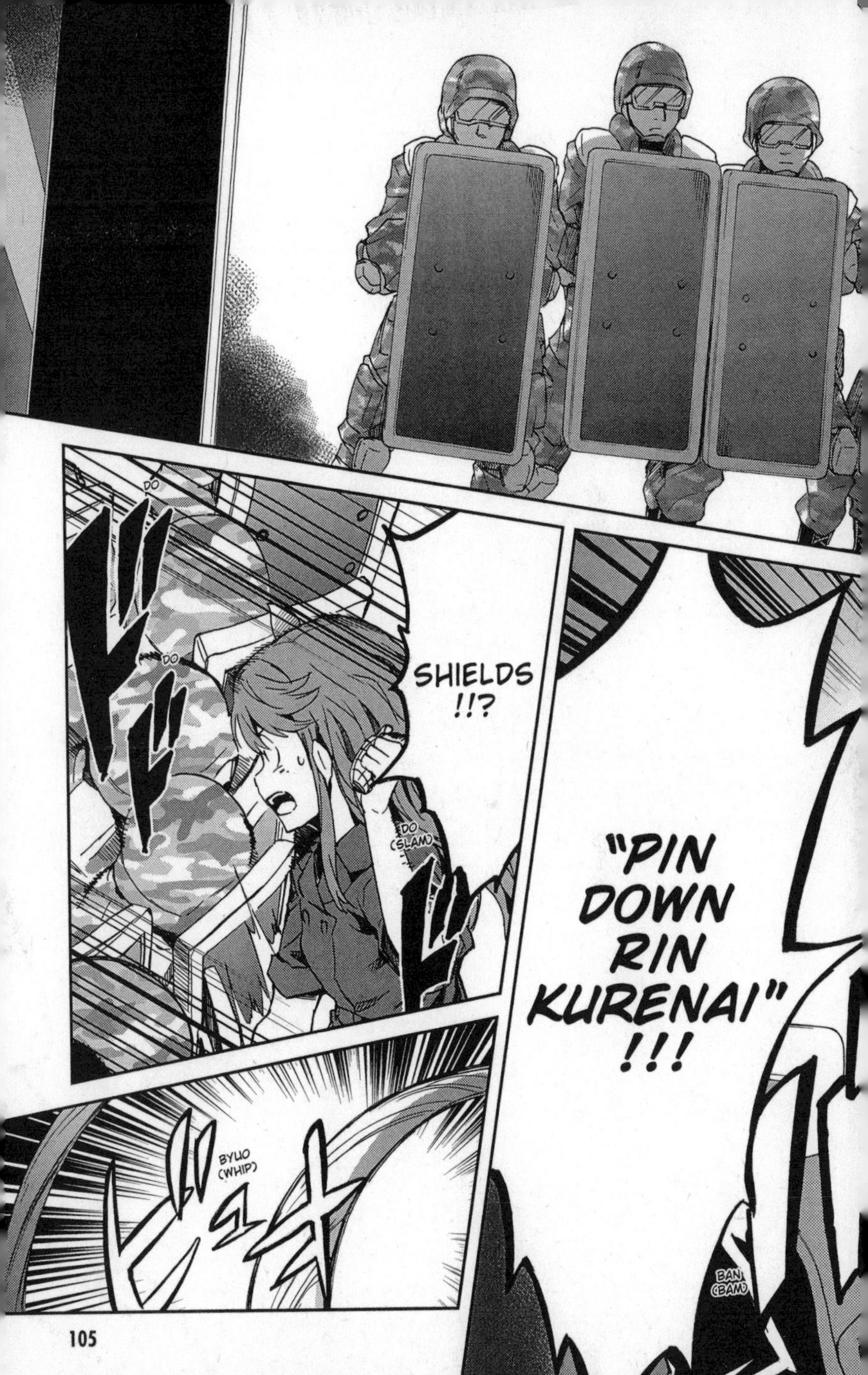
"PIN DOWN RIN KURENAI"!!!
BAN (BAM)
DO
DO
SHIELDS!!?
DO (SLAM)
BYUO (WHIP)

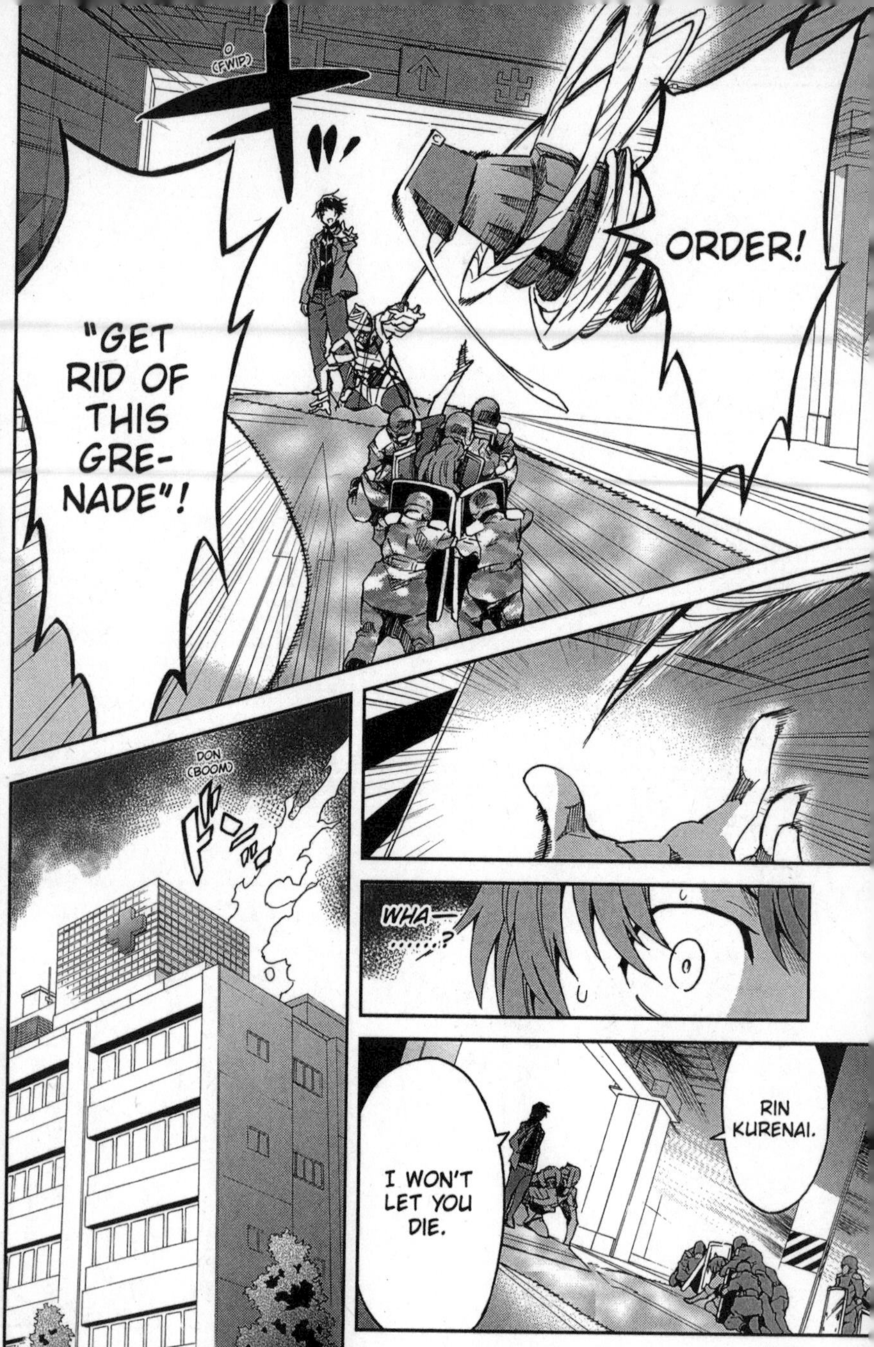
O
(FWIP)
"GET RID OF THIS GRE-NADE"!
ORDER!
WHA—......?
RIN KURENAI.
I WON'T LET YOU DIE.
DON
(BOOM)

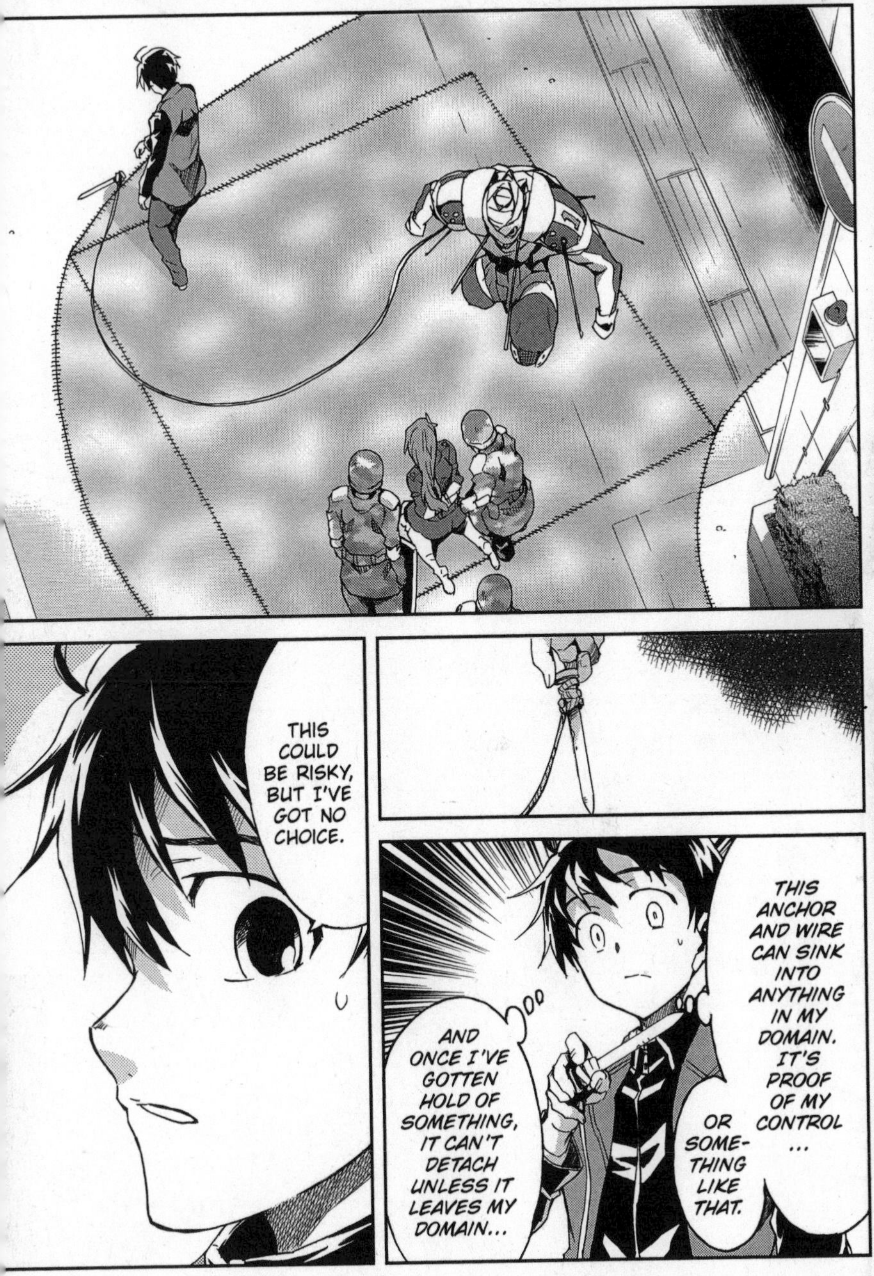
THIS ANCHOR AND WIRE CAN SINK INTO ANYTHING IN MY DOMAIN. IT'S PROOF OF MY CONTROL...
OR SOMETHING LIKE THAT.
AND ONCE I'VE GOTTEN HOLD OF SOMETHING, IT CAN'T DETACH UNLESS IT LEAVES MY DOMAIN...
THIS COULD BE RISKY, BUT I'VE GOT NO CHOICE.

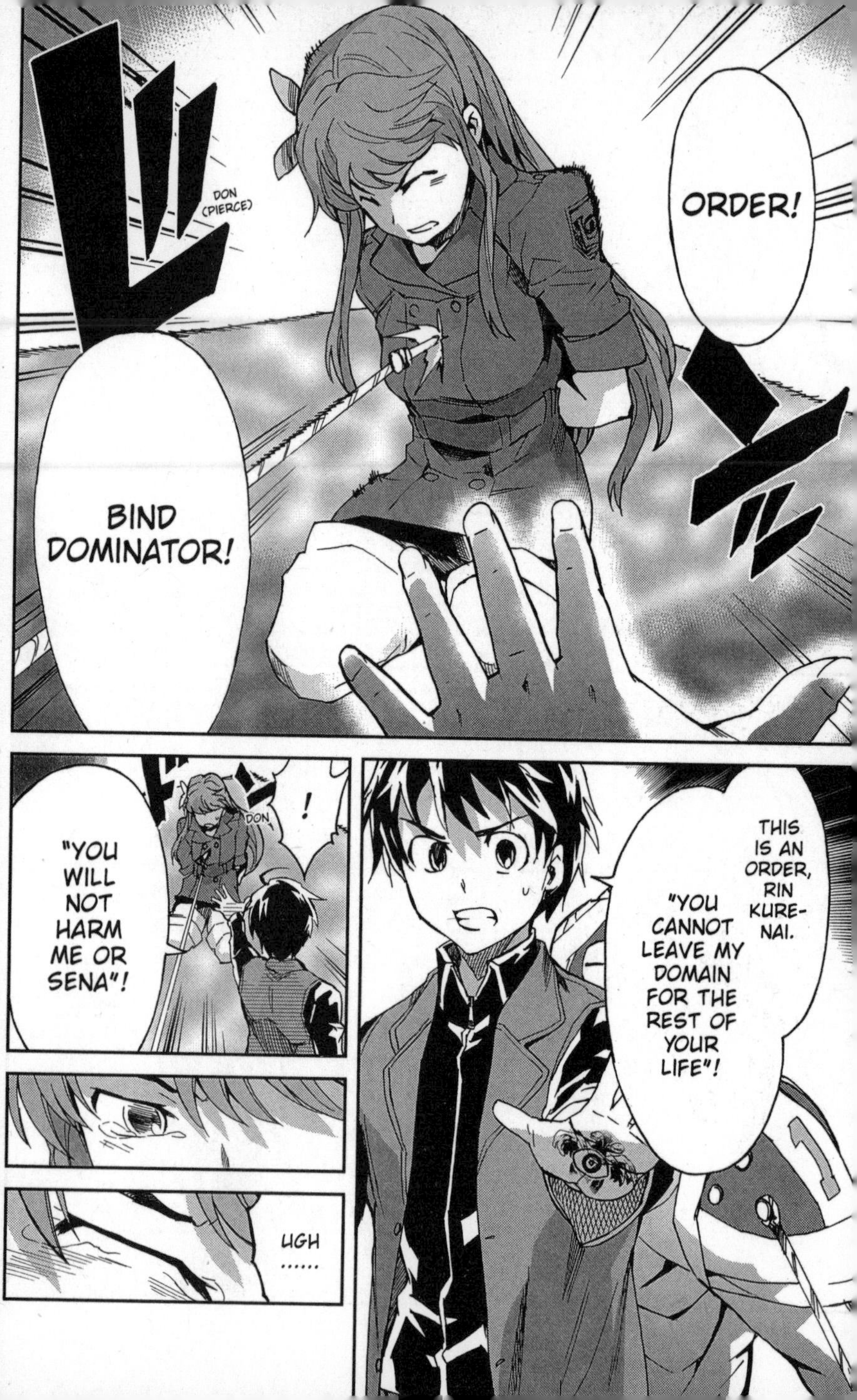
ORDER!
DON (PIERCE)
BIND DOMINATOR!
THIS IS AN ORDER, RIN KURENAI.
"YOU CANNOT LEAVE MY DOMAIN FOR THE REST OF YOUR LIFE"!
!
DON
"YOU WILL NOT HARM ME OR SENA"!
UGH ......

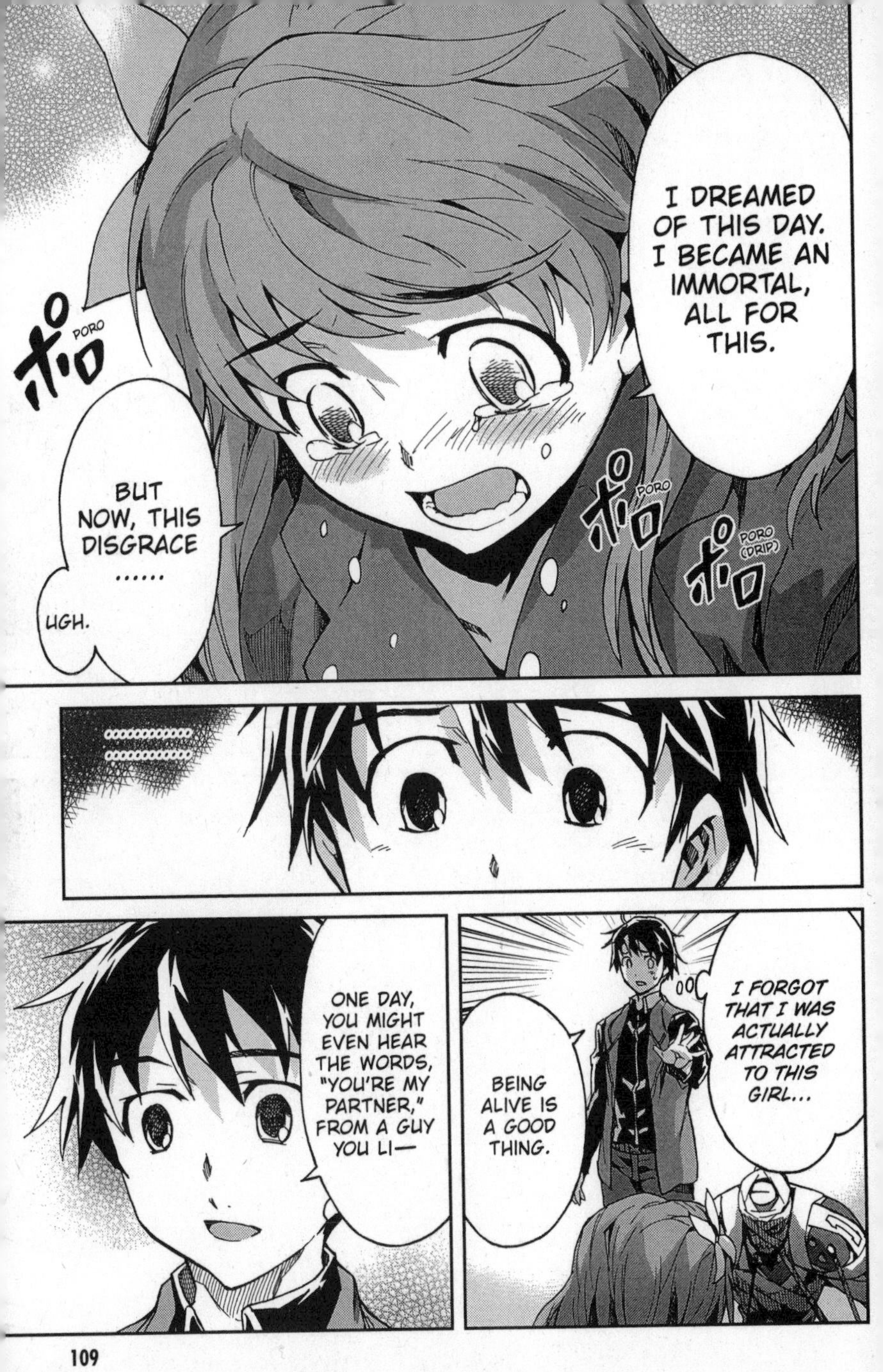
I DREAMED OF THIS DAY. I BECAME AN IMMORTAL, ALL FOR THIS.
ポロ PORO
ポロ POROポロ PORO (DRIP)
ポロ PORO
BUT NOW, THIS DISGRACE ......
UGH.
I FORGOT THAT I WAS ACTUALLY ATTRACTED TO THIS GIRL...
BEING ALIVE IS A GOOD THING.
ONE DAY, YOU MIGHT EVEN HEAR THE WORDS, "YOU'RE MY PARTNER," FROM A GUY YOU LI—

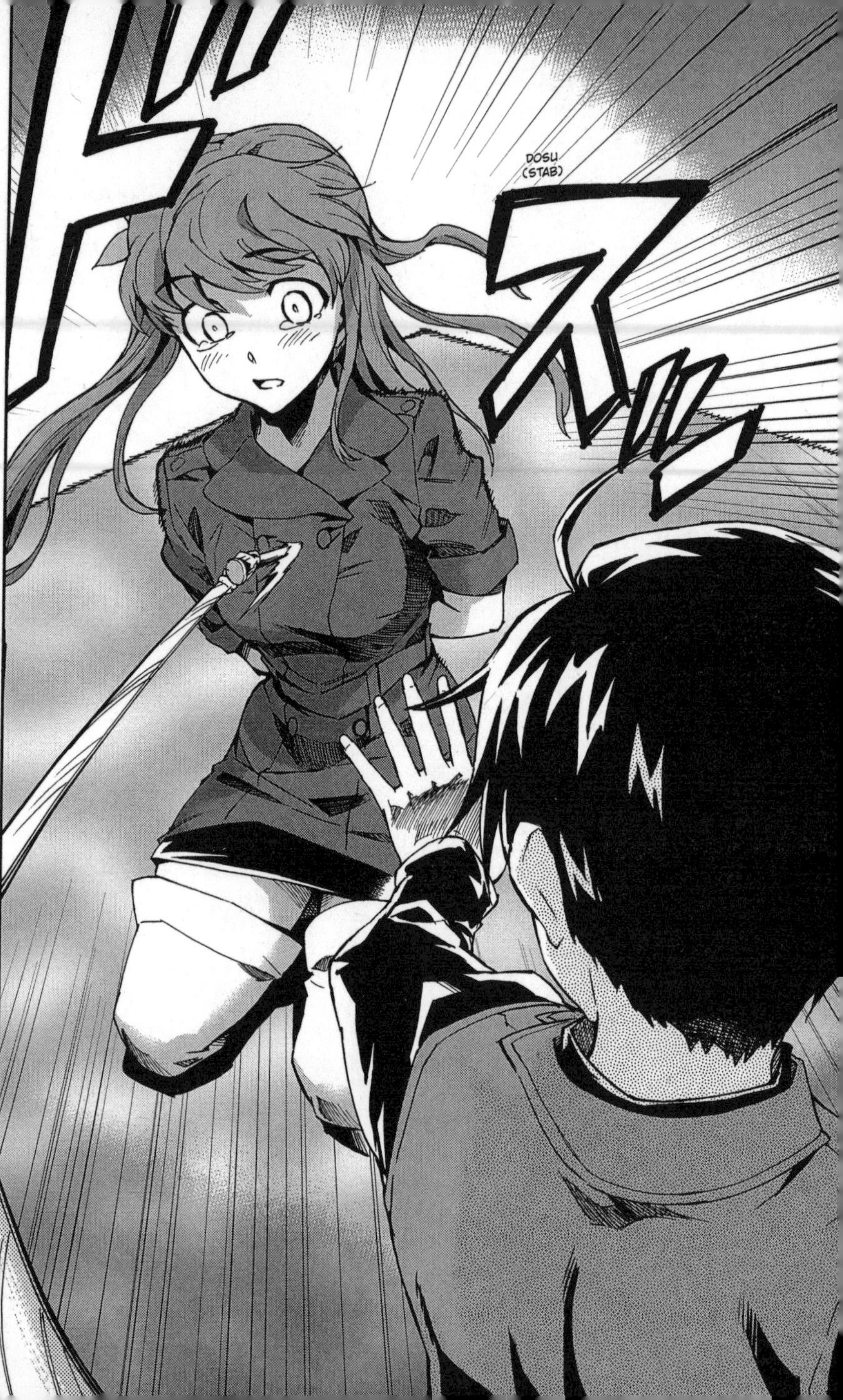
DOSU
(STAB)

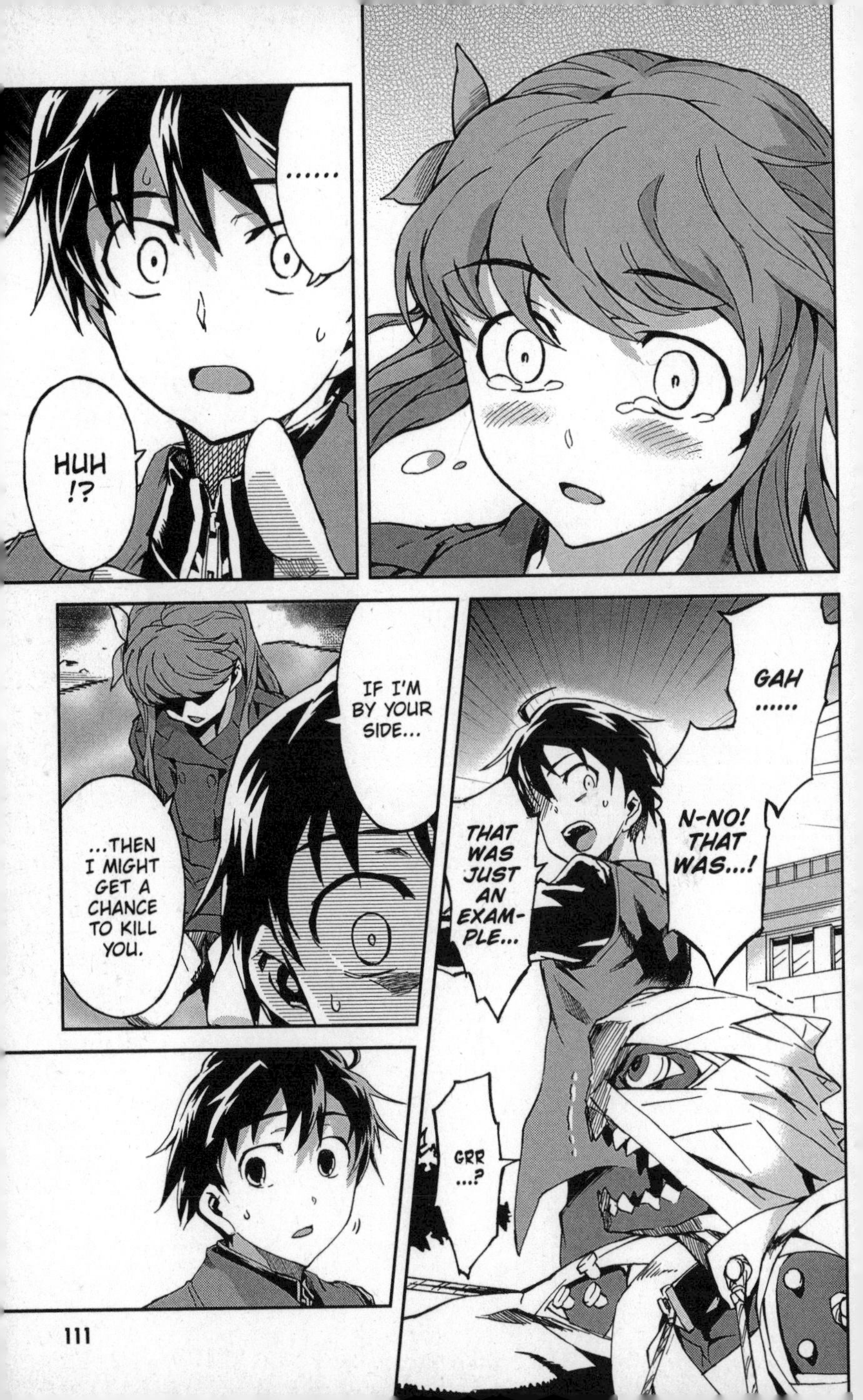
......
HUH !?
IF I'M BY YOUR SIDE...
...THEN I MIGHT GET A CHANCE TO KILL YOU.
GAH ......
N-NO! THAT WAS...!
THAT WAS JUST AN EXAM-PLE...
GRR ...?

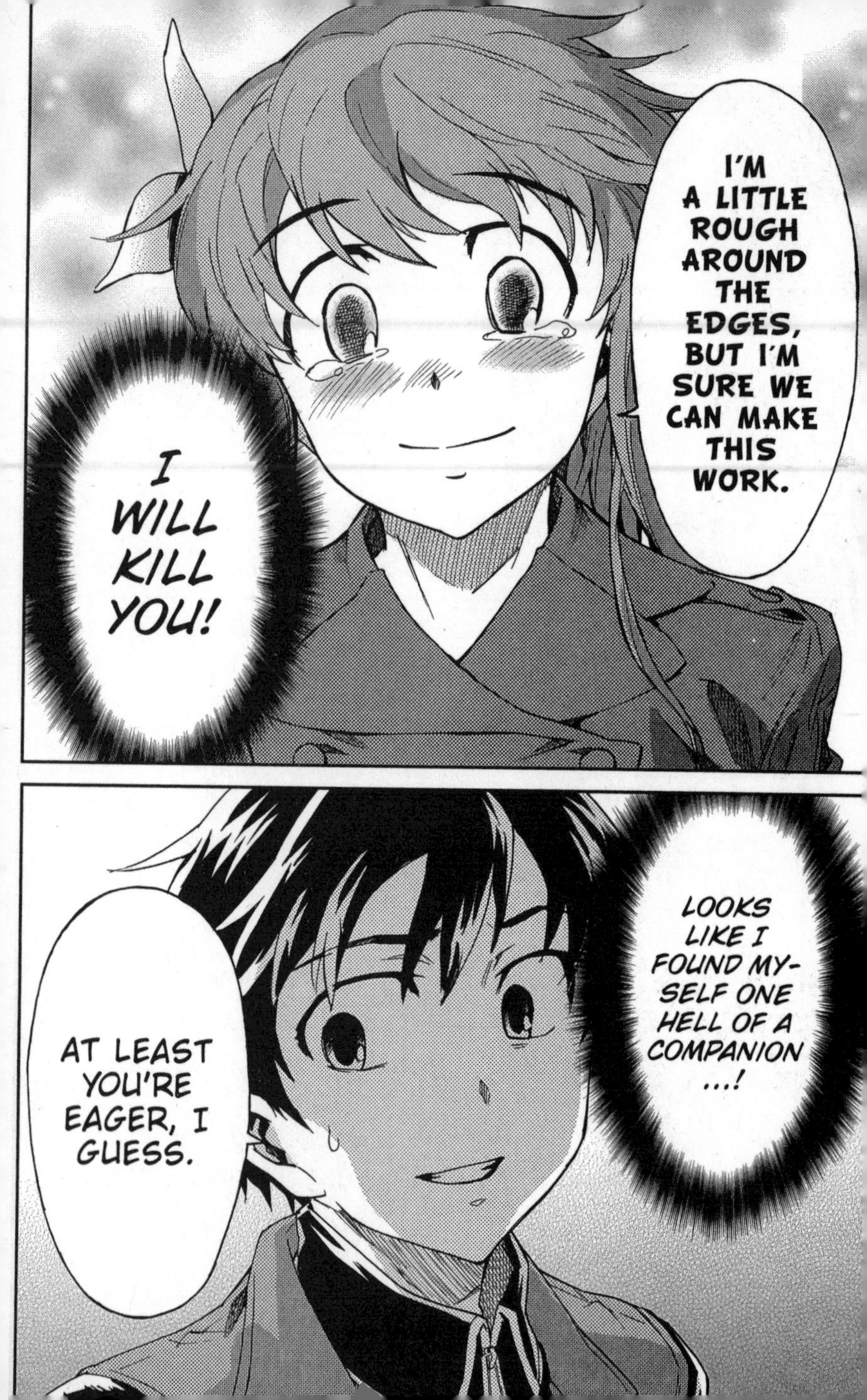
I'M A LITTLE ROUGH AROUND THE EDGES, BUT I'M SURE WE CAN MAKE THIS WORK.
I WILL KILL YOU!
LOOKS LIKE I FOUND MY-SELF ONE HELL OF A COMPANION ...!
AT LEAST YOU'RE EAGER, I GUESS.

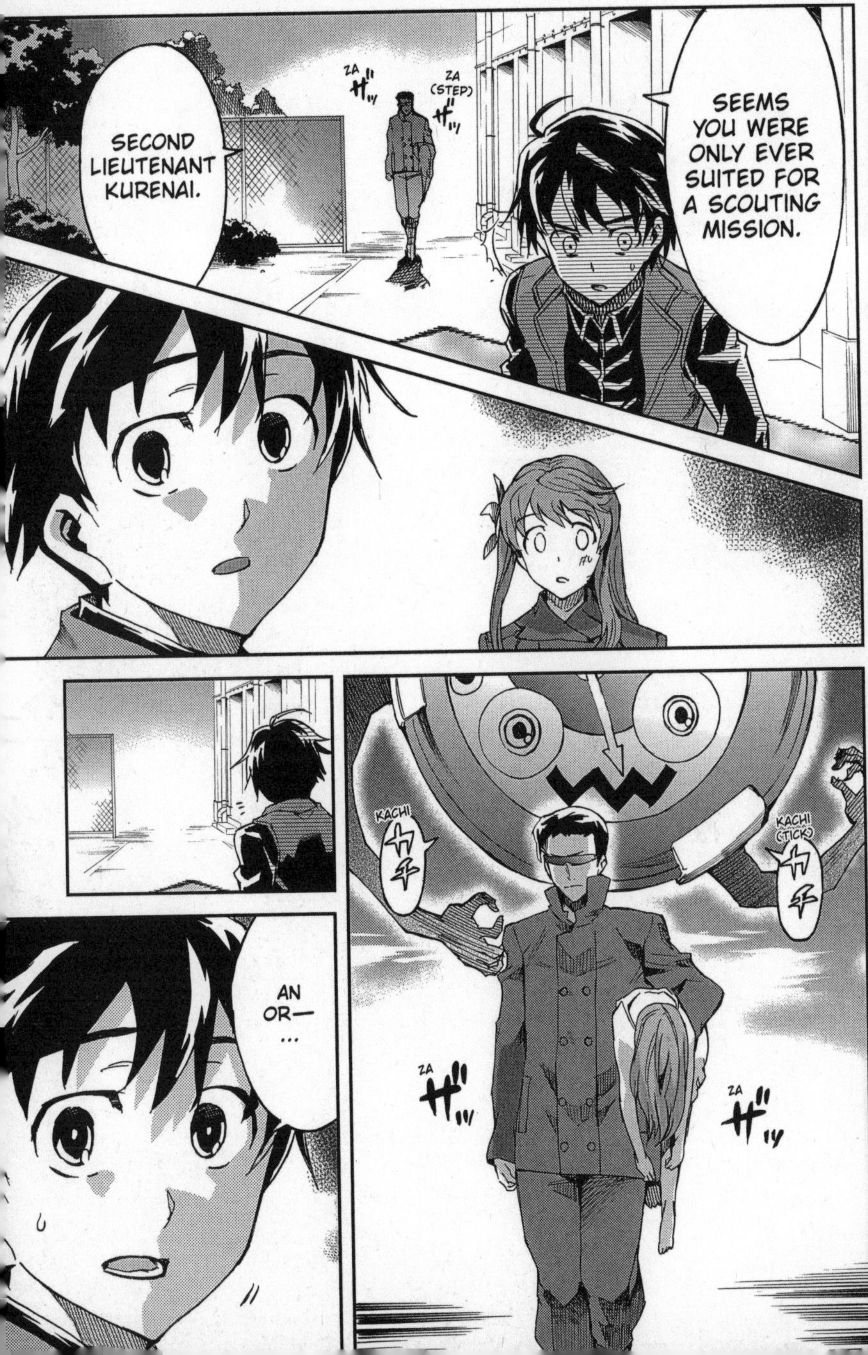
SEEMS YOU WERE ONLY EVER SUITED FOR A SCOUTING MISSION.
ZA (STEP)
ZA
SECOND LIEUTENANT KURENAI.
KACHI (TICK)
KACHI
ZA
ZA
AN OR— ...

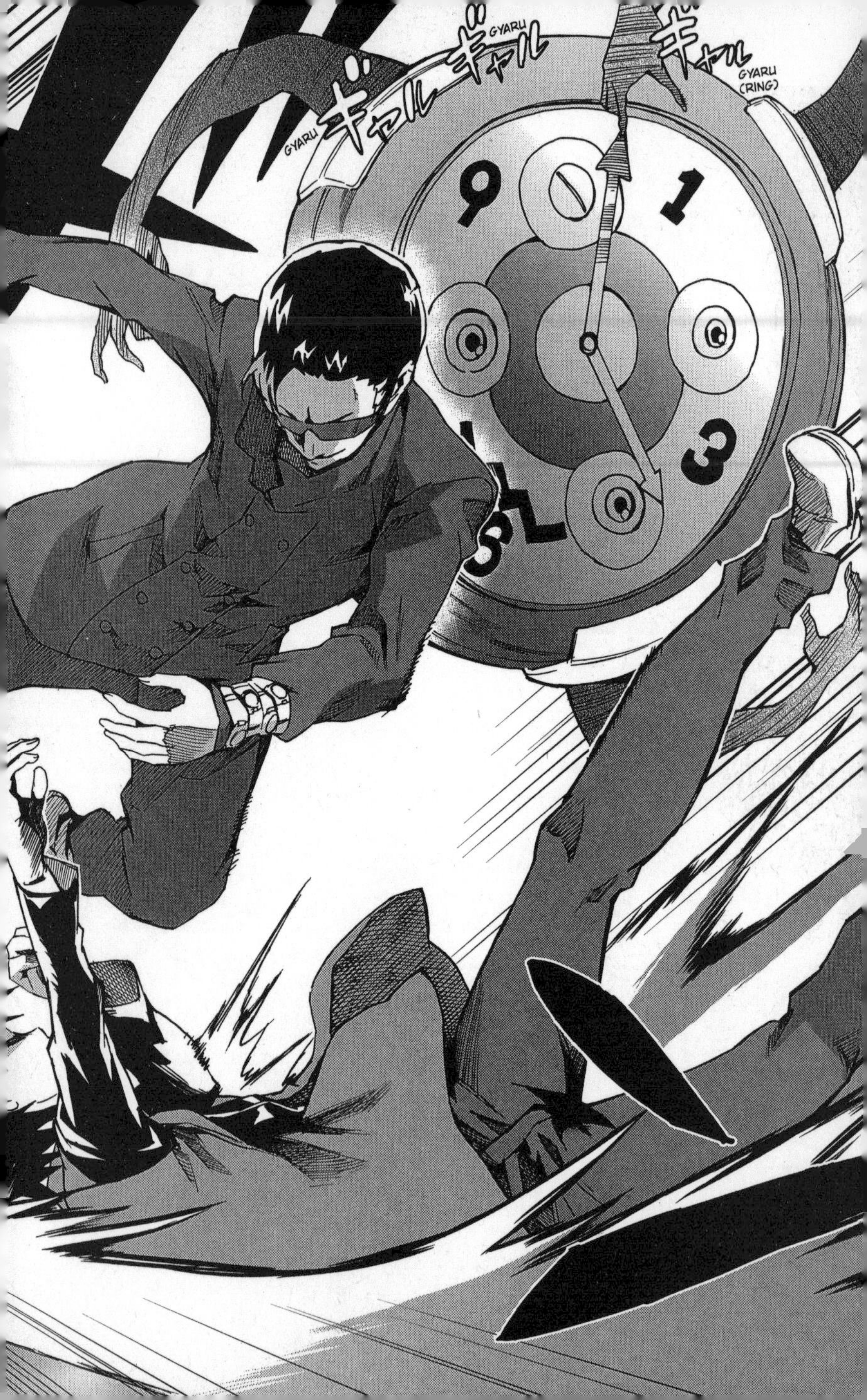
ギャル
GYARU (RING)
ギャル
GYARU
ギャル
GYARU

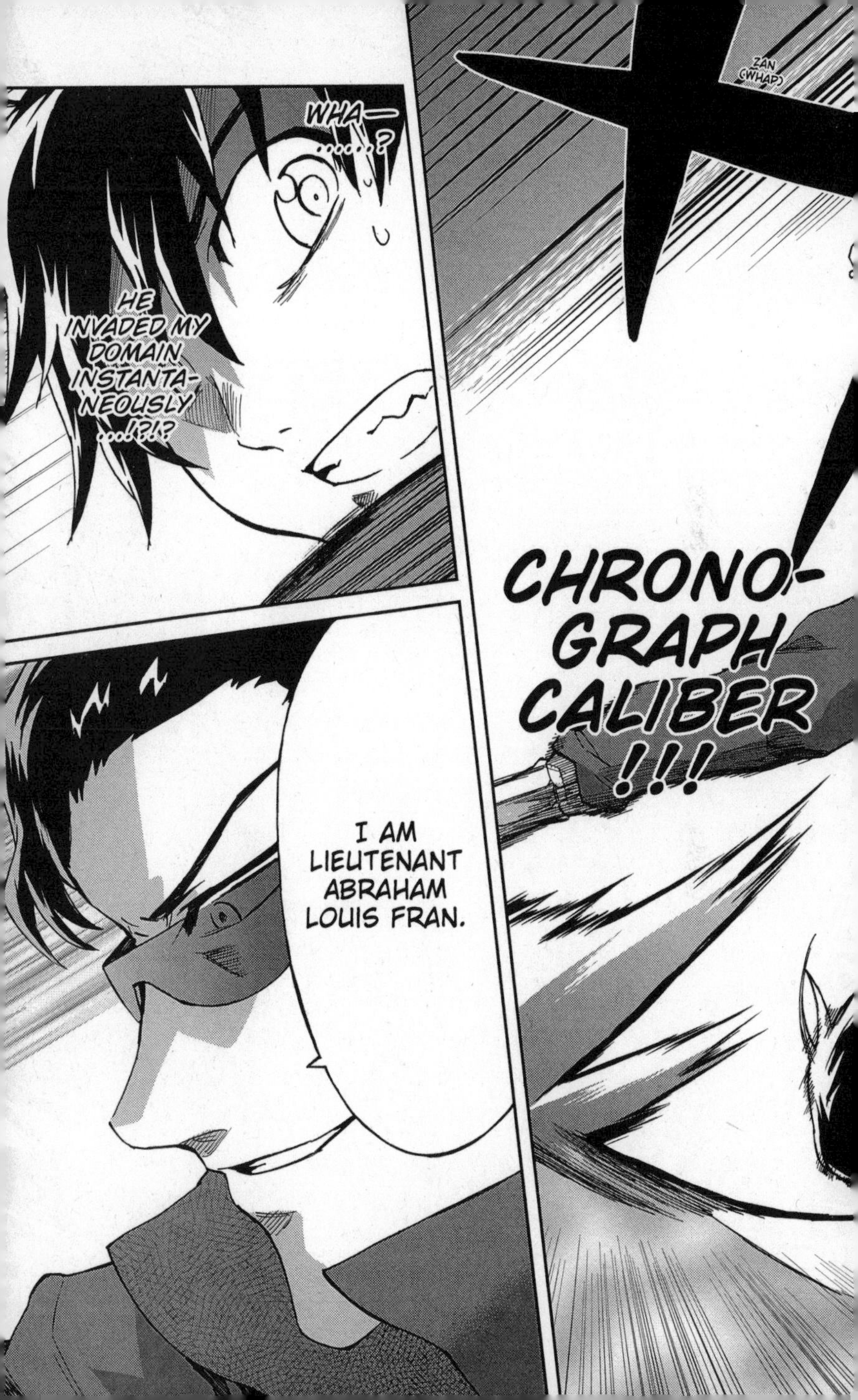
ZAN (WHAP)
CHRONO-GRAPH CALIBER!!!
WHA— ......?
HE INVADED MY DOMAIN INSTANTANEOUSLY...!?!?
I AM LIEUTENANT ABRAHAM LOUIS FRAN.

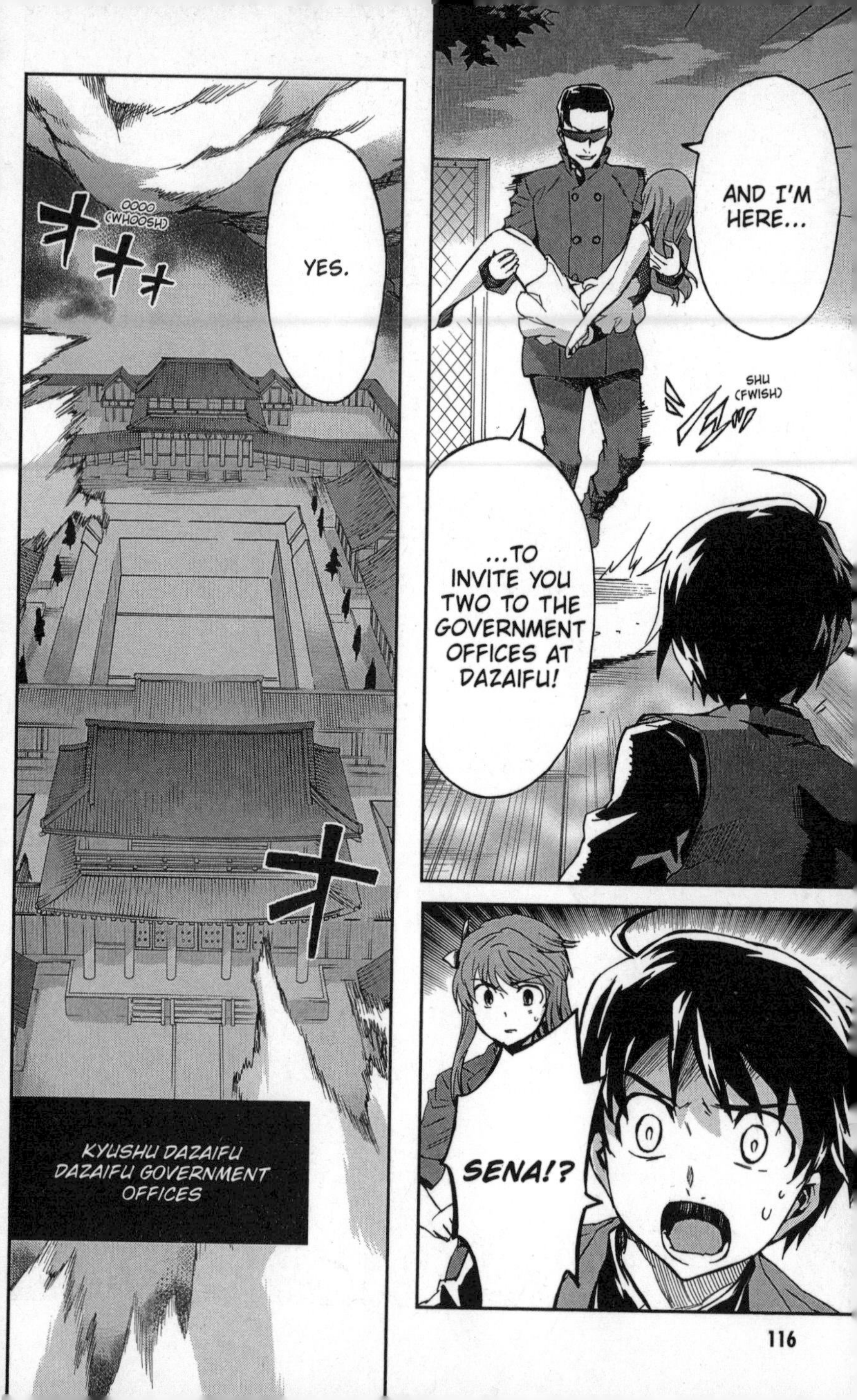
AND I'M HERE...
...TO INVITE YOU TWO TO THE GOVERNMENT OFFICES AT DAZAIFU!
SHU (FWISH)
SENA!?
YES.
OOOO (WHOOSH)
KYUSHU DAZAIFU DAZAIFU GOVERNMENT OFFICES

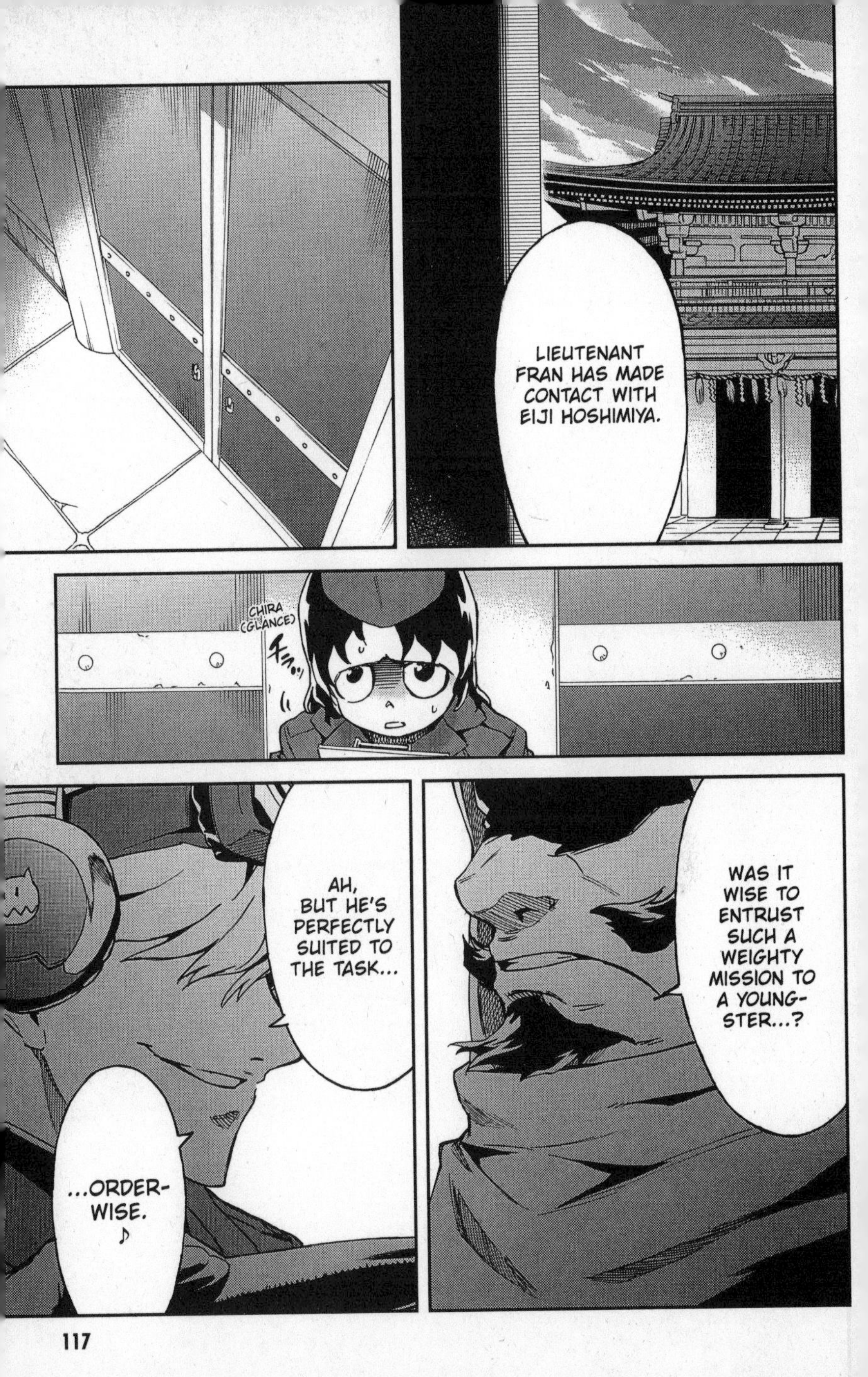
LIEUTENANT FRAN HAS MADE CONTACT WITH EIJI HOSHIMIYA.
CHIRA (GLANCE)
WAS IT WISE TO ENTRUST SUCH A WEIGHTY MISSION TO A YOUNG-STER...?
AH, BUT HE'S PERFECTLY SUITED TO THE TASK...
...ORDER-WISE. ♪

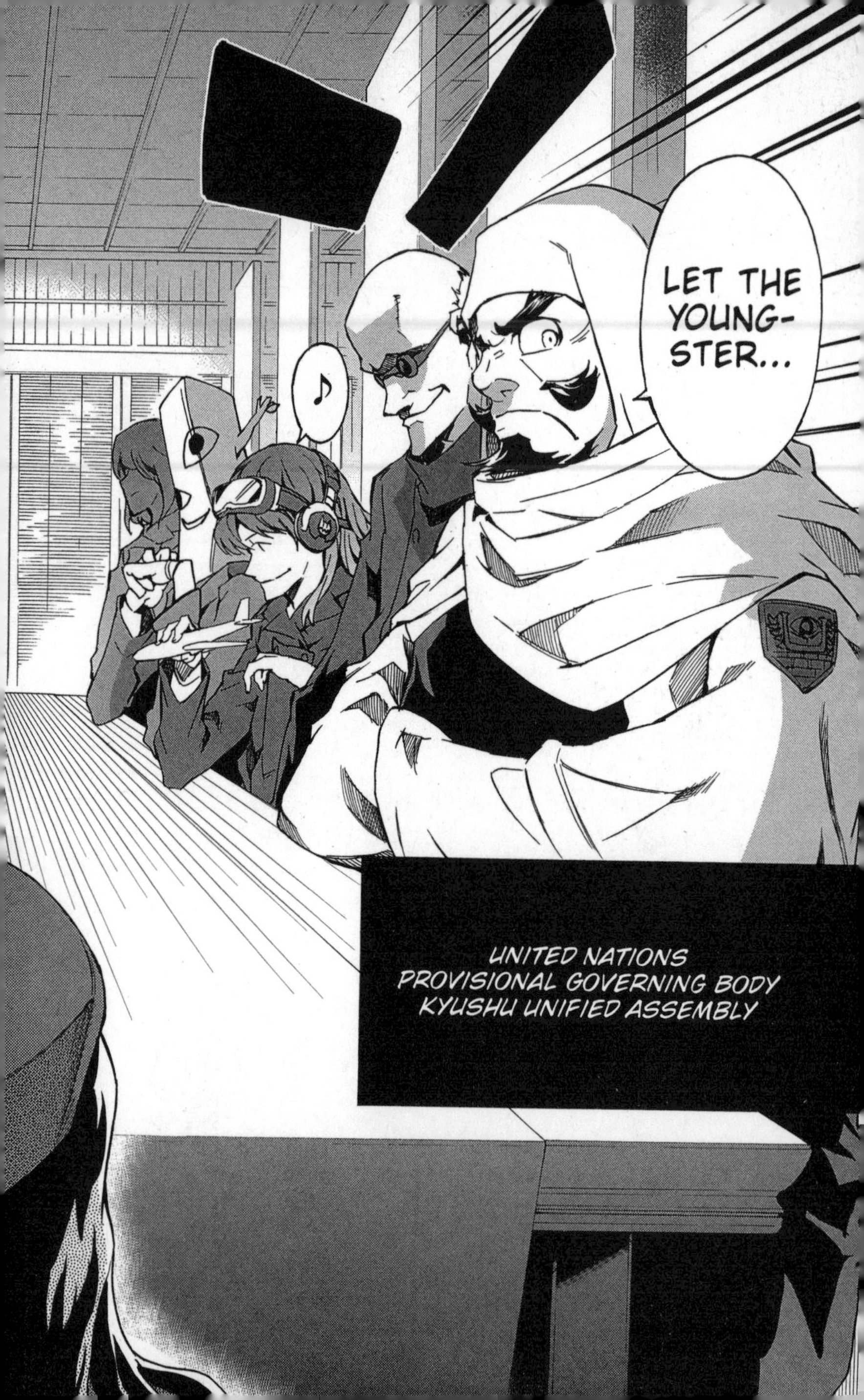
LET THE YOUNG-STER...
♪
UNITED NATIONS PROVISIONAL GOVERNING BODY KYUSHU UNIFIED ASSEMBLY

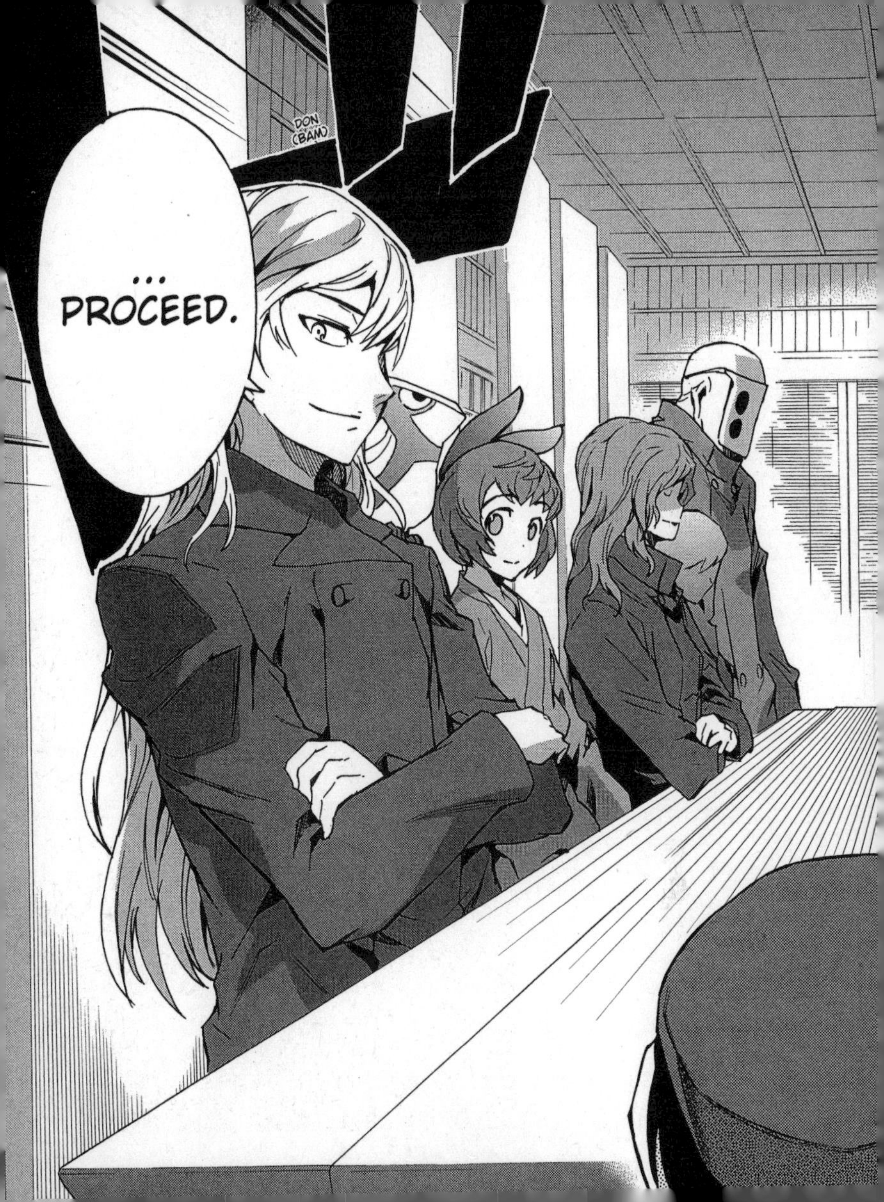
DON (BAM)
... PROCEED.

BIG ORDER

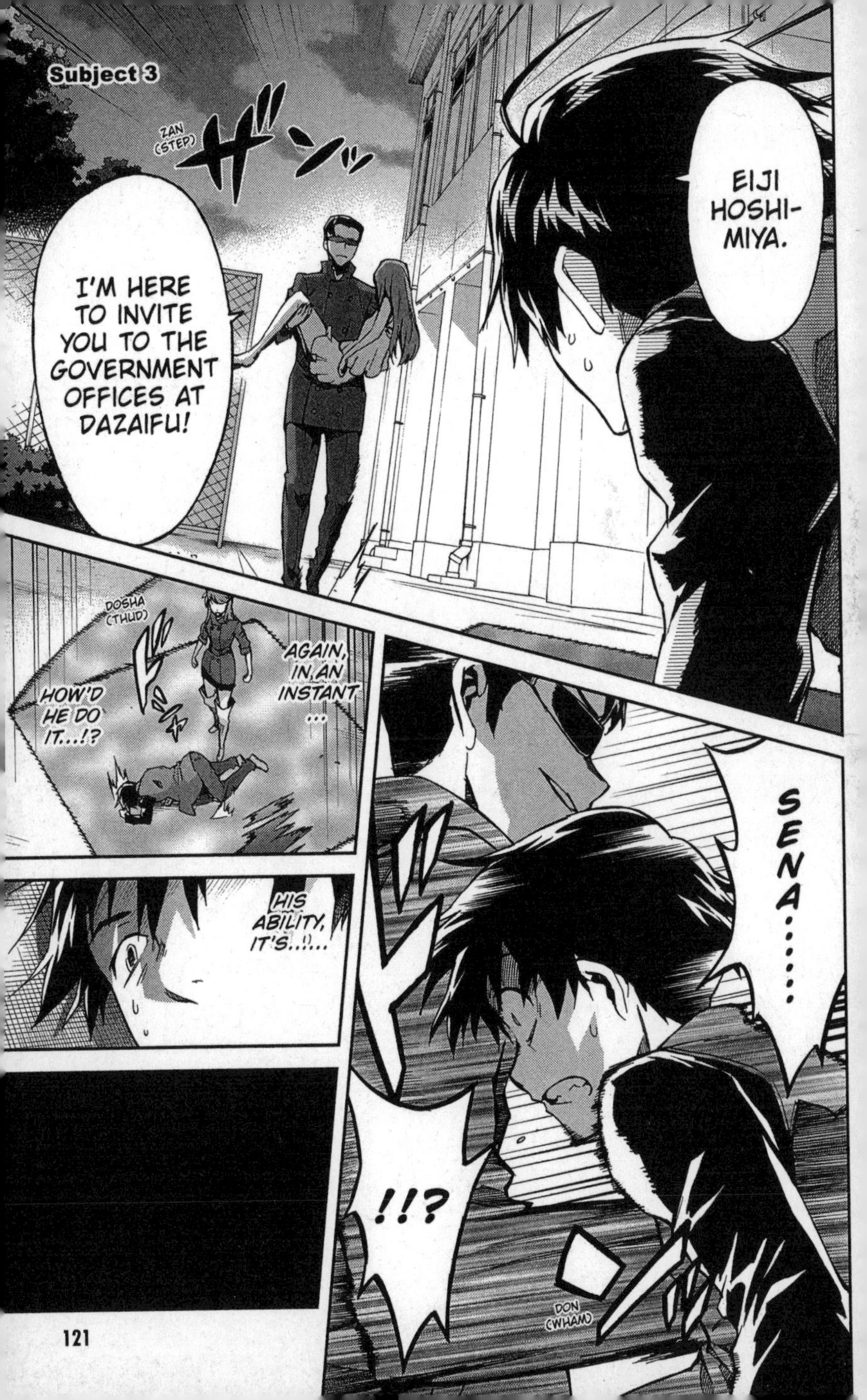
EIJI HOSHIMIYA.
ZAN (STEP)
I'M HERE TO INVITE YOU TO THE GOVERNMENT OFFICES AT DAZAIFU!
SENA......
!!?
DON (WHAM)
DOSHA (THUD)
AGAIN, IN AN INSTANT...
HOW'D HE DO IT...!?
HIS ABILITY, IT'S...!?...

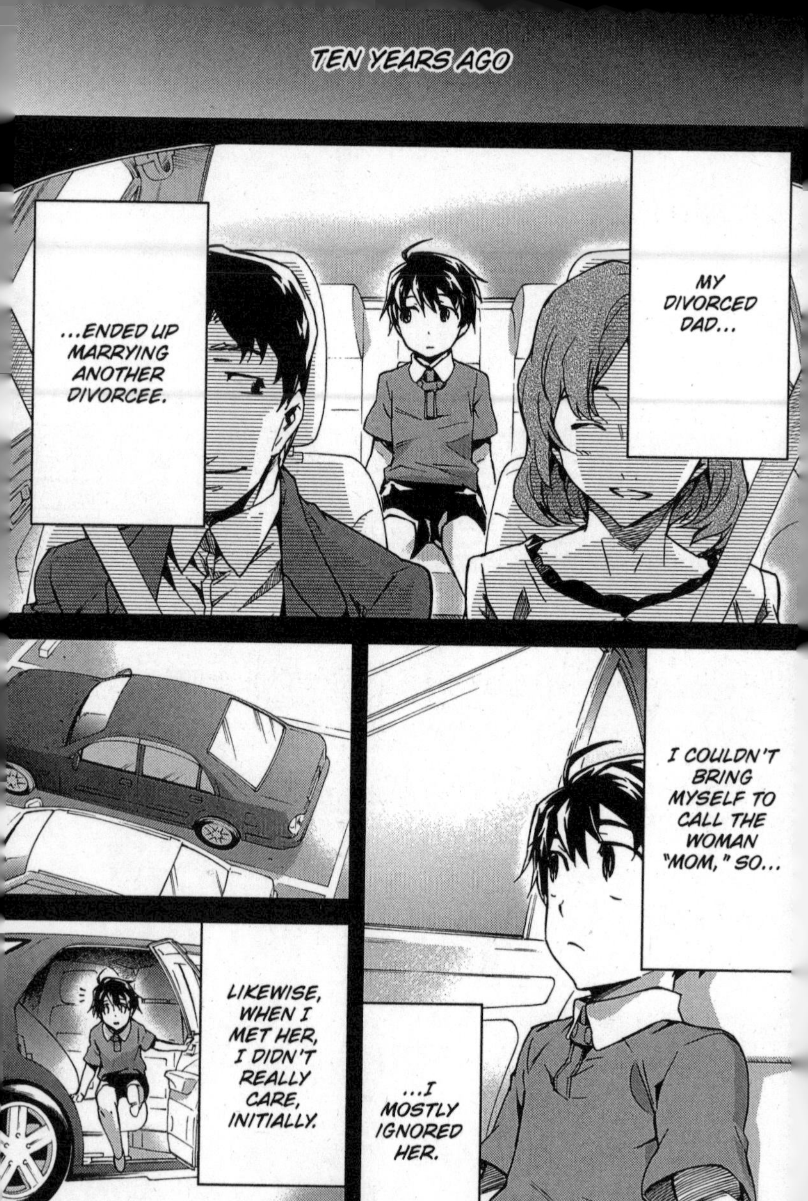
TEN YEARS AGO
MY DIVORCED DAD...
...ENDED UP MARRYING ANOTHER DIVORCEE.
I COULDN'T BRING MYSELF TO CALL THE WOMAN "MOM," SO...
...I MOSTLY IGNORED HER.
LIKEWISE, WHEN I MET HER, I DIDN'T REALLY CARE, INITIALLY.

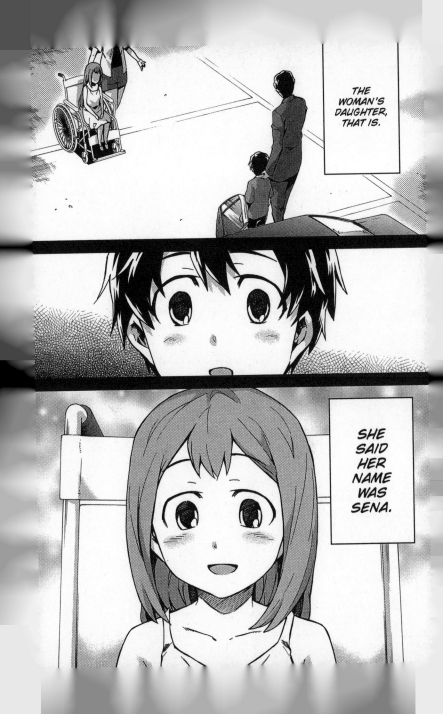

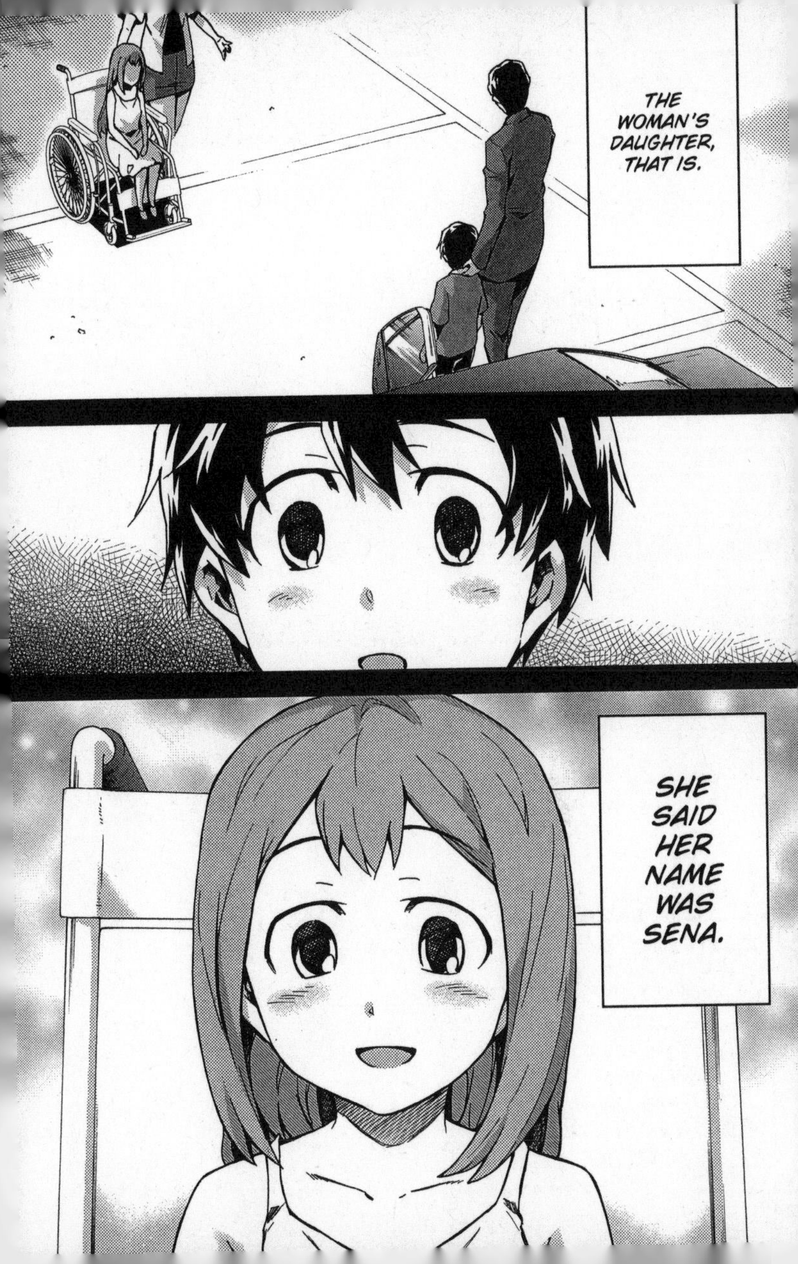
THE WOMAN'S DAUGHTER, THAT IS.
SHE SAID HER NAME WAS SENA.

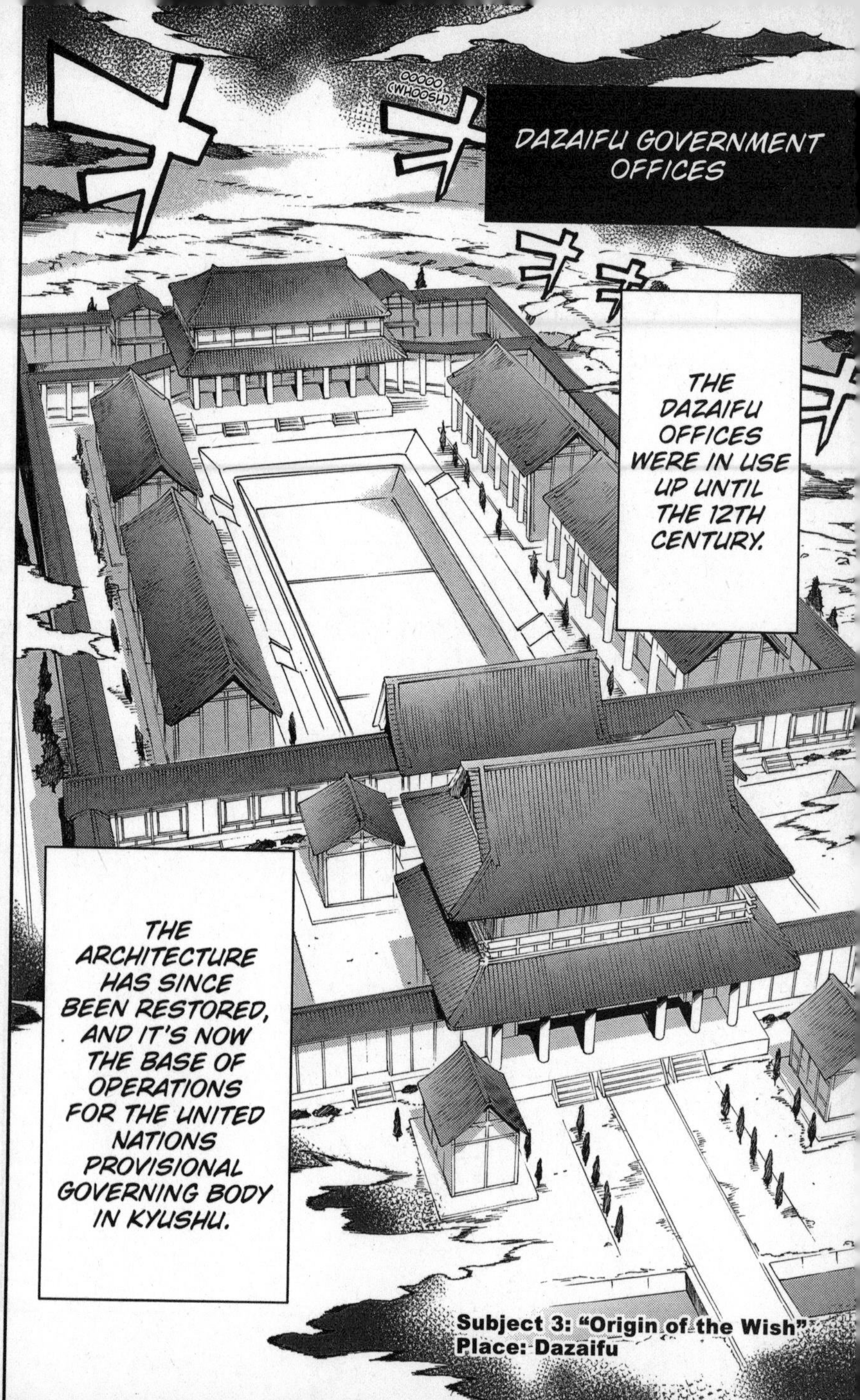
DAZAIFU GOVERNMENT OFFICES
OOOOO (WHOOSH)
THE DAZAIFU OFFICES WERE IN USE UP UNTIL THE 12TH CENTURY.
THE ARCHITECTURE HAS SINCE BEEN RESTORED, AND IT'S NOW THE BASE OF OPERATIONS FOR THE UNITED NATIONS PROVISIONAL GOVERNING BODY IN KYUSHU.
Subject 3: "Origin of the Wish"
Place: Dazaifu

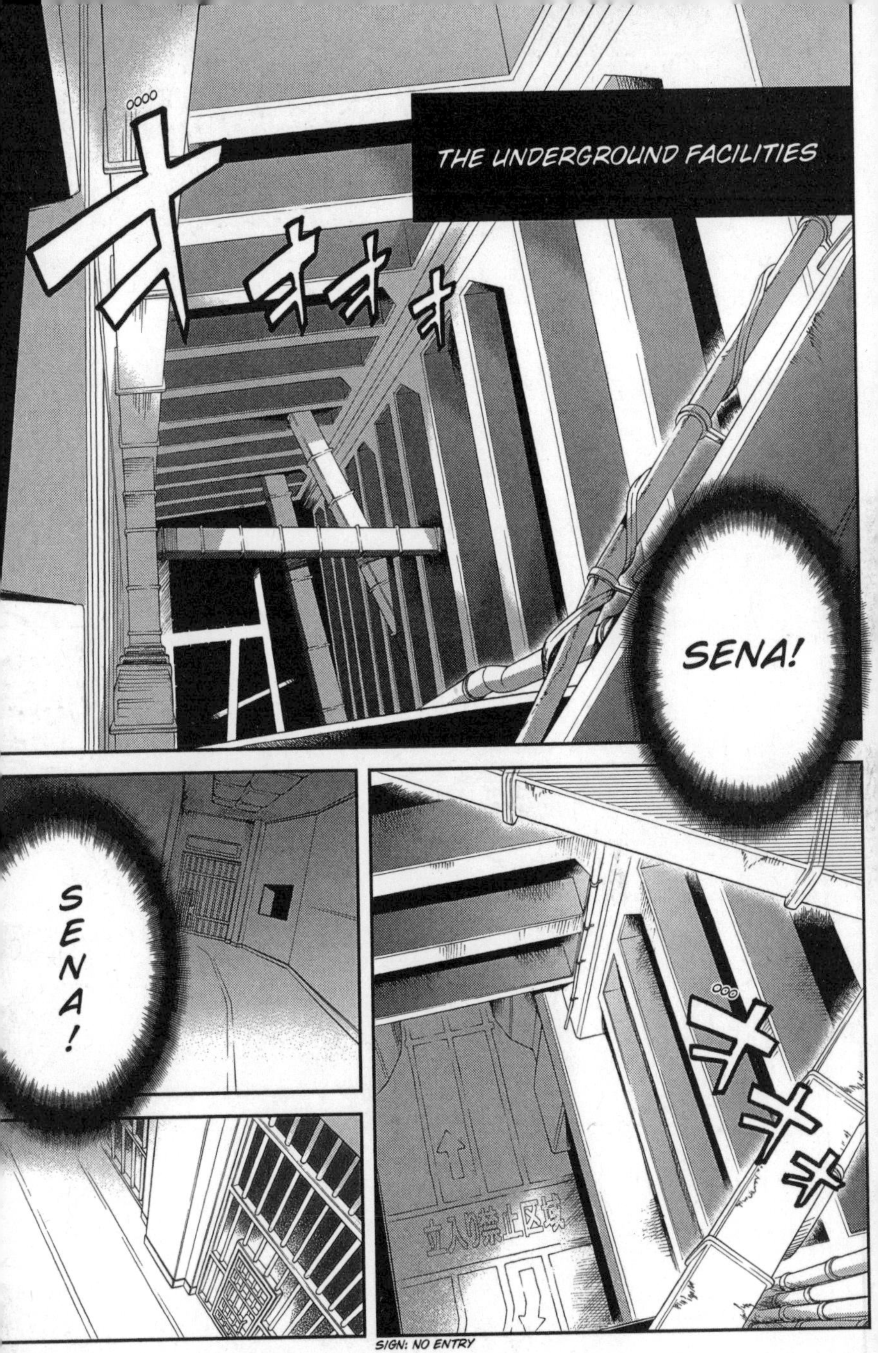
THE UNDERGROUND FACILITIES
オオオオ
SENA!
オオオ
立入り禁止区域
SENA!

SIGN: NO ENTRY

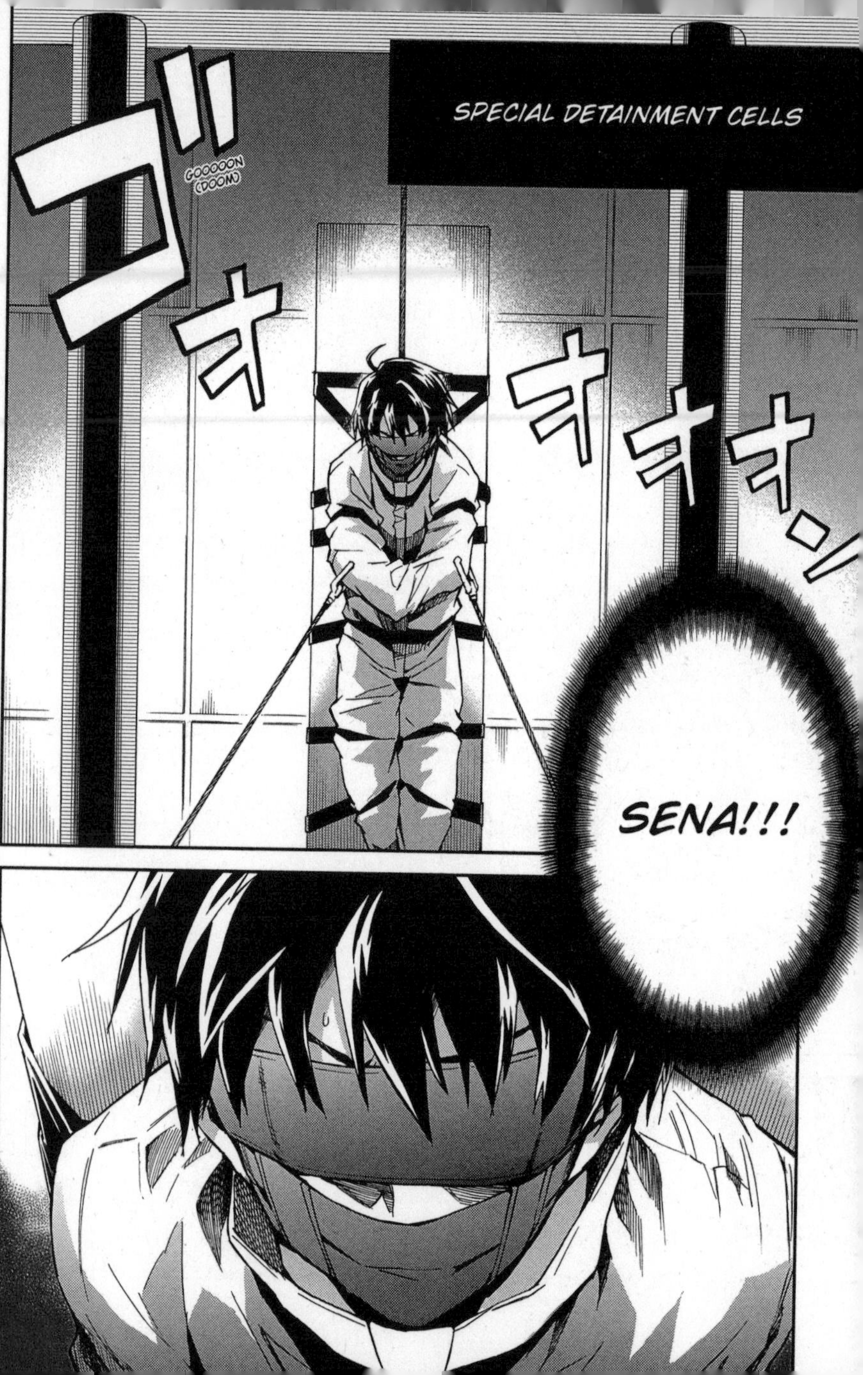
SPECIAL DETAINMENT CELLS
ゴォォォォン
GOOOOON (DOOM)
SENA!!!

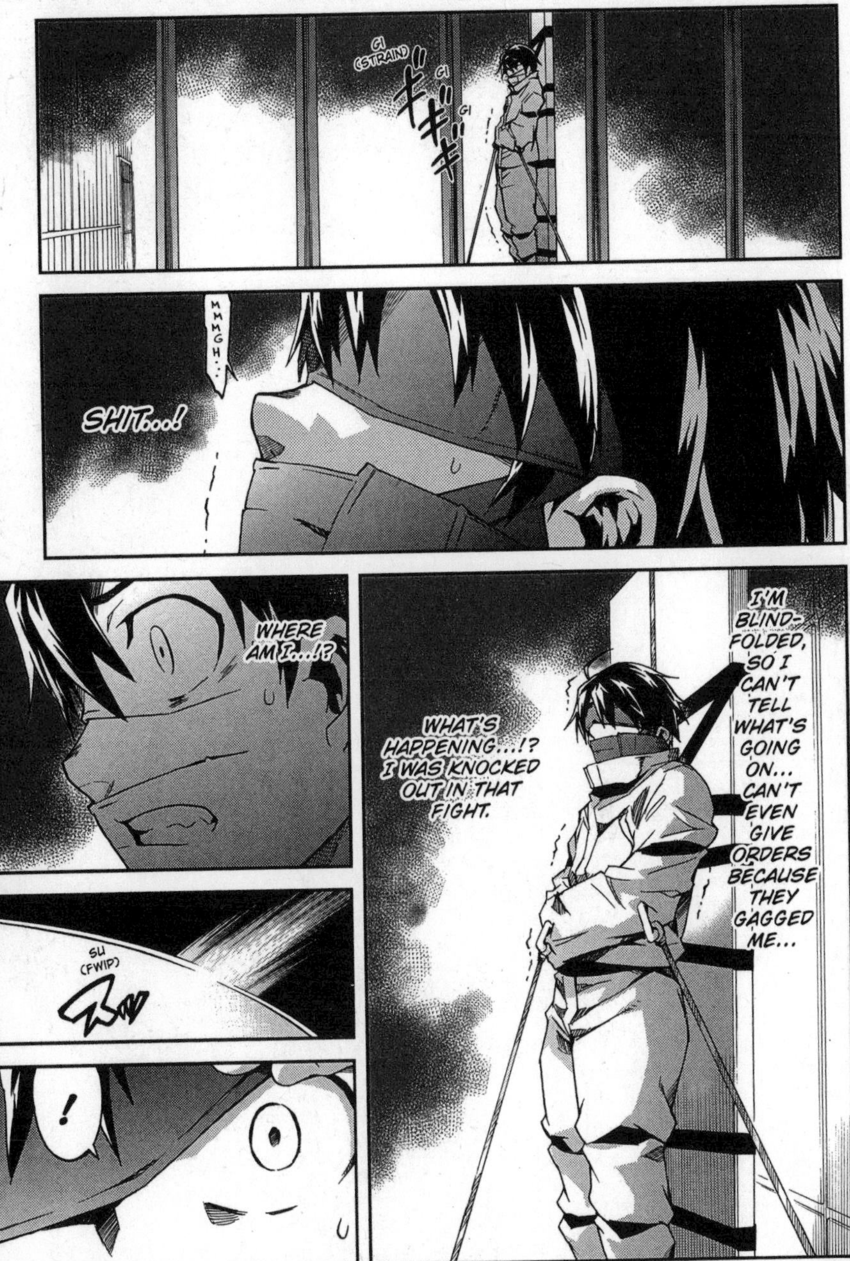
GI (STRAIN)
GI
GI
MMMGH...
SHIT...!
I'M BLIND-FOLDED, SO I CAN'T TELL WHAT'S GOING ON... CAN'T EVEN GIVE ORDERS BECAUSE THEY GAGGED ME...
WHAT'S HAPPENING...!? I WAS KNOCKED OUT IN THAT FIGHT.
WHERE AM I...!?
SU (FWIP)
!

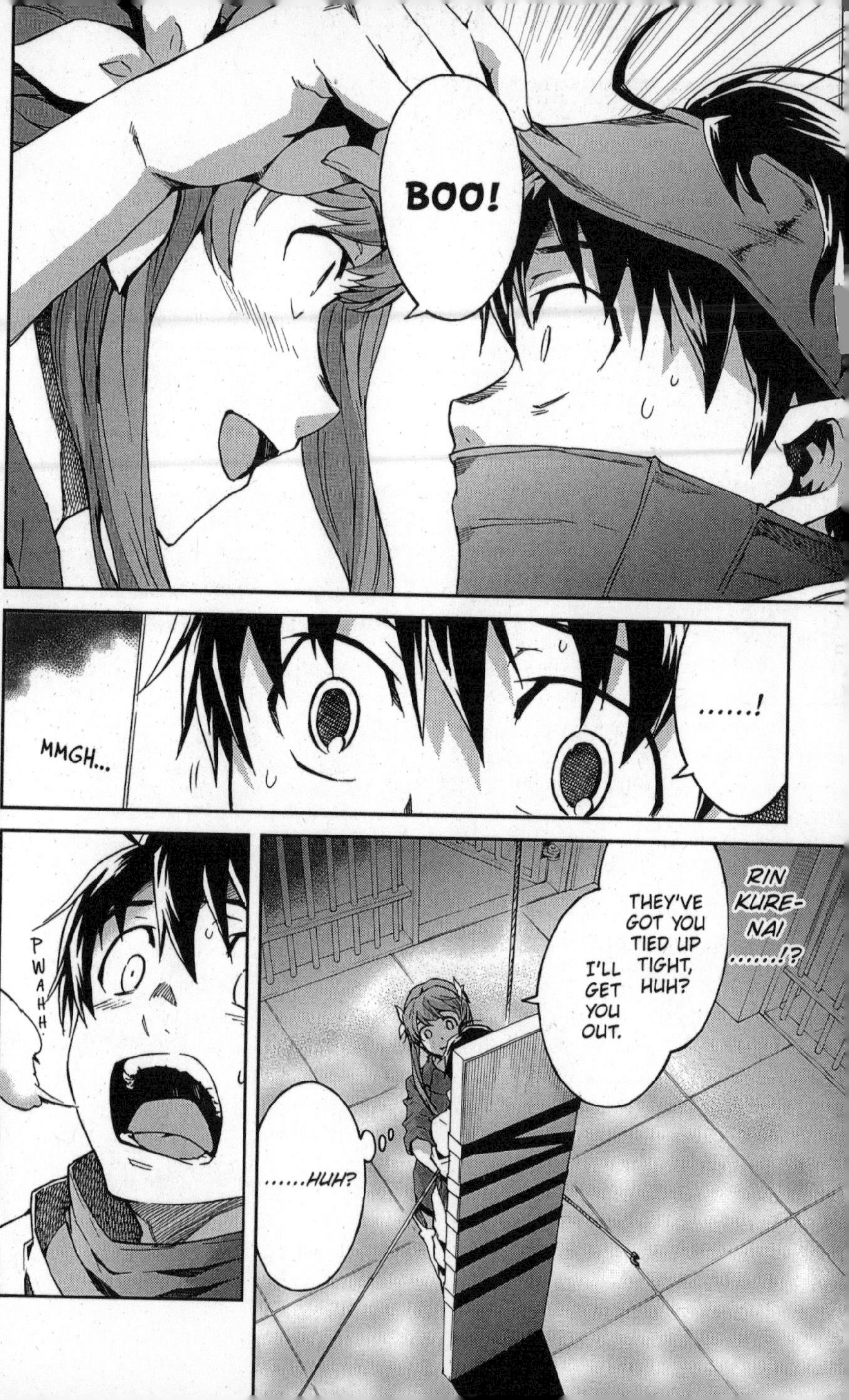
BOO!
......!
MMGH...
RIN KURE-NAI ......!?
THEY'VE GOT YOU TIED UP TIGHT, HUH?
I'LL GET YOU OUT.
......HUH?
PWAHH.

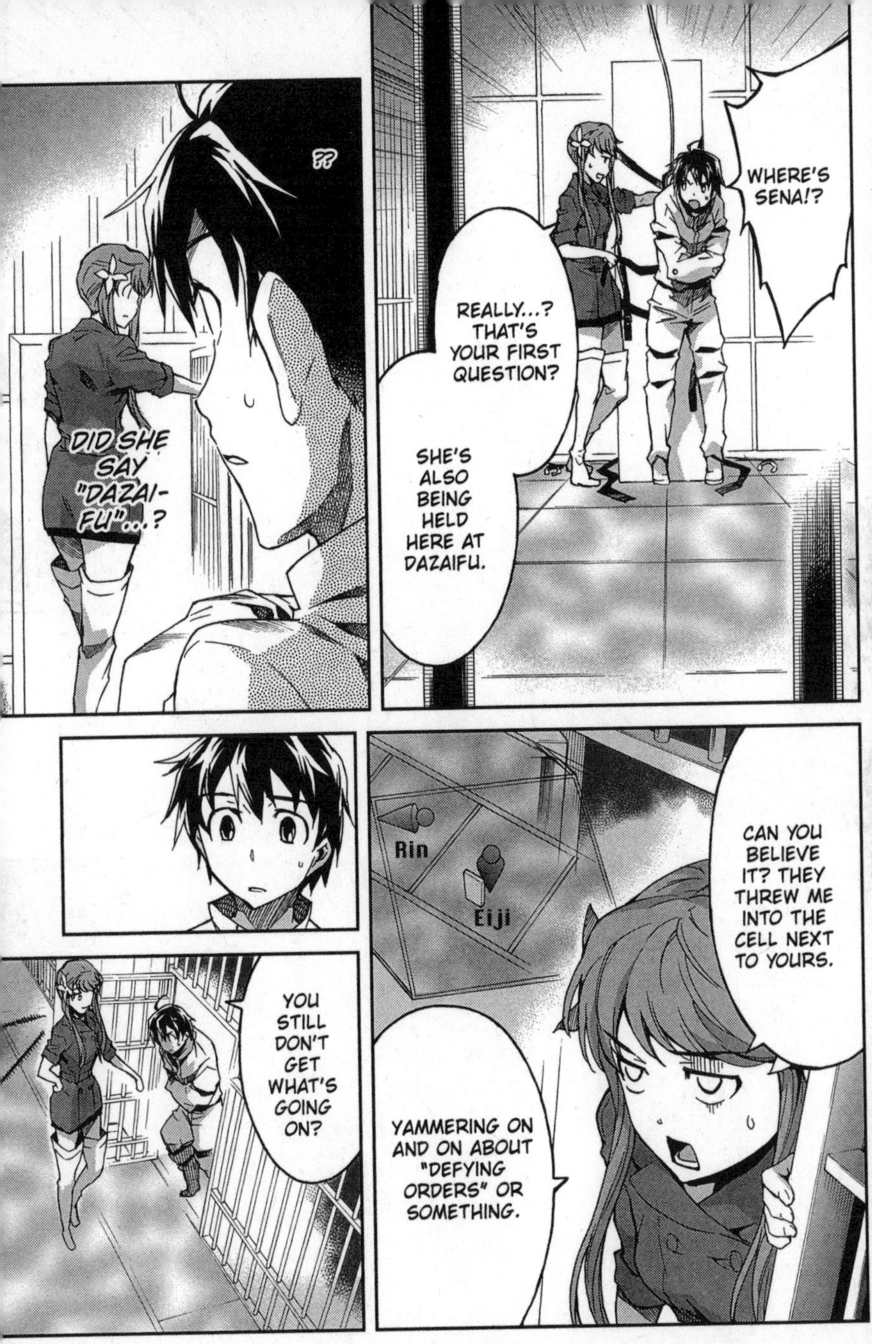
WHERE'S SENA!?
REALLY...? THAT'S YOUR FIRST QUESTION?
SHE'S ALSO BEING HELD HERE AT DAZAIFU.
??
DID SHE SAY "DAZAI-FU"...?
Rin
Eiji
CAN YOU BELIEVE IT? THEY THREW ME INTO THE CELL NEXT TO YOURS.
YAMMERING ON AND ON ABOUT "DEFYING ORDERS" OR SOMETHING.
YOU STILL DON'T GET WHAT'S GOING ON?

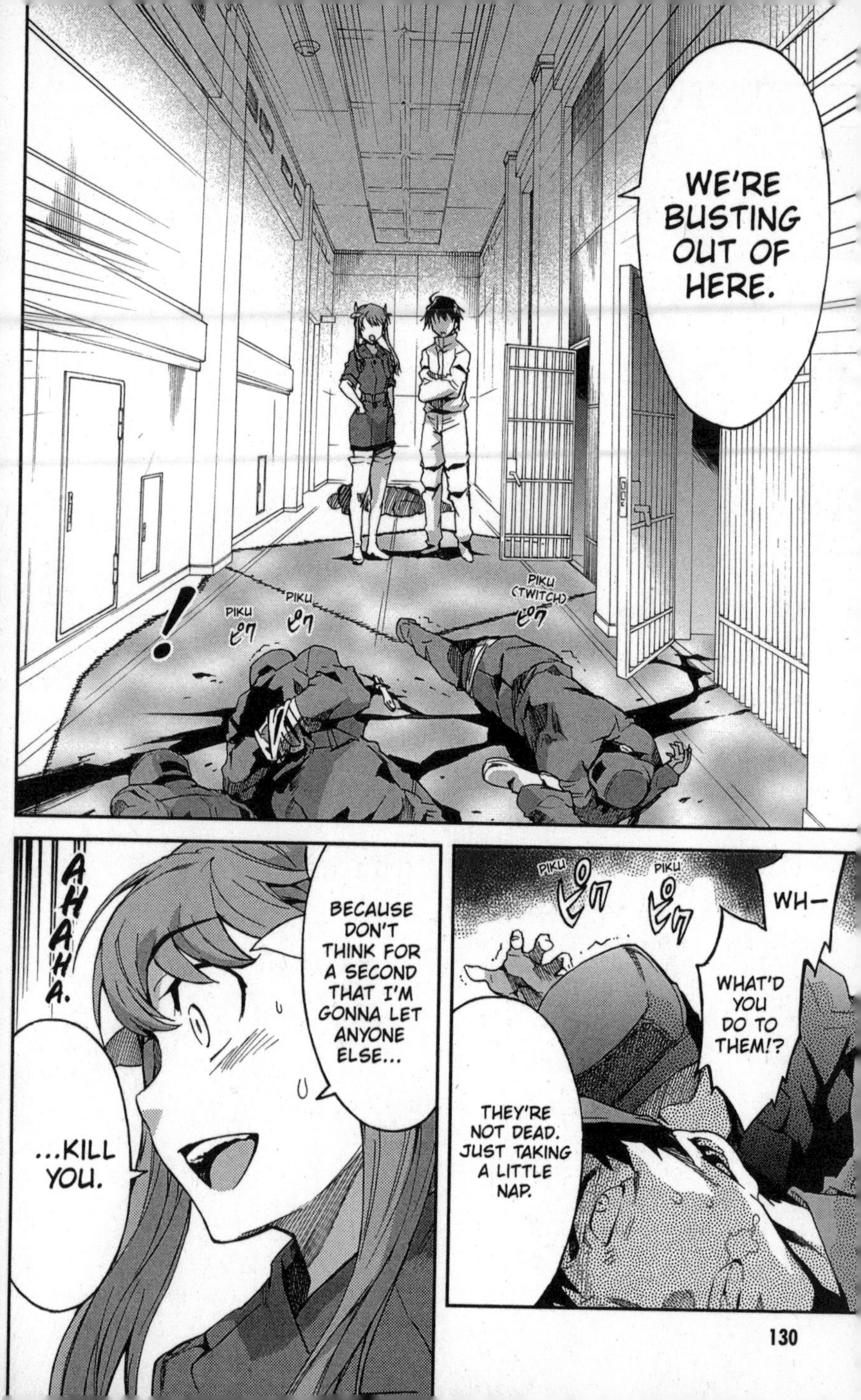
WE'RE BUSTING OUT OF HERE.
PIKU (TWITCH)
ピク
PIKU
ピク
PIKU
ピク
!
PIKU
ピク
PIKU
ピク
WH—
WHAT'D YOU DO TO THEM!?
THEY'RE NOT DEAD. JUST TAKING A LITTLE NAP.
BECAUSE DON'T THINK FOR A SECOND THAT I'M GONNA LET ANYONE ELSE...
AHAHAHA.
...KILL YOU.

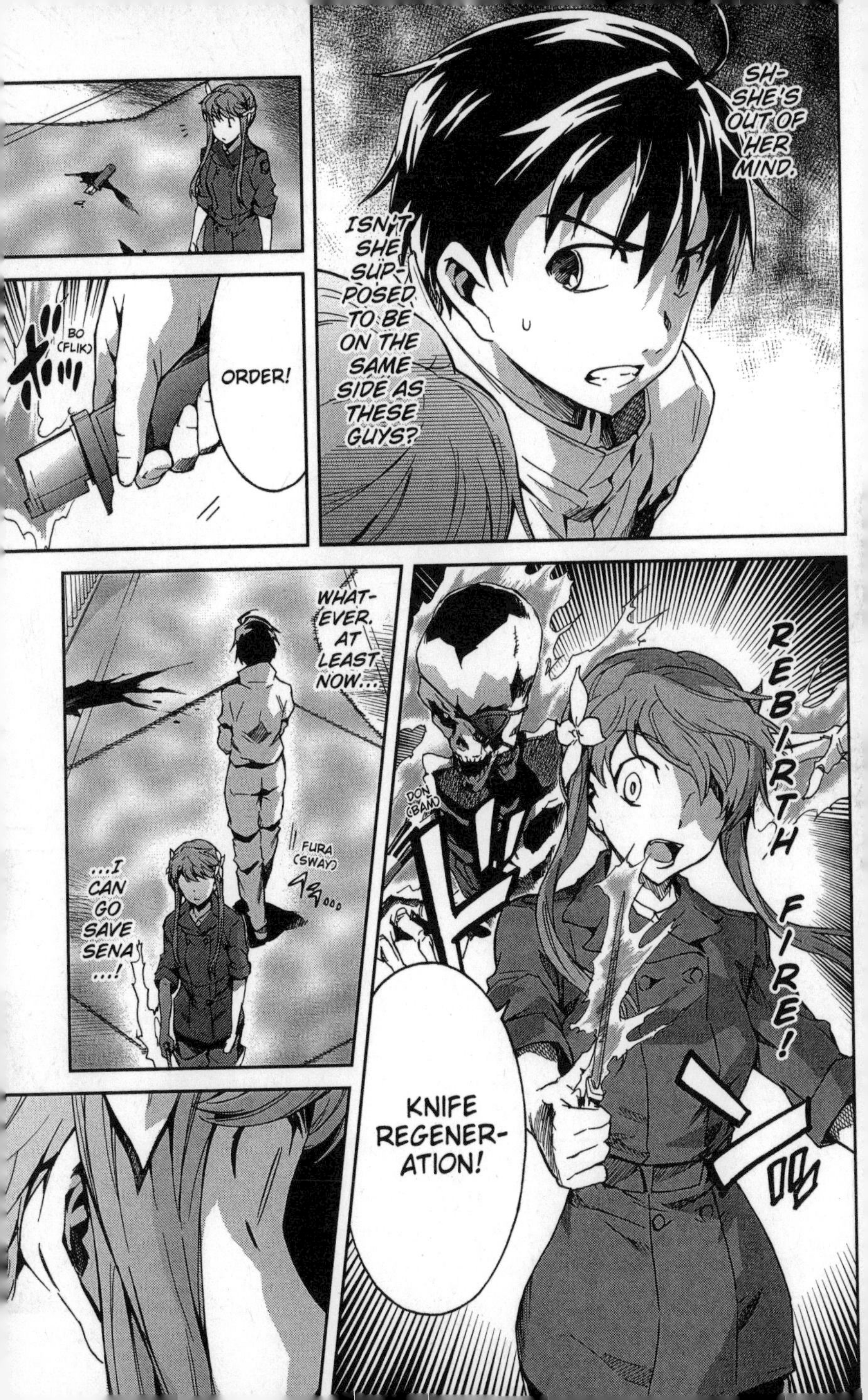
SH-SHE'S OUT OF HER MIND.
ISN'T SHE SUP-POSED TO BE ON THE SAME SIDE AS THESE GUYS?
BO (FLIK)
ORDER!
REBIRTH FIRE!
DON (BAM)
KNIFE REGENER-ATION!
WHAT-EVER. AT LEAST NOW...
FURA (SWAY)
...I CAN GO SAVE SENA...!

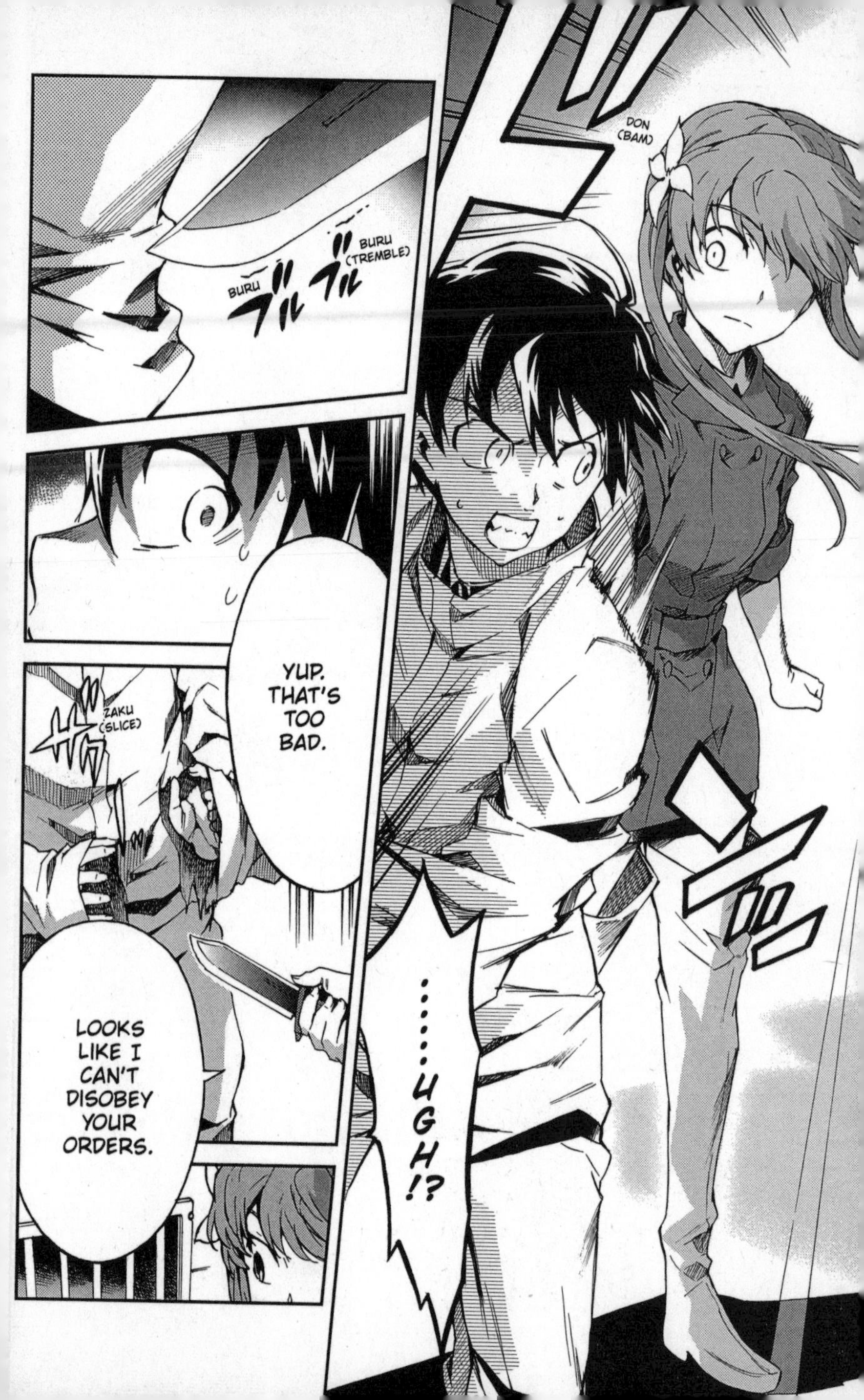

DON (BAM)
.....UGH!?
BURU (TREMBLE)
BURU
YUP. THAT'S TOO BAD.
ZAKU (SLICE)
LOOKS LIKE I CAN'T DISOBEY YOUR ORDERS.

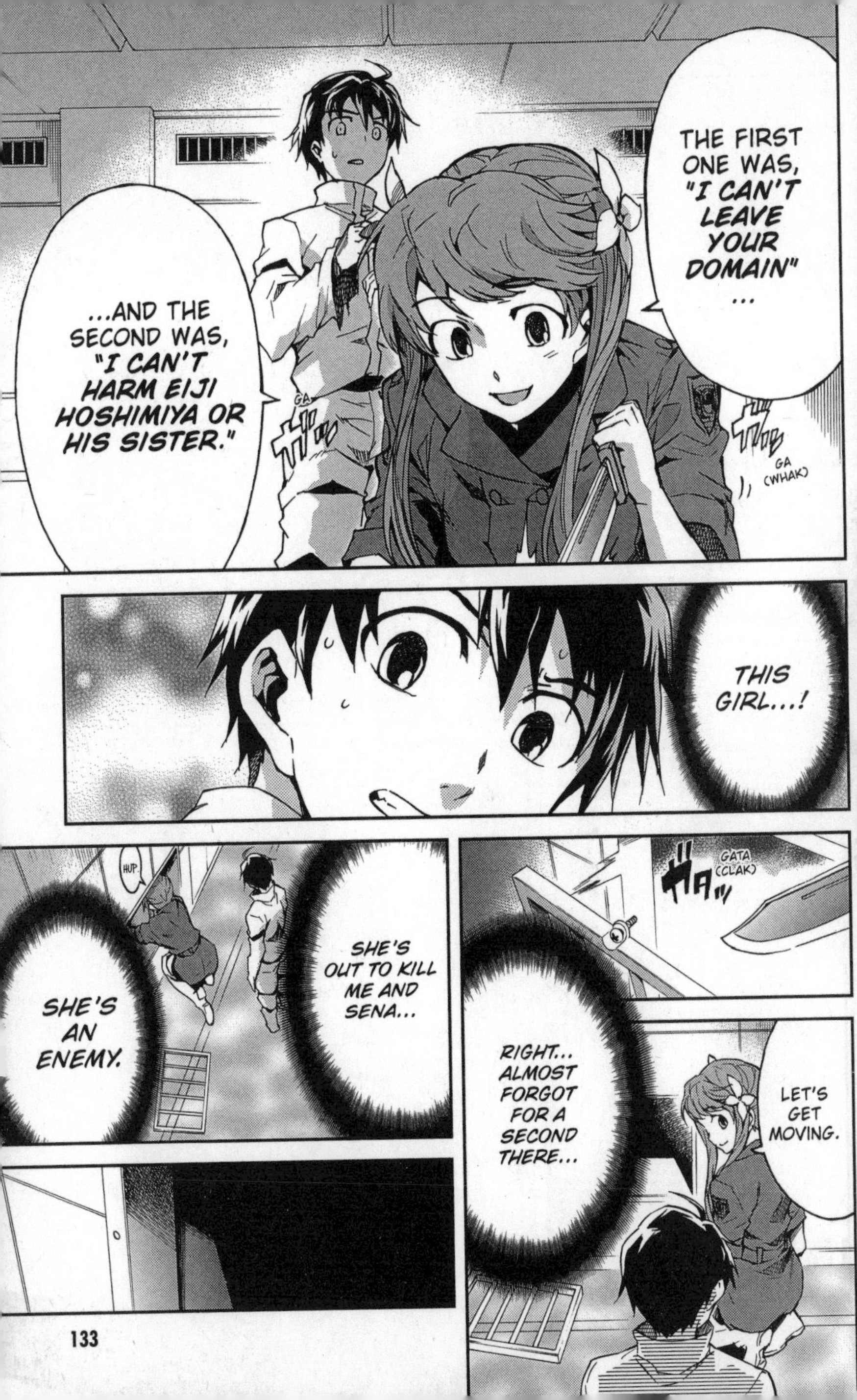
THE FIRST ONE WAS, "I CAN'T LEAVE YOUR DOMAIN"...
...AND THE SECOND WAS, "I CAN'T HARM EIJI HOSHIMIYA OR HIS SISTER."
GA
GA (WHAK)
THIS GIRL...!
GATA (CLAK)
LET'S GET MOVING.
RIGHT... ALMOST FORGOT FOR A SECOND THERE...
HUP.
SHE'S OUT TO KILL ME AND SENA...
SHE'S AN ENEMY.

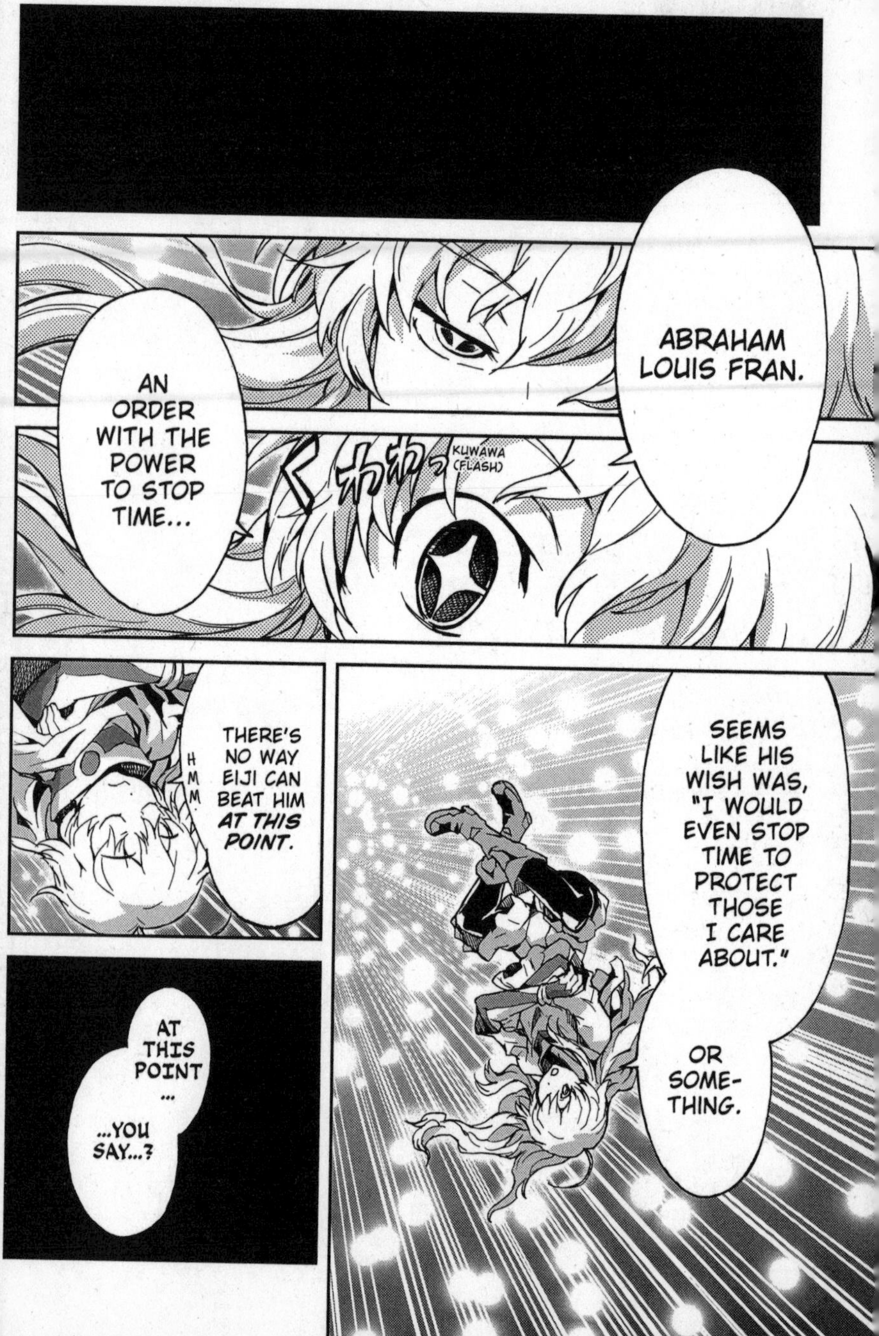
ABRAHAM LOUIS FRAN.
AN ORDER WITH THE POWER TO STOP TIME...
KUWAWA (FLASH)
SEEMS LIKE HIS WISH WAS, "I WOULD EVEN STOP TIME TO PROTECT THOSE I CARE ABOUT."
OR SOME-THING.
THERE'S NO WAY EIJI CAN BEAT HIM *AT THIS POINT*.
HMM
AT THIS POINT...
...YOU SAY...?

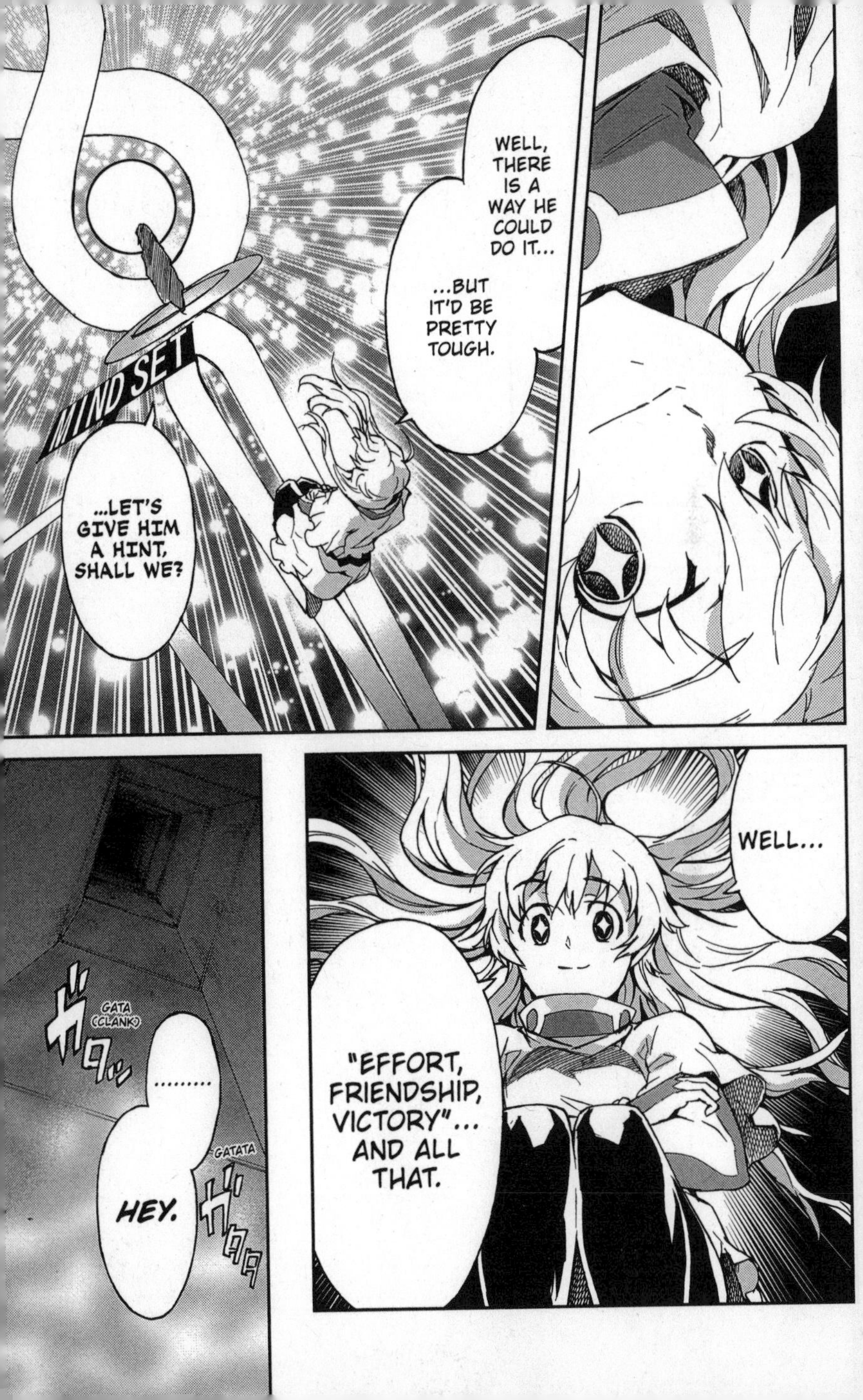

WELL, THERE IS A WAY HE COULD DO IT...
...BUT IT'D BE PRETTY TOUGH.
MIND SET
...LET'S GIVE HIM A HINT, SHALL WE?
WELL...
"EFFORT, FRIENDSHIP, VICTORY"... AND ALL THAT.
GATA (CLANK)
.........
GATATA
HEY.

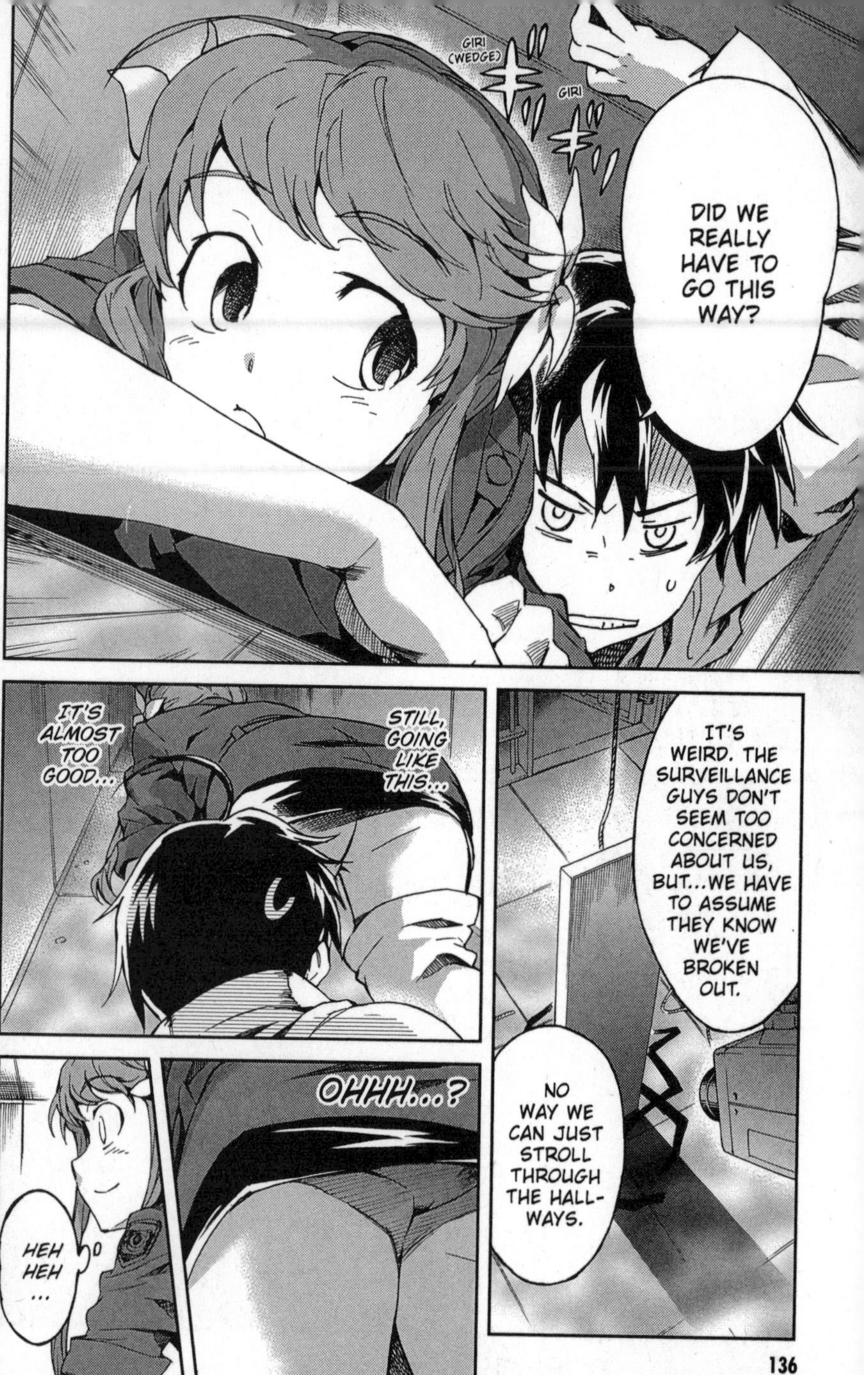
GIRI (WEDGE)
GIRI
DID WE REALLY HAVE TO GO THIS WAY?
IT'S WEIRD. THE SURVEILLANCE GUYS DON'T SEEM TOO CONCERNED ABOUT US, BUT...WE HAVE TO ASSUME THEY KNOW WE'VE BROKEN OUT.
STILL, GOING LIKE THIS...
IT'S ALMOST TOO GOOD...
NO WAY WE CAN JUST STROLL THROUGH THE HALL-WAYS.
OHHH...?
HEH HEH ...

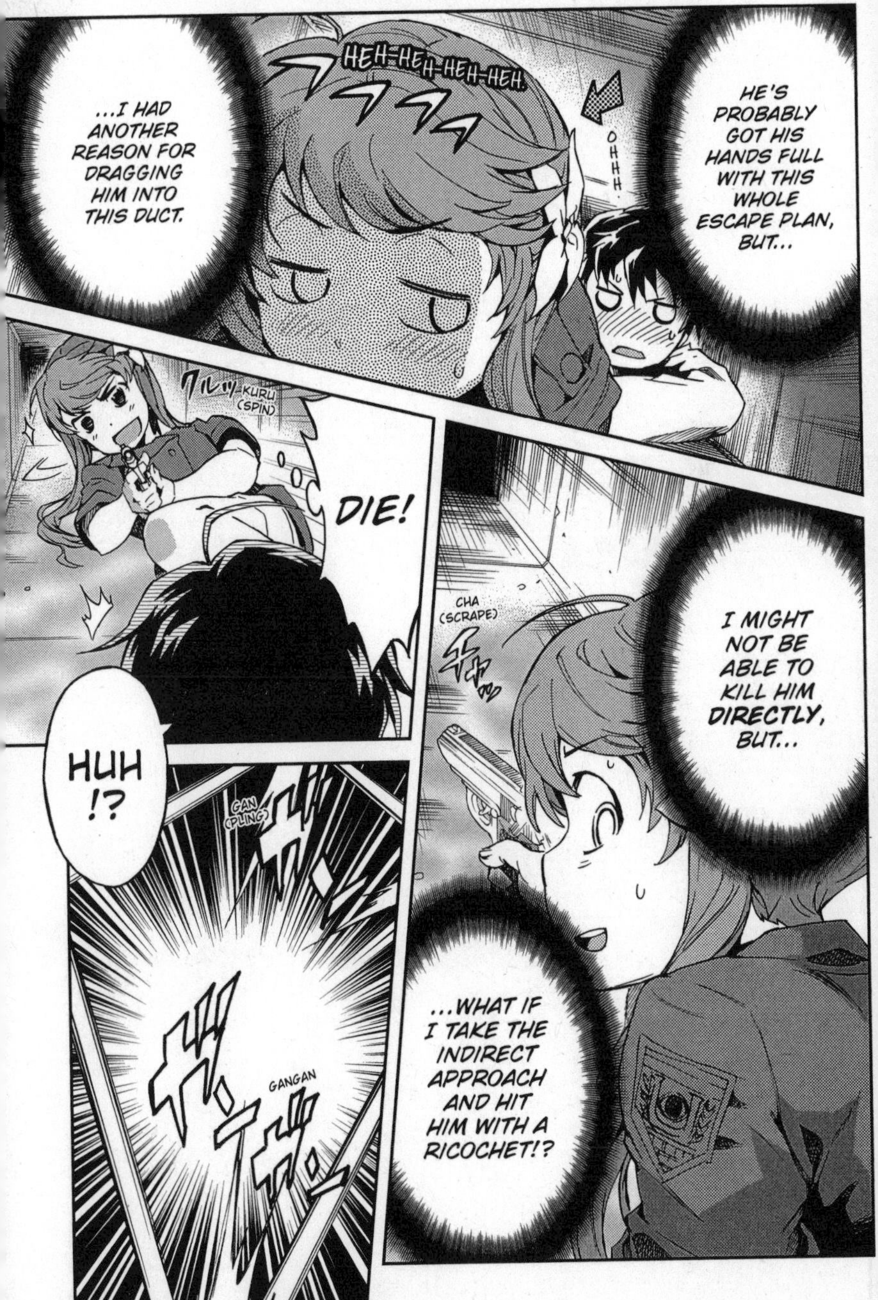

HE'S PROBABLY GOT HIS HANDS FULL WITH THIS WHOLE ESCAPE PLAN, BUT...
OHHH
HEH-HEH-HEH-HEH.
...I HAD ANOTHER REASON FOR DRAGGING HIM INTO THIS DUCT.
CHA (SCRAPE)
I MIGHT NOT BE ABLE TO KILL HIM DIRECTLY, BUT...
...WHAT IF I TAKE THE INDIRECT APPROACH AND HIT HIM WITH A RICOCHET!?
KURU (SPIN)
DIE!
HUH !?
GAN (PLING)
GANGAN

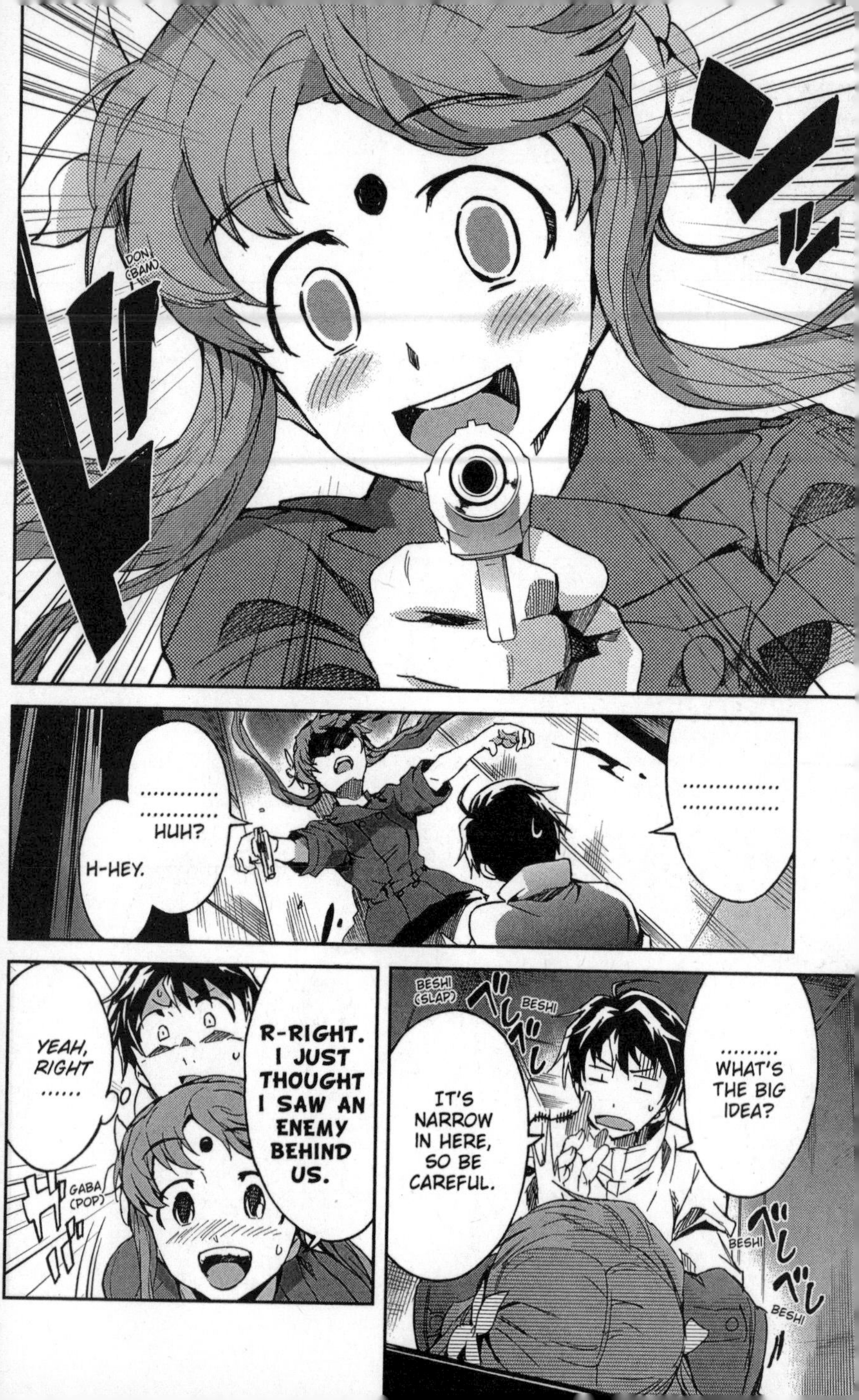
DON (BAM)
............ ............
............ ............ HUH? H-HEY.
BESHI (SLAP)
BESHI
......... WHAT'S THE BIG IDEA?
IT'S NARROW IN HERE, SO BE CAREFUL.
BESHI
BESHI
R-RIGHT. I JUST THOUGHT I SAW AN ENEMY BEHIND US.
YEAH, RIGHT ......
GABA (POP)

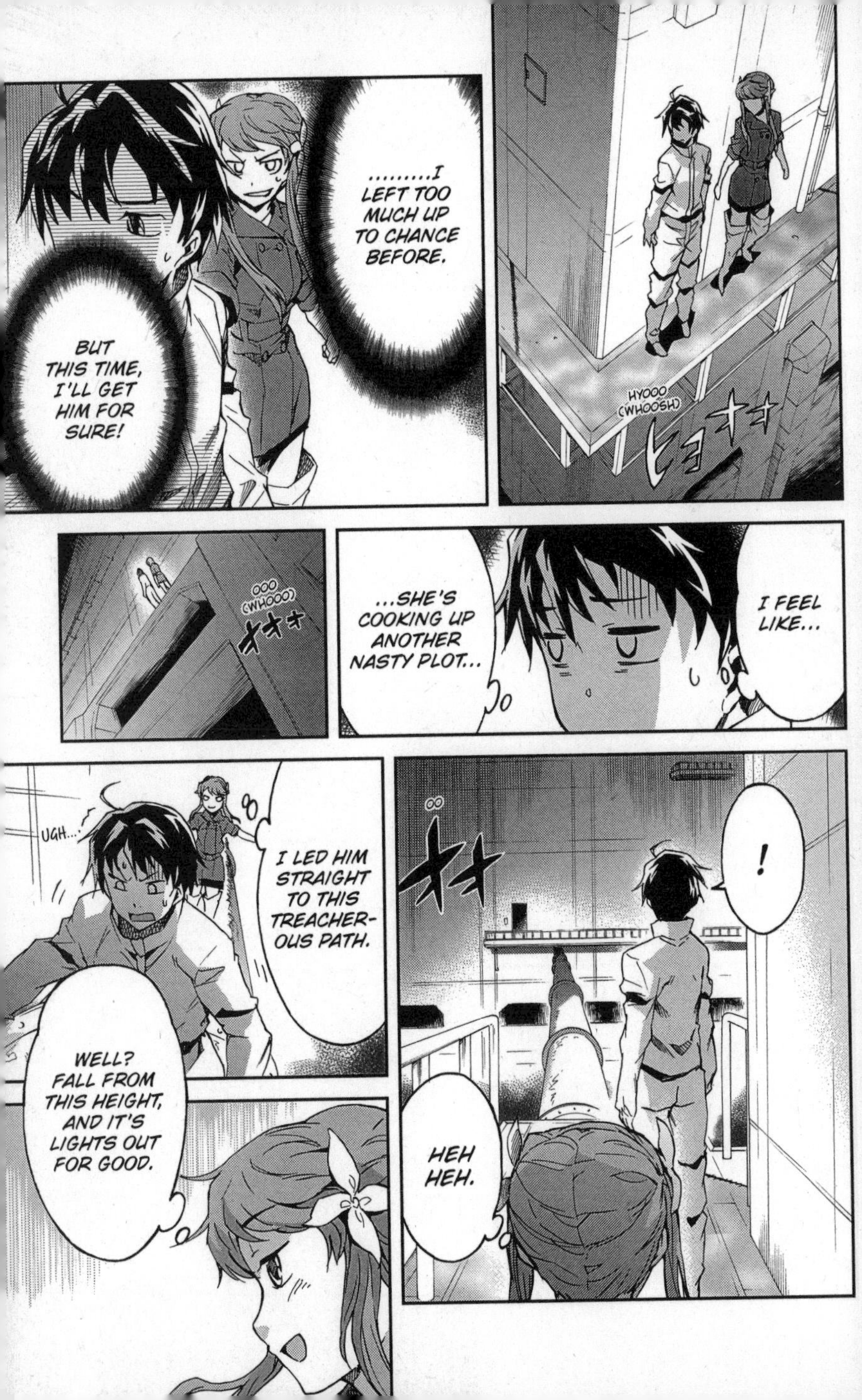
HYOOO (WHOOSH)
.........I LEFT TOO MUCH UP TO CHANCE BEFORE.
BUT THIS TIME, I'LL GET HIM FOR SURE!
I FEEL LIKE...
...SHE'S COOKING UP ANOTHER NASTY PLOT...
OOO (WHOOO)
!
HEH HEH.
UGH...
I LED HIM STRAIGHT TO THIS TREACHER-OUS PATH.
WELL? FALL FROM THIS HEIGHT, AND IT'S LIGHTS OUT FOR GOOD.

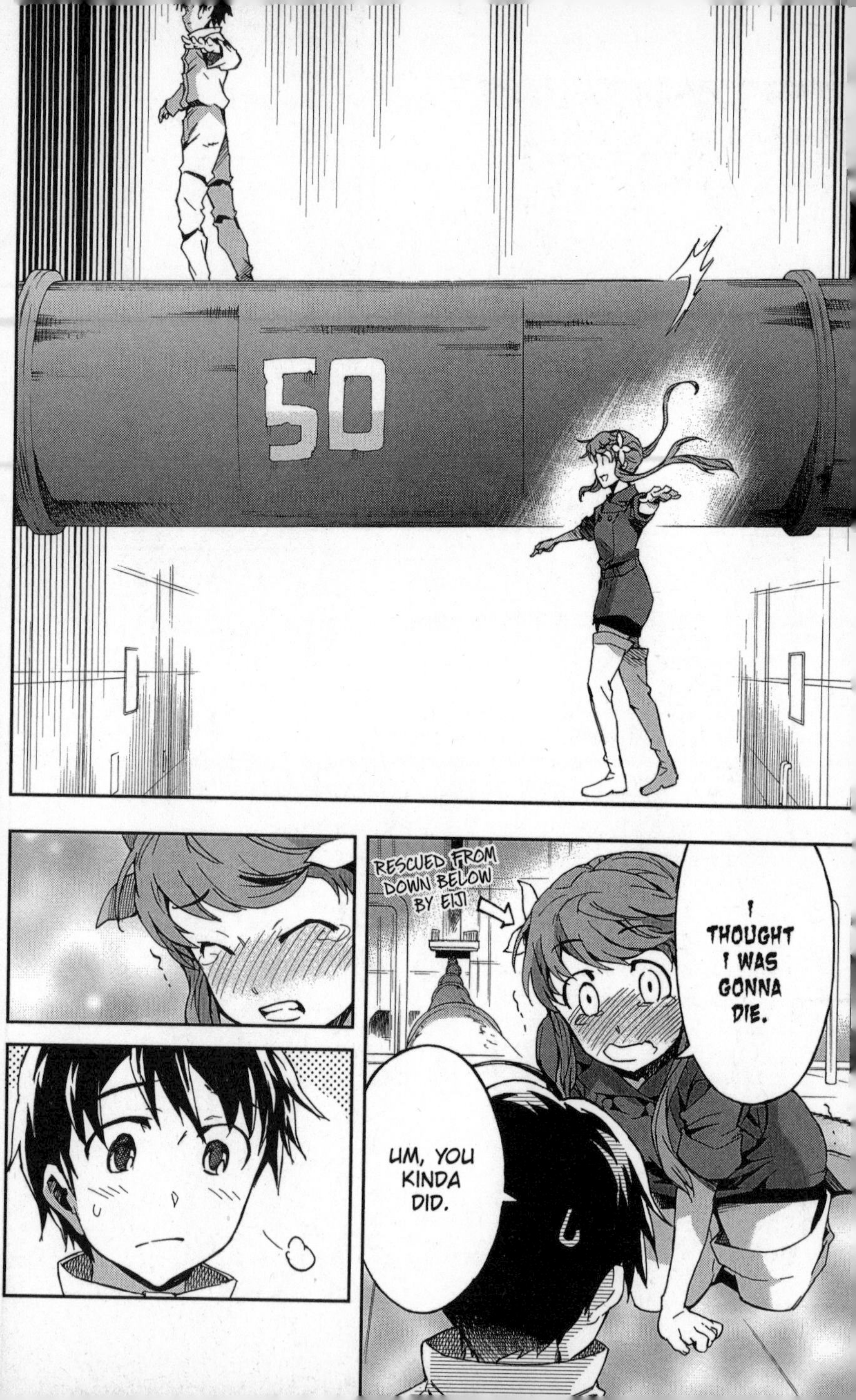

I THOUGHT I WAS GONNA DIE.
RESCUED FROM DOWN BELOW BY EIJI
UM, YOU KINDA DID.

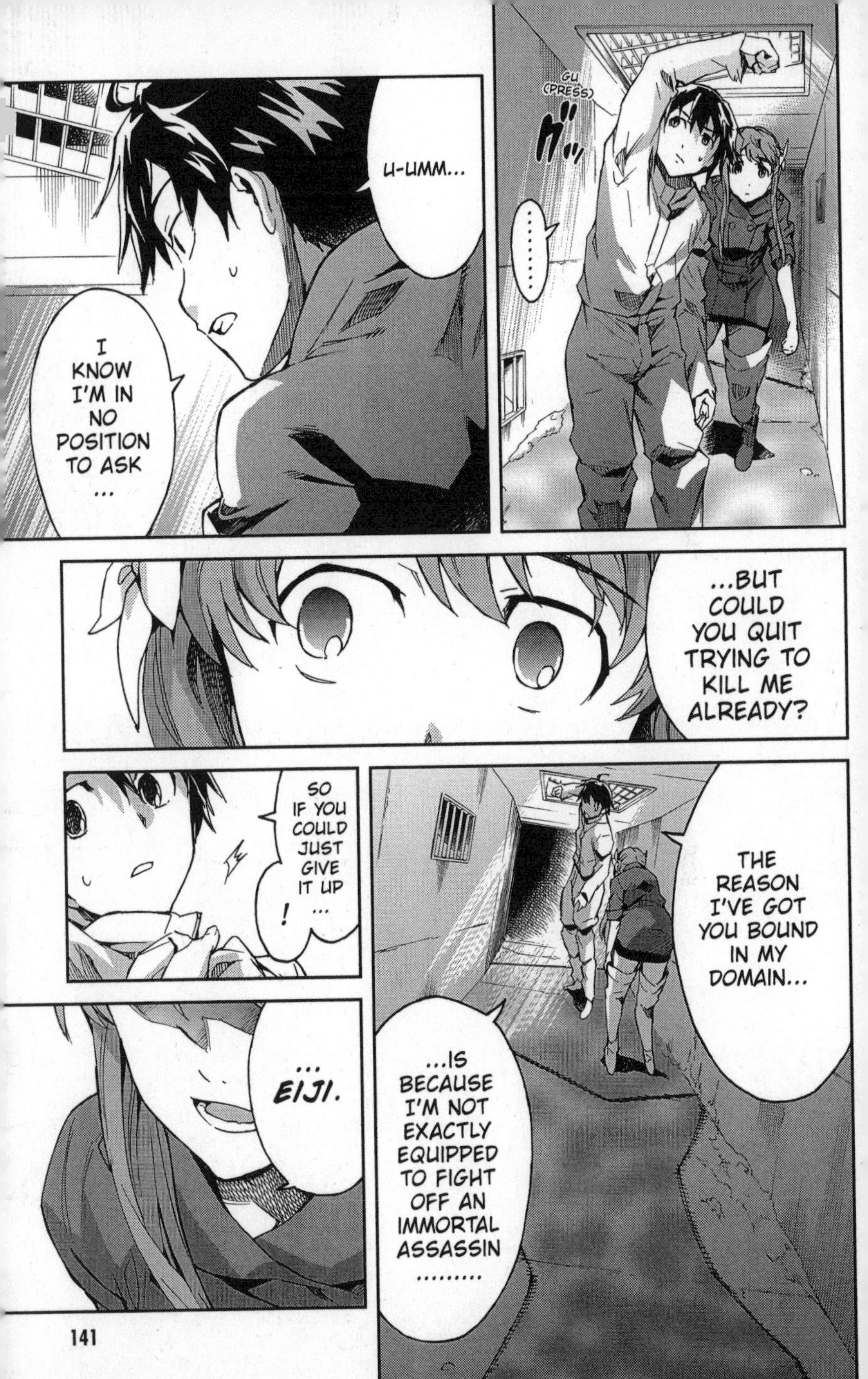

GU (PRESS)
……
U-UMM…
I KNOW I'M IN NO POSITION TO ASK …
…BUT COULD YOU QUIT TRYING TO KILL ME ALREADY?
THE REASON I'VE GOT YOU BOUND IN MY DOMAIN…
…IS BECAUSE I'M NOT EXACTLY EQUIPPED TO FIGHT OFF AN IMMORTAL ASSASSIN ………
SO IF YOU COULD JUST GIVE IT UP …
!
… EIJI.

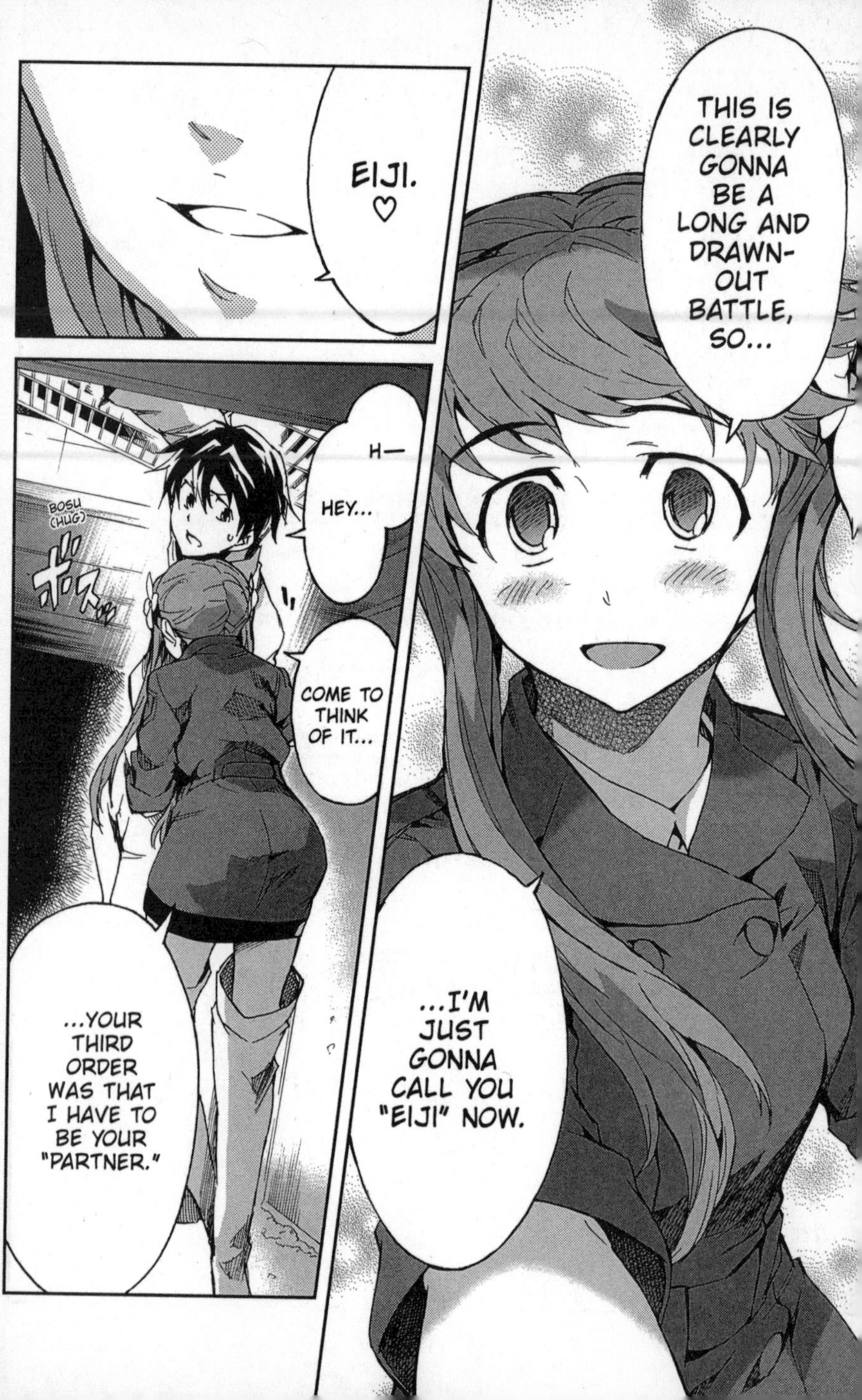
THIS IS CLEARLY GONNA BE A LONG AND DRAWN-OUT BATTLE, SO...
...I'M JUST GONNA CALL YOU "EIJI" NOW.
EIJI. ♡
H—
HEY...
BOSU (HUG)
COME TO THINK OF IT...
...YOUR THIRD ORDER WAS THAT I HAVE TO BE YOUR "PARTNER."

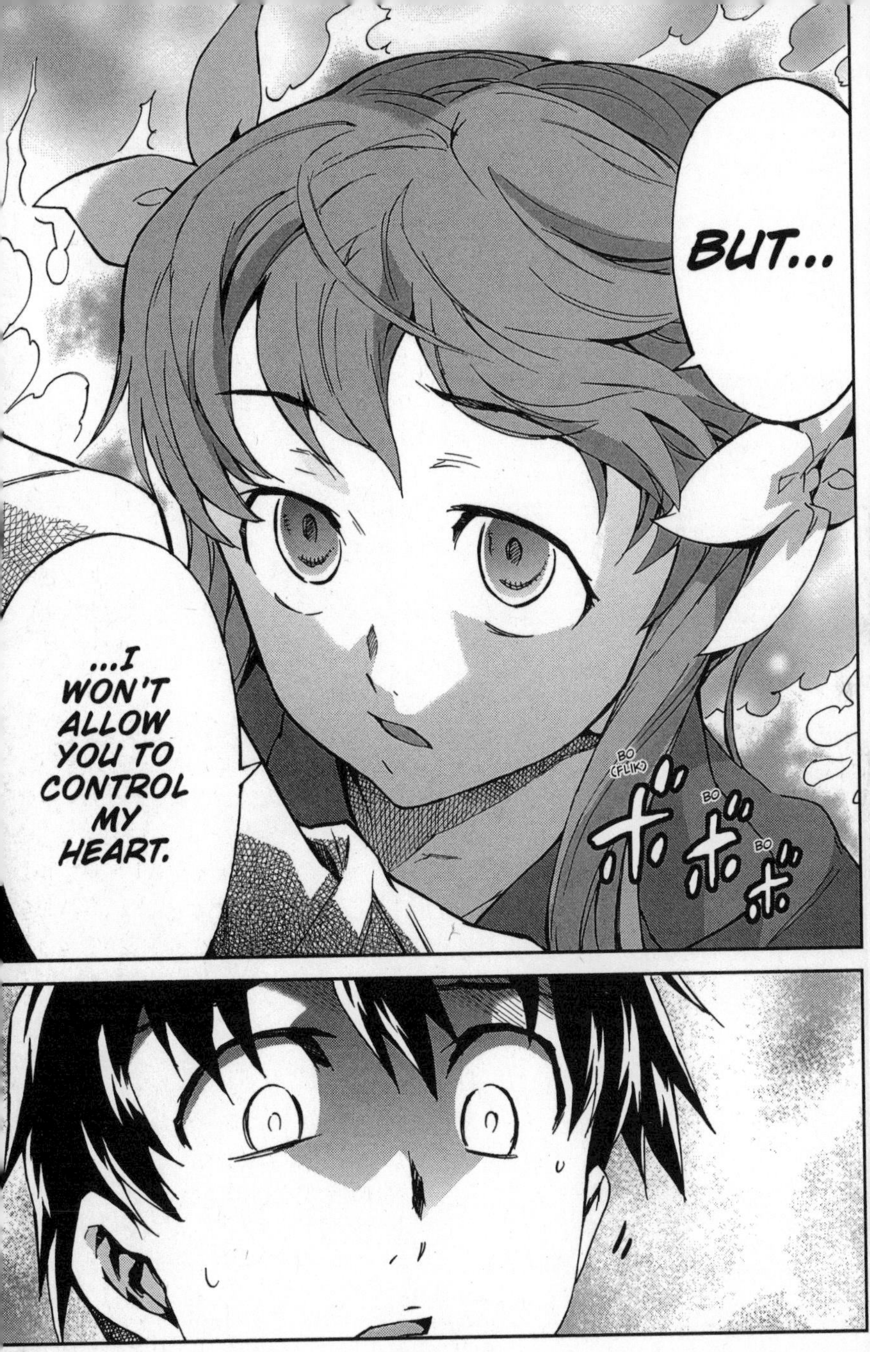
BUT...
...I WON'T ALLOW YOU TO CONTROL MY HEART.
BO (FLIK)
BO
BO

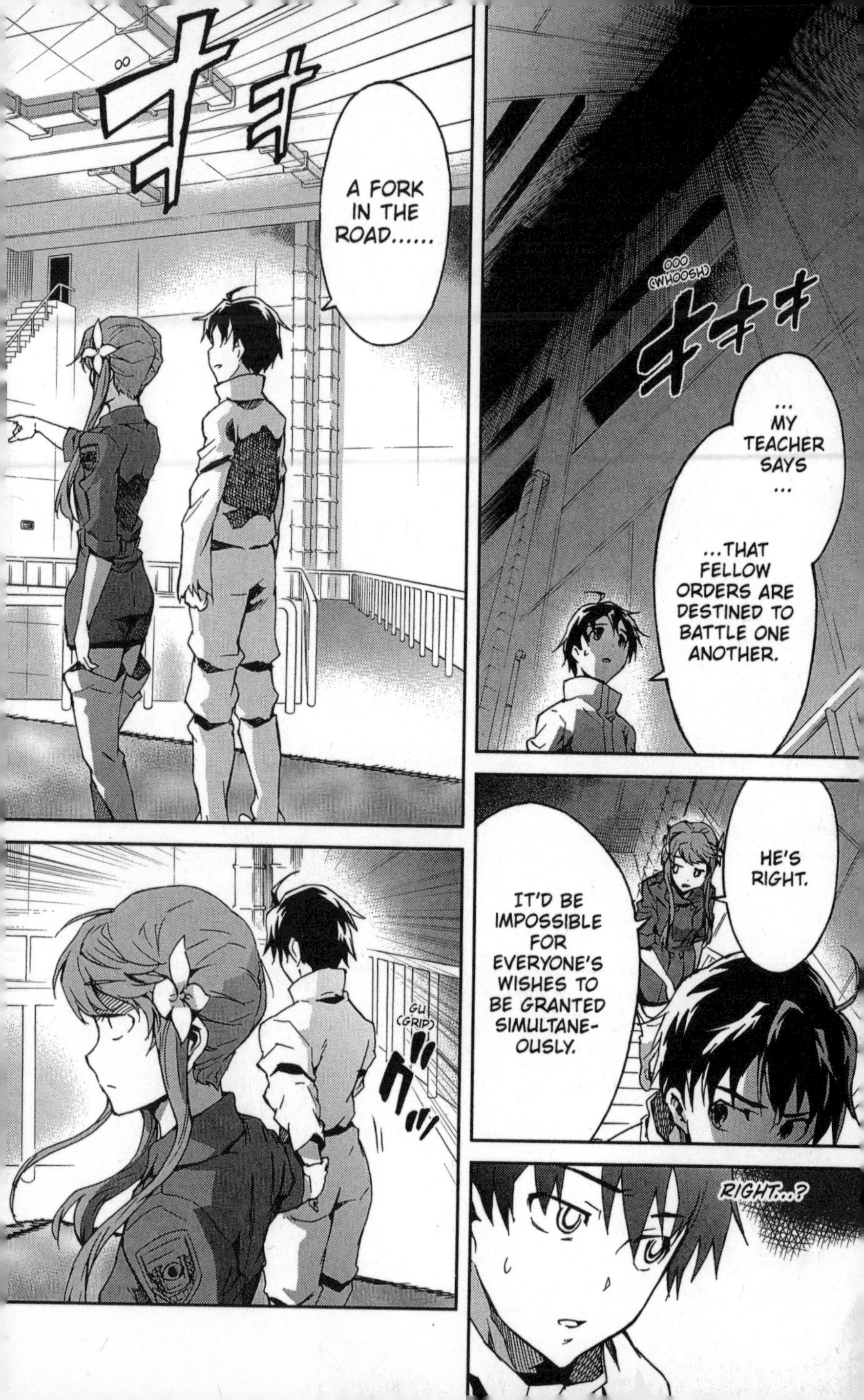
OOO (WHOOSH)
オオオ
... MY TEACHER SAYS ...
...THAT FELLOW ORDERS ARE DESTINED TO BATTLE ONE ANOTHER.
OO
オオ
A FORK IN THE ROAD......
HE'S RIGHT.
IT'D BE IMPOSSIBLE FOR EVERYONE'S WISHES TO BE GRANTED SIMULTANE-OUSLY.
RIGHT...?
GU (GRIP)
グッ

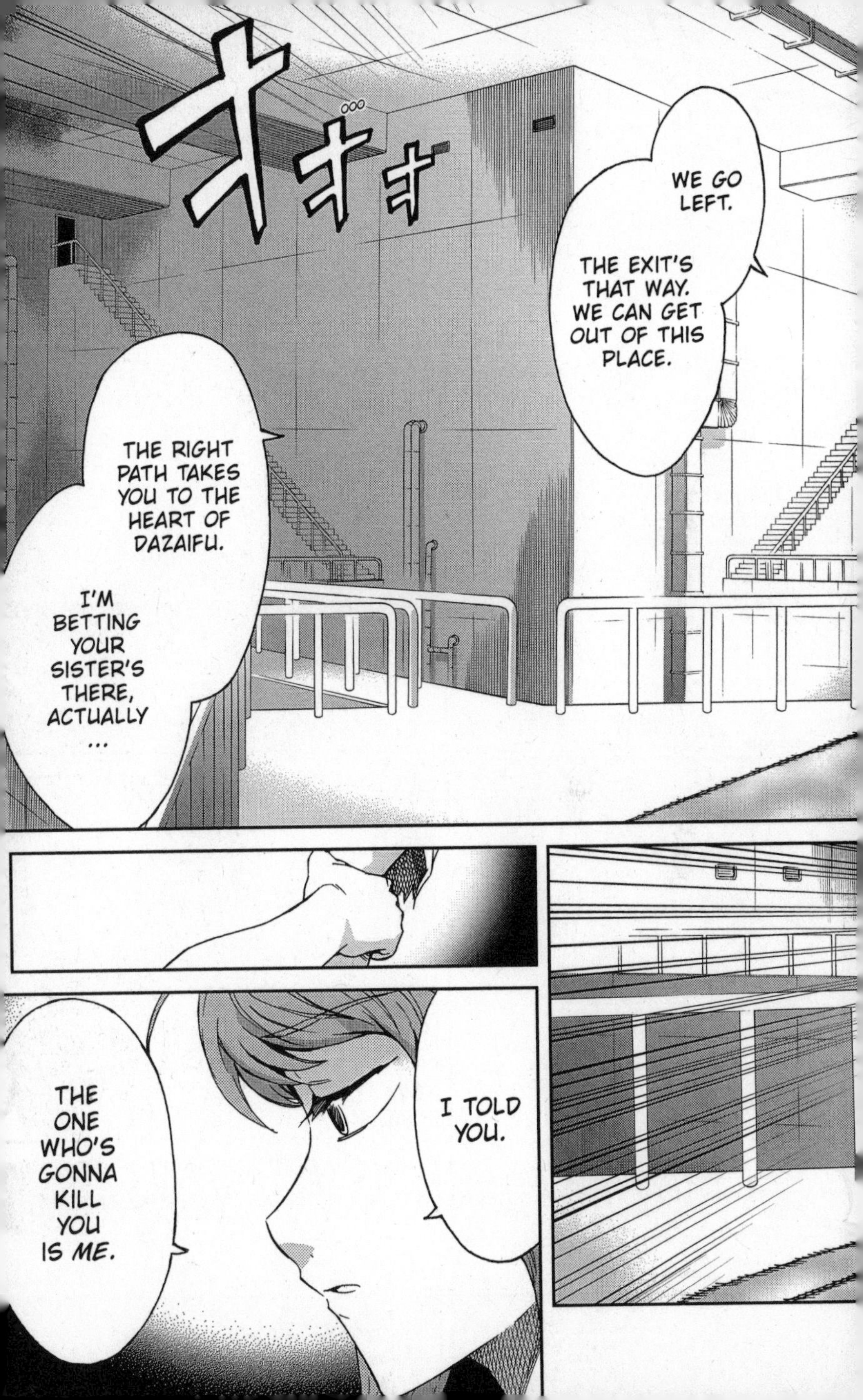
オォォ
WE GO LEFT.
THE EXIT'S THAT WAY. WE CAN GET OUT OF THIS PLACE.
THE RIGHT PATH TAKES YOU TO THE HEART OF DAZAIFU.
I'M BETTING YOUR SISTER'S THERE, ACTUALLY...
I TOLD YOU.
THE ONE WHO'S GONNA KILL YOU IS *ME*.

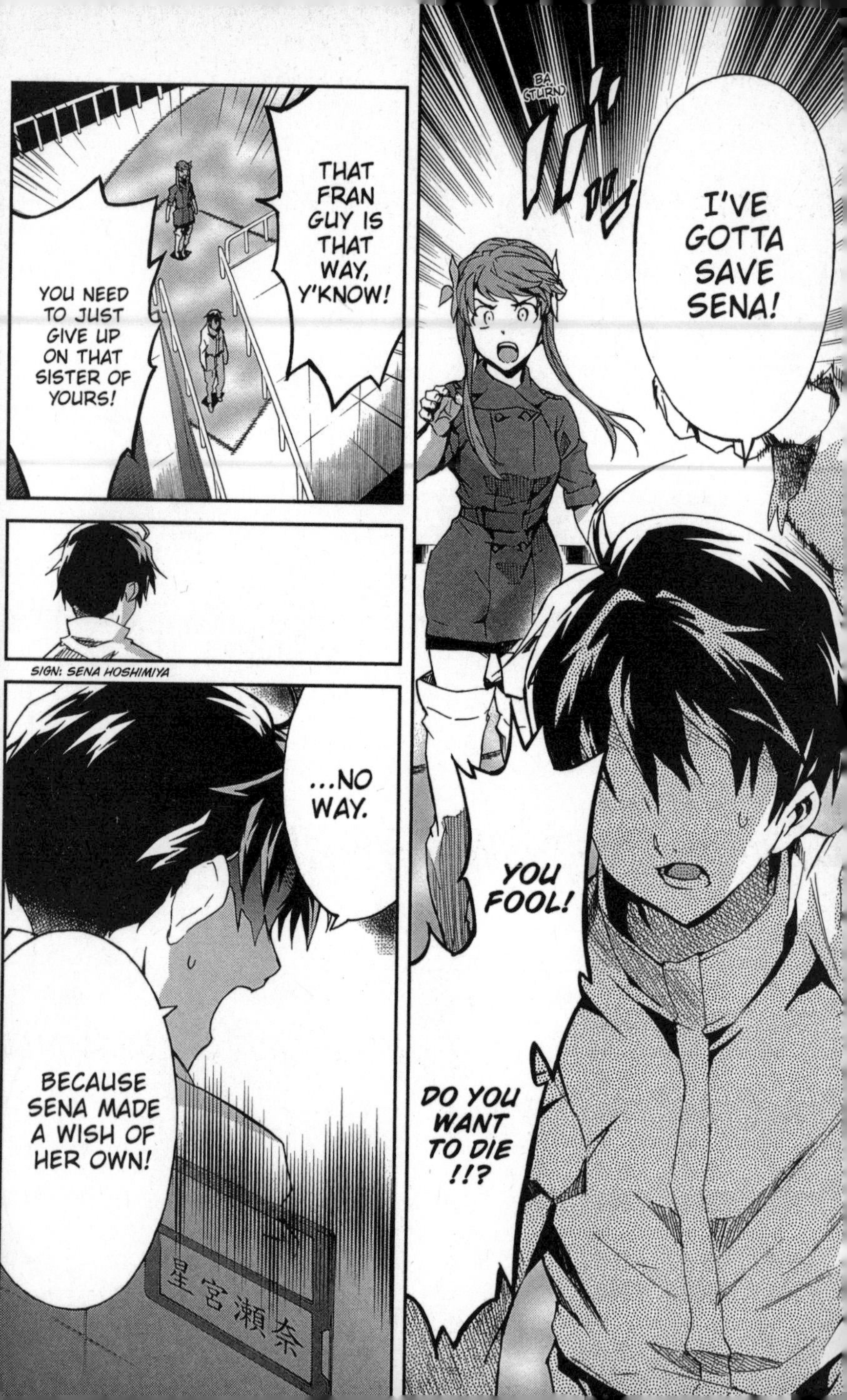
BA (STURN)
I'VE GOTTA SAVE SENA!
YOU FOOL!
DO YOU WANT TO DIE !!?
THAT FRAN GUY IS THAT WAY, Y'KNOW!
YOU NEED TO JUST GIVE UP ON THAT SISTER OF YOURS!
SIGN: SENA HOSHIMIYA
...NO WAY.
BECAUSE SENA MADE A WISH OF HER OWN!
星宮瀬奈

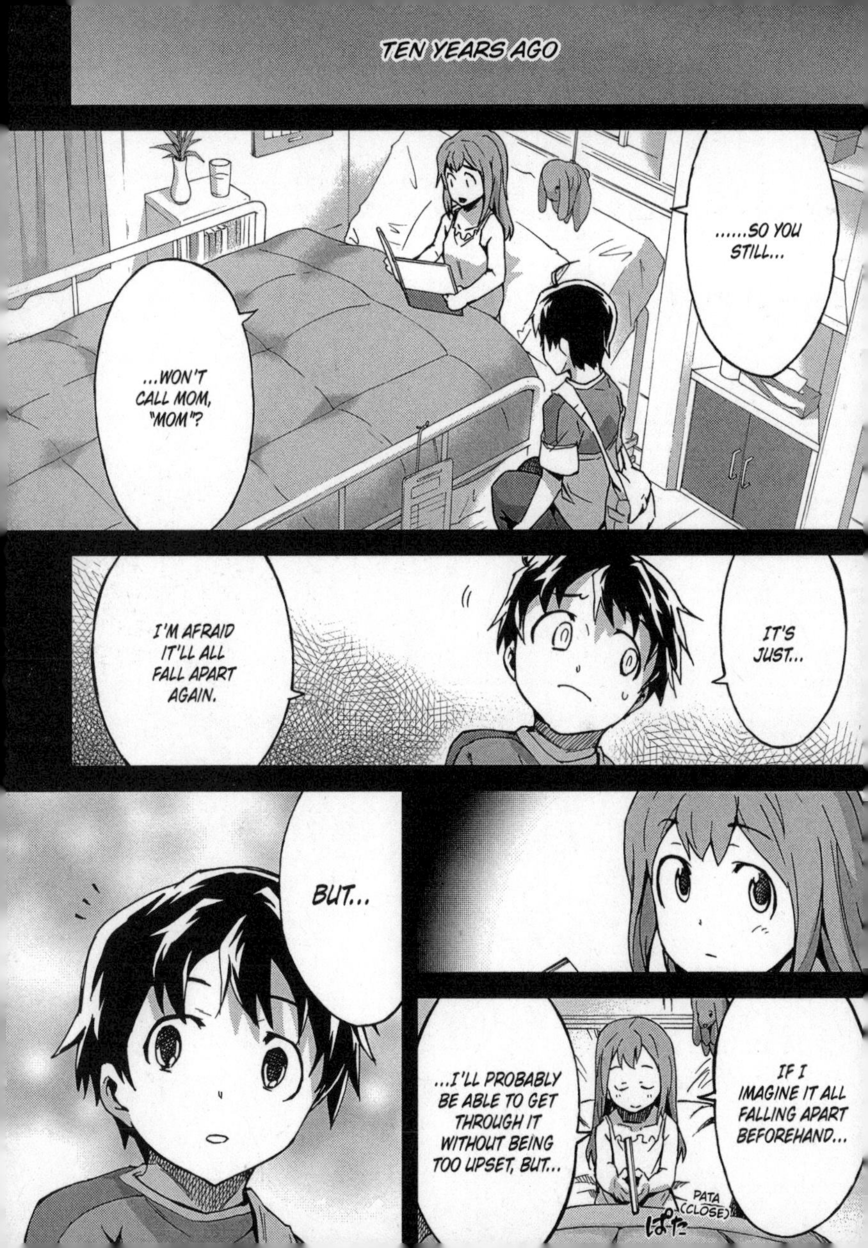
TEN YEARS AGO
......SO YOU STILL...
...WON'T CALL MOM, "MOM"?
IT'S JUST...
I'M AFRAID IT'LL ALL FALL APART AGAIN.
IF I IMAGINE IT ALL FALLING APART BEFOREHAND...
...I'LL PROBABLY BE ABLE TO GET THROUGH IT WITHOUT BEING TOO UPSET, BUT...
PATA (CLOSE)
ぱた
BUT...

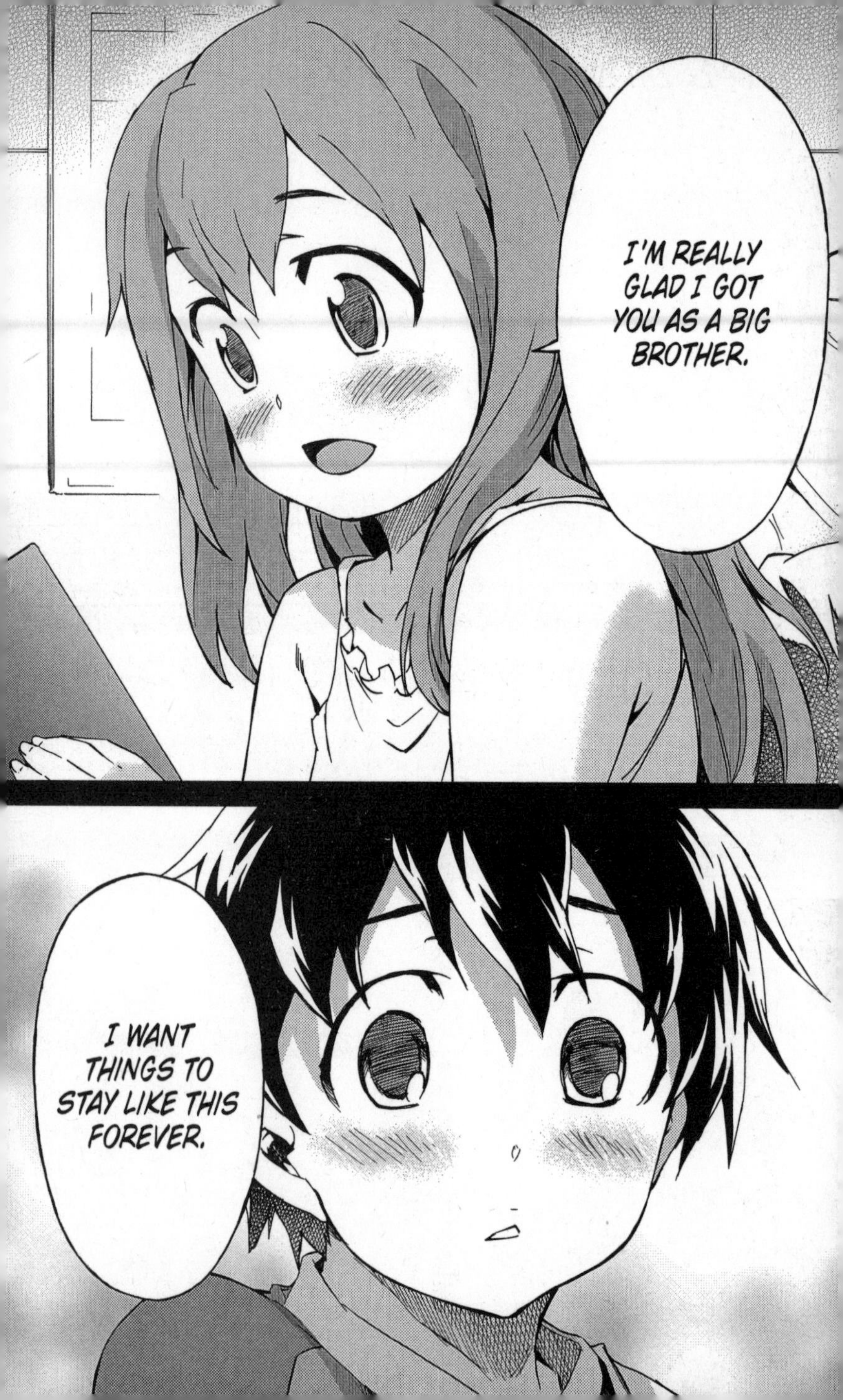
I'M REALLY GLAD I GOT YOU AS A BIG BROTHER.
I WANT THINGS TO STAY LIKE THIS FOREVER.

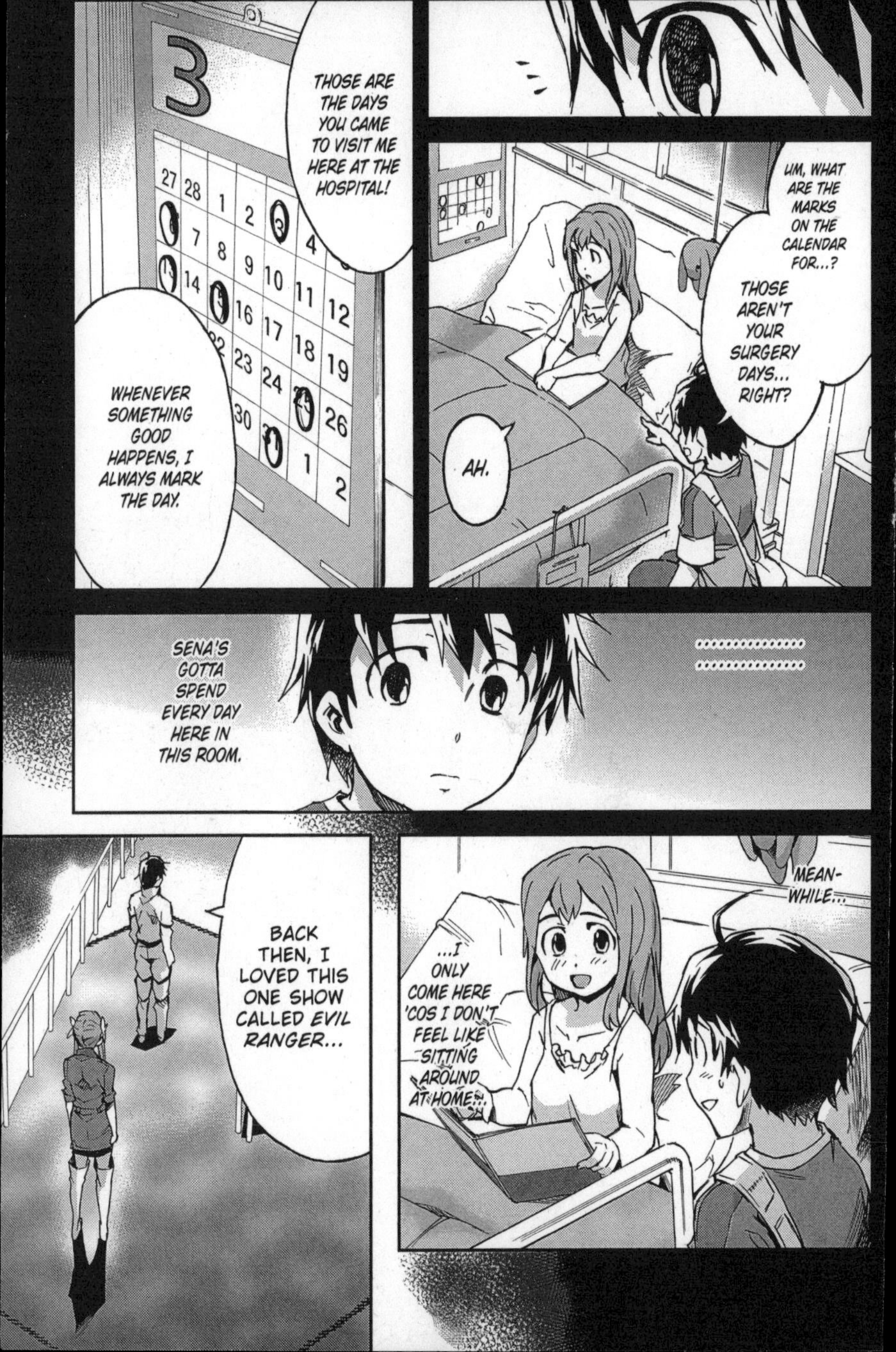
UM, WHAT ARE THE MARKS ON THE CALENDAR FOR...?
THOSE AREN'T YOUR SURGERY DAYS... RIGHT?
AH.
THOSE ARE THE DAYS YOU CAME TO VISIT ME HERE AT THE HOSPITAL!
WHENEVER SOMETHING GOOD HAPPENS, I ALWAYS MARK THE DAY.
SENA'S GOTTA SPEND EVERY DAY HERE IN THIS ROOM.
MEAN-WHILE...
...I ONLY COME HERE 'COS I DON'T FEEL LIKE SITTING AROUND AT HOME...
BACK THEN, I LOVED THIS ONE SHOW CALLED *EVIL RANGER*...

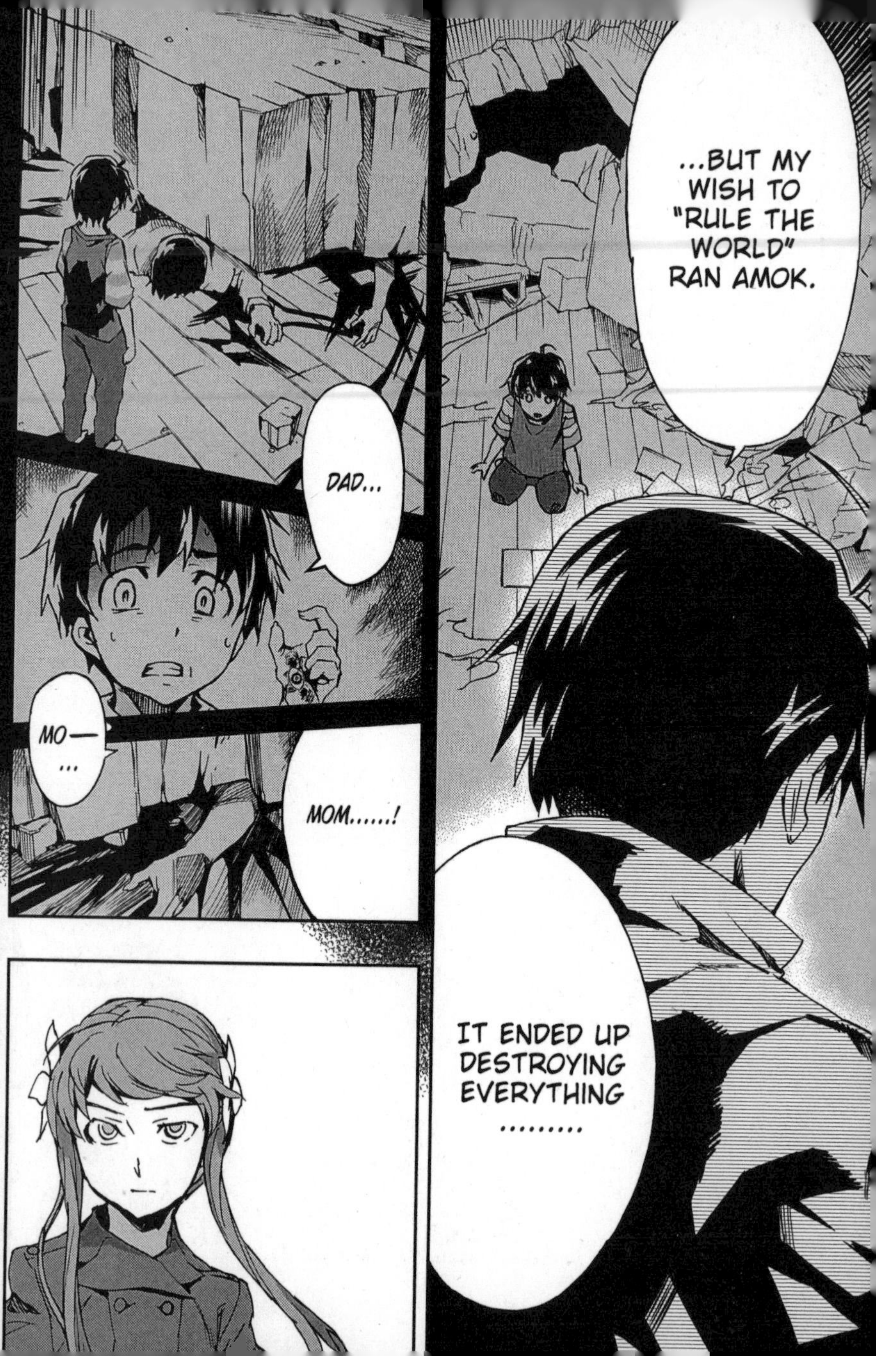
...BUT MY WISH TO "RULE THE WORLD" RAN AMOK.
IT ENDED UP DESTROYING EVERYTHING .........
DAD...
MO— ...
MOM......!

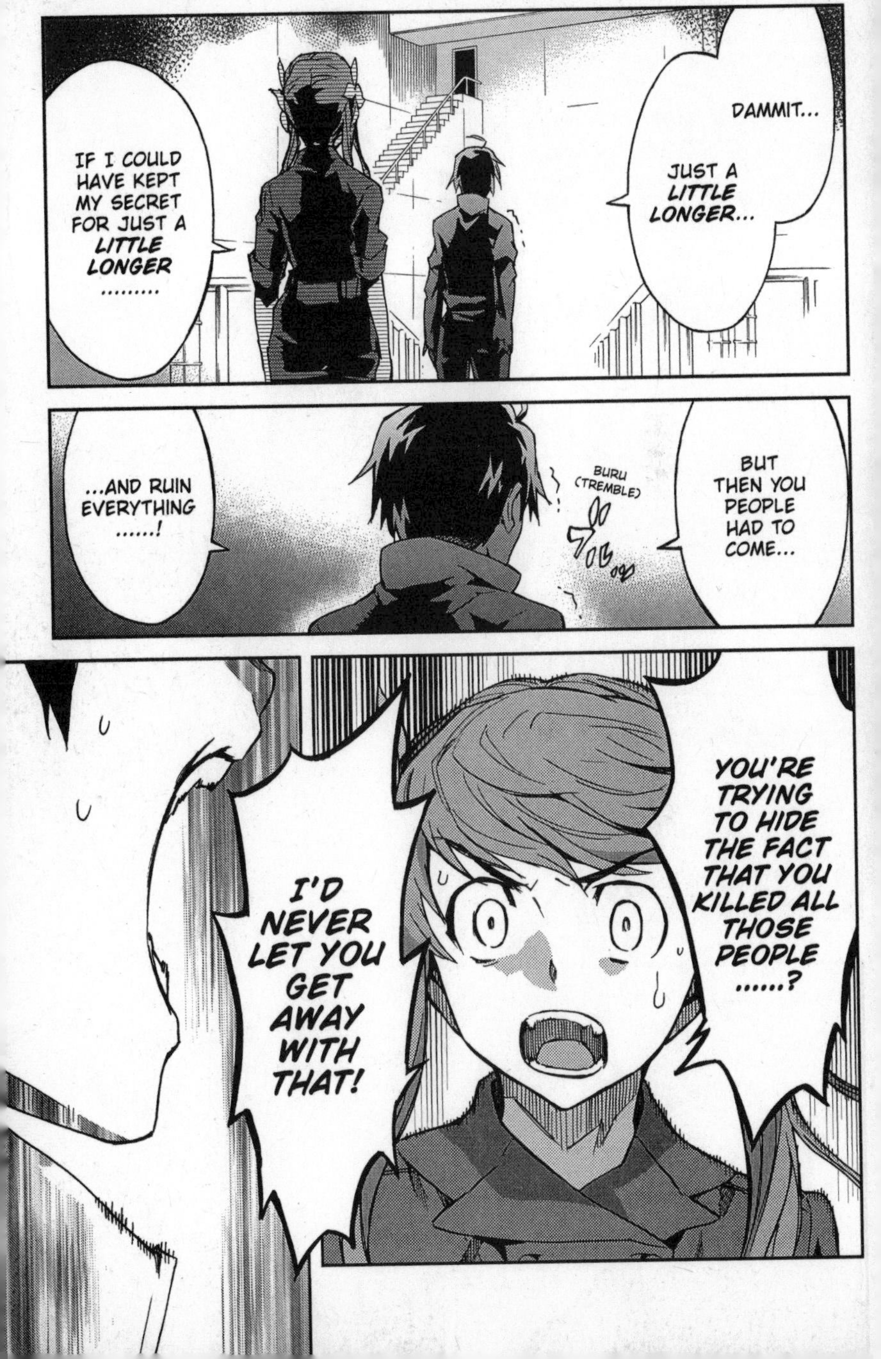
DAMMIT...
JUST A LITTLE LONGER...
IF I COULD HAVE KEPT MY SECRET FOR JUST A LITTLE LONGER .........
BUT THEN YOU PEOPLE HAD TO COME...
BURU (TREMBLE)
...AND RUIN EVERYTHING ......!
YOU'RE TRYING TO HIDE THE FACT THAT YOU KILLED ALL THOSE PEOPLE ......?
I'D NEVER LET YOU GET AWAY WITH THAT!

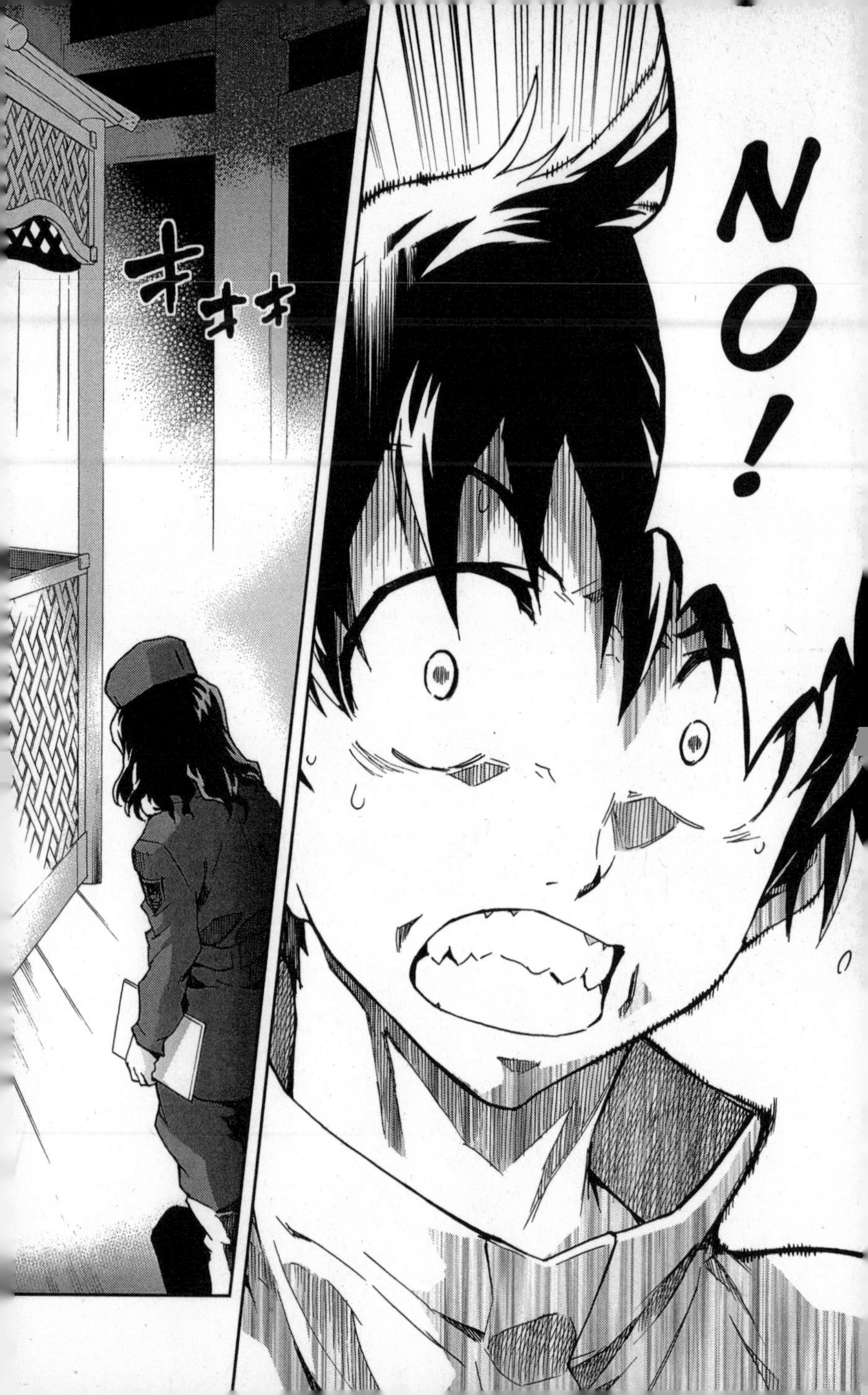
NO!
オォォ

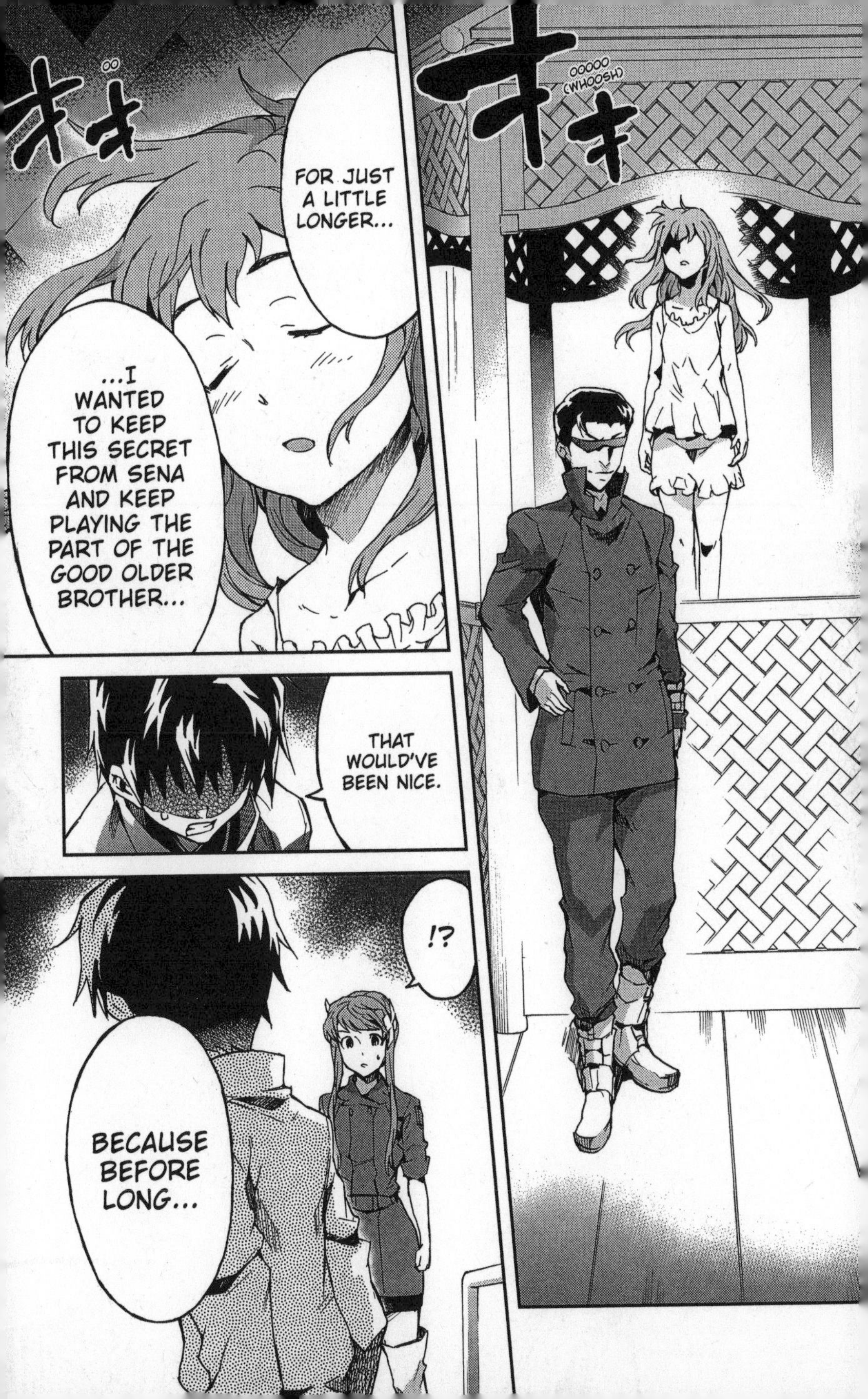
OOOOO (WHOOSH)
OO
FOR JUST A LITTLE LONGER...
...I WANTED TO KEEP THIS SECRET FROM SENA AND KEEP PLAYING THE PART OF THE GOOD OLDER BROTHER...
THAT WOULD'VE BEEN NICE.
!?
BECAUSE BEFORE LONG...

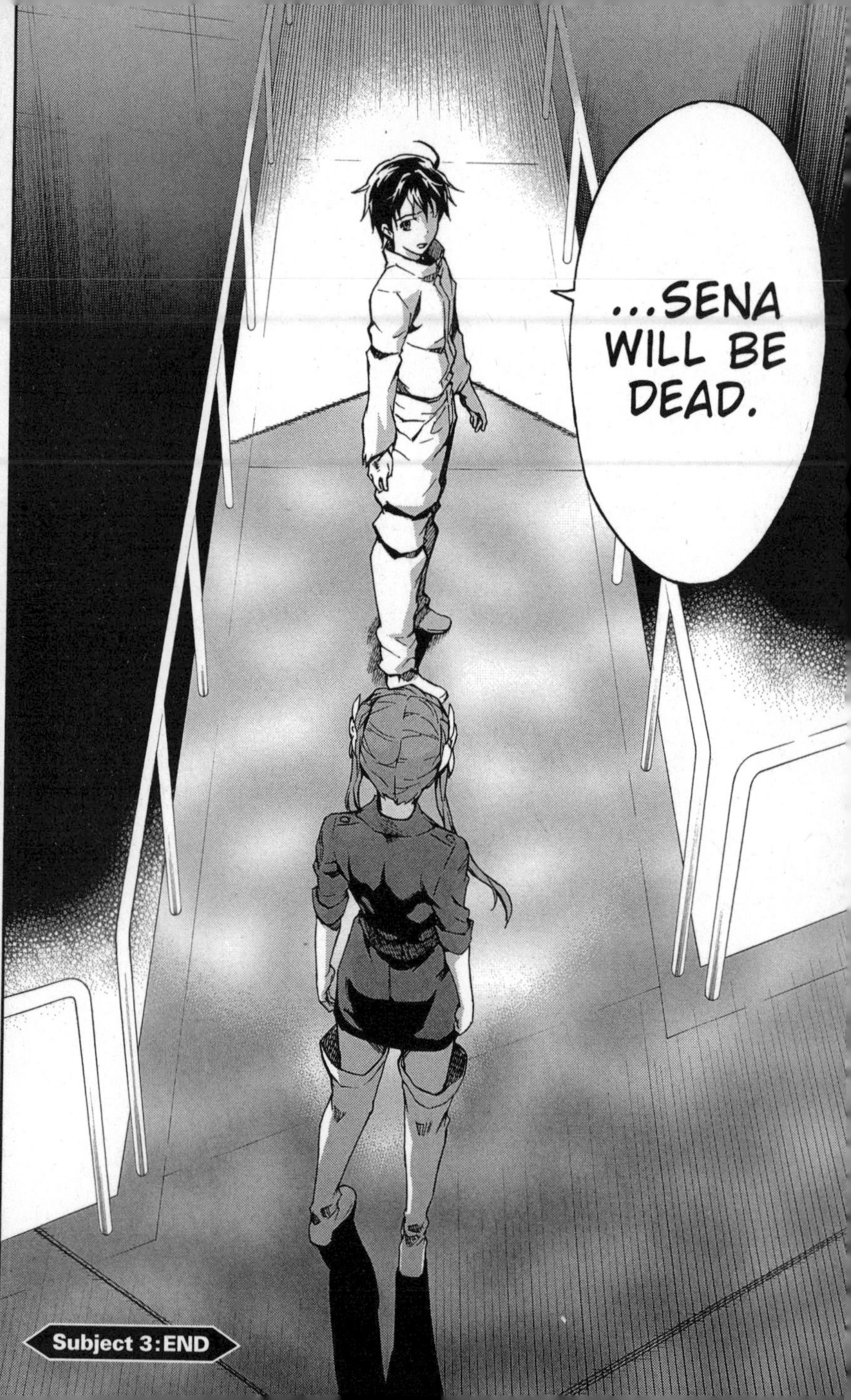
...SENA WILL BE DEAD.
Subject 3: END

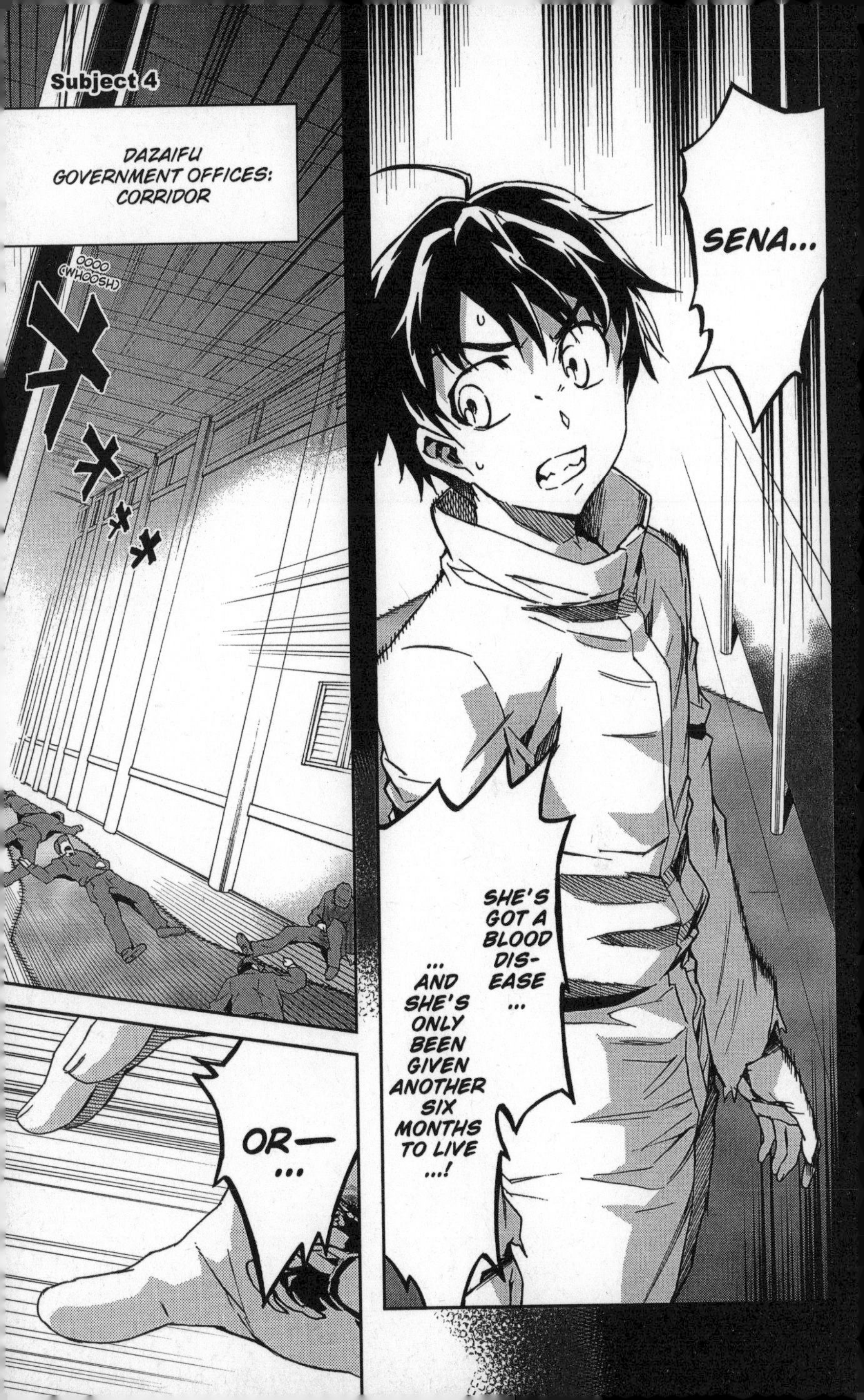
SENA...
SHE'S GOT A BLOOD DIS-EASE ...
... AND SHE'S ONLY BEEN GIVEN ANOTHER SIX MONTHS TO LIVE ...!
Subject 4
DAZAIFU GOVERNMENT OFFICES: CORRIDOR
OOOO (WHOOSH)
OR— ...

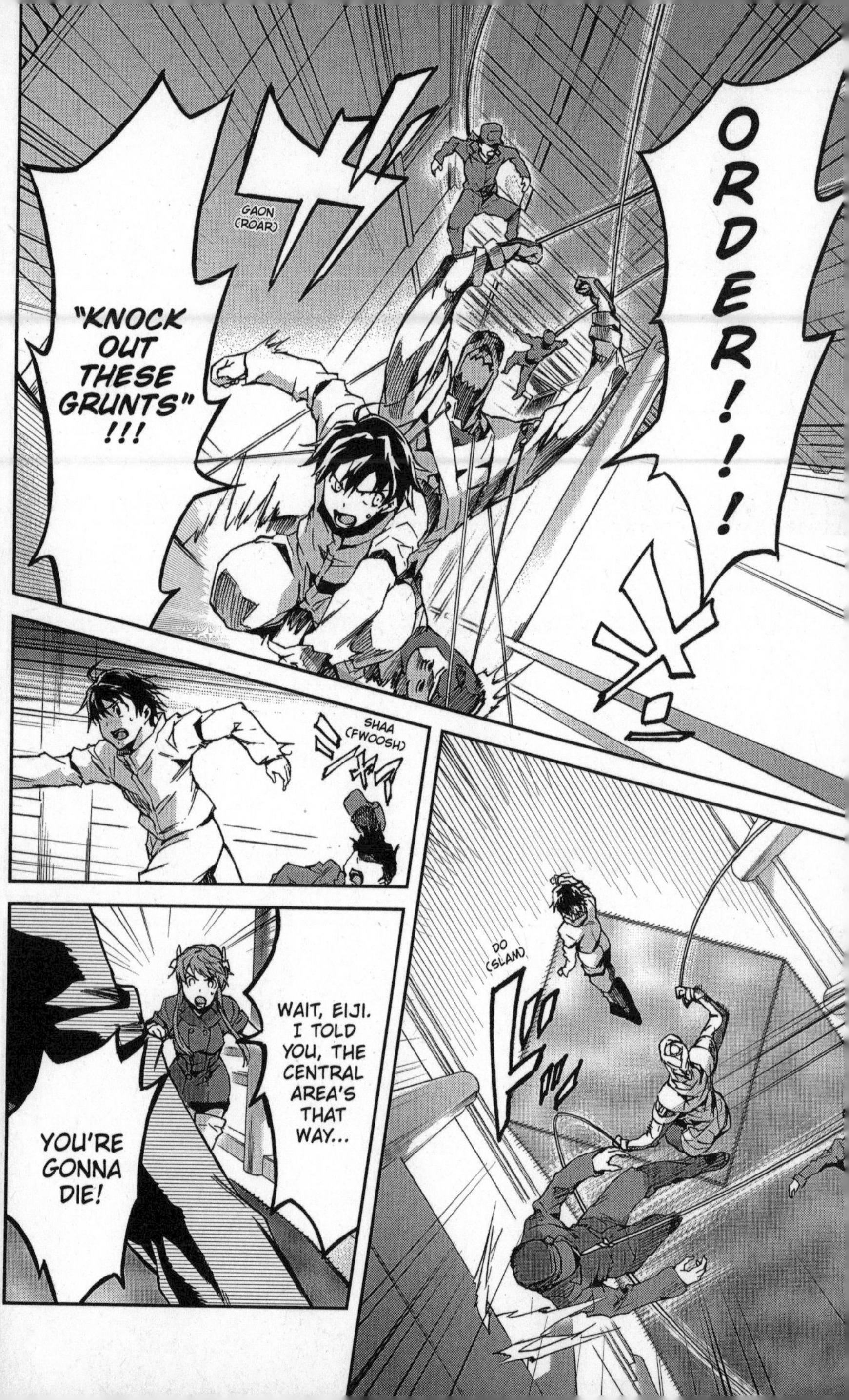
ORDER!!!
GAON (ROAR)
"KNOCK OUT THESE GRUNTS" !!!
DO (SLAM)
SHAA (FWOOSH)
WAIT, EIJI. I TOLD YOU, THE CENTRAL AREA'S THAT WAY...
YOU'RE GONNA DIE!

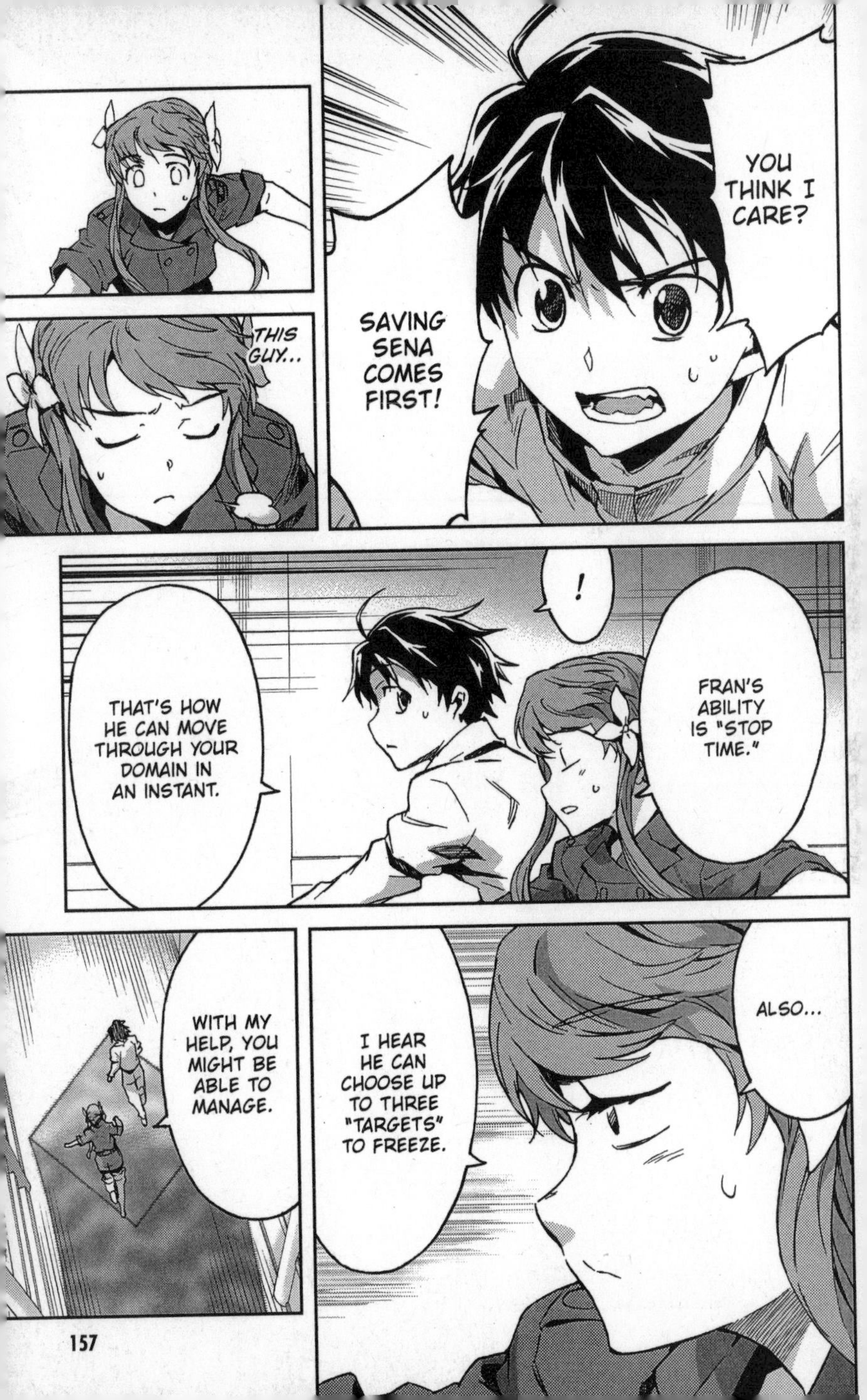

YOU THINK I CARE?
SAVING SENA COMES FIRST!
THIS GUY...
!
FRAN'S ABILITY IS "STOP TIME."
THAT'S HOW HE CAN MOVE THROUGH YOUR DOMAIN IN AN INSTANT.
ALSO...
I HEAR HE CAN CHOOSE UP TO THREE "TARGETS" TO FREEZE.
WITH MY HELP, YOU MIGHT BE ABLE TO MANAGE.

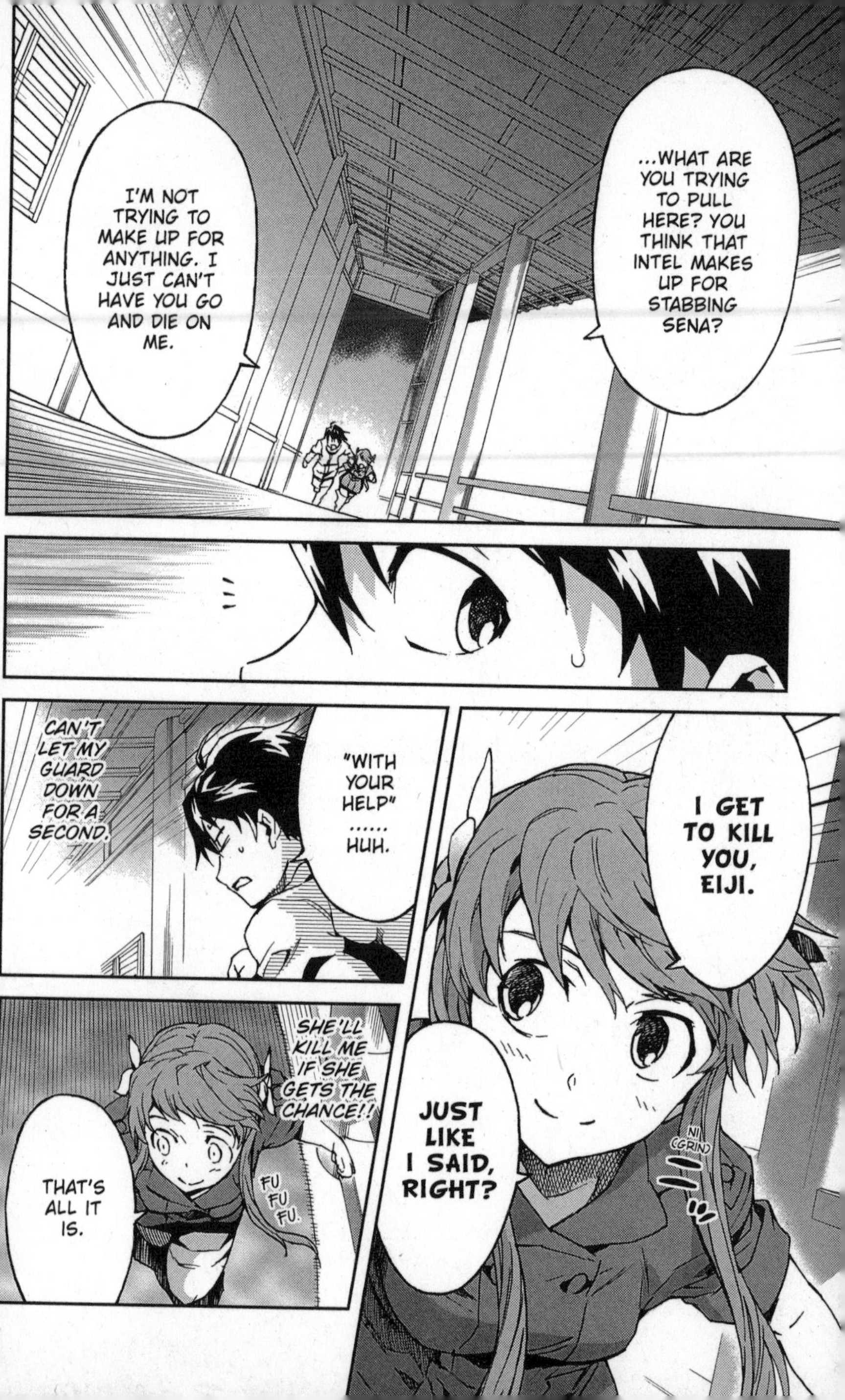
...WHAT ARE YOU TRYING TO PULL HERE? YOU THINK THAT INTEL MAKES UP FOR STABBING SENA?
I'M NOT TRYING TO MAKE UP FOR ANYTHING. I JUST CAN'T HAVE YOU GO AND DIE ON ME.
I GET TO KILL YOU, EIJI.
JUST LIKE I SAID, RIGHT?
NI (GRIN)
"WITH YOUR HELP" ...... HUH.
CAN'T LET MY GUARD DOWN FOR A SECOND.
SHE'LL KILL ME IF SHE GETS THE CHANCE!!
FU FU FU.
THAT'S ALL IT IS.

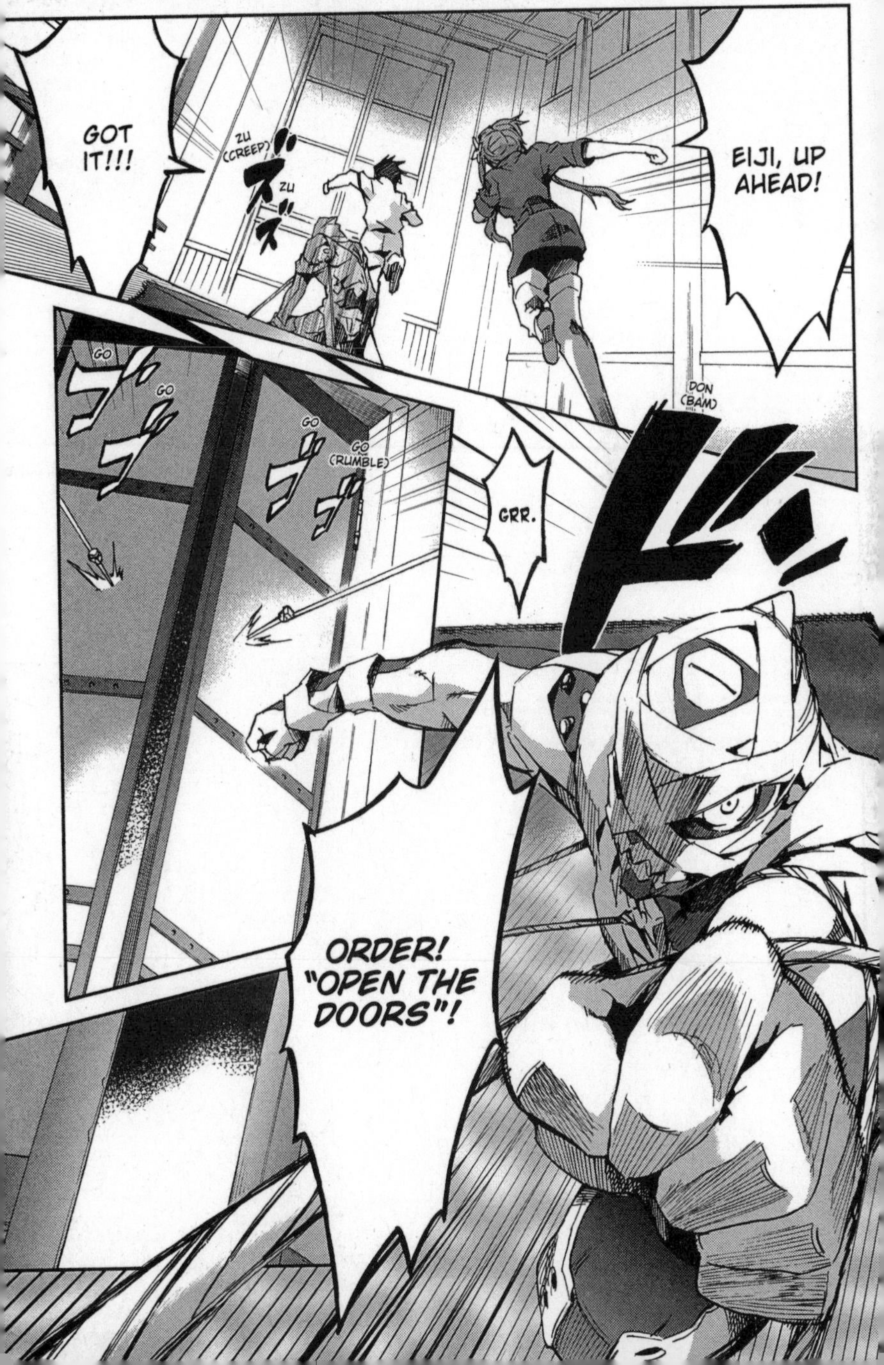
EIJI, UP AHEAD!
ZU (CREEP)
ズ
ZU
ズ
GOT IT!!!
DON (BAM)
ド
GRR.
GO
ゴ
GO
ゴ
GO
ゴ
GO (RUMBLE)
ゴ
ORDER! "OPEN THE DOORS"!

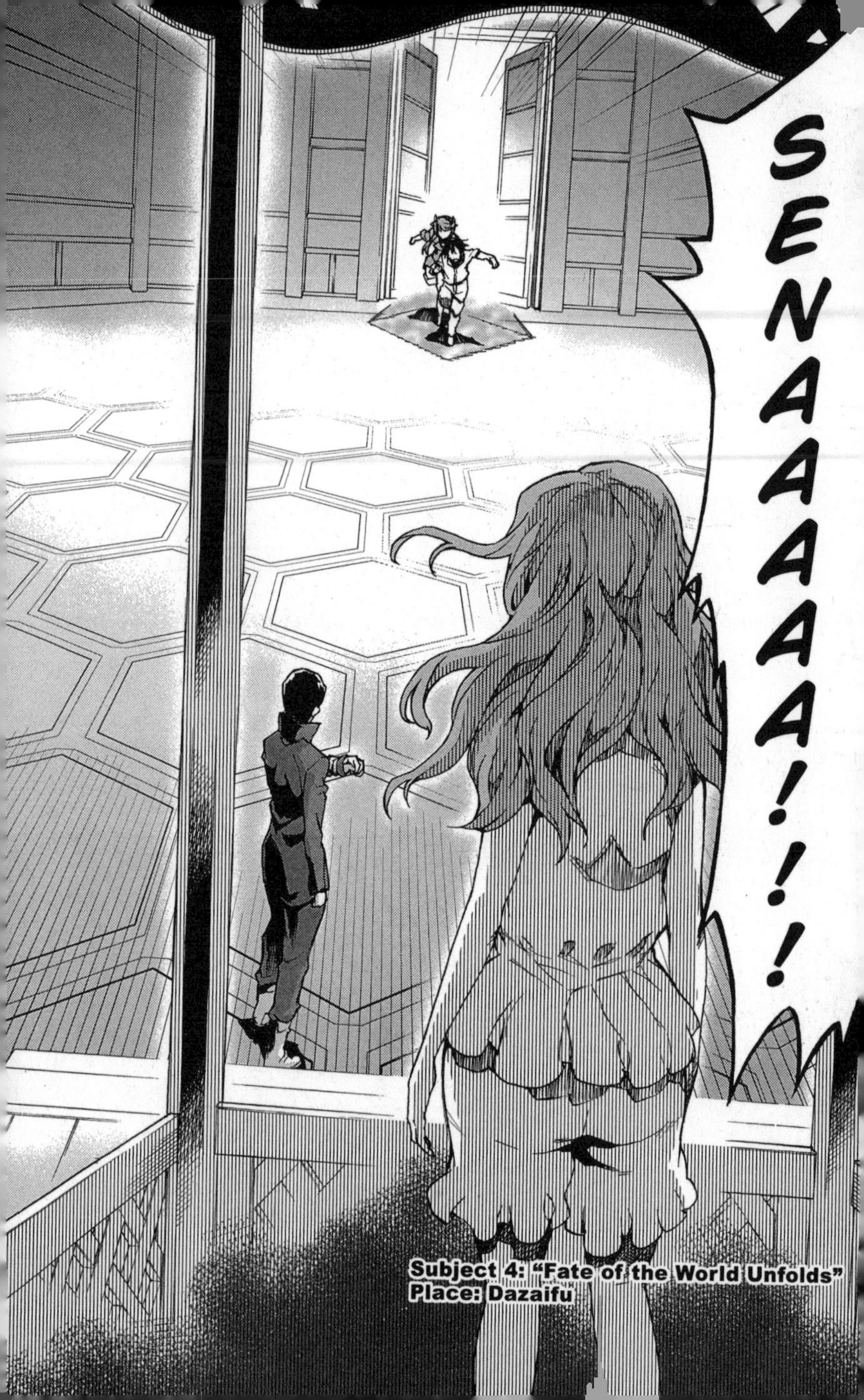
SENAAAAAA!!!!
Subject 4: "Fate of the World Unfolds"
Place: Dazaifu

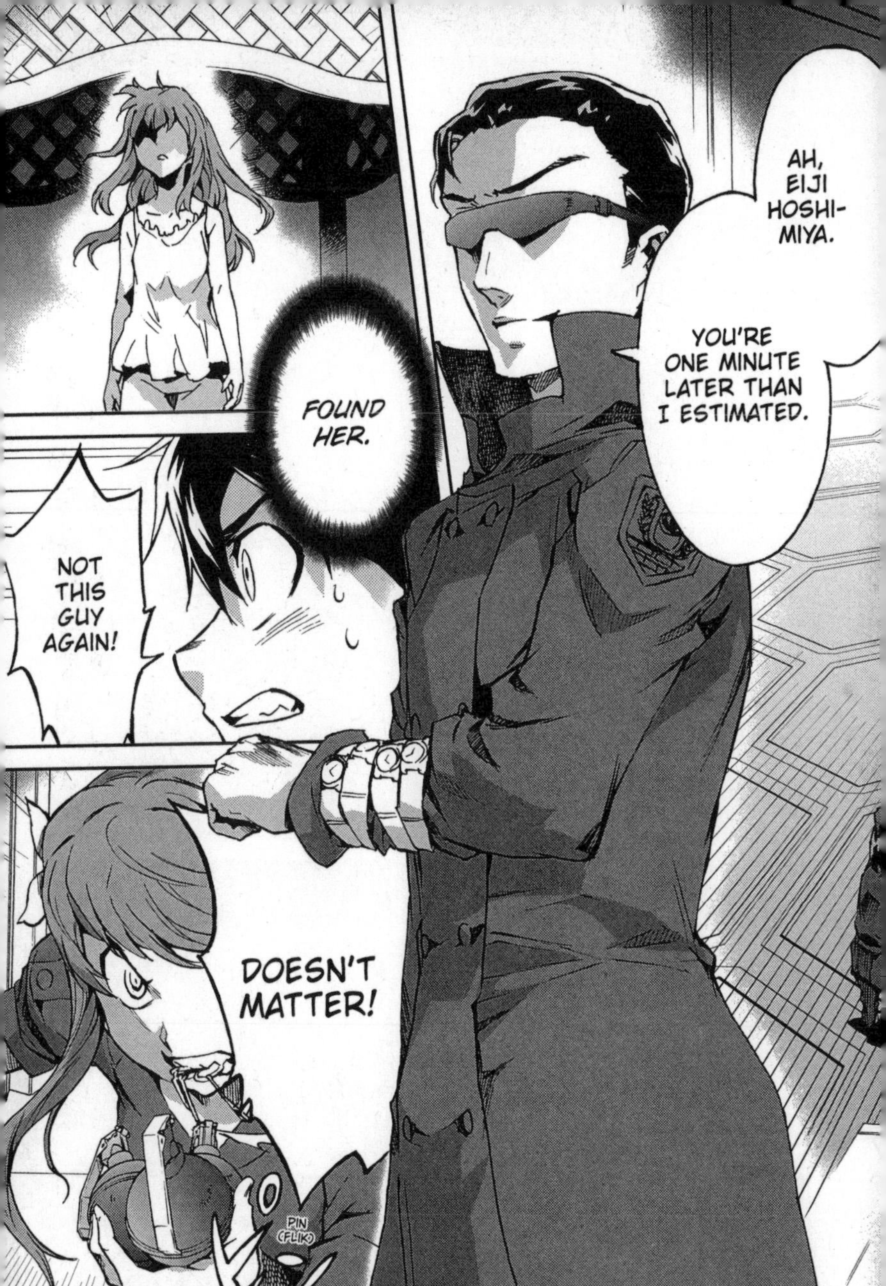

AH, EIJI HOSHI-MIYA.
YOU'RE ONE MINUTE LATER THAN I ESTIMATED.
FOUND HER.
NOT THIS GUY AGAIN!
DOESN'T MATTER!
PIN (FLIK)

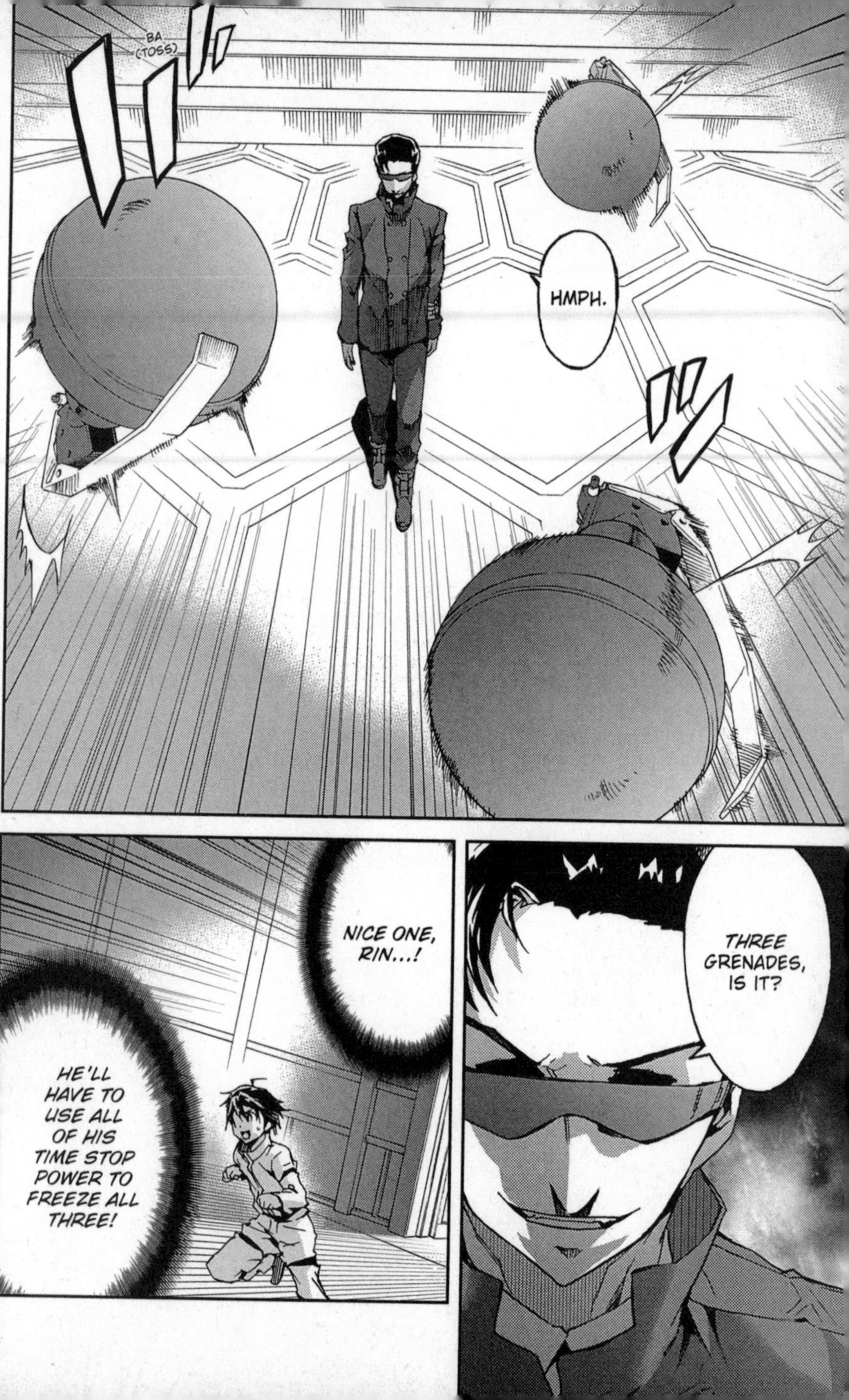
BA (TOSS)
HMPH.
THREE GRENADES, IS IT?
NICE ONE, RIN...!
HE'LL HAVE TO USE ALL OF HIS TIME STOP POWER TO FREEZE ALL THREE!

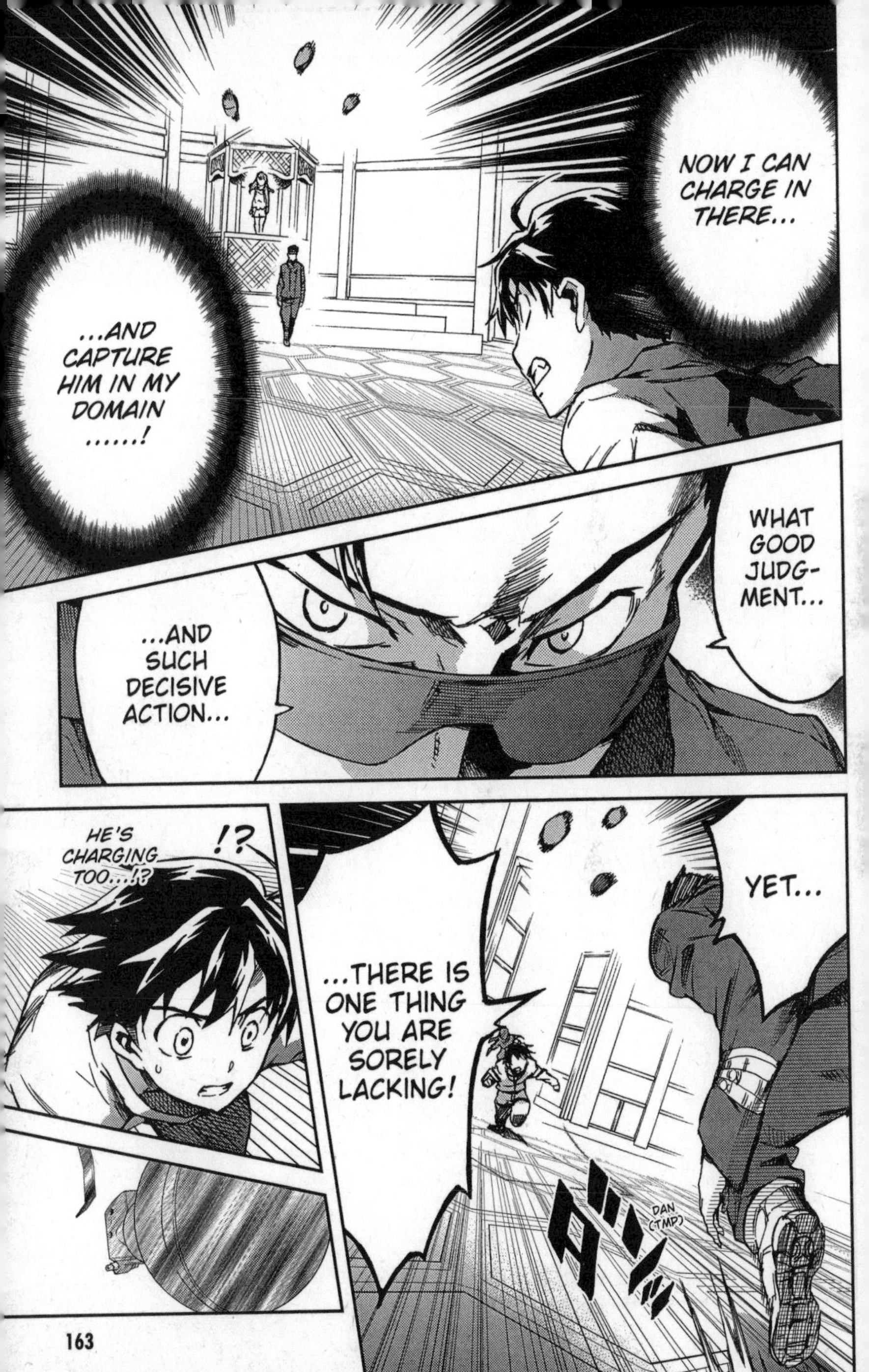
NOW I CAN CHARGE IN THERE...
...AND CAPTURE HIM IN MY DOMAIN......!
WHAT GOOD JUDG-MENT...
...AND SUCH DECISIVE ACTION...
YET...
...THERE IS ONE THING YOU ARE SORELY LACKING!
DAN (TMP)
!?
HE'S CHARGING TOO...!?

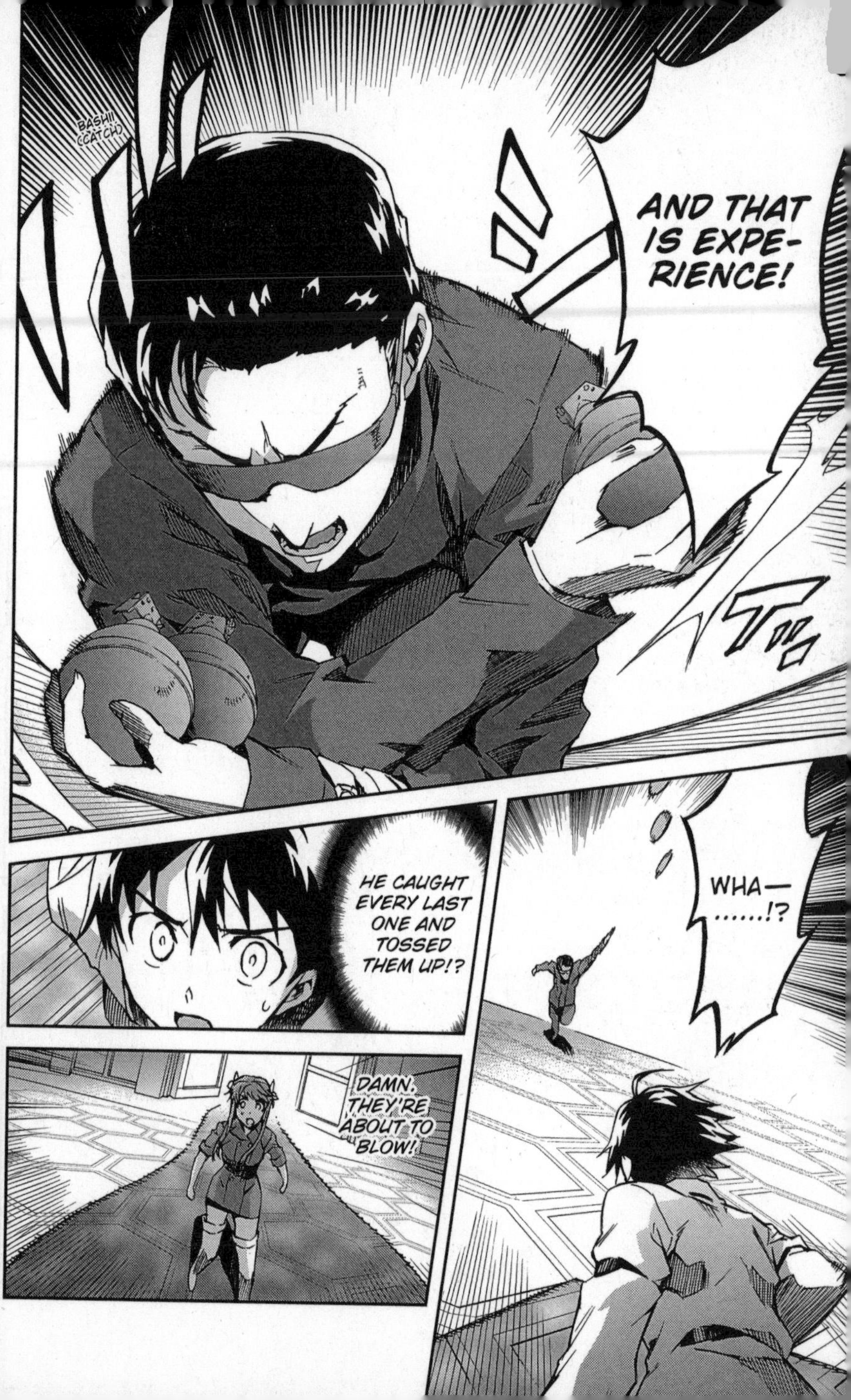
AND THAT IS EXPE-RIENCE!
BASHII (CATCH)
WHA—......!?
HE CAUGHT EVERY LAST ONE AND TOSSED THEM UP!?
DAMN. THEY'RE ABOUT TO BLOW!

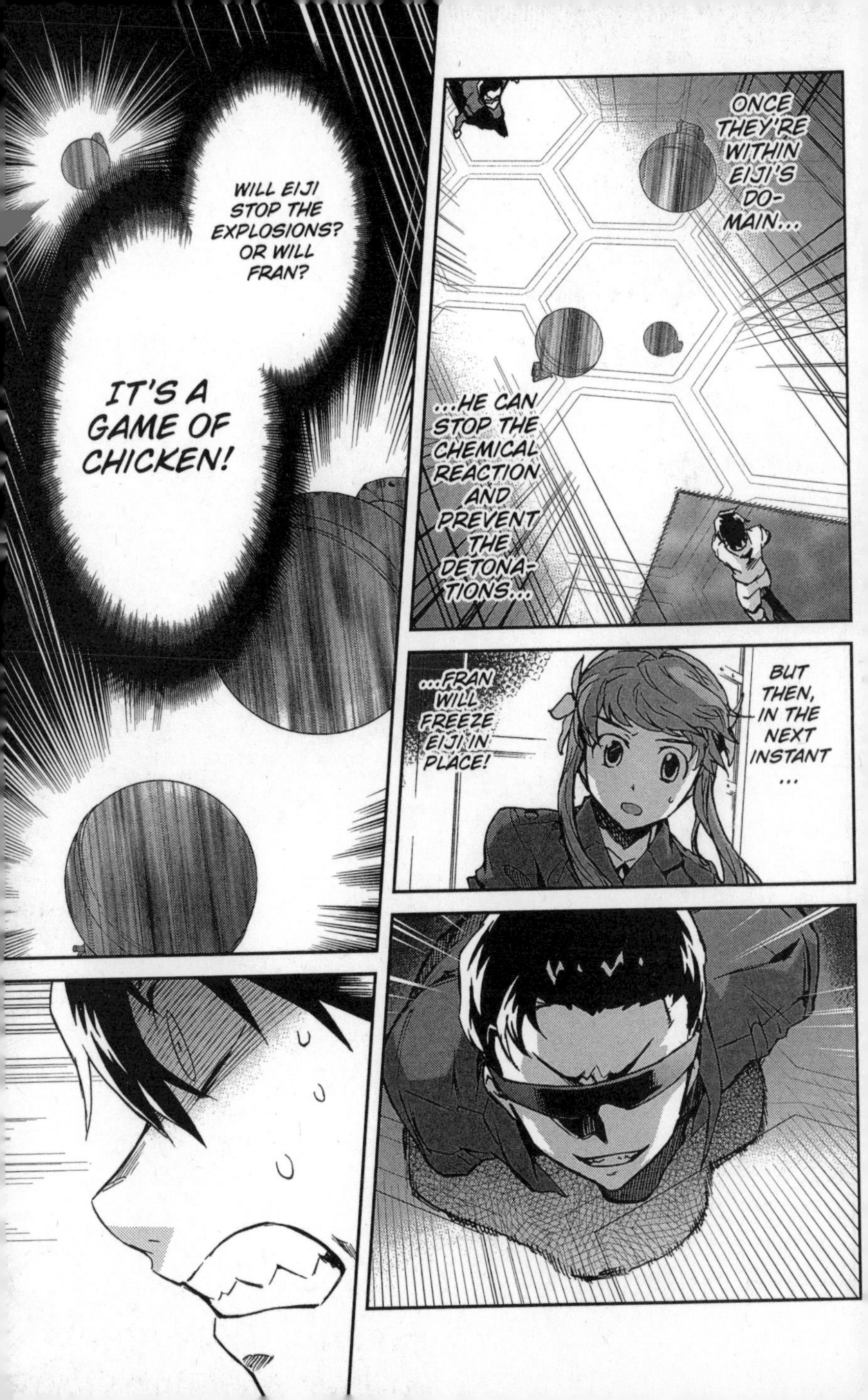
ONCE THEY'RE WITHIN EIJI'S DO-MAIN...
...HE CAN STOP THE CHEMICAL REACTION AND PREVENT THE DETONA-TIONS...
BUT THEN, IN THE NEXT INSTANT...
...FRAN WILL FREEZE EIJI IN PLACE!
WILL EIJI STOP THE EXPLOSIONS? OR WILL FRAN?
IT'S A GAME OF CHICKEN!

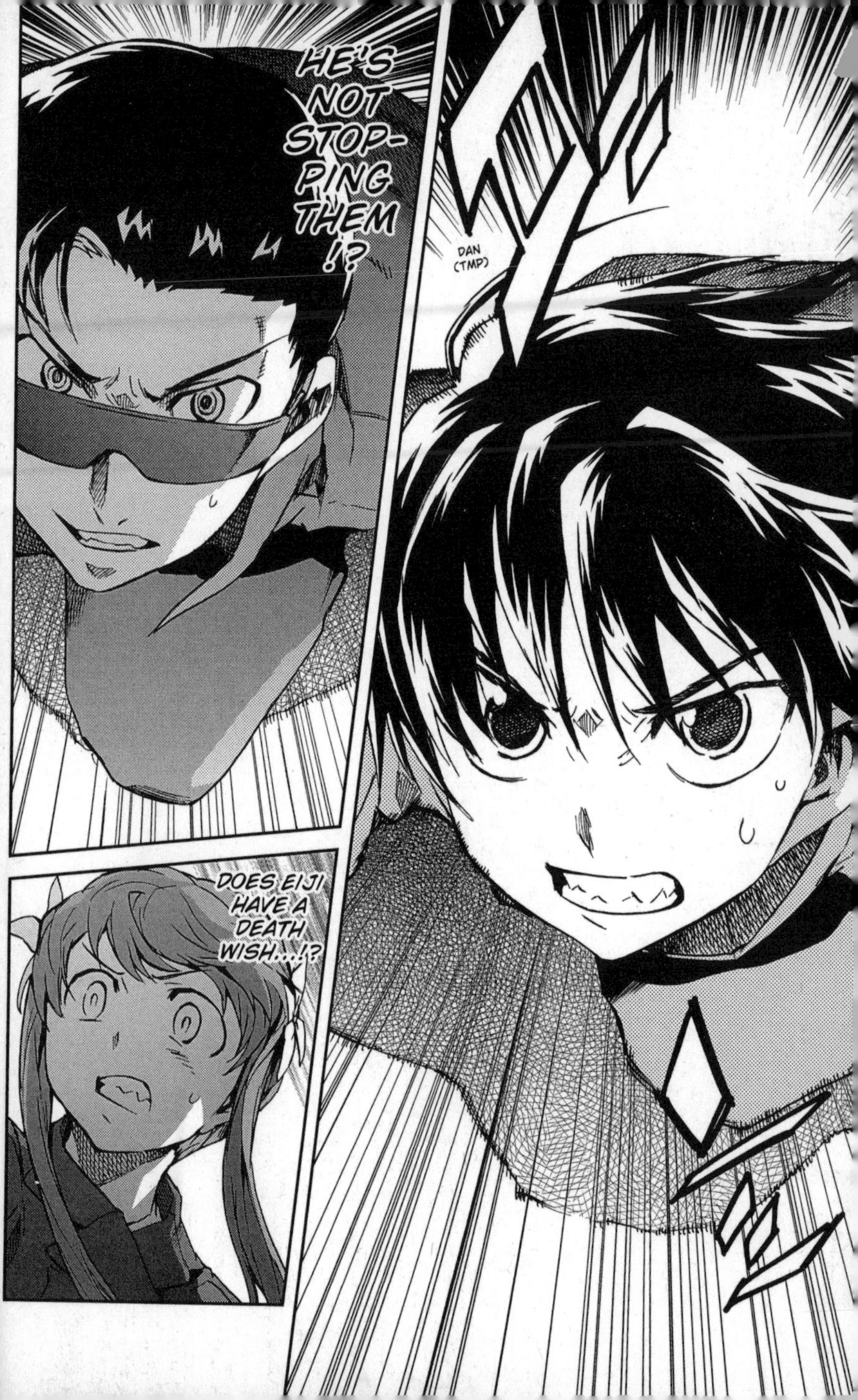
DAN (TMP)
HE'S NOT STOP-PING THEM!?
DOES EIJI HAVE A DEATH WISH...!?

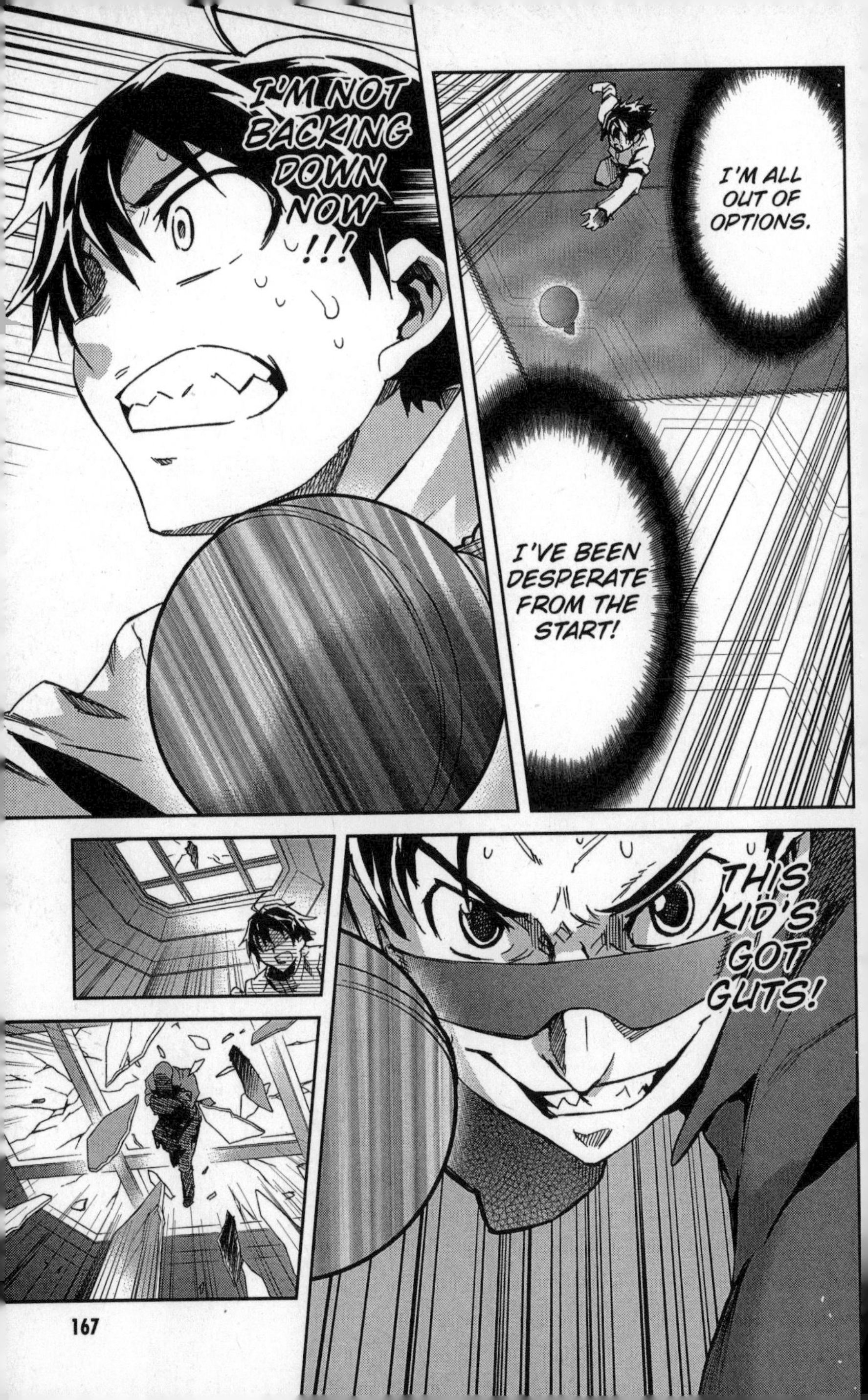
I'M ALL OUT OF OPTIONS.
I'VE BEEN DESPERATE FROM THE START!
I'M NOT BACKING DOWN NOW!!!
THIS KID'S GOT GUTS!

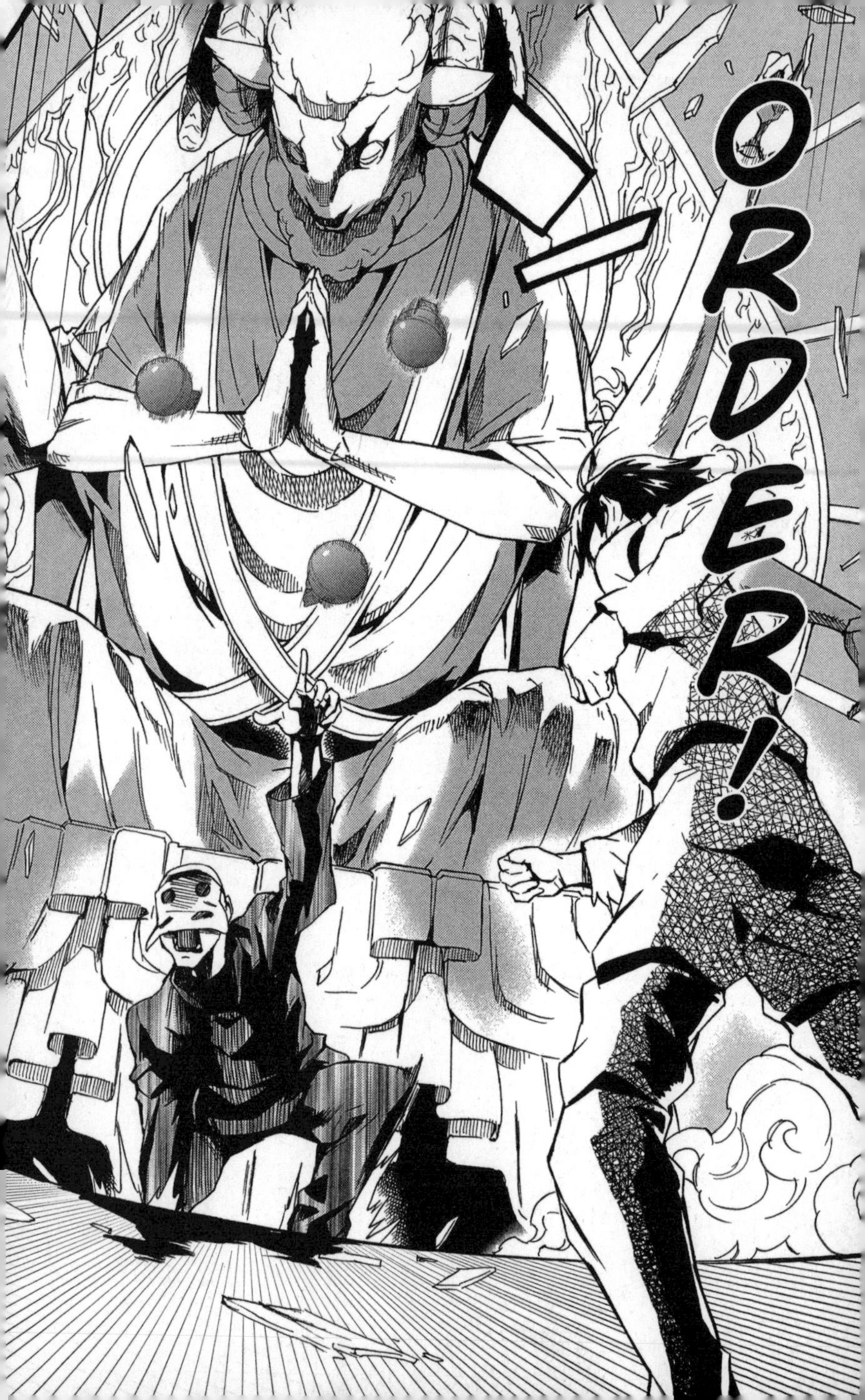
ORDER!

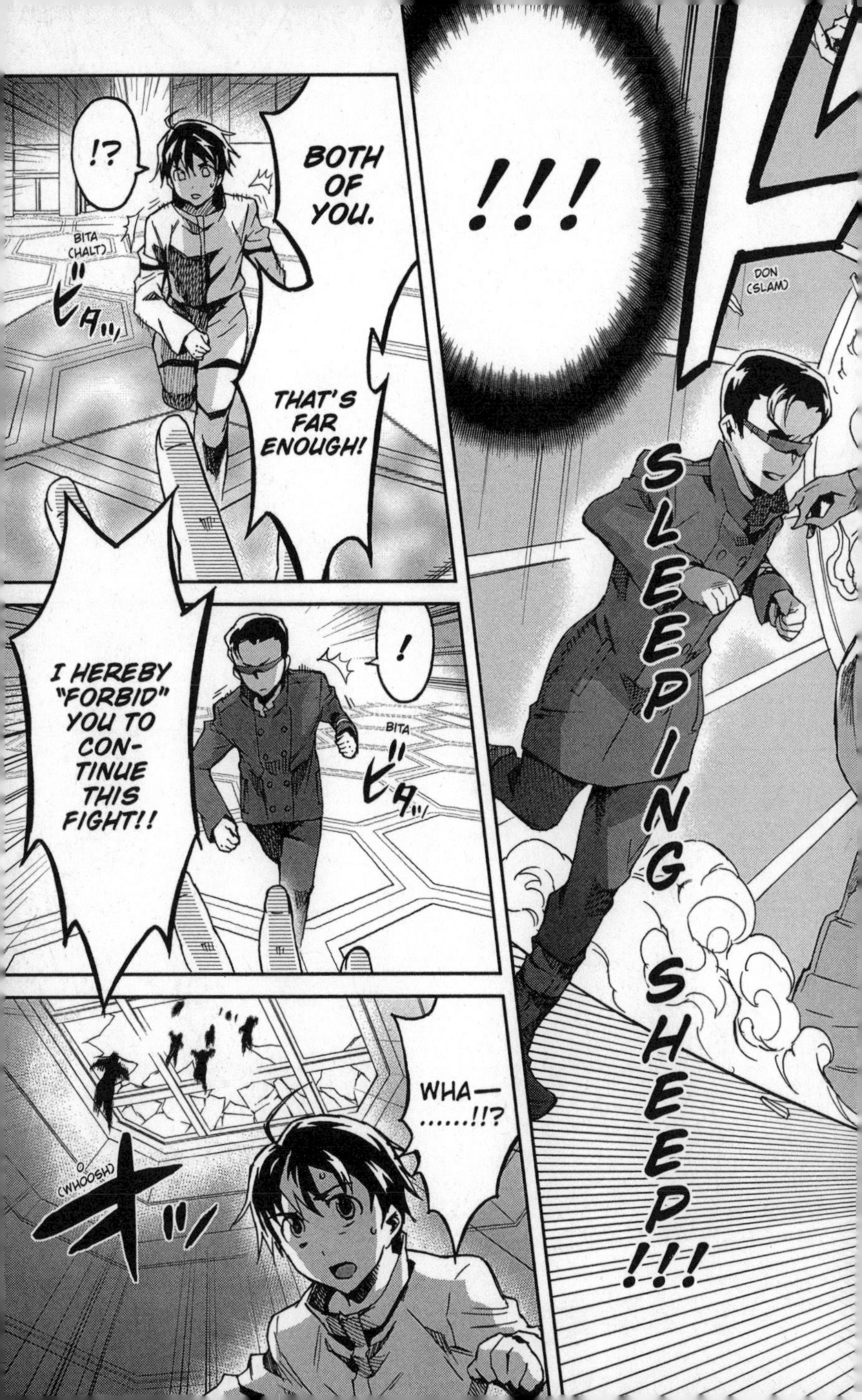
!!!
DON (SLAM)
SLEEPING SHEEP!!!
BOTH OF YOU.
THAT'S FAR ENOUGH!
!?
BITA (HALT)
I HEREBY "FORBID" YOU TO CONTINUE THIS FIGHT!!
!
BITA
WHA—......!!?
O (WHOOSH)

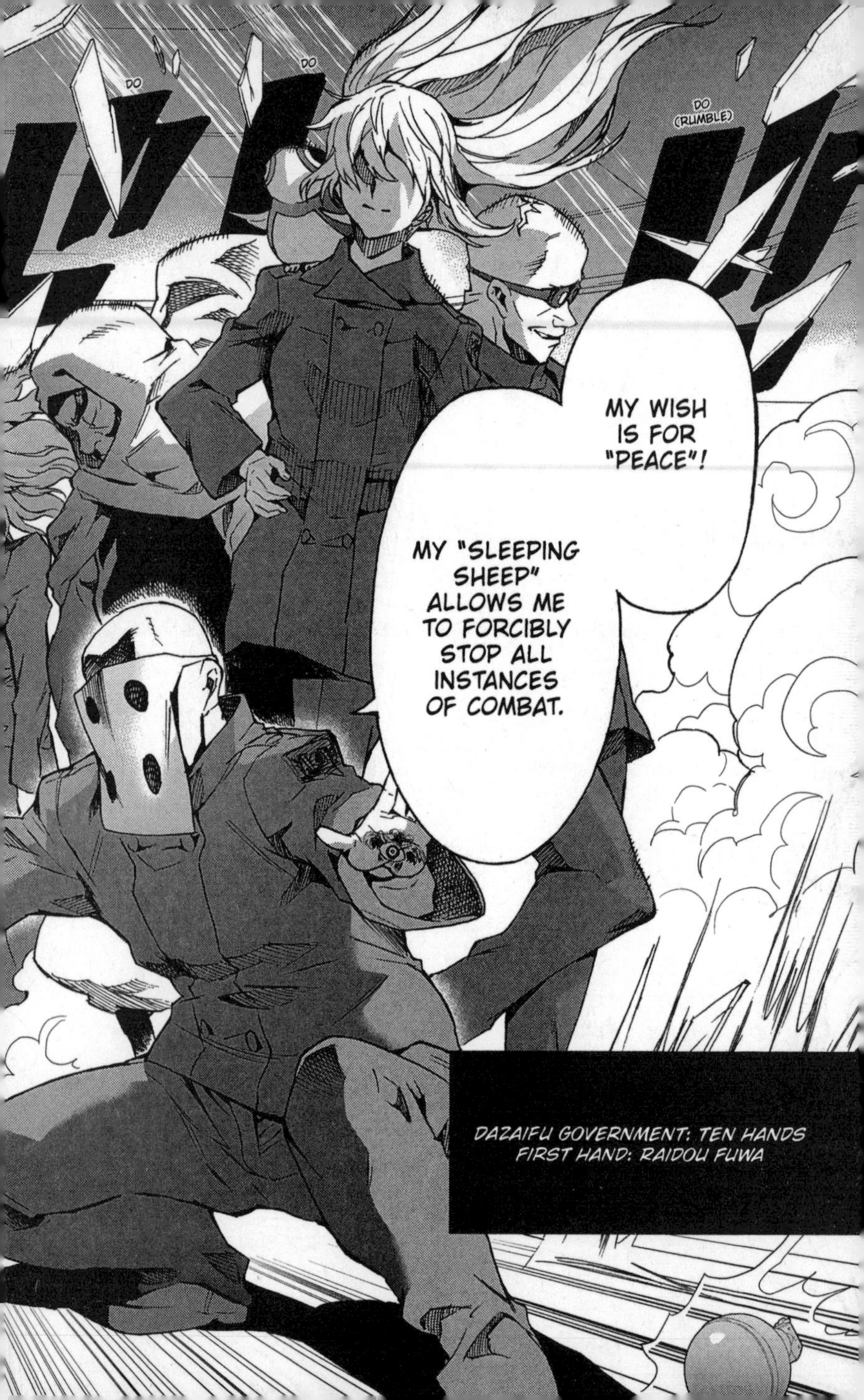
DO
(RUMBLE)
DO
DO
MY WISH IS FOR "PEACE"!
MY "SLEEPING SHEEP" ALLOWS ME TO FORCIBLY STOP ALL INSTANCES OF COMBAT.
DAZAIFU GOVERNMENT: TEN HANDS
FIRST HAND: RAIDOU FUWA

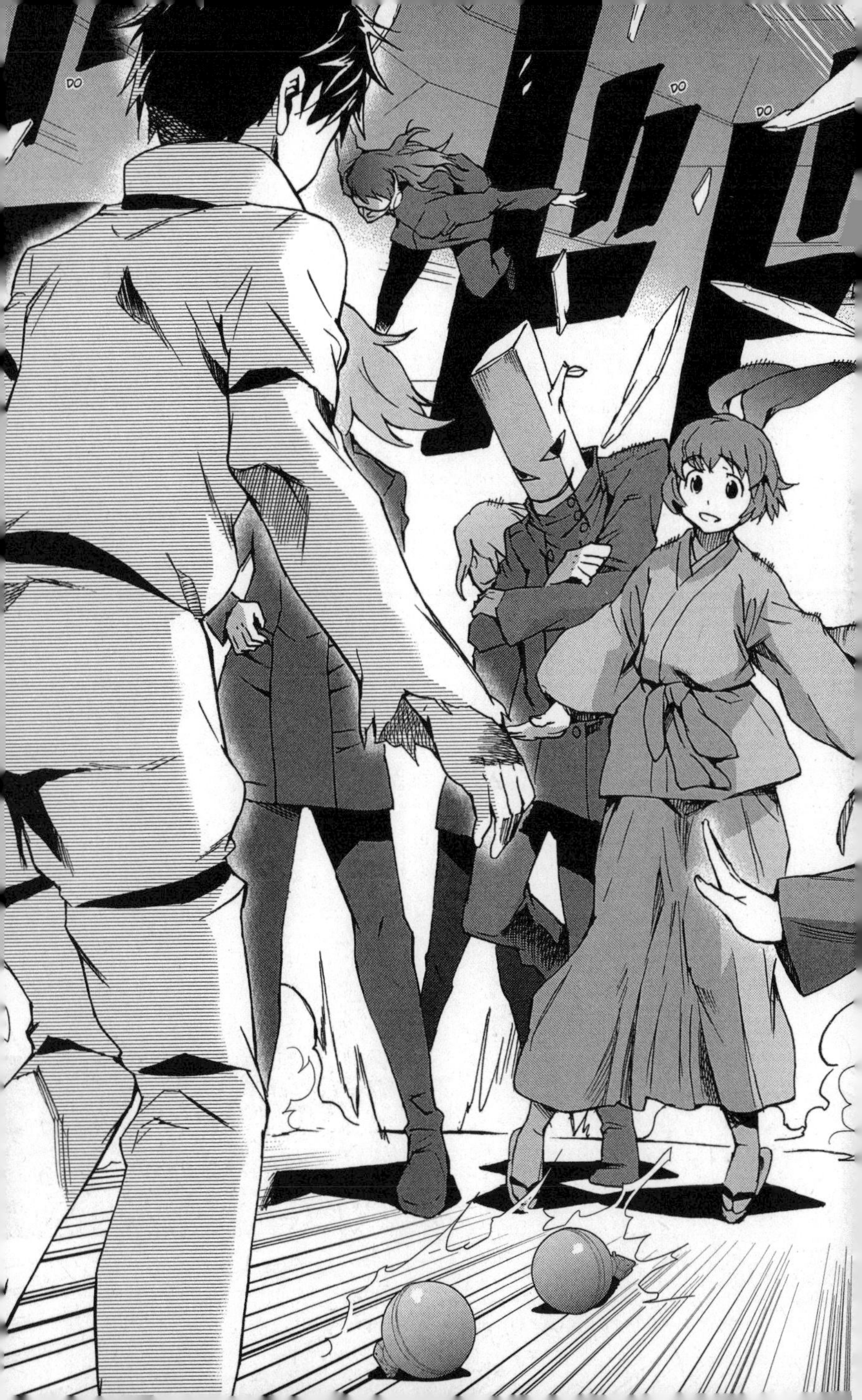
DO
DO
DO

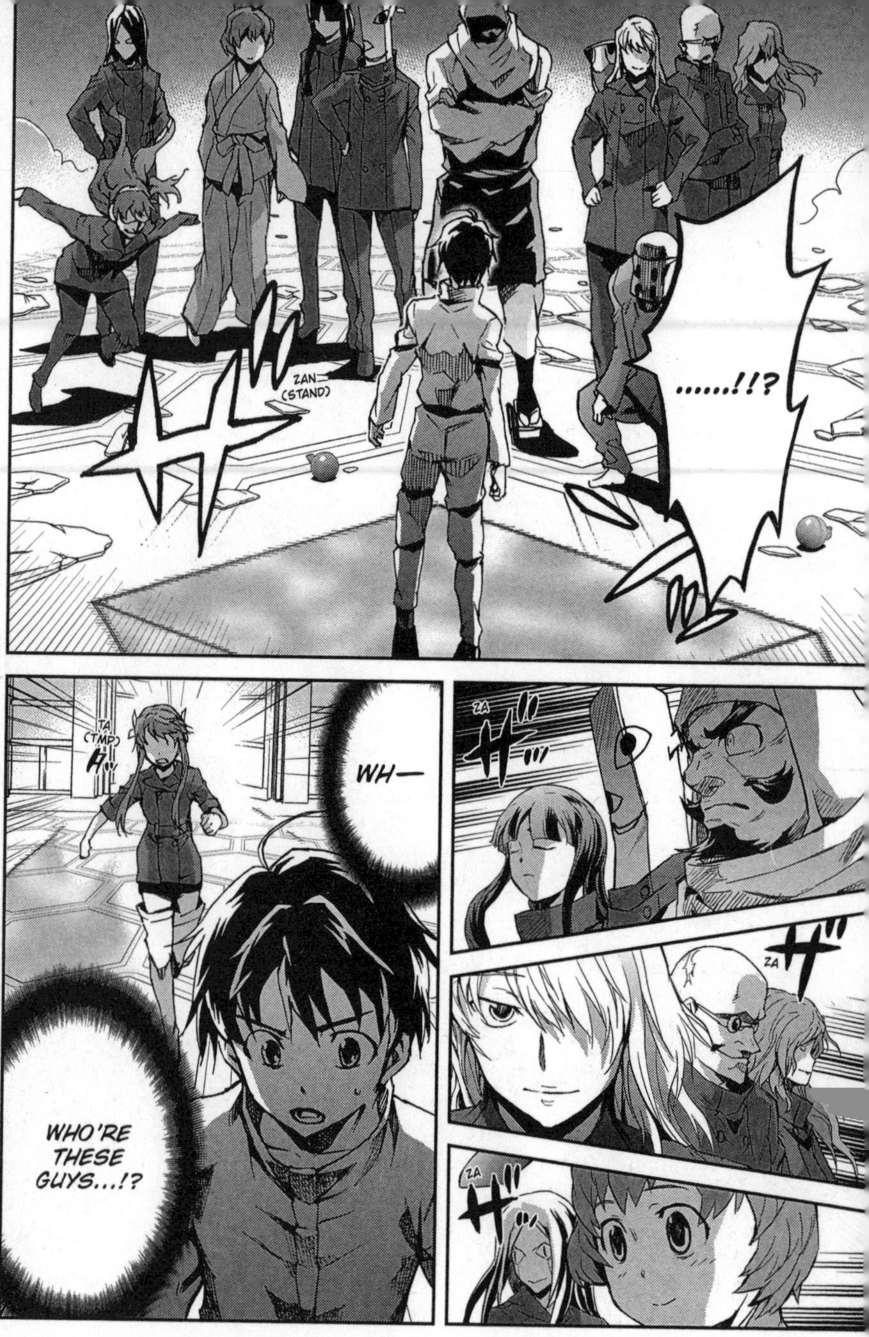
......!!?
ZAN (STAND)
ZA
ZA
ZA
TA (TMP)
WH—
WHO'RE THESE GUYS...!?

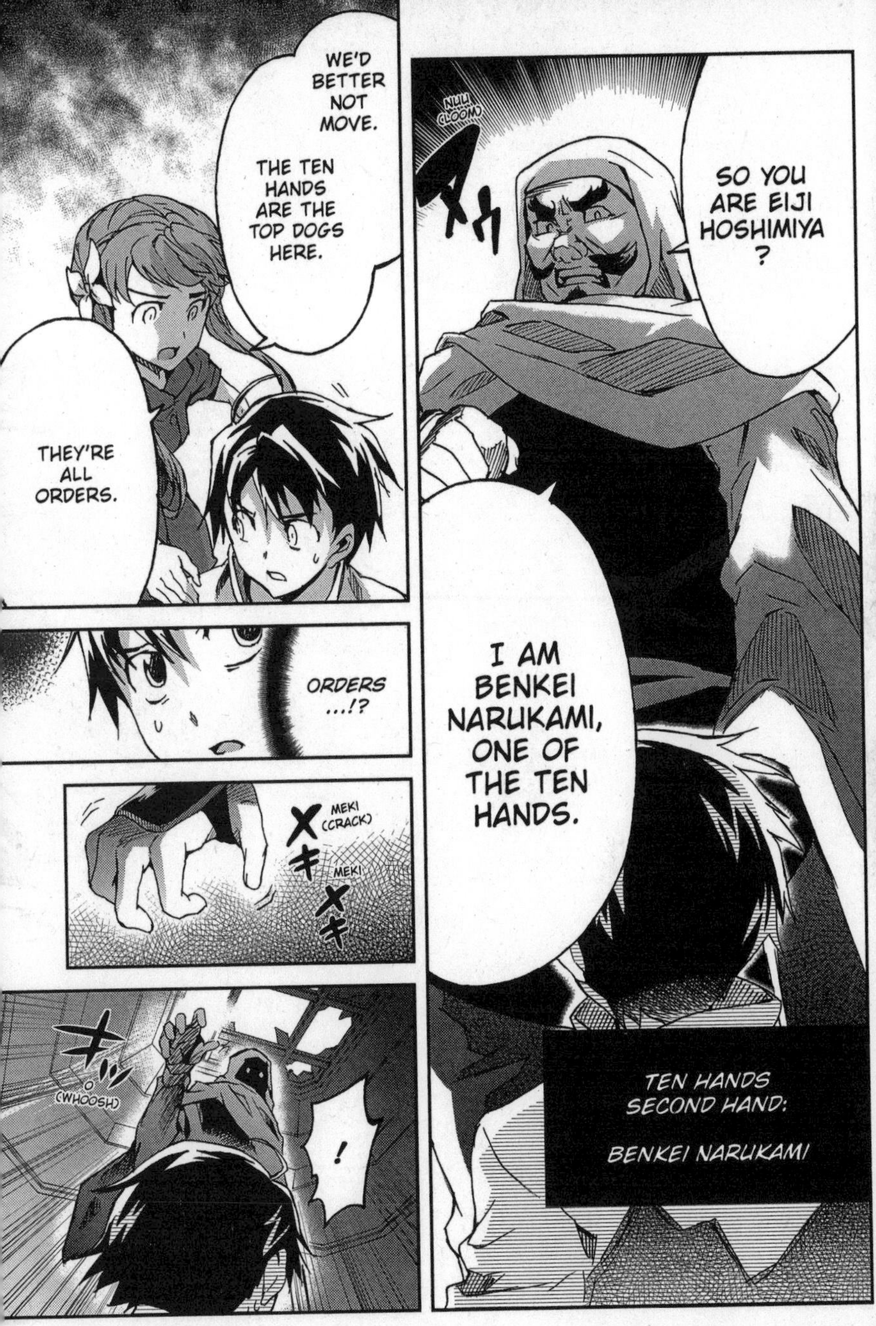
NUU (LOOM)
SO YOU ARE EIJI HOSHIMIYA ?
I AM BENKEI NARUKAMI, ONE OF THE TEN HANDS.
TEN HANDS SECOND HAND: BENKEI NARUKAMI
WE'D BETTER NOT MOVE.
THE TEN HANDS ARE THE TOP DOGS HERE.
THEY'RE ALL ORDERS.
ORDERS ...!?
MEKI (CRACK)
MEKI
O (WHOOSH)
!

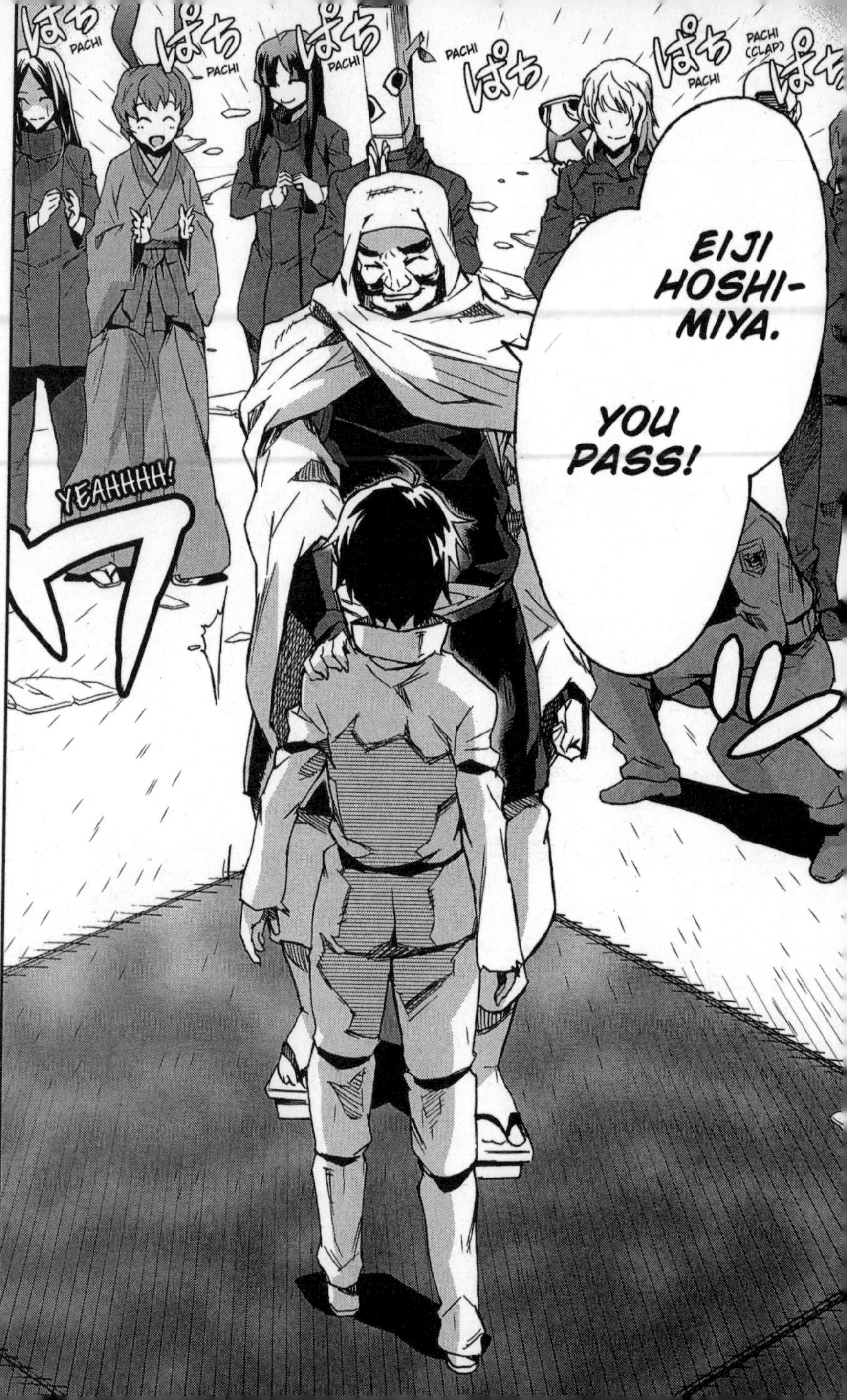
ぱち
PACHI (CLAP)
ぱち
PACHI
ぱち
PACHI
ぱち
PACHI
ぱち
PACHI
ぱち
PACHI
ぱち
PACHI
EIJI HOSHI-MIYA.
YOU PASS!
YEAHHHH!

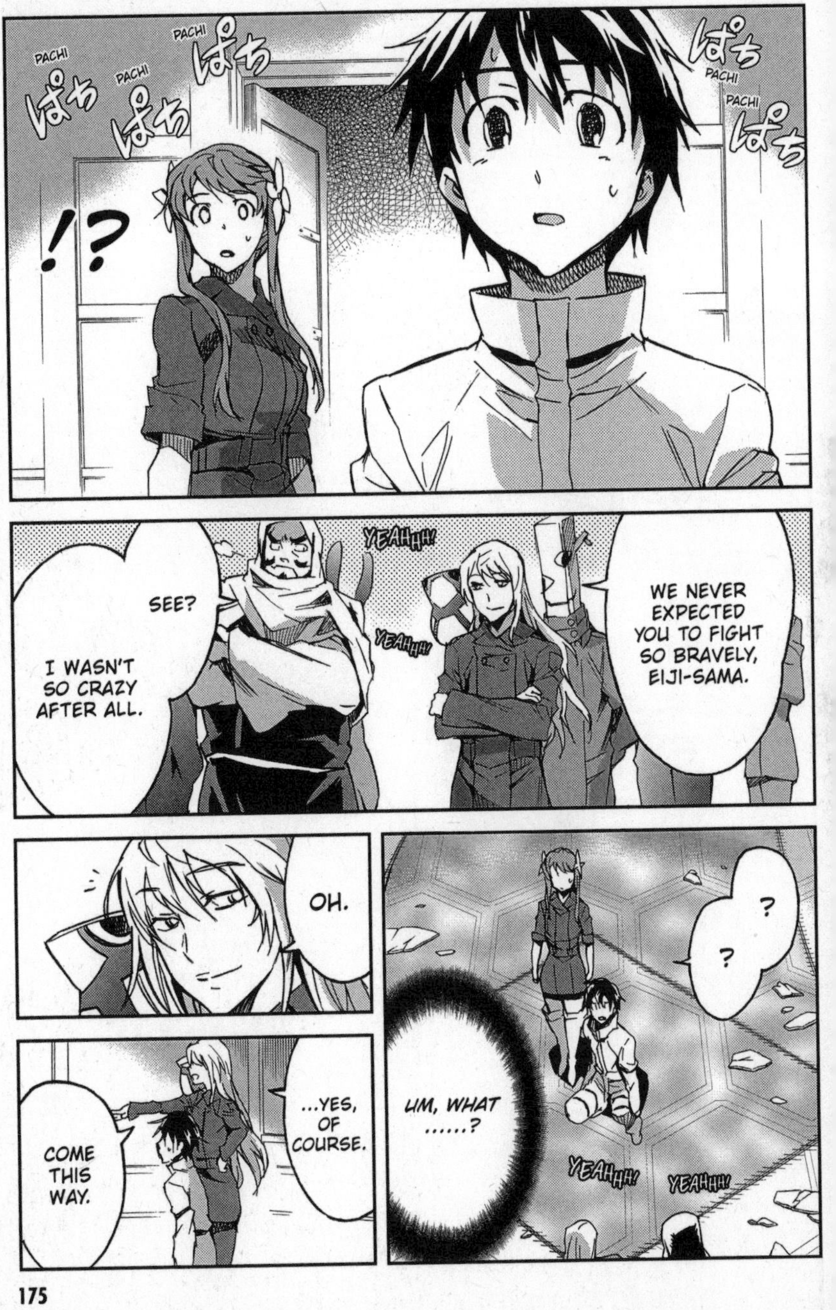
ぱち
PACHI
ぱち
PACHI
ぱち
PACHI
ぱち
PACHI
ぱち
PACHI
!?
WE NEVER EXPECTED YOU TO FIGHT SO BRAVELY, EIJI-SAMA.
YEAHHH!
YEAHHH!
SEE?
I WASN'T SO CRAZY AFTER ALL.
? ?
UM, WHAT ......?
YEAHHH!
YEAHHH!
OH.
...YES, OF COURSE.
COME THIS WAY.

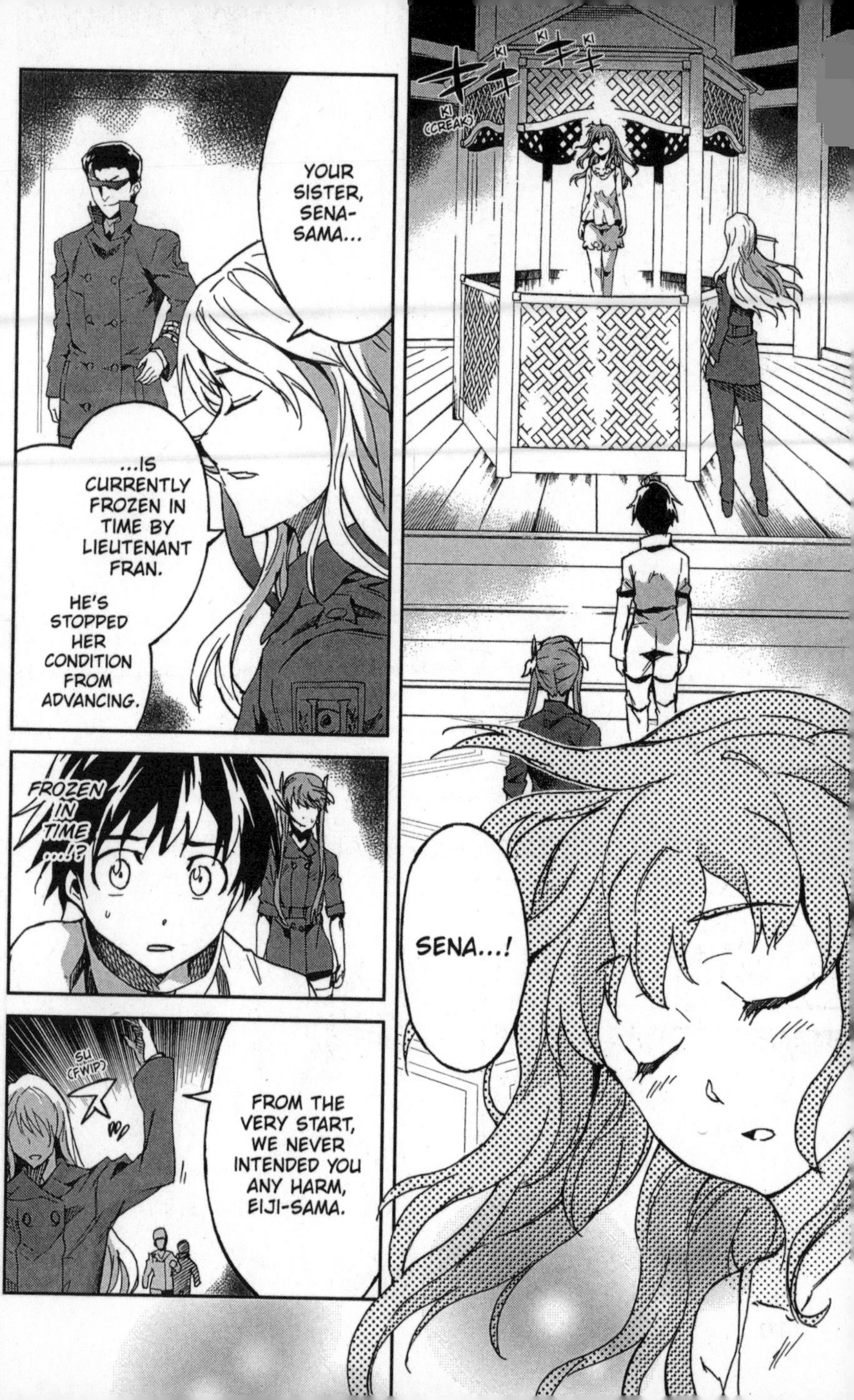
KI KI KI KI
KI (CREAK)
SENA...!
YOUR SISTER, SENA-SAMA...
...IS CURRENTLY FROZEN IN TIME BY LIEUTENANT FRAN.
HE'S STOPPED HER CONDITION FROM ADVANCING.
FROZEN IN TIME...!?
FROM THE VERY START, WE NEVER INTENDED YOU ANY HARM, EIJI-SAMA.
SU (FWIP)

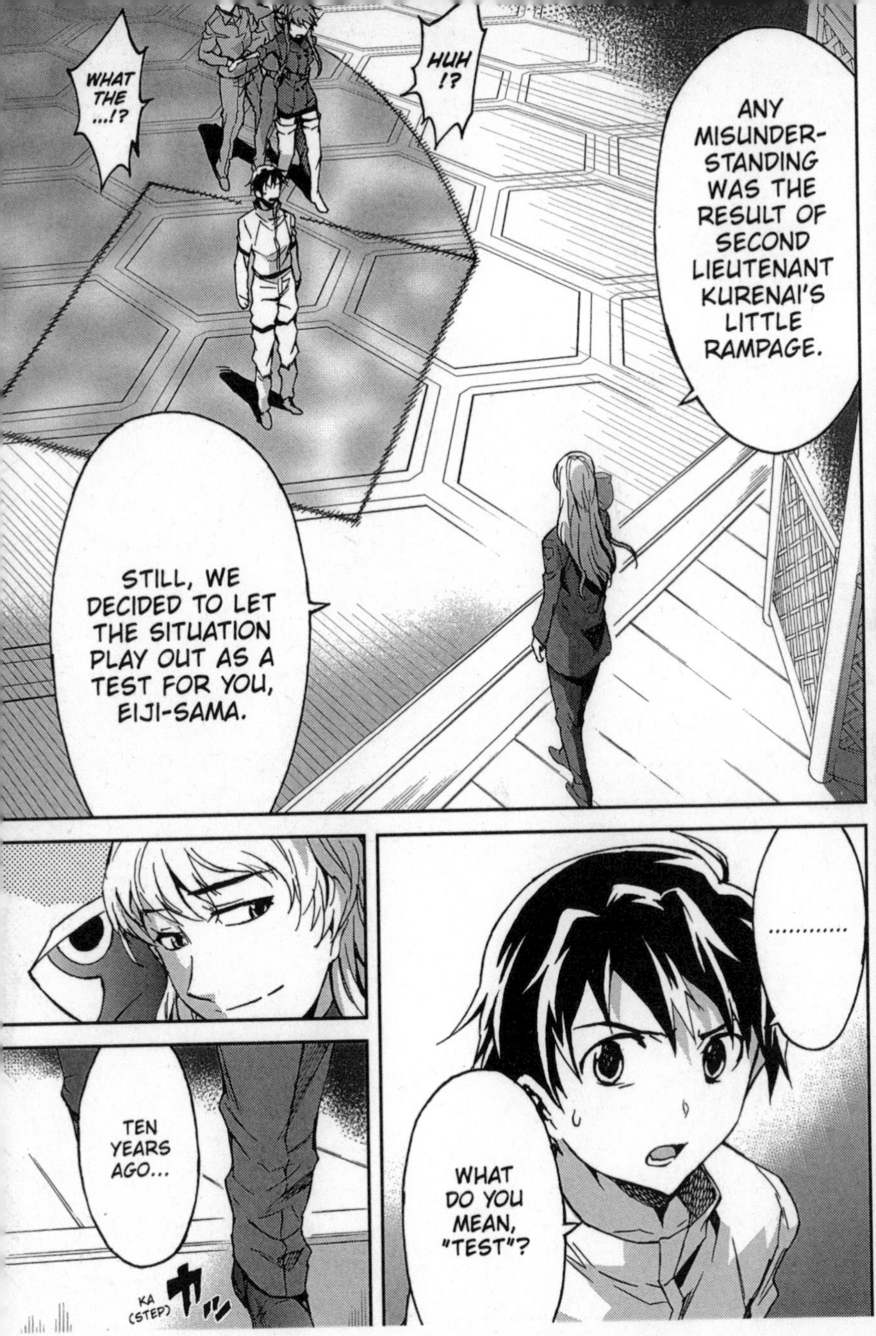
ANY MISUNDER-STANDING WAS THE RESULT OF SECOND LIEUTENANT KURENAI'S LITTLE RAMPAGE.
HUH!?
WHAT THE ...!?
STILL, WE DECIDED TO LET THE SITUATION PLAY OUT AS A TEST FOR YOU, EIJI-SAMA.
............
WHAT DO YOU MEAN, "TEST"?
TEN YEARS AGO...
KA (STEP)

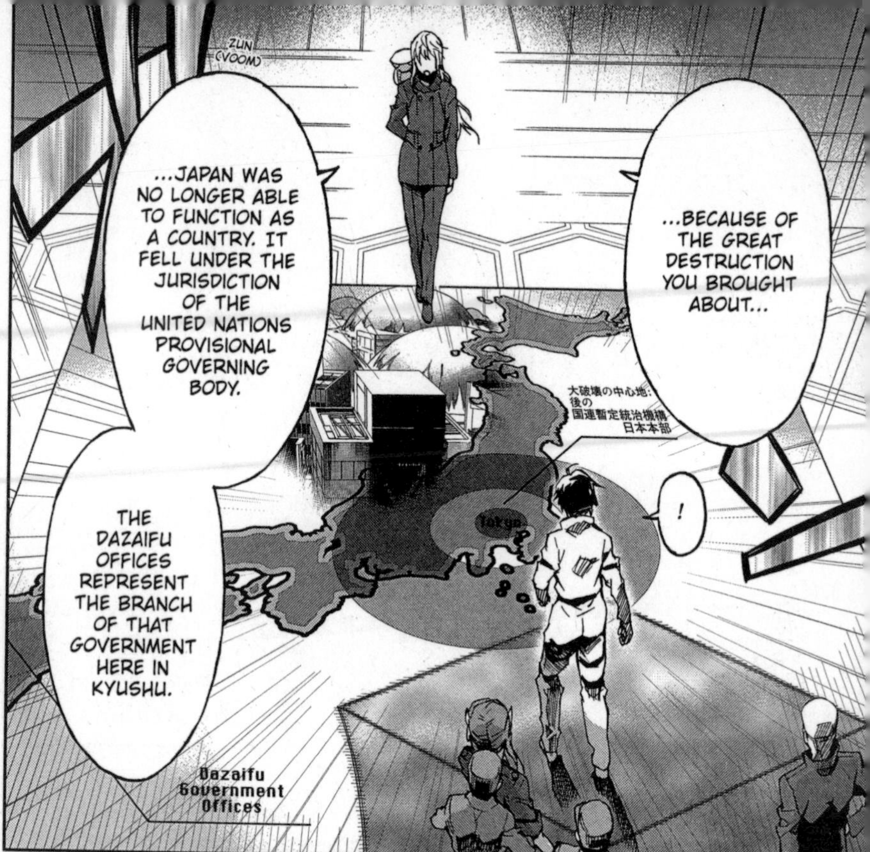
ZUN (VOOM)
...BECAUSE OF THE GREAT DESTRUCTION YOU BROUGHT ABOUT...
...JAPAN WAS NO LONGER ABLE TO FUNCTION AS A COUNTRY. IT FELL UNDER THE JURISDICTION OF THE UNITED NATIONS PROVISIONAL GOVERNING BODY.
大破壊の中心地：後の国連暫定統治機構日本本部
Tokyo
!
THE DAZAIFU OFFICES REPRESENT THE BRANCH OF THAT GOVERNMENT HERE IN KYUSHU.
Dazaifu Government Offices

*MAP: CENTER OF THE DESTRUCTION: LATER SITE OF THE UNITED NATIONS PROVISIONAL GOVERNING BODY TOKYO HQ*

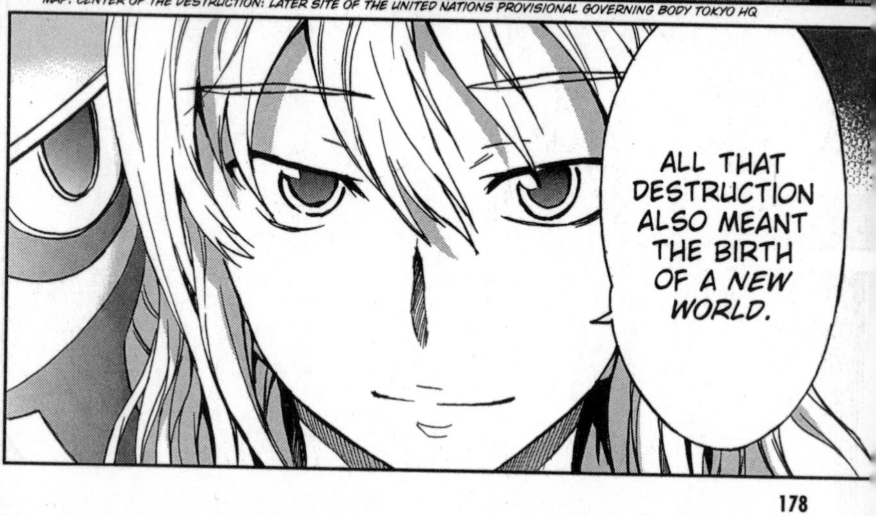
ALL THAT DESTRUCTION ALSO MEANT THE BIRTH OF A *NEW WORLD*.

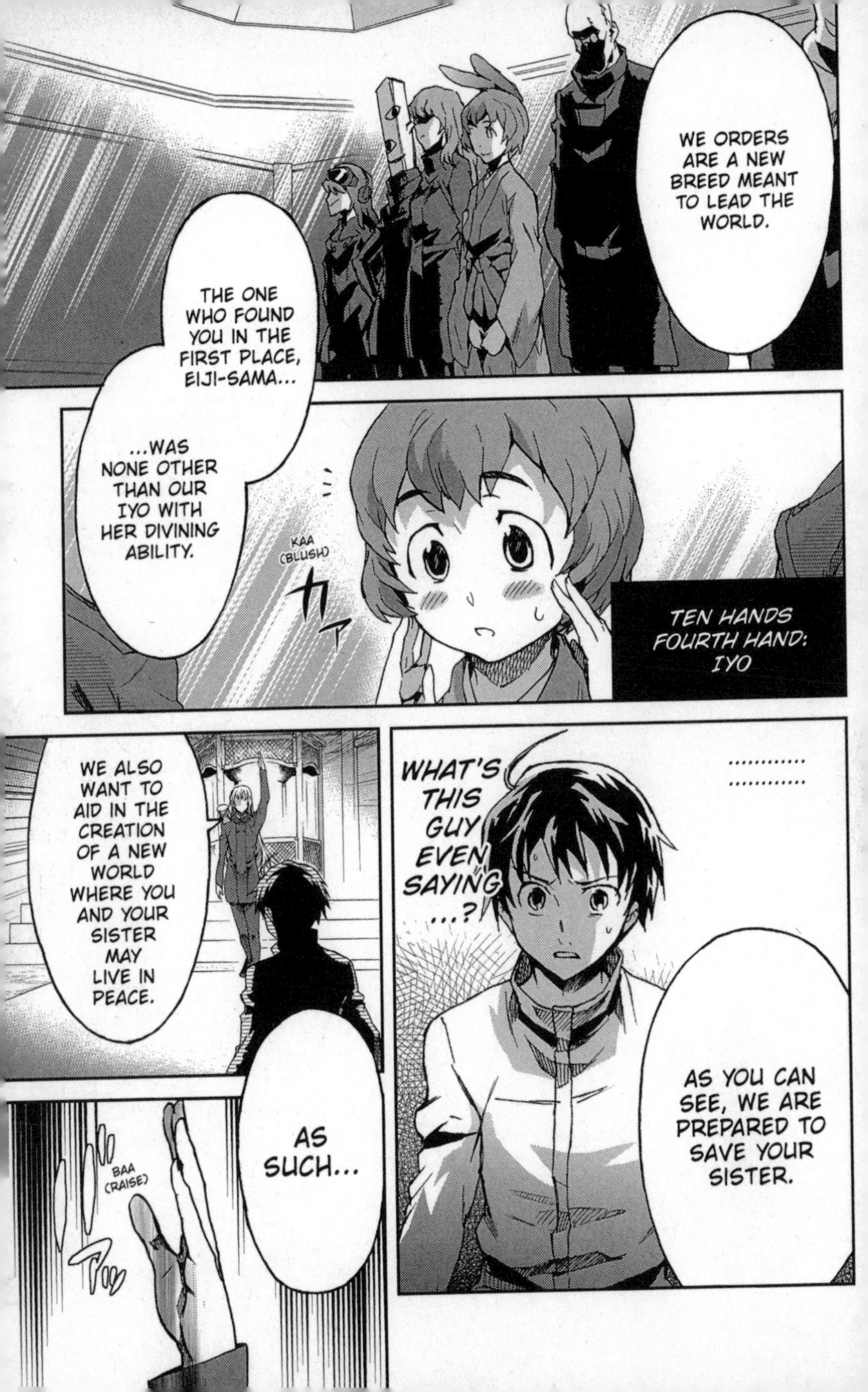
WE ORDERS ARE A NEW BREED MEANT TO LEAD THE WORLD.
THE ONE WHO FOUND YOU IN THE FIRST PLACE, EIJI-SAMA...
...WAS NONE OTHER THAN OUR IYO WITH HER DIVINING ABILITY.
KAA (BLUSH)
TEN HANDS FOURTH HAND: IYO
..........
..........
WHAT'S THIS GUY EVEN SAYING...?
AS YOU CAN SEE, WE ARE PREPARED TO SAVE YOUR SISTER.
WE ALSO WANT TO AID IN THE CREATION OF A NEW WORLD WHERE YOU AND YOUR SISTER MAY LIVE IN PEACE.
AS SUCH...
BAA (RAISE)

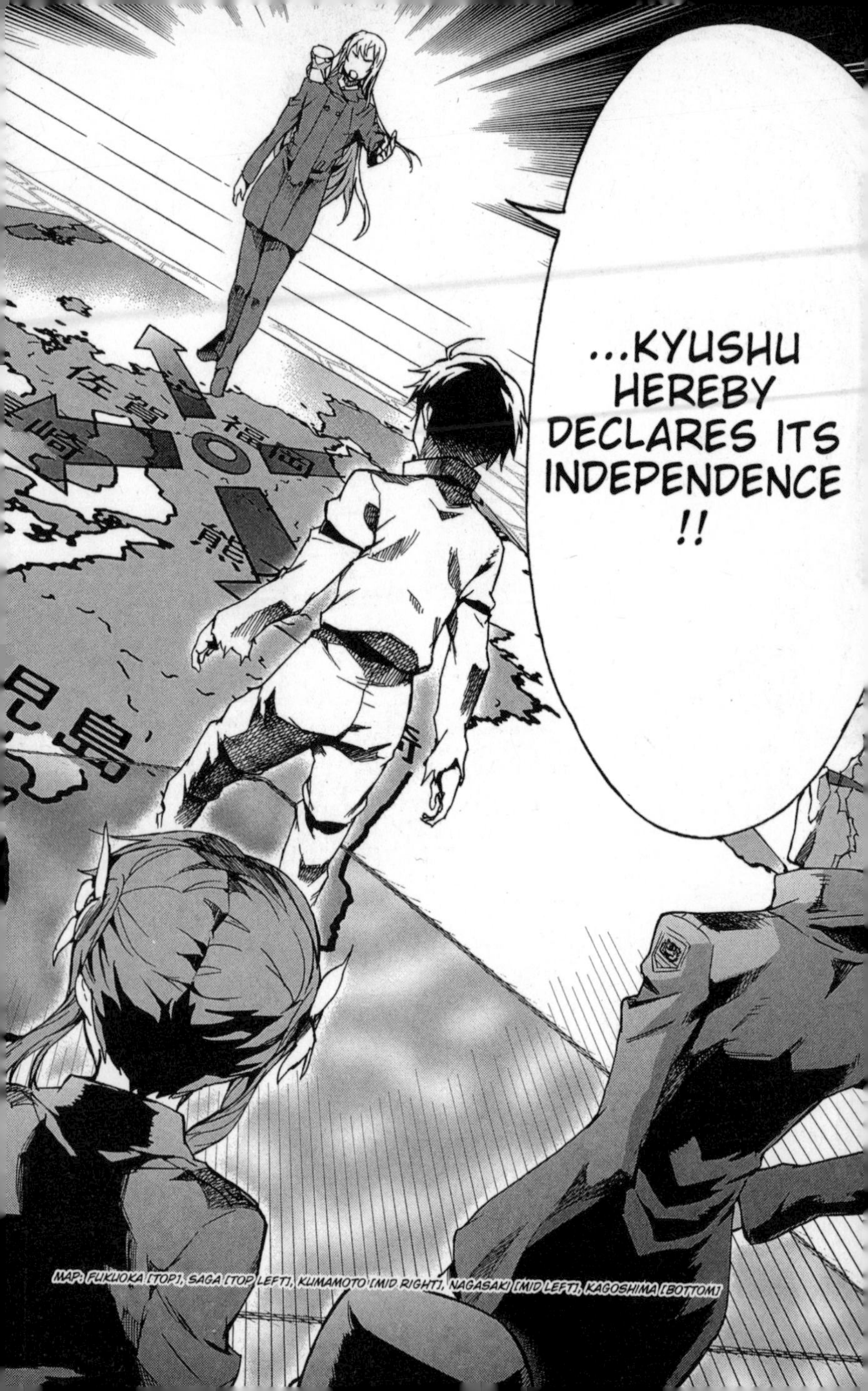
...KYUSHU HEREBY DECLARES ITS INDEPENDENCE !!
佐賀
福岡
MAP: FUKUOKA [TOP], SAGA [TOP LEFT], KUMAMOTO [MID RIGHT], NAGASAKI [MID LEFT], KAGOSHIMA [BOTTOM]

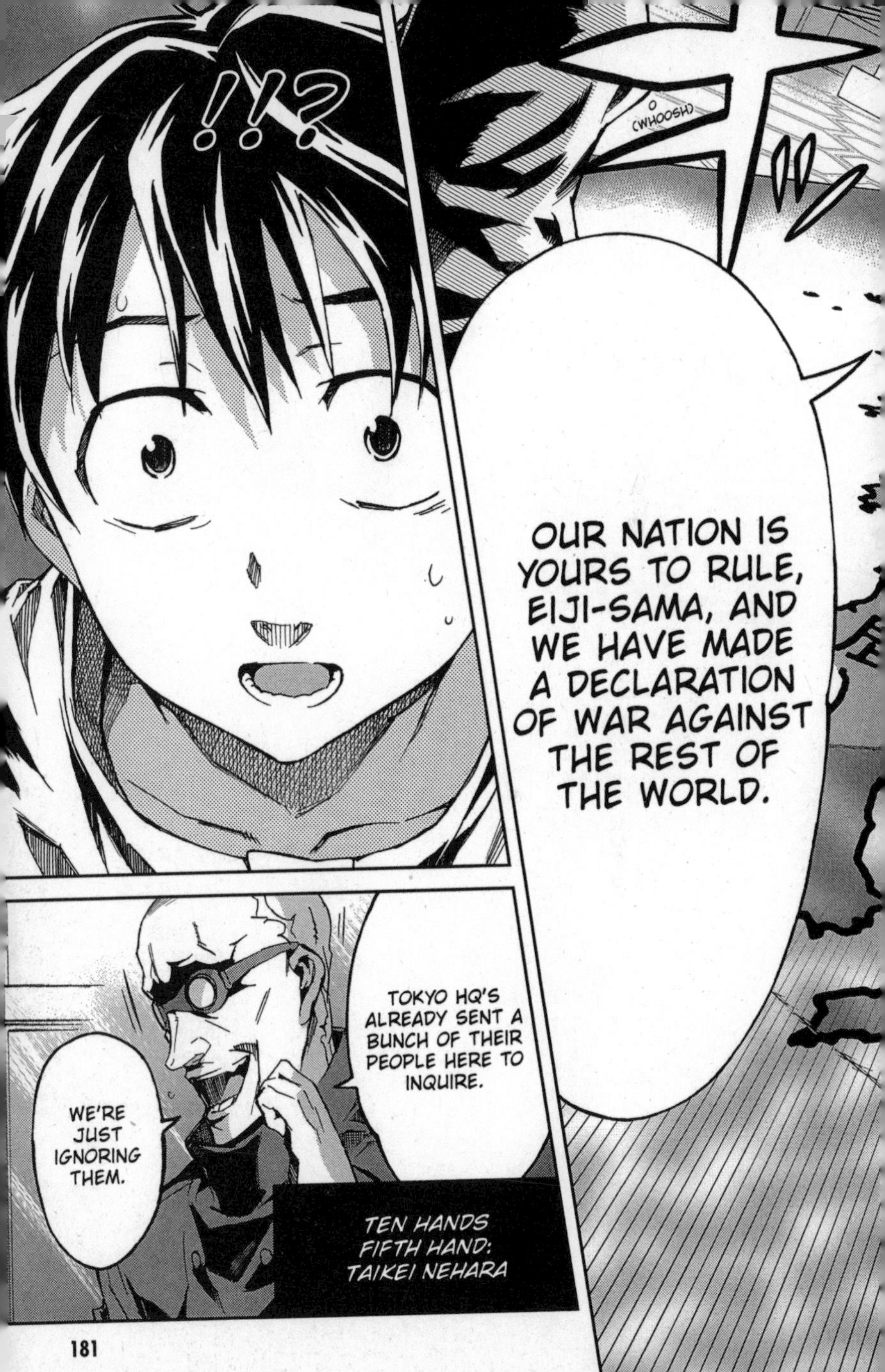
(WHOOSH)
OUR NATION IS YOURS TO RULE, EIJI-SAMA, AND WE HAVE MADE A DECLARATION OF WAR AGAINST THE REST OF THE WORLD.
!!?
TOKYO HQ'S ALREADY SENT A BUNCH OF THEIR PEOPLE HERE TO INQUIRE.
WE'RE JUST IGNORING THEM.
TEN HANDS FIFTH HAND: TAIKEI NEHARA

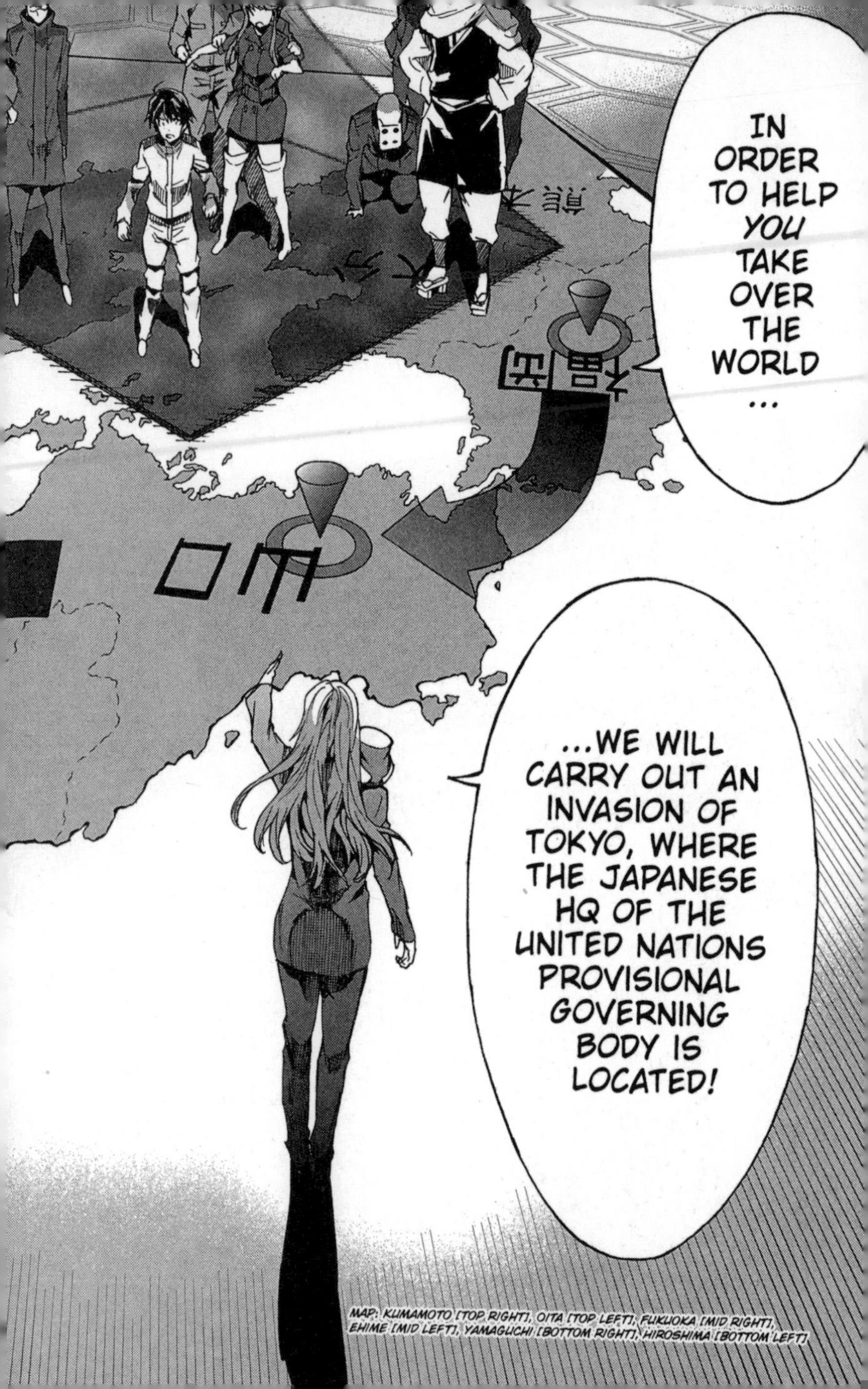
IN ORDER TO HELP *YOU* TAKE OVER THE WORLD ...
...WE WILL CARRY OUT AN INVASION OF TOKYO, WHERE THE JAPANESE HQ OF THE UNITED NATIONS PROVISIONAL GOVERNING BODY IS LOCATED!
MAP: KUMAMOTO [TOP RIGHT], OITA [TOP LEFT], FUKUOKA [MID RIGHT], EHIME [MID LEFT], YAMAGUCHI [BOTTOM RIGHT], HIROSHIMA [BOTTOM LEFT]

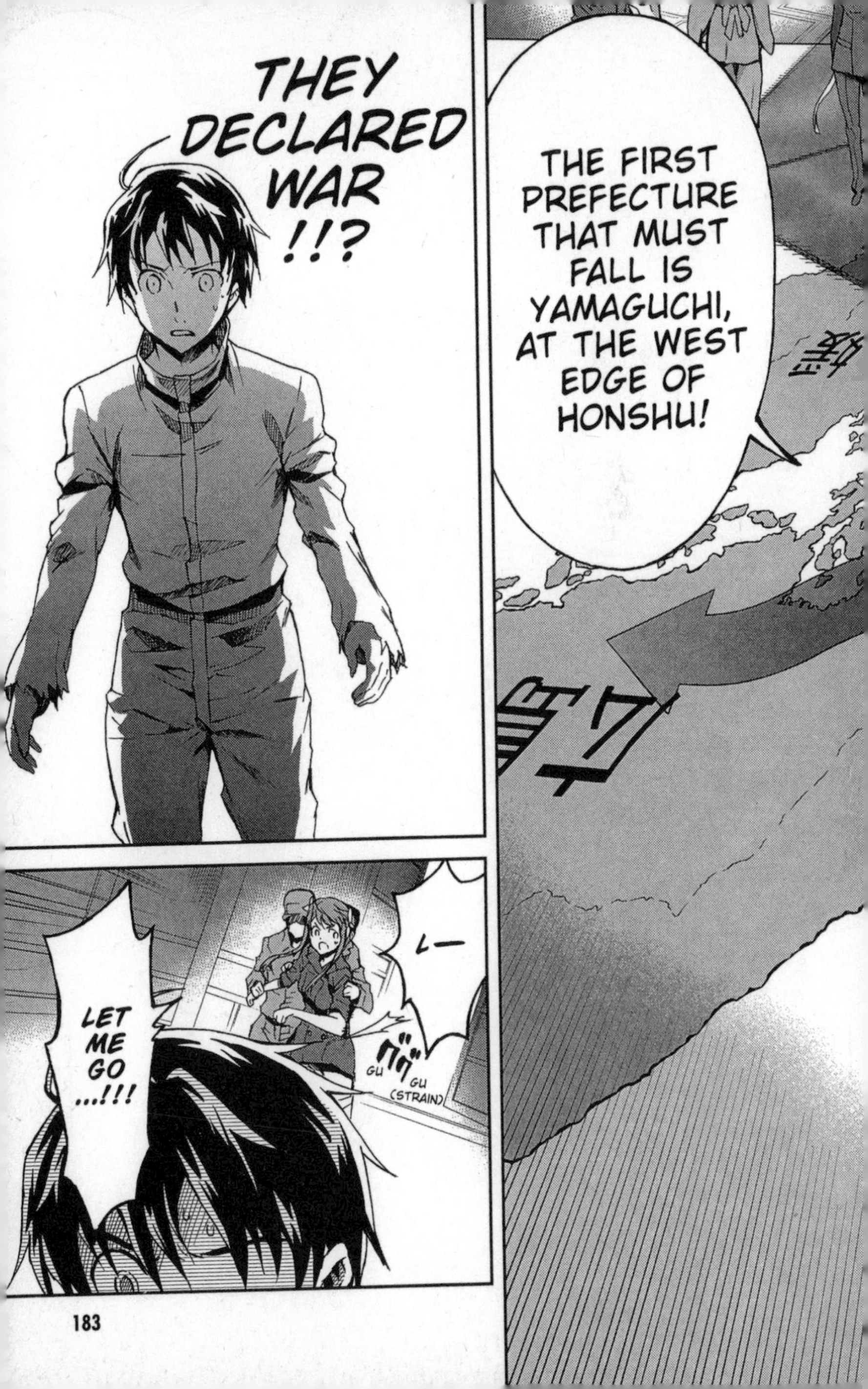
THE FIRST PREFECTURE THAT MUST FALL IS YAMAGUCHI, AT THE WEST EDGE OF HONSHU!
THEY DECLARED WAR !!?
GU GU (STRAIN)
LET ME GO ...!!!

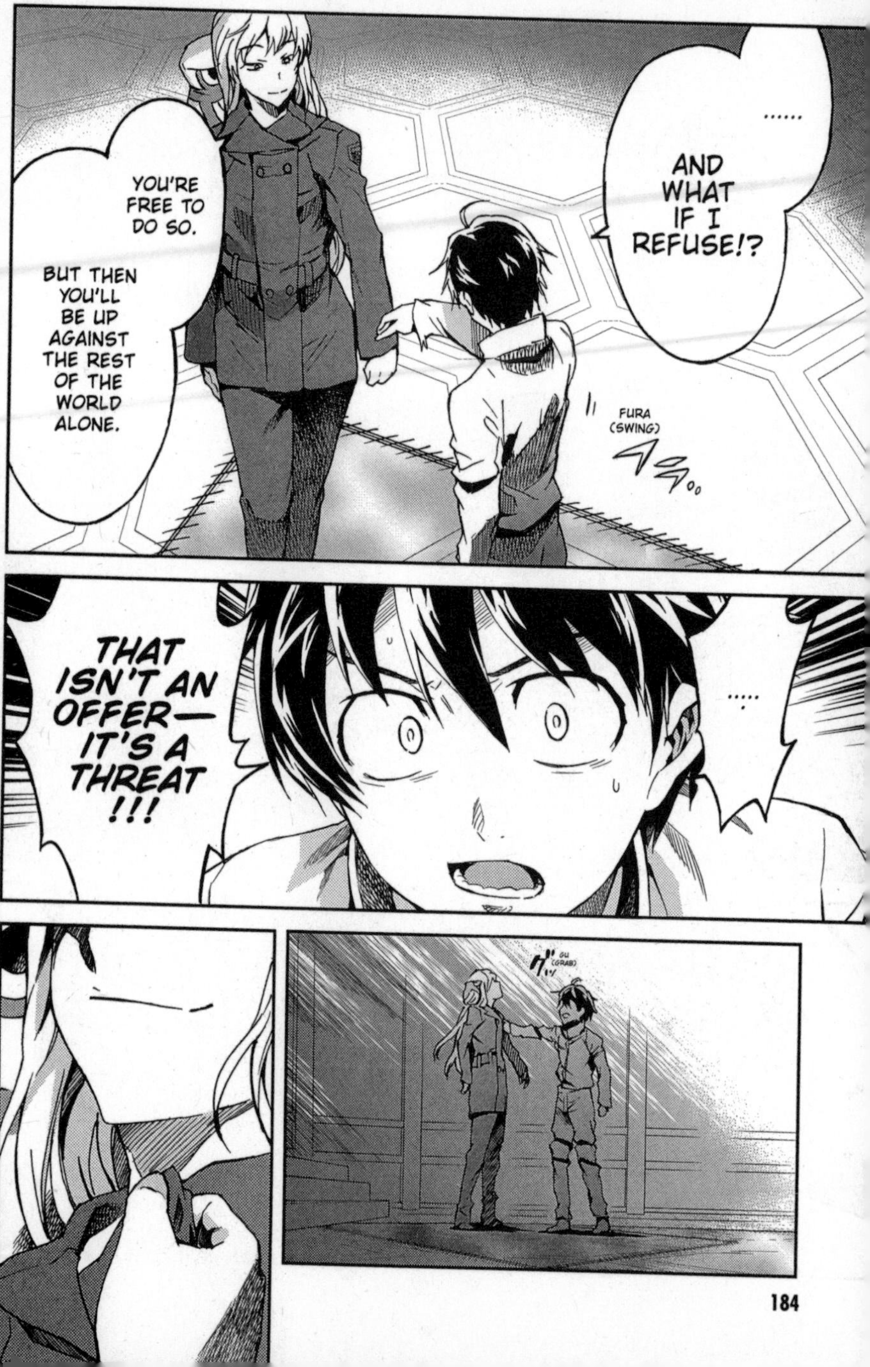
......
AND WHAT IF I REFUSE!?
YOU'RE FREE TO DO SO.
BUT THEN YOU'LL BE UP AGAINST THE REST OF THE WORLD ALONE.
FURA (SWING)
.....
THAT ISN'T AN OFFER— IT'S A THREAT!!!
GU (GRAB)

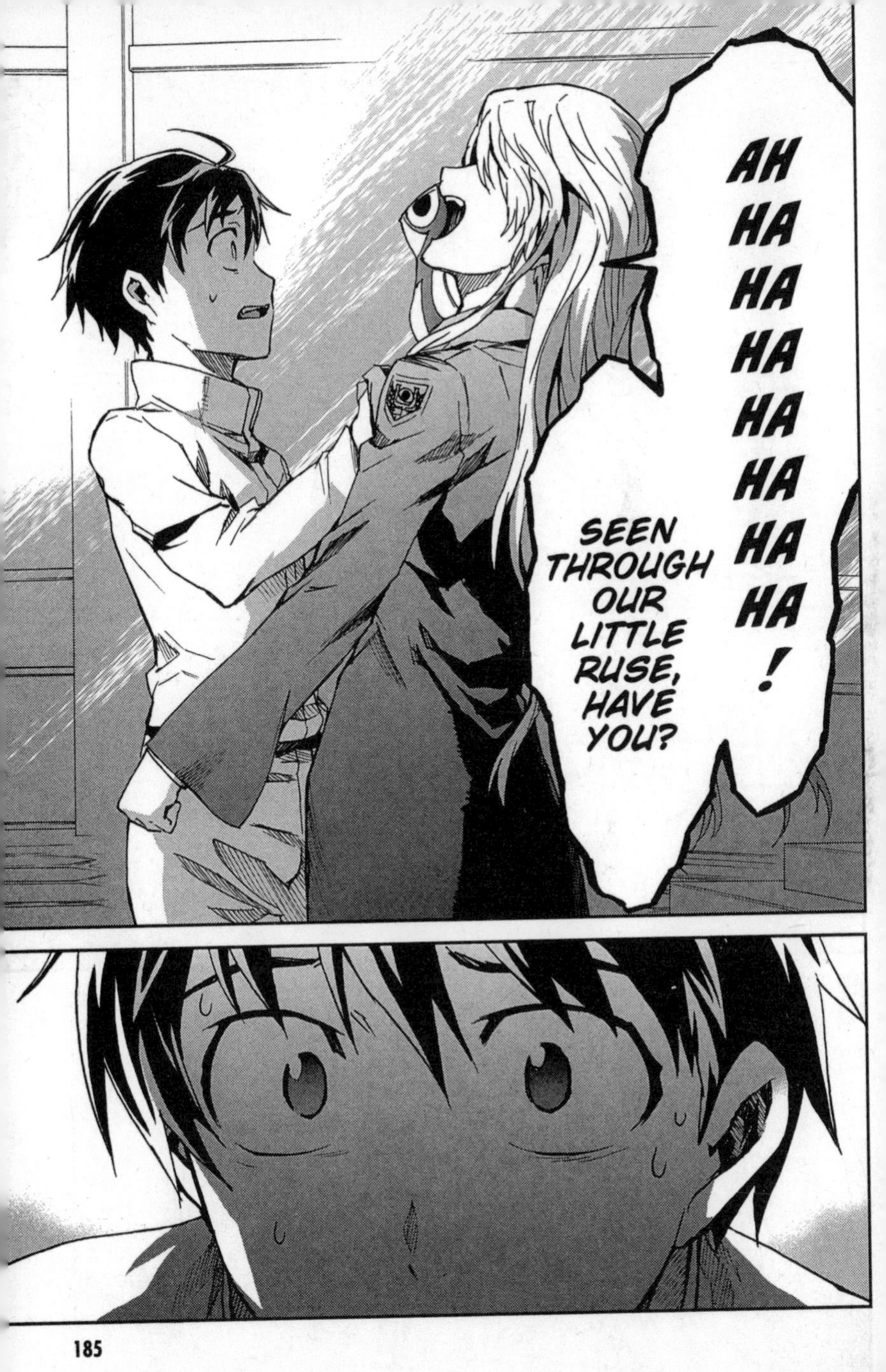
AH HA HA HA HA HA HA HA HA!
SEEN THROUGH OUR LITTLE RUSE, HAVE YOU?

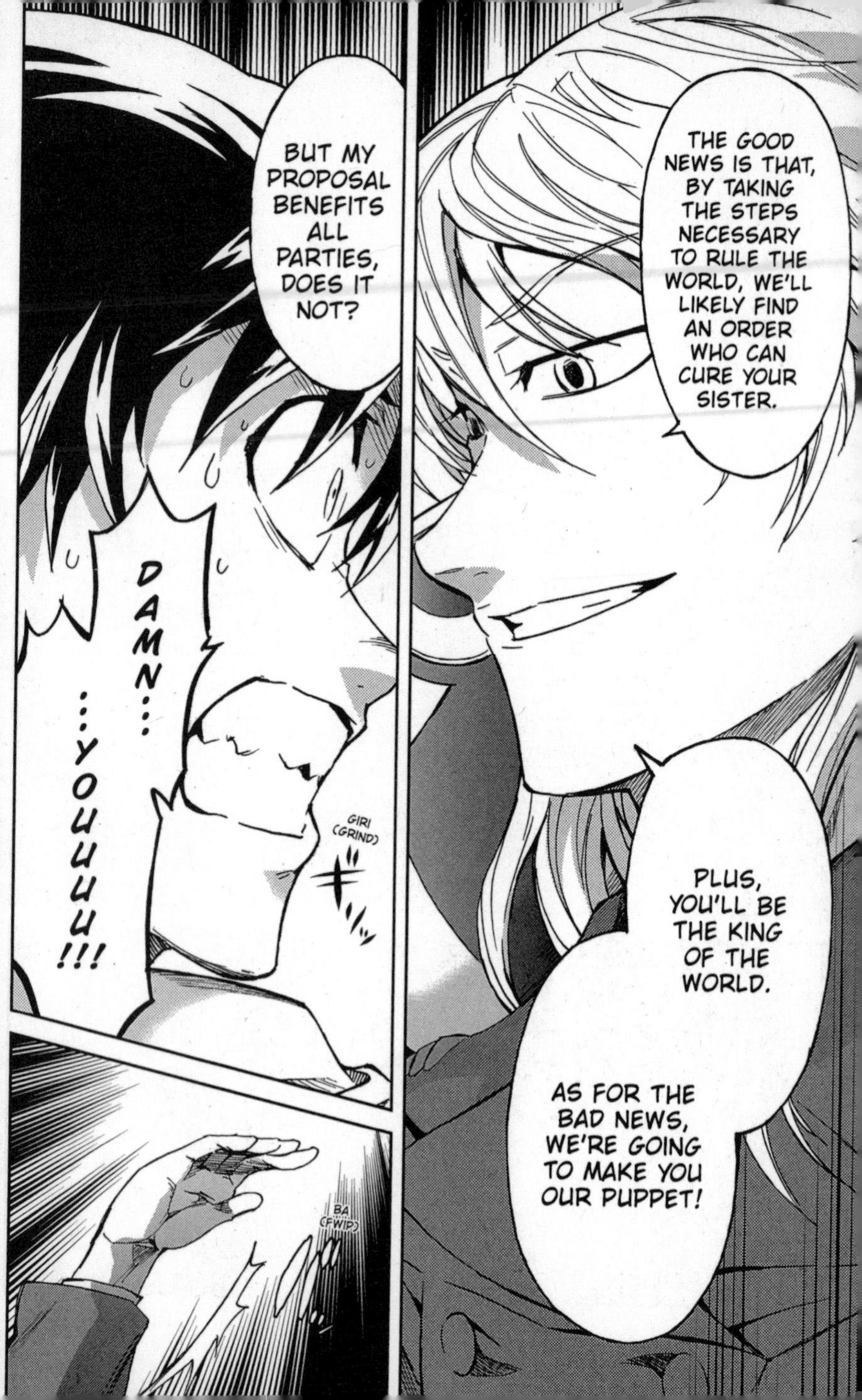
THE GOOD NEWS IS THAT, BY TAKING THE STEPS NECESSARY TO RULE THE WORLD, WE'LL LIKELY FIND AN ORDER WHO CAN CURE YOUR SISTER.
PLUS, YOU'LL BE THE KING OF THE WORLD.
AS FOR THE BAD NEWS, WE'RE GOING TO MAKE YOU OUR PUPPET!
BUT MY PROPOSAL BENEFITS ALL PARTIES, DOES IT NOT?
DAMN...
...YOUUUUU!!!
GIRI (GRIND)
BA (FWIP)

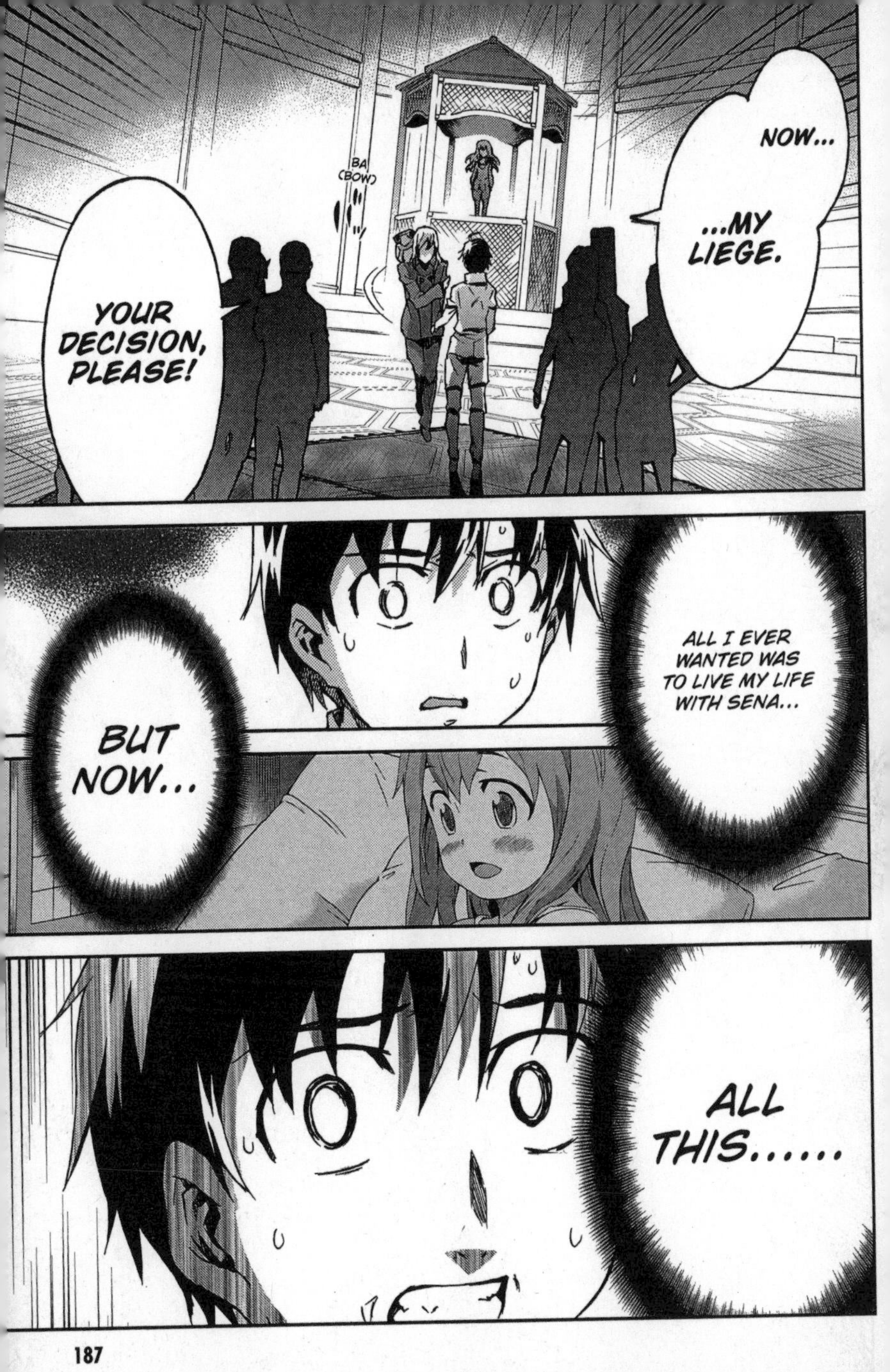
NOW...
...MY LIEGE.
BA (BOW)
YOUR DECISION, PLEASE!
ALL I EVER WANTED WAS TO LIVE MY LIFE WITH SENA...
BUT NOW...
ALL THIS......

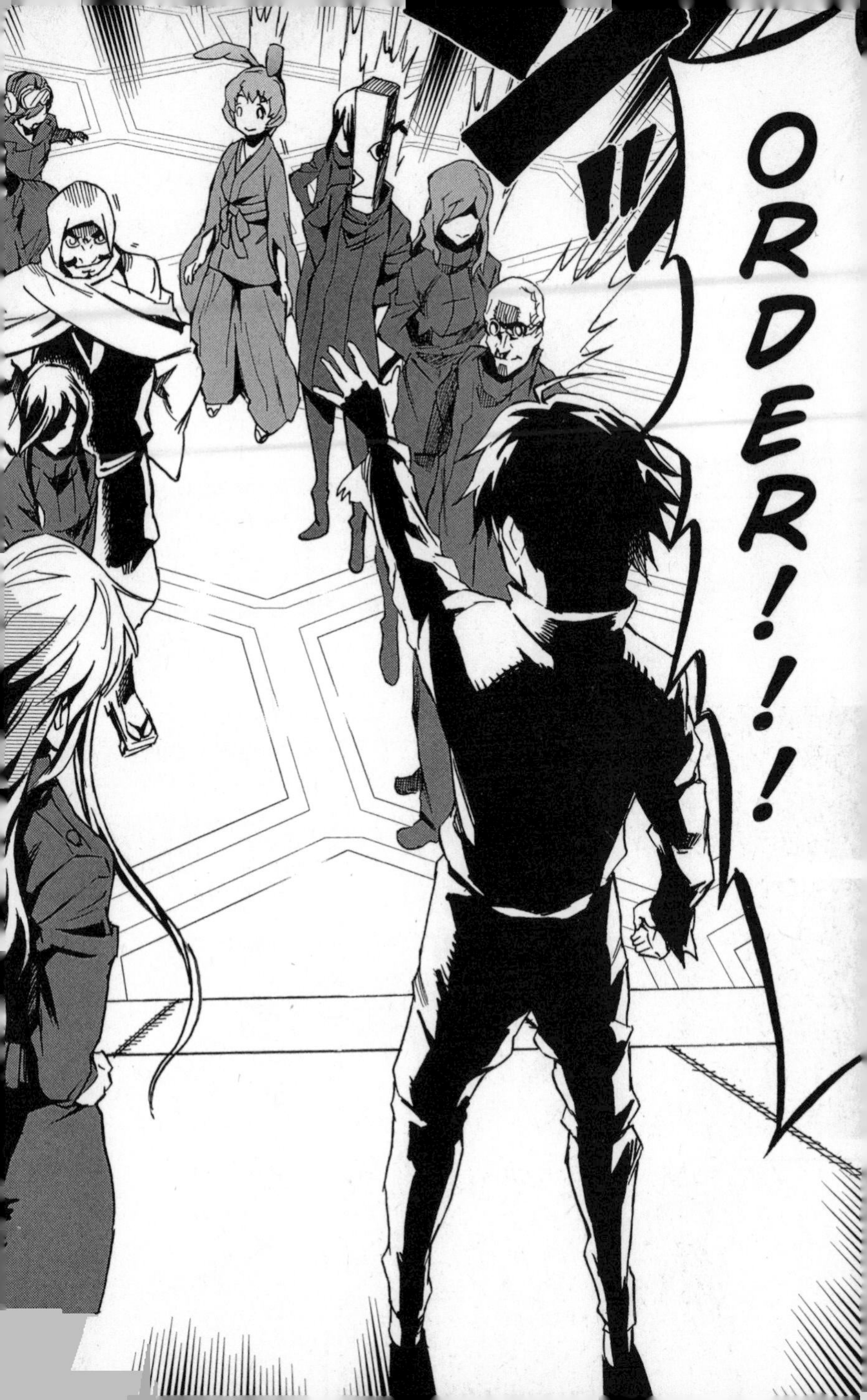
ORDER!!!

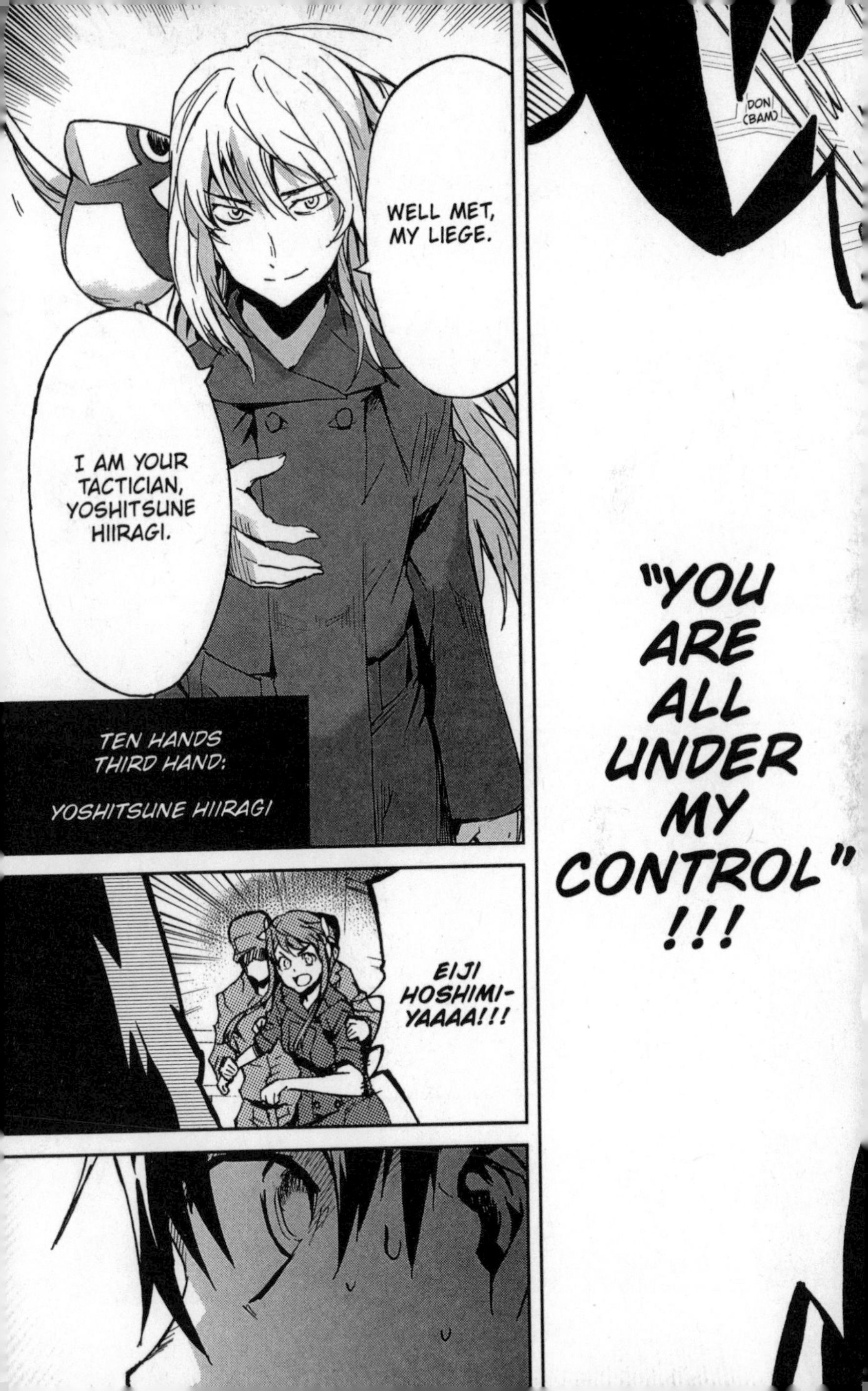
DON (BAM)
"YOU ARE ALL UNDER MY CONTROL"!!!
WELL MET, MY LIEGE.
I AM YOUR TACTICIAN, YOSHITSUNE HIIRAGI.
TEN HANDS THIRD HAND:
YOSHITSUNE HIIRAGI
EIJI HOSHIMI-YAAAA!!!

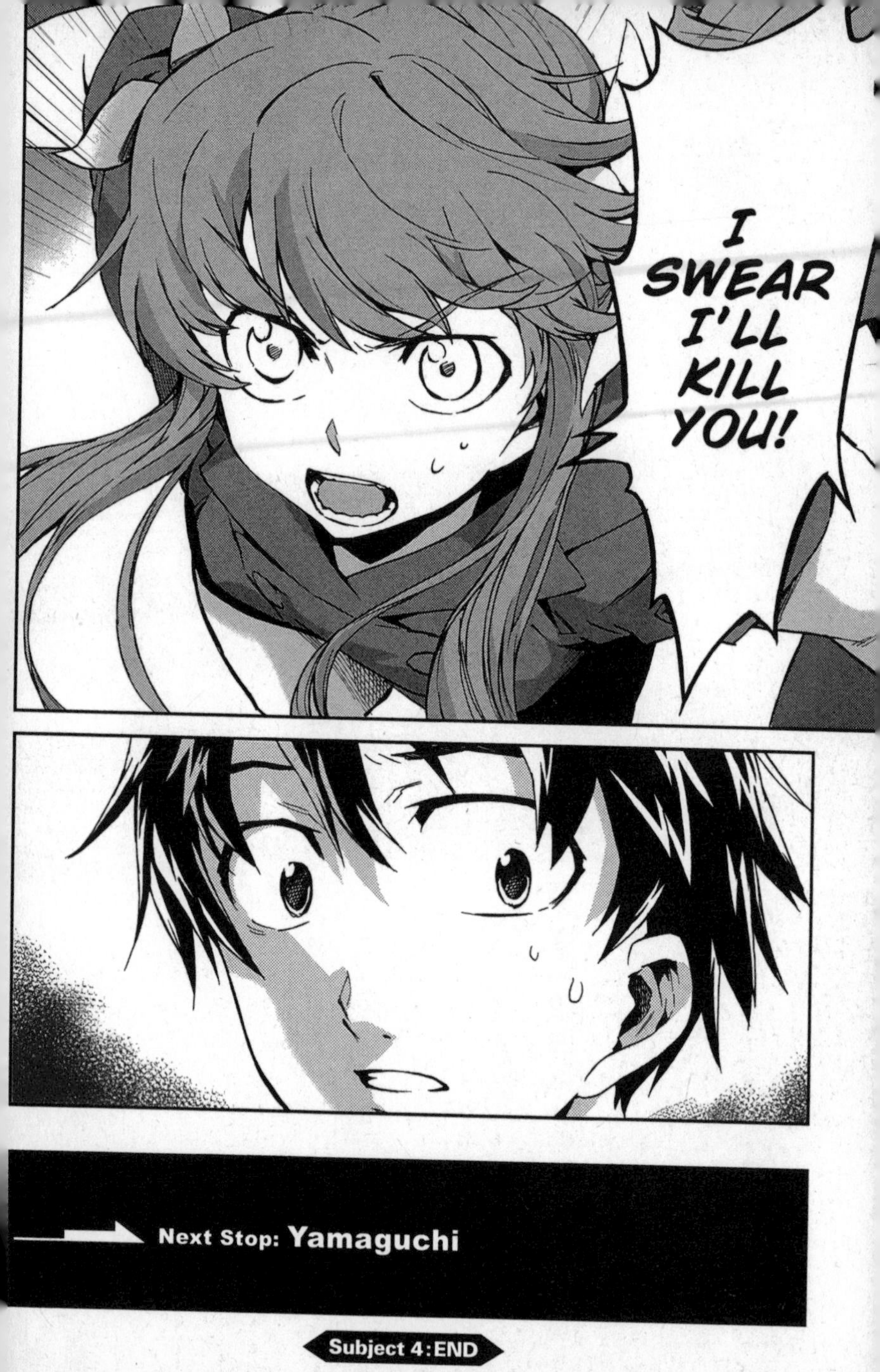
I SWEAR I'LL KILL YOU!

Next Stop: **Yamaguchi**

**Subject 4: END**

To be continued...

# 001

## ❯❯❯ "Abilities" received from Daisy

These ability users, who had their wishes made into superpowers by the mysterious entity known as Daisy, are called Orders. There are thought to be approximately two thousand Orders worldwide, though that number is steadily increasing.

## BIND DOMINATOR

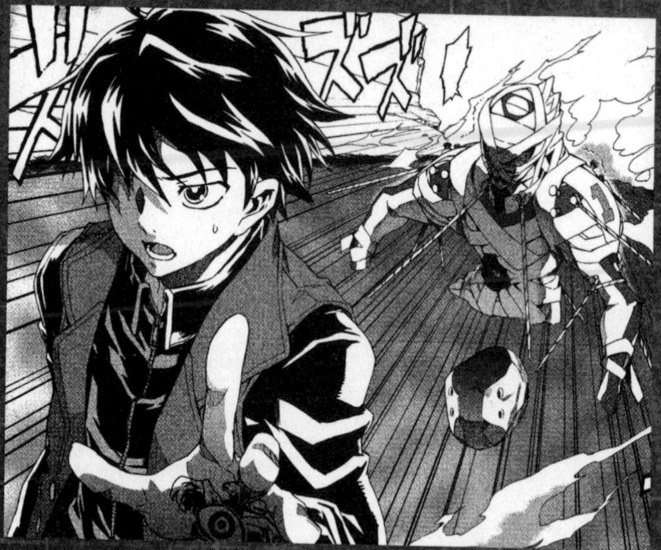

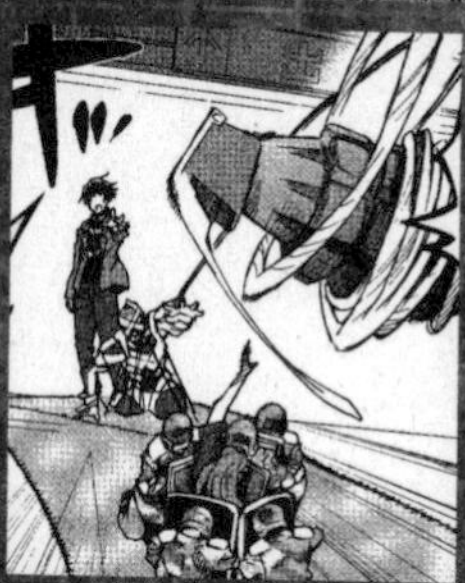

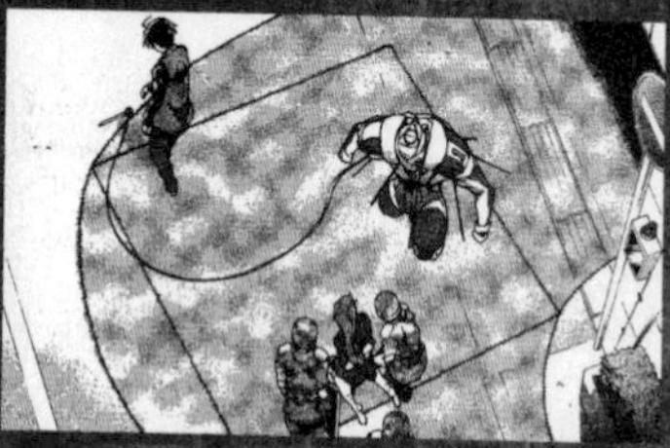

**User:** **Eiji Hoshimiya**

**Wish:** **World Domination**

**Ability:** **Complete physical control over everything within his domain**

Eiji has physical control over all objects, people, and "targets" that fall within his domain. Any area he walks over becomes part of his domain, giving him even more control. Orders must be given verbally, and the anchor and wire that plunge into the target are proof of Eiji's control. The anchor will not dislodge itself after a command is given, so long as the target is still in his domain. However, as the nature of Eiji's control only extends to the physical, he cannot manipulate the hearts and minds of others. Ten years ago, his newfound power ran rampant and caused the Great Destruction, though the process by which it occurred still isn't clear.

► Order Ability Profiles

# 002

# REBIRTH FIRE

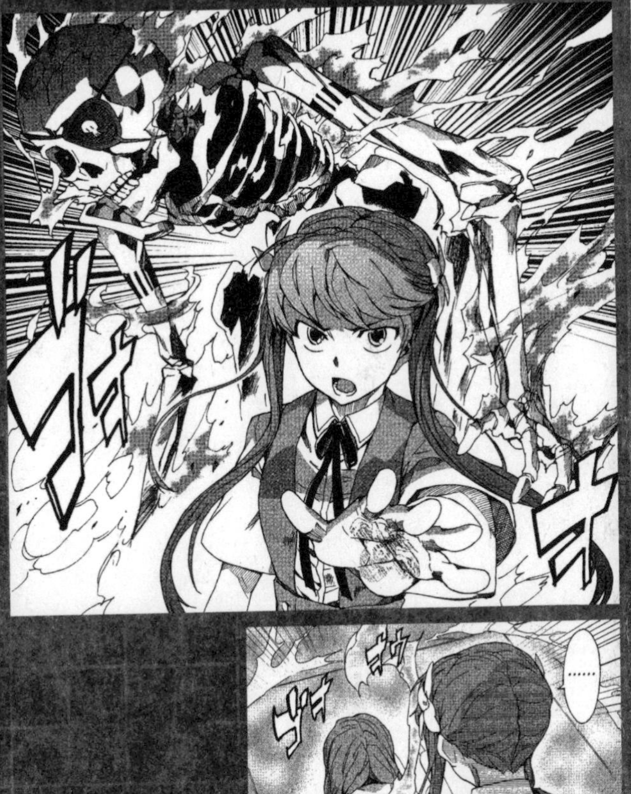

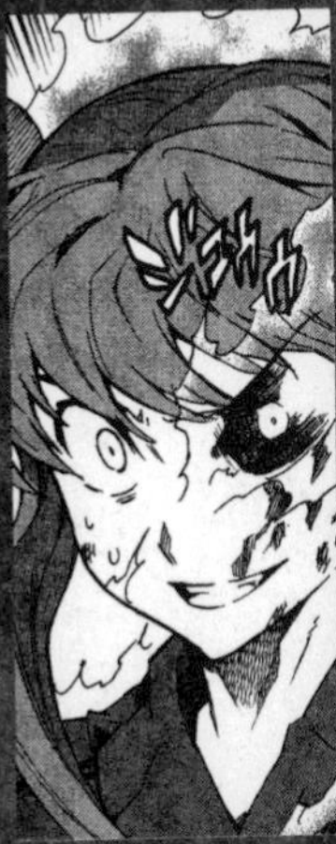

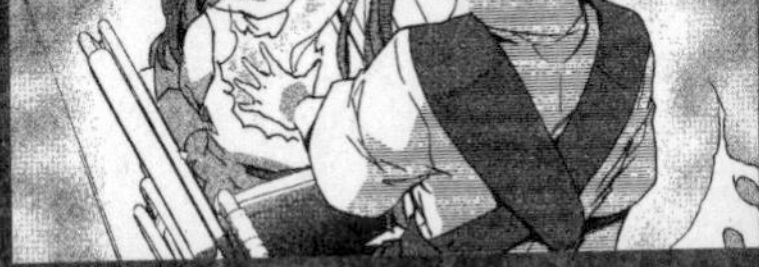
……

**User:** **Rin Kurenai**

**Wish:** **Regeneration**

**Ability:** **Immortality via regenerative powers**

Rin is essentially immortal thanks to her strong regenerative powers, which also allow her to "heal" other people and objects. The ability activates automatically for Rin herself, which means she can recover from nearly any situation—even if her head is destroyed or her heart is stopped. This means that Rin cannot truly be killed. When she wishes to speed up her own recovery or heal someone else, she has to actively use her Order ability. However, it doesn't seem as though she can heal old scars or internal illnesses. The power only works to "rewind" the effects of recent physical damage.

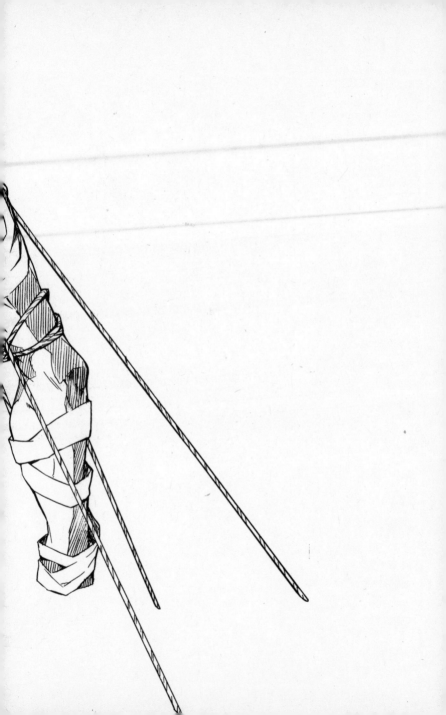

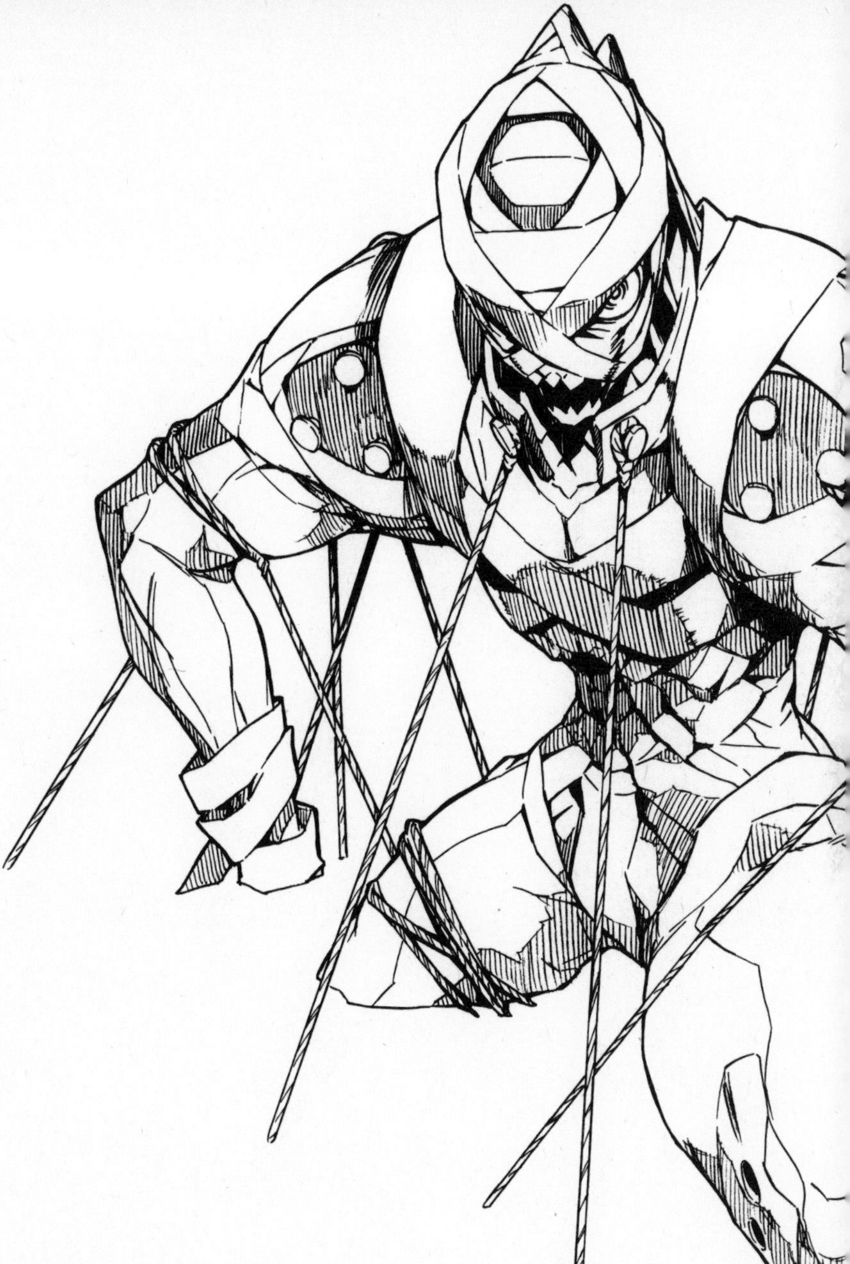

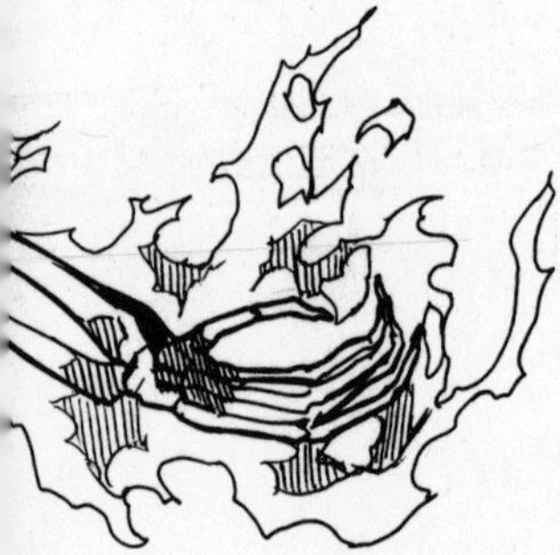

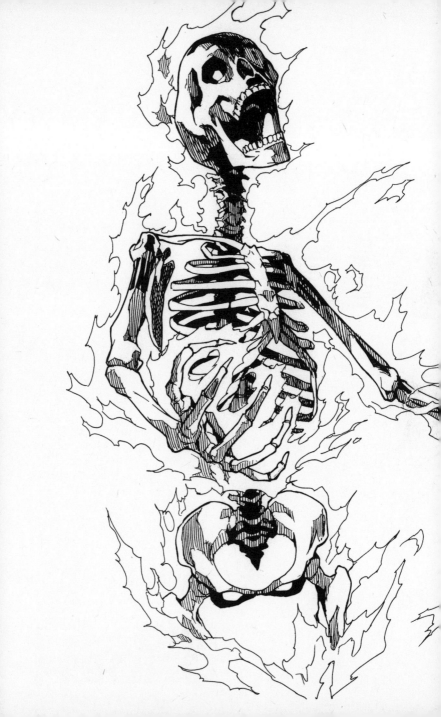

**BIG
ORDER**

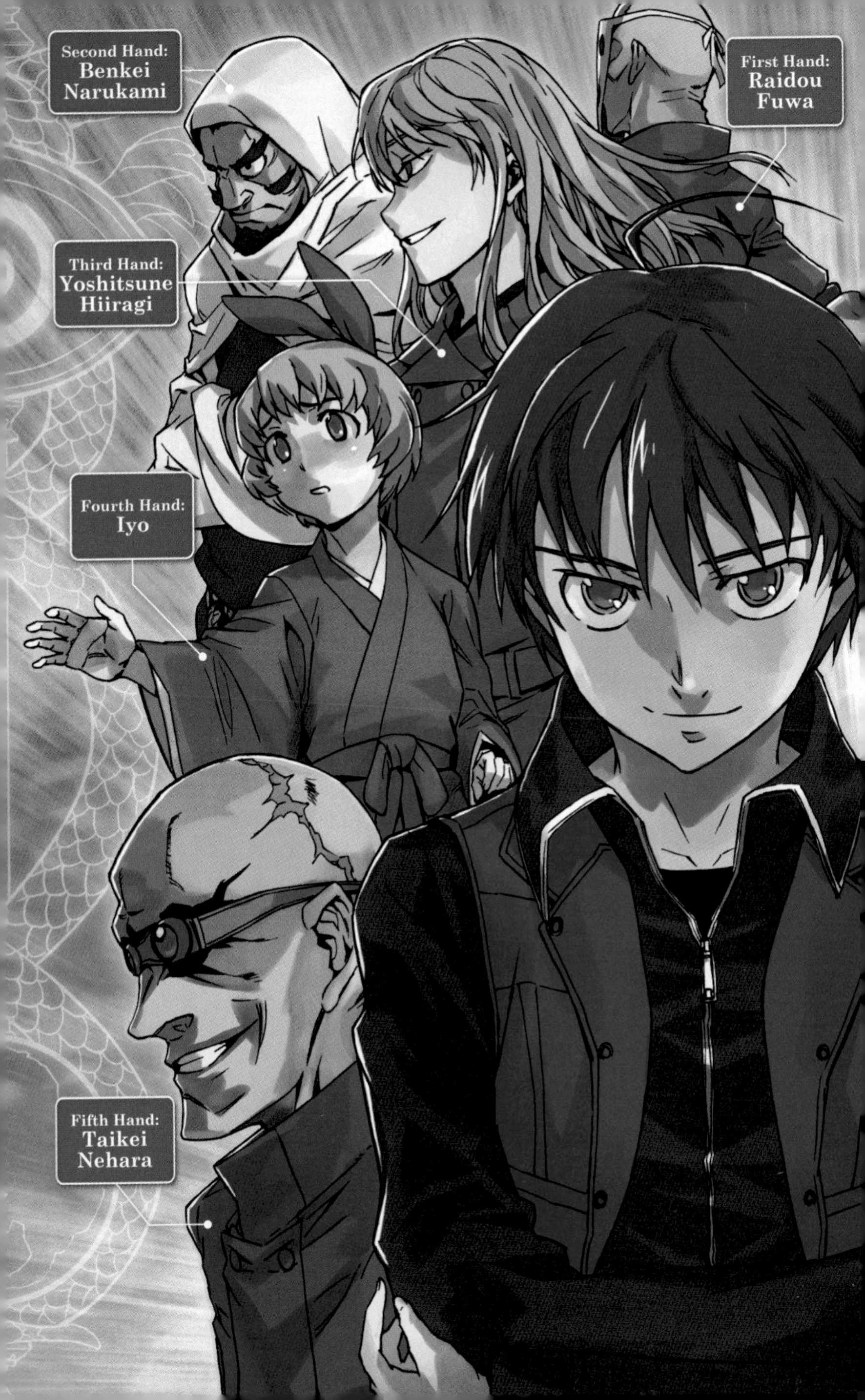
First Hand:
Raidou Fuwa
Second Hand:
Benkei Narukami
Third Hand:
Yoshitsune Hiiragi
Fourth Hand:
Iyo
Fifth Hand:
Taikei Nehara

BIG
ORDER

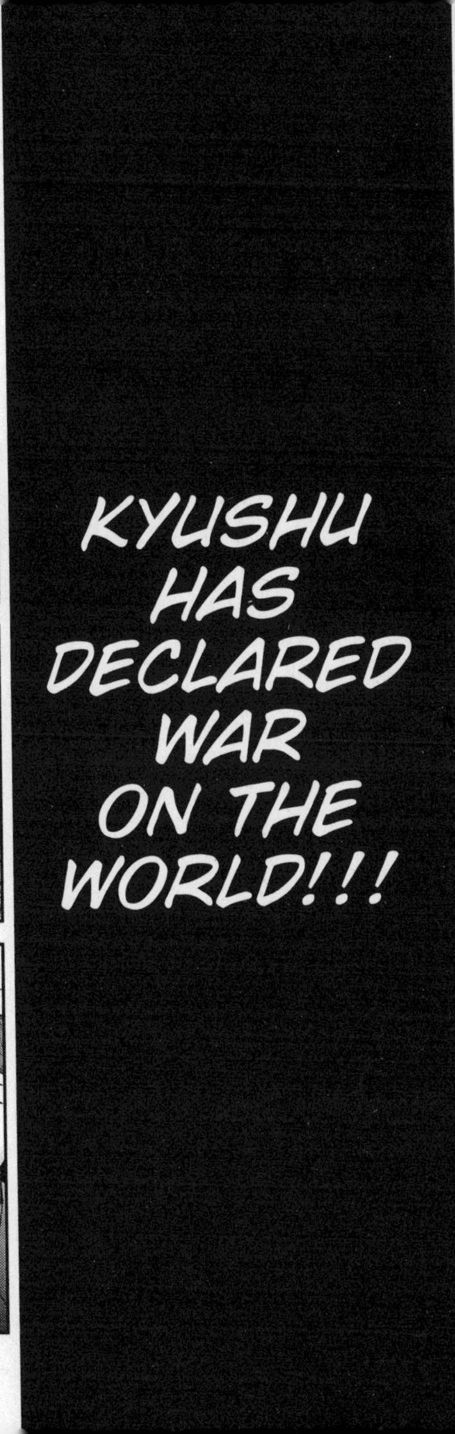
KYUSHU HAS DECLARED WAR ON THE WORLD!!!
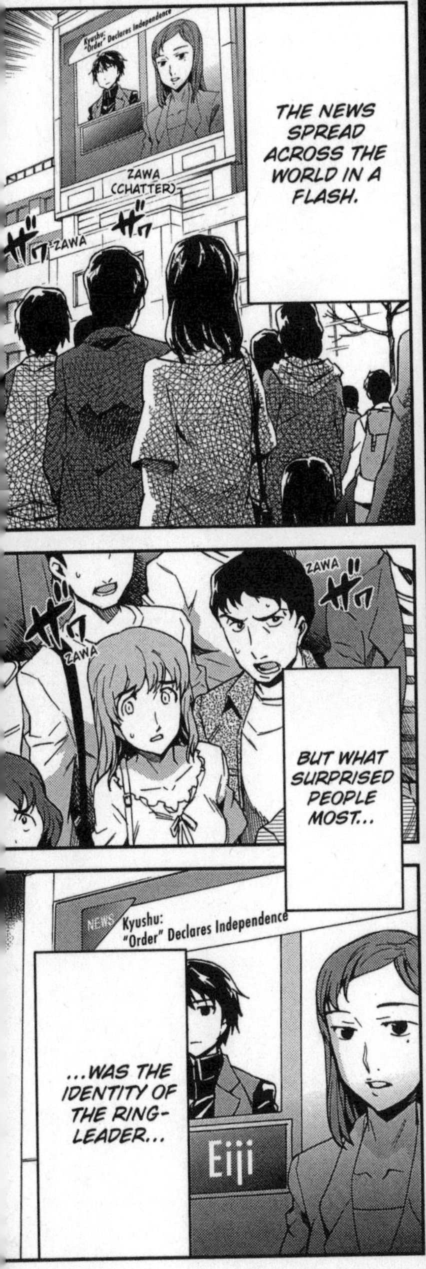
THE NEWS SPREAD ACROSS THE WORLD IN A FLASH.
Kyushu: "Order" Declares Independence
ZAWA (CHATTER)
ZAWA
ZAWA
ZAWA
BUT WHAT SURPRISED PEOPLE MOST...
NEWS
Kyushu: "Order" Declares Independence
...WAS THE IDENTITY OF THE RING-LEADER...
Eiji

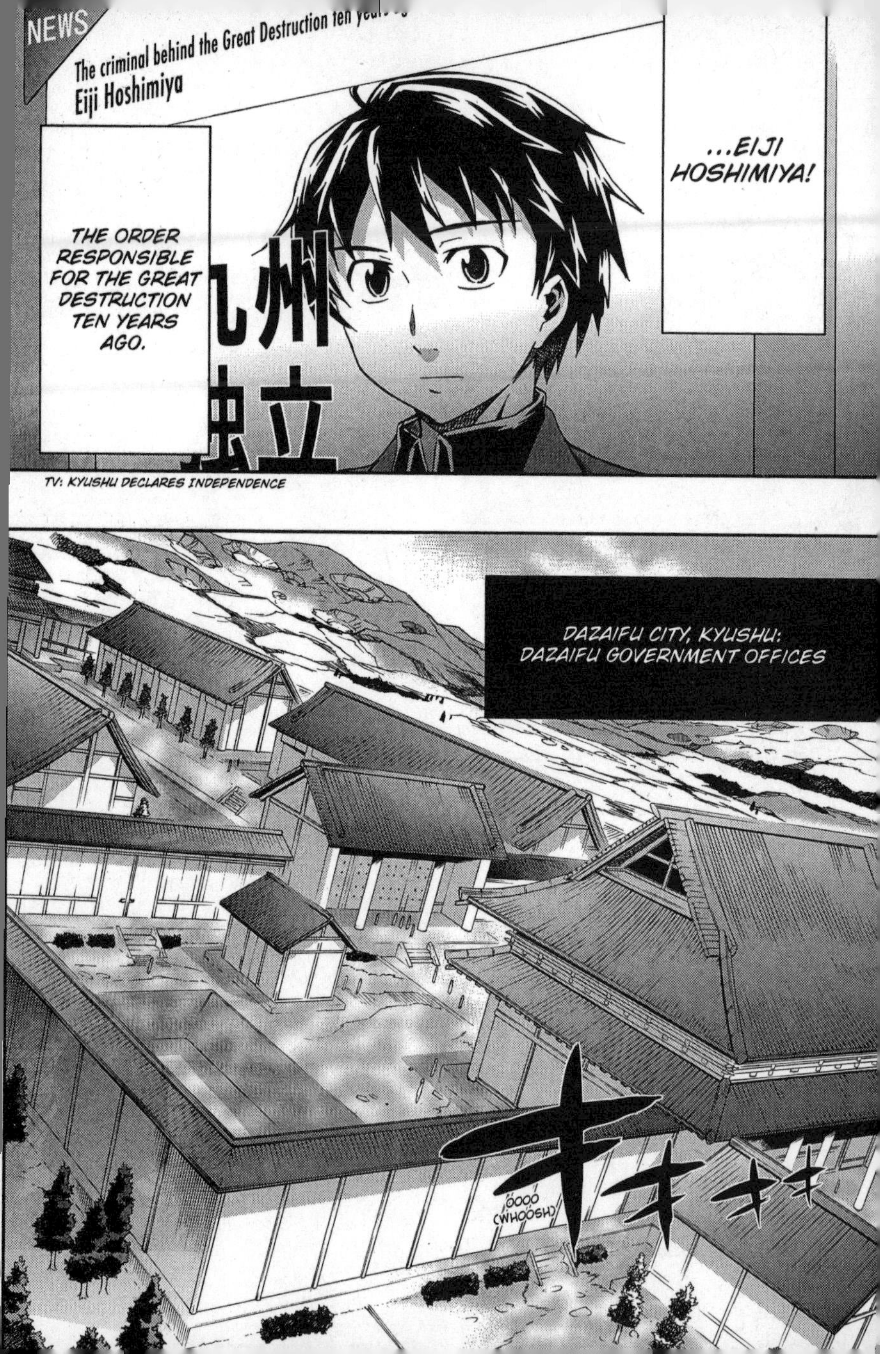
NEWS
The criminal behind the Great Destruction ten years
Eiji Hoshimiya
...EIJI HOSHIMIYA!
THE ORDER RESPONSIBLE FOR THE GREAT DESTRUCTION TEN YEARS AGO.
TV: KYUSHU DECLARES INDEPENDENCE
DAZAIFU CITY, KYUSHU: DAZAIFU GOVERNMENT OFFICES
OOOO (WHOOSH)

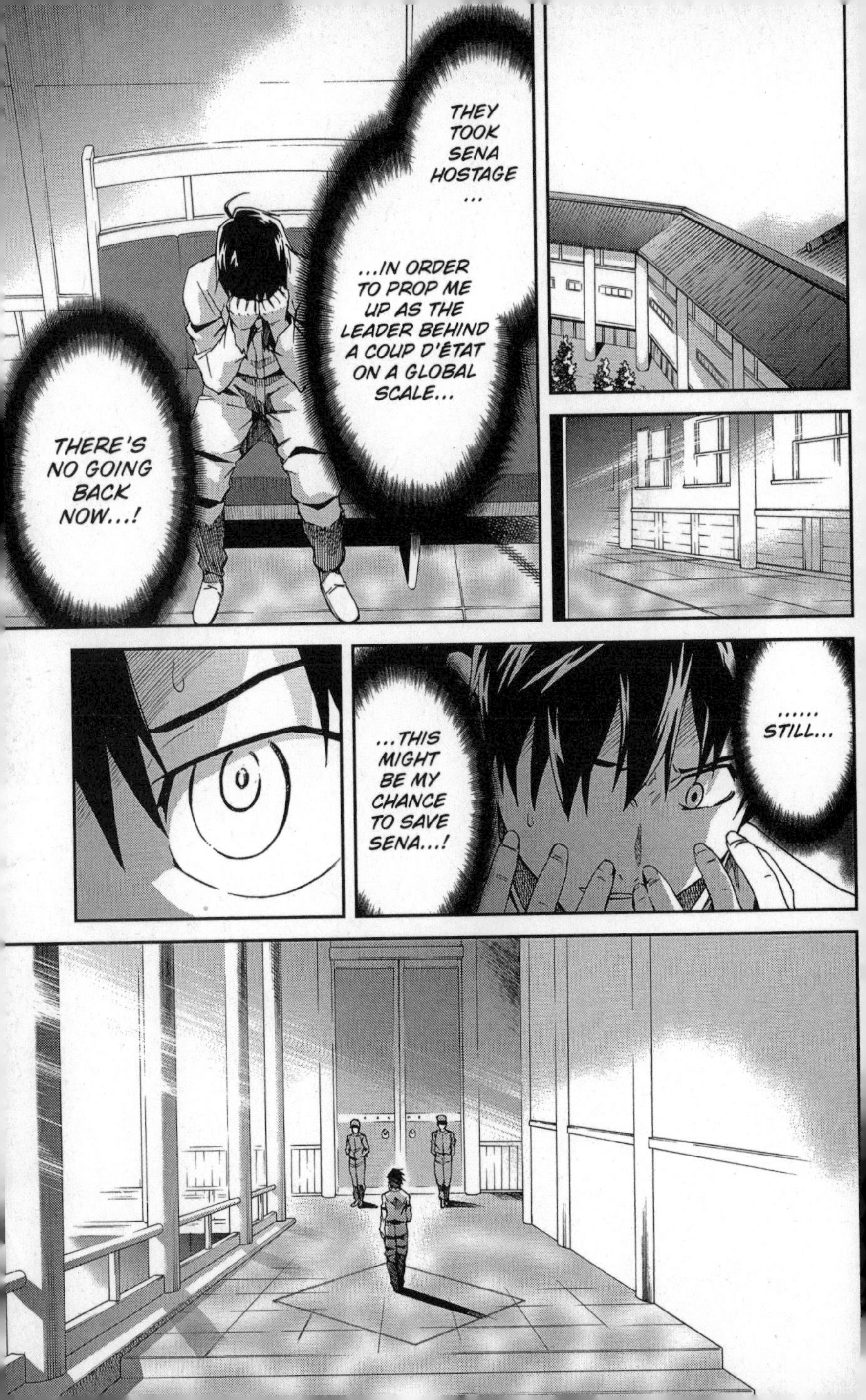
THEY TOOK SENA HOSTAGE ...
...IN ORDER TO PROP ME UP AS THE LEADER BEHIND A COUP D'ÉTAT ON A GLOBAL SCALE...
THERE'S NO GOING BACK NOW...!
...... STILL...
...THIS MIGHT BE MY CHANCE TO SAVE SENA...!

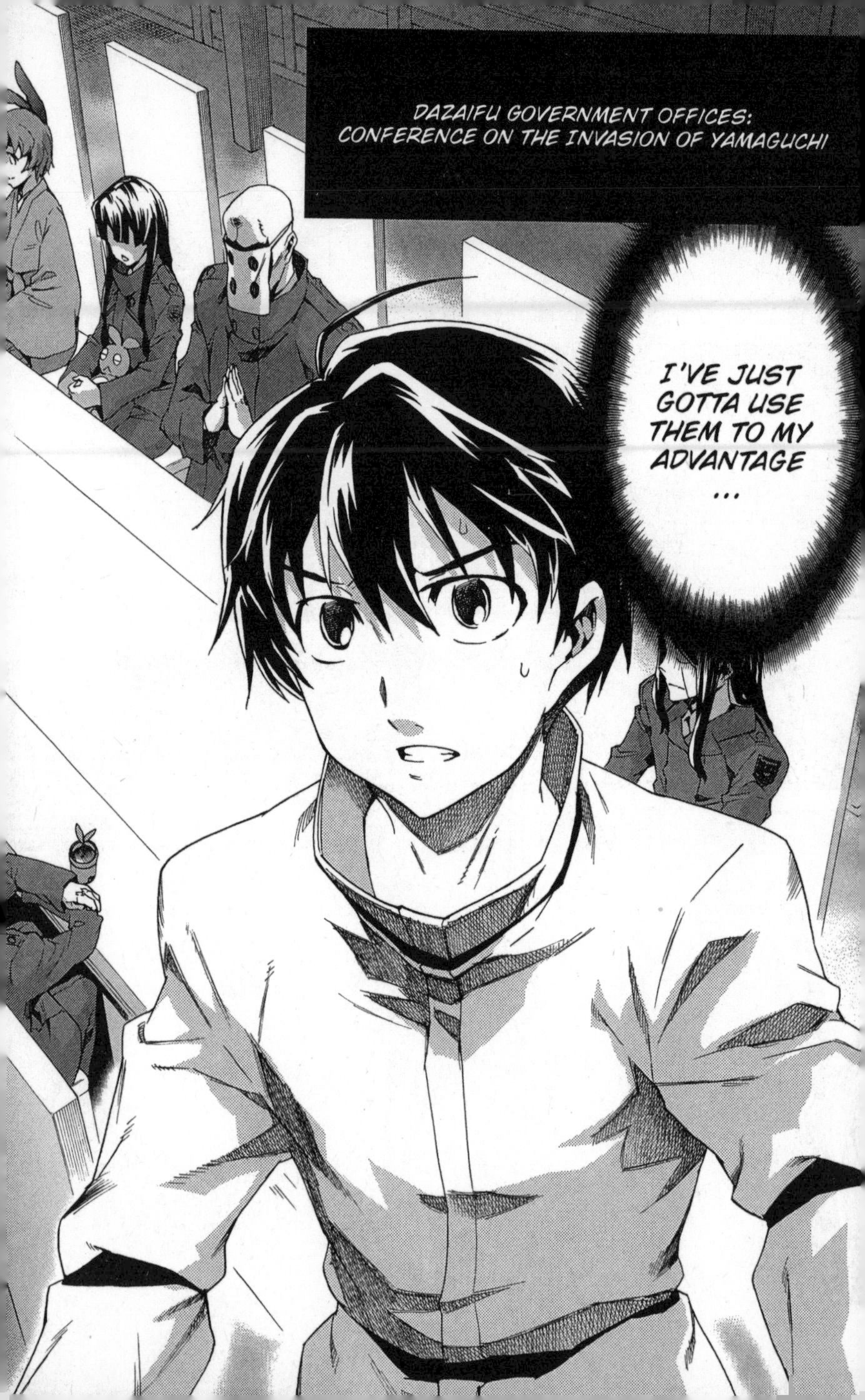
DAZAIFU GOVERNMENT OFFICES:
CONFERENCE ON THE INVASION OF YAMAGUCHI
I'VE JUST GOTTA USE THEM TO MY ADVANTAGE ...

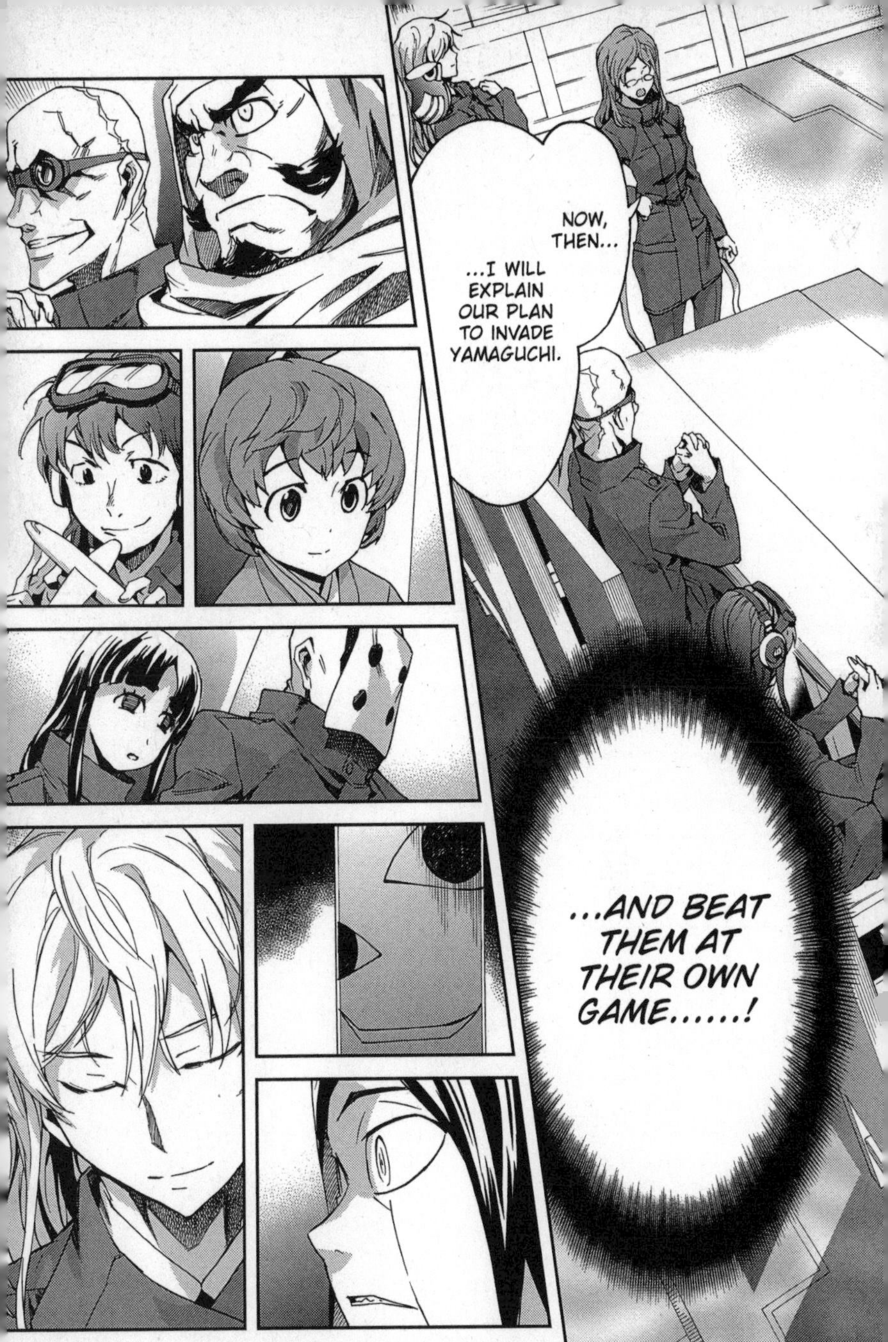
NOW, THEN...
...I WILL EXPLAIN OUR PLAN TO INVADE YAMAGUCHI.
...AND BEAT THEM AT THEIR OWN GAME......!

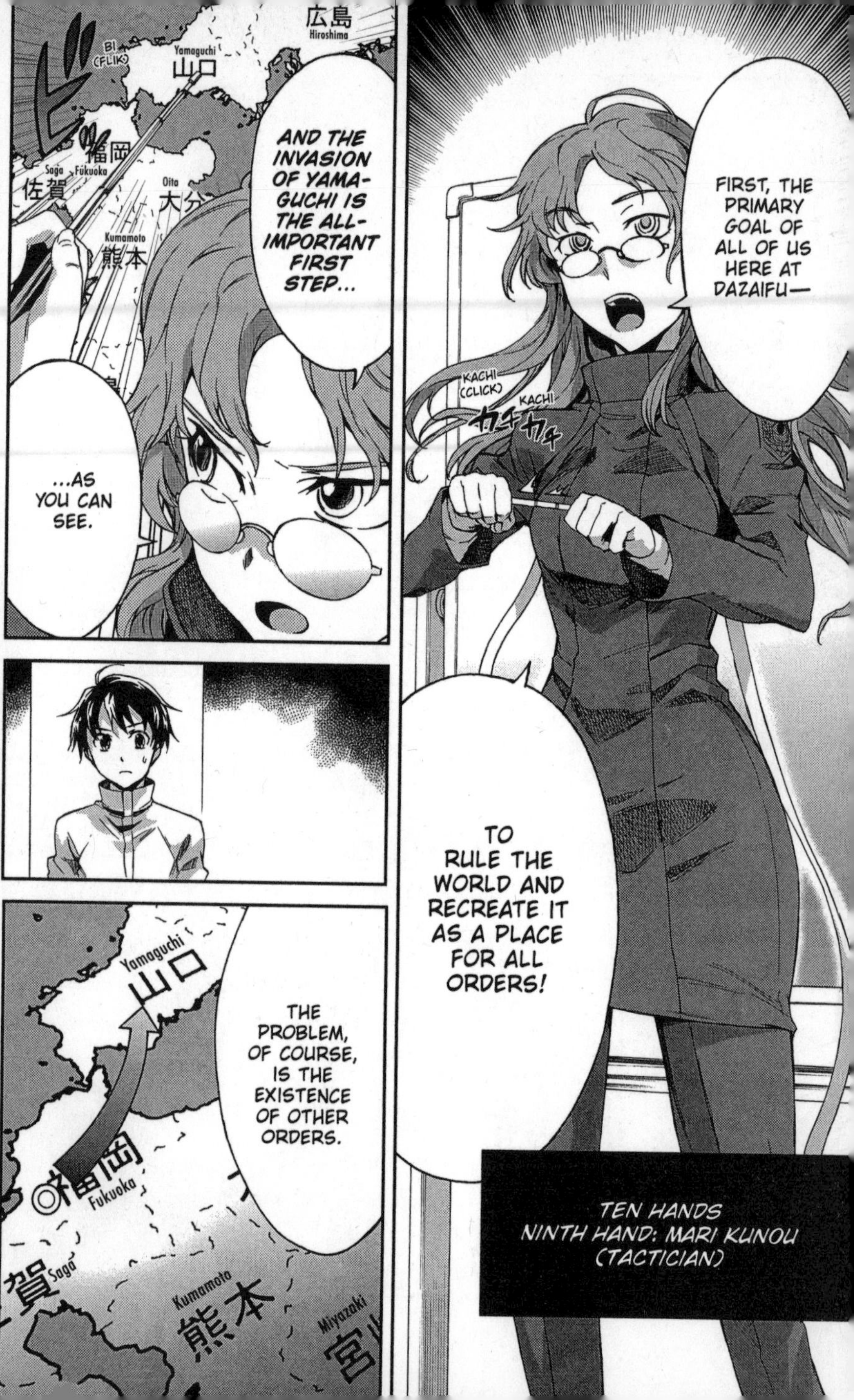
FIRST, THE PRIMARY GOAL OF ALL OF US HERE AT DAZAIFU—
KACHI (CLICK) KACHI
カチカチ
TO RULE THE WORLD AND RECREATE IT AS A PLACE FOR ALL ORDERS!
TEN HANDS
NINTH HAND: MARI KUNOU
(TACTICIAN)
広島 Hiroshima
山口 Yamaguchi
福岡 Fukuoka
佐賀 Saga
大分 Oita
熊本 Kumamoto
BI (FLIK)
AND THE INVASION OF YAMAGUCHI IS THE ALL-IMPORTANT FIRST STEP...
...AS YOU CAN SEE.
Yamaguchi 山口
Fukuoka
Saga
Kumamoto 熊本
Miyazaki
THE PROBLEM, OF COURSE, IS THE EXISTENCE OF OTHER ORDERS.

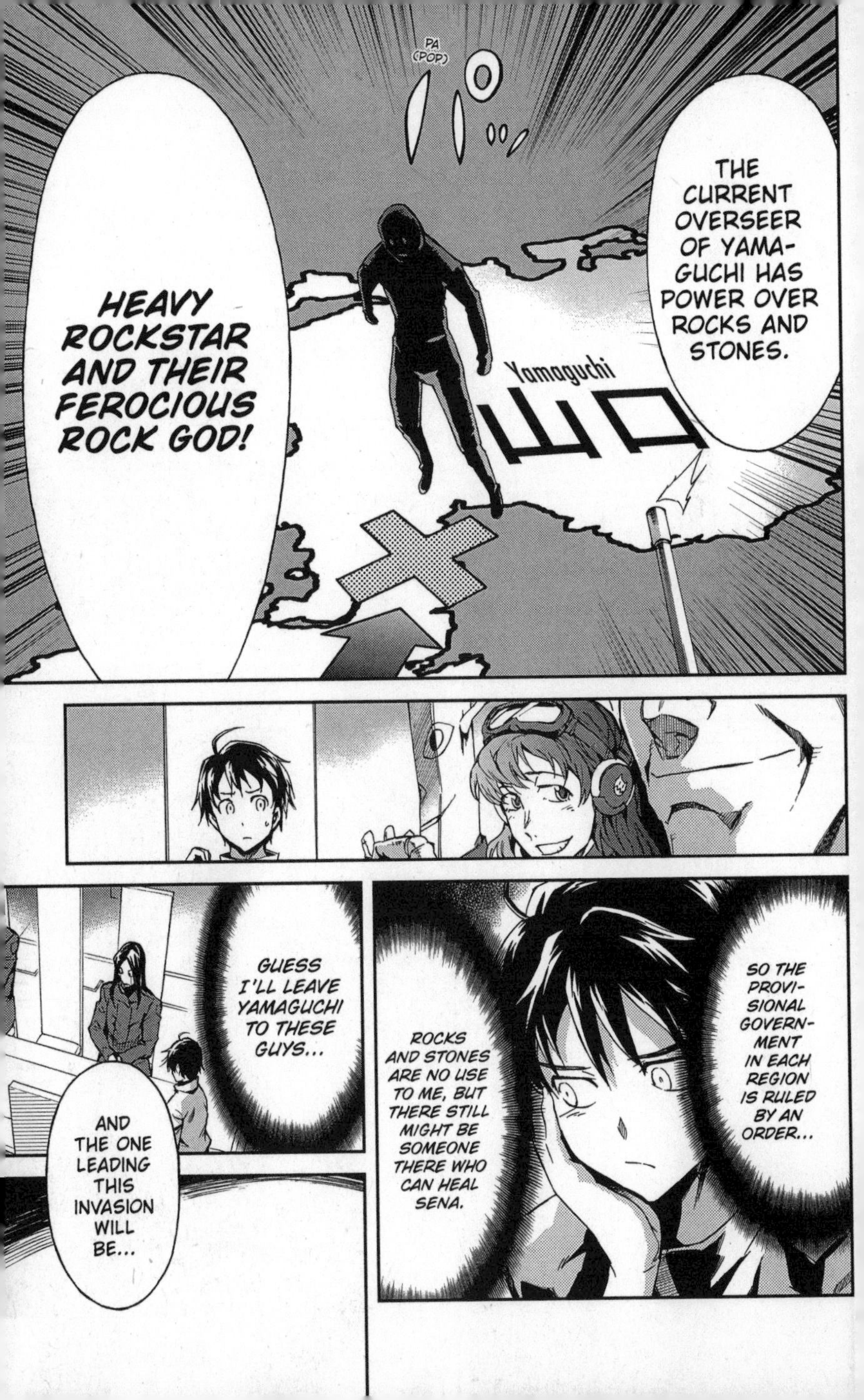
THE CURRENT OVERSEER OF YAMAGUCHI HAS POWER OVER ROCKS AND STONES.
PA (POP)
Yamaguchi
HEAVY ROCKSTAR AND THEIR FEROCIOUS ROCK GOD!
SO THE PROVISIONAL GOVERNMENT IN EACH REGION IS RULED BY AN ORDER...
ROCKS AND STONES ARE NO USE TO ME, BUT THERE STILL MIGHT BE SOMEONE THERE WHO CAN HEAL SENA.
GUESS I'LL LEAVE YAMAGUCHI TO THESE GUYS...
AND THE ONE LEADING THIS INVASION WILL BE...

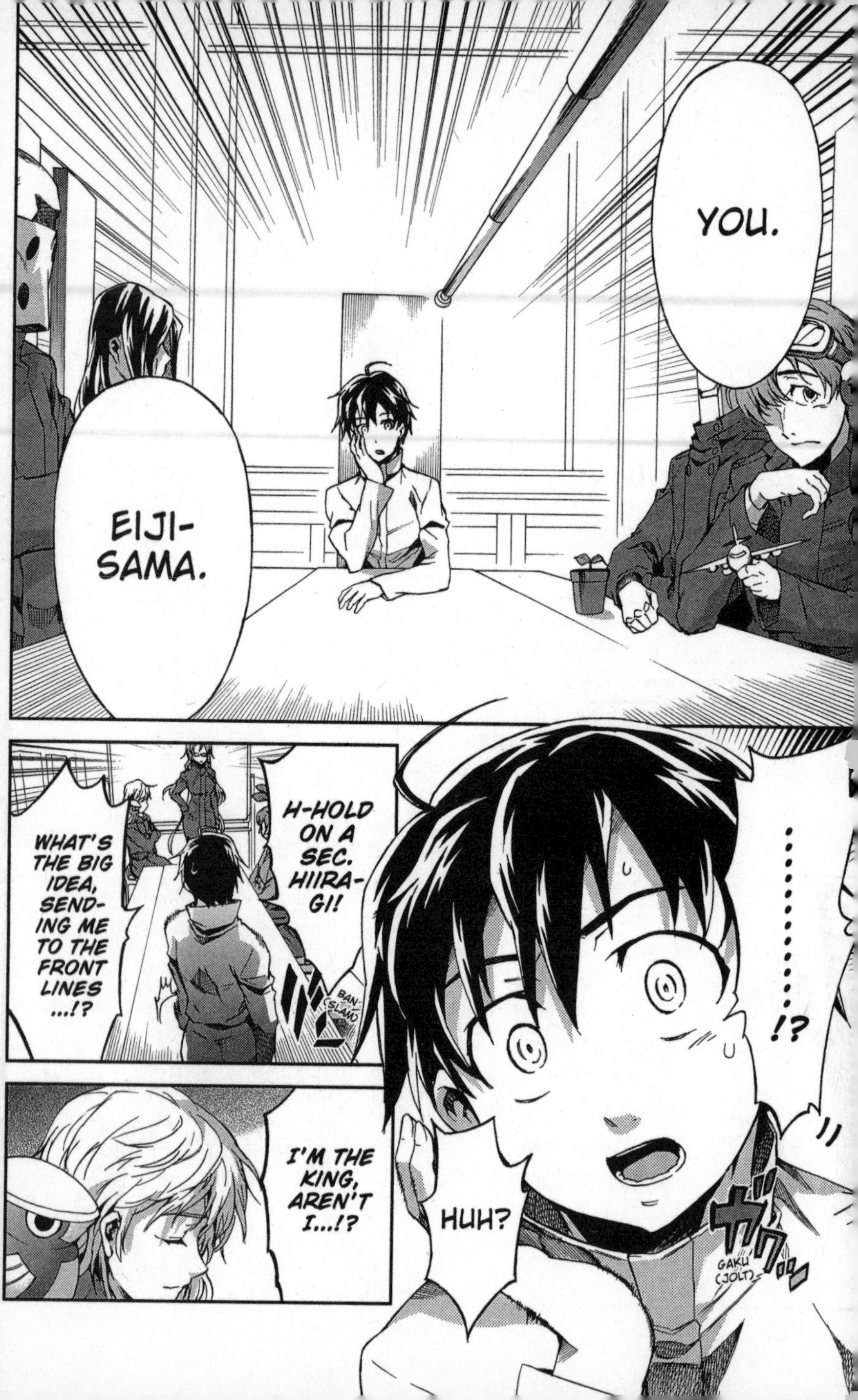
YOU.
EIJI-SAMA.
......!?
HUH?
GAKU (JOLT)
H-HOLD ON A SEC. HIIRAGI!
WHAT'S THE BIG IDEA, SENDING ME TO THE FRONT LINES ...!?
BAN (SLAM)
I'M THE KING, AREN'T I...!?

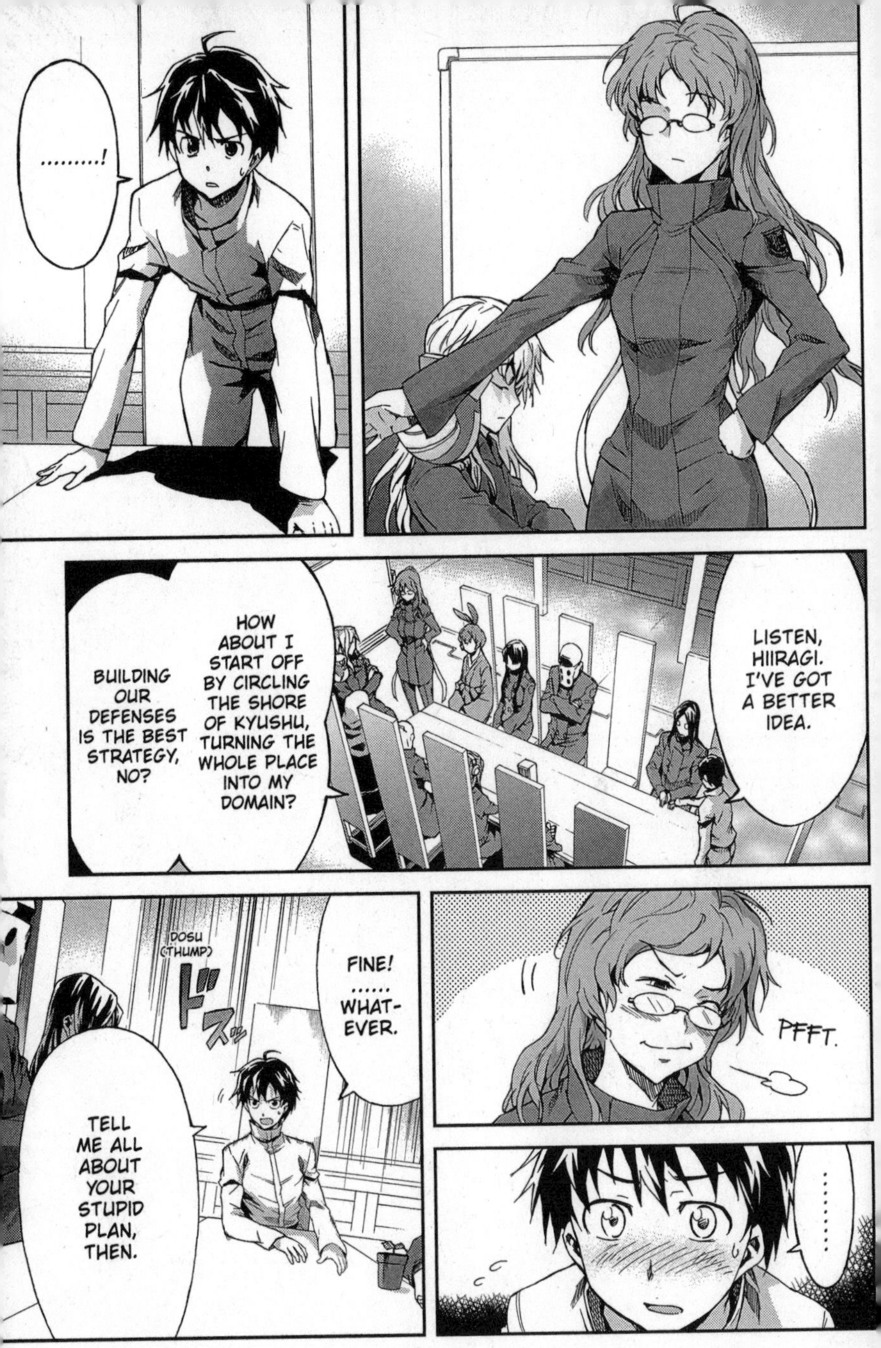
.........!
LISTEN, HIIRAGI. I'VE GOT A BETTER IDEA.
HOW ABOUT I START OFF BY CIRCLING THE SHORE OF KYUSHU, TURNING THE WHOLE PLACE INTO MY DOMAIN?
BUILDING OUR DEFENSES IS THE BEST STRATEGY, NO?
PFFT.
......
FINE! ...... WHAT-EVER.
DOSU (THUMP)
ドス
TELL ME ALL ABOUT YOUR STUPID PLAN, THEN.

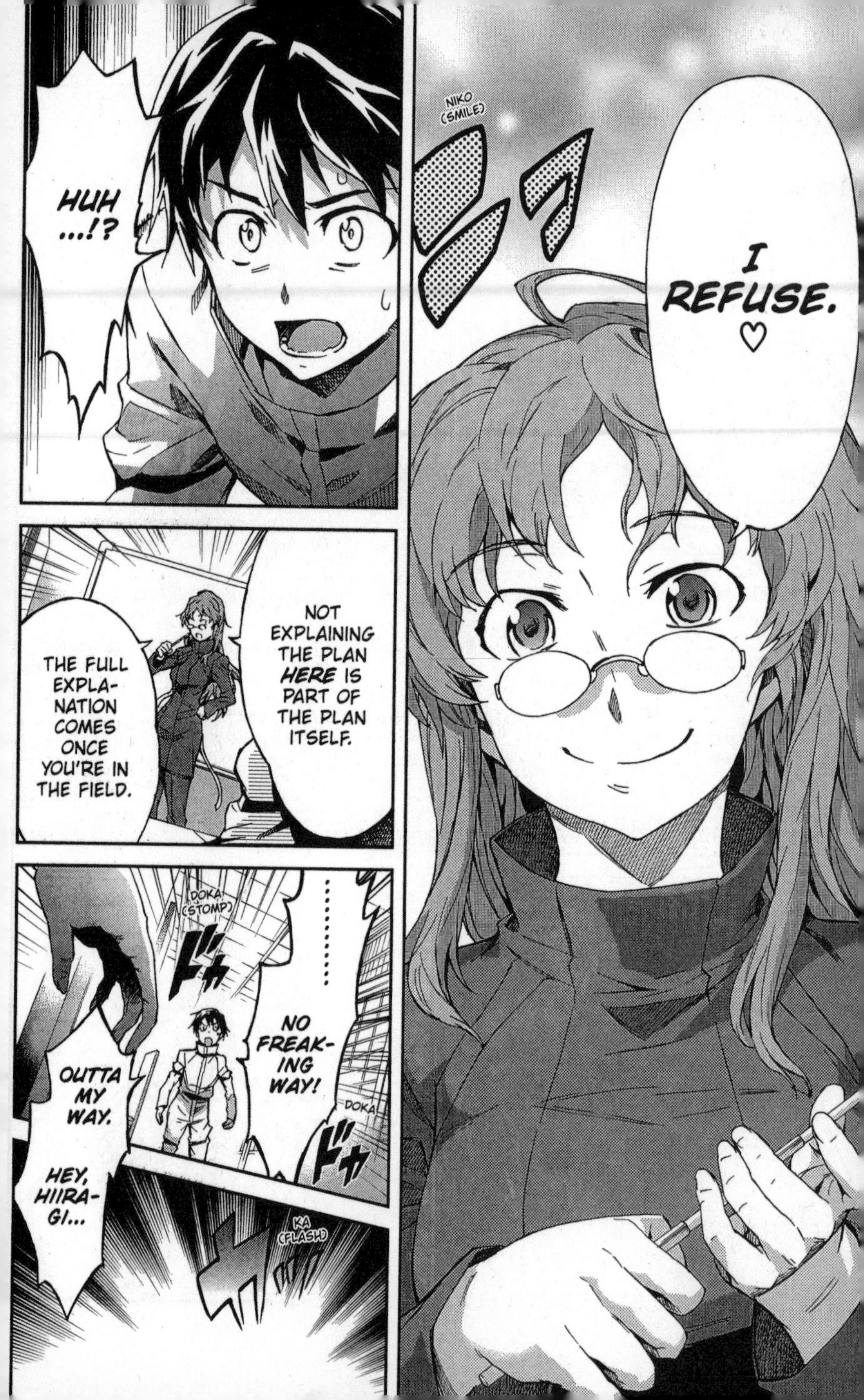
NIKO (SMILE)
I REFUSE. ♡
HUH ...!?
NOT EXPLAINING THE PLAN HERE IS PART OF THE PLAN ITSELF.
THE FULL EXPLA-NATION COMES ONCE YOU'RE IN THE FIELD.
......
DOKA (STOMP)
NO FREAK-ING WAY!
DOKA
OUTTA MY WAY.
HEY, HIIRA-GI...
KA (FLASH)

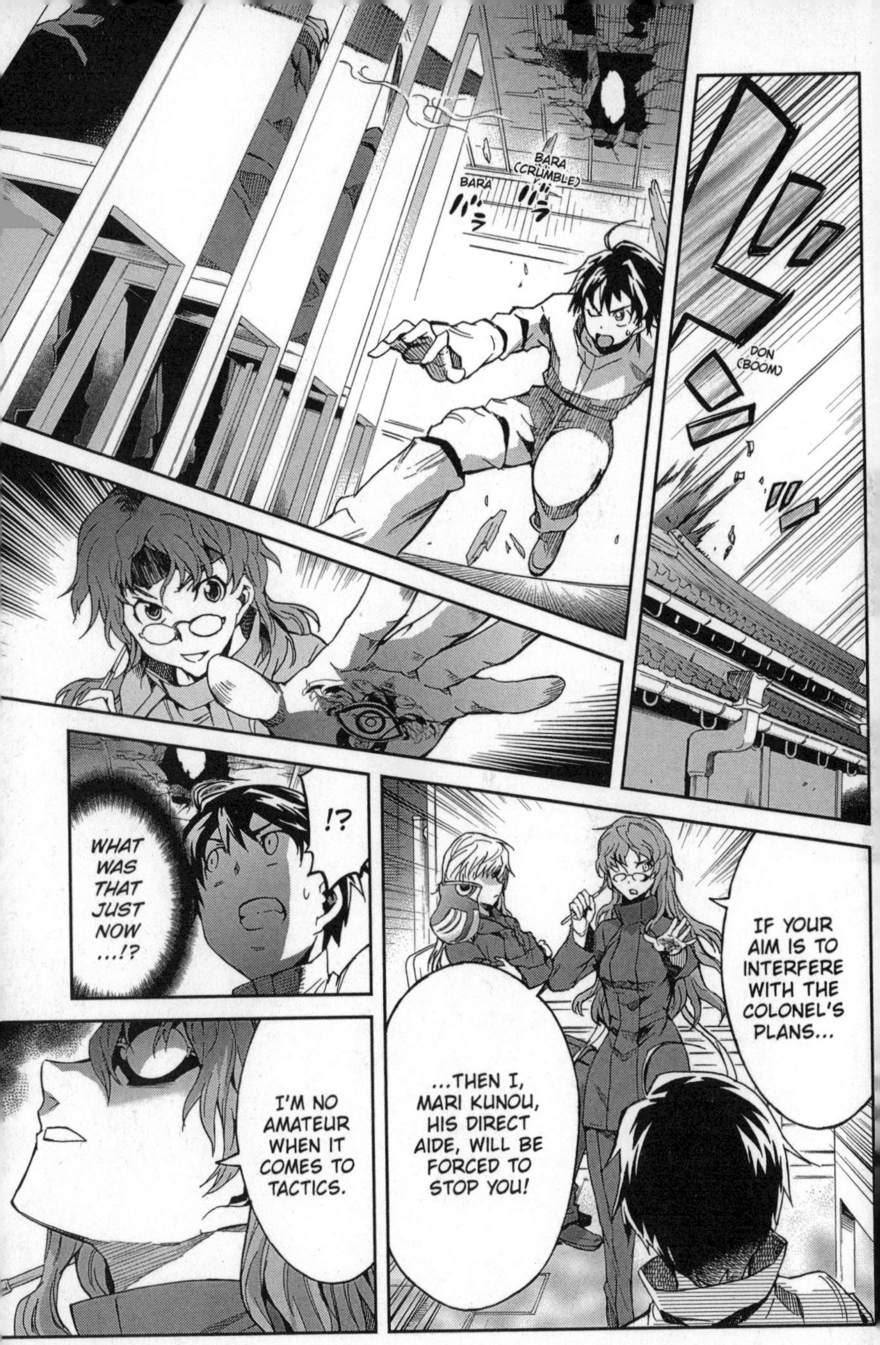

DON (BOOM)
BARA (CRUMBLE)
BARA
IF YOUR AIM IS TO INTERFERE WITH THE COLONEL'S PLANS...
...THEN I, MARI KUNOU, HIS DIRECT AIDE, WILL BE FORCED TO STOP YOU!
!?
WHAT WAS THAT JUST NOW ...!?
I'M NO AMATEUR WHEN IT COMES TO TACTICS.

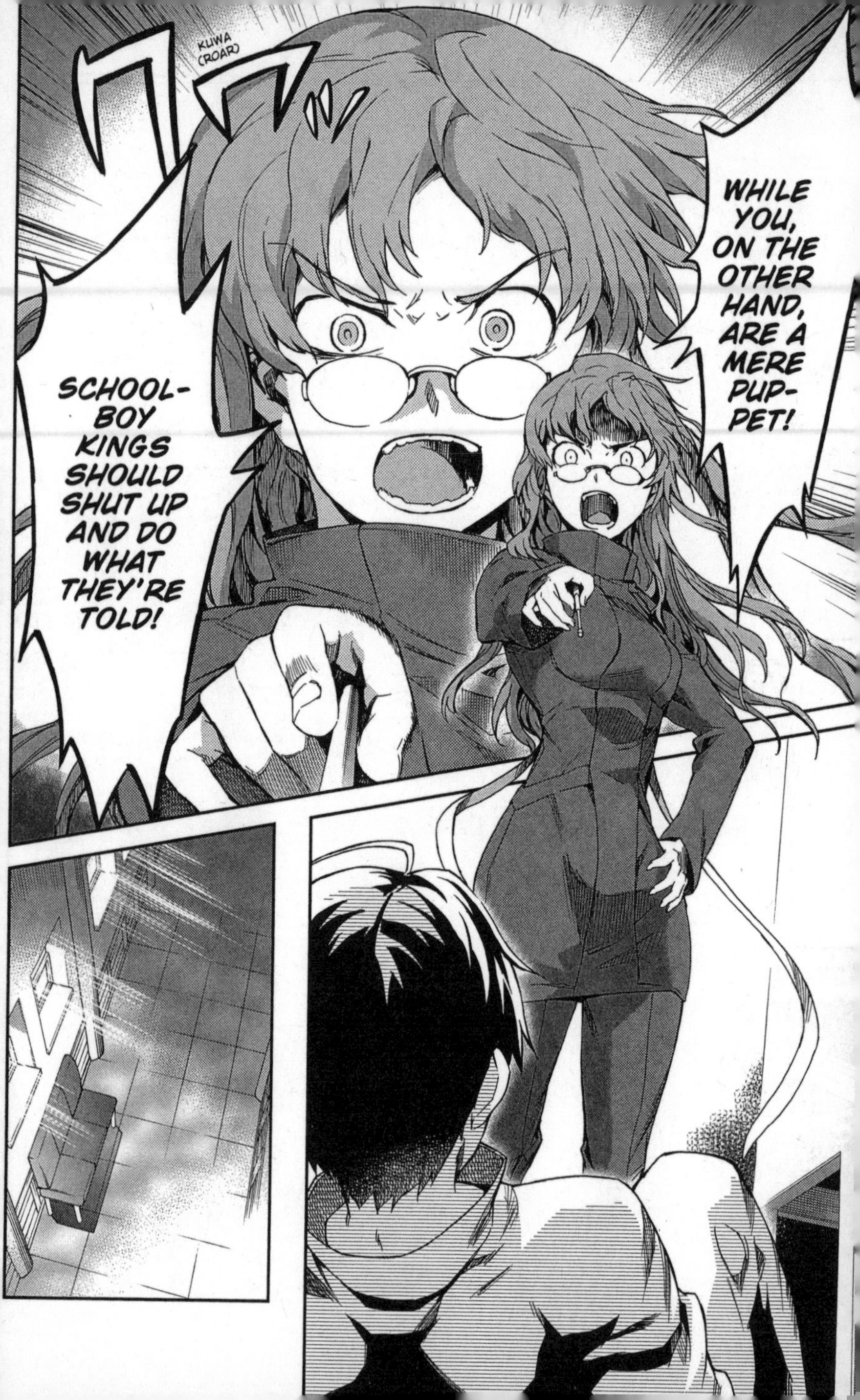
KUWA (ROAR)
WHILE YOU, ON THE OTHER HAND, ARE A MERE PUP-PET!
SCHOOL-BOY KINGS SHOULD SHUT UP AND DO WHAT THEY'RE TOLD!

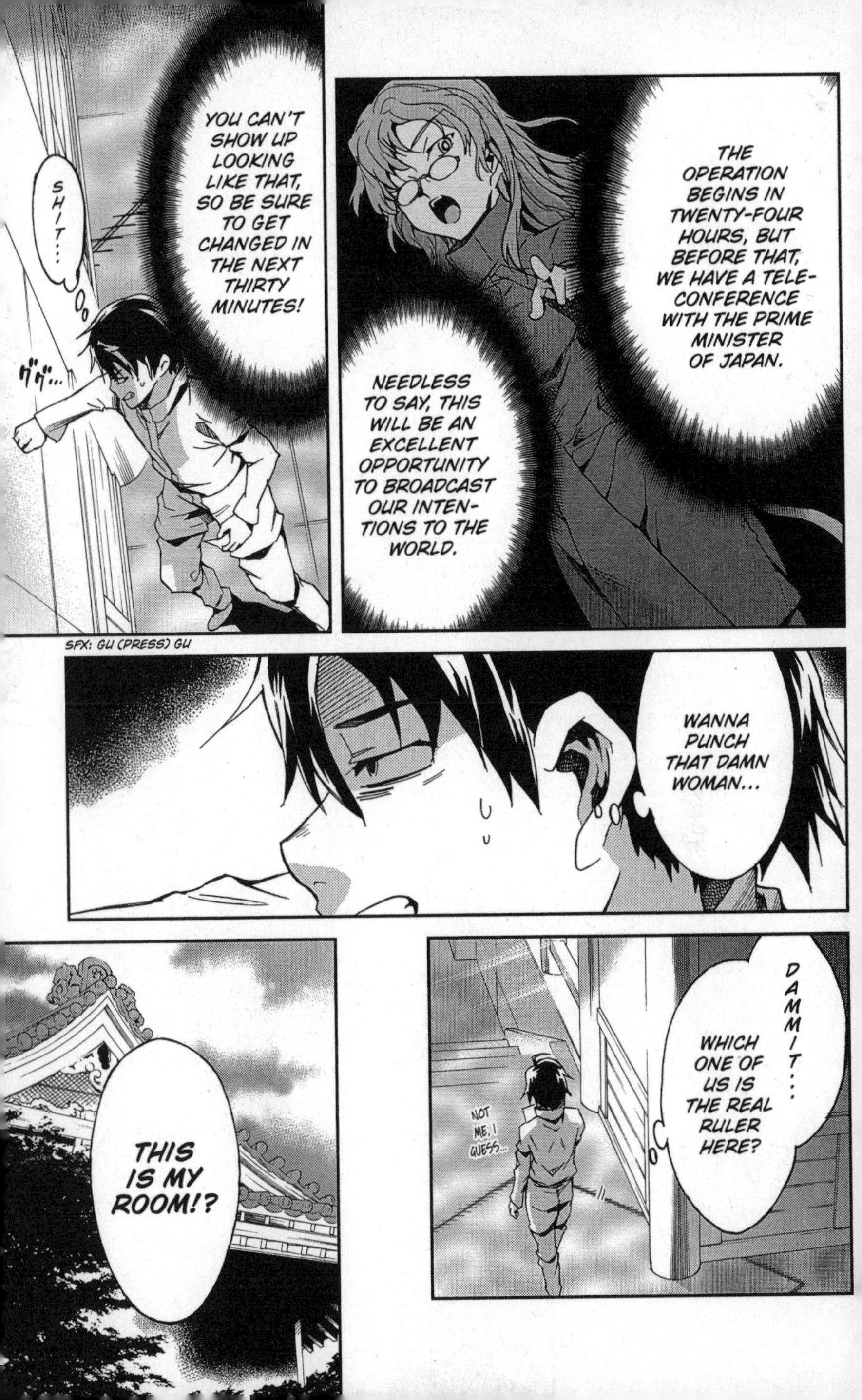
THE OPERATION BEGINS IN TWENTY-FOUR HOURS, BUT BEFORE THAT, WE HAVE A TELE-CONFERENCE WITH THE PRIME MINISTER OF JAPAN.
NEEDLESS TO SAY, THIS WILL BE AN EXCELLENT OPPORTUNITY TO BROADCAST OUR INTEN-TIONS TO THE WORLD.
YOU CAN'T SHOW UP LOOKING LIKE THAT, SO BE SURE TO GET CHANGED IN THE NEXT THIRTY MINUTES!
SHIT...
SFX: GU (PRESS) GU
WANNA PUNCH THAT DAMN WOMAN...
DAMMIT...
WHICH ONE OF US IS THE REAL RULER HERE?
NOT ME, I GUESS...
THIS IS MY ROOM!?

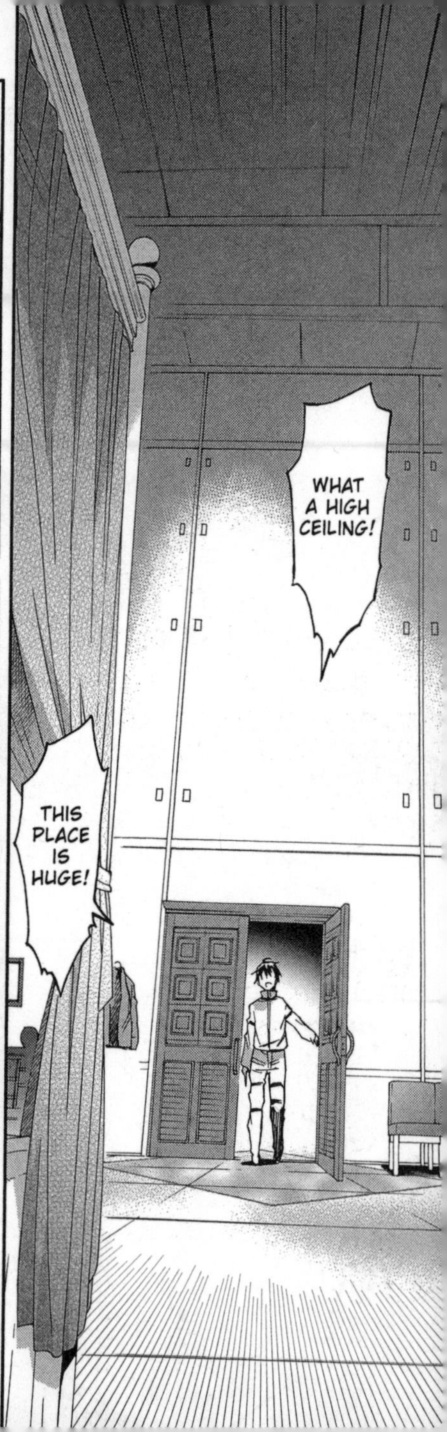
WHAT A HIGH CEILING!
THIS PLACE IS HUGE!
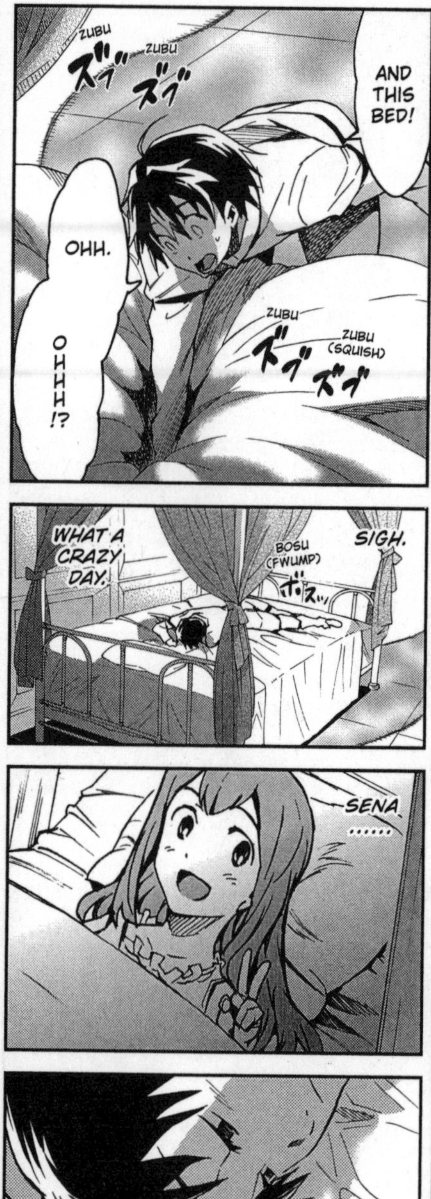
AND THIS BED!
ZUBU ZUBU
OHH.
OHHH!?
ZUBU ZUBU (SQUISH)
SIGH.
BOSU (FWUMP)
WHAT A CRAZY DAY.
SENA .......

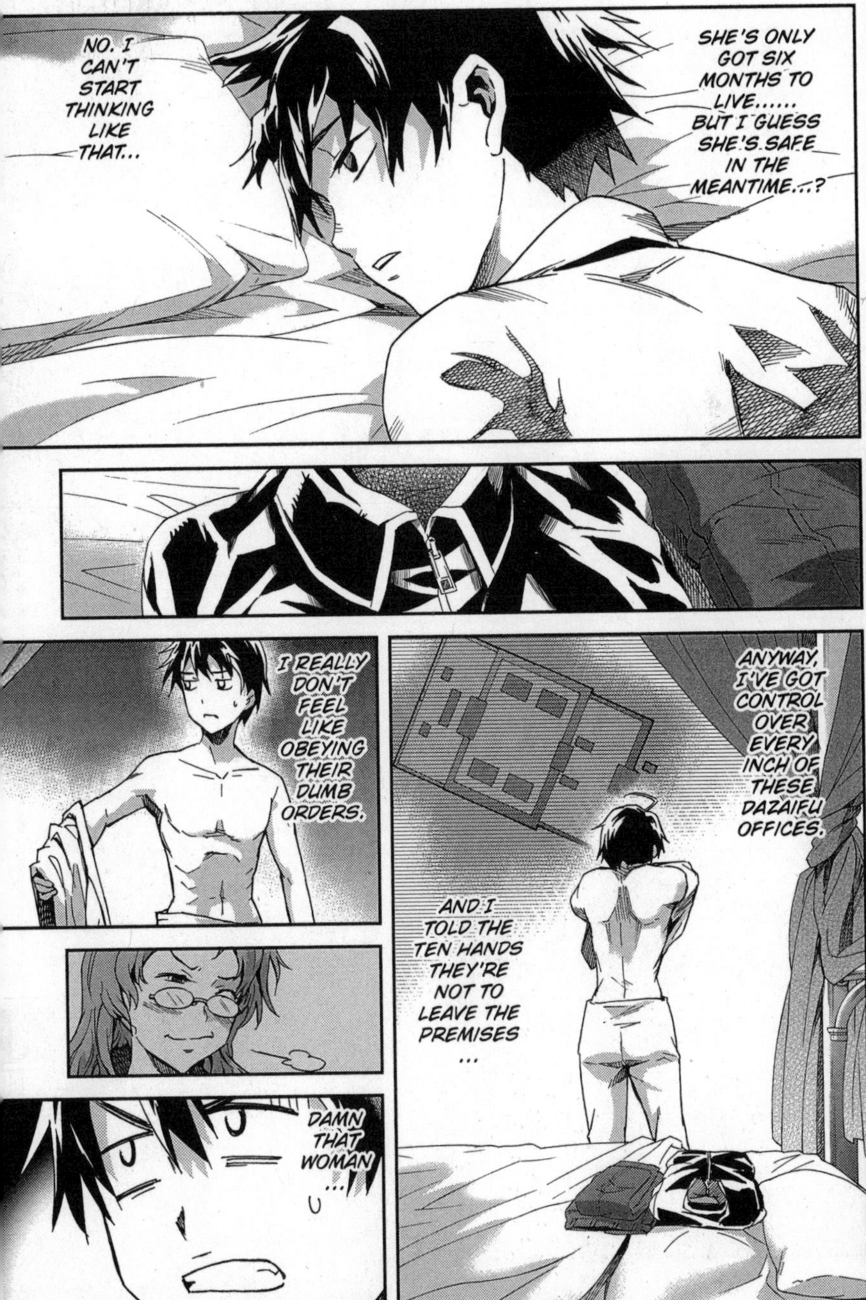
SHE'S ONLY GOT SIX MONTHS TO LIVE...... BUT I GUESS SHE'S SAFE IN THE MEANTIME...?
NO. I CAN'T START THINKING LIKE THAT...
ANYWAY, I'VE GOT CONTROL OVER EVERY INCH OF THESE DAZAIFU OFFICES.
AND I TOLD THE TEN HANDS THEY'RE NOT TO LEAVE THE PREMISES ...
I REALLY DON'T FEEL LIKE OBEYING THEIR DUMB ORDERS.
DAMN THAT WOMAN ...

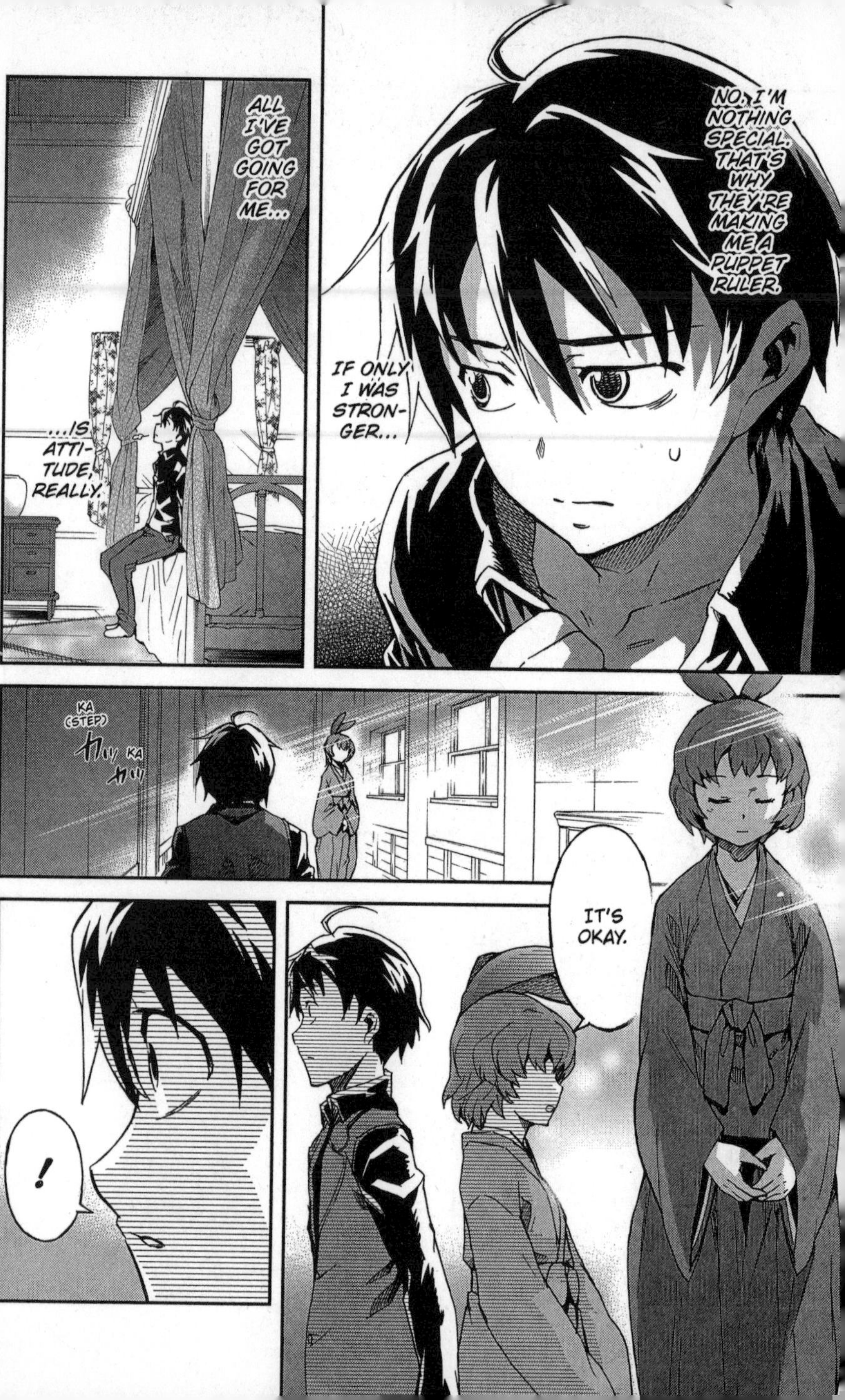

NO, I'M NOTHING SPECIAL. THAT'S WHY THEY'RE MAKING ME A PUPPET RULER.
IF ONLY I WAS STRONGER...
ALL I'VE GOT GOING FOR ME...
...IS ATTITUDE, REALLY.
KA (STEP)
KA
IT'S OKAY.
!

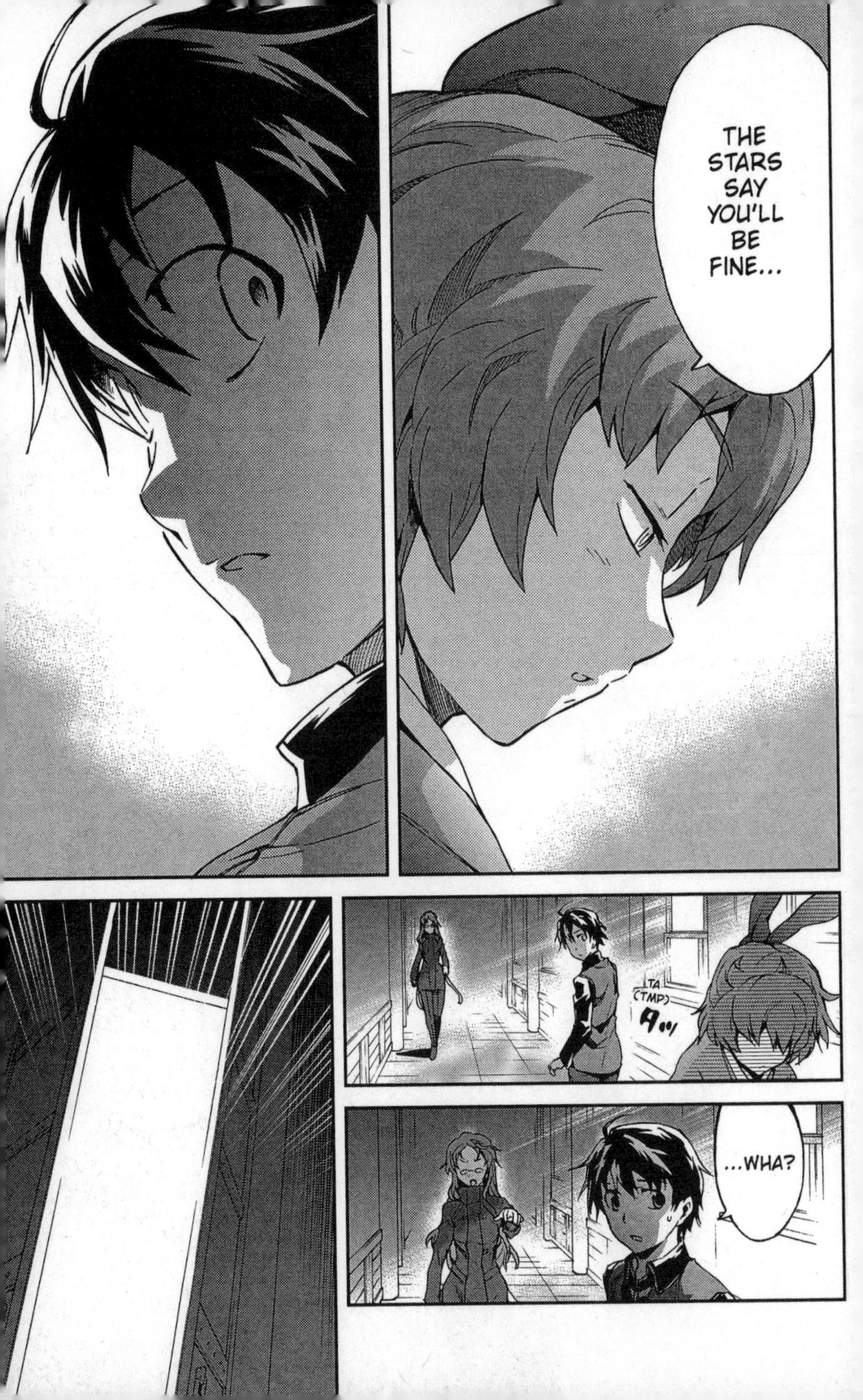
THE STARS SAY YOU'LL BE FINE...
TA (TMP)
...WHA?

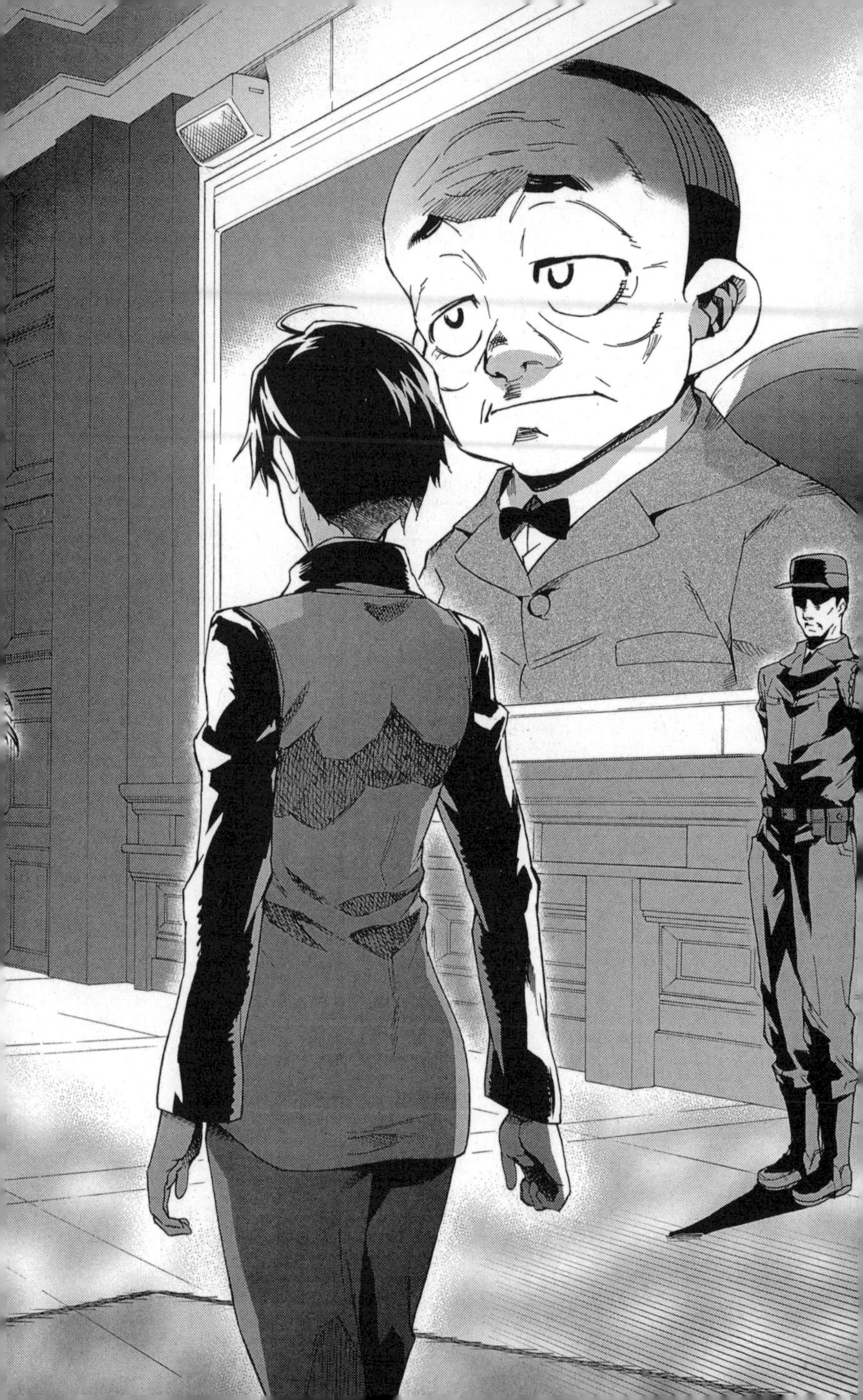

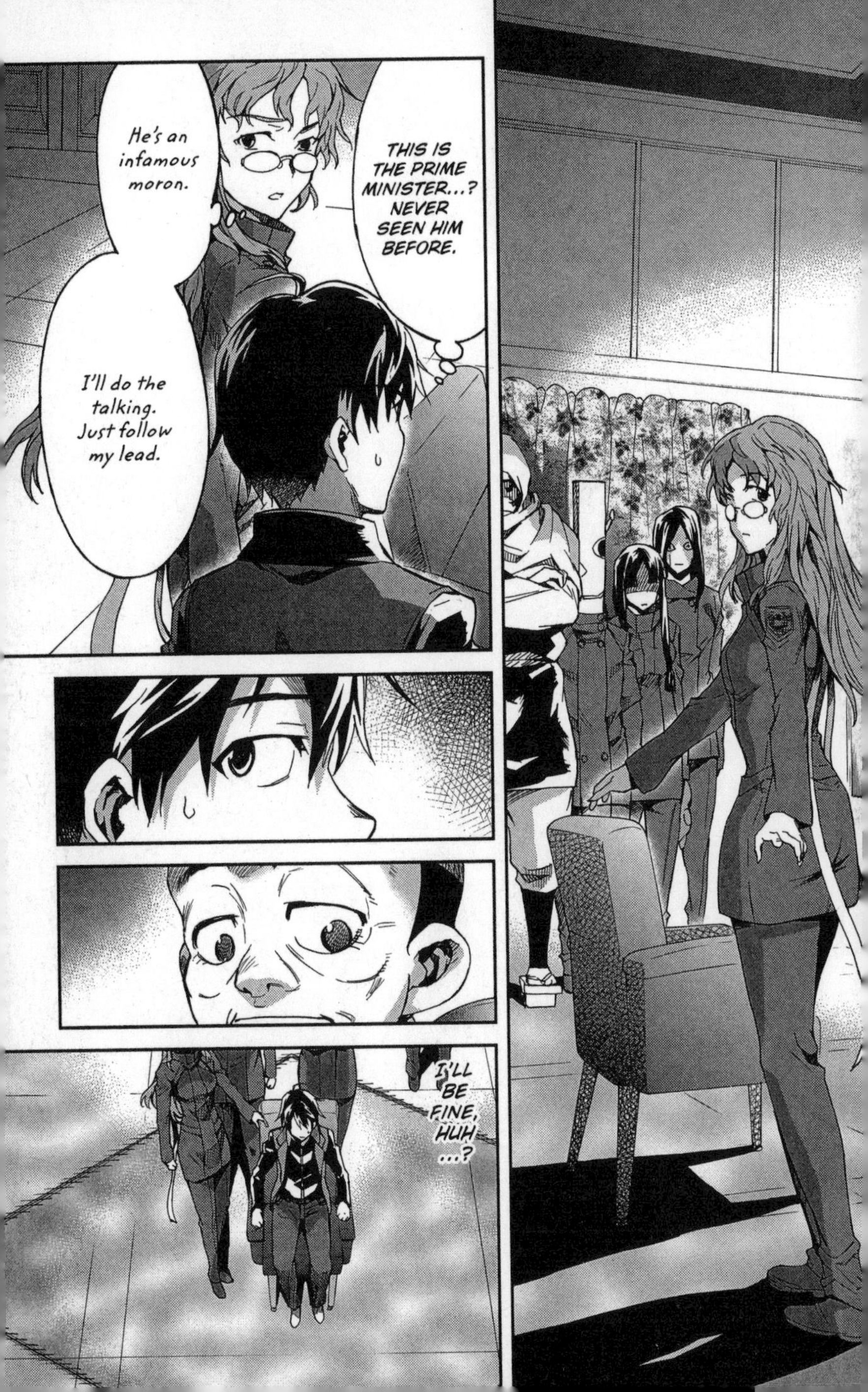
THIS IS THE PRIME MINISTER...? NEVER SEEN HIM BEFORE.
He's an infamous moron.
I'll do the talking. Just follow my lead.
I'LL BE FINE, HUH...?

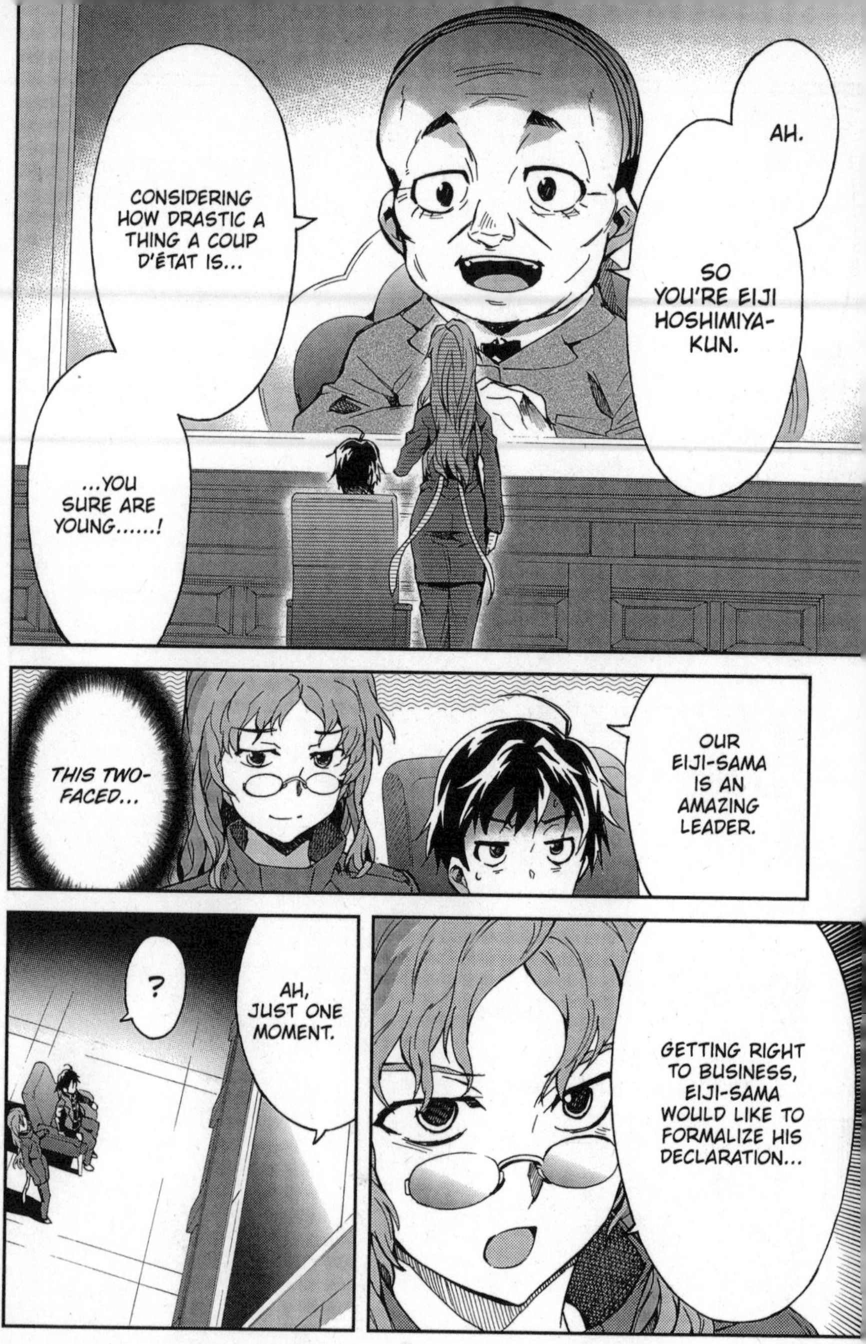
AH.
SO YOU'RE EIJI HOSHIMIYA-KUN.
CONSIDERING HOW DRASTIC A THING A COUP D'ÉTAT IS...
...YOU SURE ARE YOUNG......!
OUR EIJI-SAMA IS AN AMAZING LEADER.
THIS TWO-FACED...
GETTING RIGHT TO BUSINESS, EIJI-SAMA WOULD LIKE TO FORMALIZE HIS DECLARATION...
AH, JUST ONE MOMENT.
?

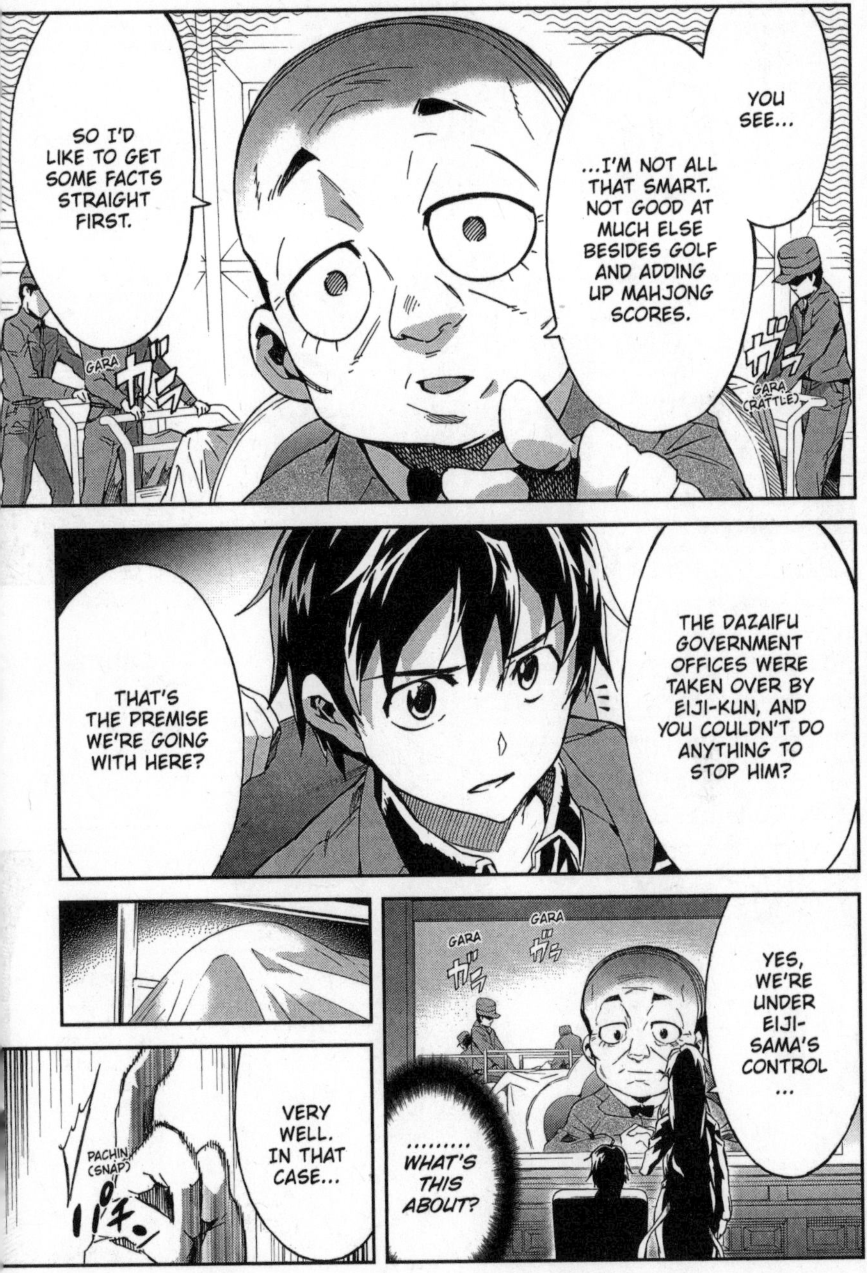
YOU SEE...
...I'M NOT ALL THAT SMART. NOT GOOD AT MUCH ELSE BESIDES GOLF AND ADDING UP MAHJONG SCORES.
GARA (RATTLE)
SO I'D LIKE TO GET SOME FACTS STRAIGHT FIRST.
GARA
THE DAZAIFU GOVERNMENT OFFICES WERE TAKEN OVER BY EIJI-KUN, AND YOU COULDN'T DO ANYTHING TO STOP HIM?
THAT'S THE PREMISE WE'RE GOING WITH HERE?
YES, WE'RE UNDER EIJI-SAMA'S CONTROL ...
GARA
GARA
.......... WHAT'S THIS ABOUT?
VERY WELL. IN THAT CASE...
PACHIN (SNAP)

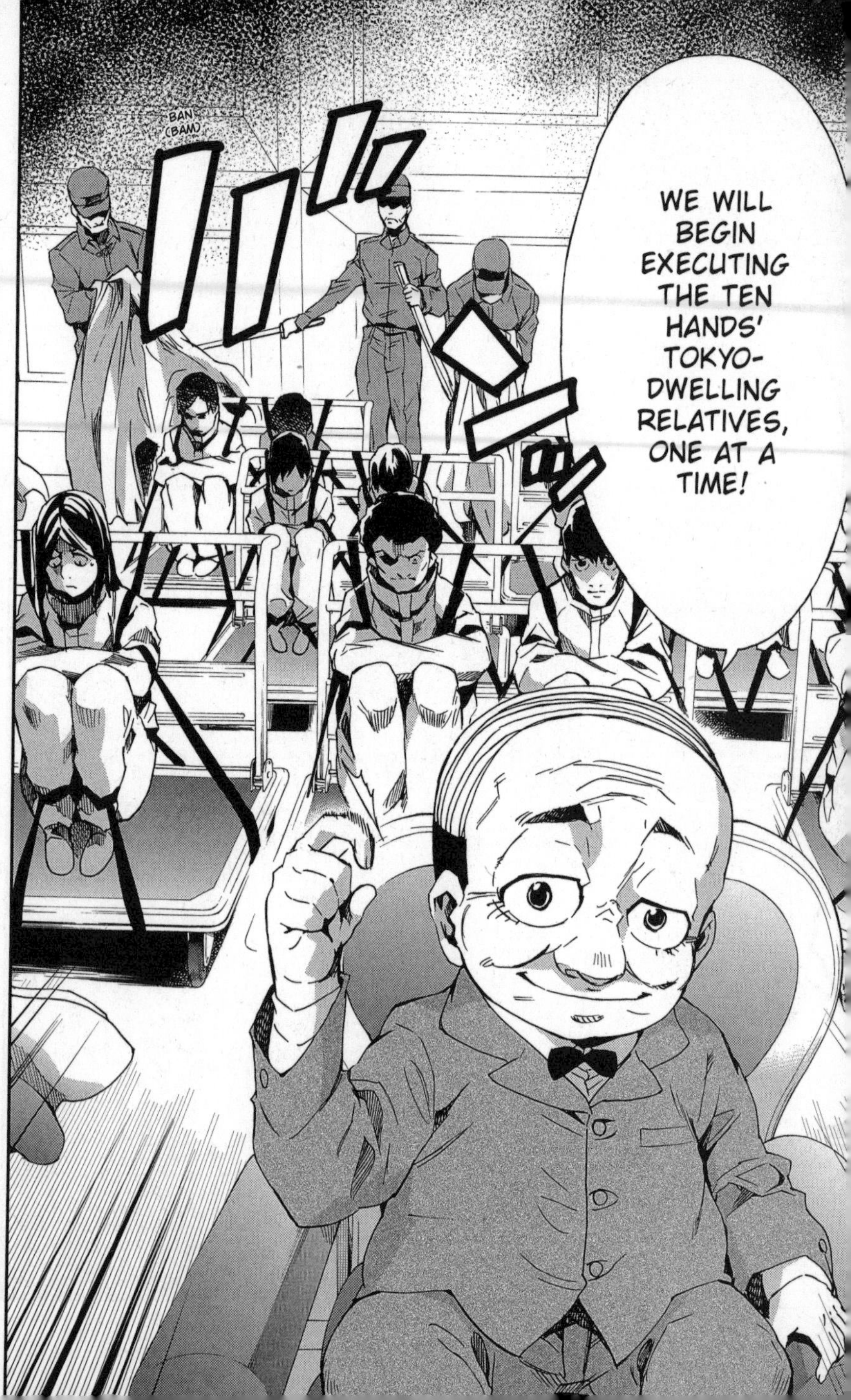
BAN (BAM)
WE WILL BEGIN EXECUTING THE TEN HANDS' TOKYO-DWELLING RELATIVES, ONE AT A TIME!

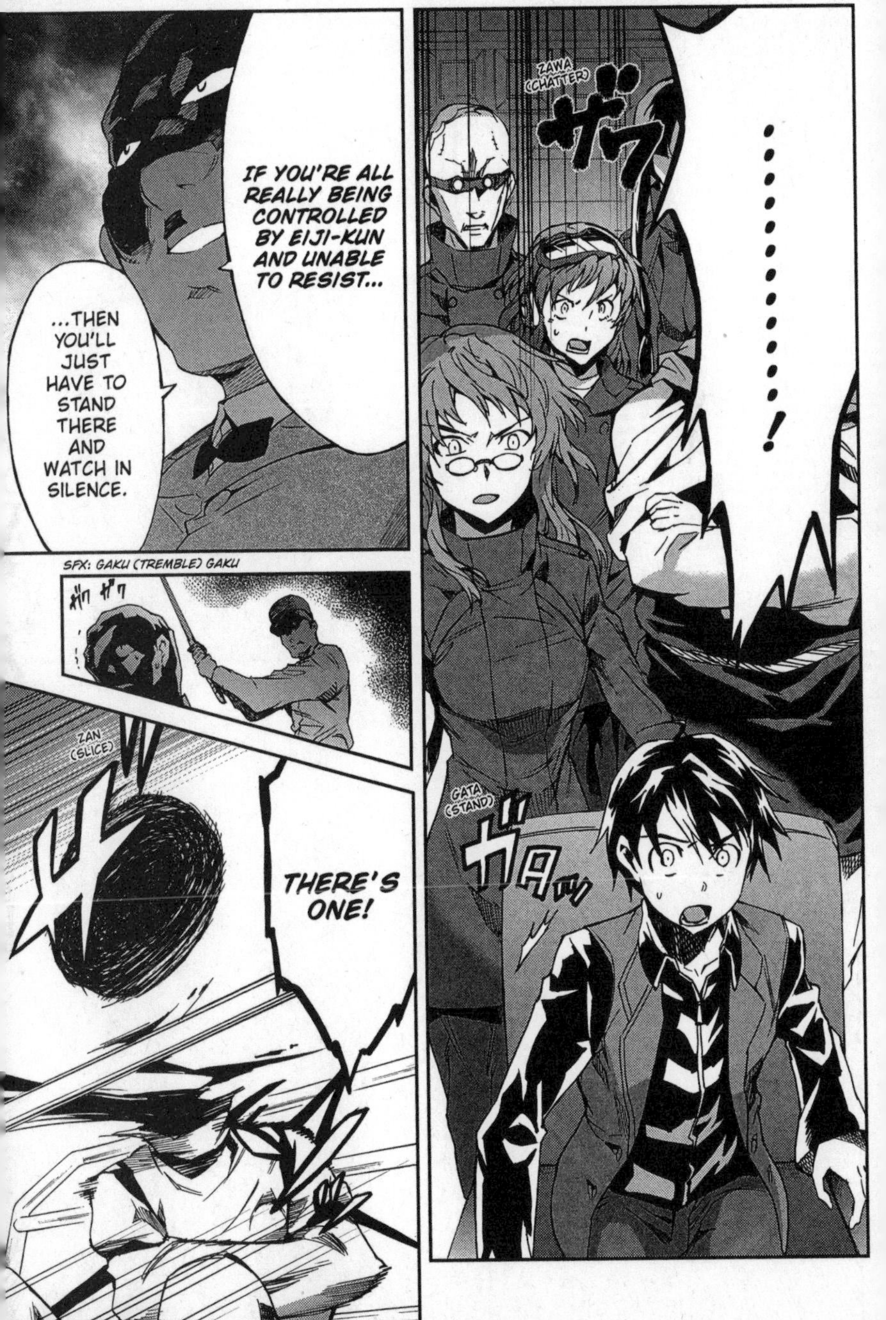
ZAWA (CHATTER)
..........!
GATA (STAND)
IF YOU'RE ALL REALLY BEING CONTROLLED BY EIJI-KUN AND UNABLE TO RESIST...
...THEN YOU'LL JUST HAVE TO STAND THERE AND WATCH IN SILENCE.
SFX: GAKU (TREMBLE) GAKU
ZAN (SLICE)
THERE'S ONE!

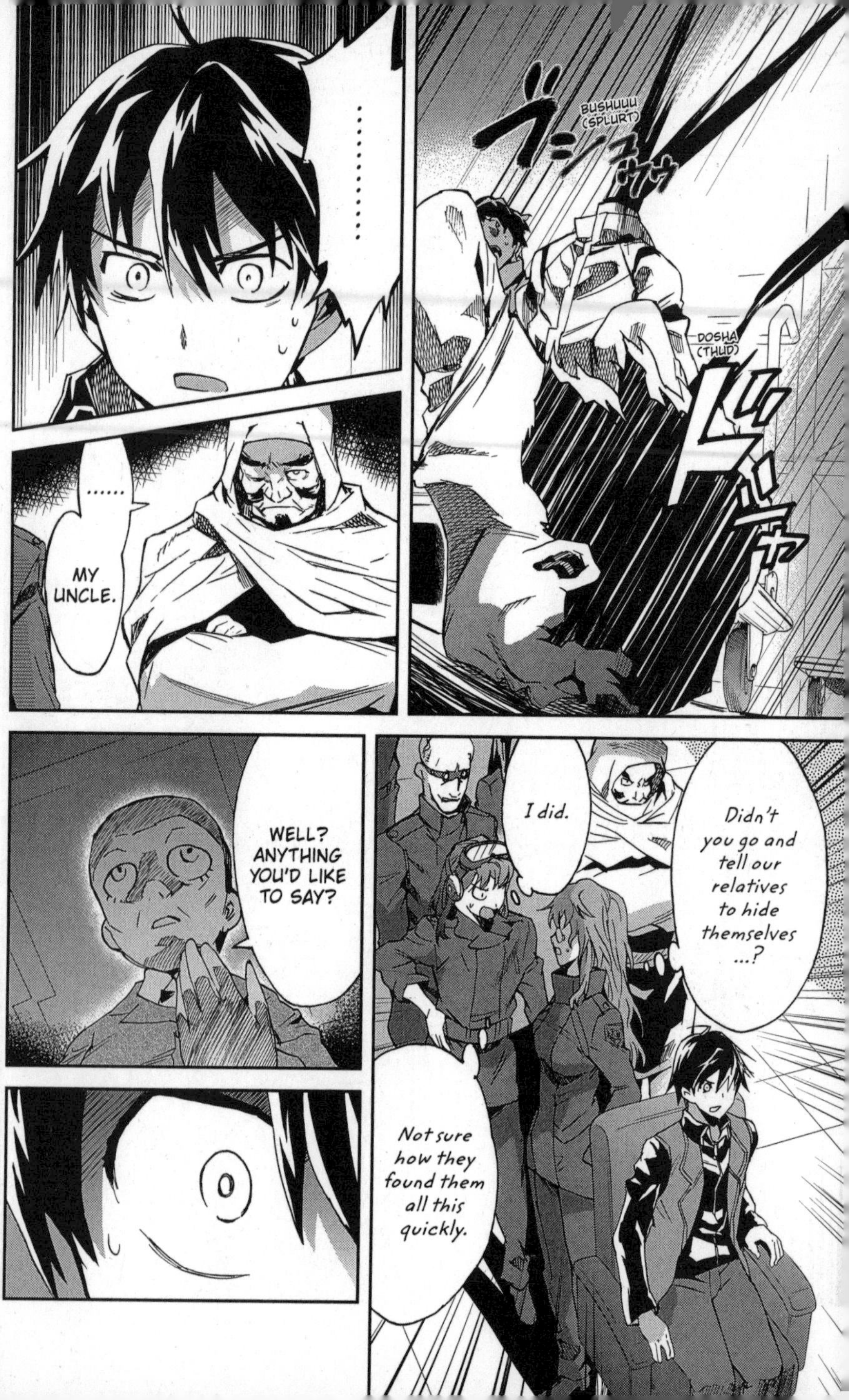
BUSHUUU (SPLURT)
DOSHA (THUD)
......
...... MY UNCLE.
Didn't you go and tell our relatives to hide themselves ...?
I did.
Not sure how they found them all this quickly.
WELL? ANYTHING YOU'D LIKE TO SAY?

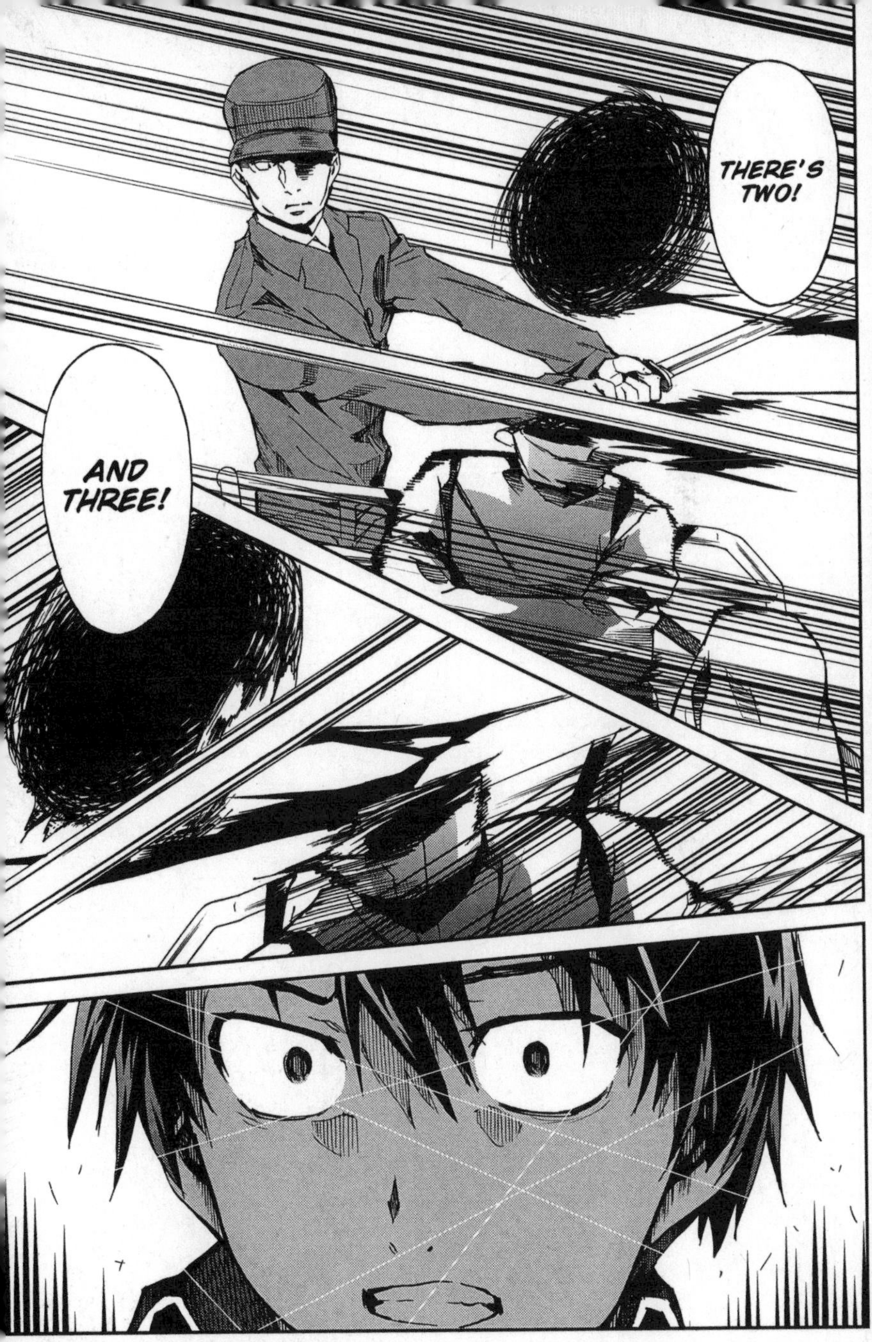
THERE'S TWO!
AND THREE!

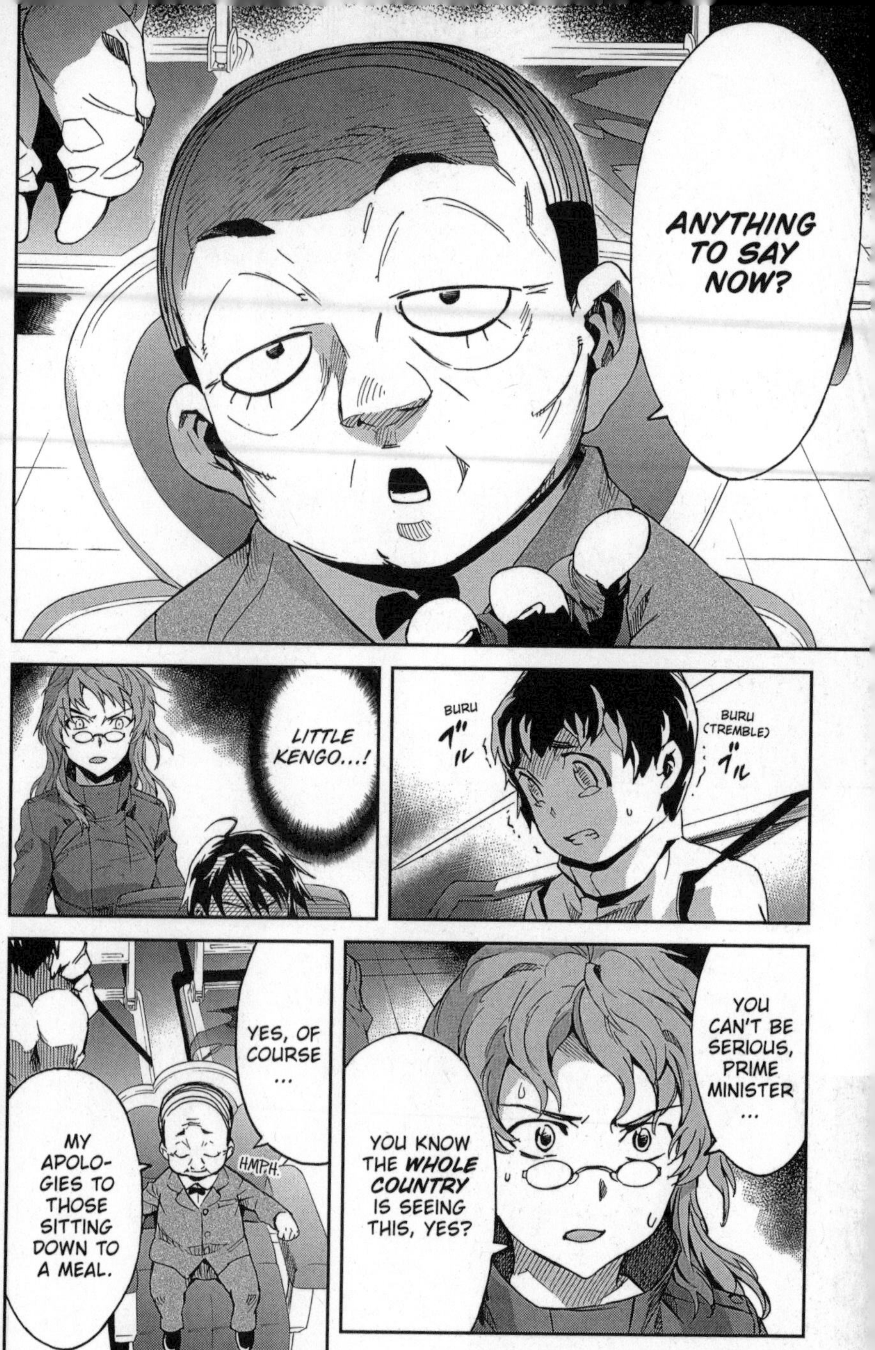
ANYTHING TO SAY NOW?
BURU ブル
BURU (TREMBLE) ブル
LITTLE KENGO...!
YOU CAN'T BE SERIOUS, PRIME MINISTER...
YOU KNOW THE **WHOLE COUNTRY** IS SEEING THIS, YES?
YES, OF COURSE...
HMPH.
MY APOLOGIES TO THOSE SITTING DOWN TO A MEAL.

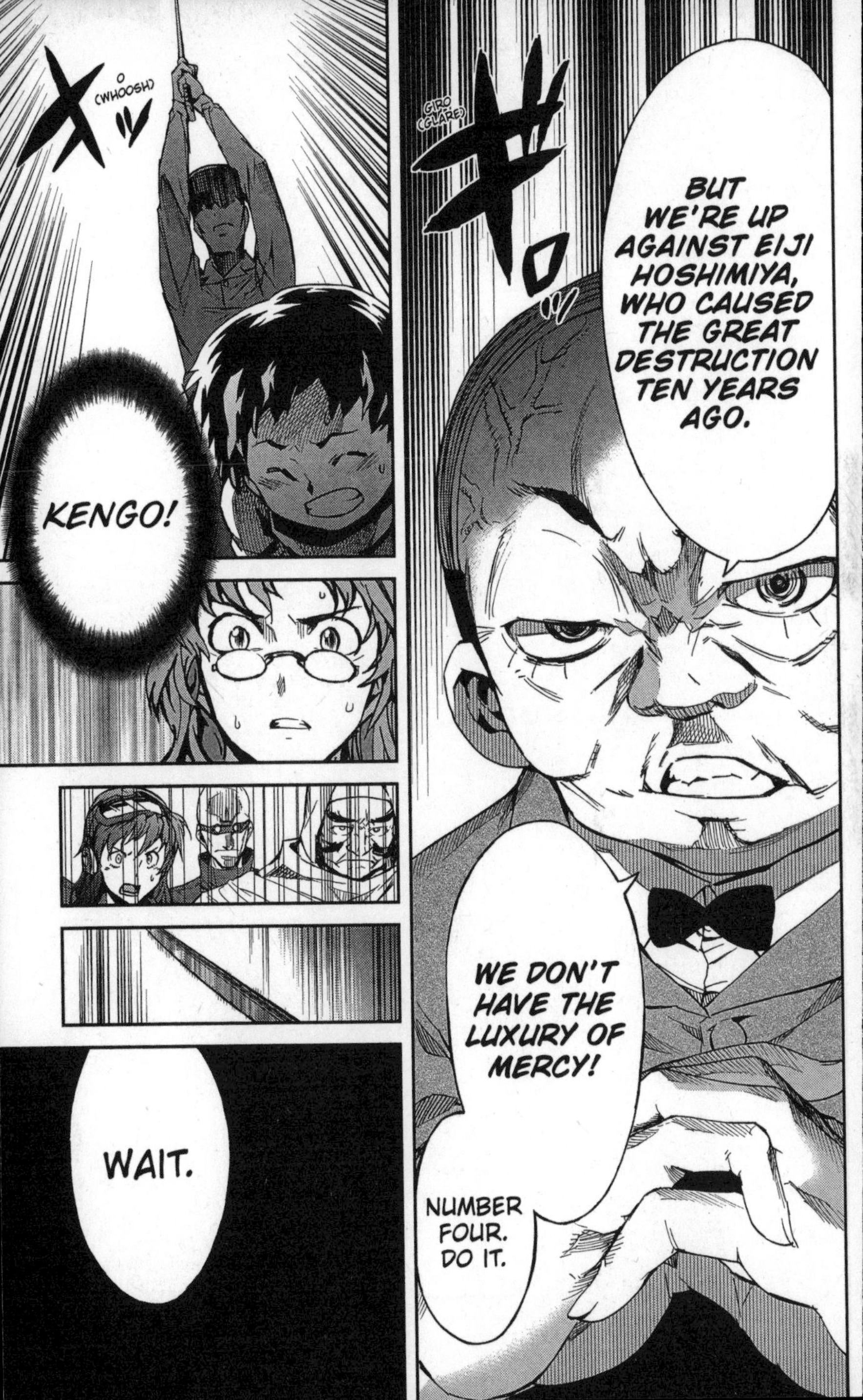
GIRO (GLARE)
BUT WE'RE UP AGAINST EIJI HOSHIMIYA, WHO CAUSED THE GREAT DESTRUCTION TEN YEARS AGO.
WE DON'T HAVE THE LUXURY OF MERCY!
NUMBER FOUR. DO IT.
O (WHOOSH)
KENGO!
WAIT.

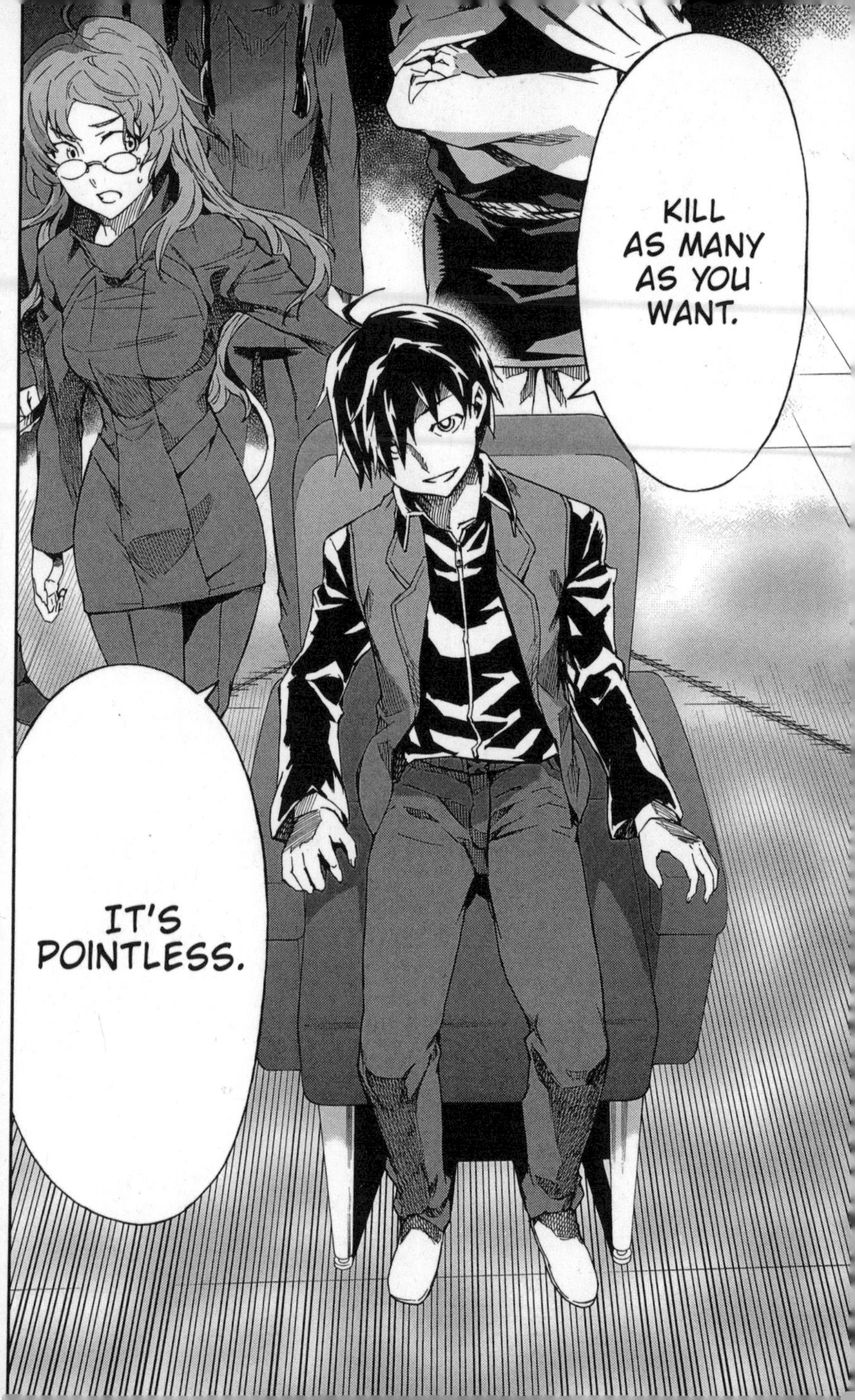
KILL AS MANY AS YOU WANT.
IT'S POINTLESS.

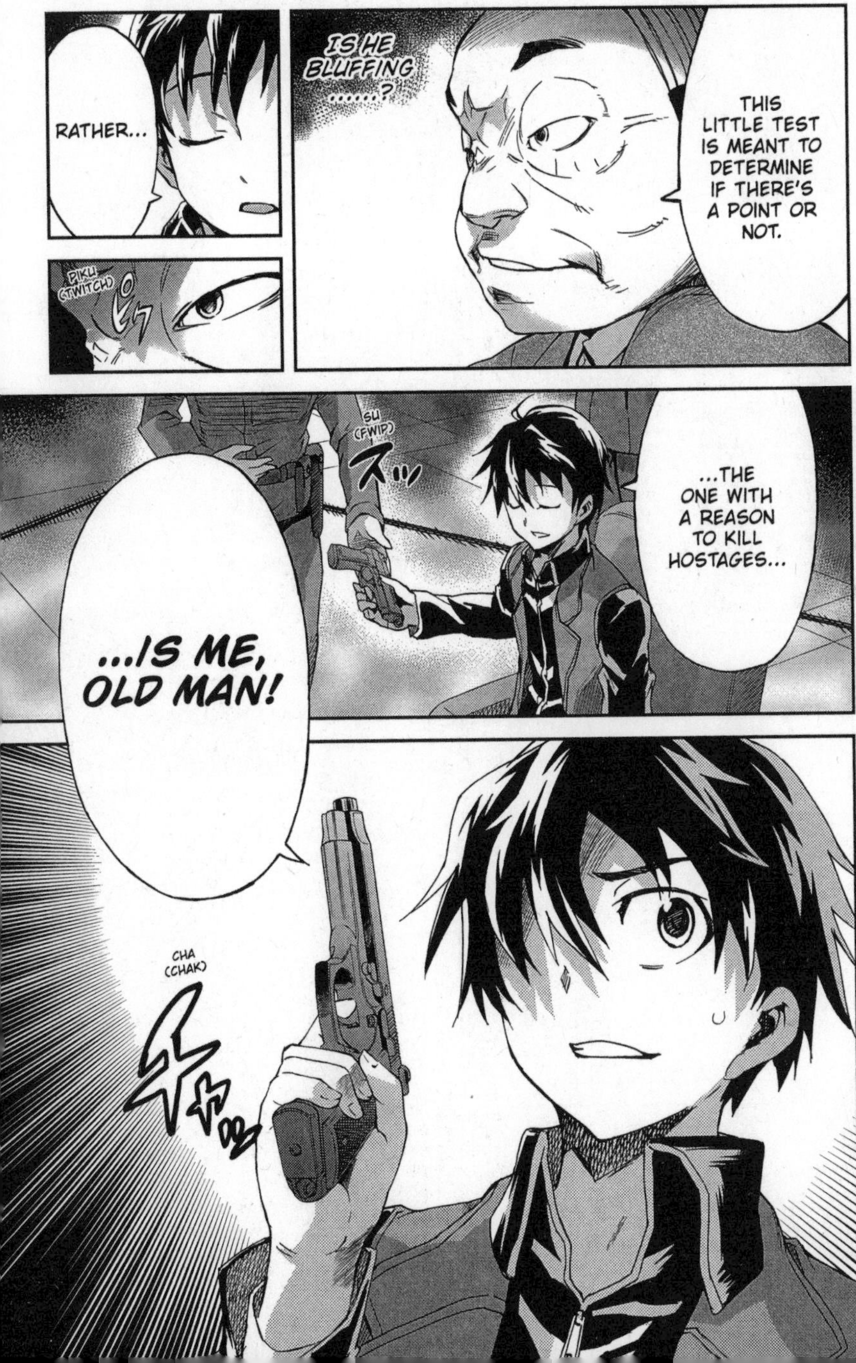
THIS LITTLE TEST IS MEANT TO DETERMINE IF THERE'S A POINT OR NOT.
IS HE BLUFFING ......?
RATHER...
PIKU (TWITCH)
...THE ONE WITH A REASON TO KILL HOSTAGES...
SU (FWIP)
...IS ME, OLD MAN!
CHA (CHAK)

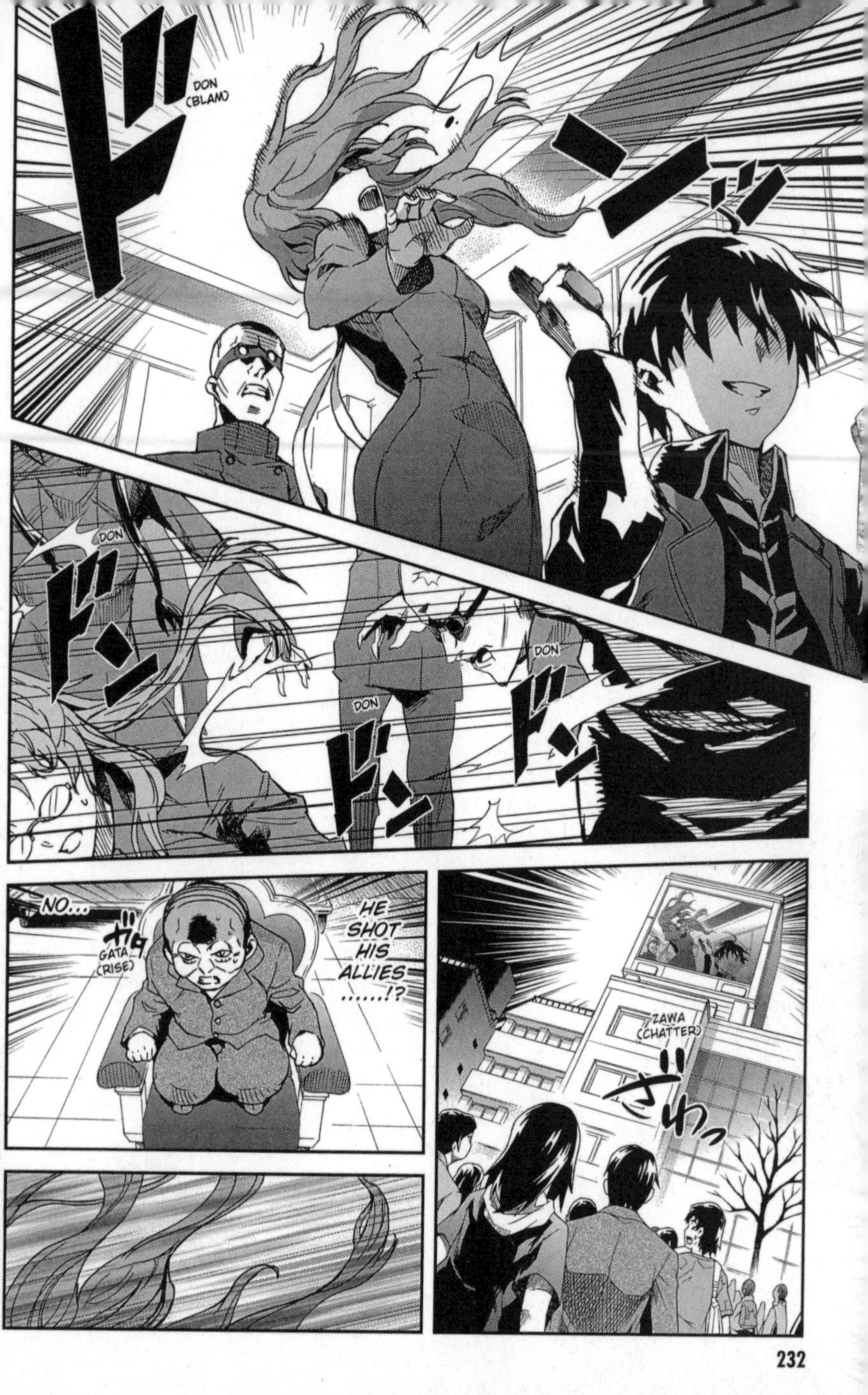
ドーン
DON (BLAM)
ドン
DON
ドン
DON
ドン
DON
ざわっ
ZAWA (CHATTER)
HE SHOT HIS ALLIES ......!?
ガタ
GATA (RISE)
NO...

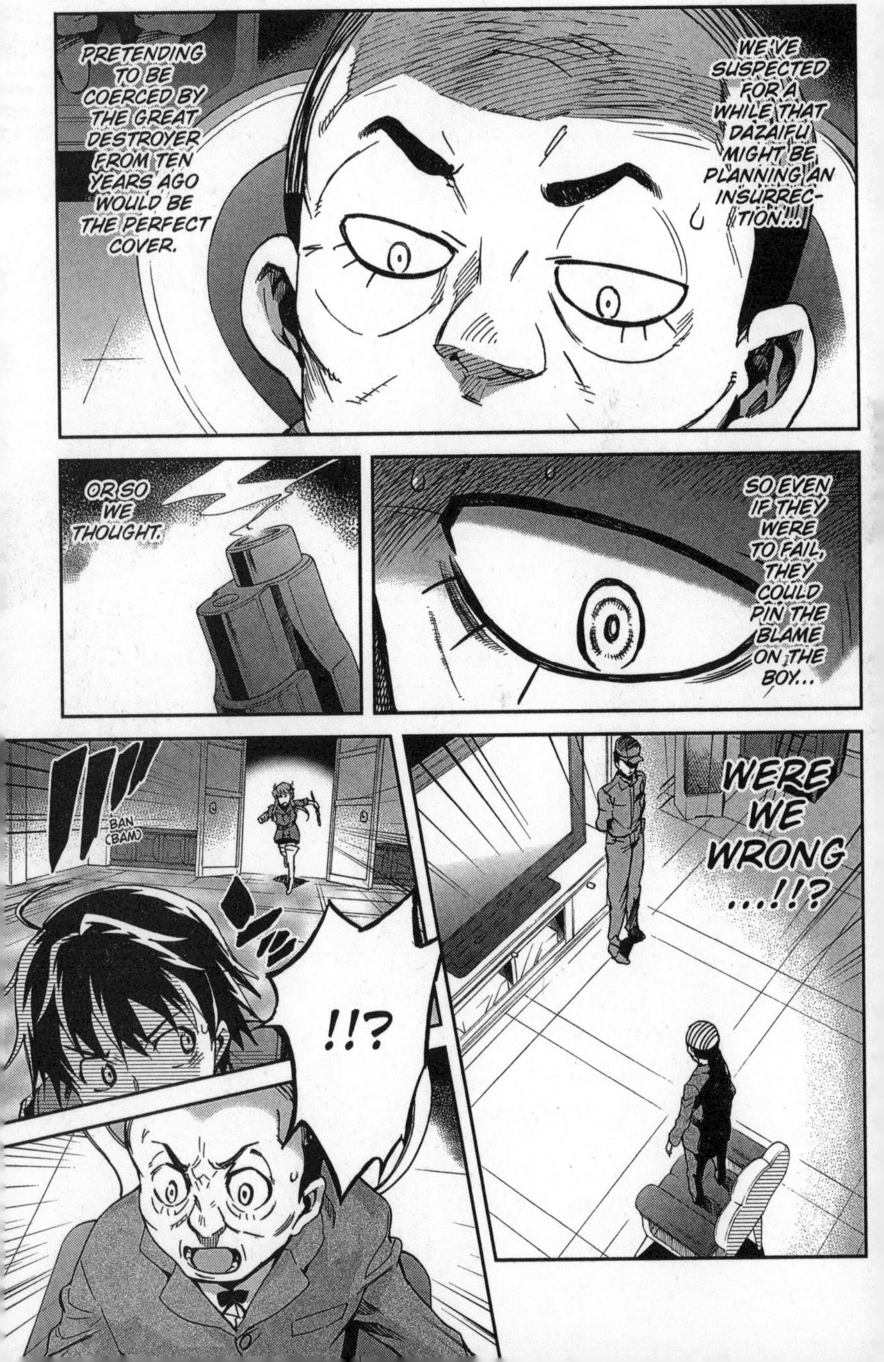
WE'VE SUSPECTED FOR A WHILE THAT DAZAIFU MIGHT BE PLANNING AN INSURRECTION...!
PRETENDING TO BE COERCED BY THE GREAT DESTROYER FROM TEN YEARS AGO WOULD BE THE PERFECT COVER.
SO EVEN IF THEY WERE TO FAIL, THEY COULD PIN THE BLAME ON THE BOY...
OR SO WE THOUGHT.
WERE WE WRONG ...!!?
BAN (BAM)
!!?

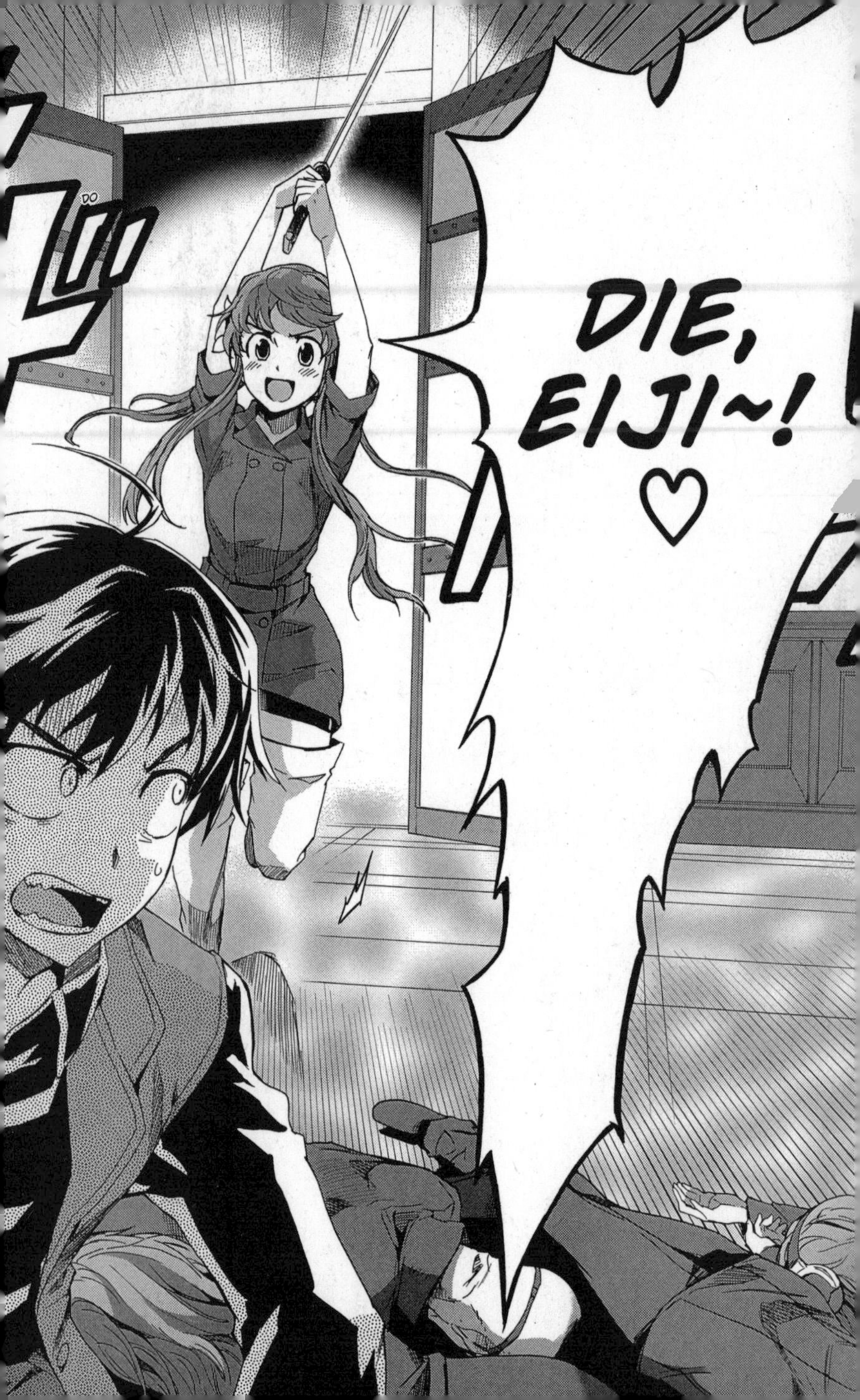
DO
DIE, EIJI~! ♡

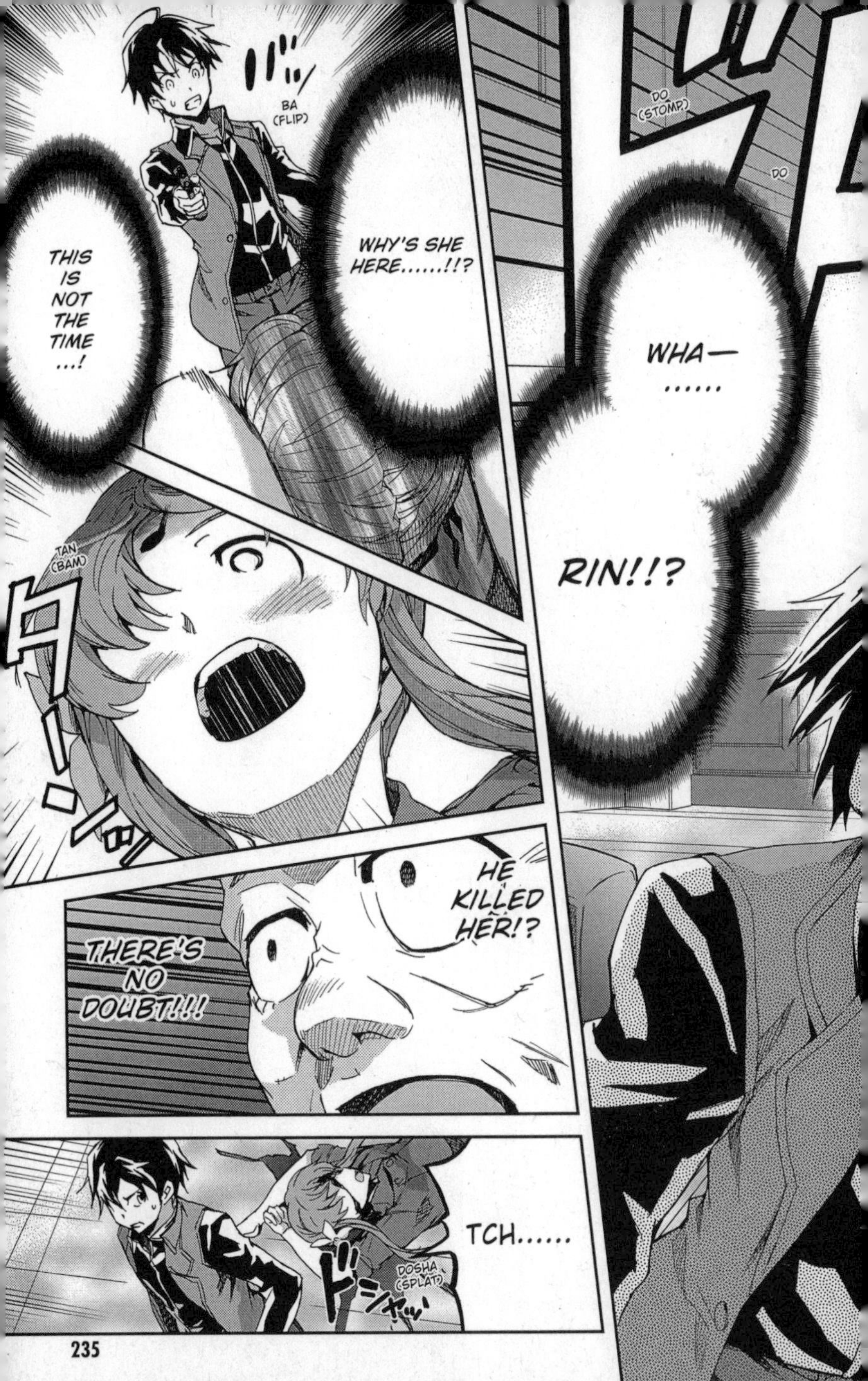
DO (STOMP)
DO
WHA— ......
RIN!!?
BA (FLIP)
WHY'S SHE HERE......!!?
THIS IS NOT THE TIME ...!
TAN (BAM)
HE KILLED HER!?
THERE'S NO DOUBT!!!
TCH......
DOSHA (SPLAT)

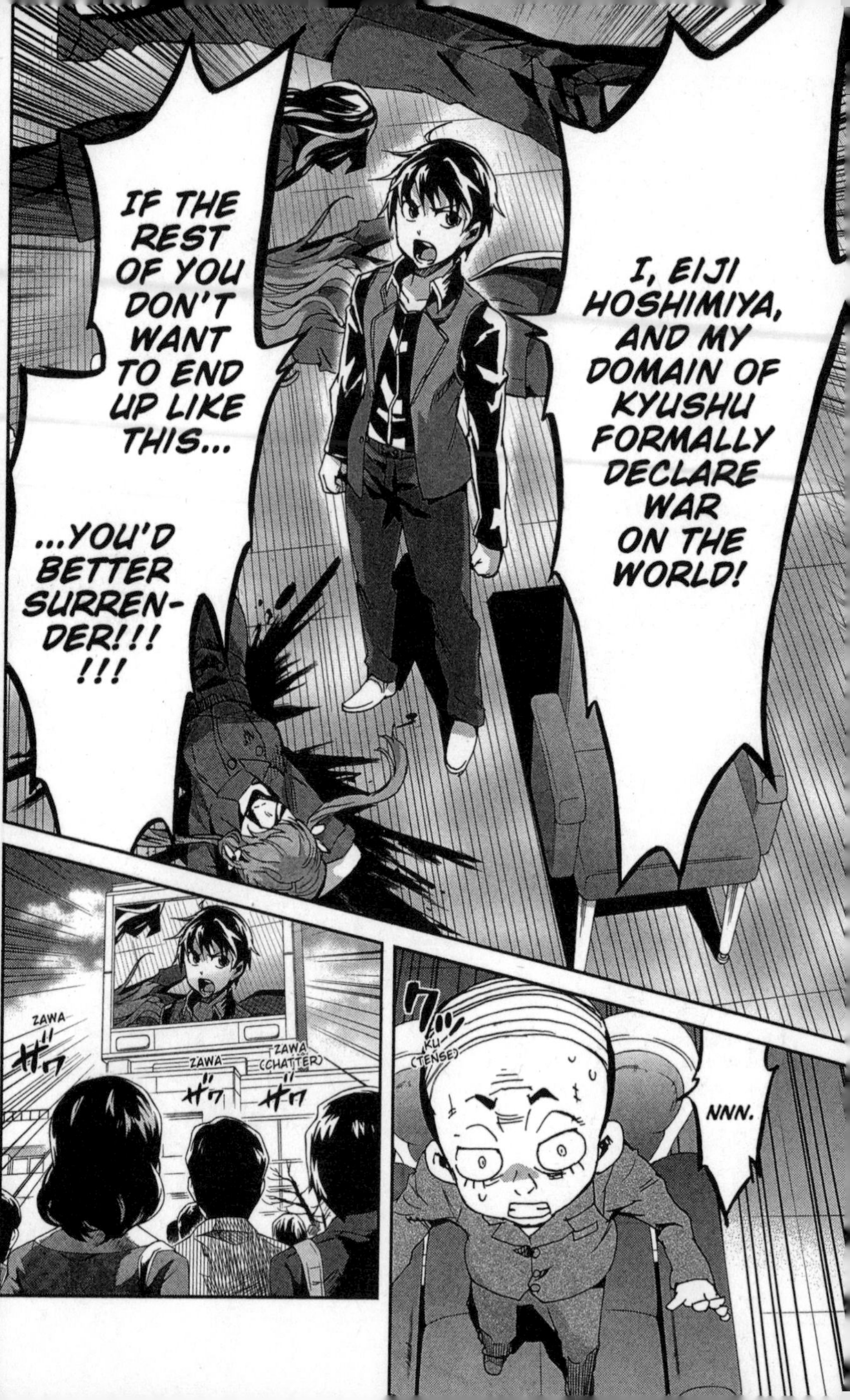
I, EIJI HOSHIMIYA, AND MY DOMAIN OF KYUSHU FORMALLY DECLARE WAR ON THE WORLD!
IF THE REST OF YOU DON'T WANT TO END UP LIKE THIS...
...YOU'D BETTER SURREN-DER!!! !!!
KU (TENSE)
NNN.
ZAWA
ZAWA
ZAWA (CHATTER)

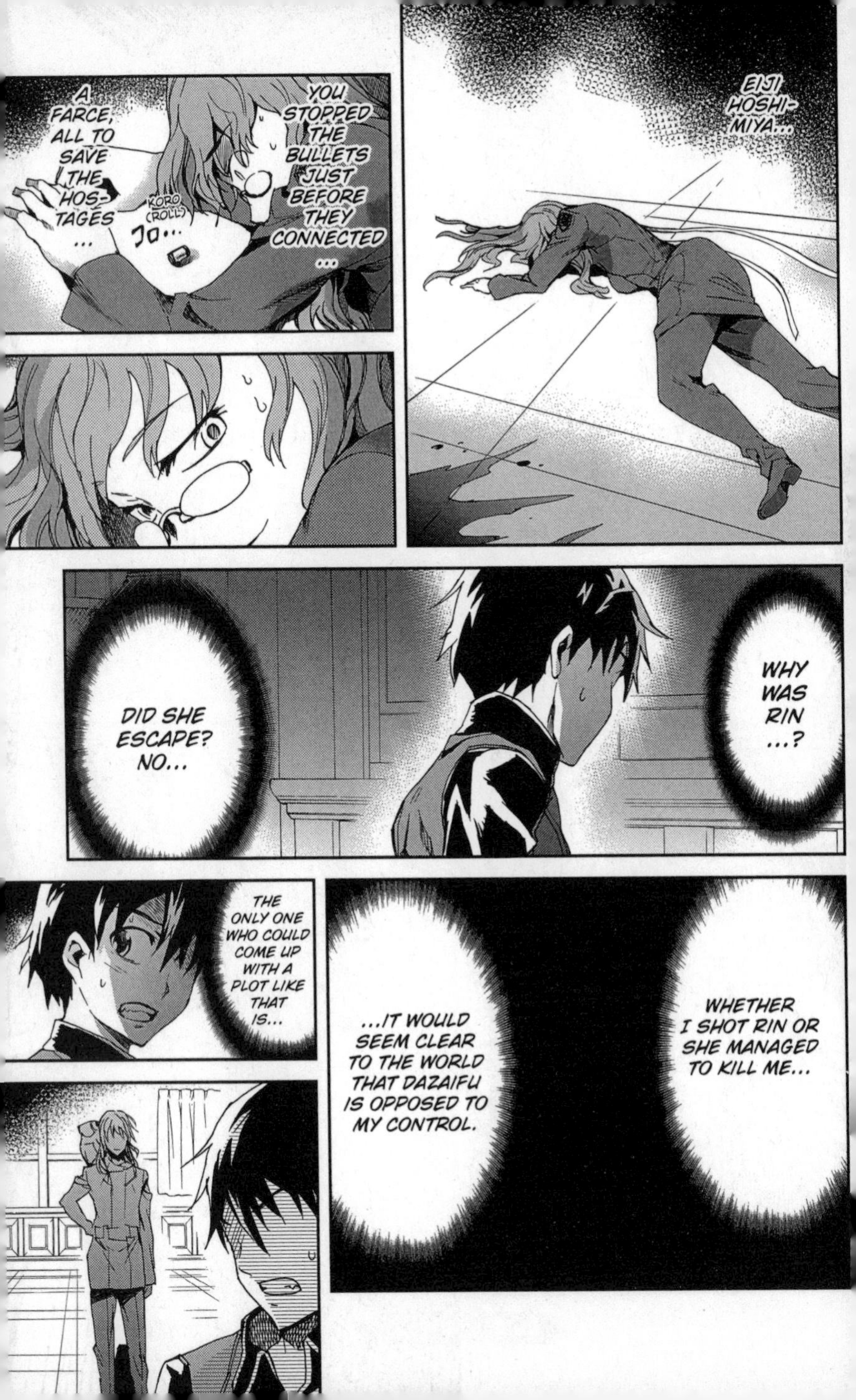
EIJI HOSHIMIYA...
YOU STOPPED THE BULLETS JUST BEFORE THEY CONNECTED...
KORO (ROLL)
コロ...
A FARCE, ALL TO SAVE THE HOSTAGES...
WHY WAS RIN...?
DID SHE ESCAPE? NO...
WHETHER I SHOT RIN OR SHE MANAGED TO KILL ME...
...IT WOULD SEEM CLEAR TO THE WORLD THAT DAZAIFU IS OPPOSED TO MY CONTROL.
THE ONLY ONE WHO COULD COME UP WITH A PLOT LIKE THAT IS...

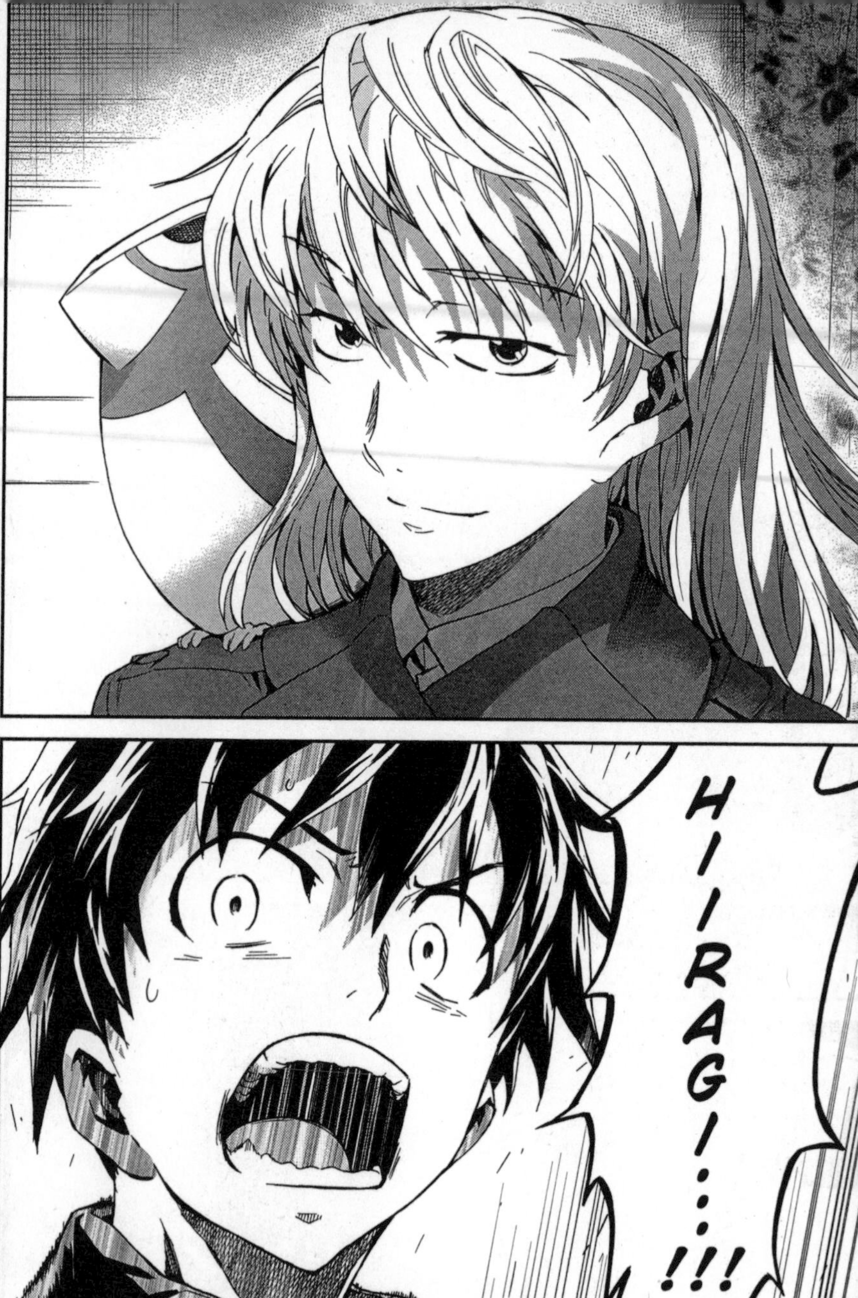
HIIRAGI...!!!

Subject 5: END

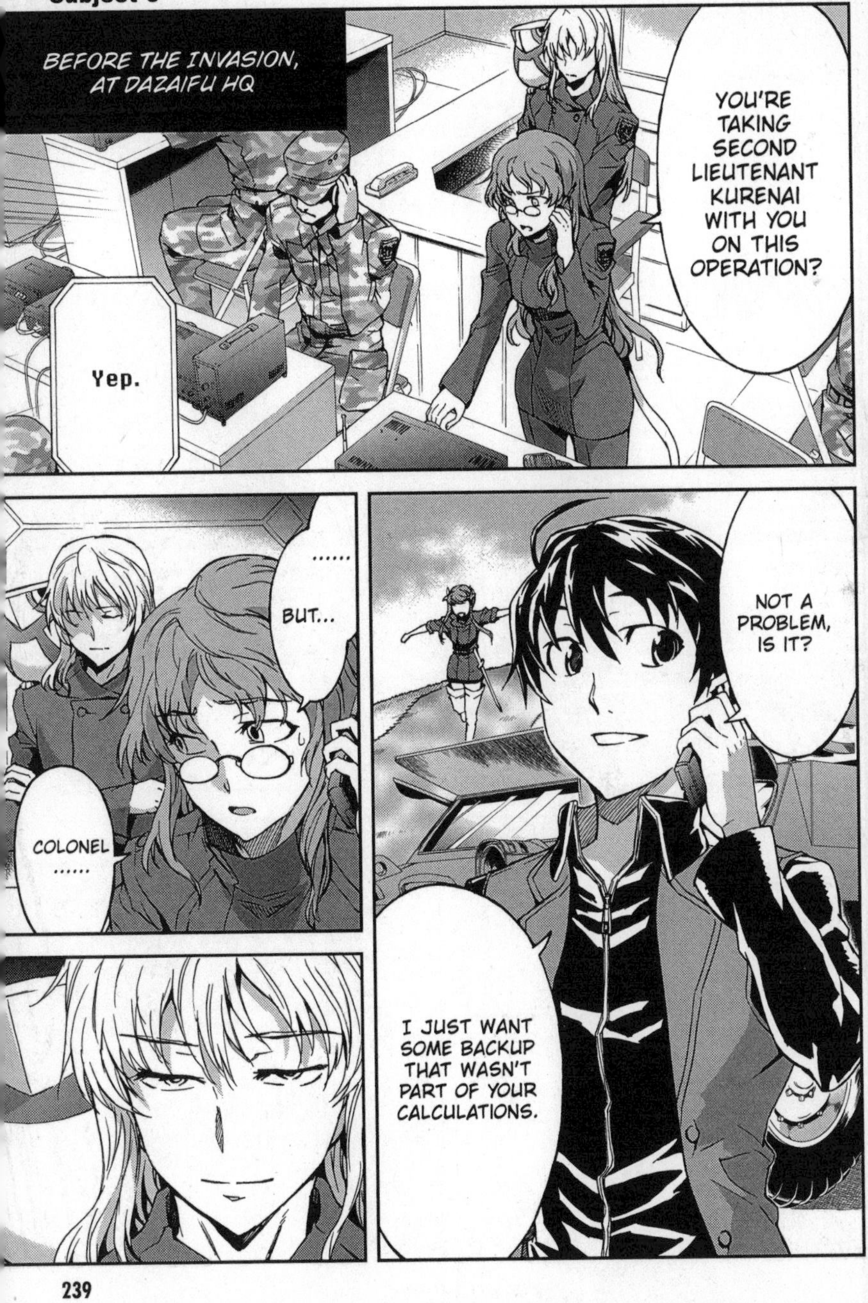
YOU'RE TAKING SECOND LIEUTENANT KURENAI WITH YOU ON THIS OPERATION?
BEFORE THE INVASION, AT DAZAIFU HQ
Yep.
NOT A PROBLEM, IS IT?
I JUST WANT SOME BACKUP THAT WASN'T PART OF YOUR CALCULATIONS.
......
BUT...
COLONEL ......

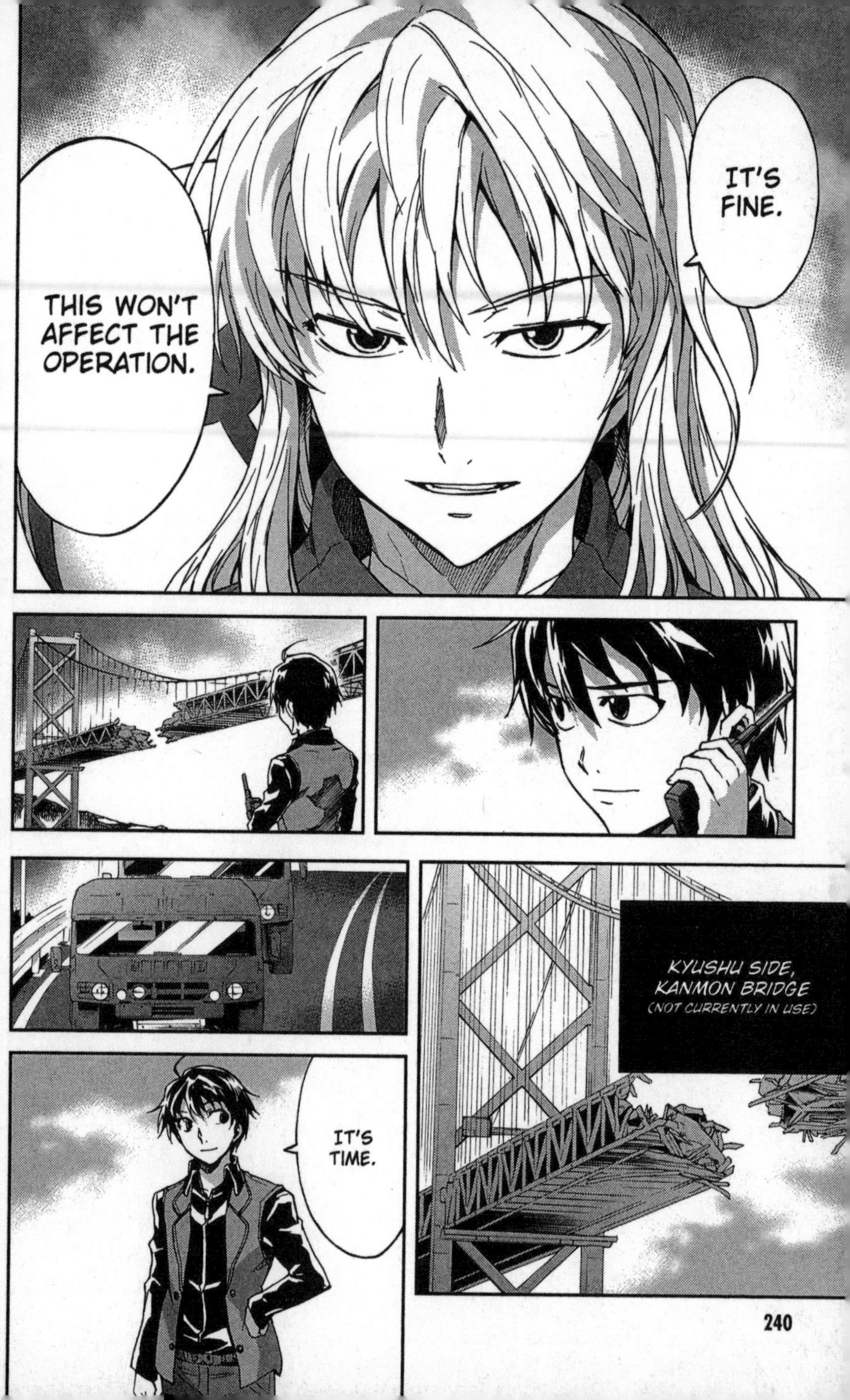
IT'S FINE.
THIS WON'T AFFECT THE OPERATION.
KYUSHU SIDE, KANMON BRIDGE (NOT CURRENTLY IN USE)
IT'S TIME.

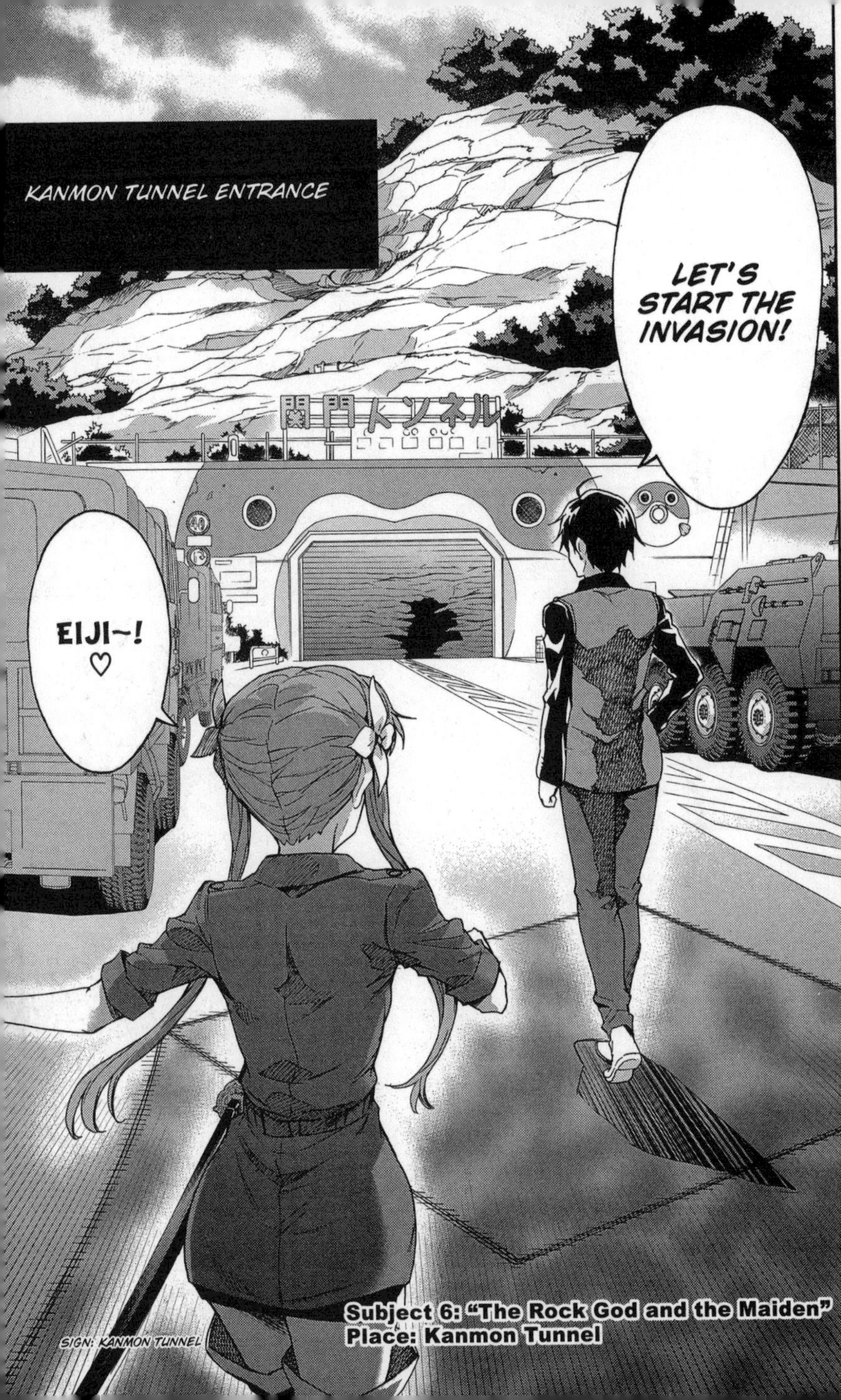
LET'S START THE INVASION!
KANMON TUNNEL ENTRANCE
関門トンネル
EIJI~! ♡
Subject 6: "The Rock God and the Maiden"
Place: Kanmon Tunnel
SIGN: KANMON TUNNEL

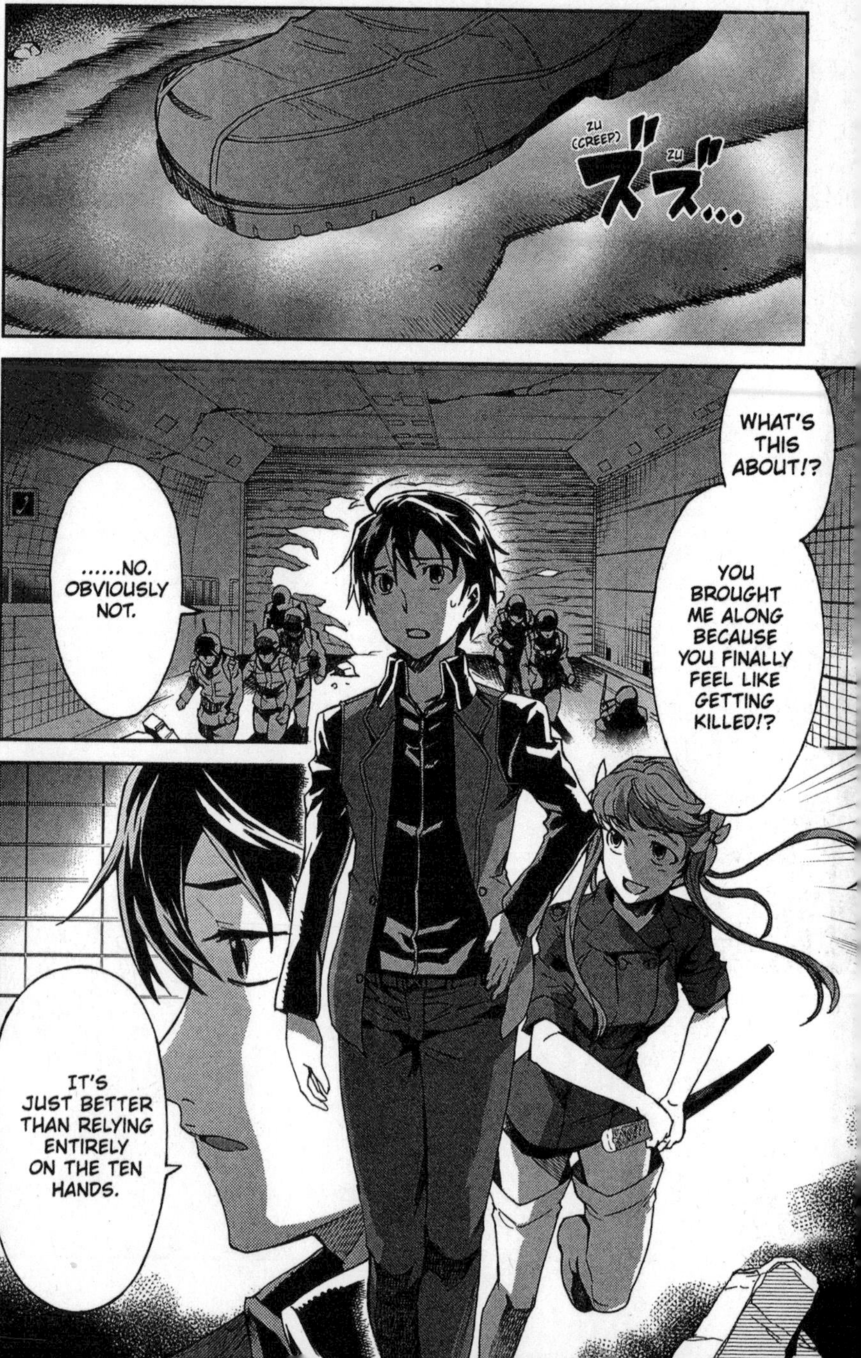
ZU (CREEP) ZU
ズズ...
WHAT'S THIS ABOUT!?
YOU BROUGHT ME ALONG BECAUSE YOU FINALLY FEEL LIKE GETTING KILLED!?
......NO. OBVIOUSLY NOT.
IT'S JUST BETTER THAN RELYING ENTIRELY ON THE TEN HANDS.

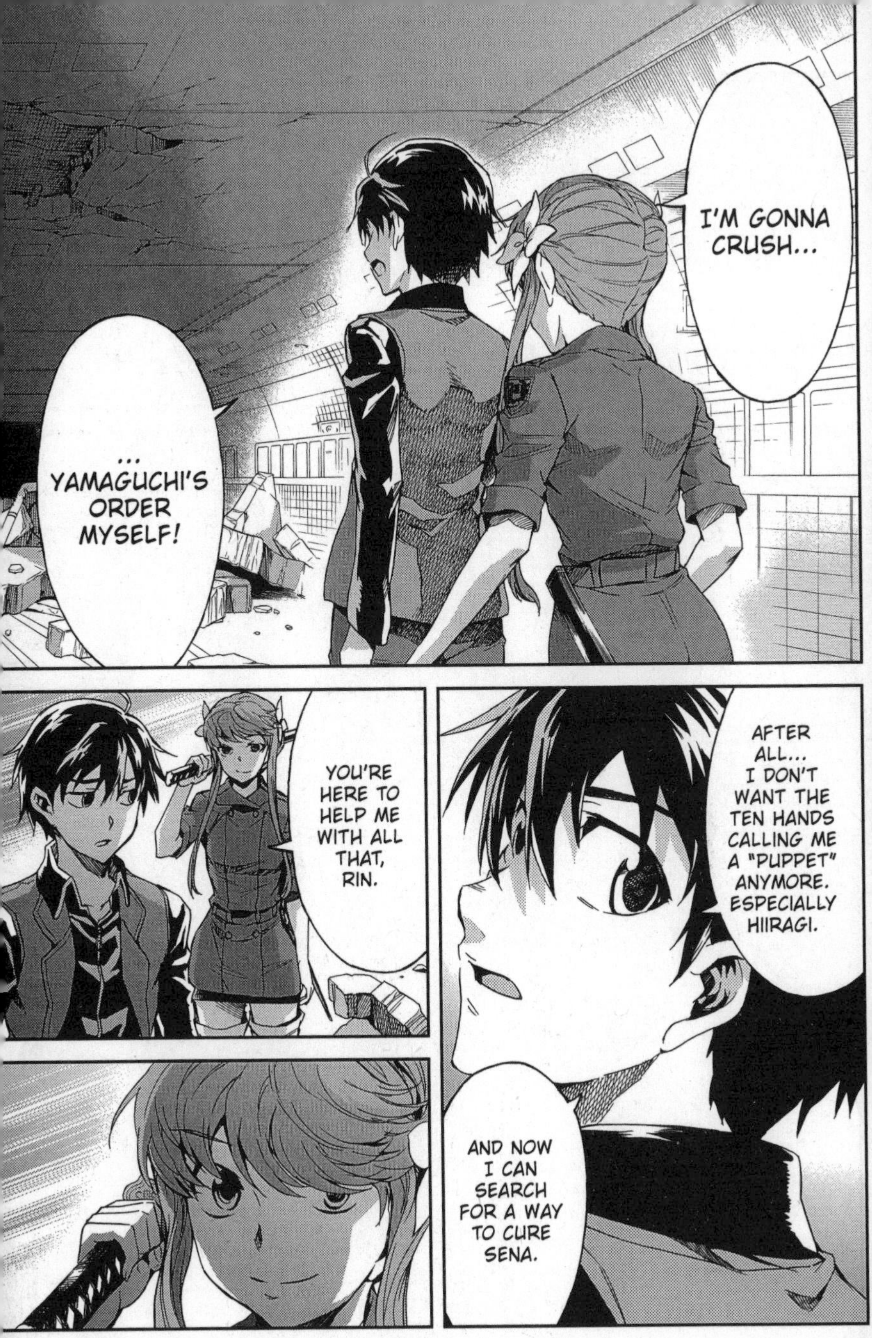
I'M GONNA CRUSH...
...YAMAGUCHI'S ORDER MYSELF!
AFTER ALL... I DON'T WANT THE TEN HANDS CALLING ME A "PUPPET" ANYMORE. ESPECIALLY HIIRAGI.
AND NOW I CAN SEARCH FOR A WAY TO CURE SENA.
YOU'RE HERE TO HELP ME WITH ALL THAT, RIN.

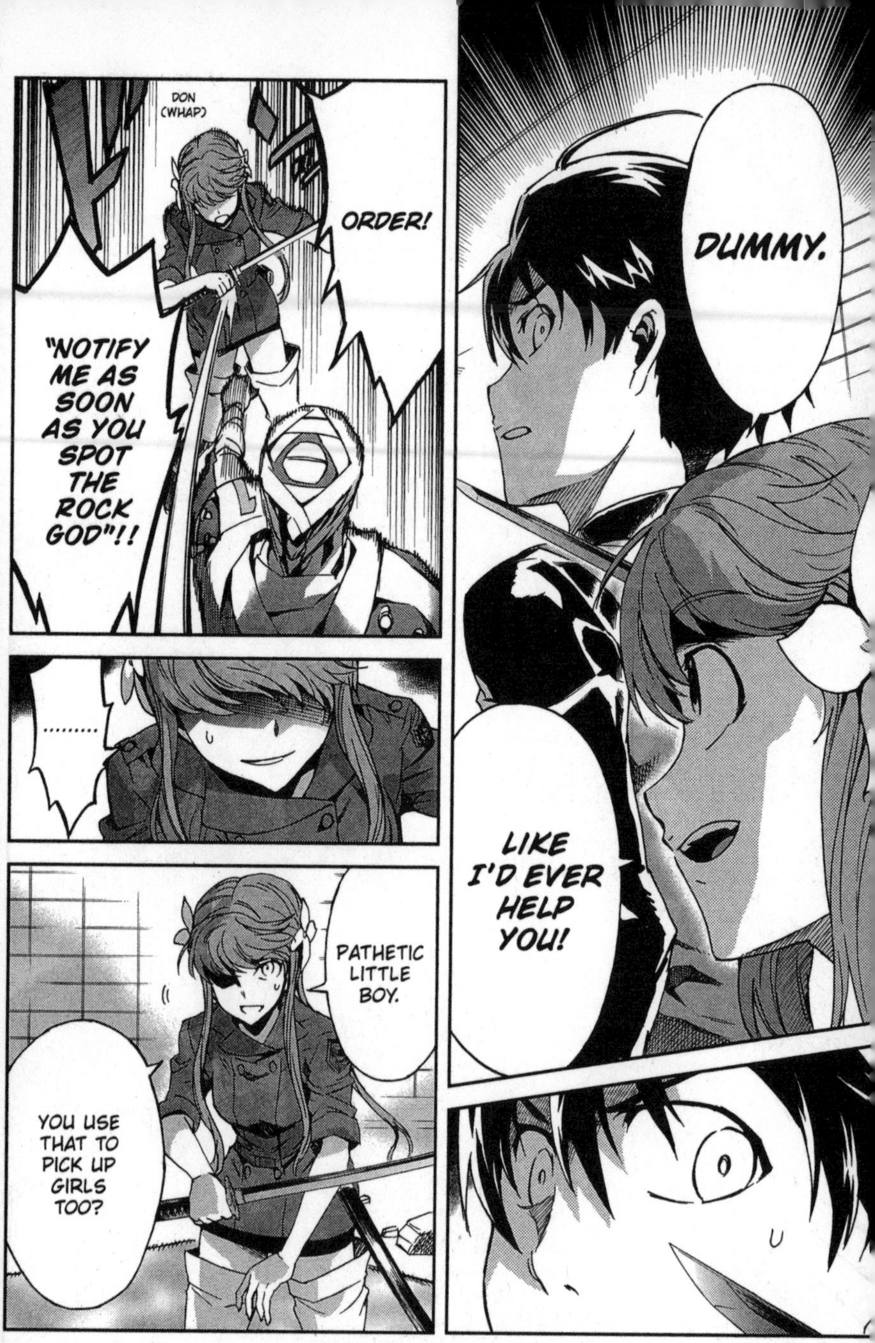
DUMMY.
LIKE I'D EVER HELP YOU!
DON (WHAP)
ORDER!
"NOTIFY ME AS SOON AS YOU SPOT THE ROCK GOD"!!
.........
PATHETIC LITTLE BOY.
YOU USE THAT TO PICK UP GIRLS TOO?

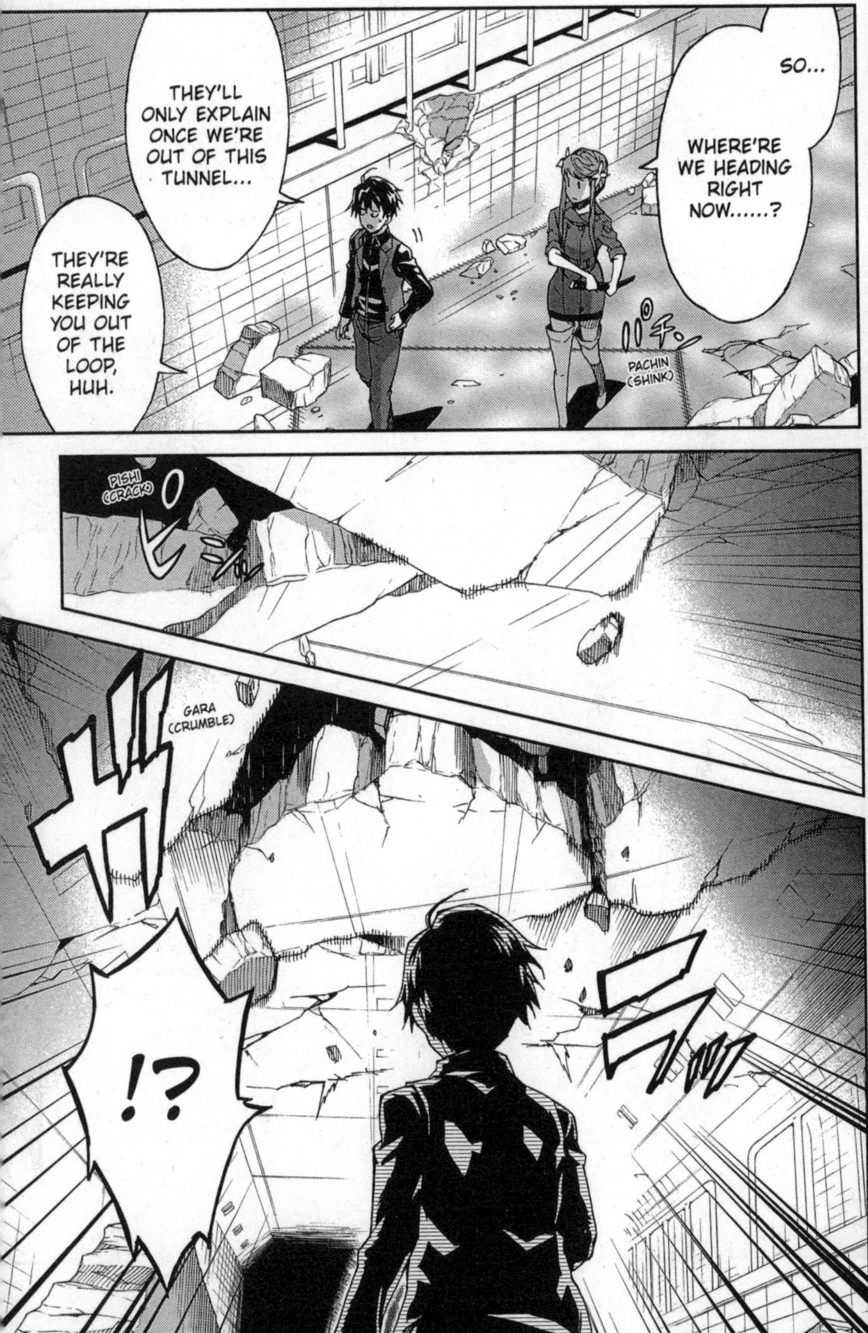
SO...
WHERE'RE WE HEADING RIGHT NOW......?
PACHIN (SHINK)
THEY'LL ONLY EXPLAIN ONCE WE'RE OUT OF THIS TUNNEL...
THEY'RE REALLY KEEPING YOU OUT OF THE LOOP, HUH.
PISHI (CRACK)
GARA (CRUMBLE)
!?

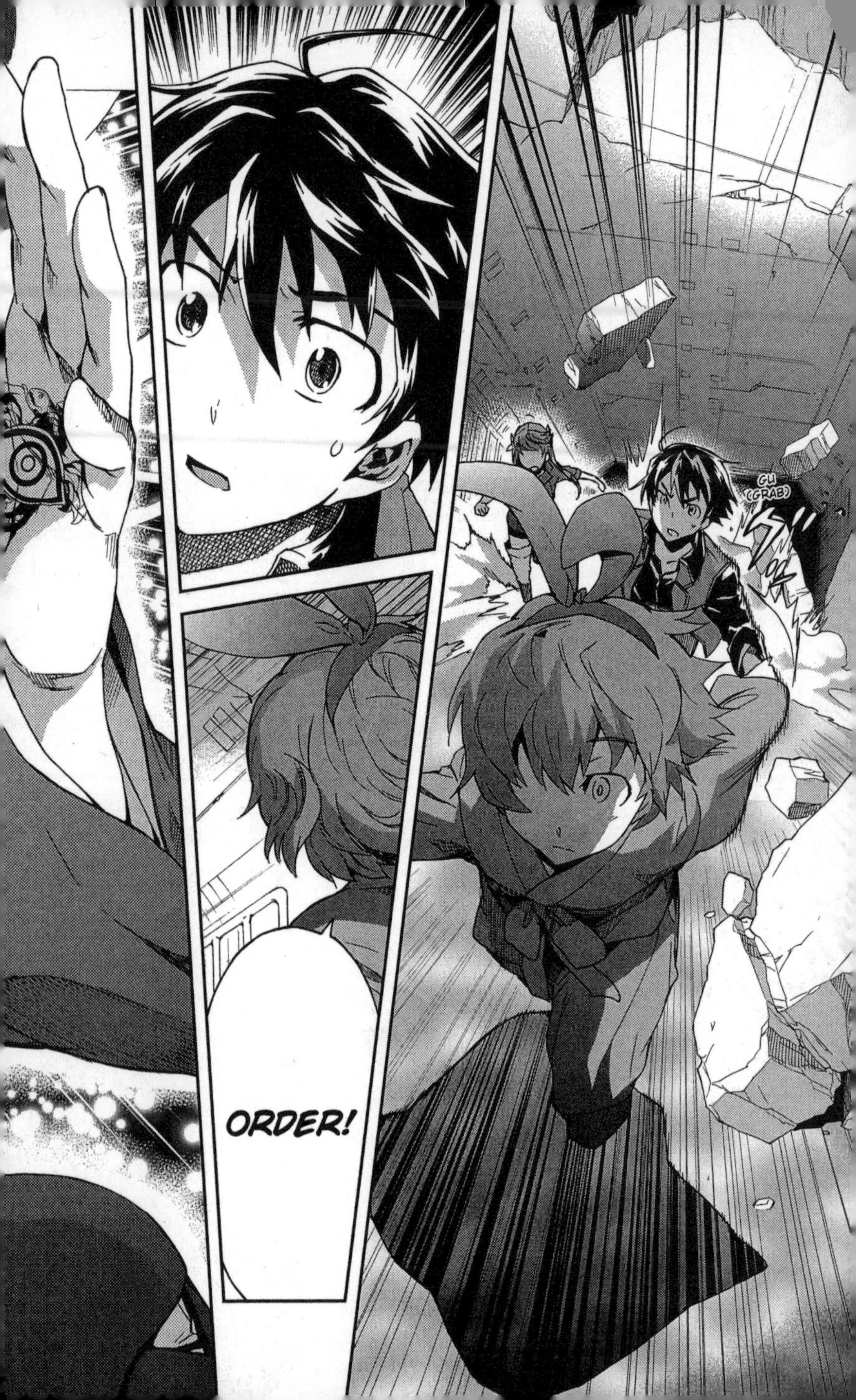
GU (GRAB)
ORDER!

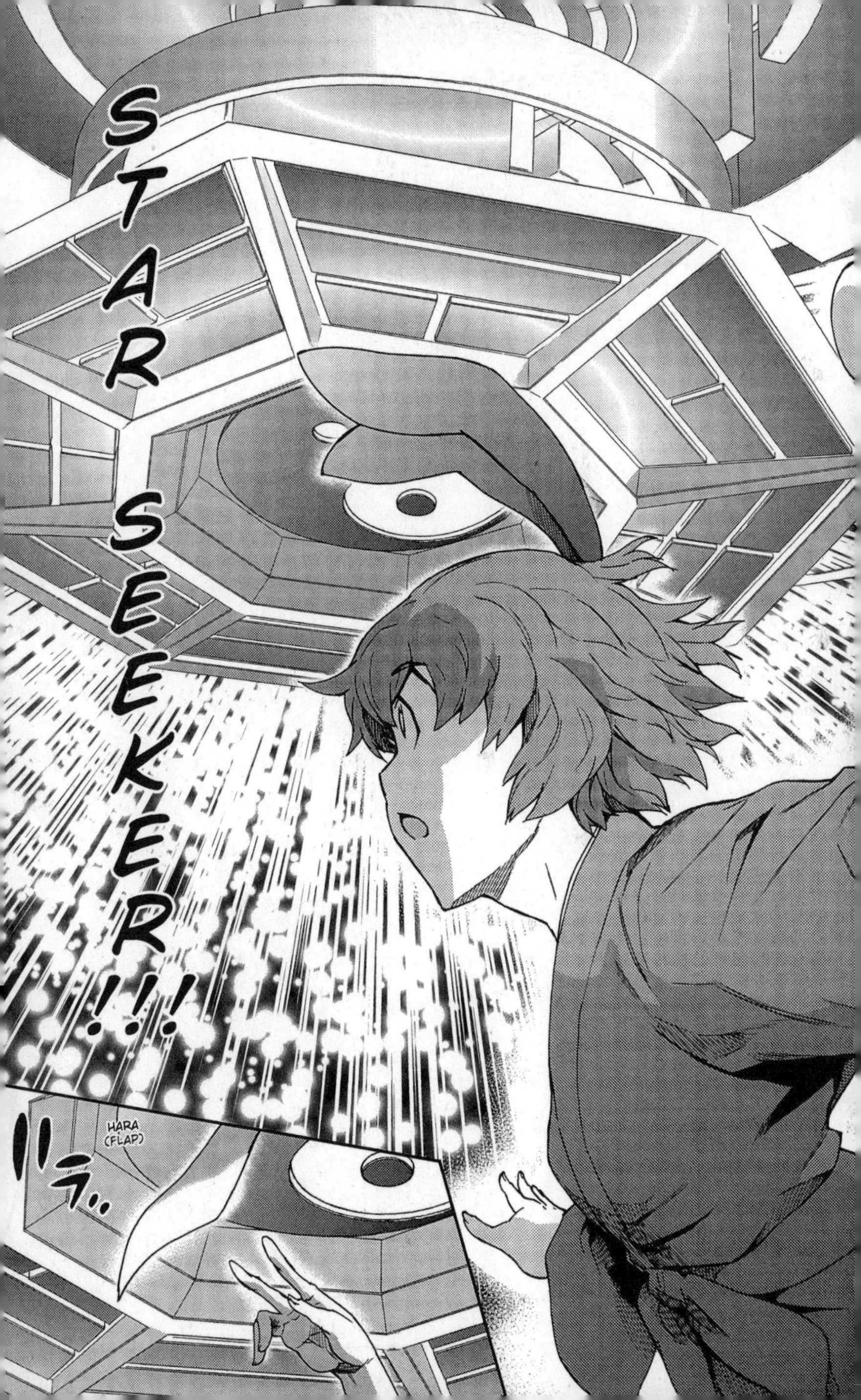
STAR SEEKER!!!
ハラ..
HARA (FLAP)

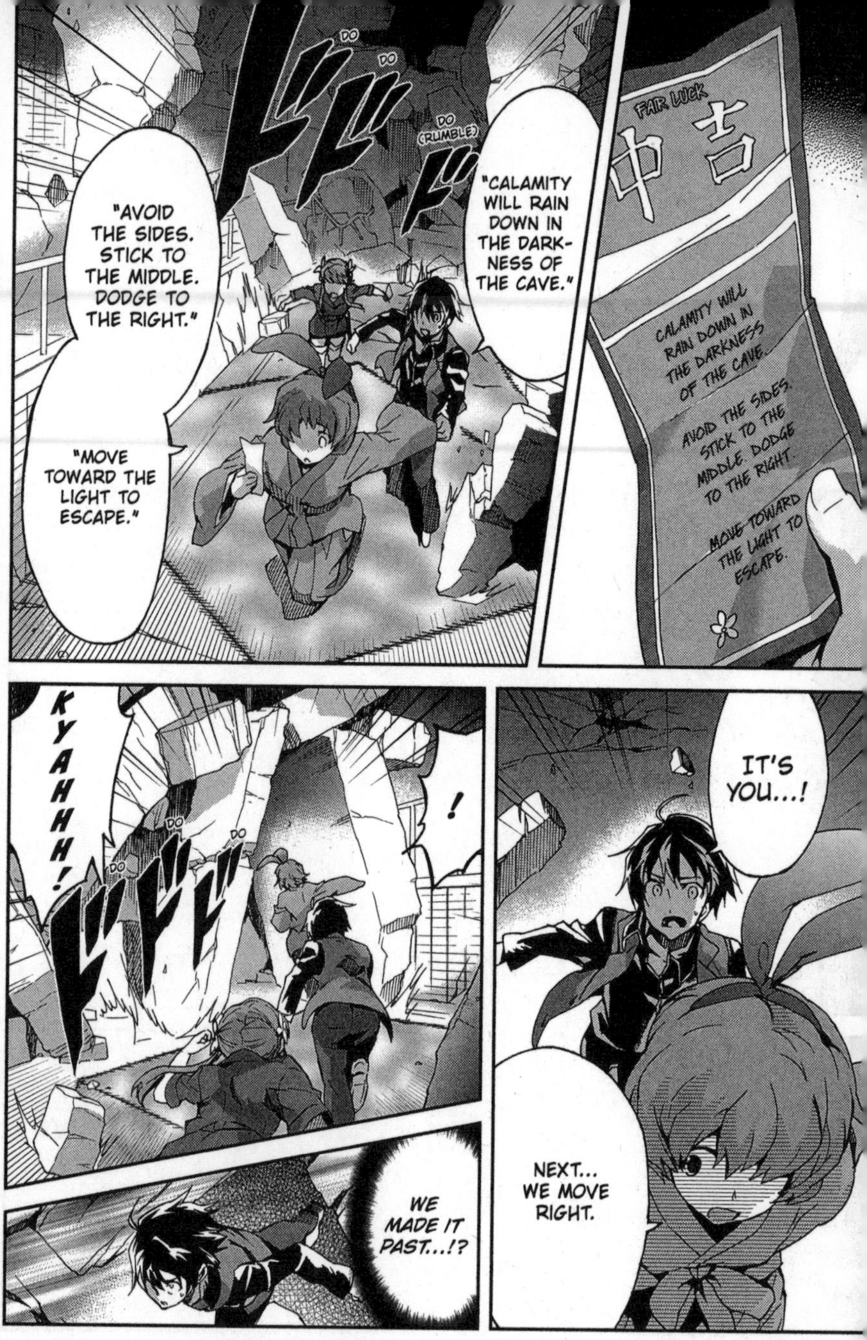
FAIR LUCK
中吉
CALAMITY WILL RAIN DOWN IN THE DARKNESS OF THE CAVE.
AVOID THE SIDES. STICK TO THE MIDDLE. DODGE TO THE RIGHT.
MOVE TOWARD THE LIGHT TO ESCAPE.
DO DO DO (RUMBLE)
"CALAMITY WILL RAIN DOWN IN THE DARK-NESS OF THE CAVE."
"AVOID THE SIDES. STICK TO THE MIDDLE. DODGE TO THE RIGHT."
"MOVE TOWARD THE LIGHT TO ESCAPE."
IT'S YOU...!
NEXT... WE MOVE RIGHT.
KYAHHHH!
DO DO DO
!
WE MADE IT PAST...!?

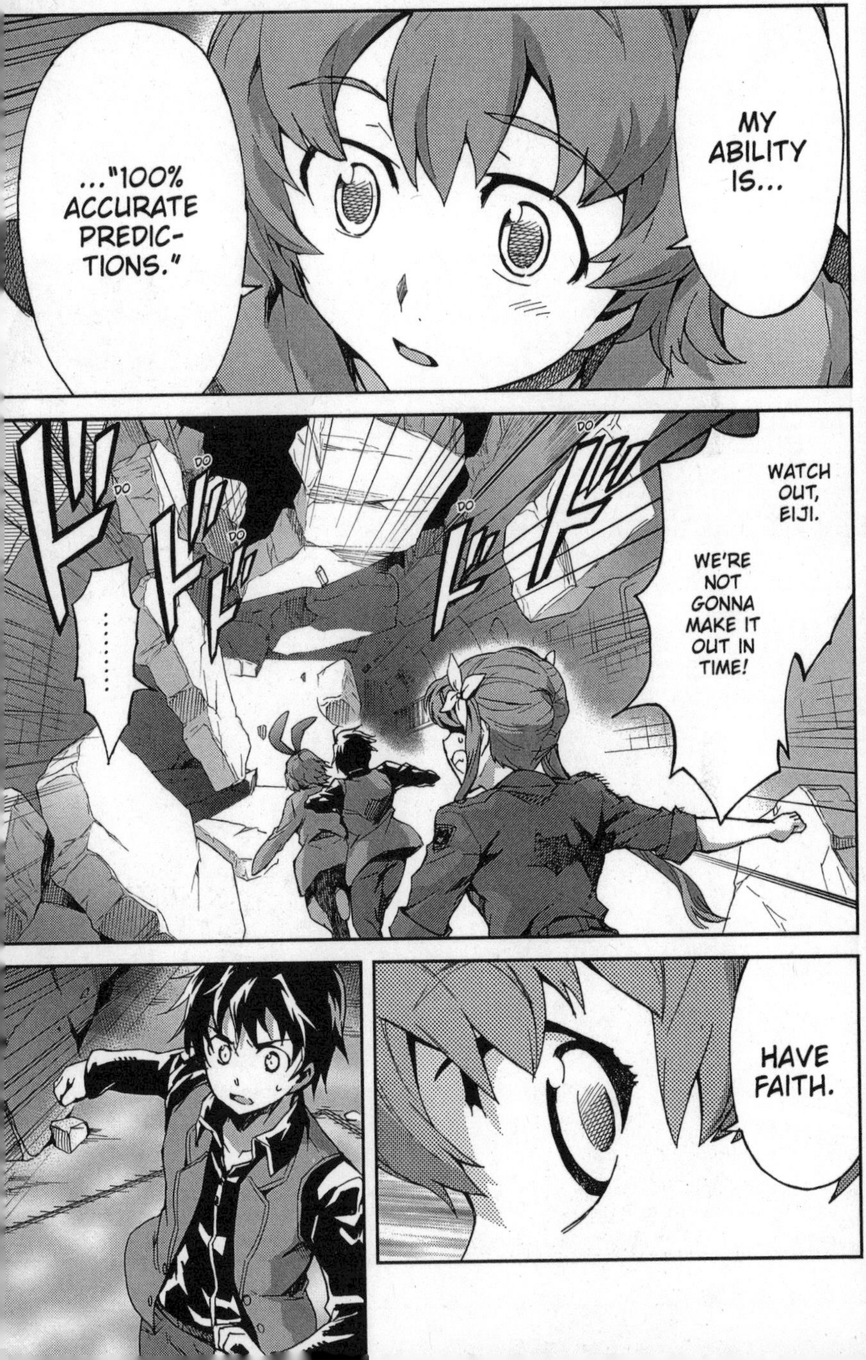
MY ABILITY IS...
..."100% ACCURATE PREDICTIONS."
DO
WATCH OUT, EIJI.
WE'RE NOT GONNA MAKE IT OUT IN TIME!
DO
DO
DO
DO
......
HAVE FAITH.

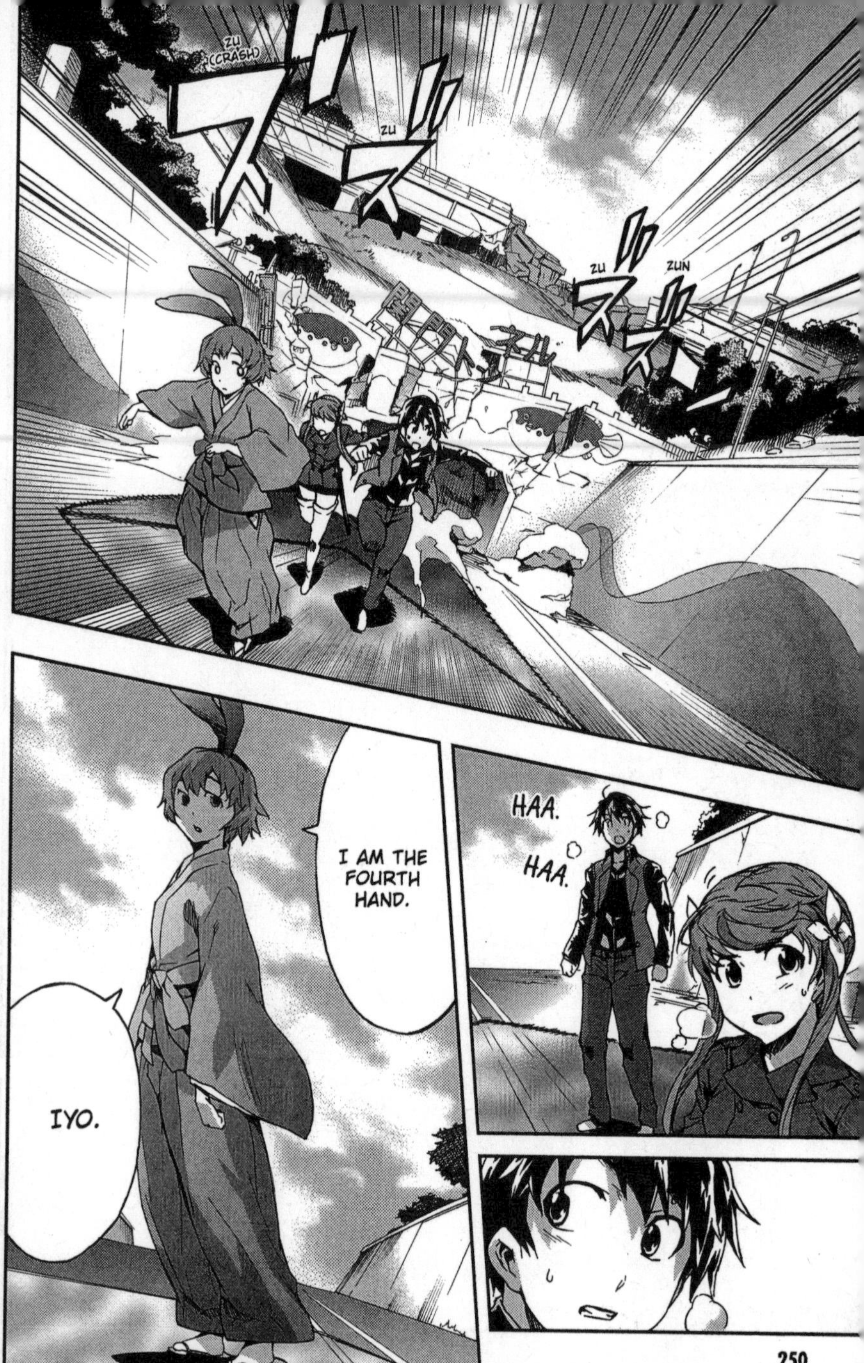

ZU (CRASH)
ZU
ZUN
ZU
HAA.
HAA.
I AM THE FOURTH HAND.
IYO.

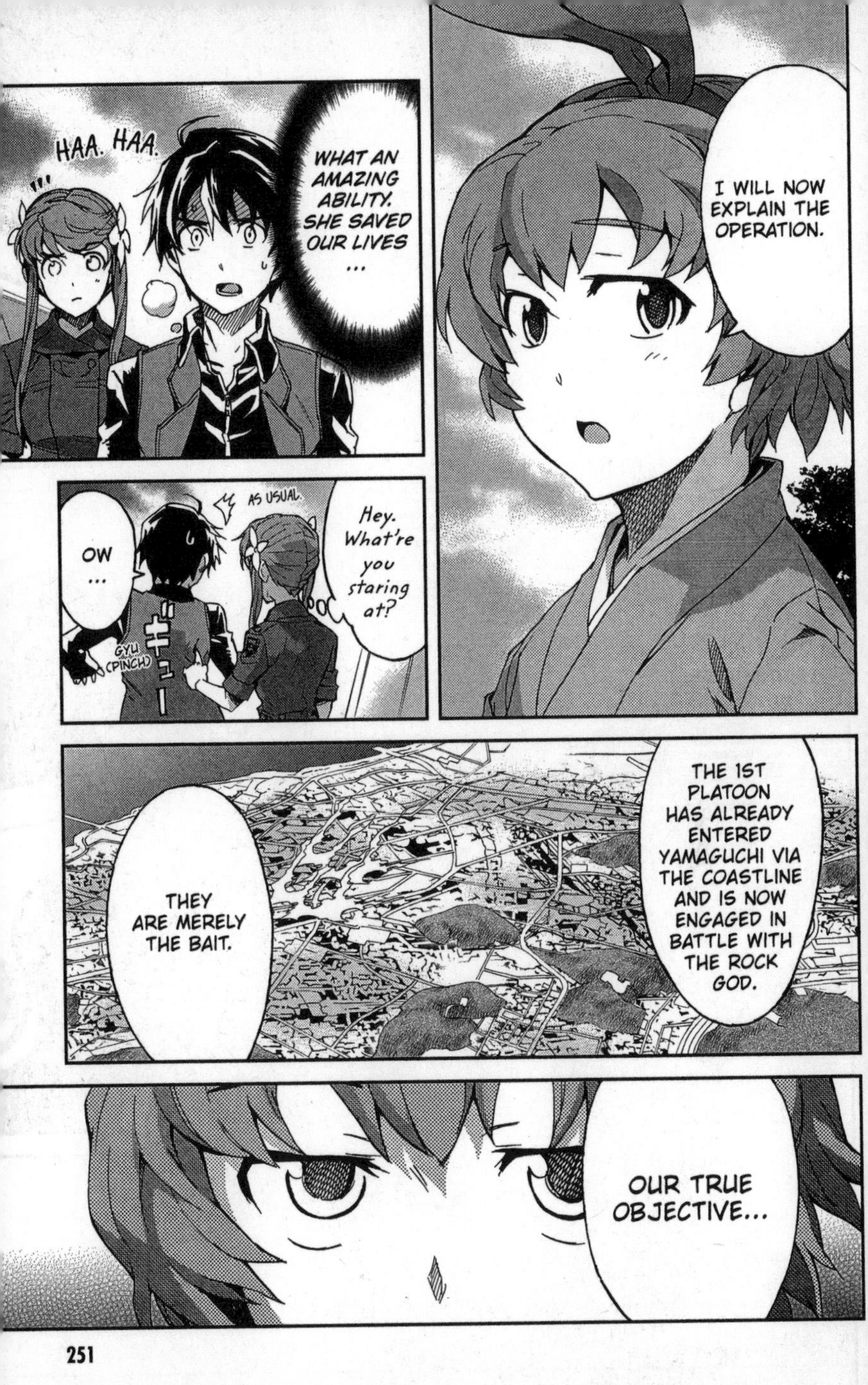

I WILL NOW EXPLAIN THE OPERATION.
WHAT AN AMAZING ABILITY. SHE SAVED OUR LIVES ...
HAA. HAA.
AS USUAL.
Hey. What're you staring at?
OW ...
GYU (PINCH)
THE 1ST PLATOON HAS ALREADY ENTERED YAMAGUCHI VIA THE COASTLINE AND IS NOW ENGAGED IN BATTLE WITH THE ROCK GOD.
THEY ARE MERELY THE BAIT.
OUR TRUE OBJECTIVE...

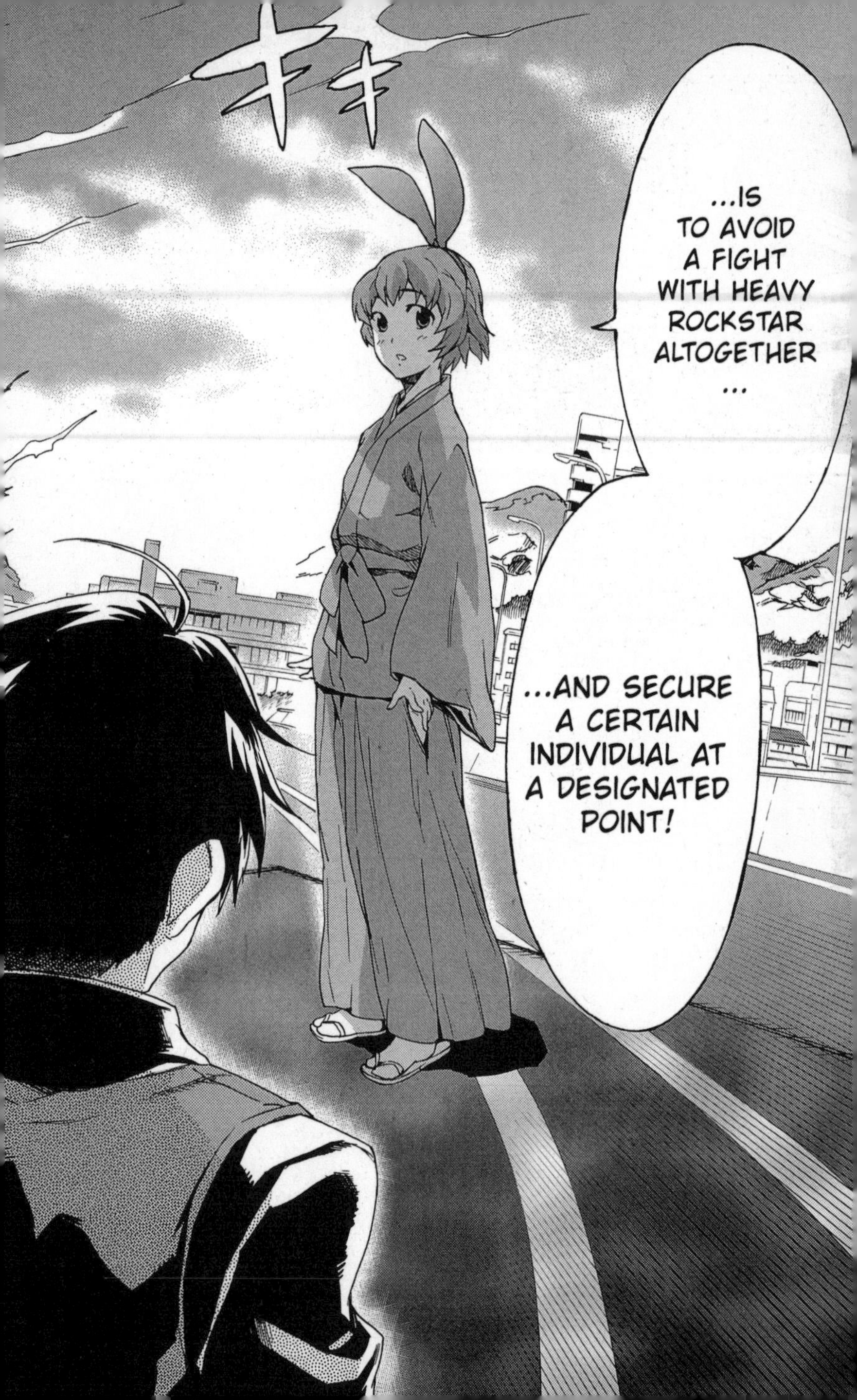
キキ
...IS TO AVOID A FIGHT WITH HEAVY ROCKSTAR ALTOGETHER ...
...AND SECURE A CERTAIN INDIVIDUAL AT A DESIGNATED POINT!

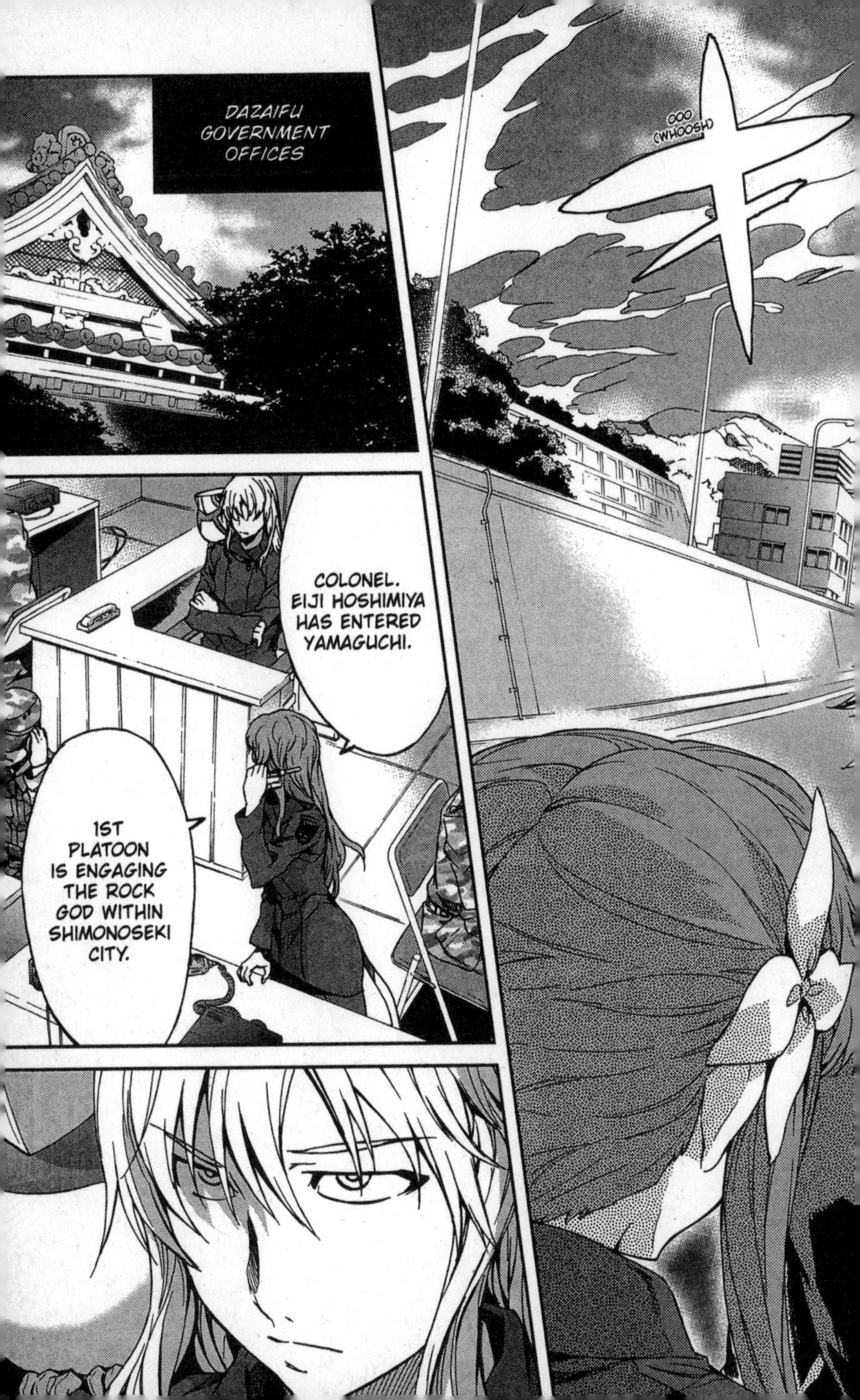
OOO (WHOOSH)
DAZAIFU GOVERNMENT OFFICES
COLONEL. EIJI HOSHIMIYA HAS ENTERED YAMAGUCHI.
1ST PLATOON IS ENGAGING THE ROCK GOD WITHIN SHIMONOSEKI CITY.

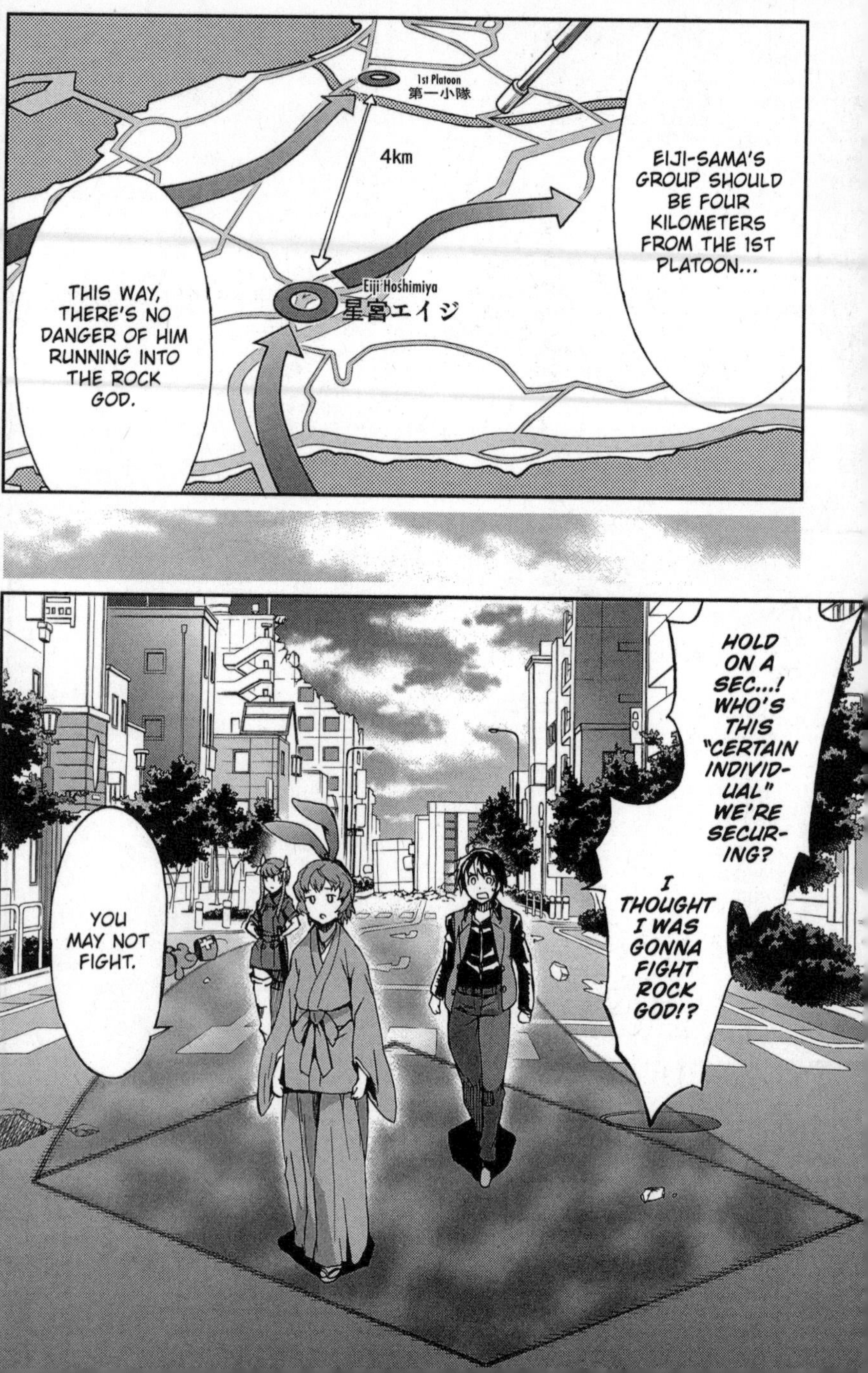
EIJI-SAMA'S GROUP SHOULD BE FOUR KILOMETERS FROM THE 1ST PLATOON...
1st Platoon
第一小隊
4km
Eiji Hoshimiya
星宮エイジ
THIS WAY, THERE'S NO DANGER OF HIM RUNNING INTO THE ROCK GOD.
HOLD ON A SEC...! WHO'S THIS "CERTAIN INDIVIDUAL" WE'RE SECURING?
I THOUGHT I WAS GONNA FIGHT ROCK GOD!?
YOU MAY NOT FIGHT.

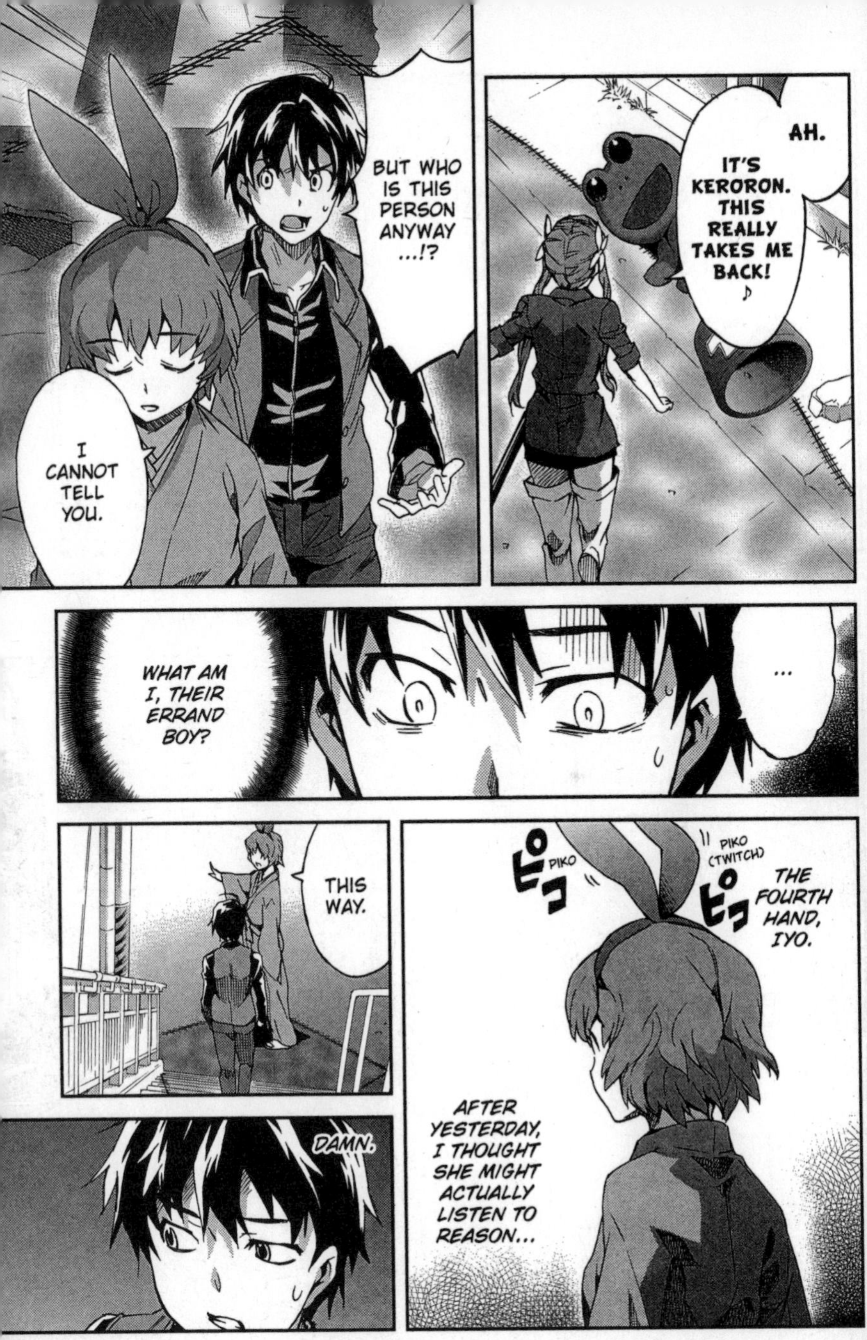
AH.
IT'S KERORON. THIS REALLY TAKES ME BACK! ♪
BUT WHO IS THIS PERSON ANYWAY ...!?
I CANNOT TELL YOU.
...
WHAT AM I, THEIR ERRAND BOY?
ピコ PIKO (TWITCH)
THE FOURTH HAND, IYO.
ピコ PIKO
AFTER YESTERDAY, I THOUGHT SHE MIGHT ACTUALLY LISTEN TO REASON...
THIS WAY.
DAMN.

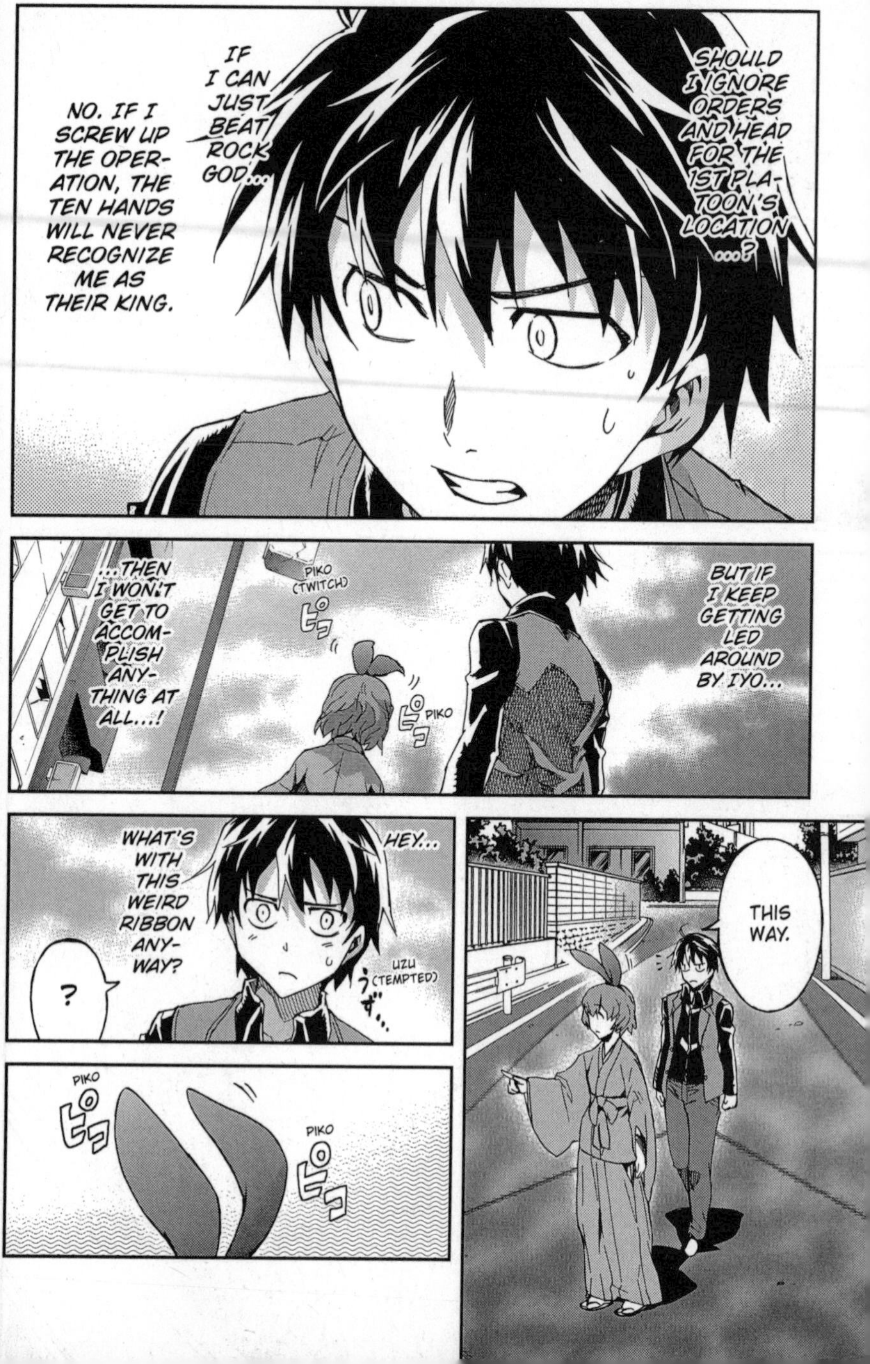
SHOULD I IGNORE ORDERS AND HEAD FOR THE 1ST PLATOON'S LOCATION...?
IF I CAN JUST BEAT ROCK GOD...
NO. IF I SCREW UP THE OPERATION, THE TEN HANDS WILL NEVER RECOGNIZE ME AS THEIR KING.
BUT IF I KEEP GETTING LED AROUND BY IYO...
PIKO (TWITCH)
ピコッ
PIKO
ピコッ
...THEN I WON'T GET TO ACCOMPLISH ANYTHING AT ALL...!
THIS WAY.
HEY...
WHAT'S WITH THIS WEIRD RIBBON ANYWAY?
UZU (TEMPTED)
うず...
?
PIKO
ピコッ
PIKO
ピコッ

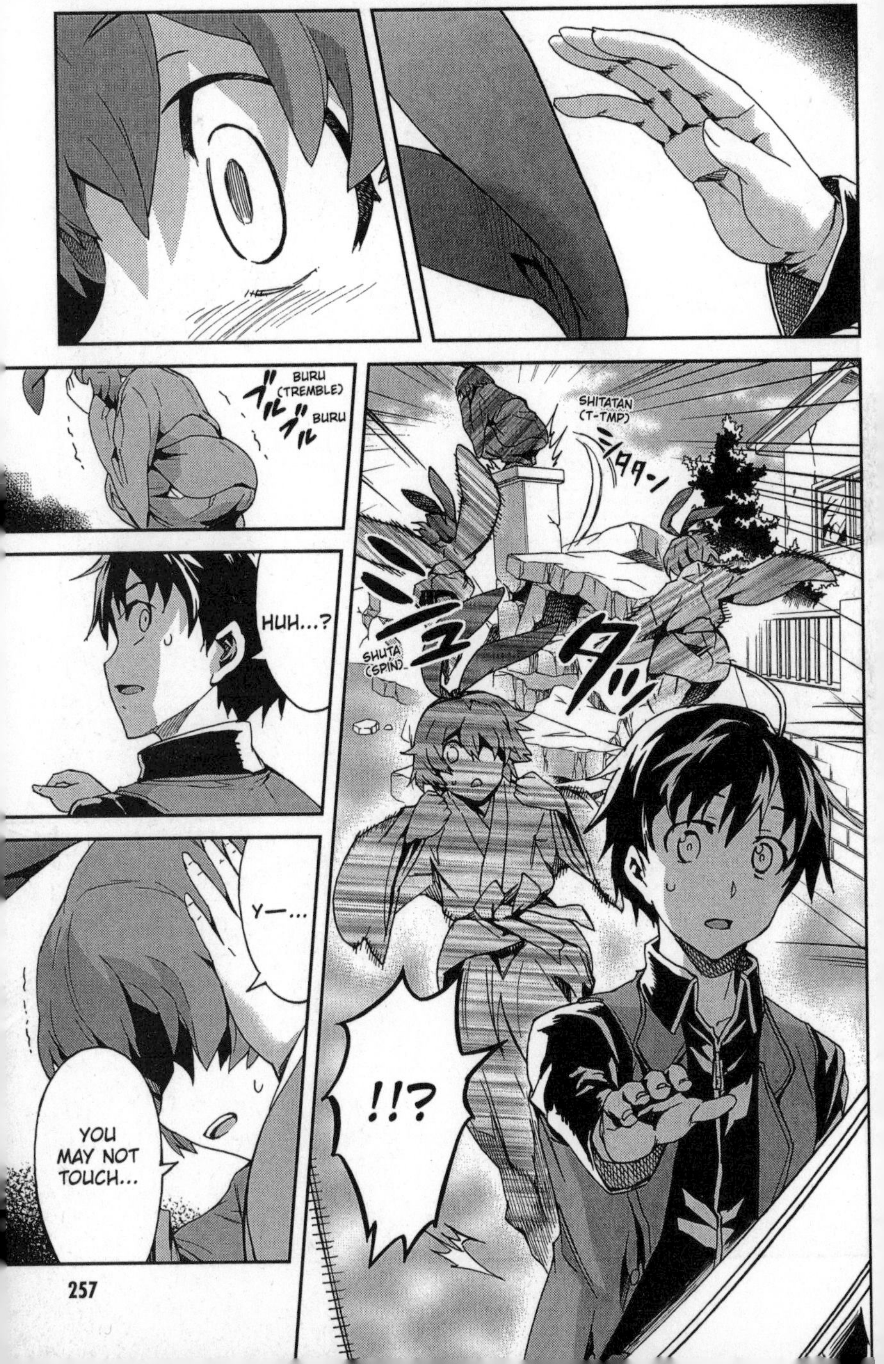
SHITATAN (T-TMP)
SHUTA (SPIN)
!!?
BURU (TREMBLE) BURU
HUH...?
Y—...
YOU MAY NOT TOUCH...

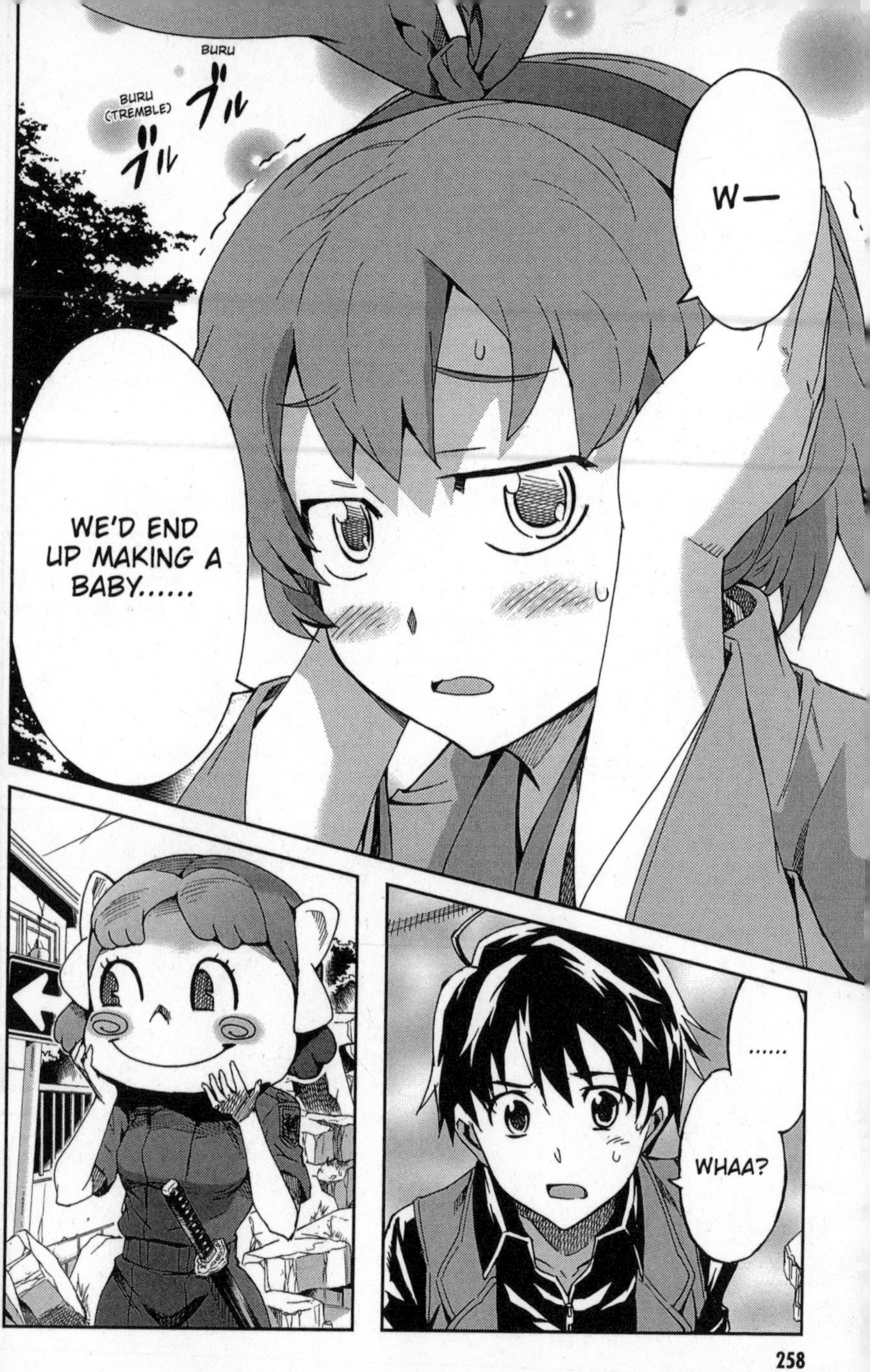
W—
BURU
ブル
BURU (TREMBLE)
ブル
WE'D END UP MAKING A BABY......
......
WHAA?

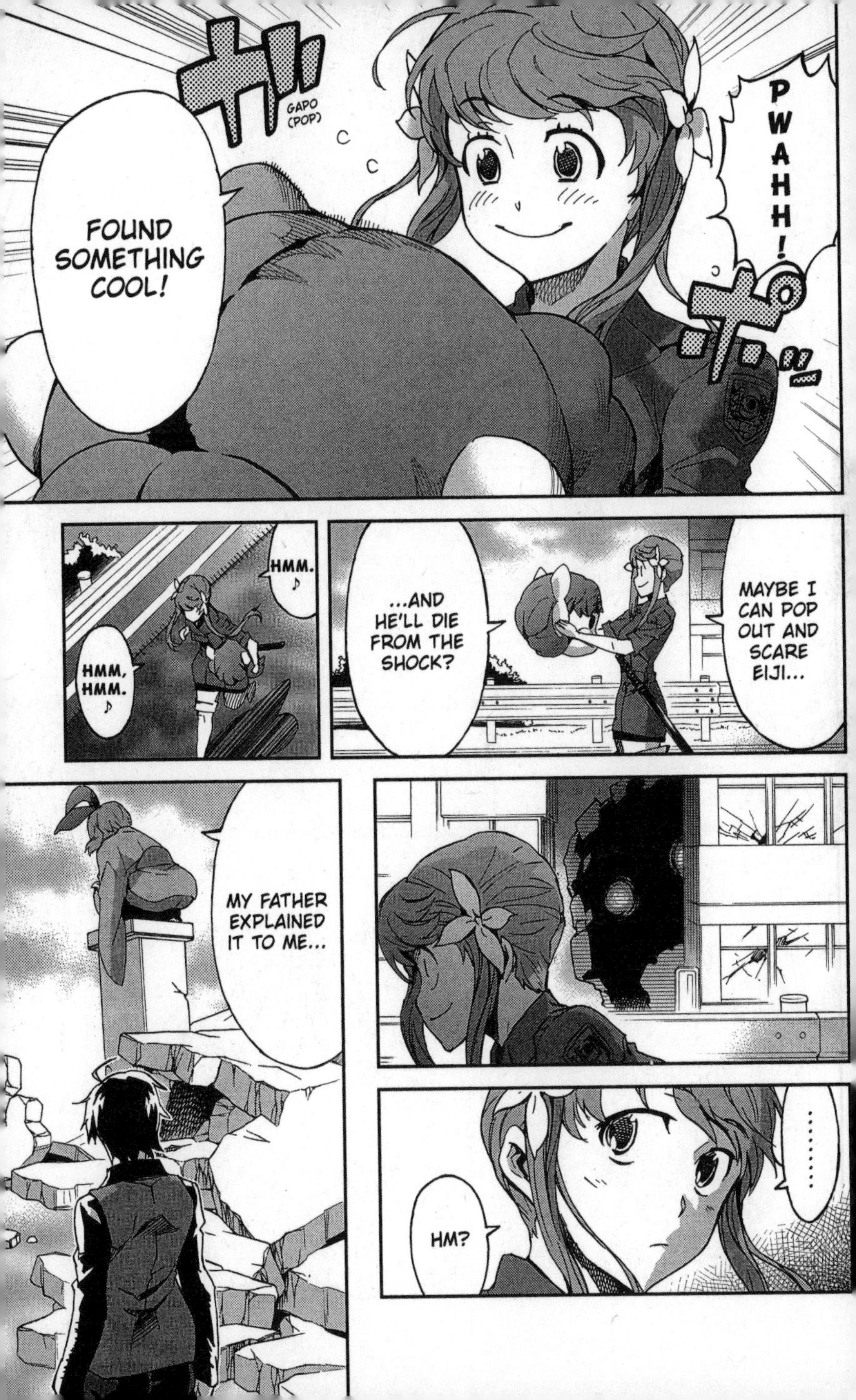
PWAHH!
GAPO (POP)
FOUND SOMETHING COOL!
MAYBE I CAN POP OUT AND SCARE EIJI...
...AND HE'LL DIE FROM THE SHOCK?
HMM. ♪
HMM, HMM. ♪
......
HM?
MY FATHER EXPLAINED IT TO ME...

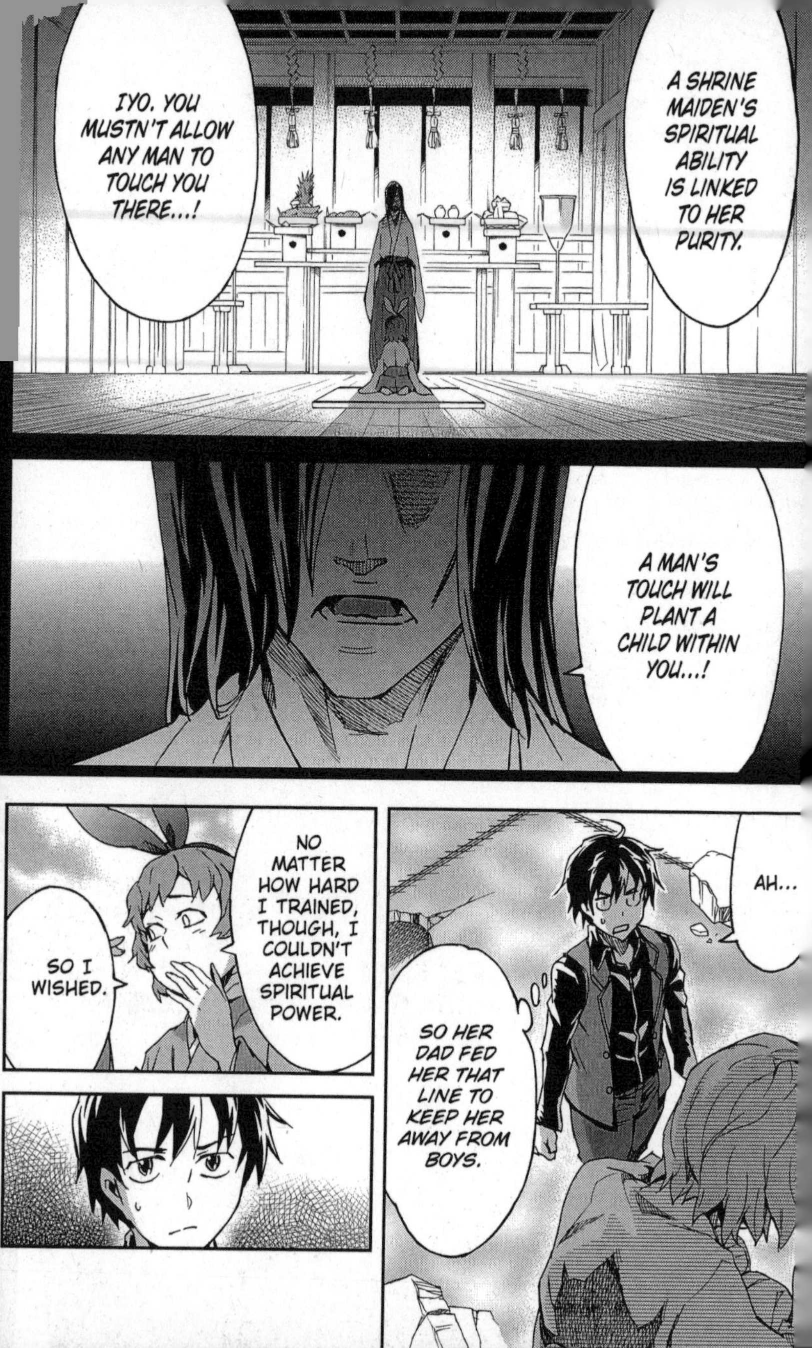
A SHRINE MAIDEN'S SPIRITUAL ABILITY IS LINKED TO HER PURITY.
IYO. YOU MUSTN'T ALLOW ANY MAN TO TOUCH YOU THERE...!
A MAN'S TOUCH WILL PLANT A CHILD WITHIN YOU...!
AH...
SO HER DAD FED HER THAT LINE TO KEEP HER AWAY FROM BOYS.
NO MATTER HOW HARD I TRAINED, THOUGH, I COULDN'T ACHIEVE SPIRITUAL POWER.
SO I WISHED.

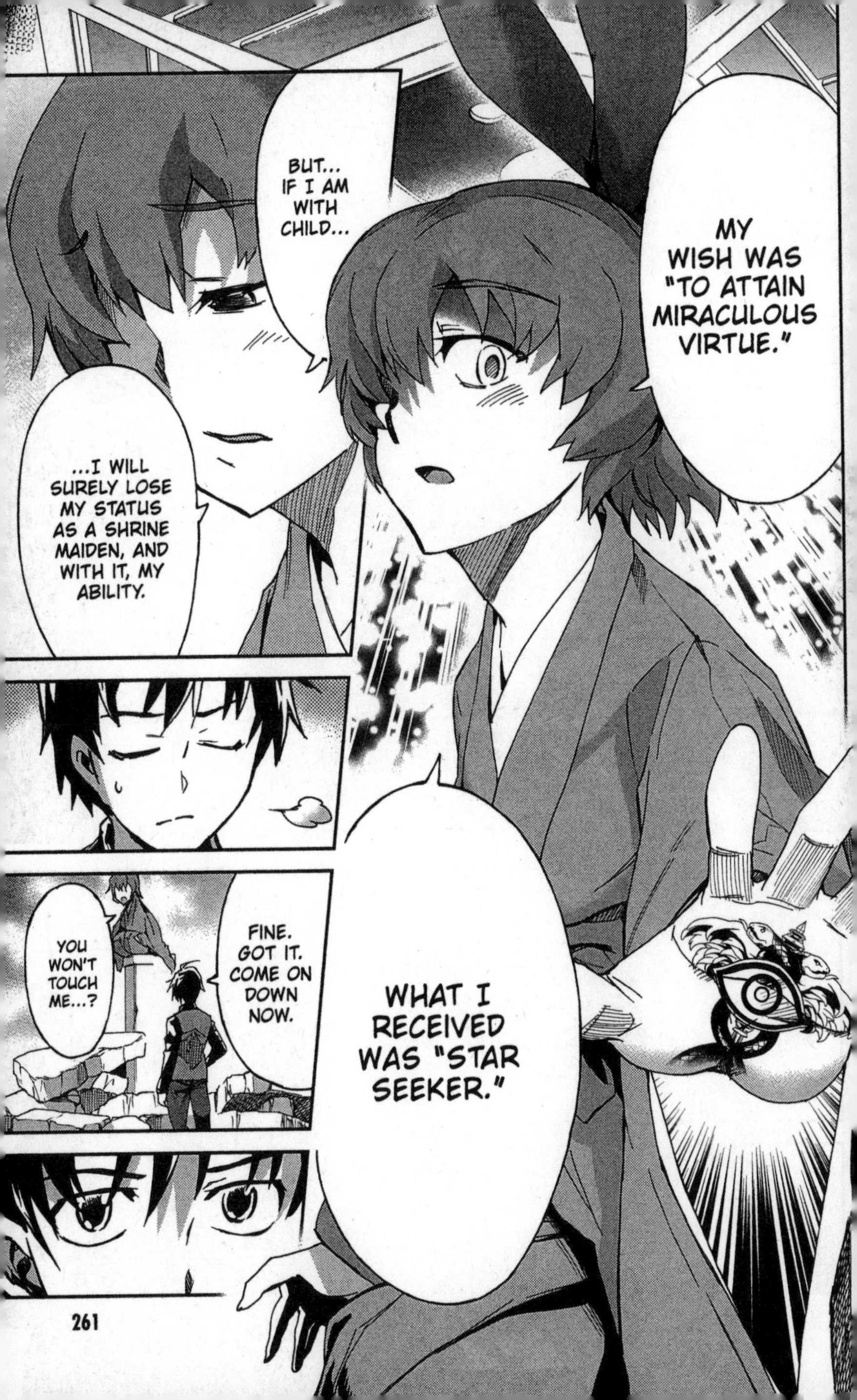
MY WISH WAS "TO ATTAIN MIRACULOUS VIRTUE."
WHAT I RECEIVED WAS "STAR SEEKER."
BUT... IF I AM WITH CHILD...
...I WILL SURELY LOSE MY STATUS AS A SHRINE MAIDEN, AND WITH IT, MY ABILITY.
FINE. GOT IT. COME ON DOWN NOW.
YOU WON'T TOUCH ME...?

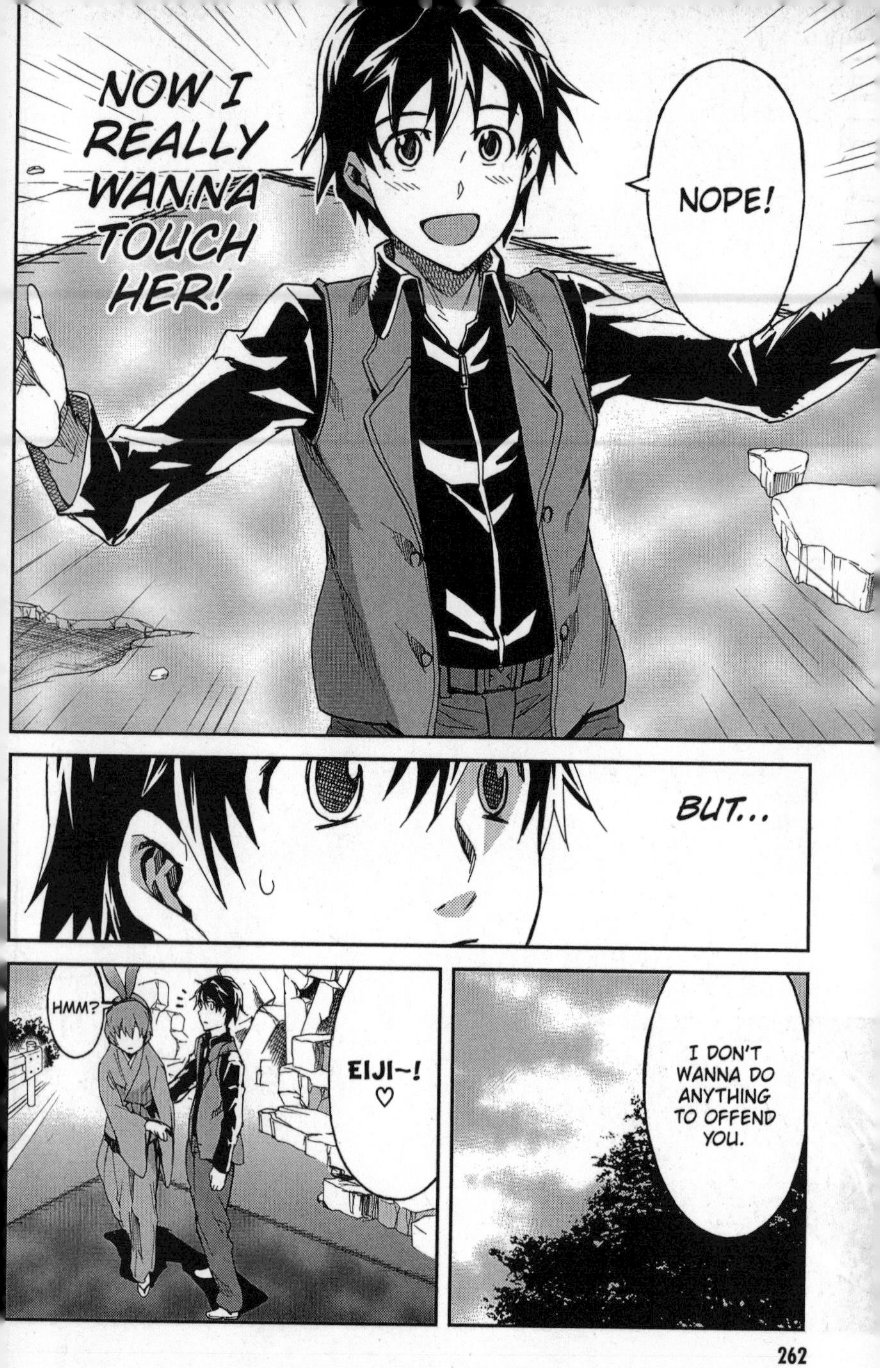
NOPE!
NOW I REALLY WANNA TOUCH HER!
BUT...
I DON'T WANNA DO ANYTHING TO OFFEND YOU.
EIJI~! ♡
HMM?

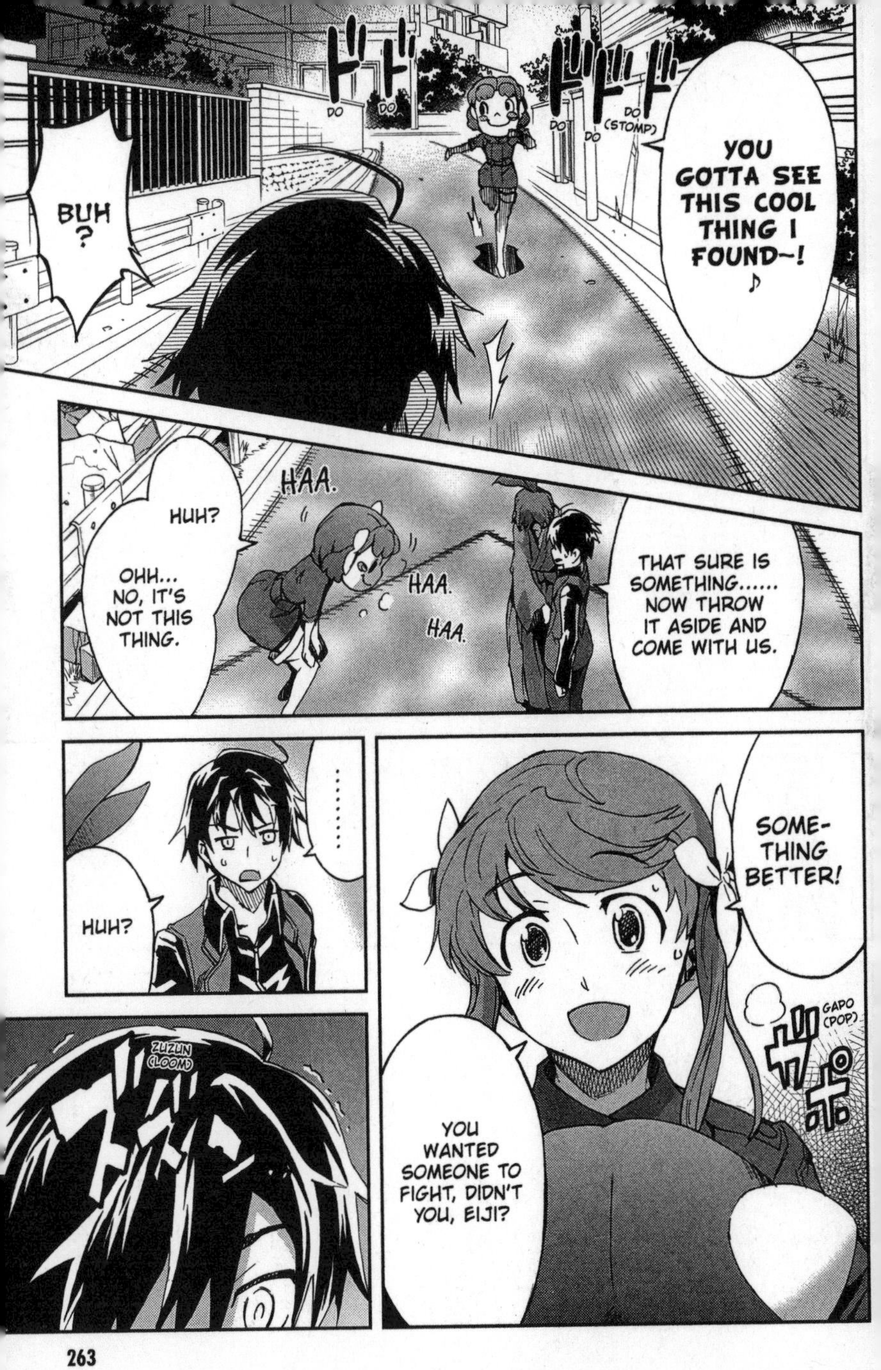
DO DO DO (STOMP)
YOU GOTTA SEE THIS COOL THING I FOUND~! ♪
DO DO
BUH?
THAT SURE IS SOMETHING...... NOW THROW IT ASIDE AND COME WITH US.
HAA.
HAA.
HAA.
HUH?
OHH... NO, IT'S NOT THIS THING.
SOME-THING BETTER!
GAPO (POP)
YOU WANTED SOMEONE TO FIGHT, DIDN'T YOU, EIJI?
......
HUH?
ZUZUN (LOOM)

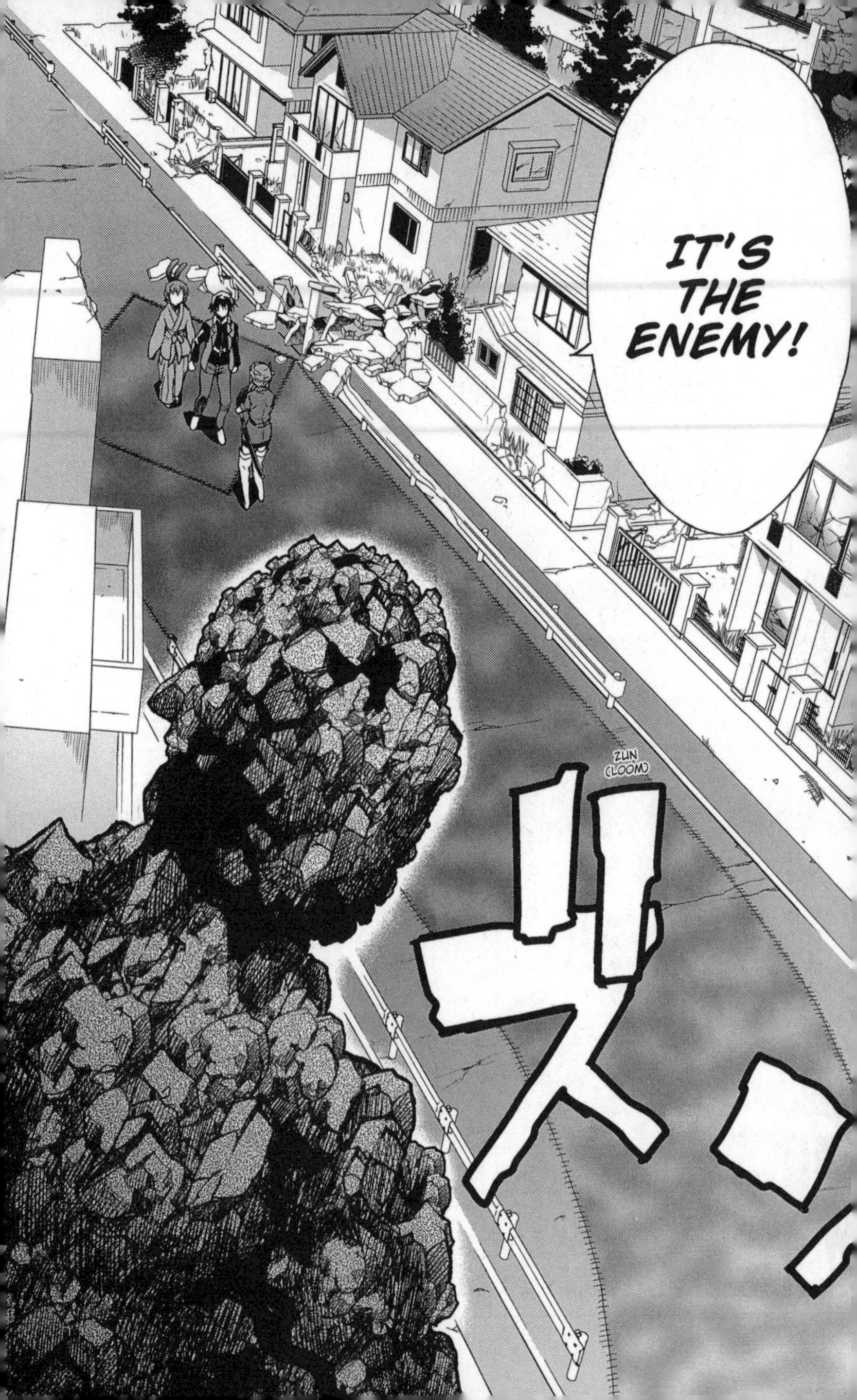
IT'S THE ENEMY!
ZUN (LOOM)

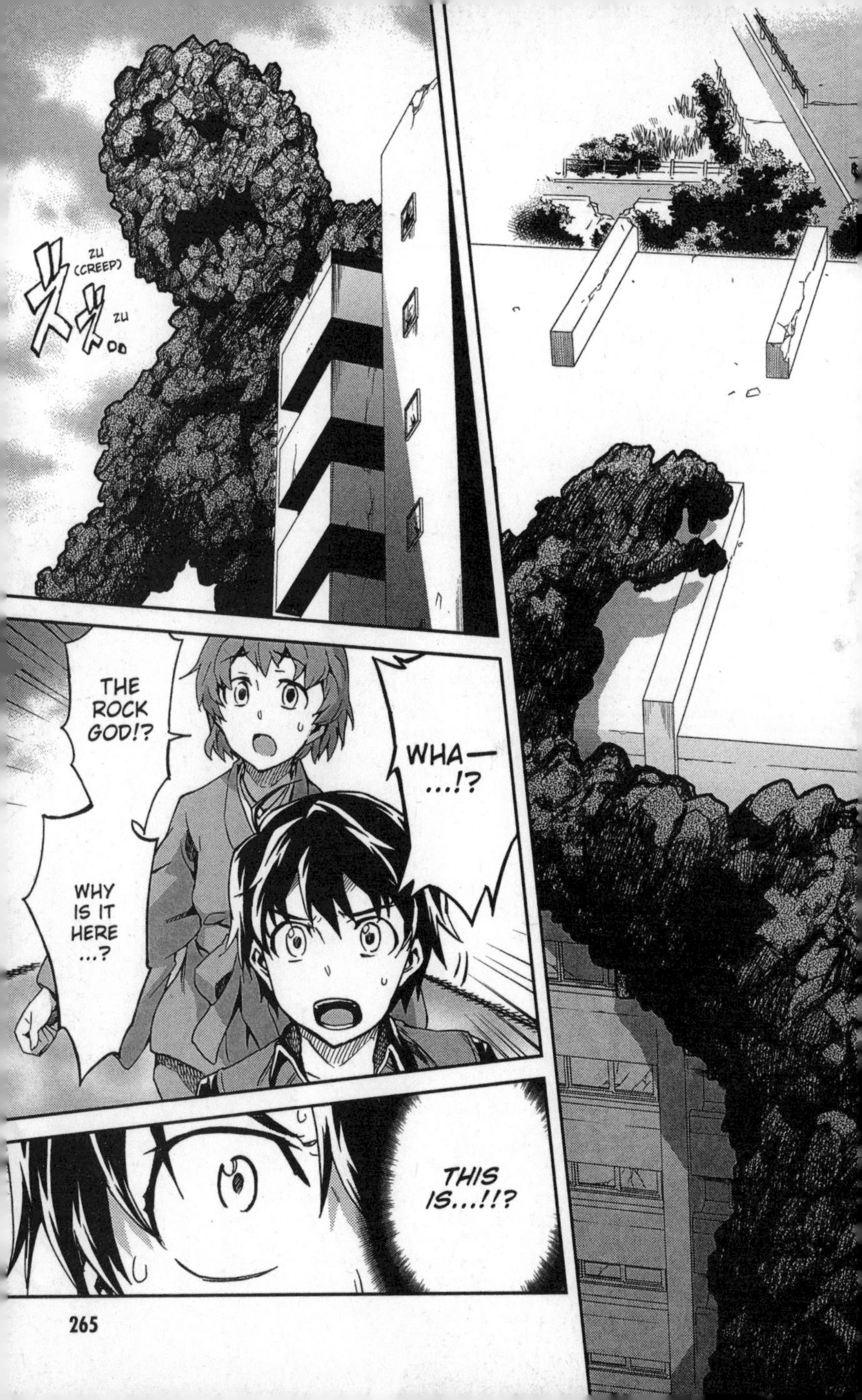
ZU (CREEP) ZU ZU
THE ROCK GOD!?
WHY IS IT HERE ...?
WHA— ...!?
THIS IS...!!?

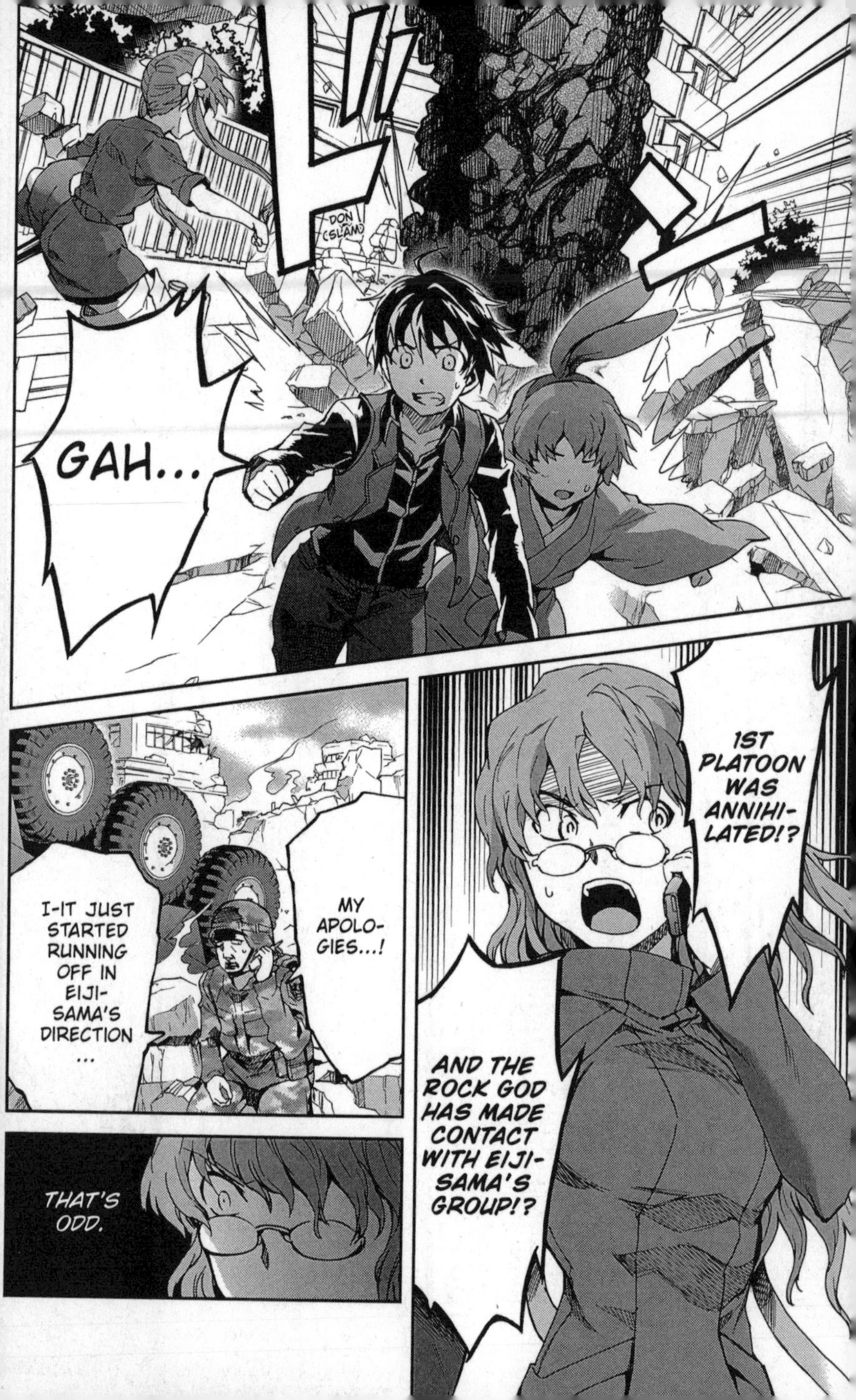
DON (SLAM)
GAH...
1ST PLATOON WAS ANNIHILATED!?
AND THE ROCK GOD HAS MADE CONTACT WITH EIJI-SAMA'S GROUP!?
MY APOLOGIES...!
I-IT JUST STARTED RUNNING OFF IN EIJI-SAMA'S DIRECTION...
THAT'S ODD.

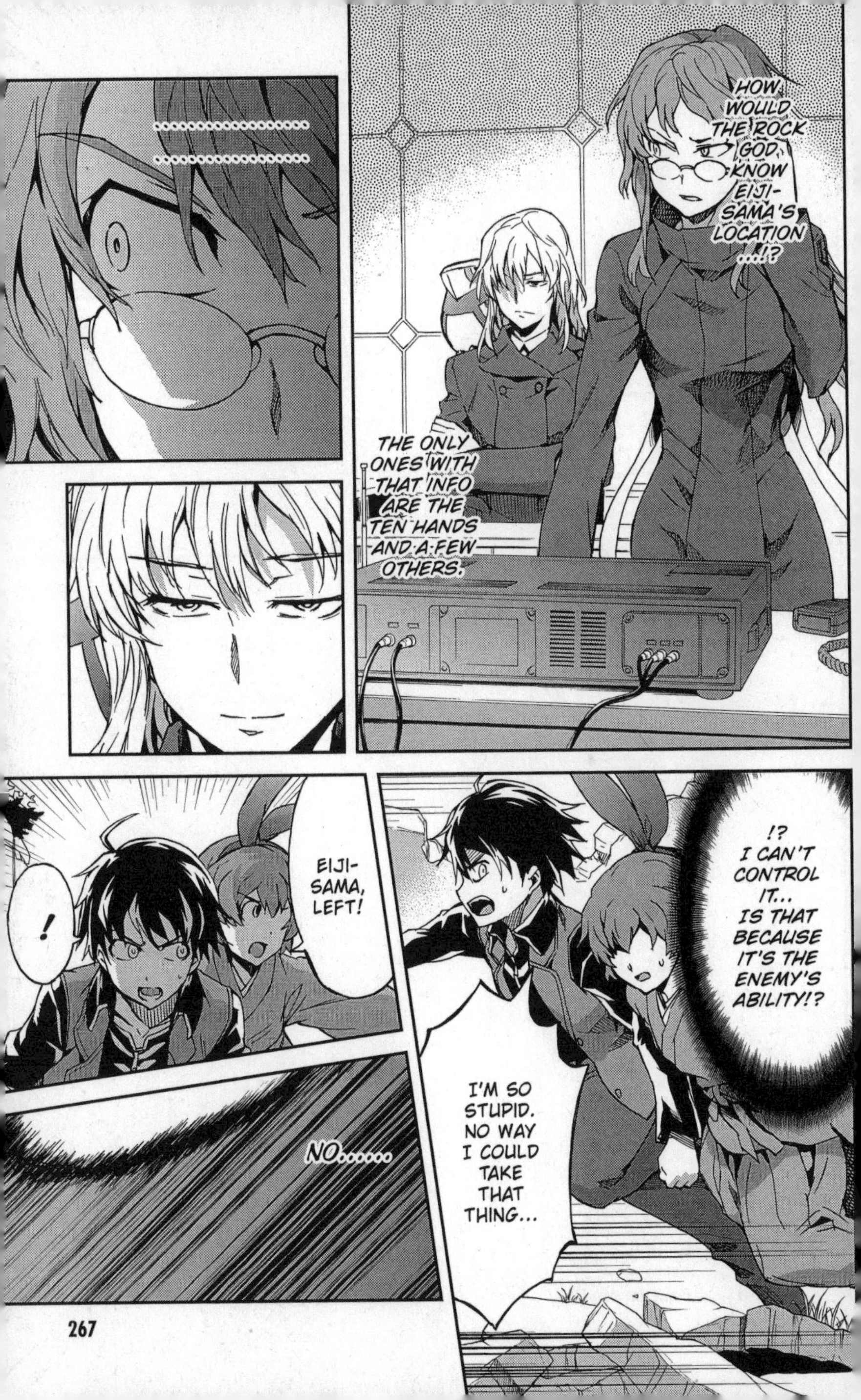
HOW WOULD THE ROCK GOD KNOW EIJI-SAMA'S LOCATION......!?
THE ONLY ONES WITH THAT INFO ARE THE TEN HANDS AND A FEW OTHERS.
..................
..................
!? I CAN'T CONTROL IT... IS THAT BECAUSE IT'S THE ENEMY'S ABILITY!?
I'M SO STUPID. NO WAY I COULD TAKE THAT THING...
EIJI-SAMA, LEFT!
!
NO......

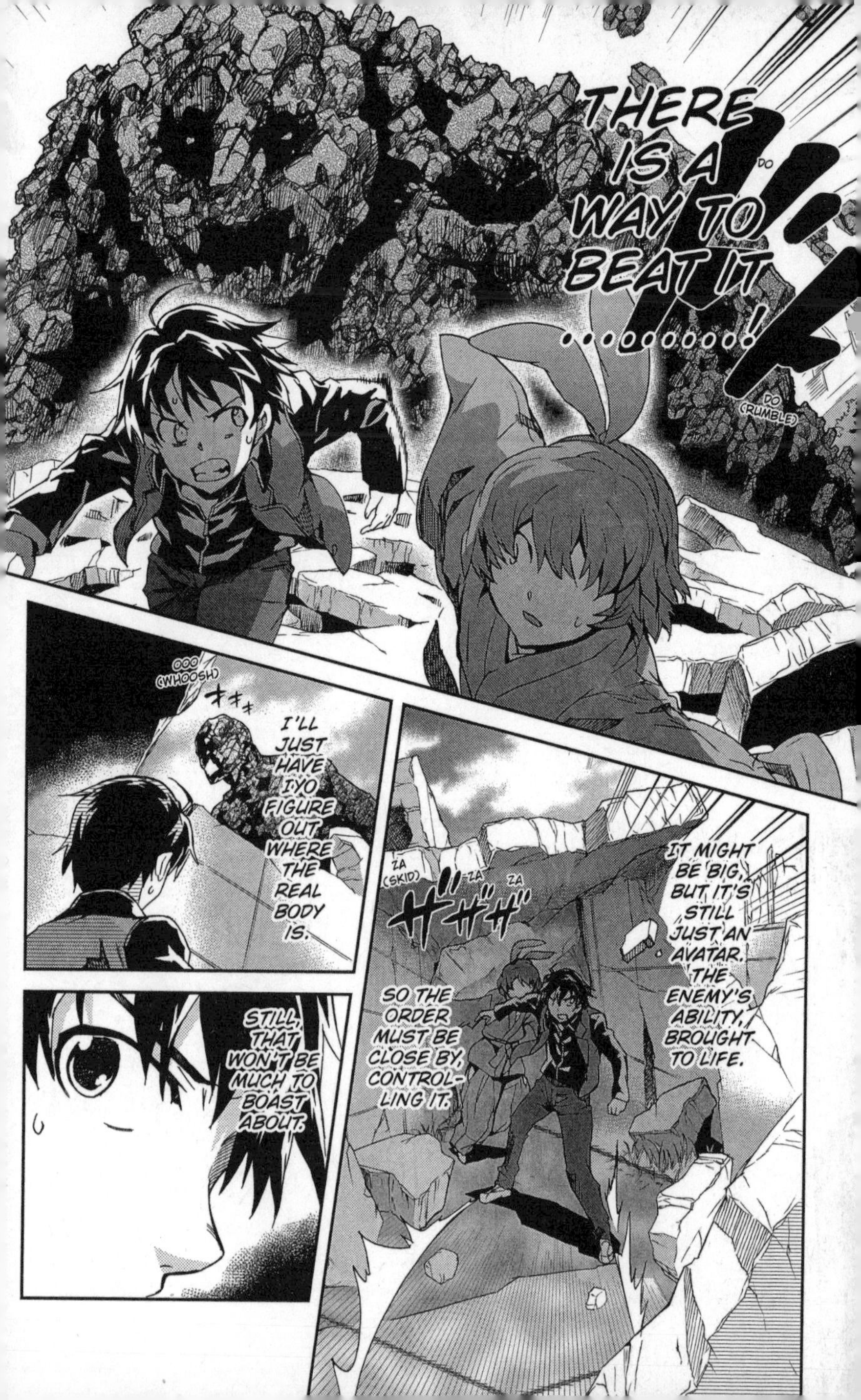
THERE IS A WAY TO BEAT IT..........!
DO
DO (RUMBLE)
ZA (SKID) ZA ZA
IT MIGHT BE BIG, BUT IT'S STILL JUST AN AVATAR. THE ENEMY'S ABILITY, BROUGHT TO LIFE.
SO THE ORDER MUST BE CLOSE BY, CONTROL-LING IT.
OOO (WHOOSH)
I'LL JUST HAVE IYO FIGURE OUT WHERE THE REAL BODY IS.
STILL, THAT WON'T BE MUCH TO BOAST ABOUT.

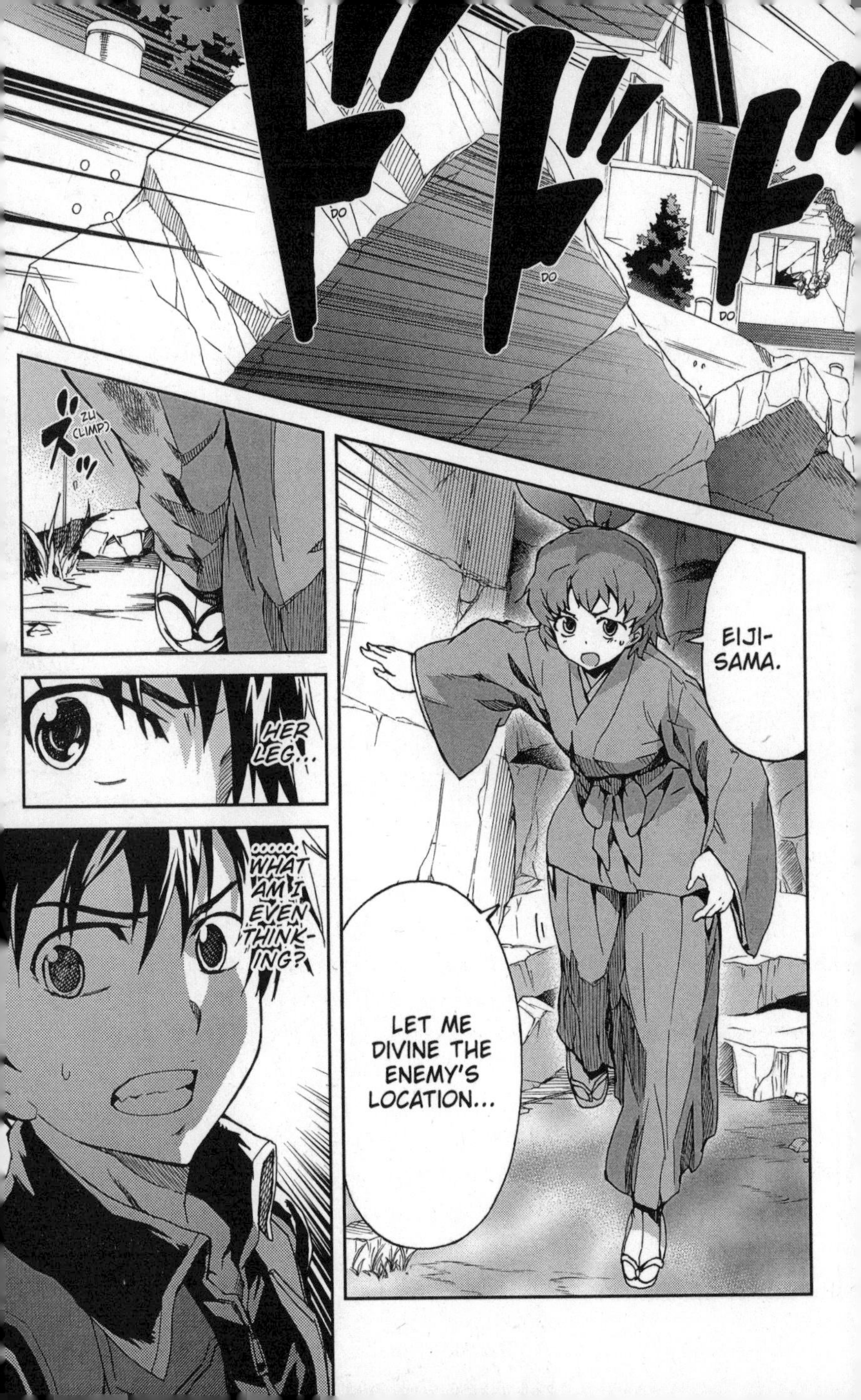
DO
DO
DO
EIJI-SAMA.
LET ME DIVINE THE ENEMY'S LOCATION...
ZU (LIMP)
HER LEG...
......WHAT AM I EVEN THINKING?

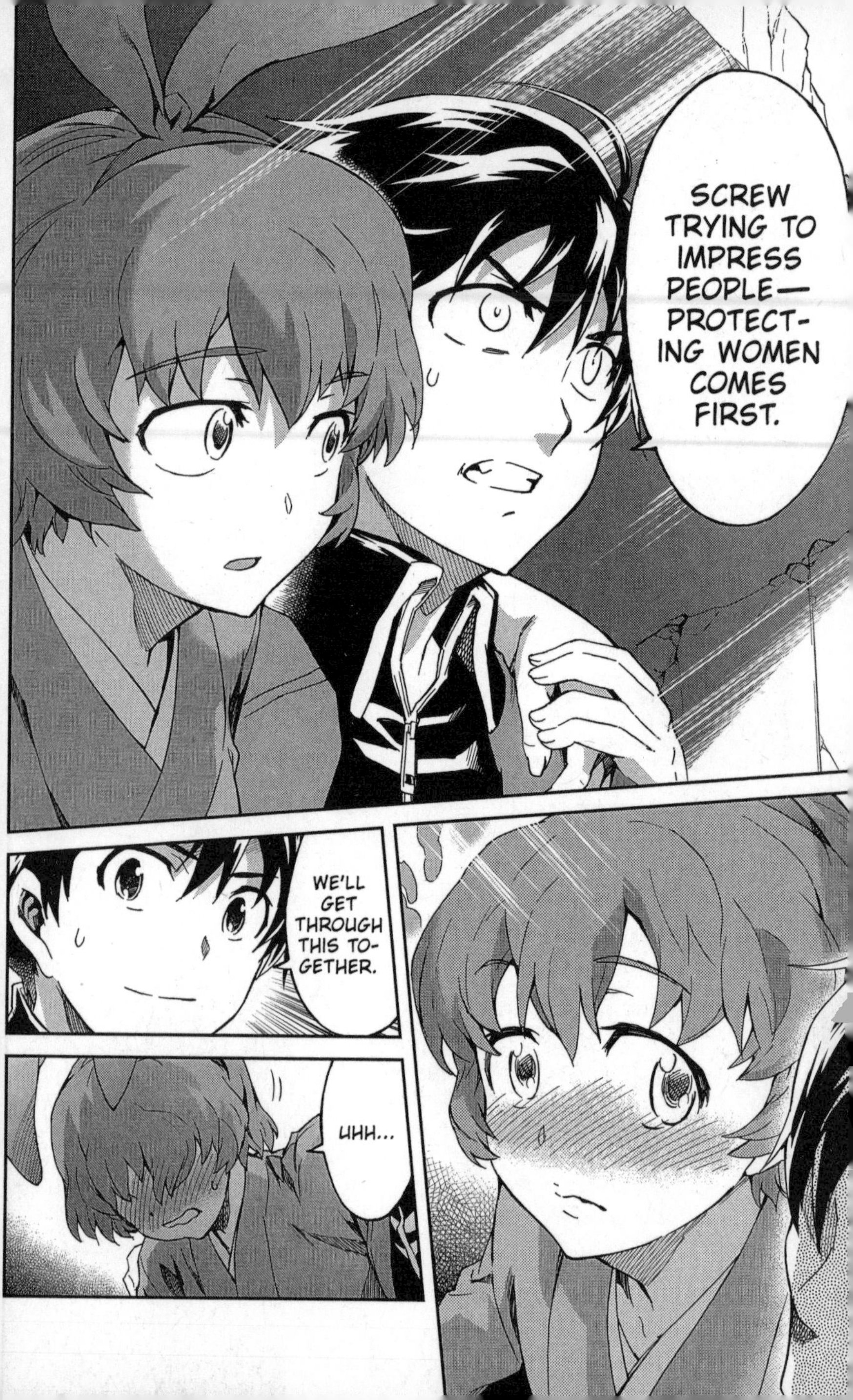
SCREW TRYING TO IMPRESS PEOPLE—PROTECTING WOMEN COMES FIRST.
WE'LL GET THROUGH THIS TOGETHER.
UHH...

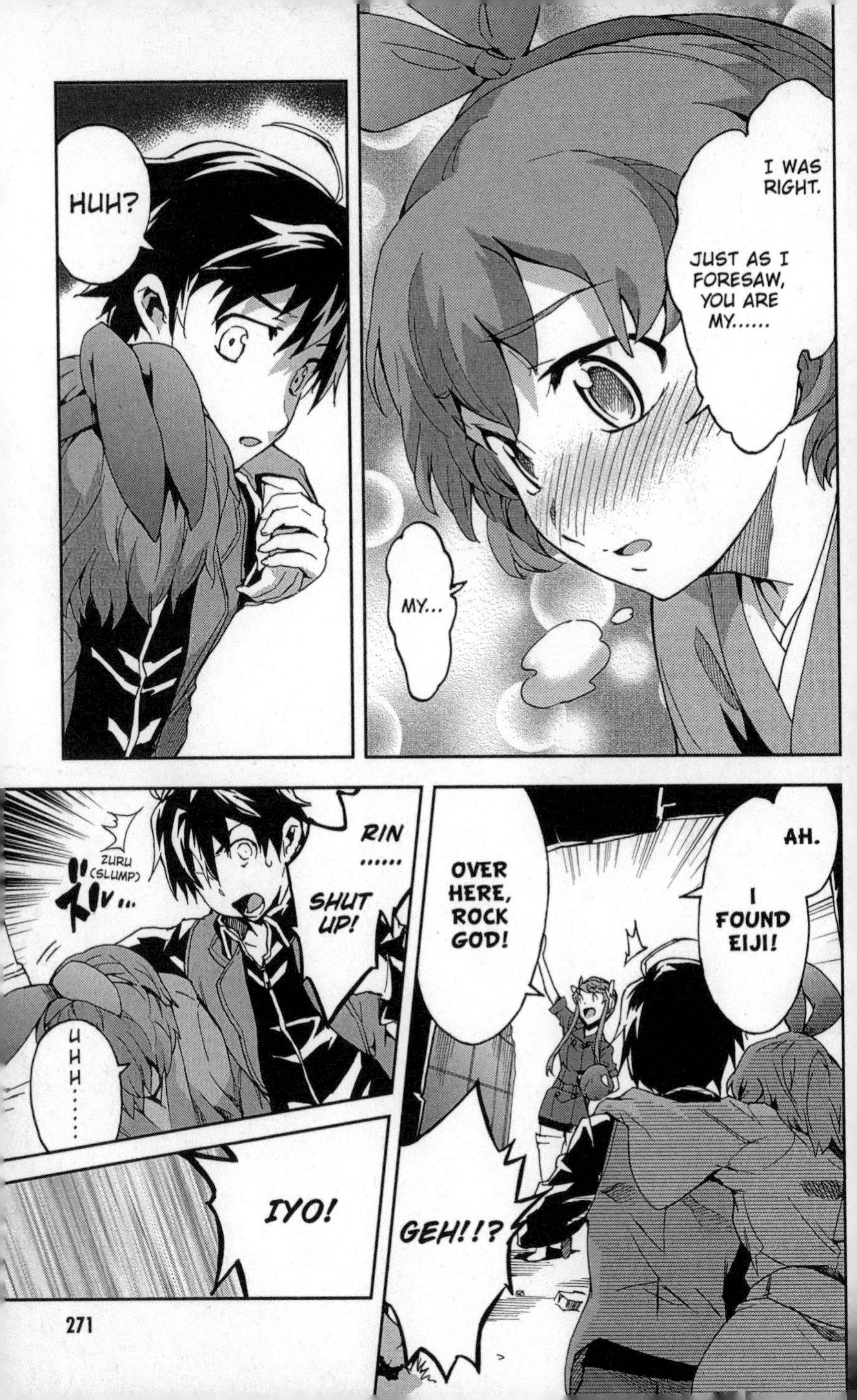
I WAS RIGHT.
JUST AS I FORESAW, YOU ARE MY......
MY...
HUH?
AH.
I FOUND EIJI!
OVER HERE, ROCK GOD!
GEH!!?
RIN ......
SHUT UP!
ズルッ...
ZURU (SLUMP)
UHH......
IYO!

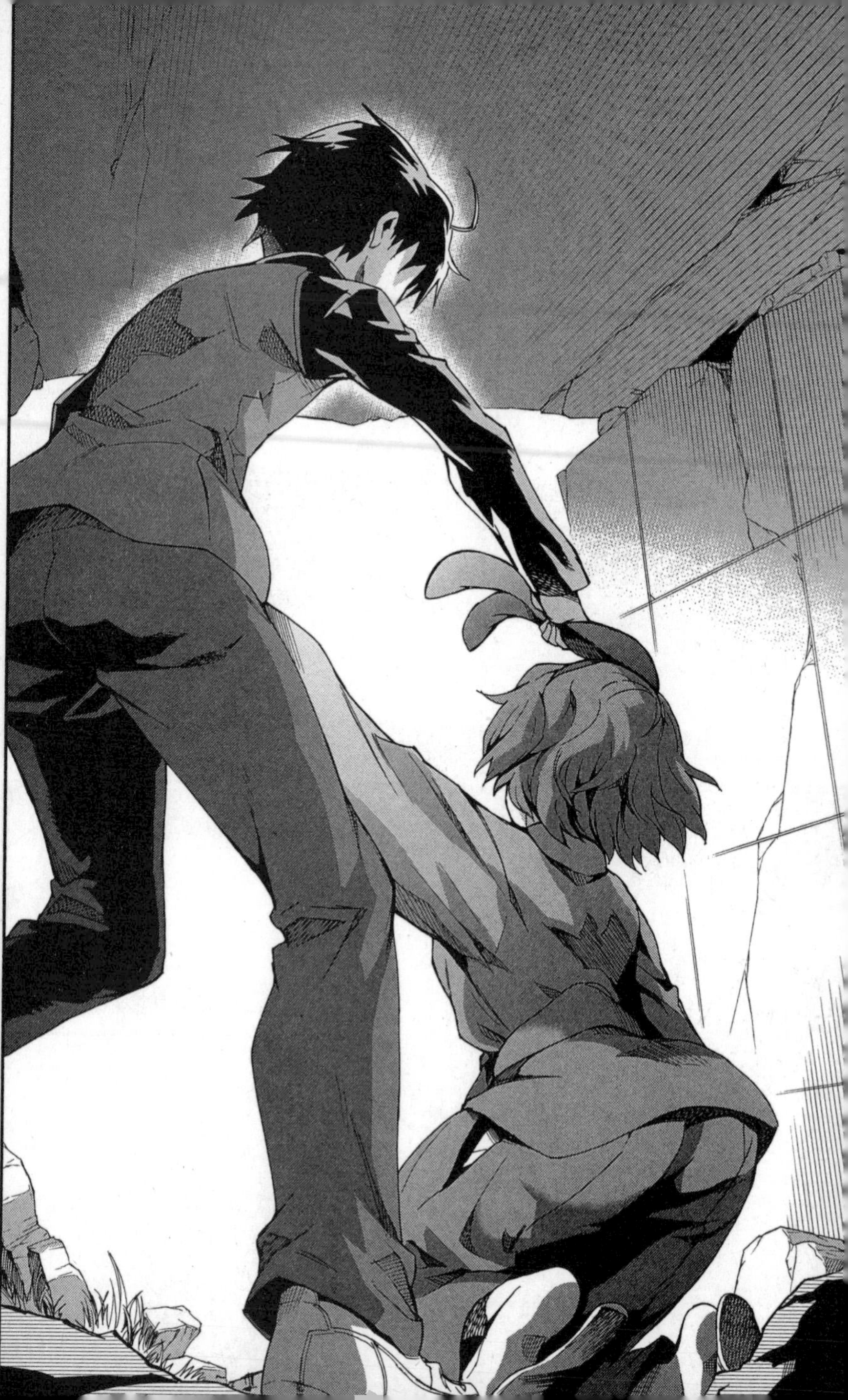

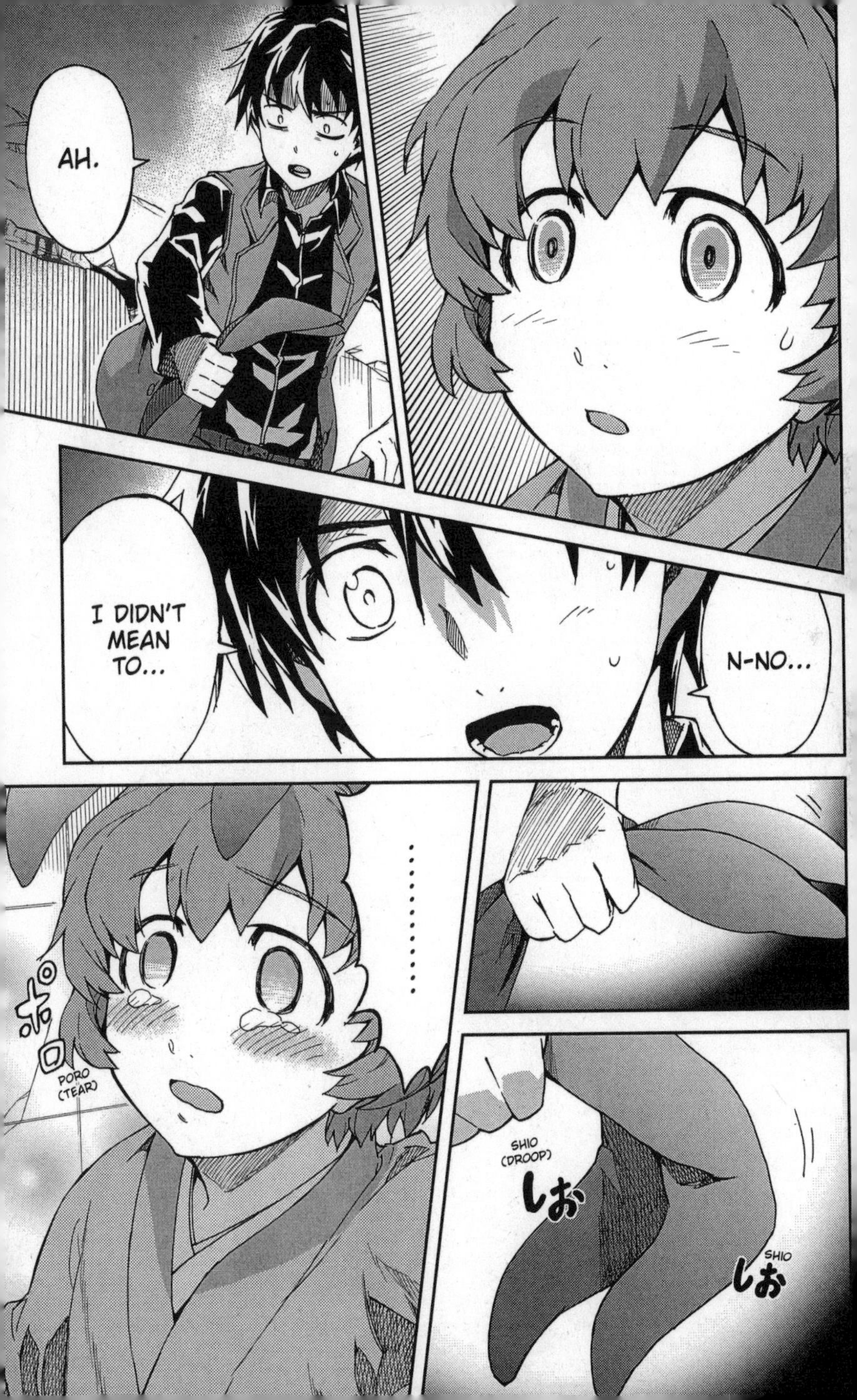
AH.
N-NO...
I DIDN'T MEAN TO...
しお
SHIO (DROOP)
しお
SHIO
......
ポロ
PORO (TEAR)

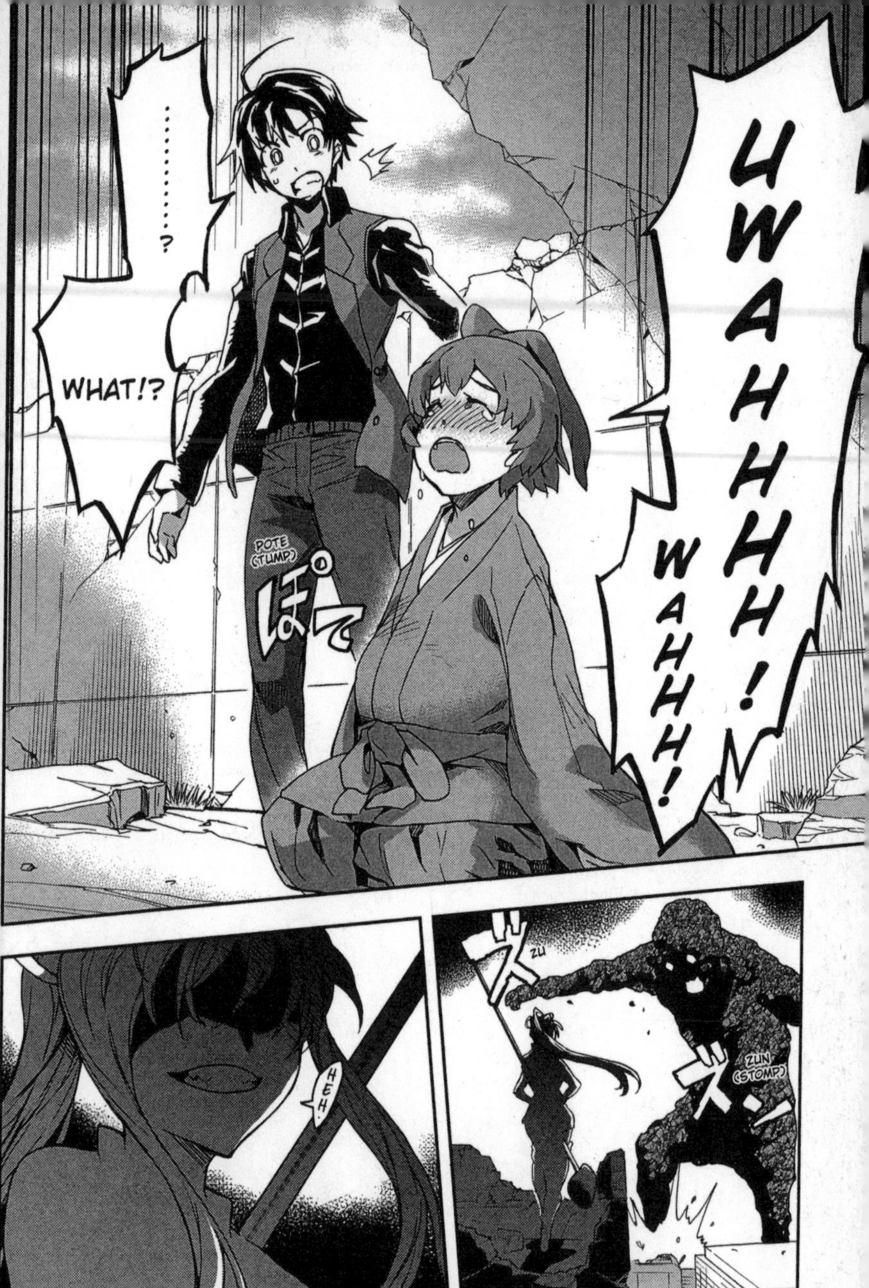
UWAHHHH!
WAHHHH!
......?
WHAT!?
POTE (TUMP)
ぽて
ZU
ZUN (STOMP)
HEH.

Subject 6: END

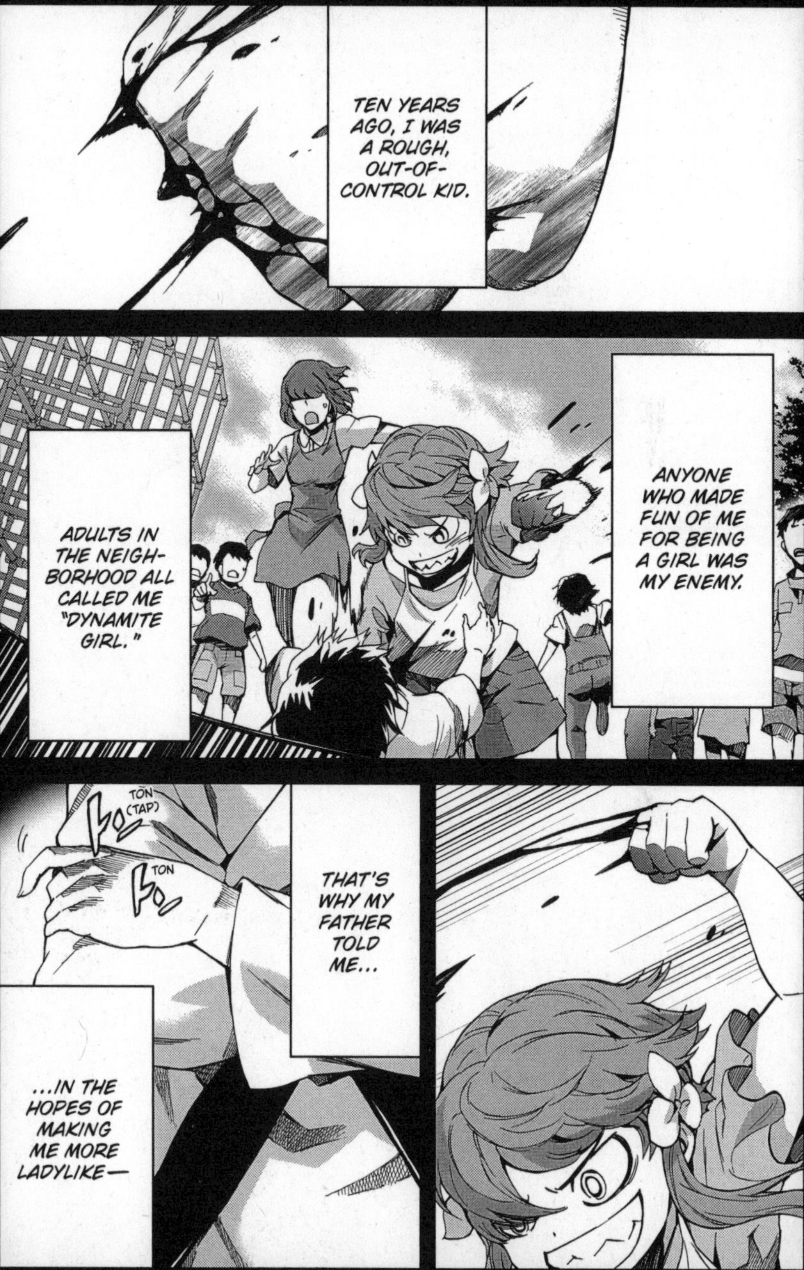
TEN YEARS AGO, I WAS A ROUGH, OUT-OF-CONTROL KID.
ANYONE WHO MADE FUN OF ME FOR BEING A GIRL WAS MY ENEMY.
ADULTS IN THE NEIGH-BORHOOD ALL CALLED ME "DYNAMITE GIRL."
THAT'S WHY MY FATHER TOLD ME...
TON (TAP)
TON
...IN THE HOPES OF MAKING ME MORE LADYLIKE—

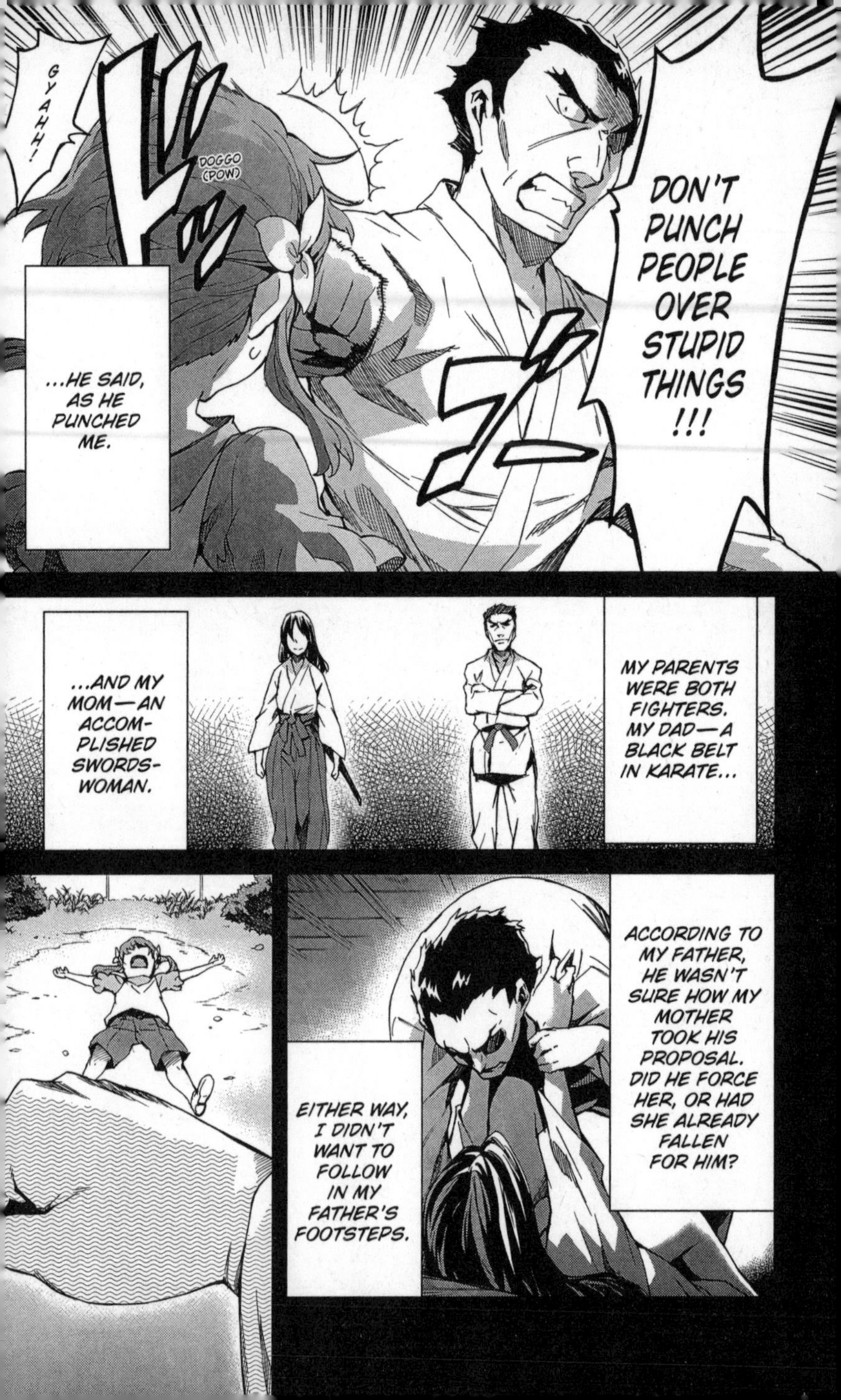
DON'T PUNCH PEOPLE OVER STUPID THINGS!!!
GYAHH!
DOGGO (POW)
...HE SAID, AS HE PUNCHED ME.
MY PARENTS WERE BOTH FIGHTERS. MY DAD—A BLACK BELT IN KARATE...
...AND MY MOM—AN ACCOMPLISHED SWORDSWOMAN.
ACCORDING TO MY FATHER, HE WASN'T SURE HOW MY MOTHER TOOK HIS PROPOSAL. DID HE FORCE HER, OR HAD SHE ALREADY FALLEN FOR HIM?
EITHER WAY, I DIDN'T WANT TO FOLLOW IN MY FATHER'S FOOTSTEPS.

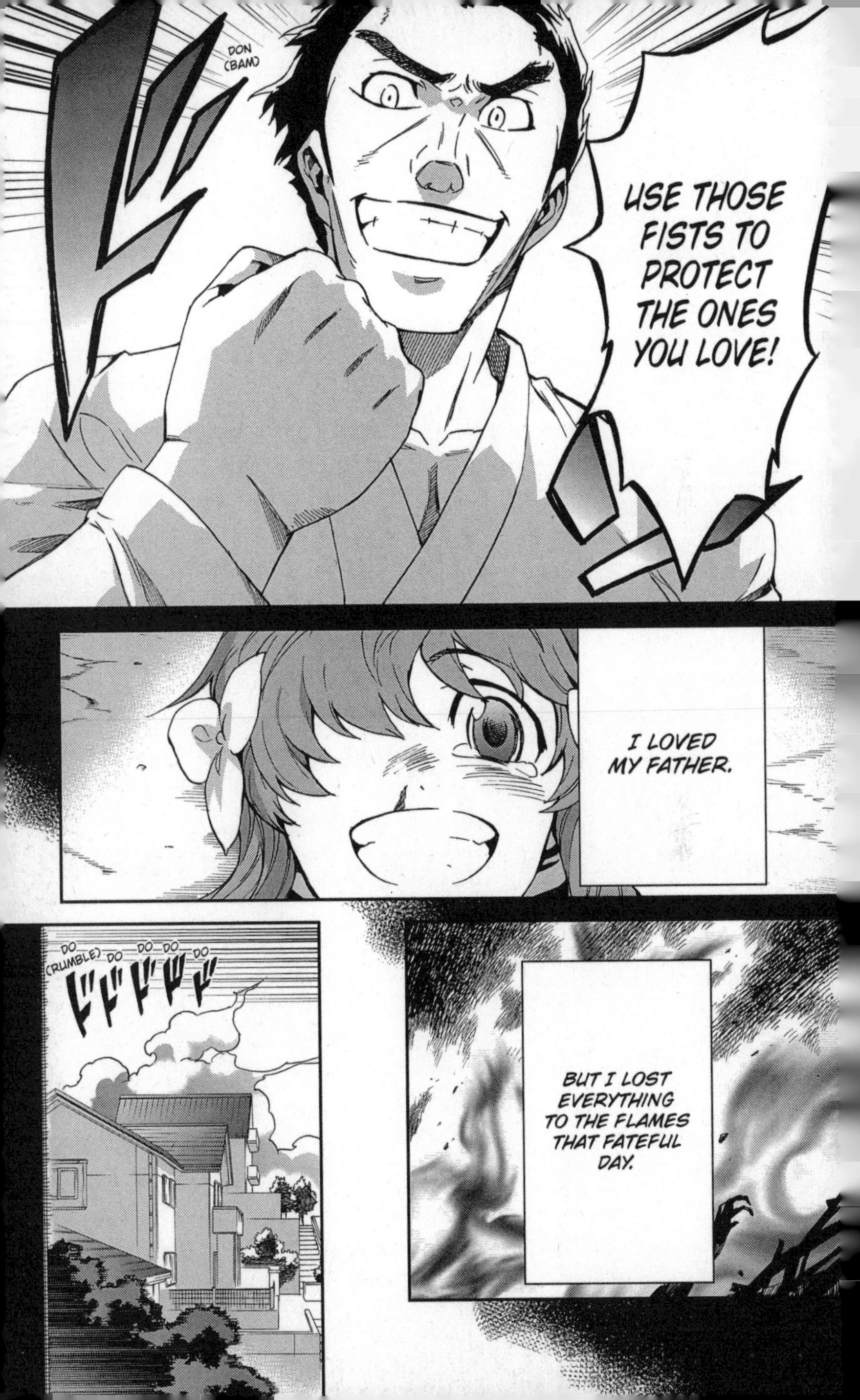

DON (BAM)
USE THOSE FISTS TO PROTECT THE ONES YOU LOVE!
I LOVED MY FATHER.
BUT I LOST EVERYTHING TO THE FLAMES THAT FATEFUL DAY.
DO (RUMBLE) DO DO DO DO
ドドドドド

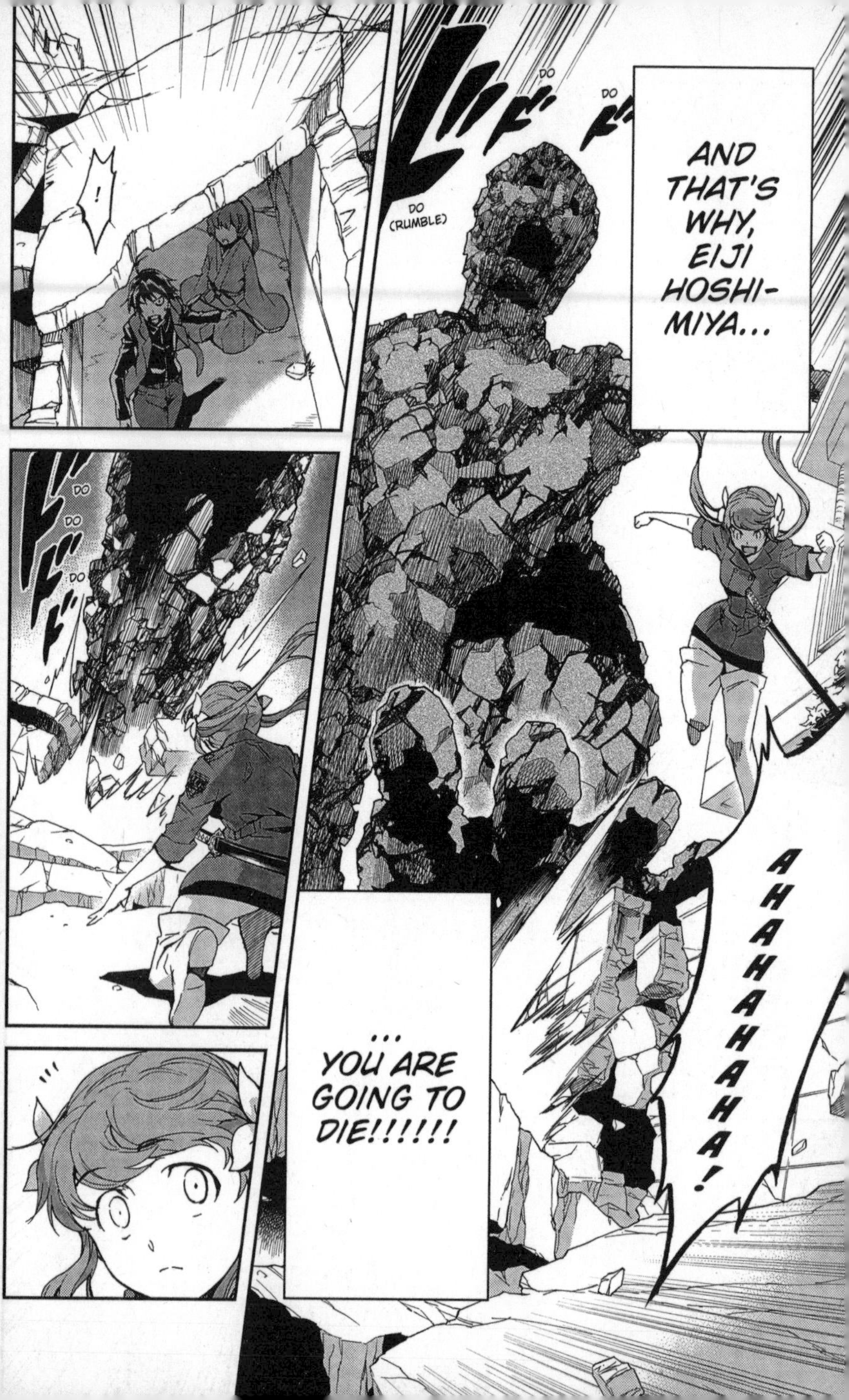
DO
DO
AND THAT'S WHY, EIJI HOSHI-MIYA...
DO (RUMBLE)
AHAHAHAHAHA!
... YOU ARE GOING TO DIE!!!!!!
!
DO
DO
DO
!!

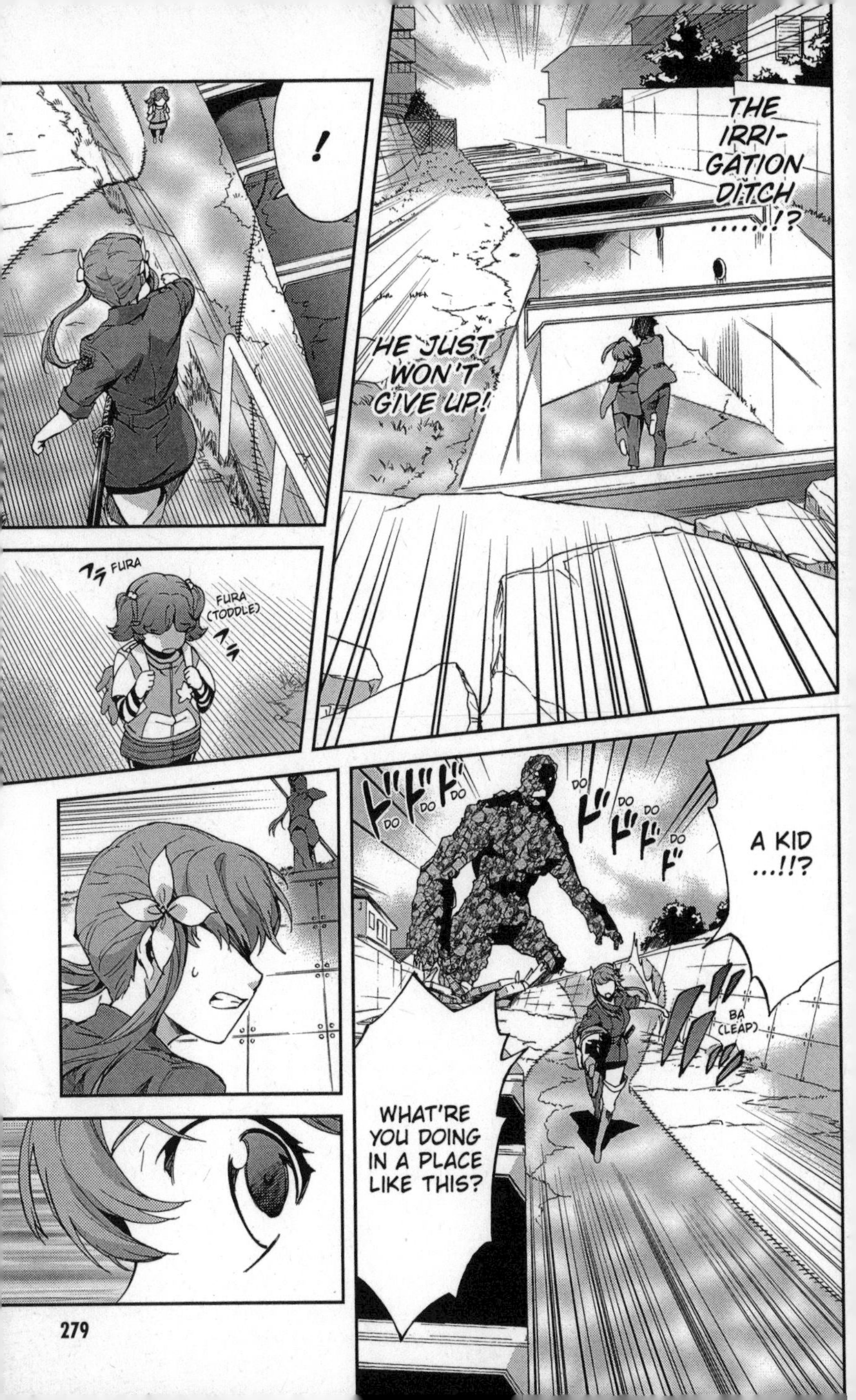
THE IRRI-GATION DITCH ......!?
HE JUST WON'T GIVE UP!
!
FURA
FURA (TODDLE)
DO DO DO
DO DO DO DO
A KID ...!!?
BA (LEAP)
WHAT'RE YOU DOING IN A PLACE LIKE THIS?

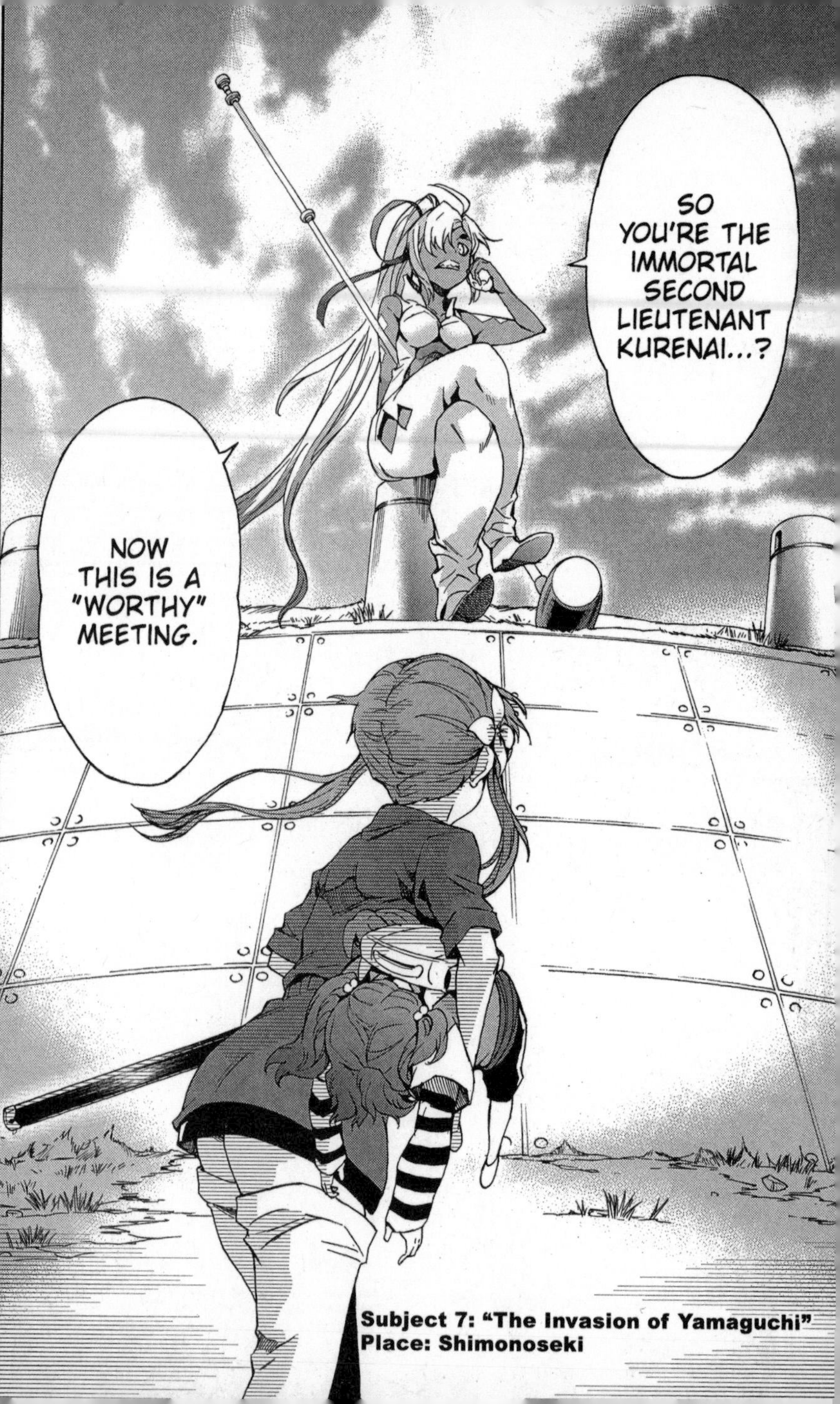
SO YOU'RE THE IMMORTAL SECOND LIEUTENANT KURENAI...?
NOW THIS IS A "WORTHY" MEETING.
Subject 7: "The Invasion of Yamaguchi"
Place: Shimonoseki

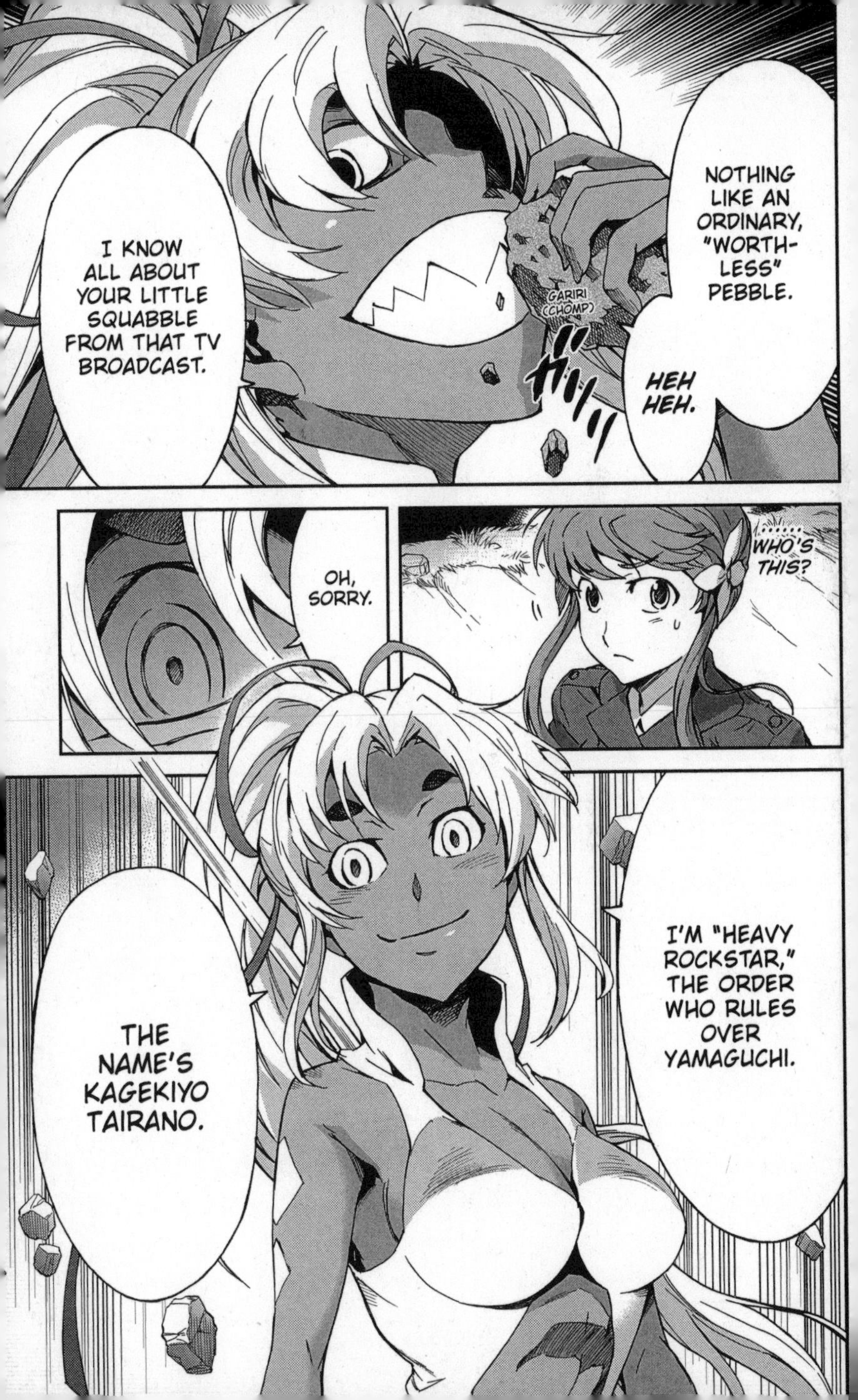
NOTHING LIKE AN ORDINARY, "WORTH-LESS" PEBBLE.
HEH HEH.
GARIRI (CHOMP)
I KNOW ALL ABOUT YOUR LITTLE SQUABBLE FROM THAT TV BROADCAST.
......WHO'S THIS?
OH, SORRY.
I'M "HEAVY ROCKSTAR," THE ORDER WHO RULES OVER YAMAGUCHI.
THE NAME'S KAGEKIYO TAIRANO.

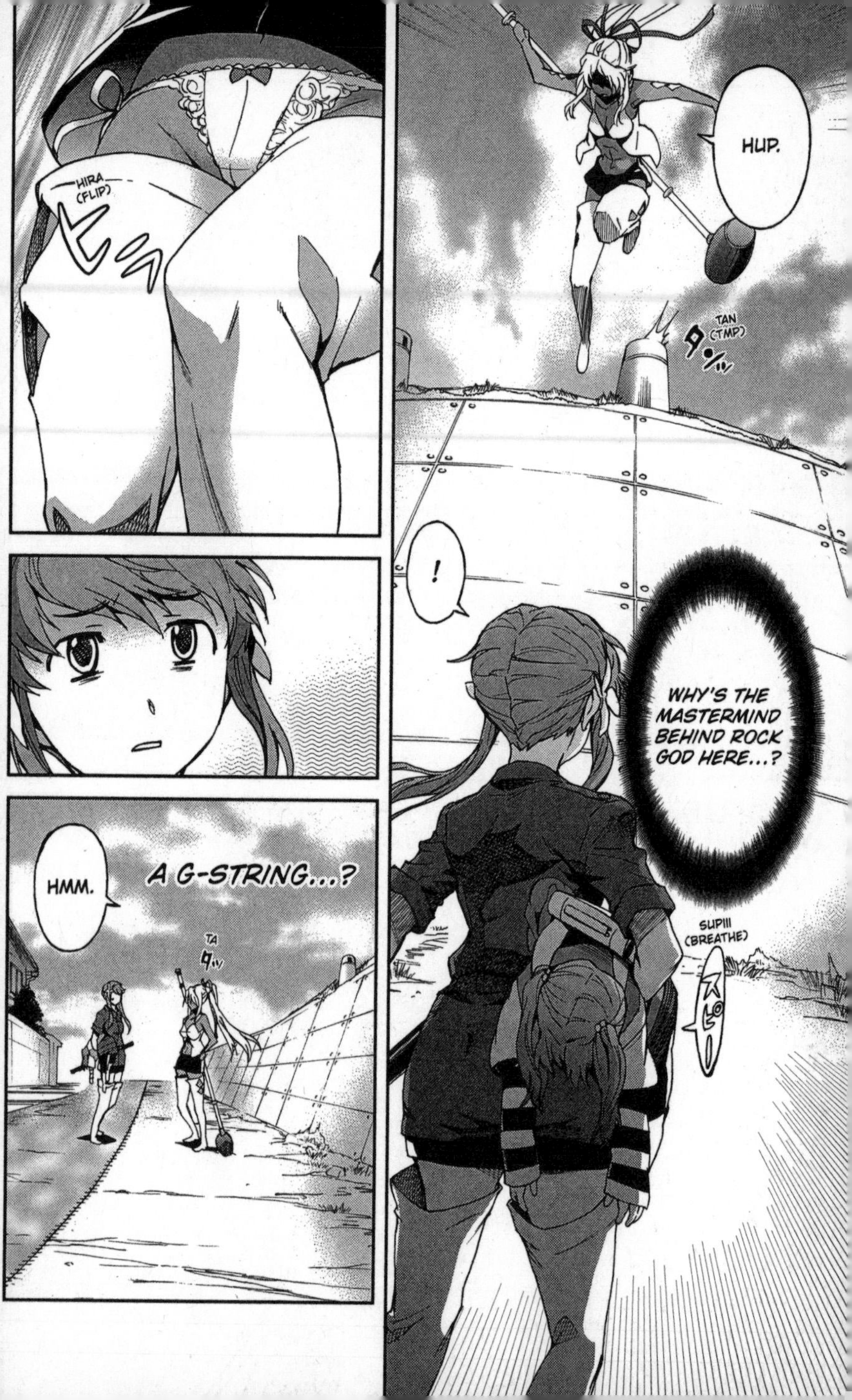
HUP.
TAN (TMP)
!
WHY'S THE MASTERMIND BEHIND ROCK GOD HERE...?
SUPIII (BREATHE)
HIRA (FLIP)
HMM.
A G-STRING...?
TA

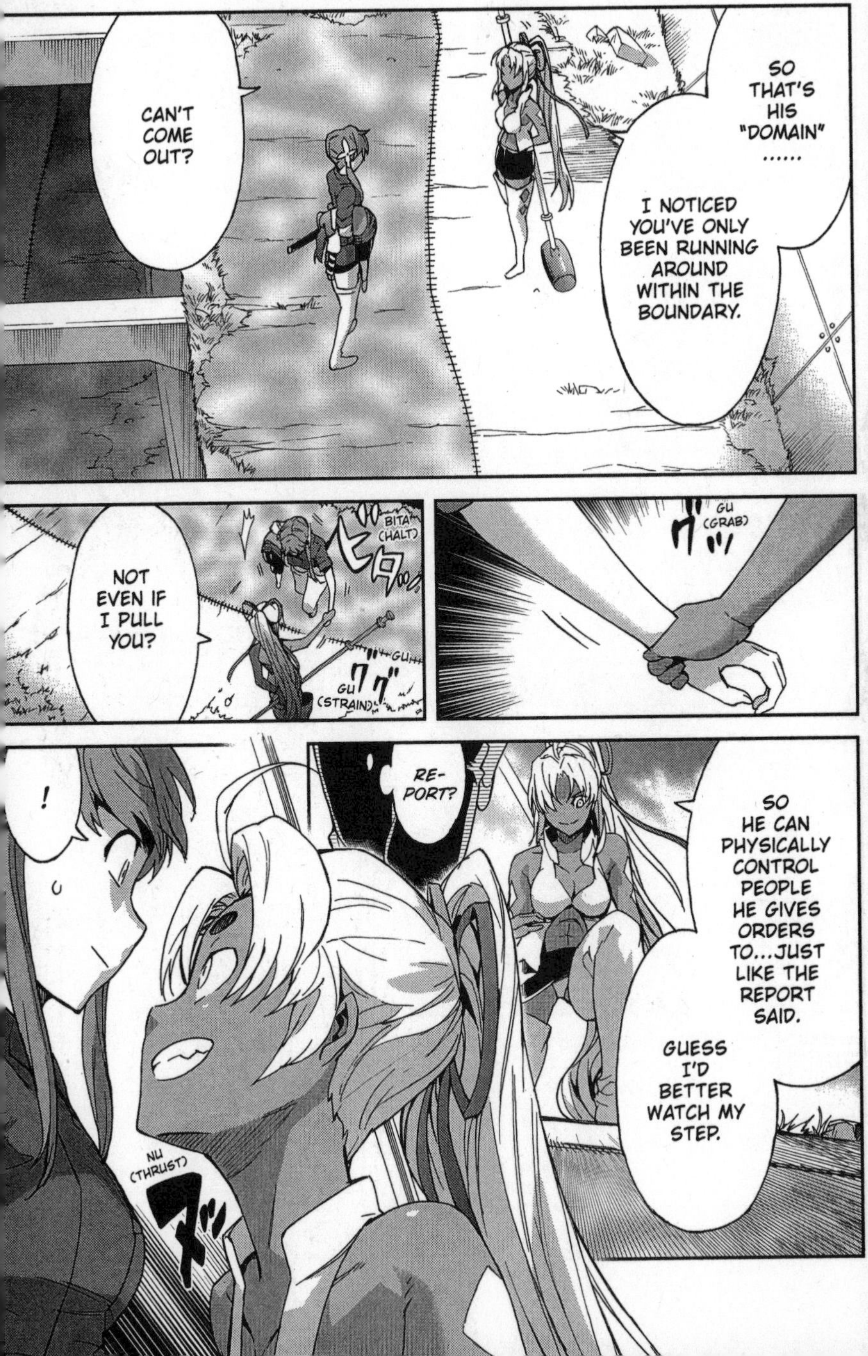
SO THAT'S HIS "DOMAIN" ......
I NOTICED YOU'VE ONLY BEEN RUNNING AROUND WITHIN THE BOUNDARY.
CAN'T COME OUT?
GU (GRAB)
BITA (HALT)
NOT EVEN IF I PULL YOU?
GU GU (STRAIN)
SO HE CAN PHYSICALLY CONTROL PEOPLE HE GIVES ORDERS TO...JUST LIKE THE REPORT SAID.
GUESS I'D BETTER WATCH MY STEP.
RE-PORT?
!
NU (THRUST)

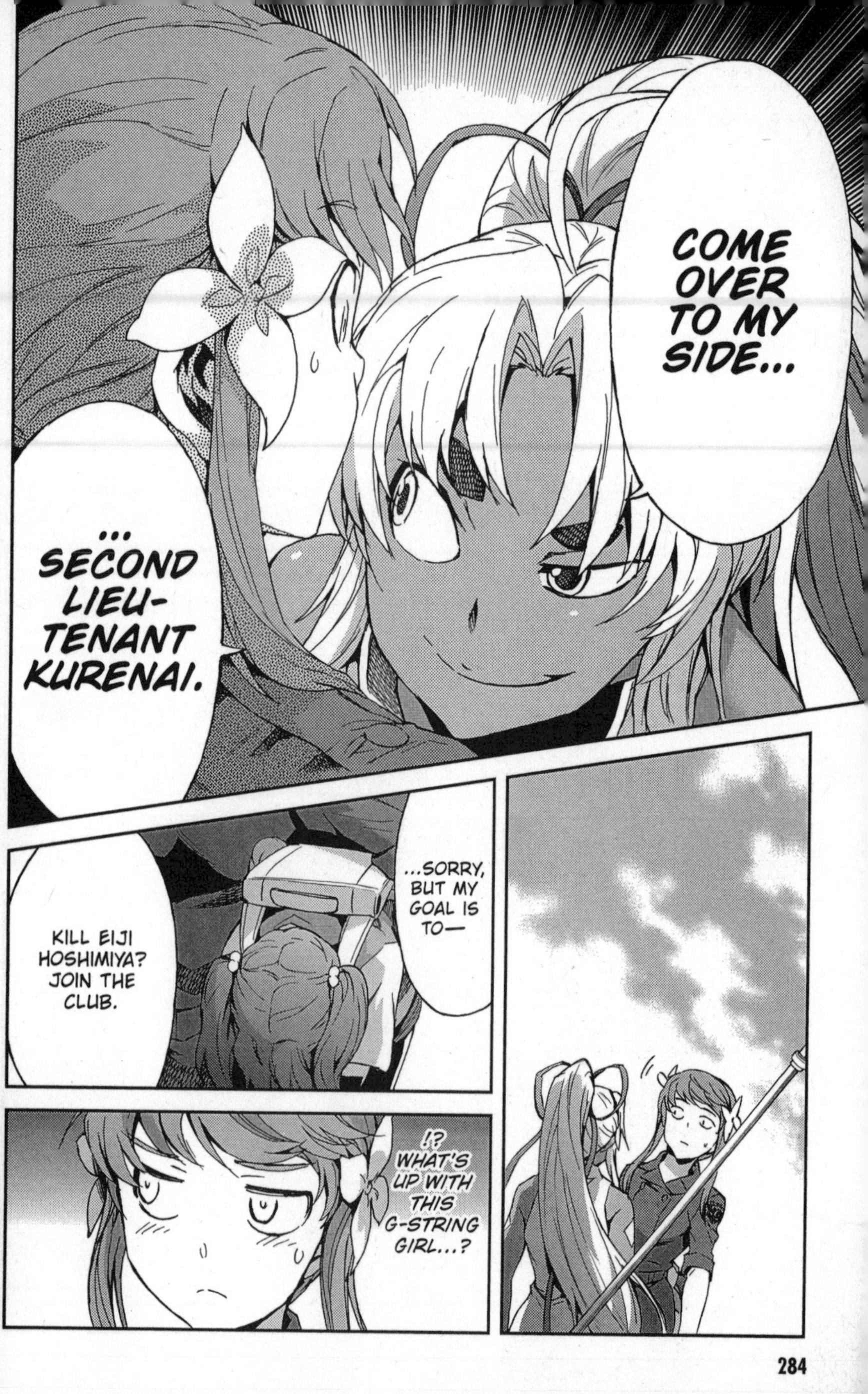
COME OVER TO MY SIDE...
...SECOND LIEU-TENANT KURENAI.
...SORRY, BUT MY GOAL IS TO—
KILL EIJI HOSHIMIYA? JOIN THE CLUB.
!? WHAT'S UP WITH THIS G-STRING GIRL...?

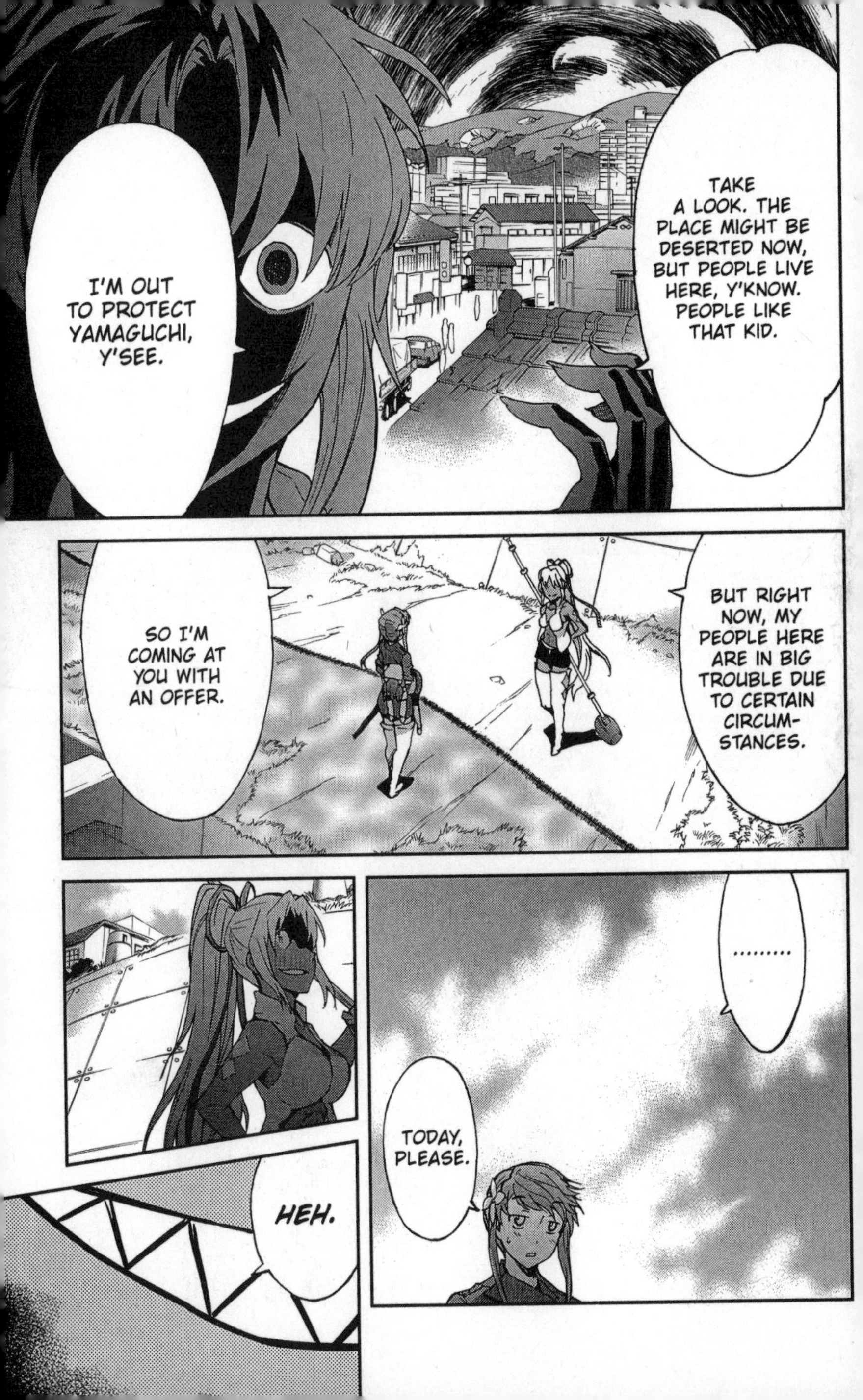
TAKE A LOOK. THE PLACE MIGHT BE DESERTED NOW, BUT PEOPLE LIVE HERE, Y'KNOW. PEOPLE LIKE THAT KID.
I'M OUT TO PROTECT YAMAGUCHI, Y'SEE.
BUT RIGHT NOW, MY PEOPLE HERE ARE IN BIG TROUBLE DUE TO CERTAIN CIRCUM-STANCES.
SO I'M COMING AT YOU WITH AN OFFER.
.........
TODAY, PLEASE.
HEH.

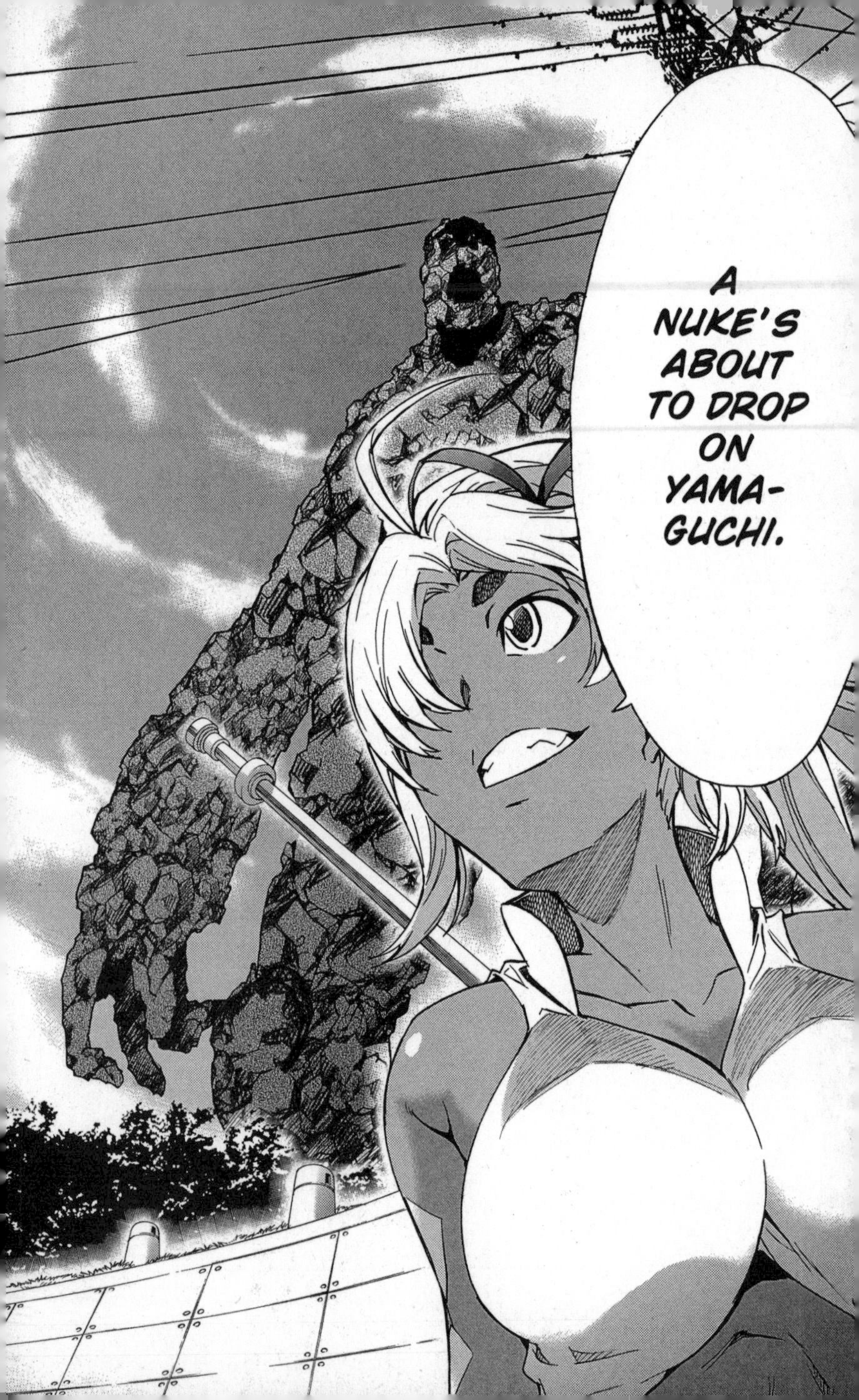
A NUKE'S ABOUT TO DROP ON YAMA-GUCHI.

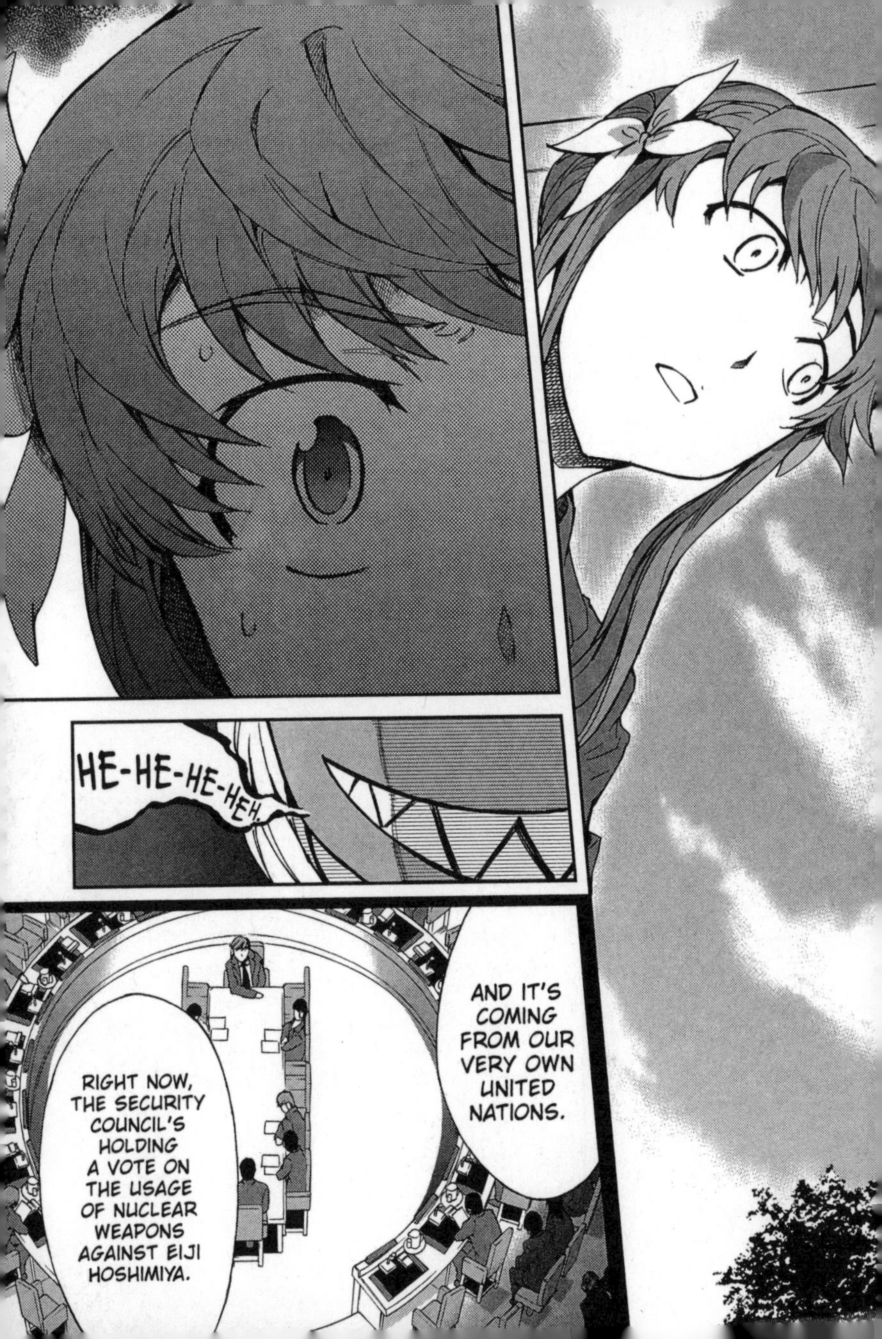
HE-HE-HE-HEH.
AND IT'S COMING FROM OUR VERY OWN UNITED NATIONS.
RIGHT NOW, THE SECURITY COUNCIL'S HOLDING A VOTE ON THE USAGE OF NUCLEAR WEAPONS AGAINST EIJI HOSHIMIYA.

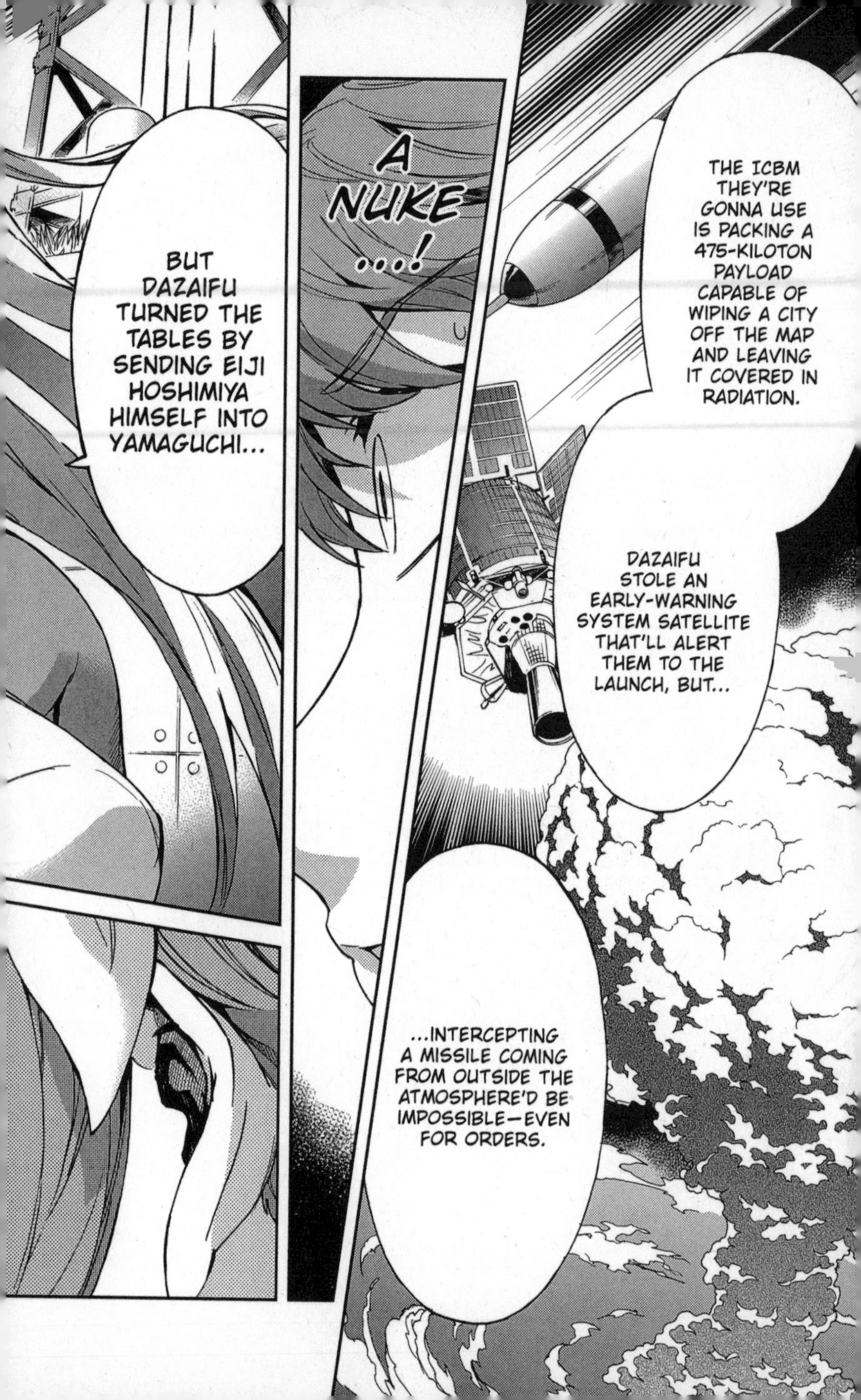
THE ICBM THEY'RE GONNA USE IS PACKING A 475-KILOTON PAYLOAD CAPABLE OF WIPING A CITY OFF THE MAP AND LEAVING IT COVERED IN RADIATION.
DAZAIFU STOLE AN EARLY-WARNING SYSTEM SATELLITE THAT'LL ALERT THEM TO THE LAUNCH, BUT...
...INTERCEPTING A MISSILE COMING FROM OUTSIDE THE ATMOSPHERE'D BE IMPOSSIBLE—EVEN FOR ORDERS.
A NUKE ...!
BUT DAZAIFU TURNED THE TABLES BY SENDING EIJI HOSHIMIYA HIMSELF INTO YAMAGUCHI...

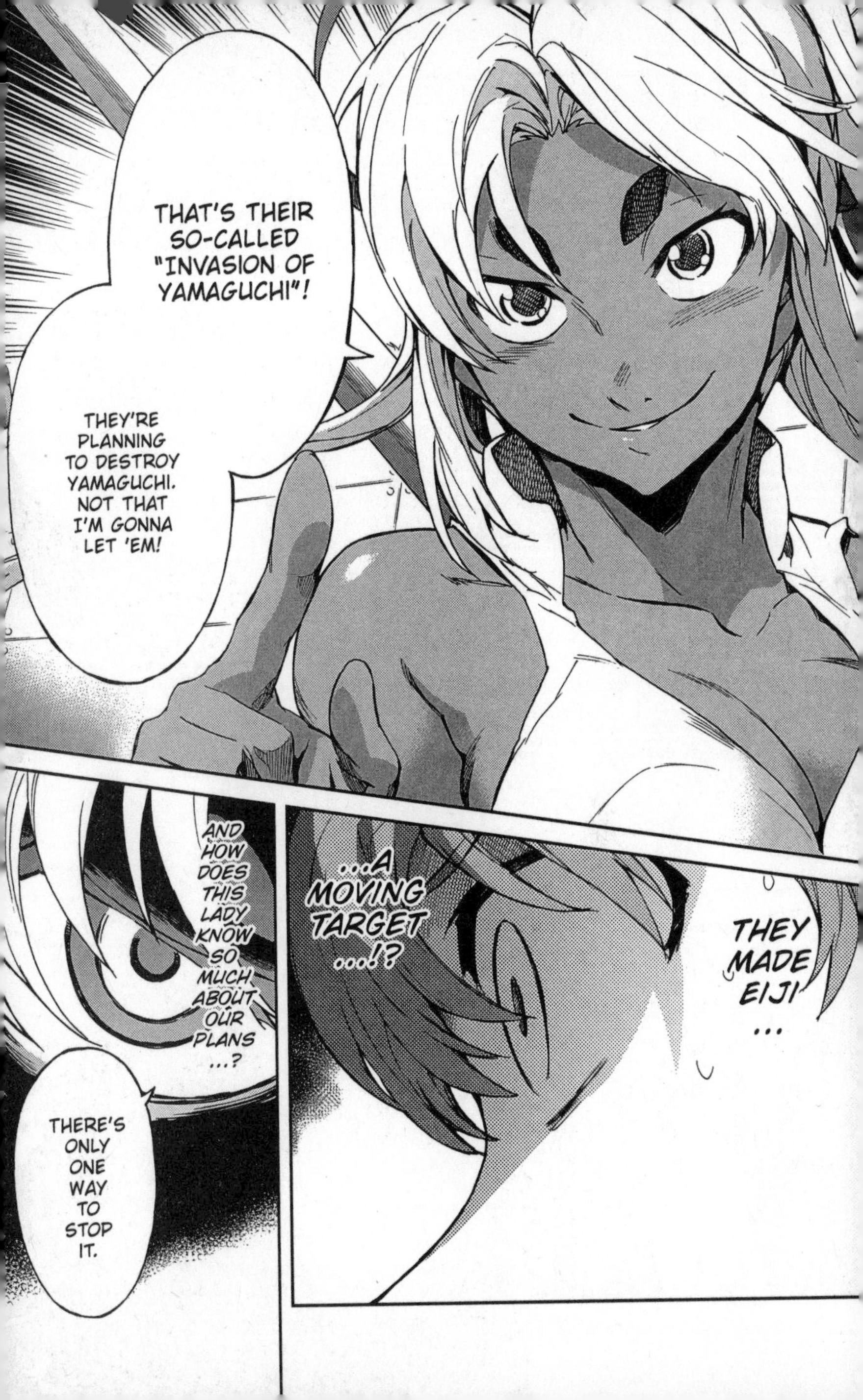
THAT'S THEIR SO-CALLED "INVASION OF YAMAGUCHI"!
THEY'RE PLANNING TO DESTROY YAMAGUCHI. NOT THAT I'M GONNA LET 'EM!
THEY MADE EIJI...
...A MOVING TARGET...!?
AND HOW DOES THIS LADY KNOW SO MUCH ABOUT OUR PLANS...?
THERE'S ONLY ONE WAY TO STOP IT.

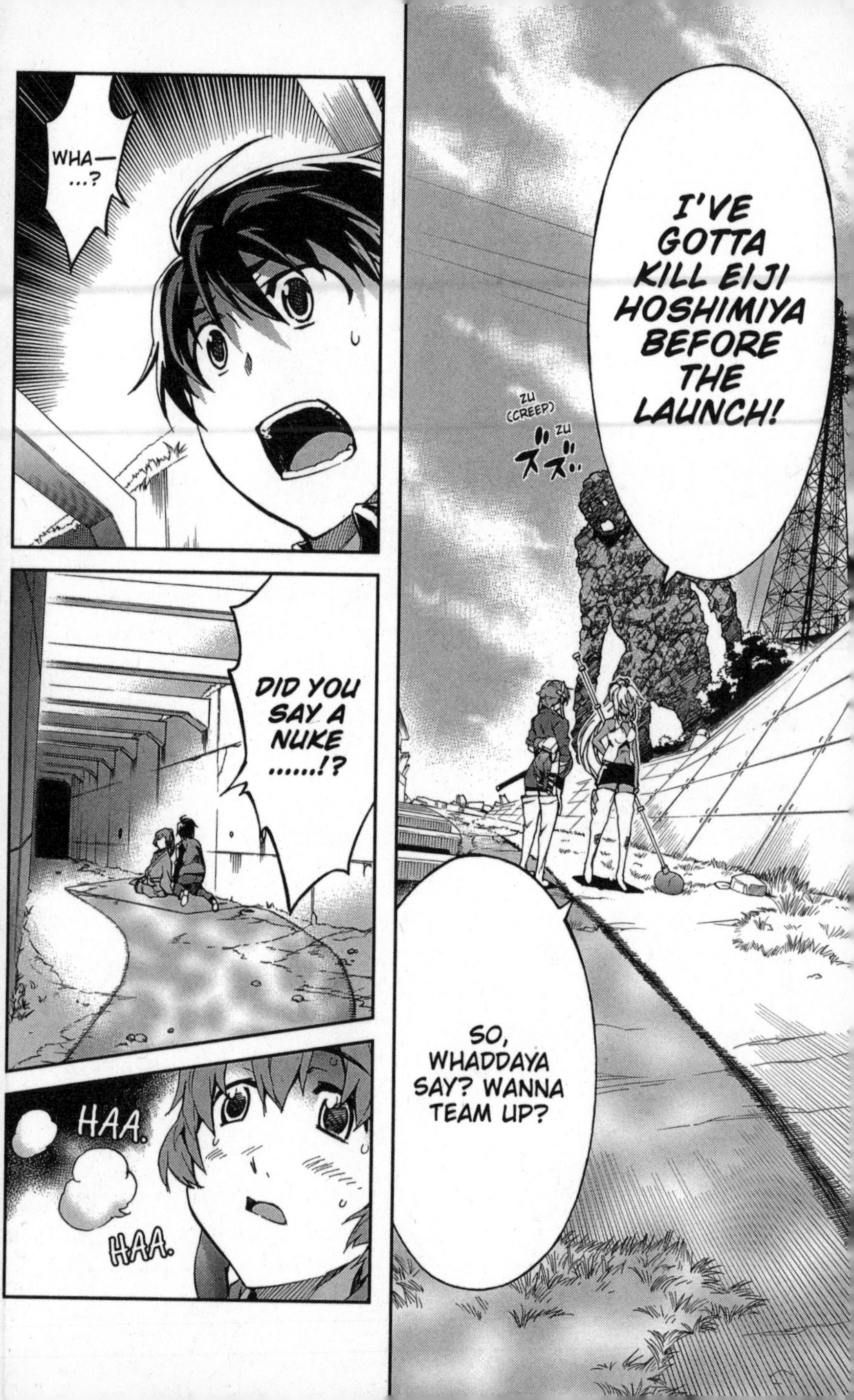
I'VE GOTTA KILL EIJI HOSHIMIYA BEFORE THE LAUNCH!
ZU (CREEP) ZU
ズズ
SO, WHADDAYA SAY? WANNA TEAM UP?
WHA— ...?
DID YOU SAY A NUKE ......!?
HAA.
HAA.

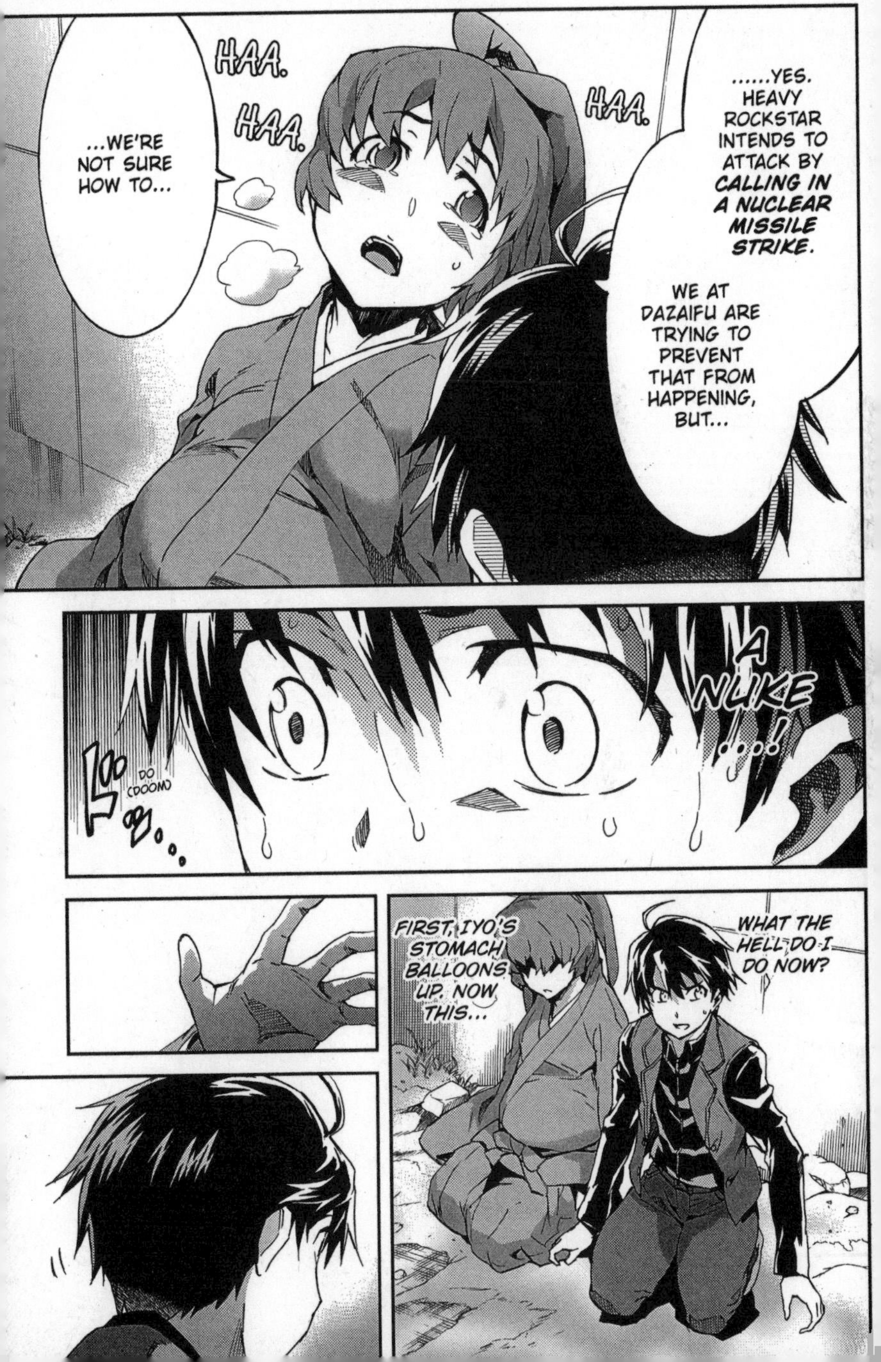
......YES. HEAVY ROCKSTAR INTENDS TO ATTACK BY CALLING IN A NUCLEAR MISSILE STRIKE.
WE AT DAZAIFU ARE TRYING TO PREVENT THAT FROM HAPPENING, BUT...
HAA.
HAA.
HAA.
...WE'RE NOT SURE HOW TO...
A NUKE ...!
DO (DOOM)
WHAT THE HELL DO I DO NOW?
FIRST, IYO'S STOMACH BALLOONS UP. NOW THIS...

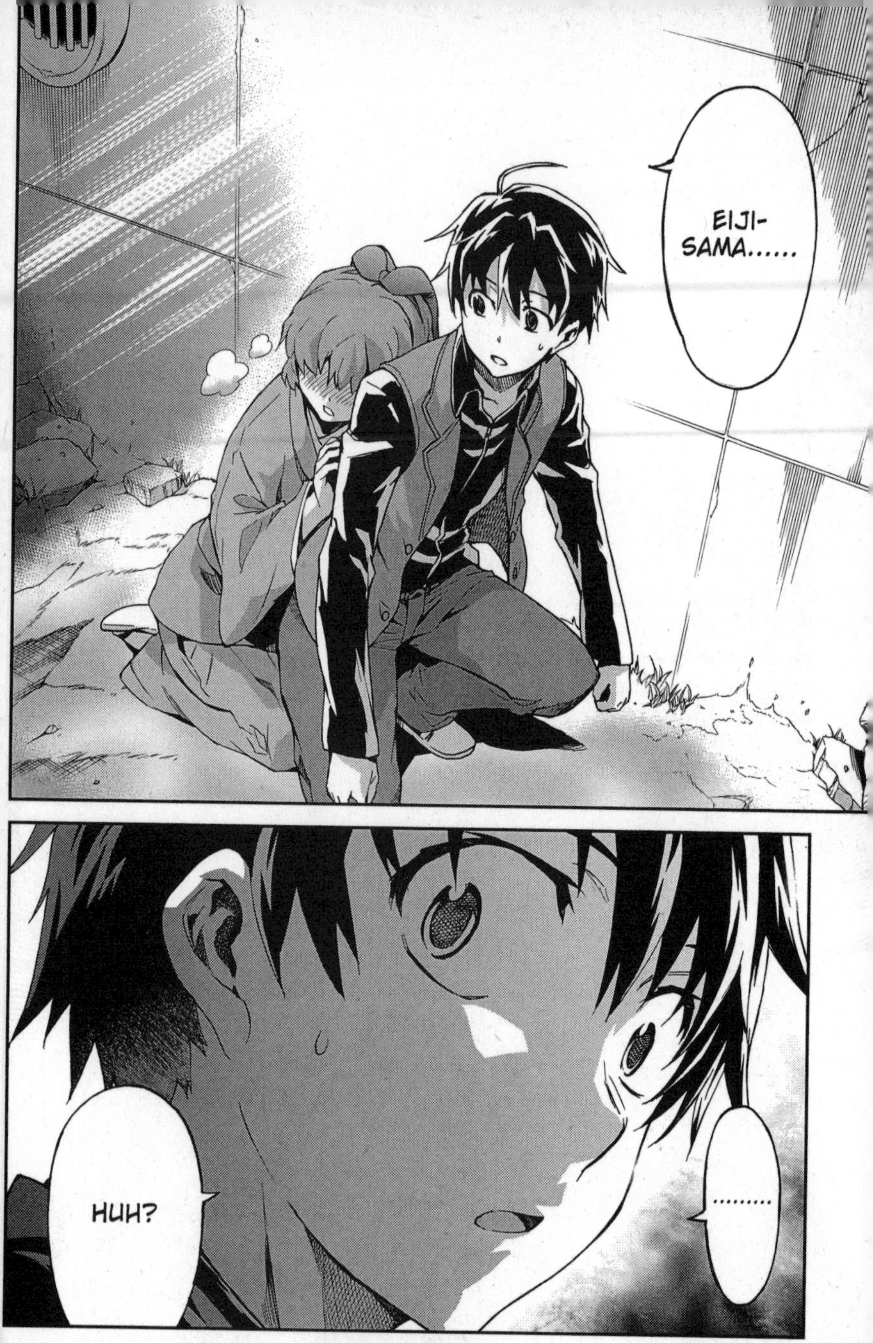
EIJI-SAMA......
.........
HUH?

**Subject 7: END**

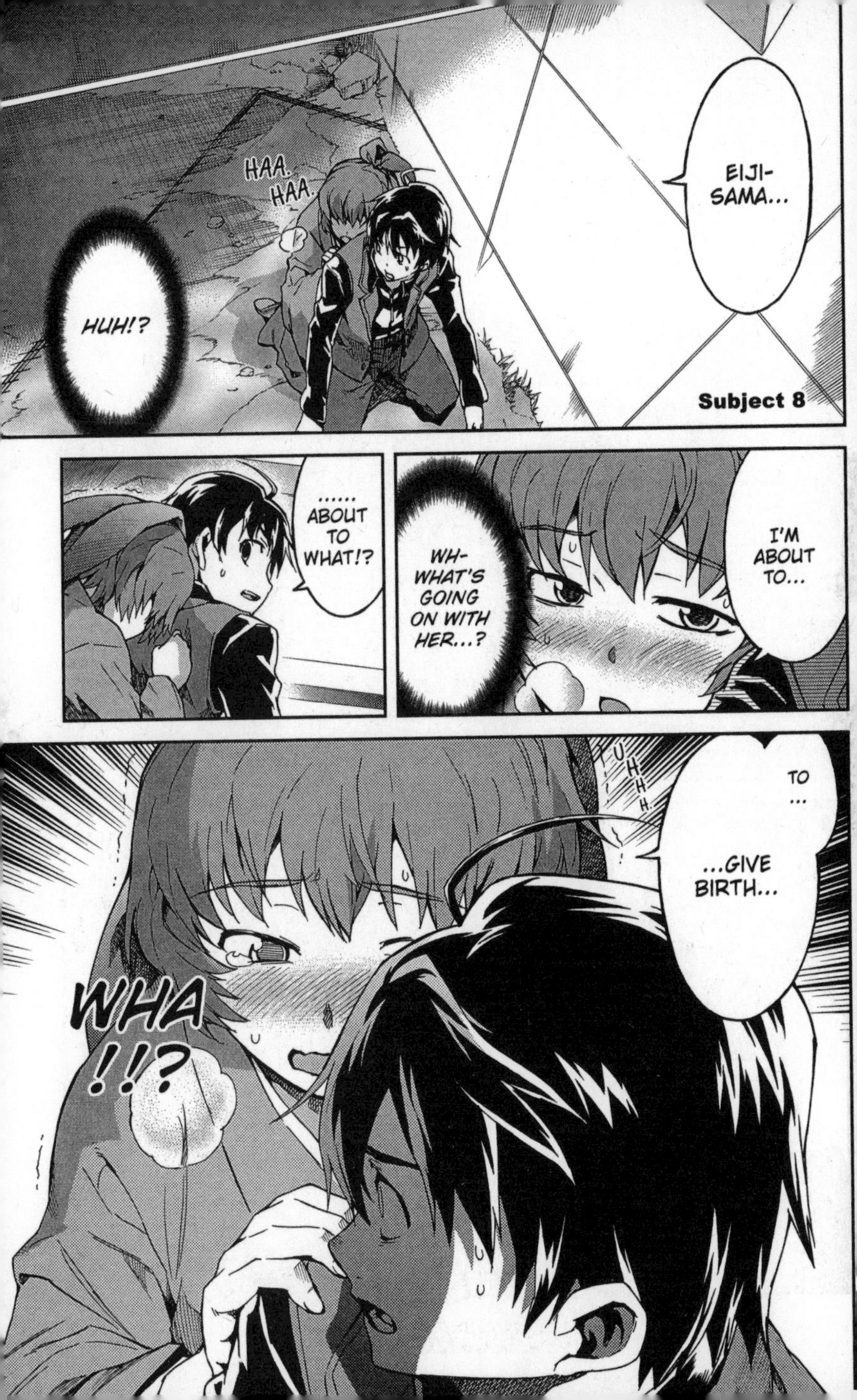
EIJI-SAMA...
Subject 8
HAA. HAA.
HUH!?
I'M ABOUT TO...
WH-WHAT'S GOING ON WITH HER...?
...... ABOUT TO WHAT!?
TO...
...GIVE BIRTH...
UHHH
WHA!!?

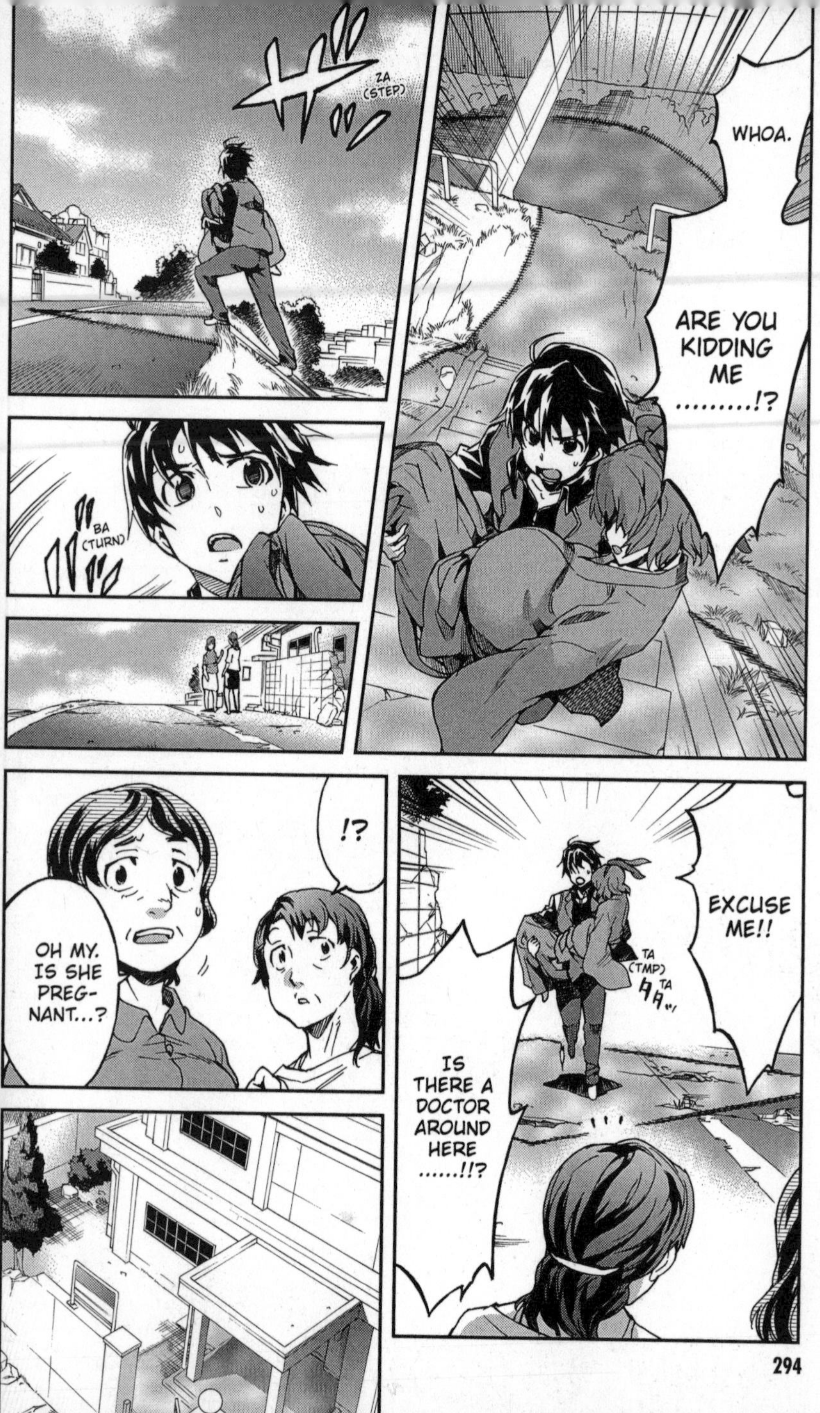
WHOA.
ARE YOU KIDDING ME .........!?
ZA (STEP)
BA (TURN)
EXCUSE ME!!
TA (TMP) TA
IS THERE A DOCTOR AROUND HERE ......!!?
!?
OH MY. IS SHE PREG- NANT...?

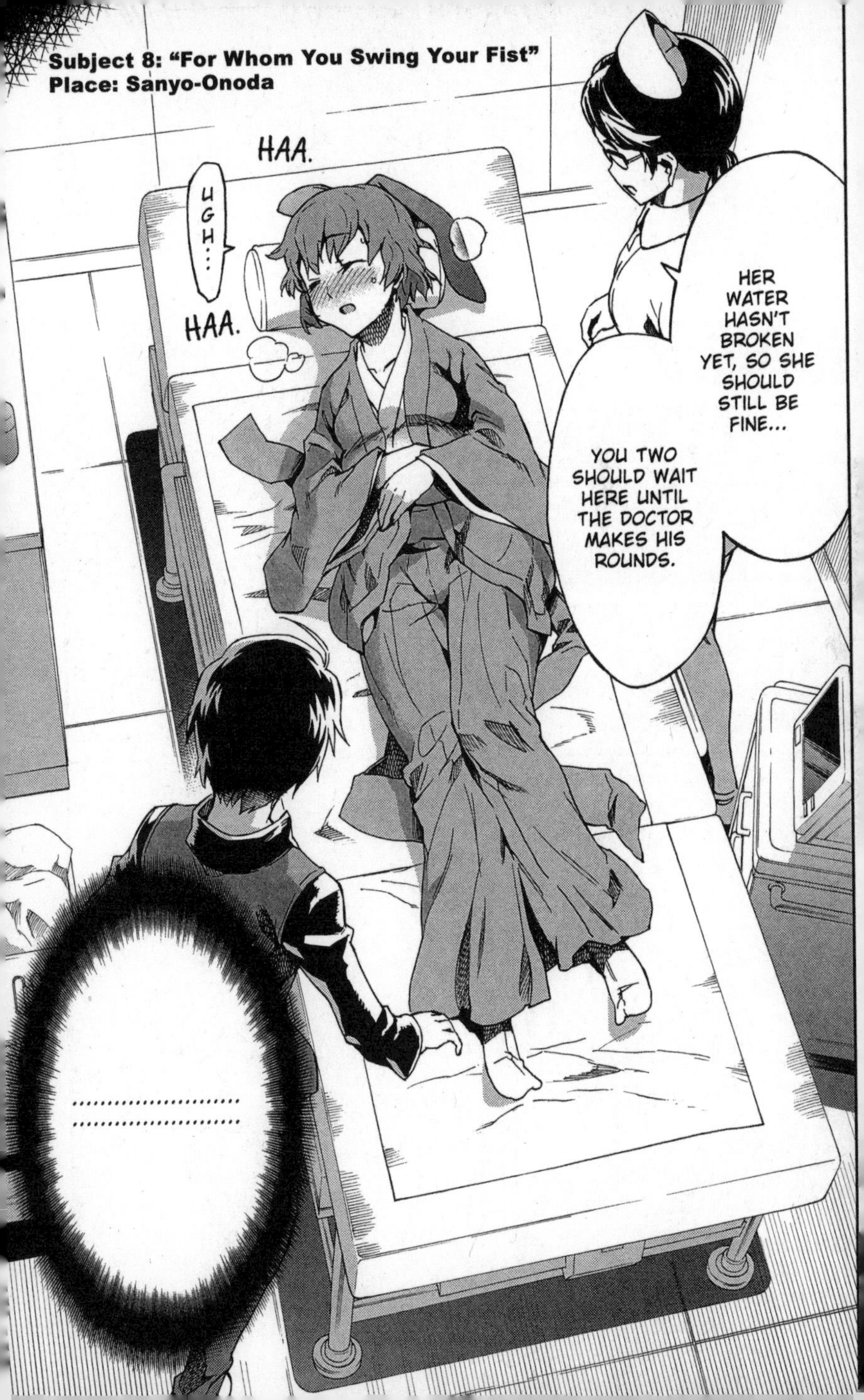
Subject 8: "For Whom You Swing Your Fist"
Place: Sanyo-Onoda
HER WATER HASN'T BROKEN YET, SO SHE SHOULD STILL BE FINE...
YOU TWO SHOULD WAIT HERE UNTIL THE DOCTOR MAKES HIS ROUNDS.
HAA.
UGH...
HAA.
........................
........................

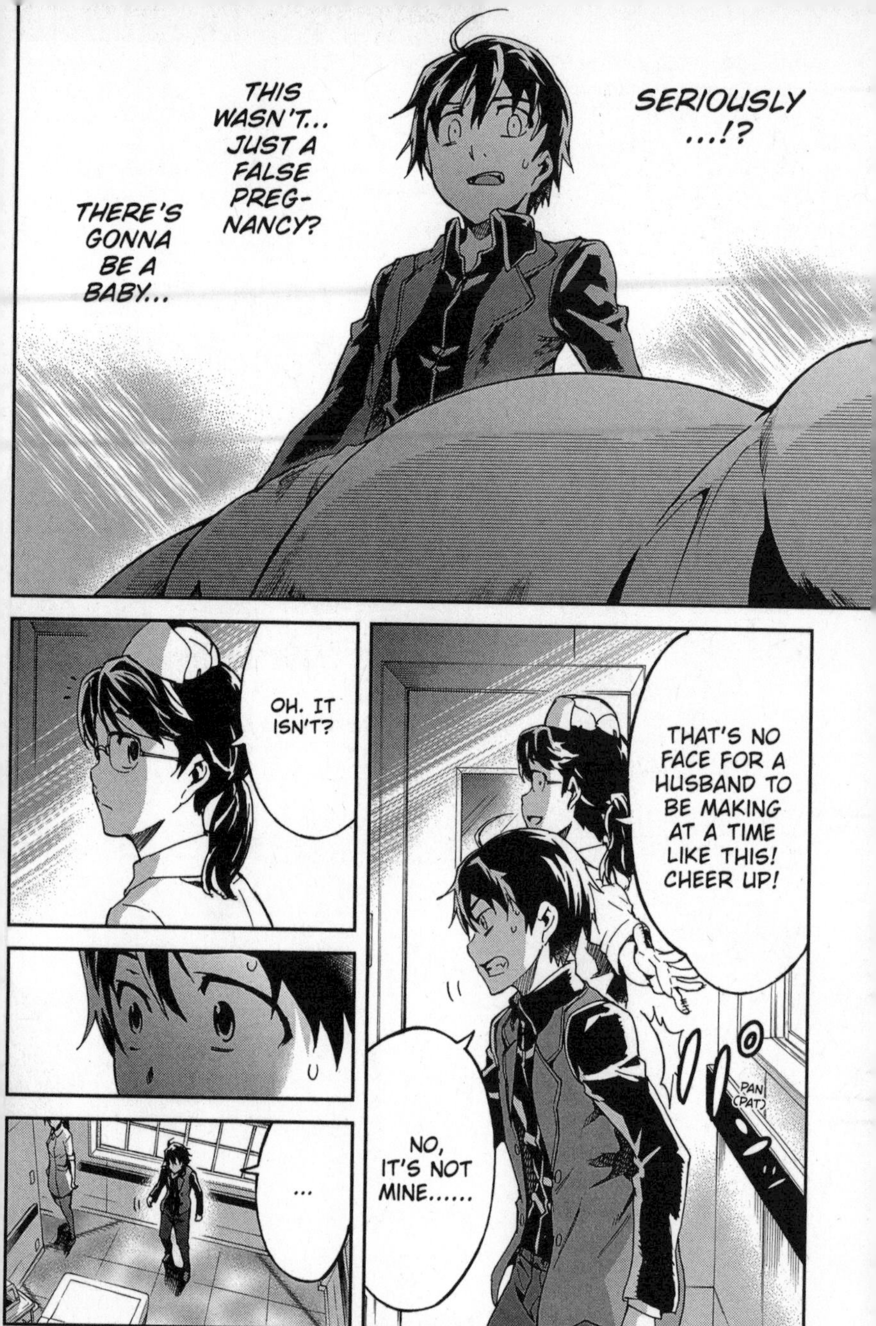
SERIOUSLY ...!?
THIS WASN'T... JUST A FALSE PREGNANCY?
THERE'S GONNA BE A BABY...
THAT'S NO FACE FOR A HUSBAND TO BE MAKING AT A TIME LIKE THIS! CHEER UP!
PAN (PAT)
NO, IT'S NOT MINE......
OH. IT ISN'T?
...

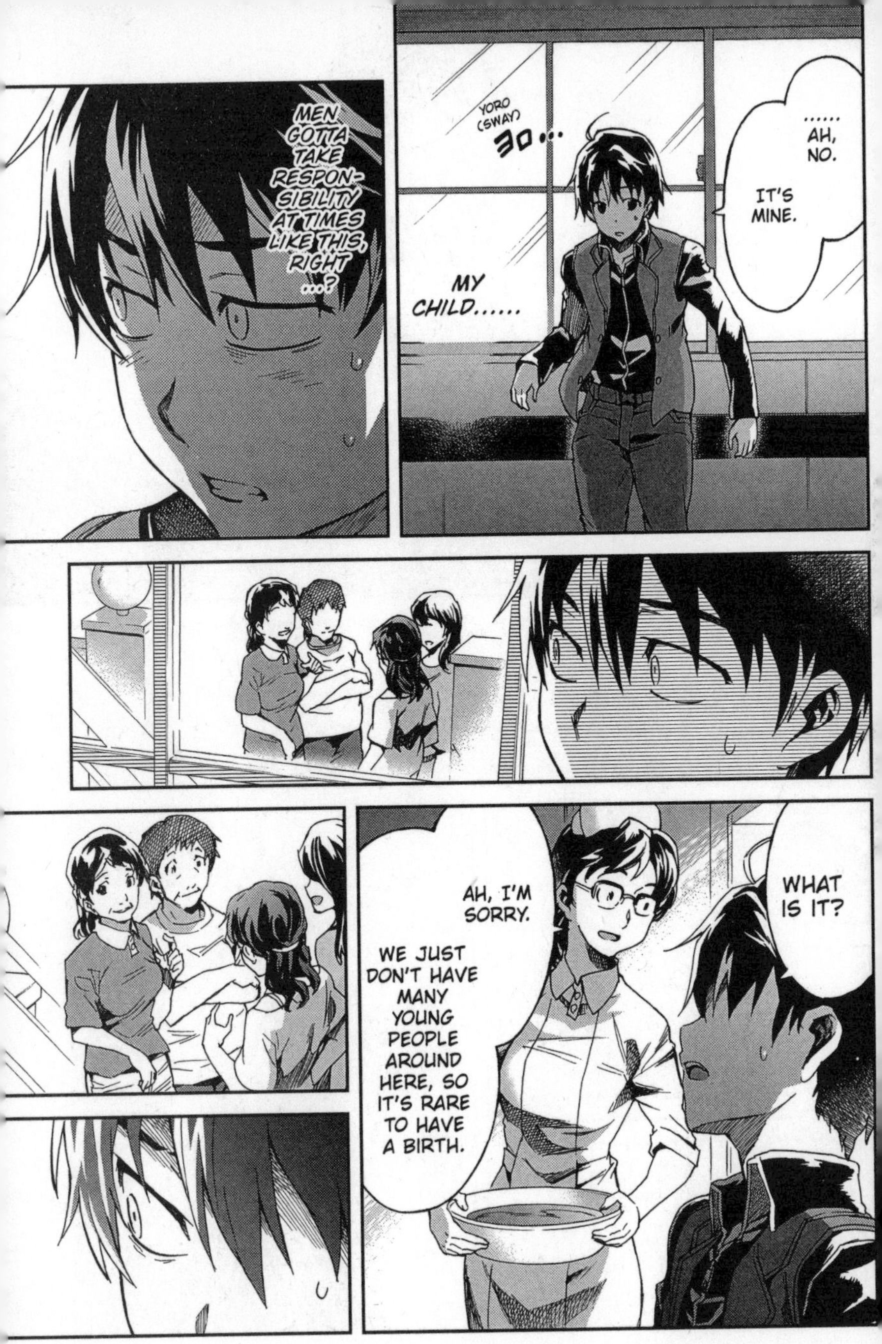
......AH, NO.
IT'S MINE.
YORO (SWAY) ヨロ...
MY CHILD......
MEN GOTTA TAKE RESPON-SIBILITY AT TIMES LIKE THIS, RIGHT ...?
WHAT IS IT?
AH, I'M SORRY.
WE JUST DON'T HAVE MANY YOUNG PEOPLE AROUND HERE, SO IT'S RARE TO HAVE A BIRTH.

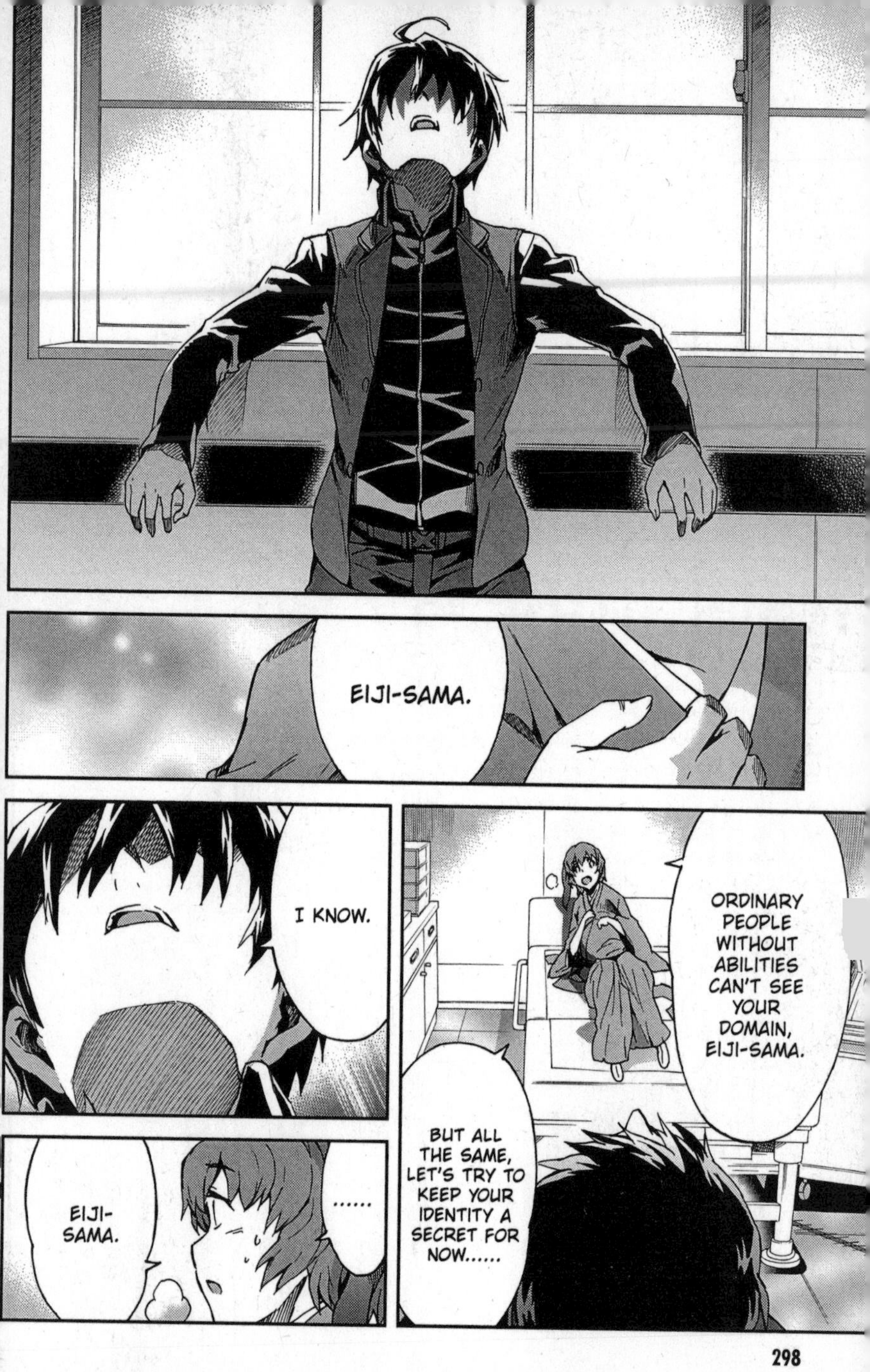
EIJI-SAMA.
ORDINARY PEOPLE WITHOUT ABILITIES CAN'T SEE YOUR DOMAIN, EIJI-SAMA.
BUT ALL THE SAME, LET'S TRY TO KEEP YOUR IDENTITY A SECRET FOR NOW......
I KNOW.
......
EIJI-SAMA.

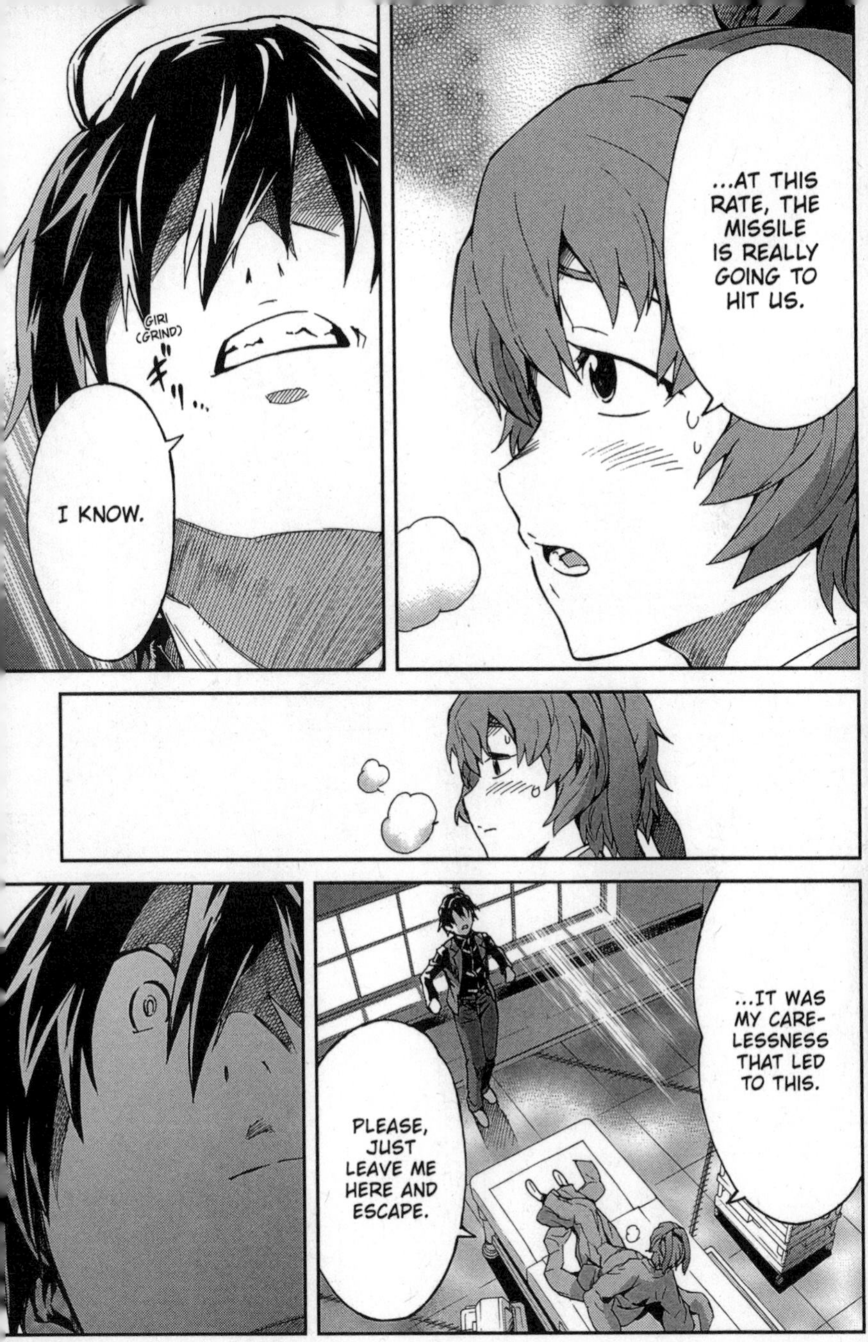
...AT THIS RATE, THE MISSILE IS REALLY GOING TO HIT US.
GIRI (GRIND)
ギリ...
I KNOW.
...IT WAS MY CARELESSNESS THAT LED TO THIS.
PLEASE, JUST LEAVE ME HERE AND ESCAPE.

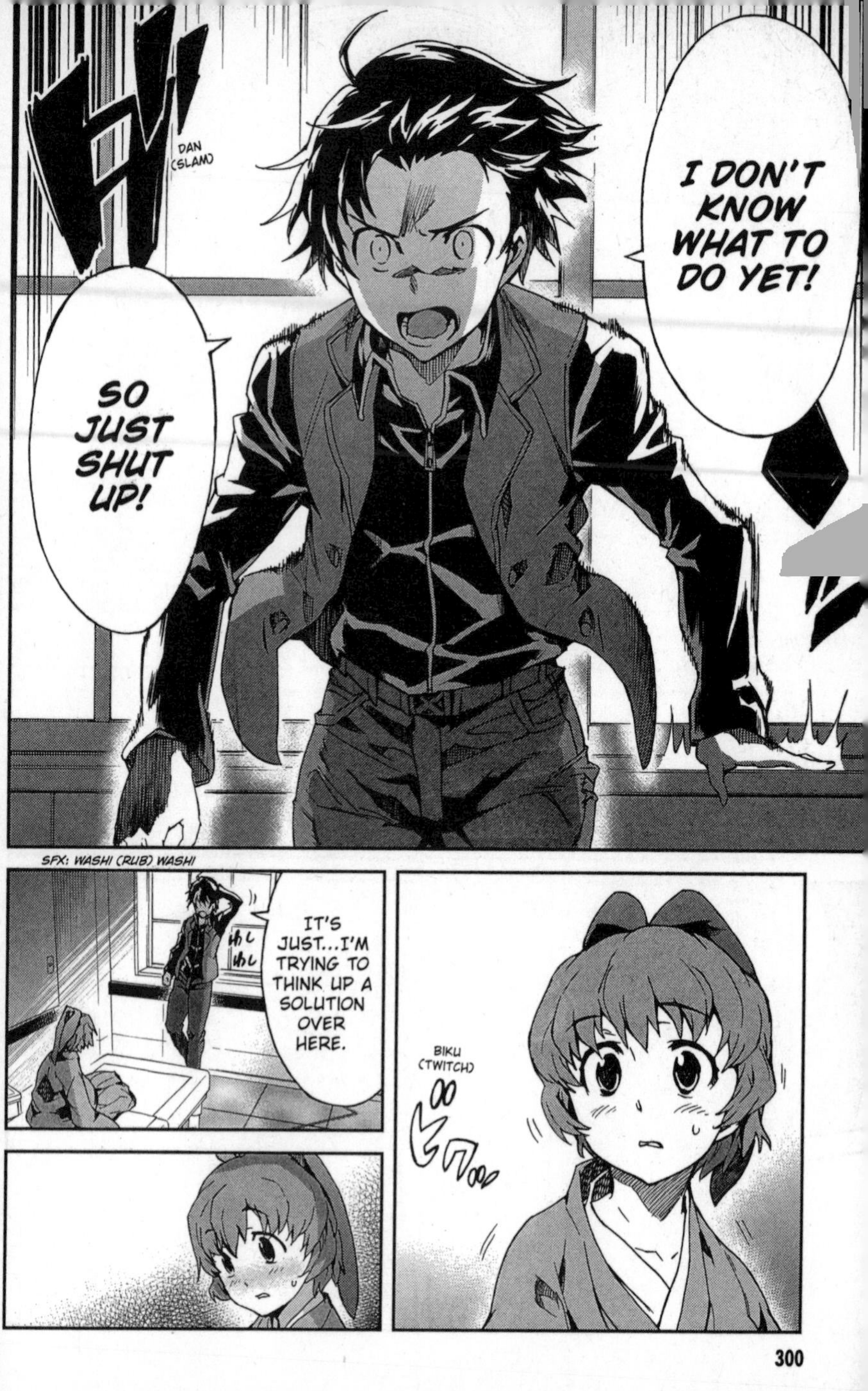
I DON'T KNOW WHAT TO DO YET!
DAN (SLAM)
SO JUST SHUT UP!
SFX: WASHI (RUB) WASHI
BIKU (TWITCH)
IT'S JUST...I'M TRYING TO THINK UP A SOLUTION OVER HERE.

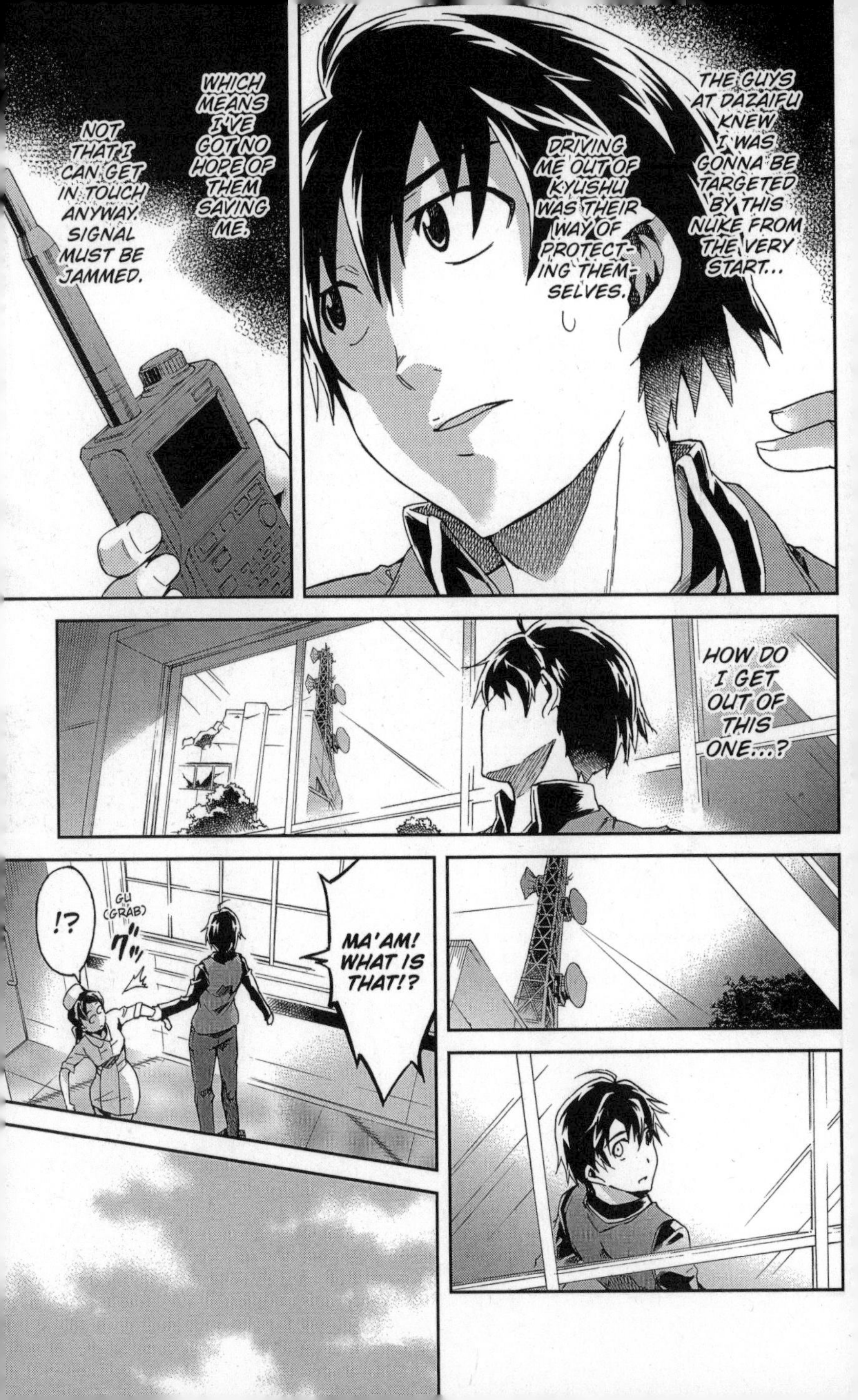
THE GUYS AT DAZAIFU KNEW I WAS GONNA BE TARGETED BY THIS NUKE FROM THE VERY START...
DRIVING ME OUT OF KYUSHU WAS THEIR WAY OF PROTECTING THEMSELVES.
WHICH MEANS I'VE GOT NO HOPE OF THEM SAVING ME.
NOT THAT I CAN GET IN TOUCH ANYWAY. SIGNAL MUST BE JAMMED.
HOW DO I GET OUT OF THIS ONE...?
MA'AM! WHAT IS THAT!?
GU (GRAB)
!?

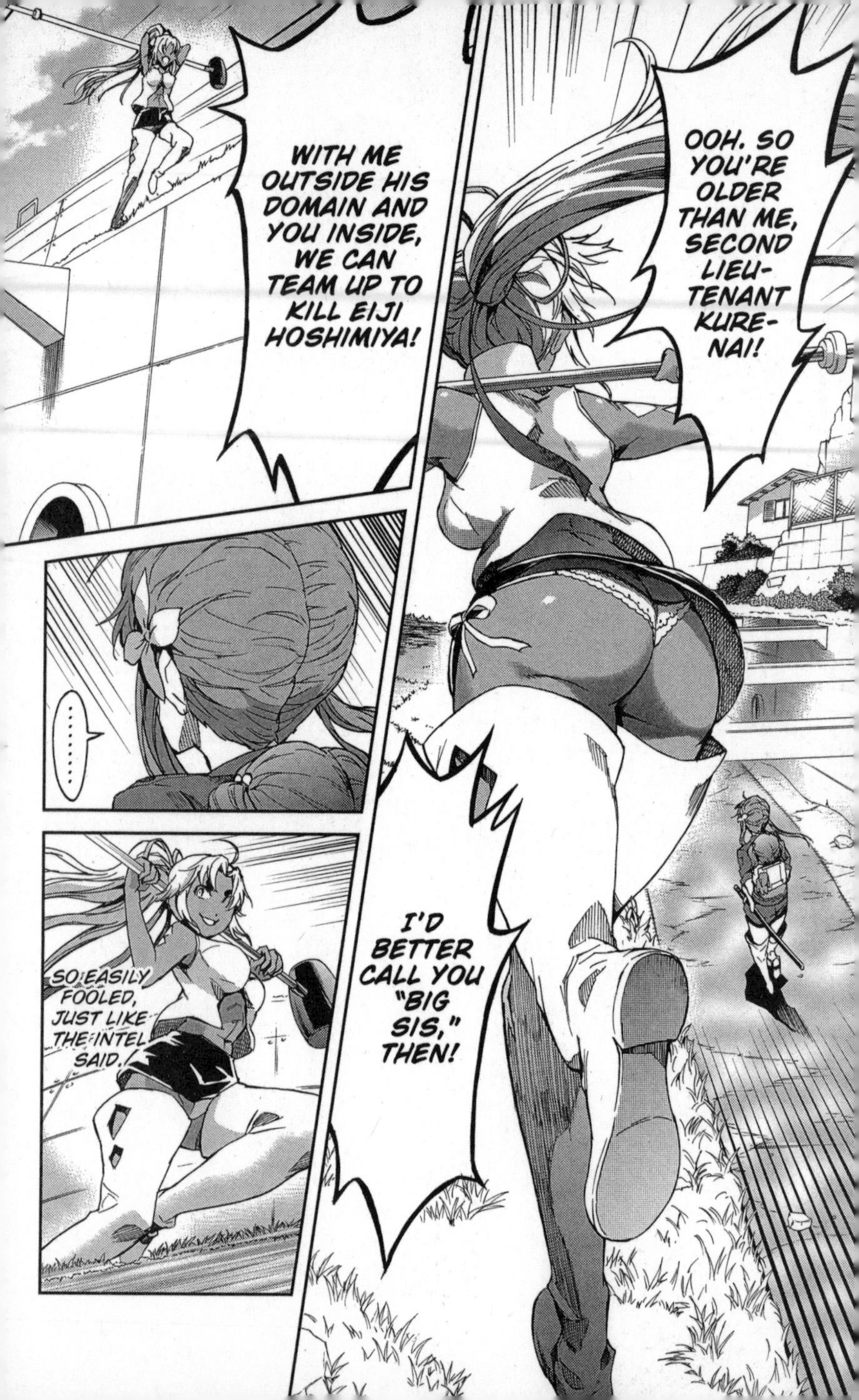
OOH. SO YOU'RE OLDER THAN ME, SECOND LIEU-TENANT KURE-NAI!
I'D BETTER CALL YOU "BIG SIS," THEN!
WITH ME OUTSIDE HIS DOMAIN AND YOU INSIDE, WE CAN TEAM UP TO KILL EIJI HOSHIMIYA!
......
SO EASILY FOOLED, JUST LIKE THE INTEL SAID.

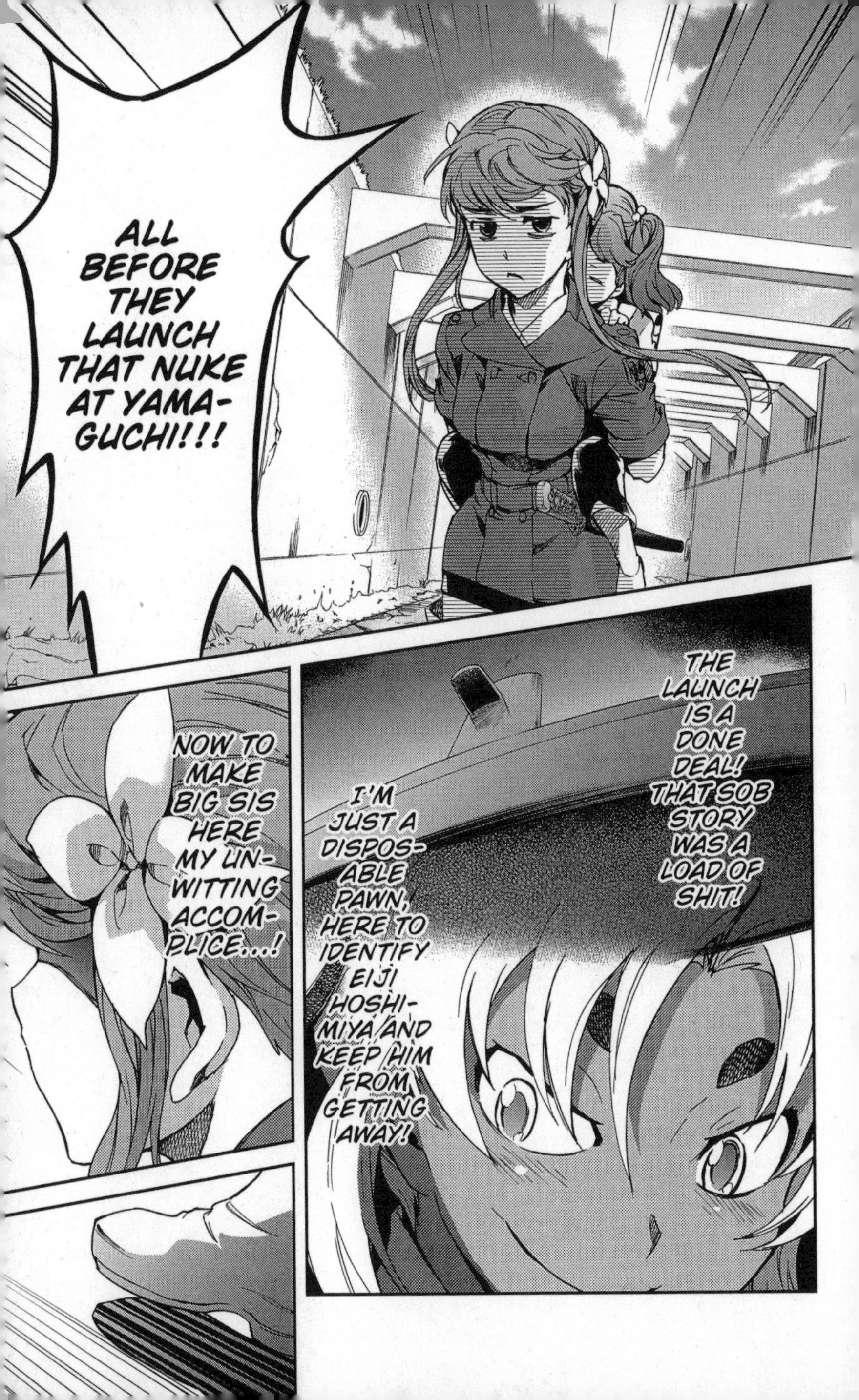
ALL BEFORE THEY LAUNCH THAT NUKE AT YAMA-GUCHI!!!
THE LAUNCH IS A DONE DEAL! THAT SOB STORY WAS A LOAD OF SHIT!
I'M JUST A DISPOS-ABLE PAWN, HERE TO IDENTIFY EIJI HOSHI-MIYA AND KEEP HIM FROM GETTING AWAY!
NOW TO MAKE BIG SIS HERE MY UN-WITTING ACCOM-PLICE...!

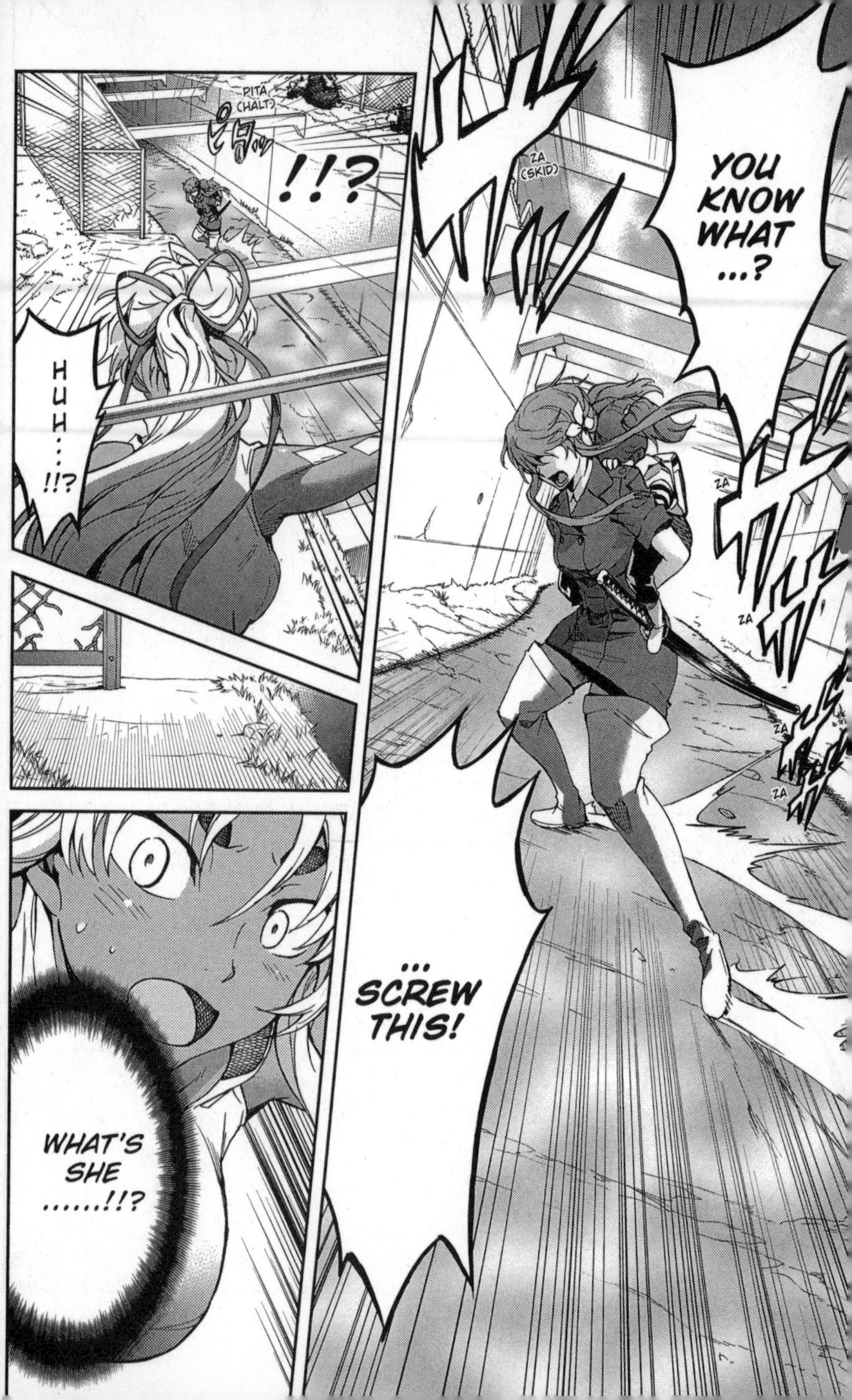
ZA (SKID)
YOU KNOW WHAT ...?
ZA
ZA
ZA
ZA
... SCREW THIS!
PITA (HALT)
!!?
HUH... !!?
WHAT'S SHE ......!!?

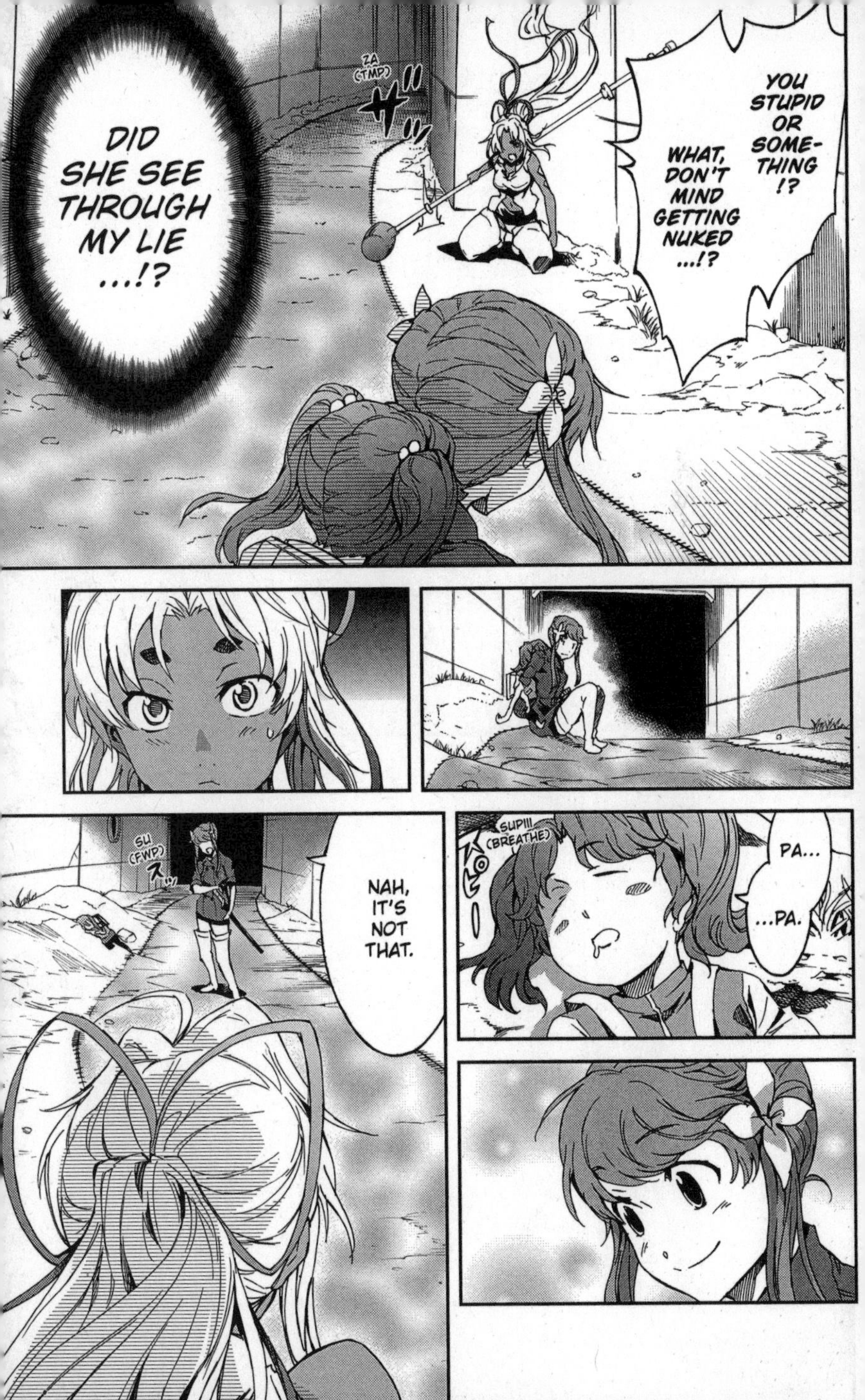
YOU STUPID OR SOME-THING!?
WHAT, DON'T MIND GETTING NUKED ...!?
ZA (TMP)
DID SHE SEE THROUGH MY LIE ...!?
SUPIII (BREATHE)
PA...
...PA.
SU (FWP)
NAH, IT'S NOT THAT.

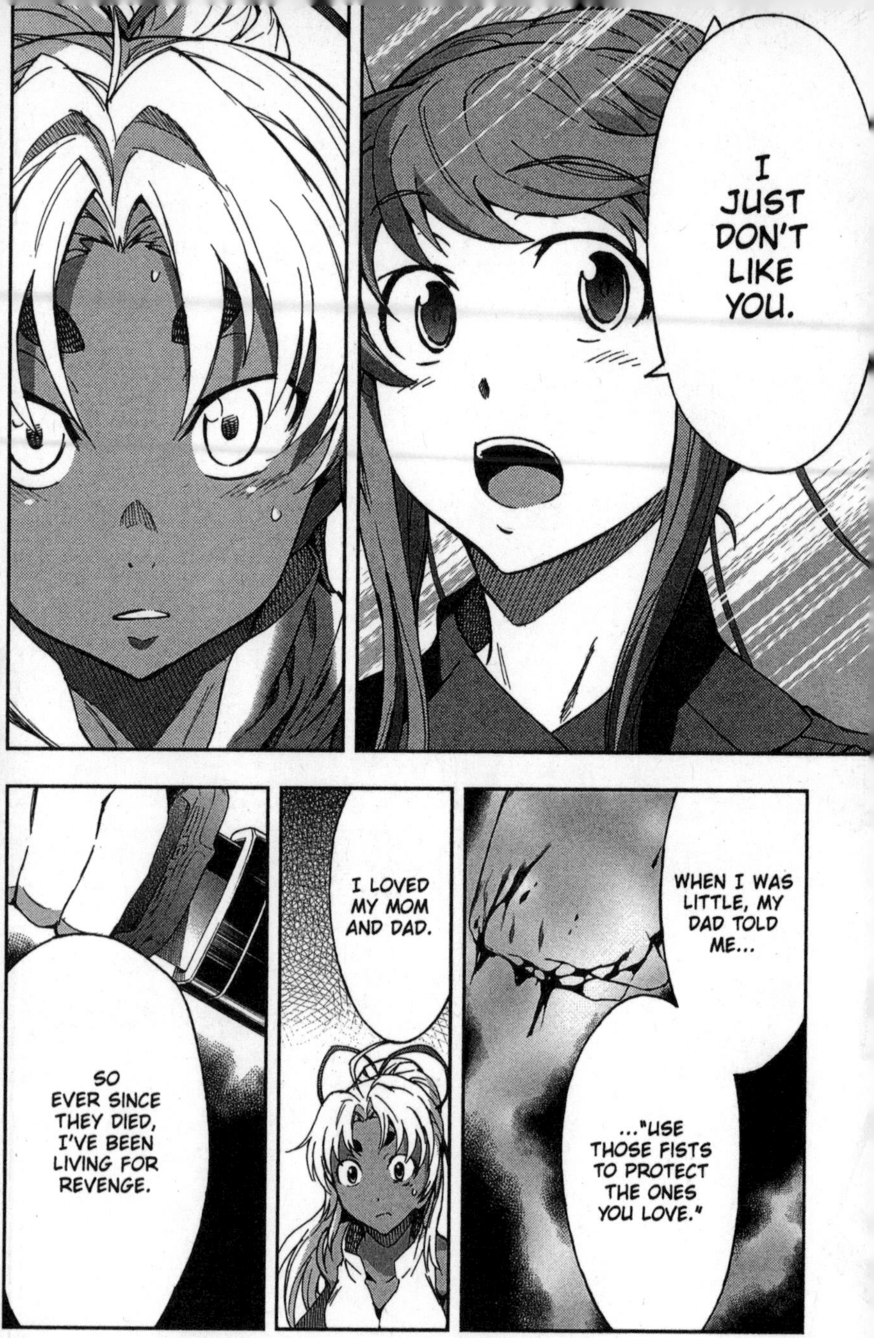
I JUST DON'T LIKE YOU.
WHEN I WAS LITTLE, MY DAD TOLD ME...
..."USE THOSE FISTS TO PROTECT THE ONES YOU LOVE."
I LOVED MY MOM AND DAD.
SO EVER SINCE THEY DIED, I'VE BEEN LIVING FOR REVENGE.

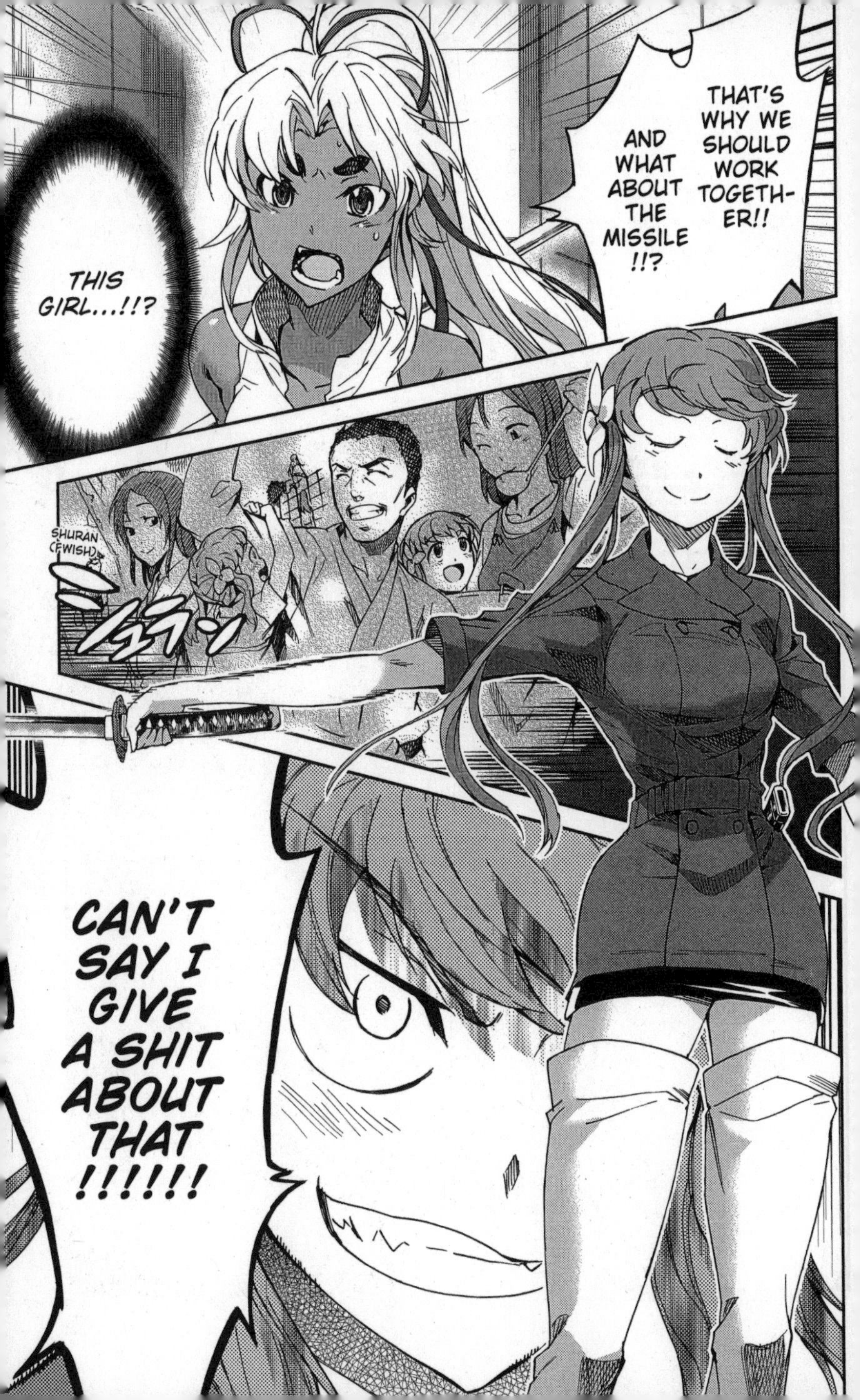
THAT'S WHY WE SHOULD WORK TOGETH-ER!!
AND WHAT ABOUT THE MISSILE !!?
THIS GIRL...!!?
SHURAN (FWISH)
CAN'T SAY I GIVE A SHIT ABOUT THAT !!!!!!

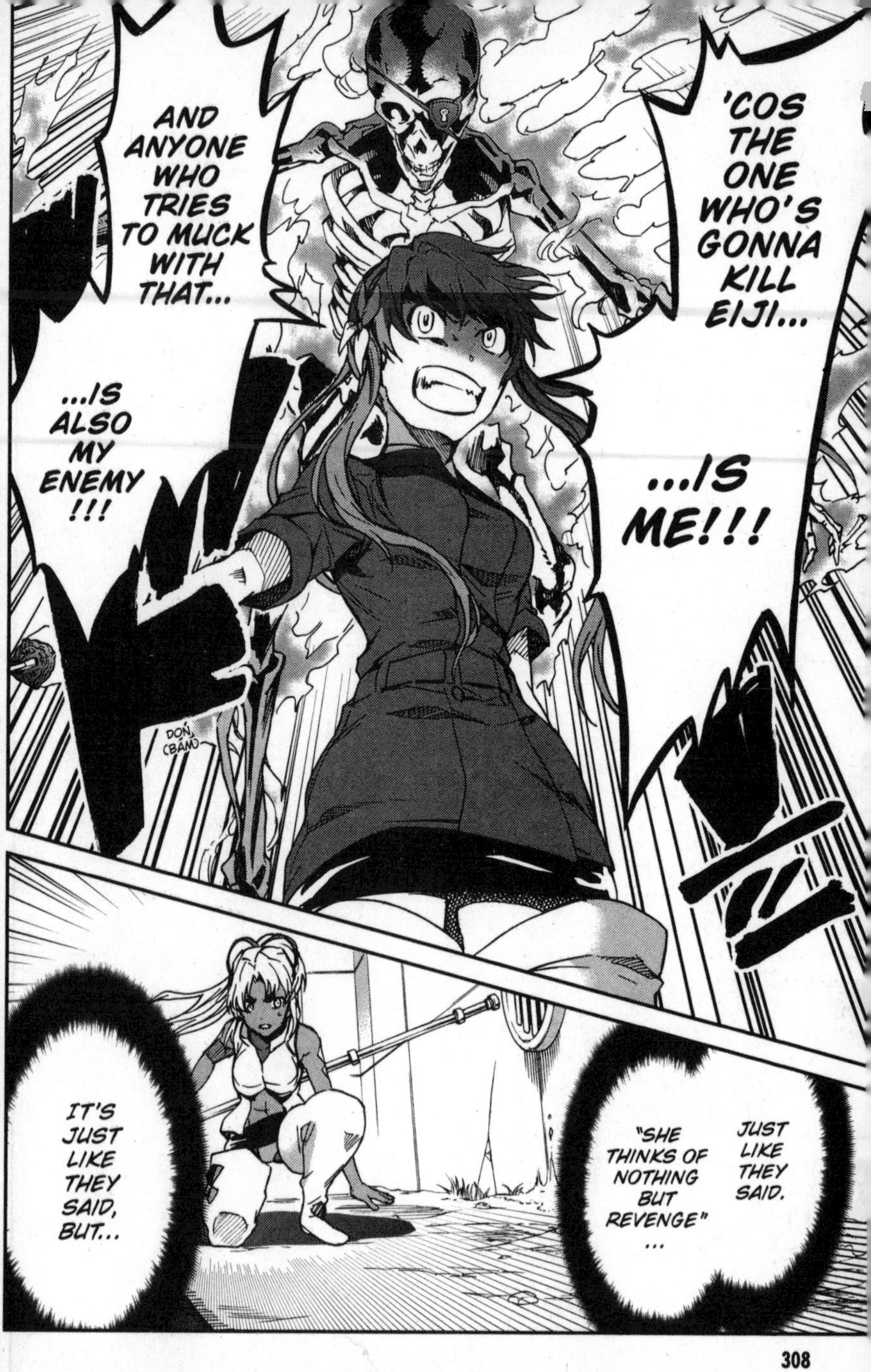
'COS THE ONE WHO'S GONNA KILL EIJI...
...IS ME!!!
AND ANYONE WHO TRIES TO MUCK WITH THAT...
...IS ALSO MY ENEMY!!!
DON (BAM)
JUST LIKE THEY SAID.
"SHE THINKS OF NOTHING BUT REVENGE"...
IT'S JUST LIKE THEY SAID, BUT...

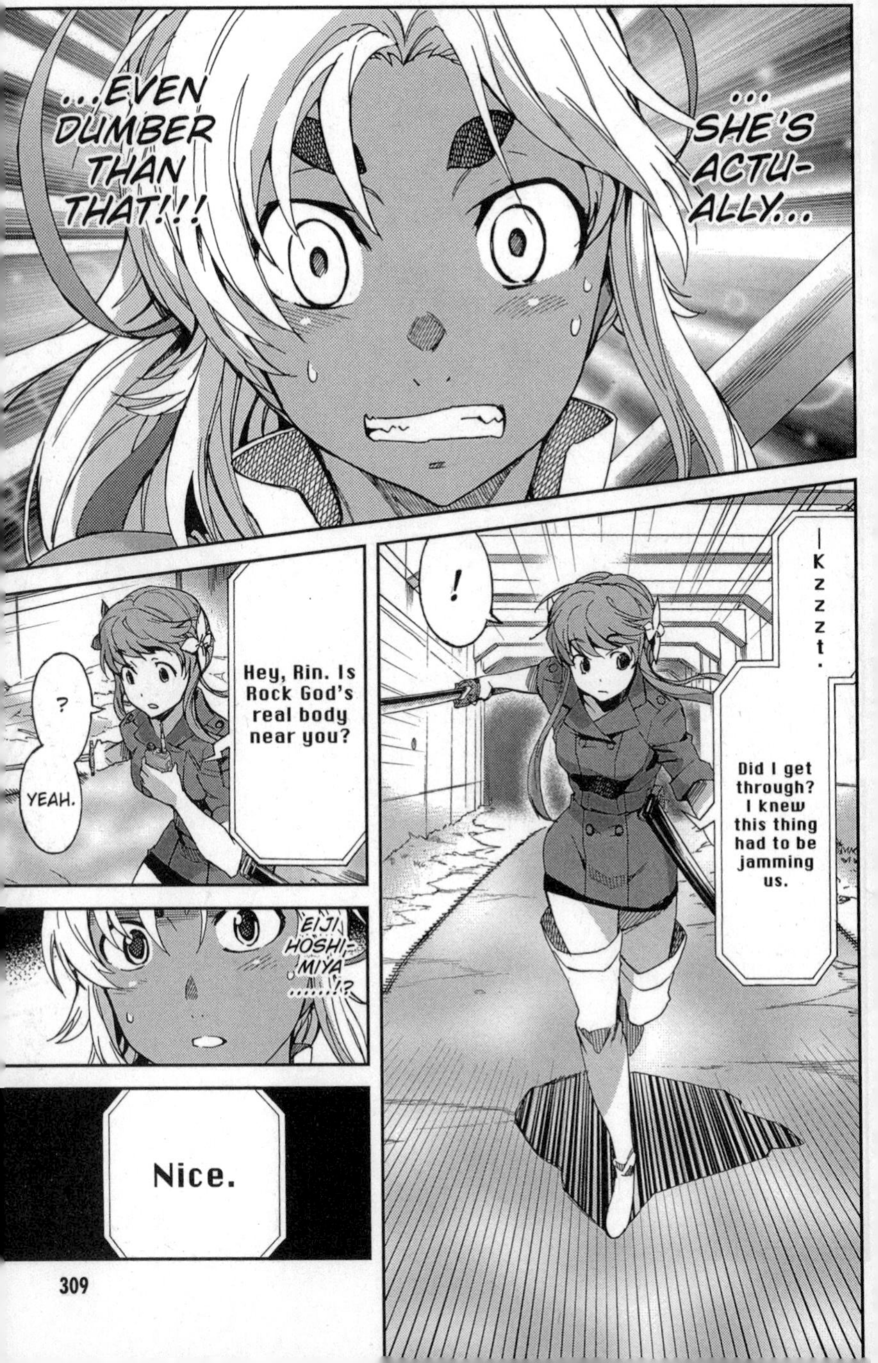
...SHE'S ACTUALLY...
...EVEN DUMBER THAN THAT!!!
!
—Kzzzt.
Did I get through? I knew this thing had to be jamming us.
Hey, Rin. Is Rock God's real body near you?
?
YEAH.
EIJI HOSHIMIYA......!?
Nice.

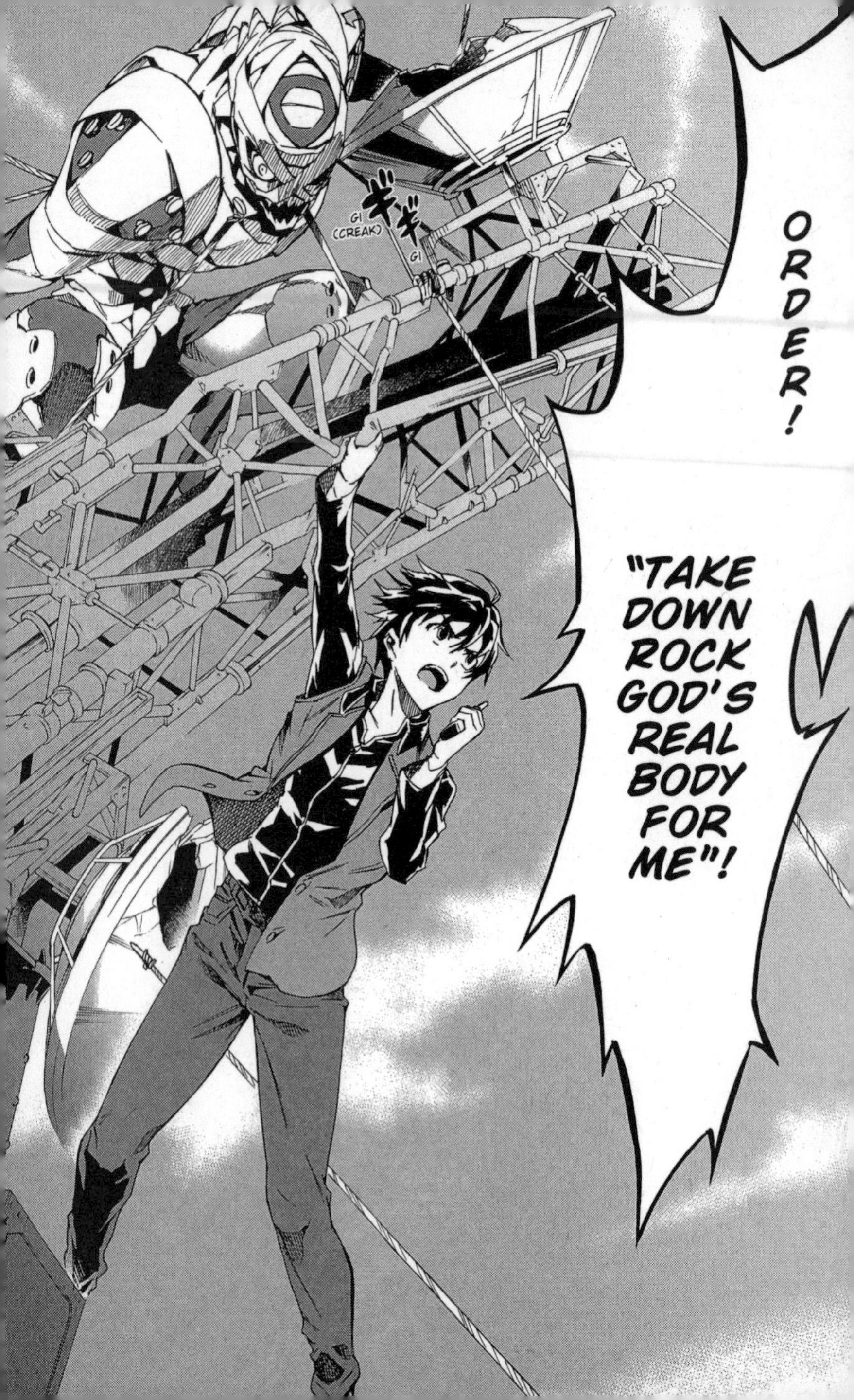
ORDER!
ギギ
GI (CREAK) GI
"TAKE DOWN ROCK GOD'S REAL BODY FOR ME"!

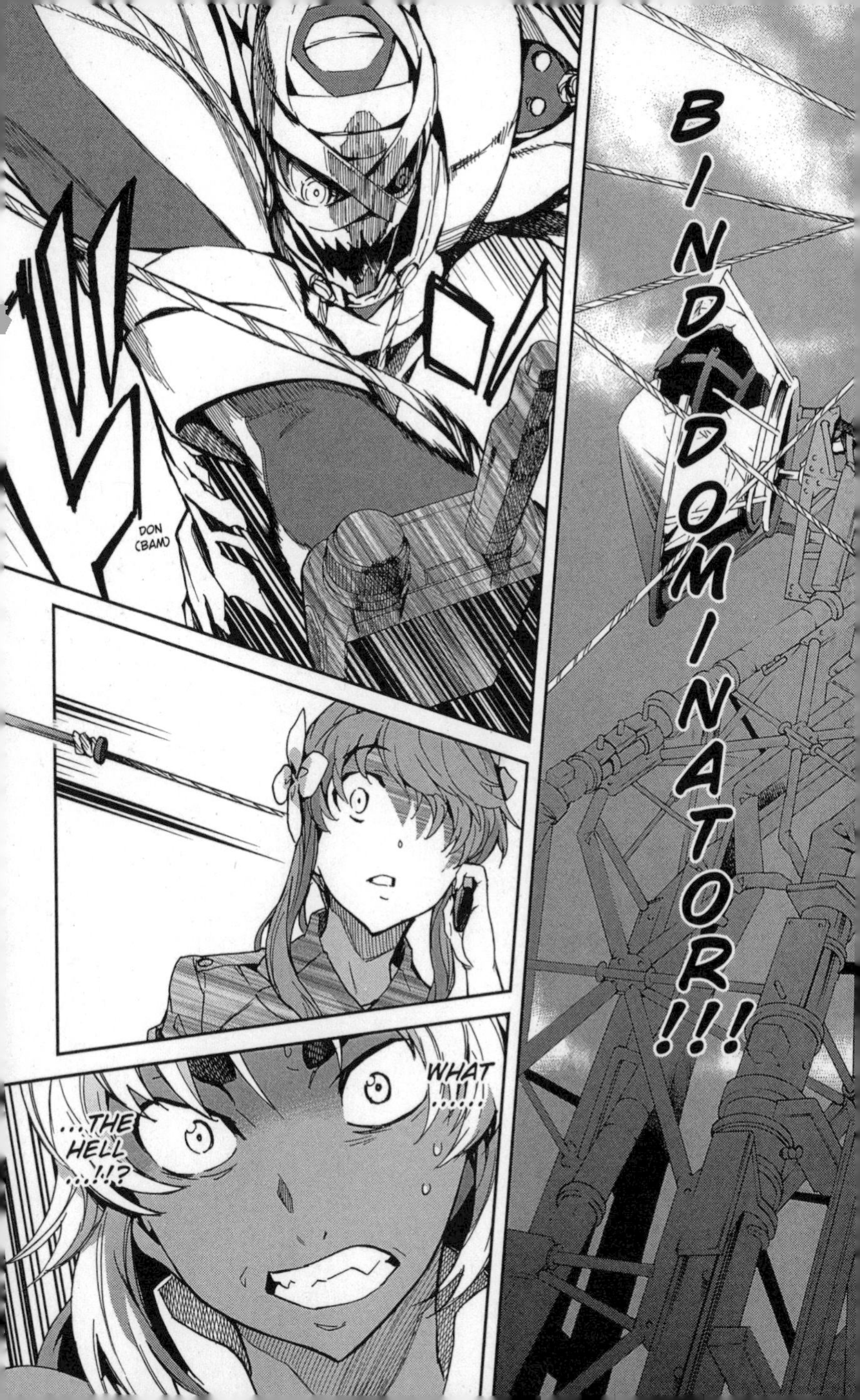
BINDDOMINATOR!!!
DON (BAM)
WHAT......
...THE HELL...!!?

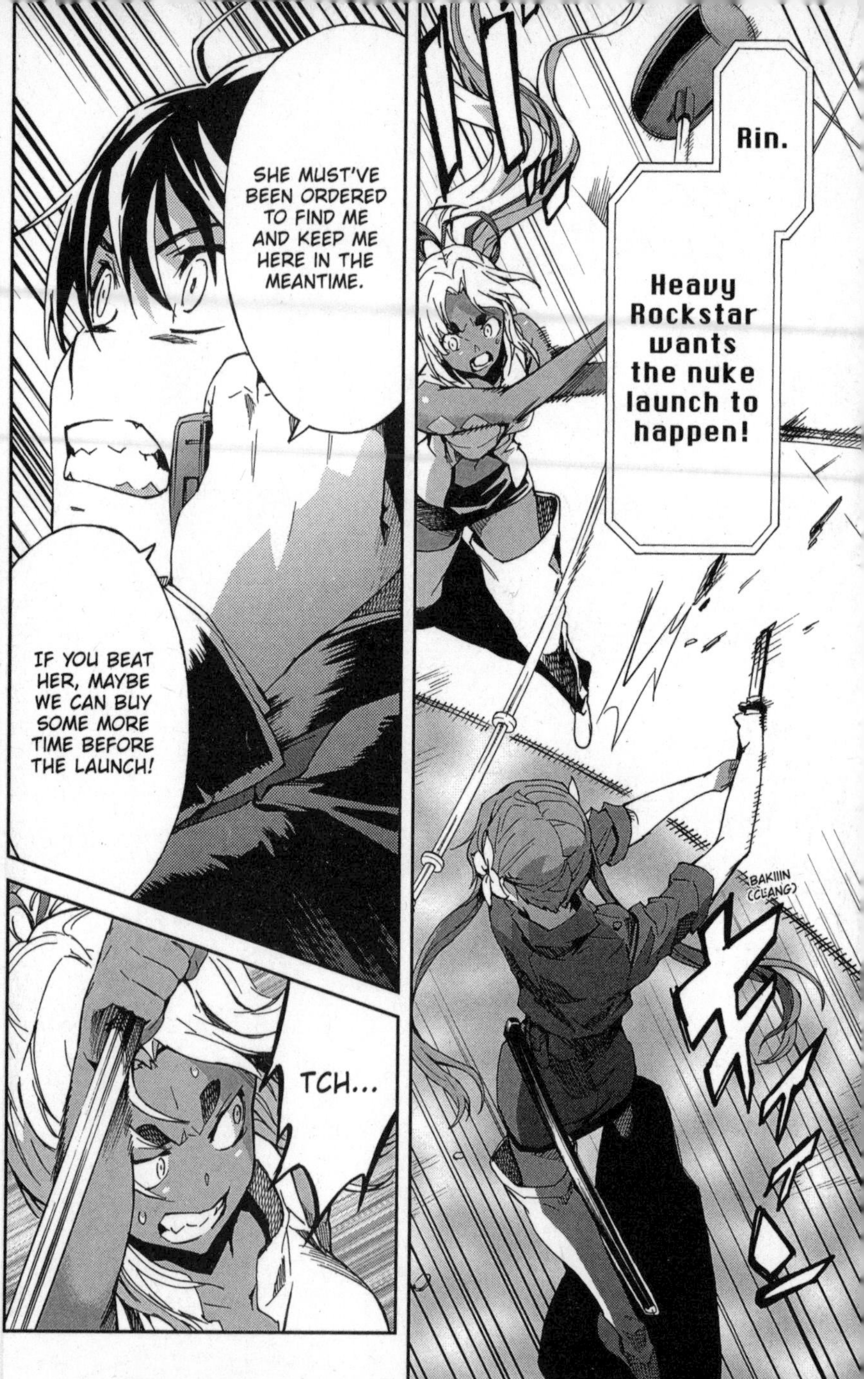
Rin.
Heavy Rockstar wants the nuke launch to happen!
BAKIIN (CLANG)
SHE MUST'VE BEEN ORDERED TO FIND ME AND KEEP ME HERE IN THE MEANTIME.
IF YOU BEAT HER, MAYBE WE CAN BUY SOME MORE TIME BEFORE THE LAUNCH!
TCH...

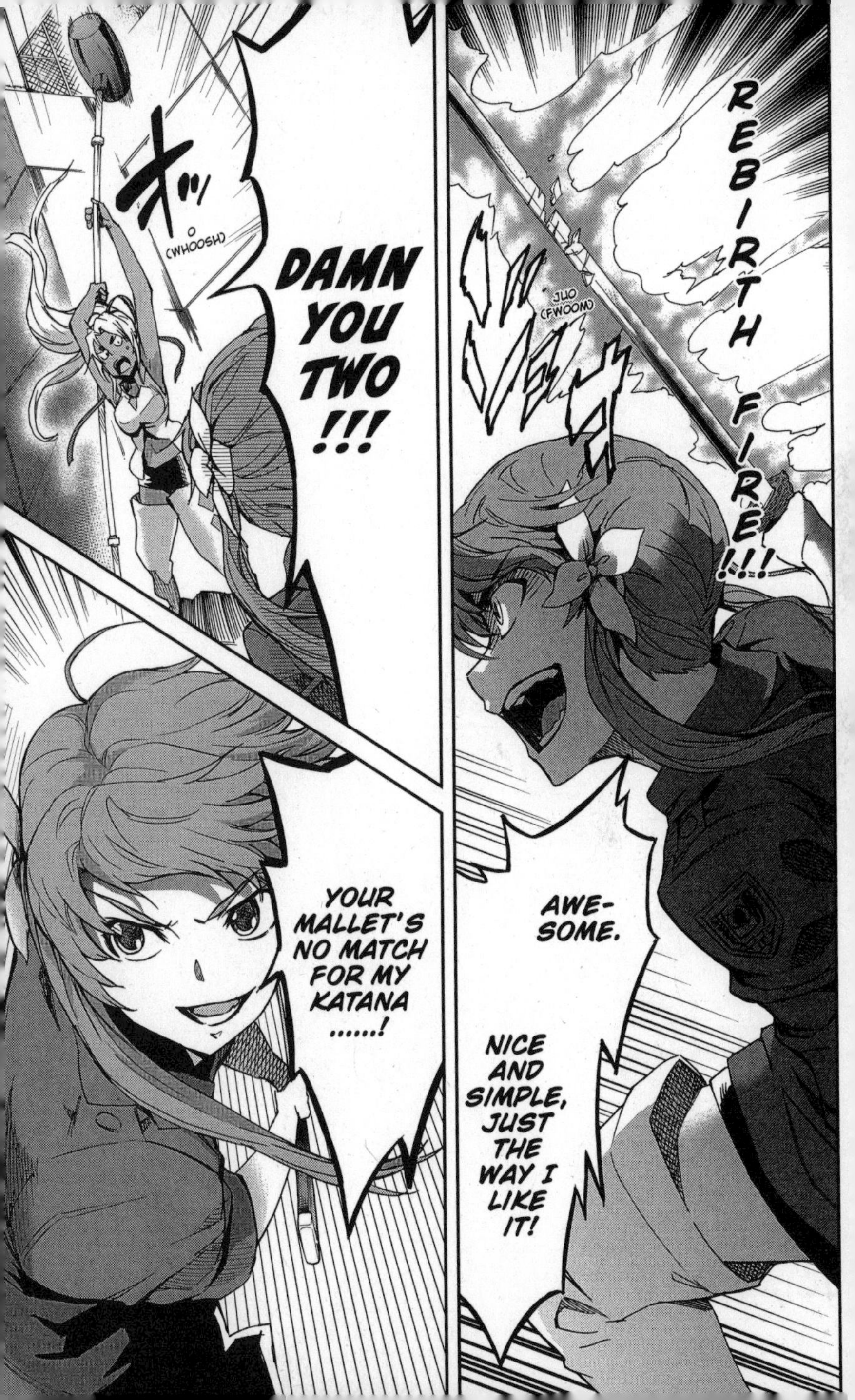
REBIRTH FIRE!!!
JUO (FWOOM)
AWE-SOME.
NICE AND SIMPLE, JUST THE WAY I LIKE IT!
O (WHOOSH)
DAMN YOU TWO!!!
YOUR MALLET'S NO MATCH FOR MY KATANA ......!

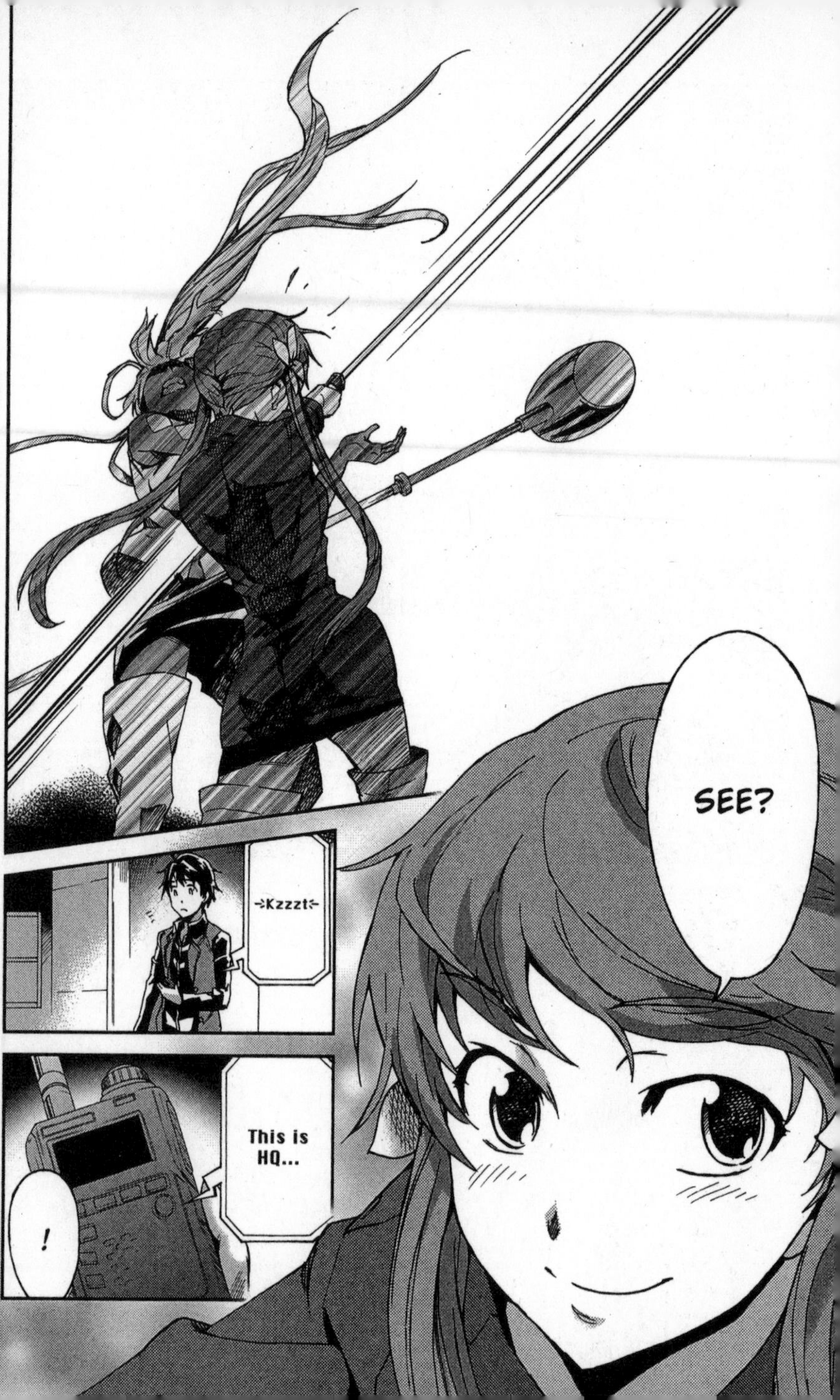
SEE?
Kzzzt
This is HQ...
!

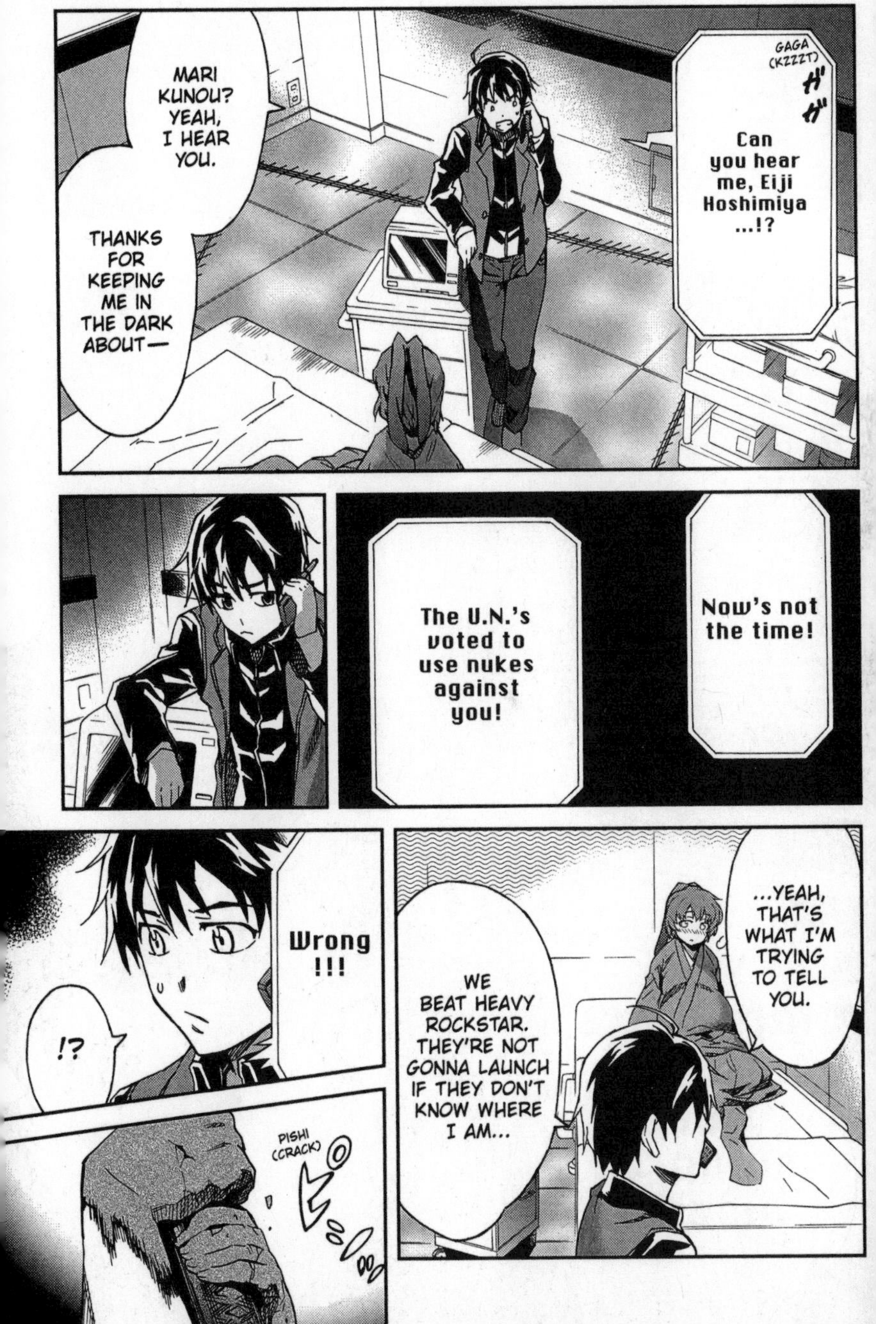
GAGA (KZZZT)
Can you hear me, Eiji Hoshimiya ...!?
MARI KUNOU? YEAH, I HEAR YOU.
THANKS FOR KEEPING ME IN THE DARK ABOUT—
Now's not the time!
The U.N.'s voted to use nukes against you!
...YEAH, THAT'S WHAT I'M TRYING TO TELL YOU.
WE BEAT HEAVY ROCKSTAR. THEY'RE NOT GONNA LAUNCH IF THEY DON'T KNOW WHERE I AM...
Wrong !!!
!?
PISHI (CRACK)

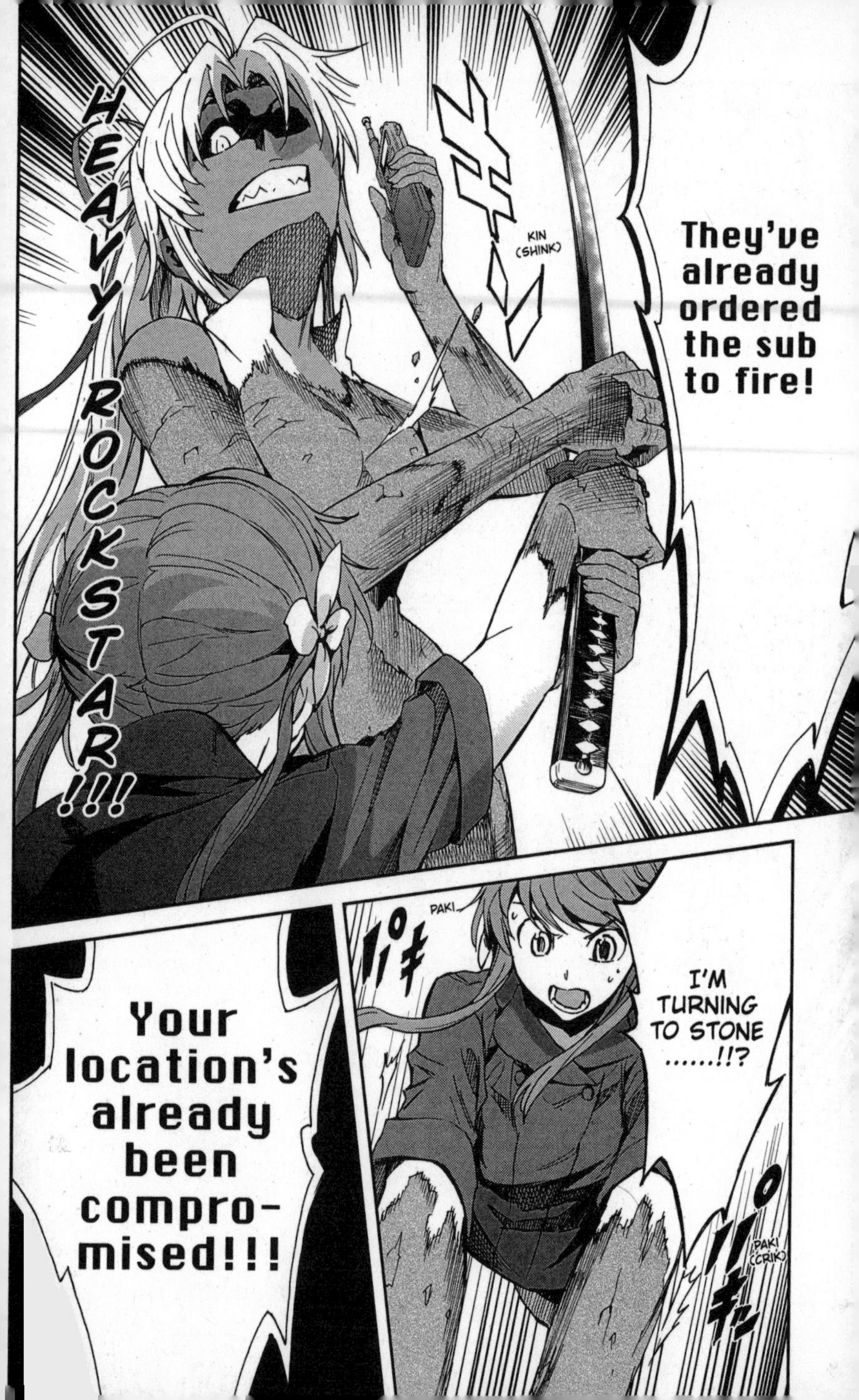
They've already ordered the sub to fire!
KIN (SHINK)
HEAVY ROCKSTAR!!!
PAKI
I'M TURNING TO STONE ......!!?
PAKI (CRIK)
Your location's already been compromised!!!

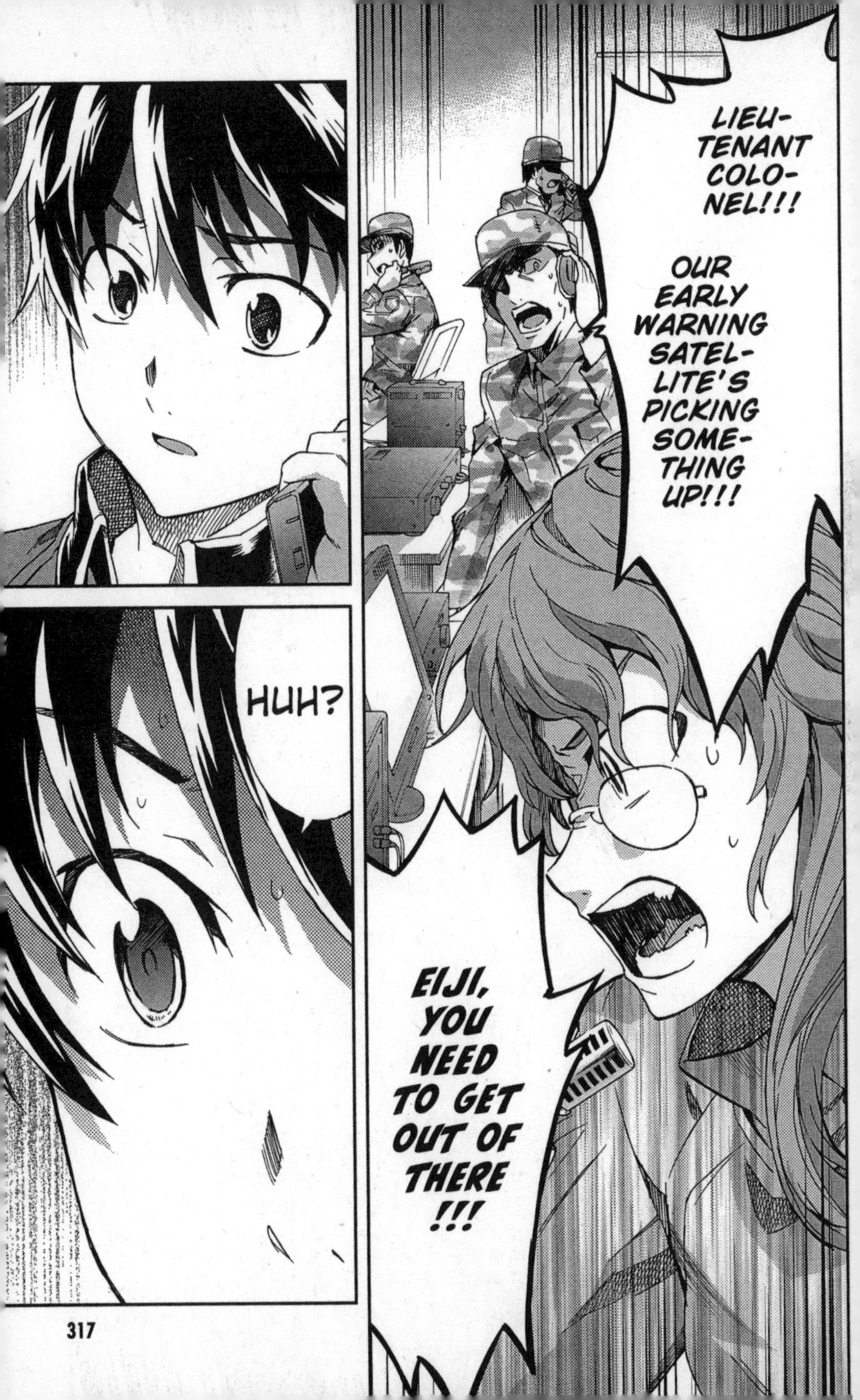
LIEU-TENANT COLO-NEL!!!
OUR EARLY WARNING SATEL-LITE'S PICKING SOME-THING UP!!!
EIJI, YOU NEED TO GET OUT OF THERE !!!
HUH?

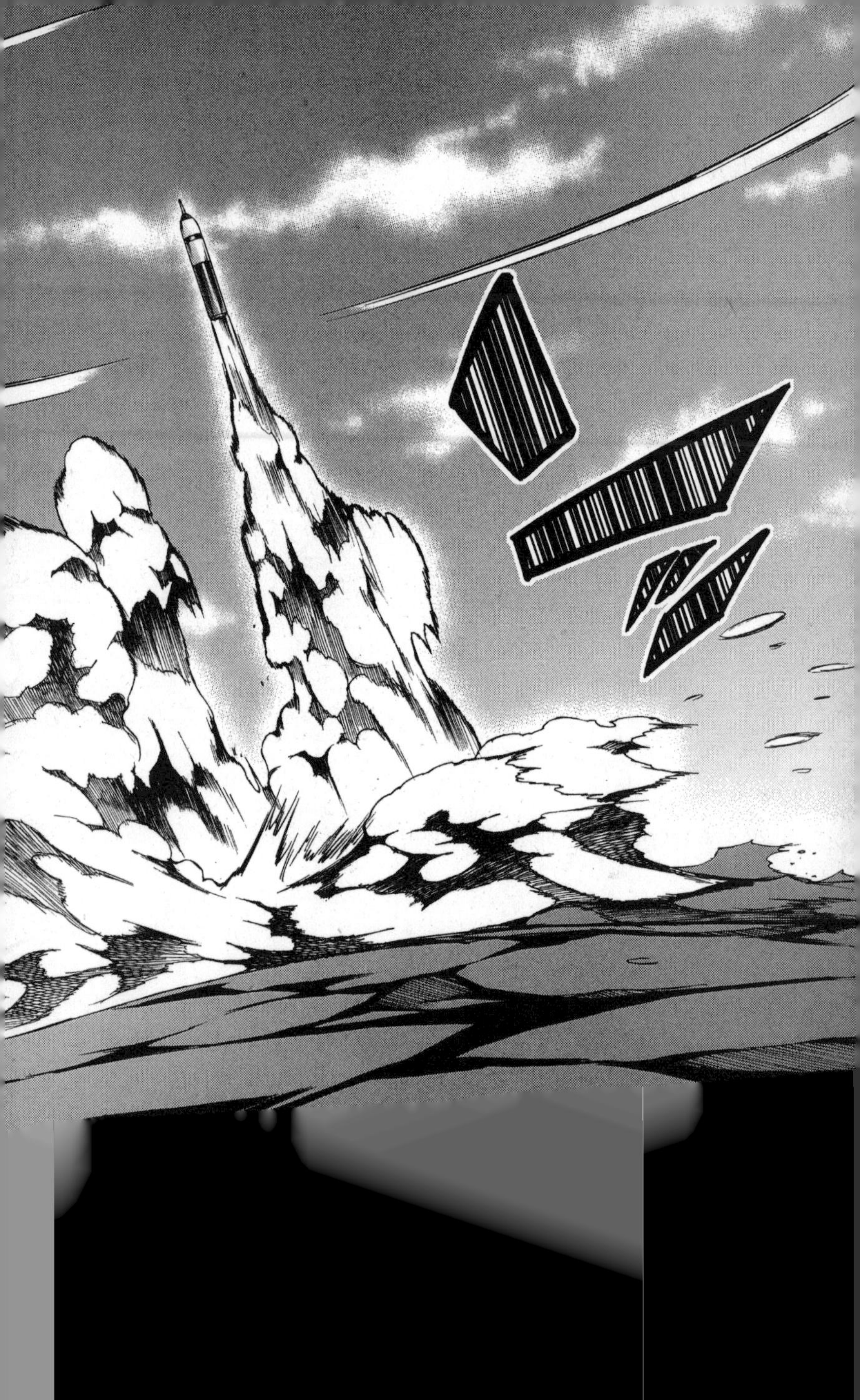

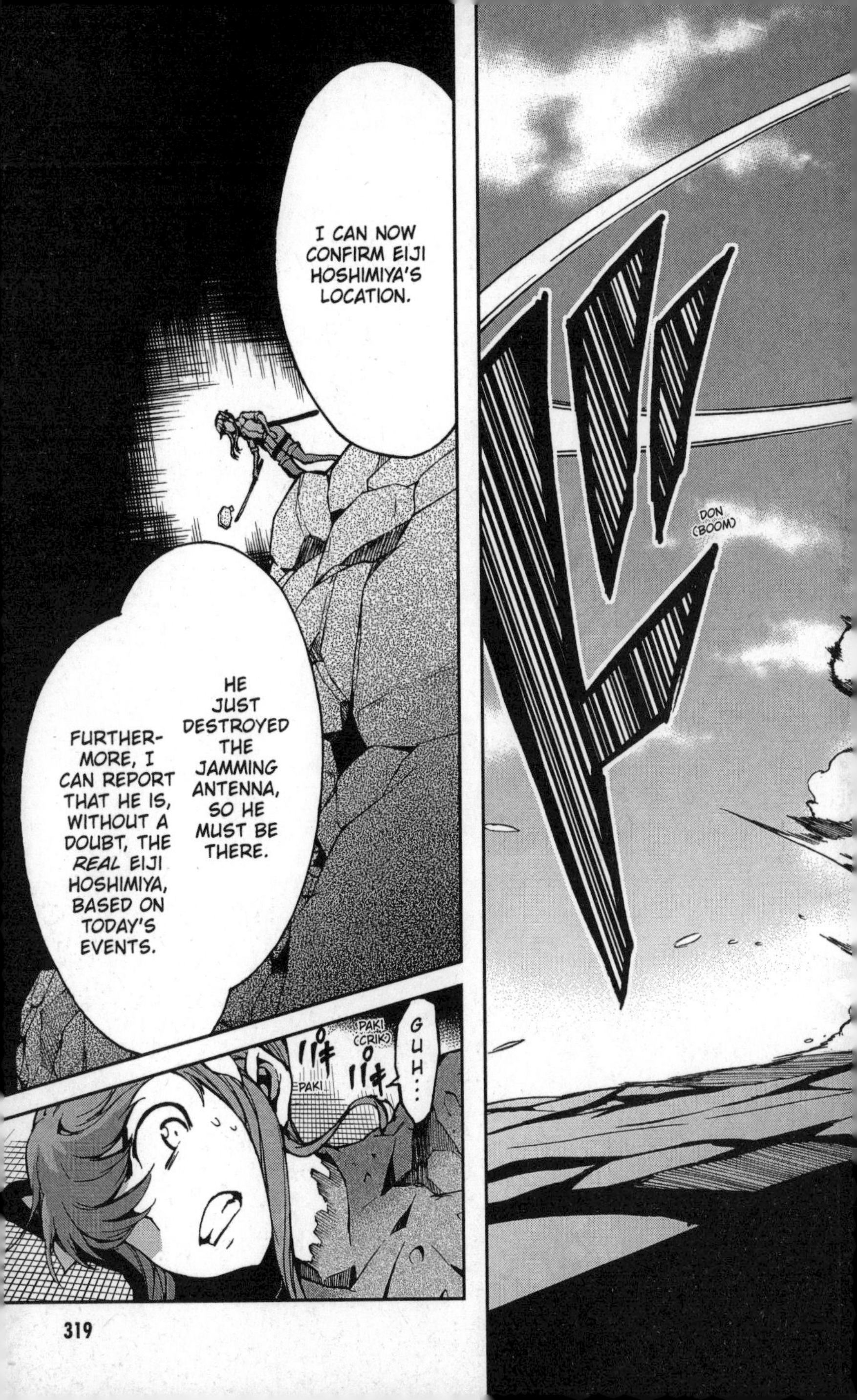
DON (BOOM)
I CAN NOW CONFIRM EIJI HOSHIMIYA'S LOCATION.
HE JUST DESTROYED THE JAMMING ANTENNA, SO HE MUST BE THERE.
FURTHERMORE, I CAN REPORT THAT HE IS, WITHOUT A DOUBT, THE *REAL* EIJI HOSHIMIYA, BASED ON TODAY'S EVENTS.
パキ PAKI (CRIK)
パキ PAKI
GUH...

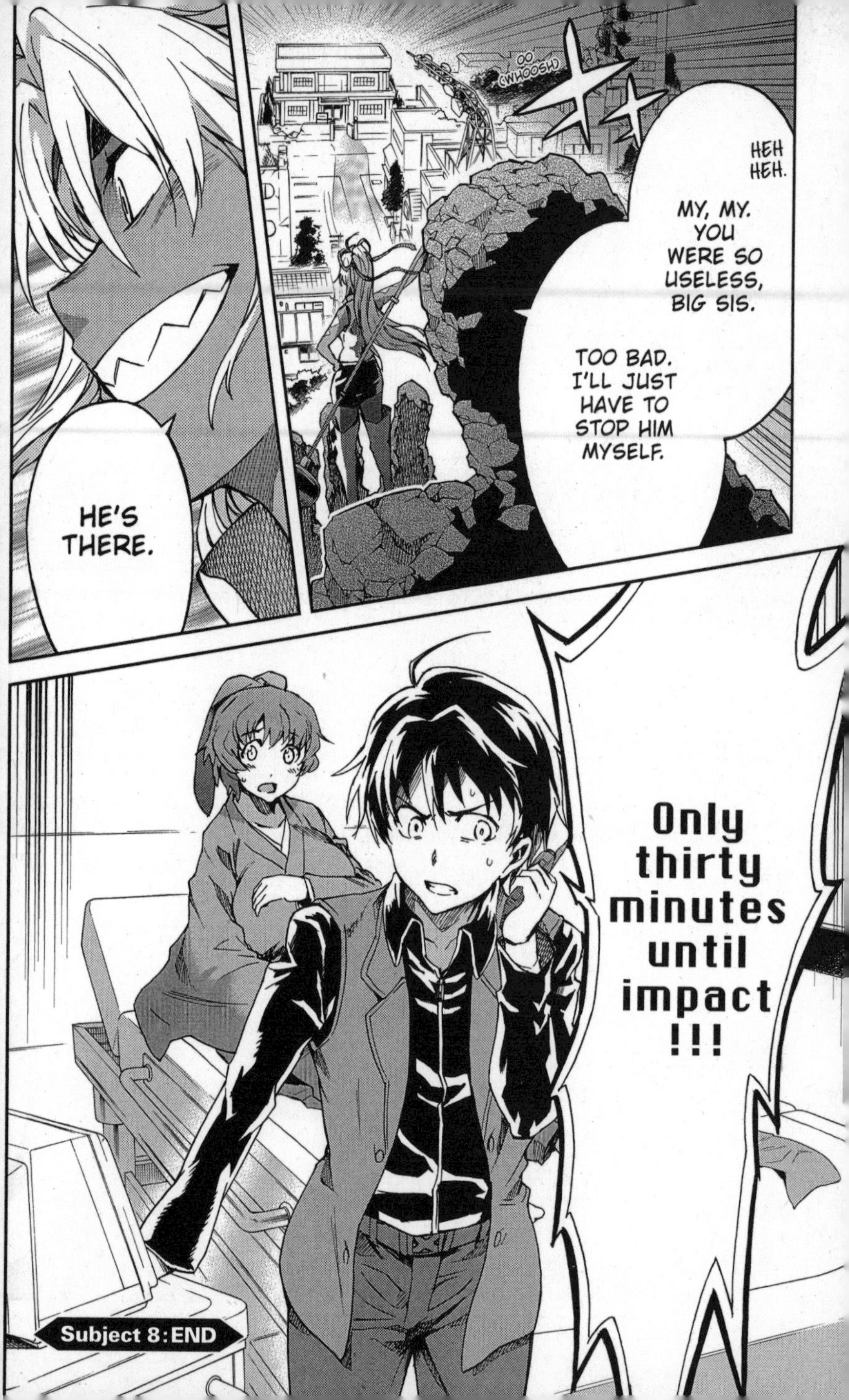
OO (WHOOSH)
HEH HEH.
MY, MY. YOU WERE SO USELESS, BIG SIS.
TOO BAD. I'LL JUST HAVE TO STOP HIM MYSELF.
HE'S THERE.
Only thirty minutes until impact!!!
Subject 8: END

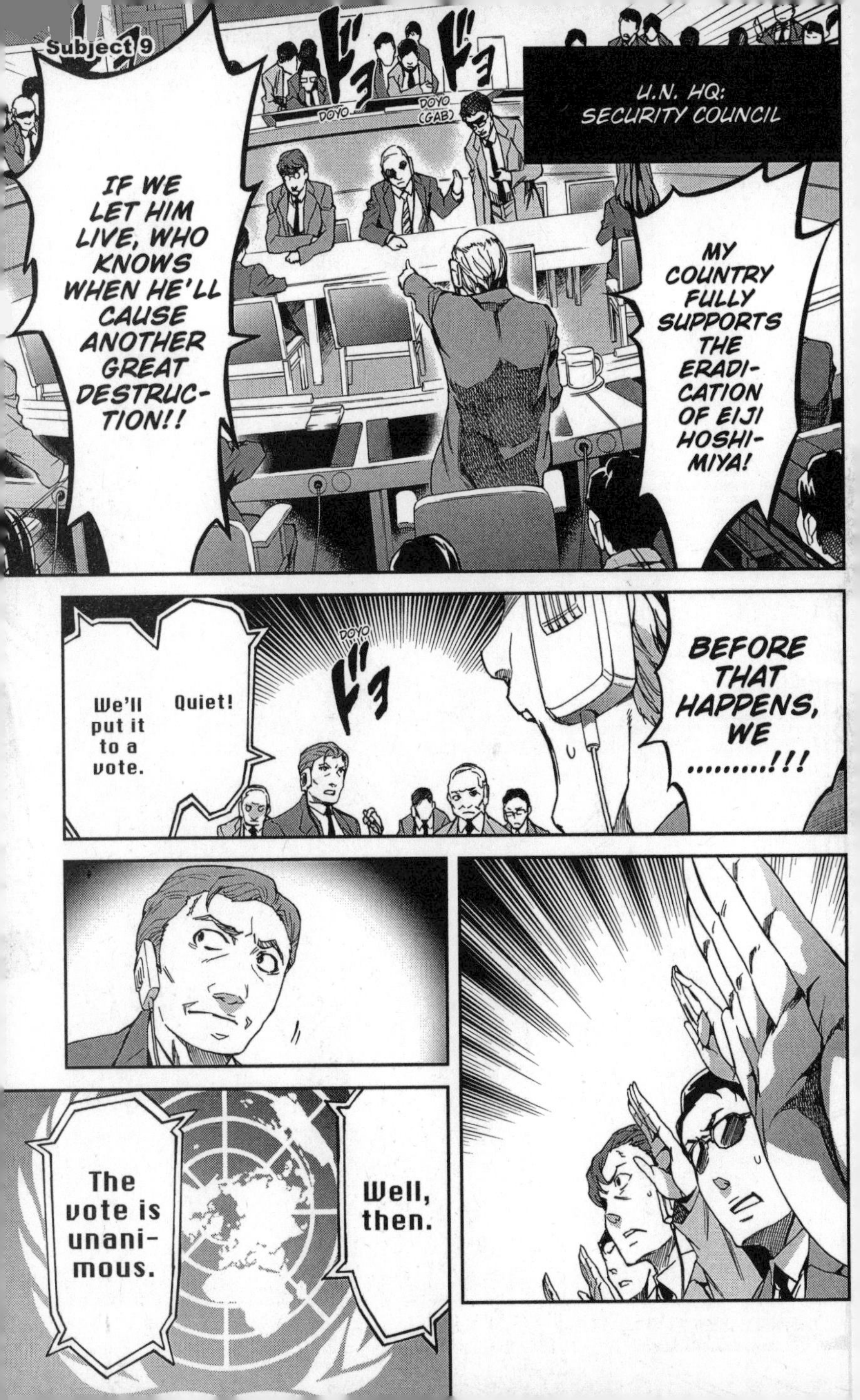
U.N. HQ:
SECURITY COUNCIL
DOYO (GAB)
DOYO
MY COUNTRY FULLY SUPPORTS THE ERADICATION OF EIJI HOSHIMIYA!
IF WE LET HIM LIVE, WHO KNOWS WHEN HE'LL CAUSE ANOTHER GREAT DESTRUCTION!!
BEFORE THAT HAPPENS, WE .........!!!
DOYO
Quiet!
We'll put it to a vote.
Well, then.
The vote is unanimous.

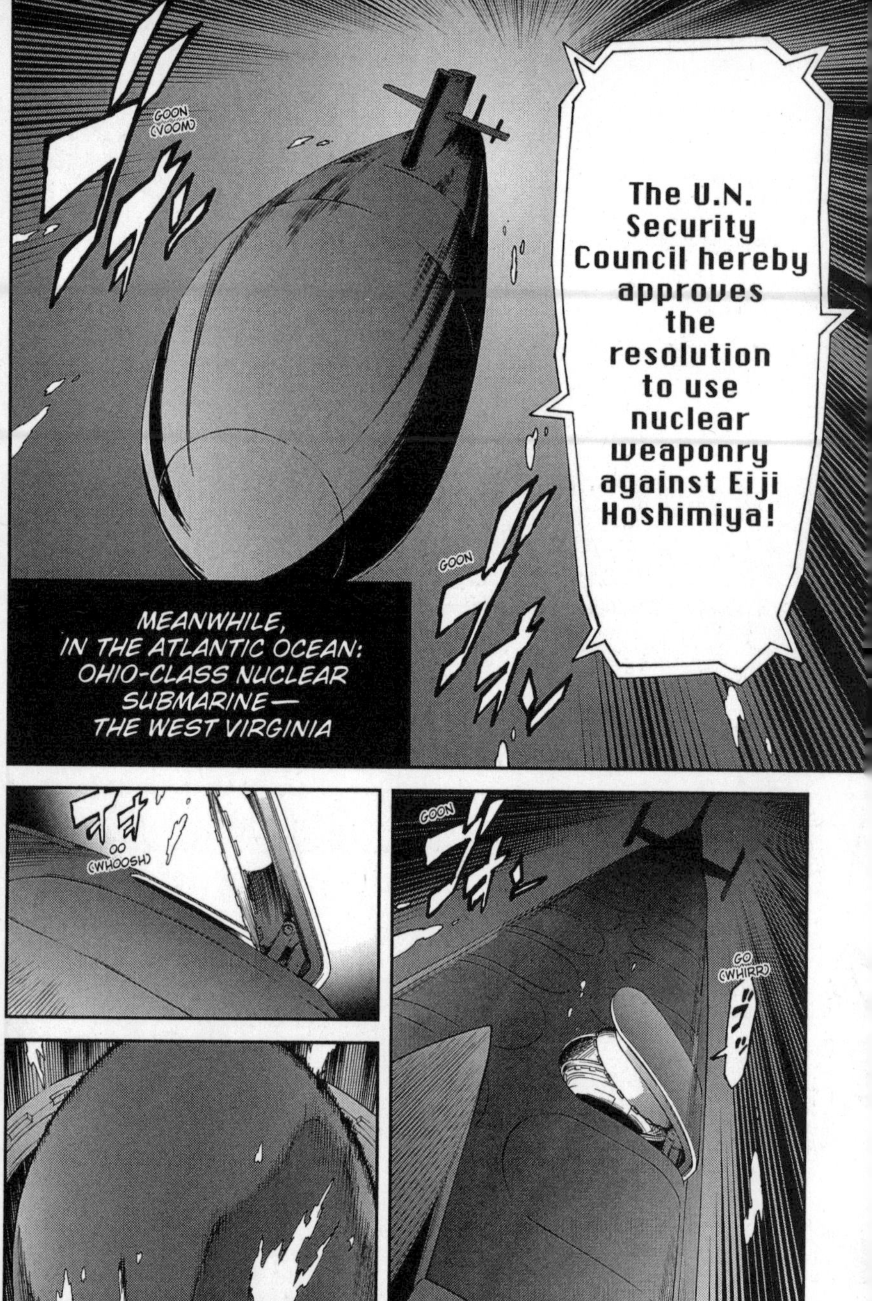
The U.N. Security Council hereby approves the resolution to use nuclear weaponry against Eiji Hoshimiya!
GOON (VOOM)
GOON
MEANWHILE, IN THE ATLANTIC OCEAN: OHIO-CLASS NUCLEAR SUBMARINE— THE WEST VIRGINIA
GOON
GO (WHIRR)
OO (WHOOSH)

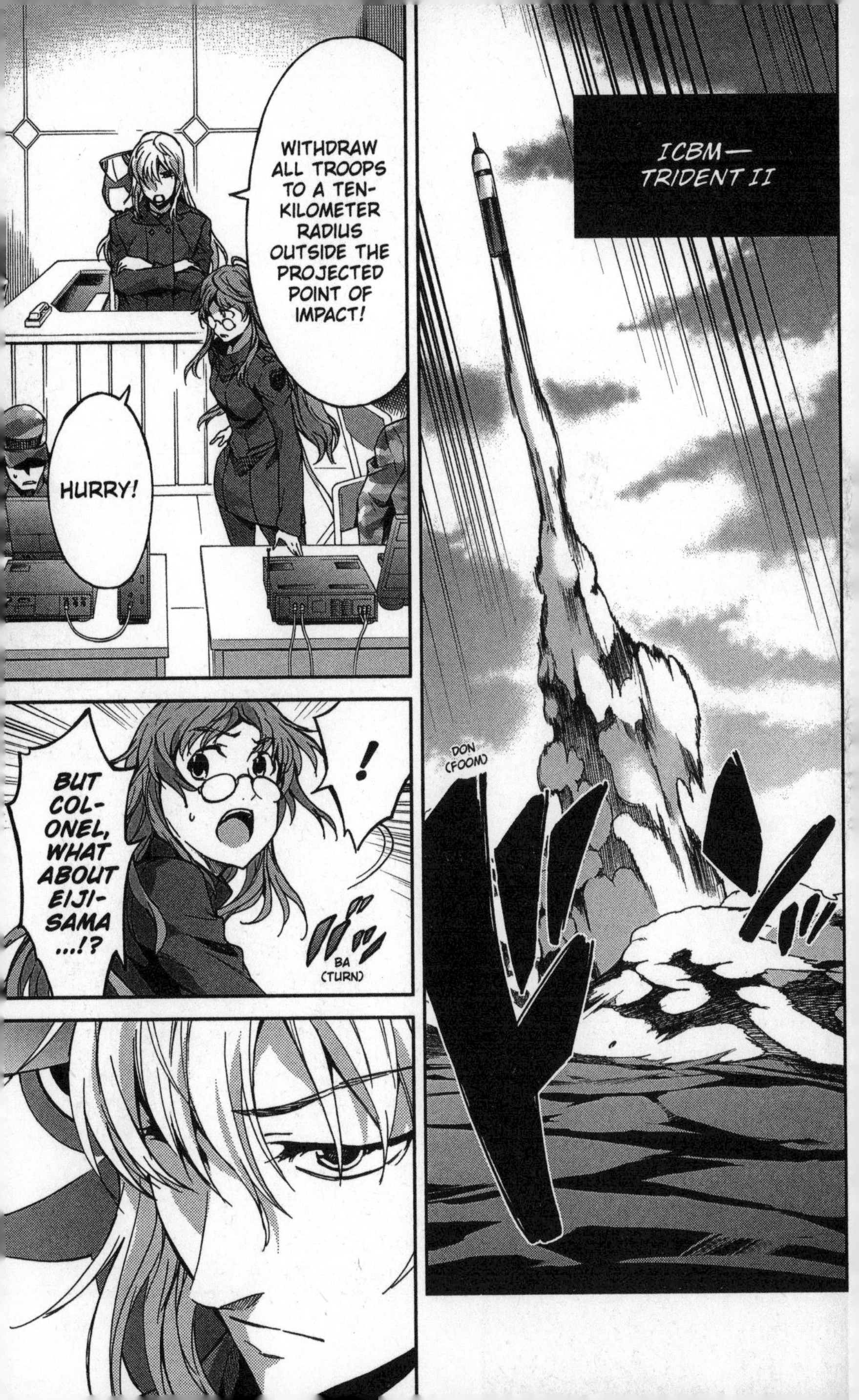
ICBM—TRIDENT II
DON (FOOM)
WITHDRAW ALL TROOPS TO A TEN-KILOMETER RADIUS OUTSIDE THE PROJECTED POINT OF IMPACT!
HURRY!
!
BUT COL-ONEL, WHAT ABOUT EIJI-SAMA ...!?
BA (TURN)

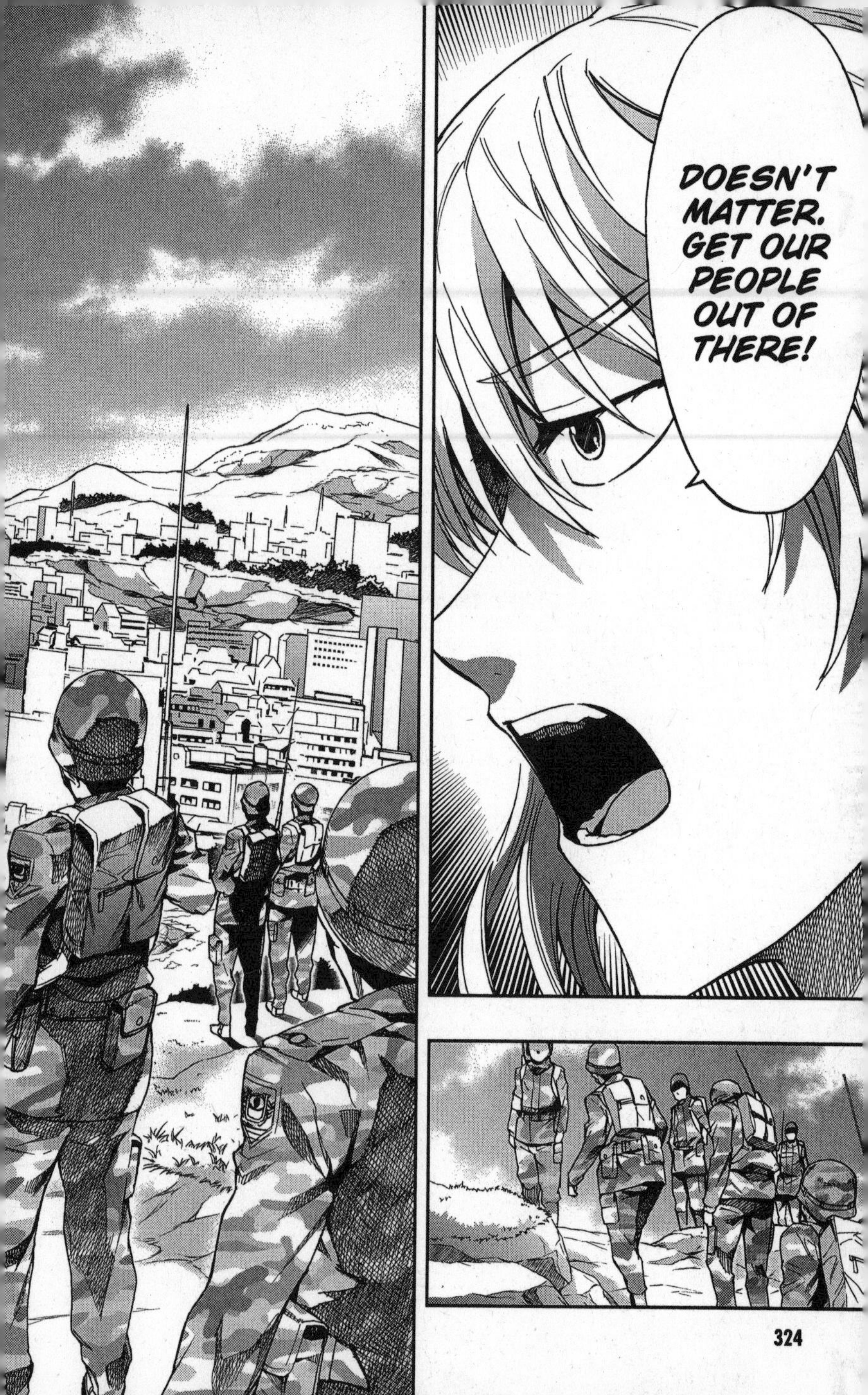
DOESN'T MATTER. GET OUR PEOPLE OUT OF THERE!

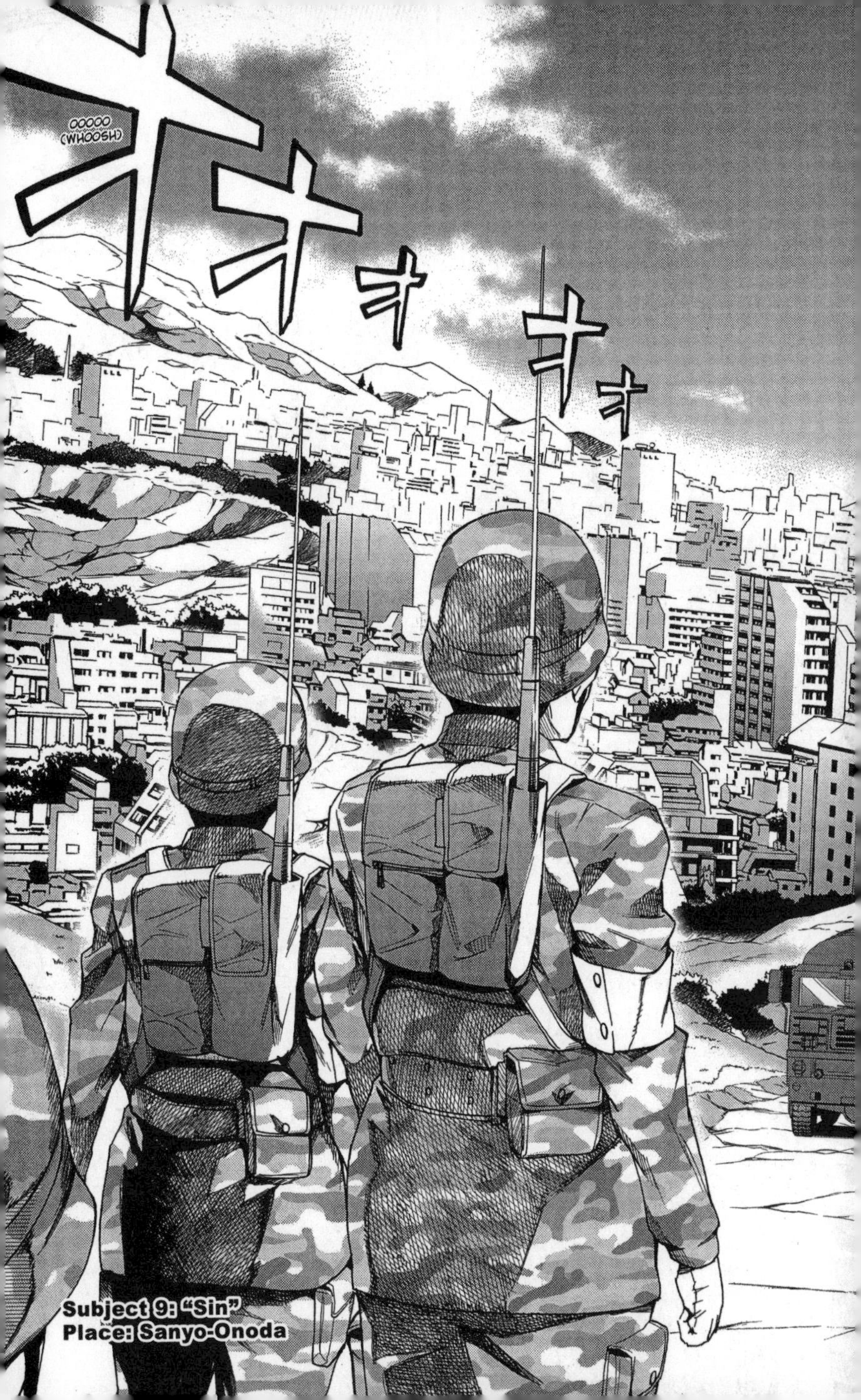
オオォォオォ
OOOOO
(WHOOSH)
Subject 9: "Sin"
Place: Sanyo-Onoda

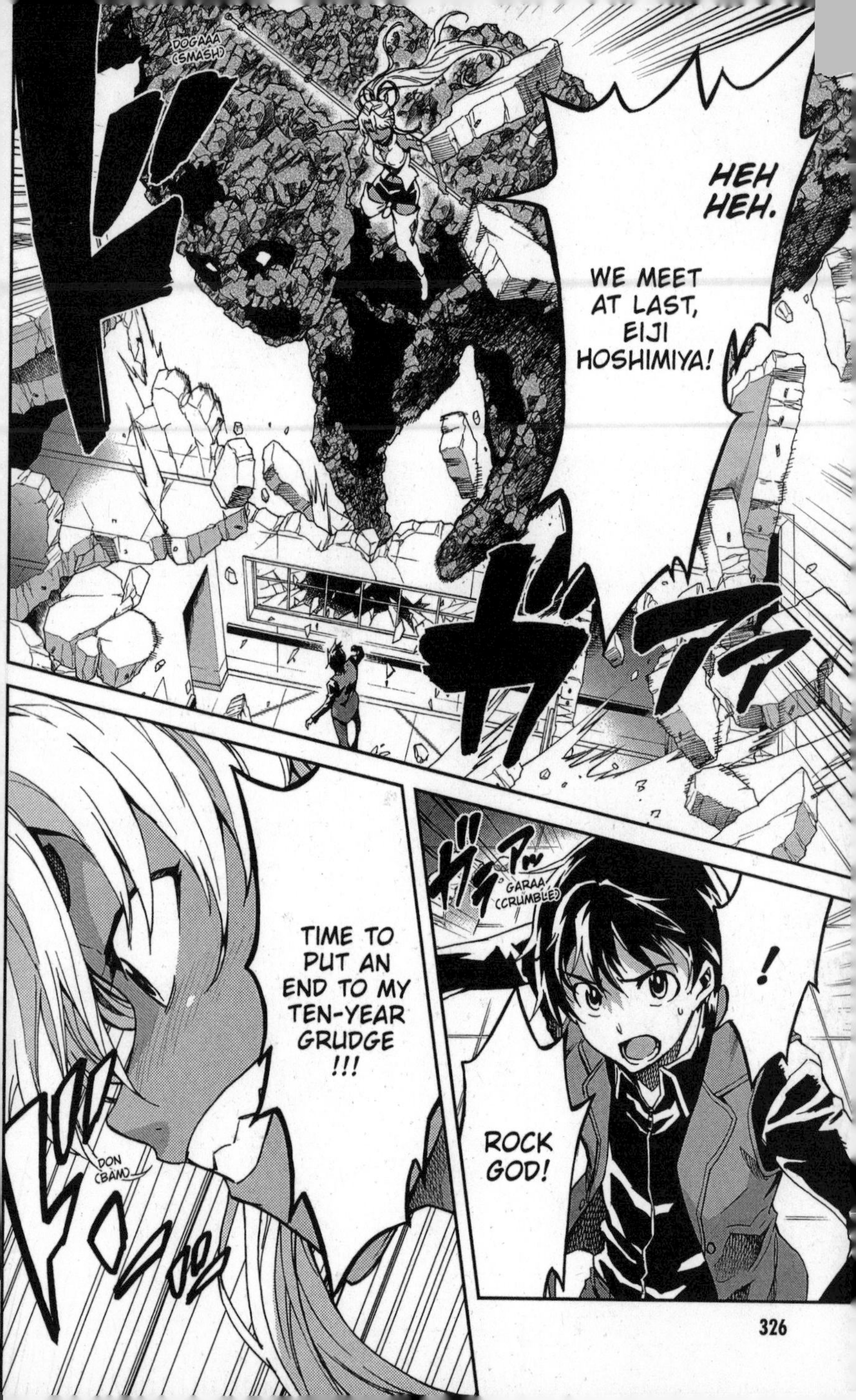
HEH HEH.
WE MEET AT LAST, EIJI HOSHIMIYA!
DOGAAA (SMASH)
GARAA (CRUMBLE)
!
ROCK GOD!
TIME TO PUT AN END TO MY TEN-YEAR GRUDGE !!!
DON (BAM)

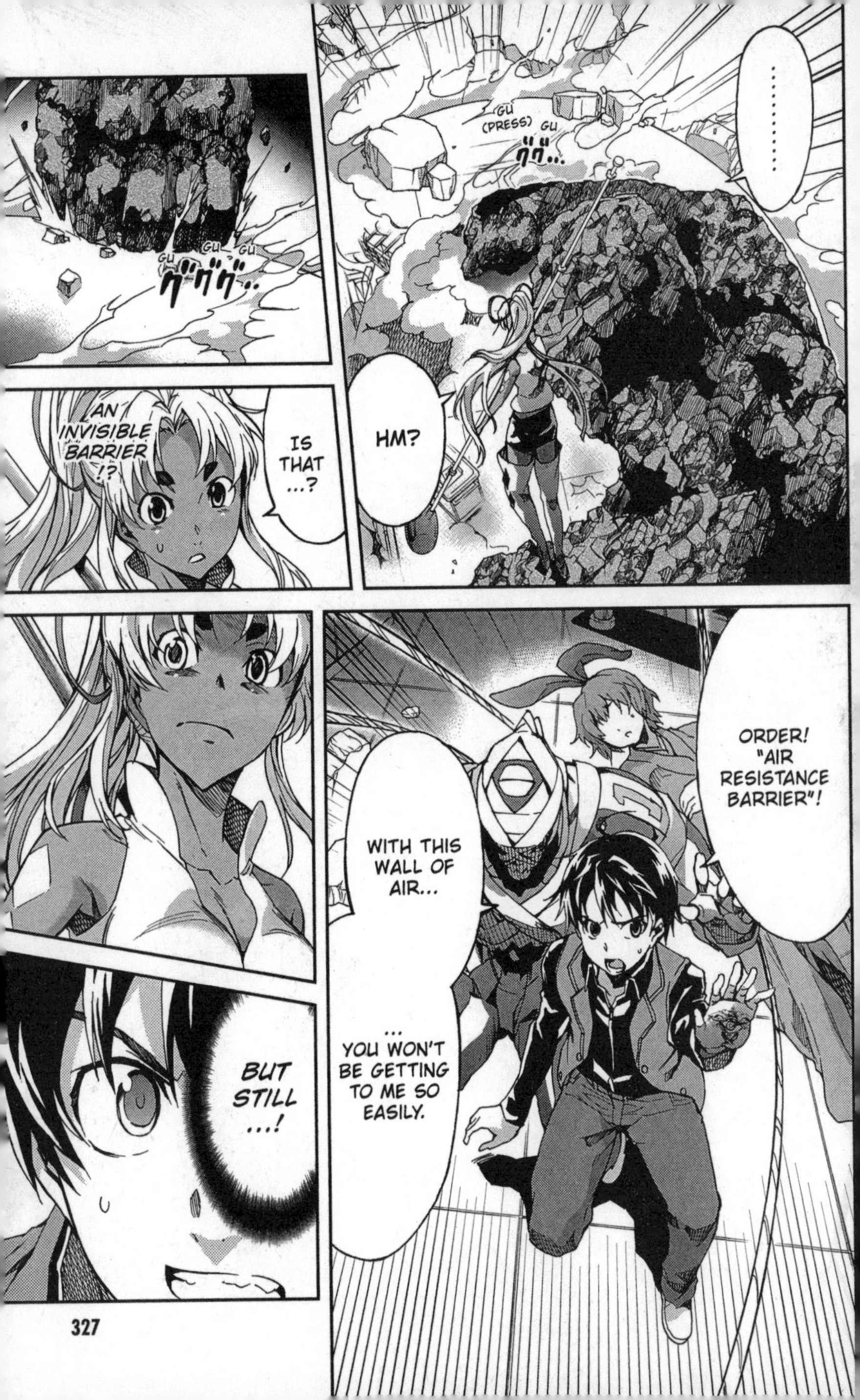

......
GU
(PRESS) GU
HM?
GU GU
IS THAT ...?
AN INVISIBLE BARRIER !?
ORDER! "AIR RESISTANCE BARRIER"!
WITH THIS WALL OF AIR...
... YOU WON'T BE GETTING TO ME SO EASILY.
BUT STILL ...!

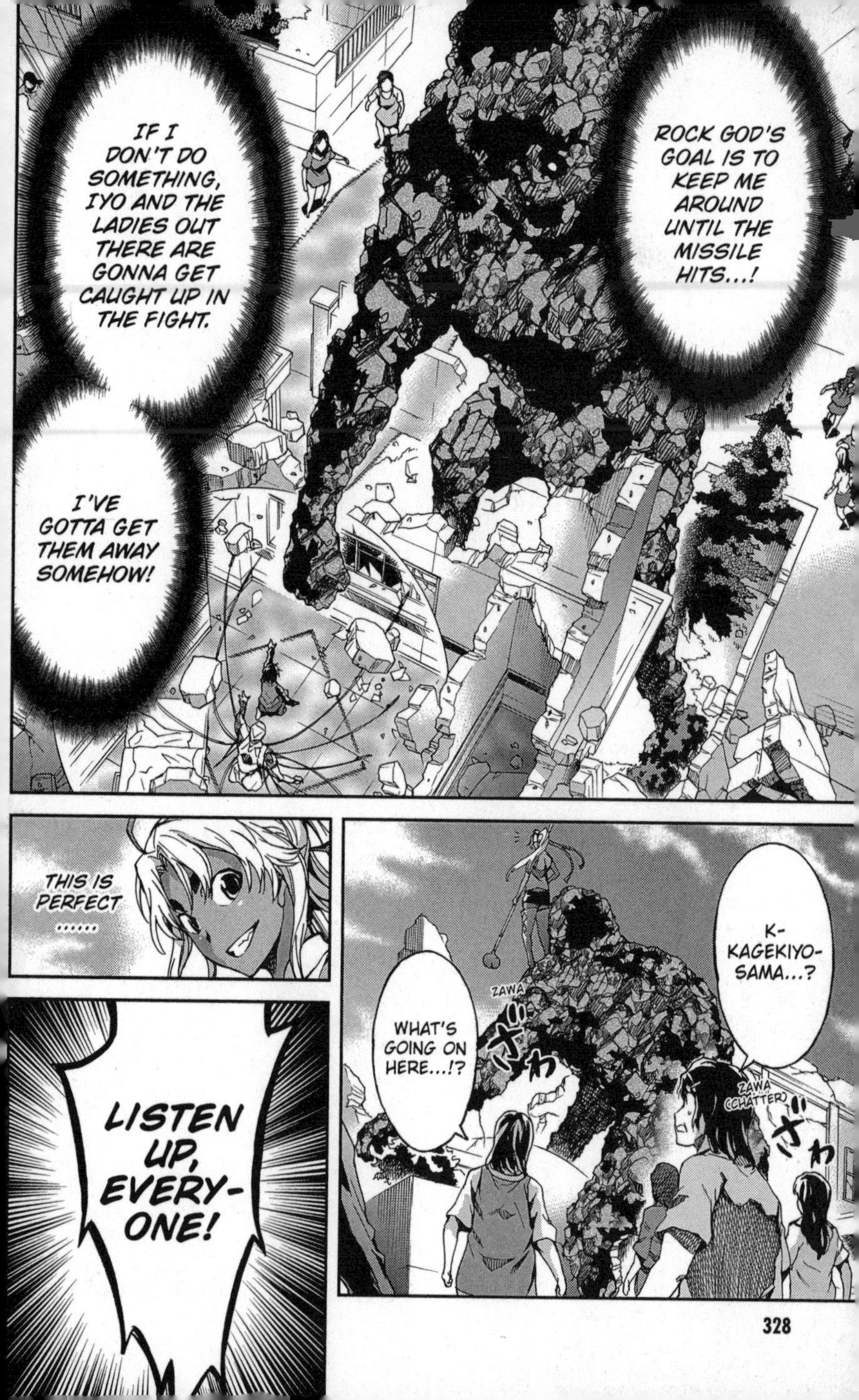
ROCK GOD'S GOAL IS TO KEEP ME AROUND UNTIL THE MISSILE HITS...!
IF I DON'T DO SOMETHING, IYO AND THE LADIES OUT THERE ARE GONNA GET CAUGHT UP IN THE FIGHT.
I'VE GOTTA GET THEM AWAY SOMEHOW!
K-KAGEKIYO-SAMA...?
ZAWA (CHATTER)
ZAWA
WHAT'S GOING ON HERE...!?
THIS IS PERFECT......
LISTEN UP, EVERY-ONE!

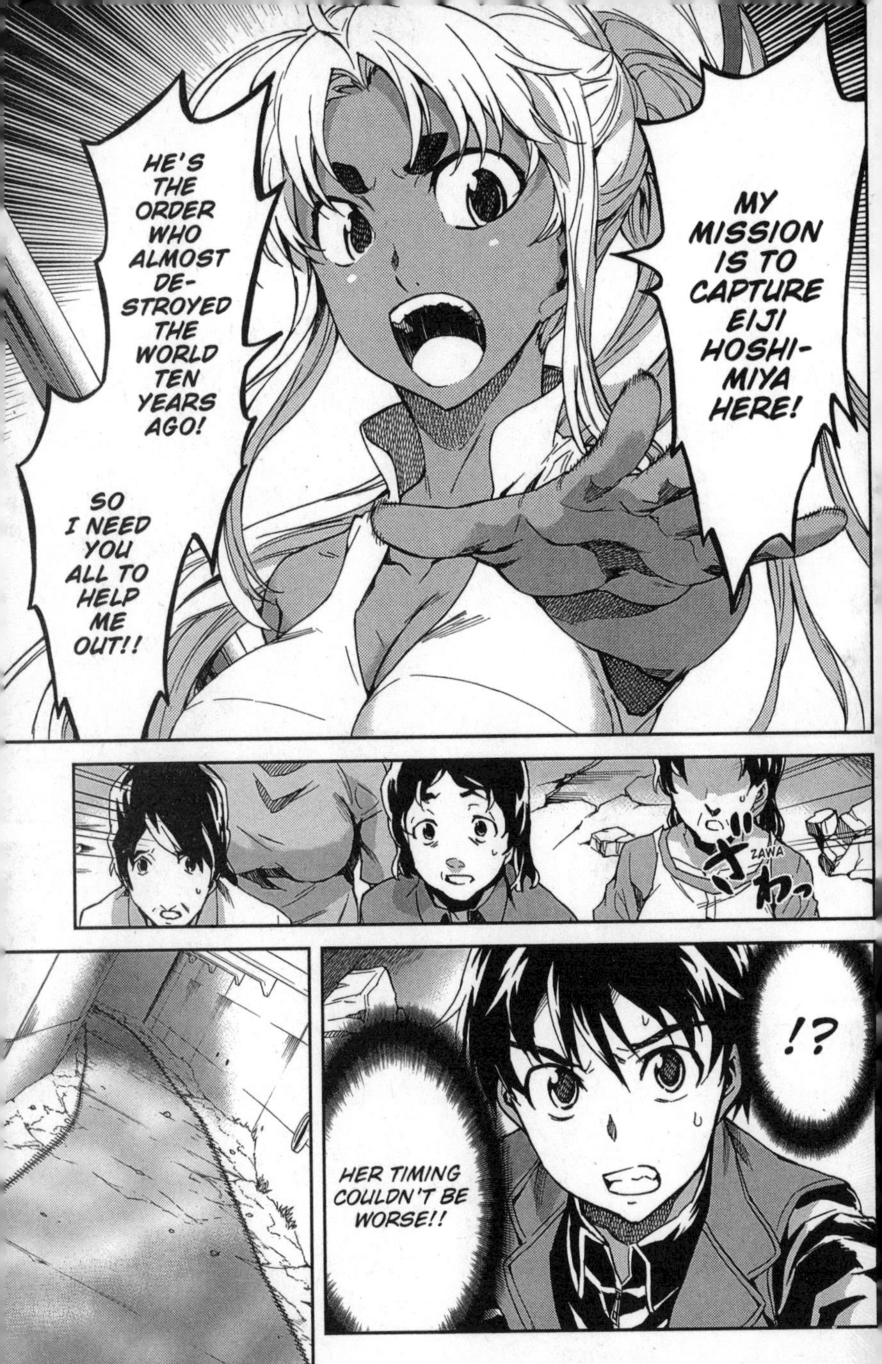
MY MISSION IS TO CAPTURE EIJI HOSHI-MIYA HERE!
HE'S THE ORDER WHO ALMOST DE-STROYED THE WORLD TEN YEARS AGO!
SO I NEED YOU ALL TO HELP ME OUT!!
ざわっ
ZAWA
!?
HER TIMING COULDN'T BE WORSE!!

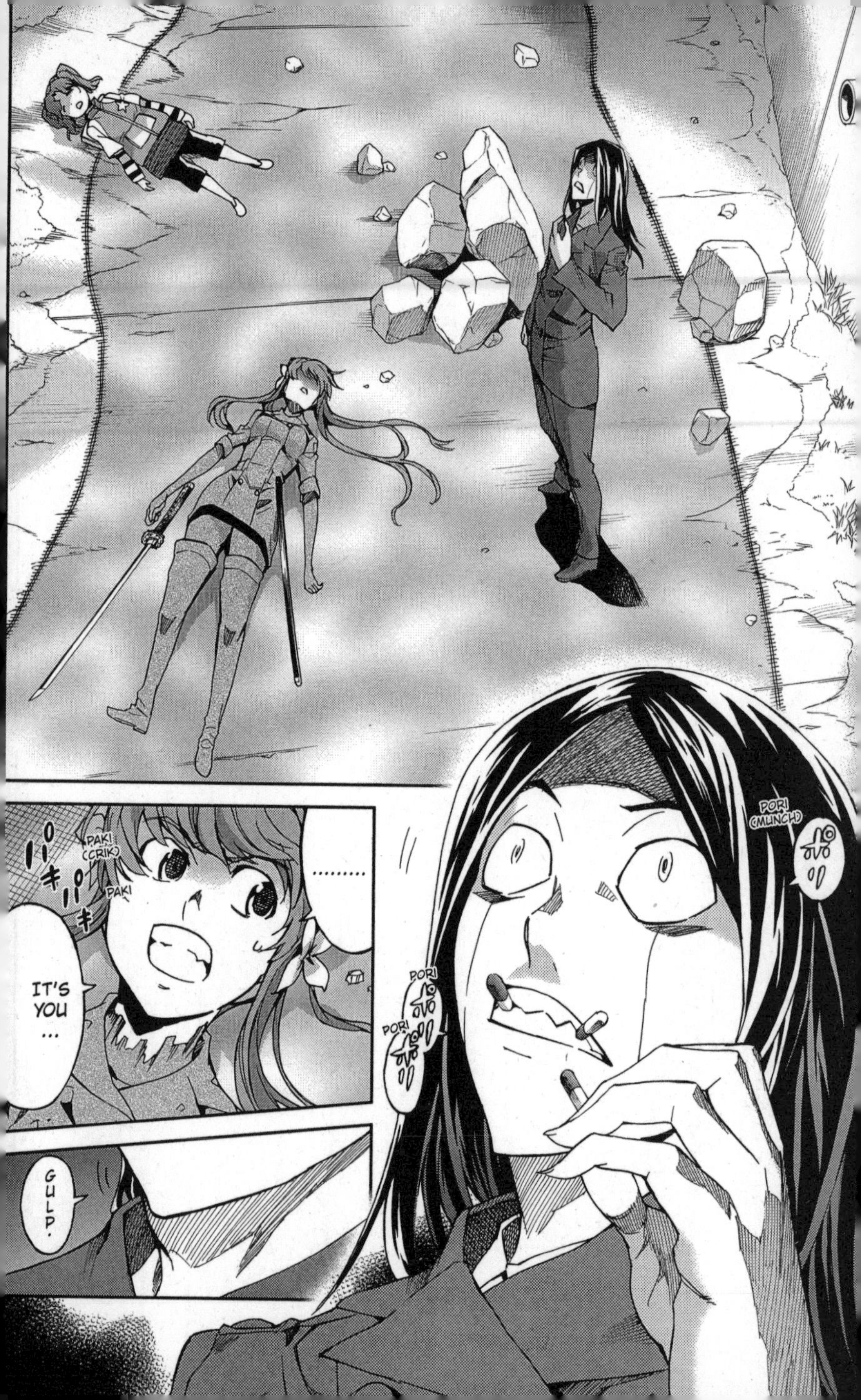
PORI (MUNCH)
PORI
PORI
........
PAKI (CRIK)
PAKI
IT'S YOU ...
GULP.

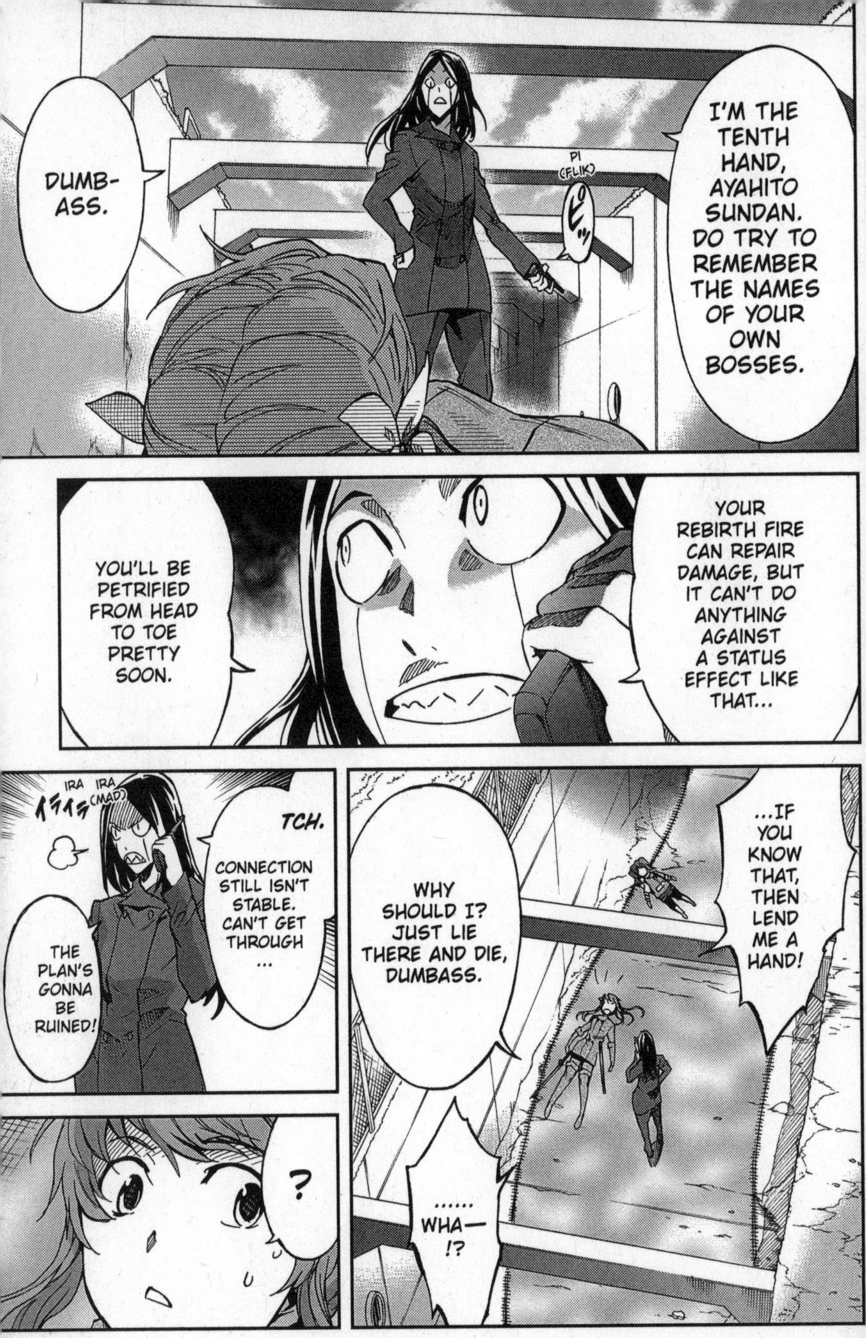
I'M THE TENTH HAND, AYAHITO SUNDAN. DO TRY TO REMEMBER THE NAMES OF YOUR OWN BOSSES.
PI (FLIK)
DUMB-ASS.
YOUR REBIRTH FIRE CAN REPAIR DAMAGE, BUT IT CAN'T DO ANYTHING AGAINST A STATUS EFFECT LIKE THAT...
YOU'LL BE PETRIFIED FROM HEAD TO TOE PRETTY SOON.
...IF YOU KNOW THAT, THEN LEND ME A HAND!
WHY SHOULD I? JUST LIE THERE AND DIE, DUMBASS.
......WHA—!?
IRA IRA (MAD)
TCH.
CONNECTION STILL ISN'T STABLE. CAN'T GET THROUGH ...
THE PLAN'S GONNA BE RUINED!
?

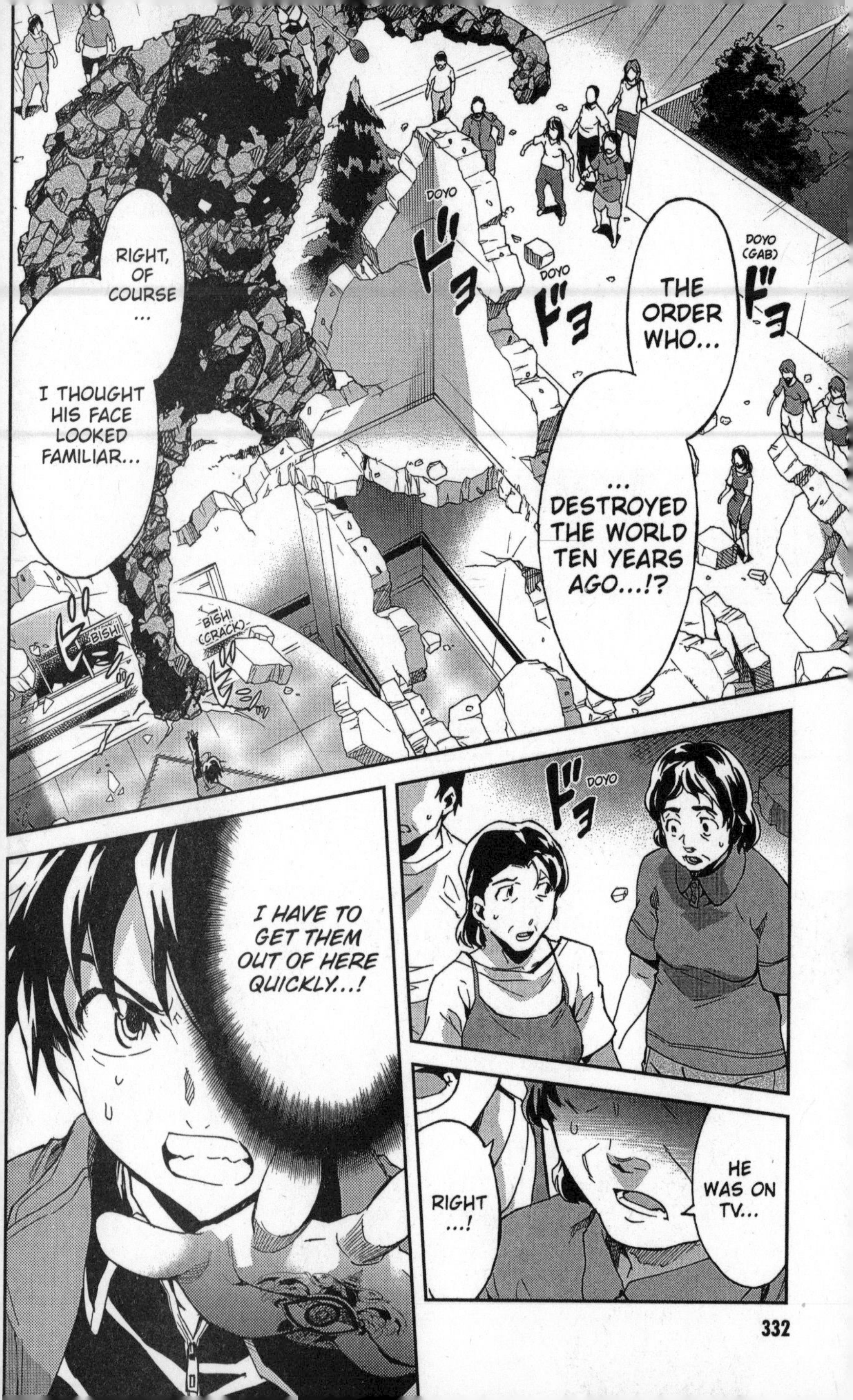
DOYO (GAB)
ドヨ
THE ORDER WHO...
... DESTROYED THE WORLD TEN YEARS AGO...!?
DOYO
ドヨ
DOYO
ドヨ
RIGHT, OF COURSE ...
I THOUGHT HIS FACE LOOKED FAMILIAR...
BISHI (CRACK)
BISHI
DOYO
ドヨ
HE WAS ON TV...
RIGHT ...!
I HAVE TO GET THEM OUT OF HERE QUICKLY...!

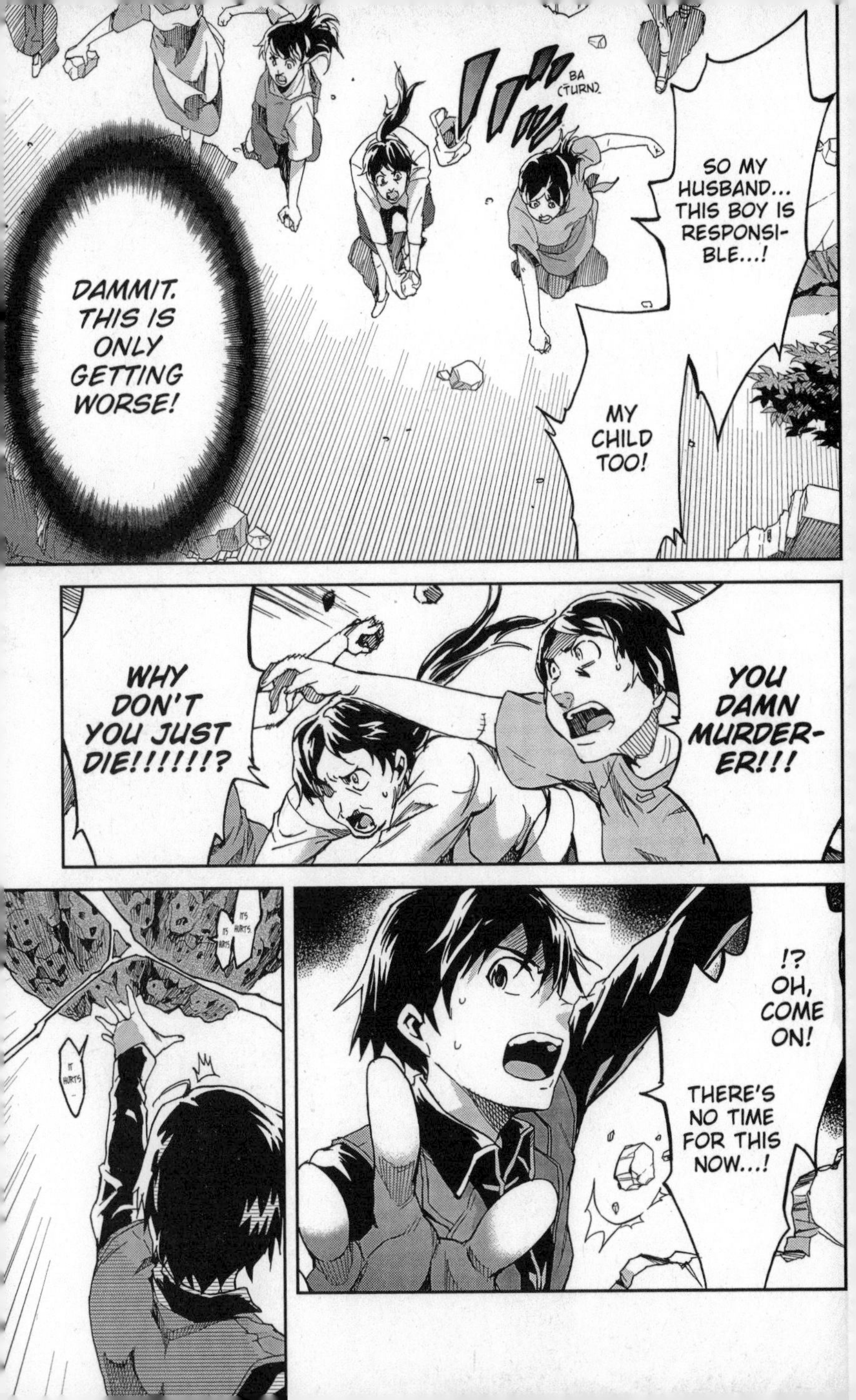
SO MY HUSBAND... THIS BOY IS RESPONSI-BLE...!
MY CHILD TOO!
BA (TURN)
DAMMIT. THIS IS ONLY GETTING WORSE!
YOU DAMN MURDER-ER!!!
WHY DON'T YOU JUST DIE!!!!!!?
!? OH, COME ON!
THERE'S NO TIME FOR THIS NOW...!
ITS HURTS.
ITS HURTS.
IT HURTS...

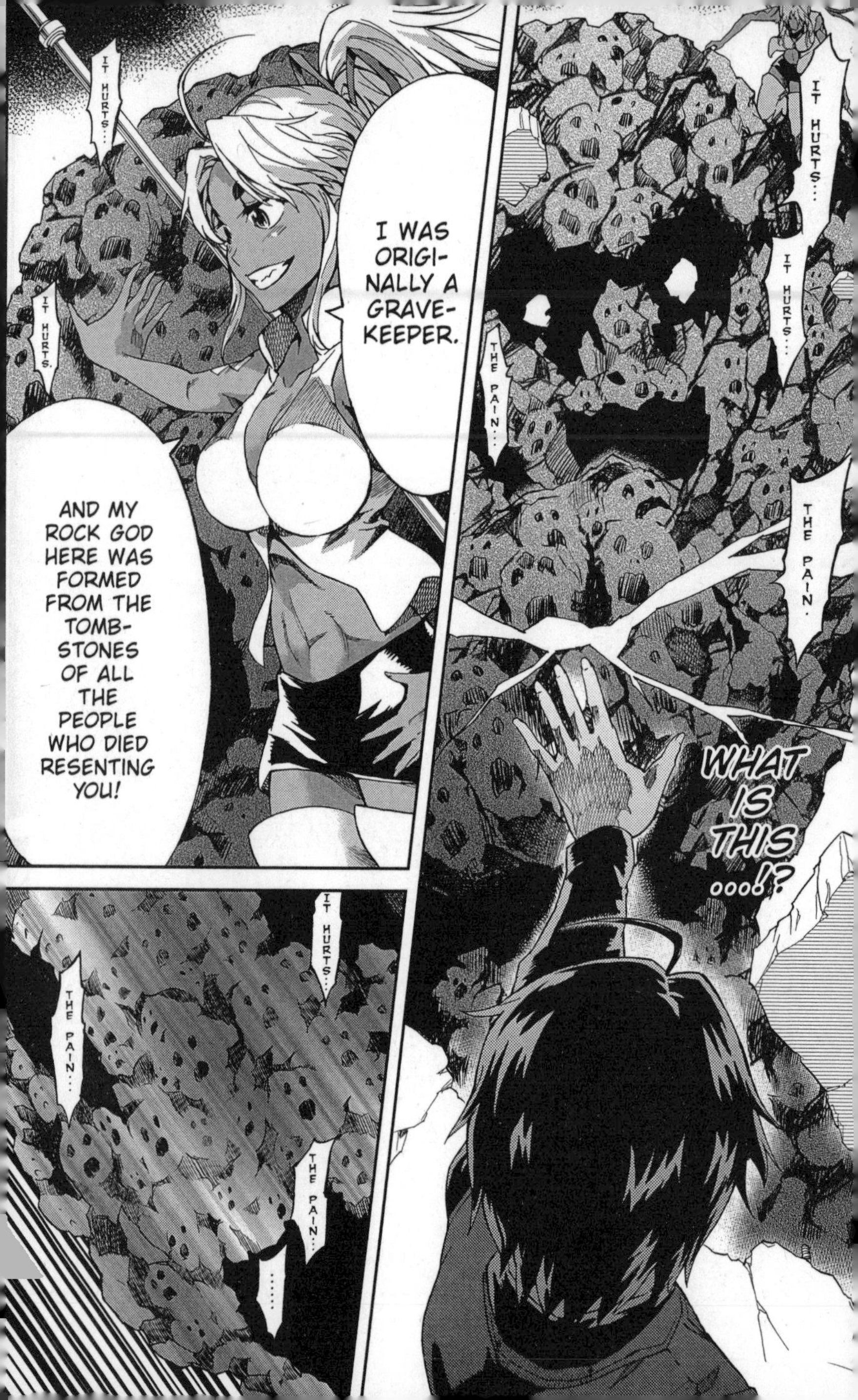
IT HURTS...
IT HURTS...
THE PAIN...
THE PAIN.
WHAT IS THIS...!?
IT HURTS...
I WAS ORIGINALLY A GRAVE-KEEPER.
IT HURTS.
AND MY ROCK GOD HERE WAS FORMED FROM THE TOMBSTONES OF ALL THE PEOPLE WHO DIED RESENTING YOU!
IT HURTS...
THE PAIN...
THE PAIN...
......

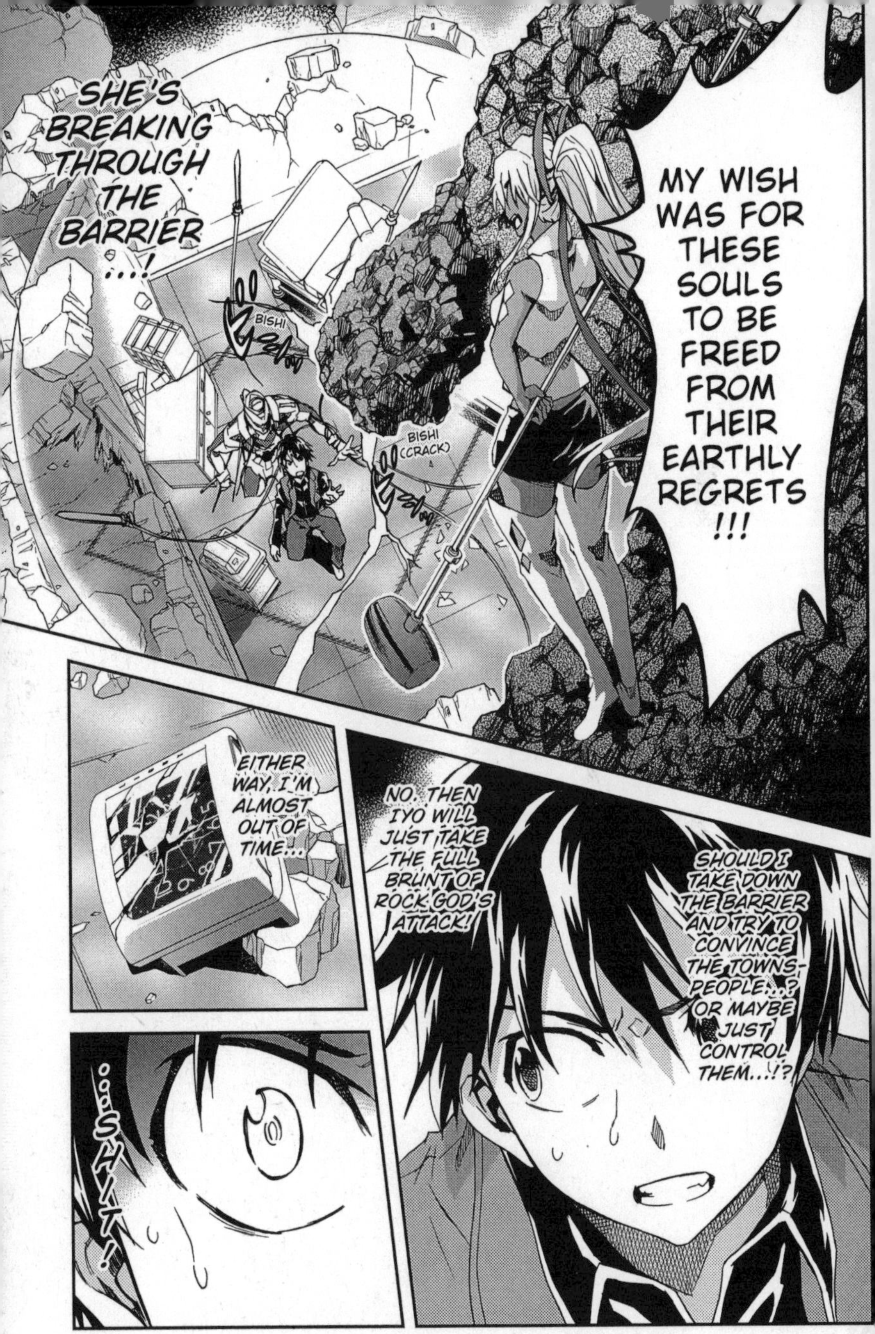
MY WISH WAS FOR THESE SOULS TO BE FREED FROM THEIR EARTHLY REGRETS !!!
SHE'S BREAKING THROUGH THE BARRIER ...!
BISHI
BISHI (CRACK)
SHOULD I TAKE DOWN THE BARRIER AND TRY TO CONVINCE THE TOWNS-PEOPLE...? OR MAYBE JUST CONTROL THEM...!?
NO. THEN IYO WILL JUST TAKE THE FULL BRUNT OF ROCK GOD'S ATTACK!
EITHER WAY, I'M ALMOST OUT OF TIME...
...SHIT!

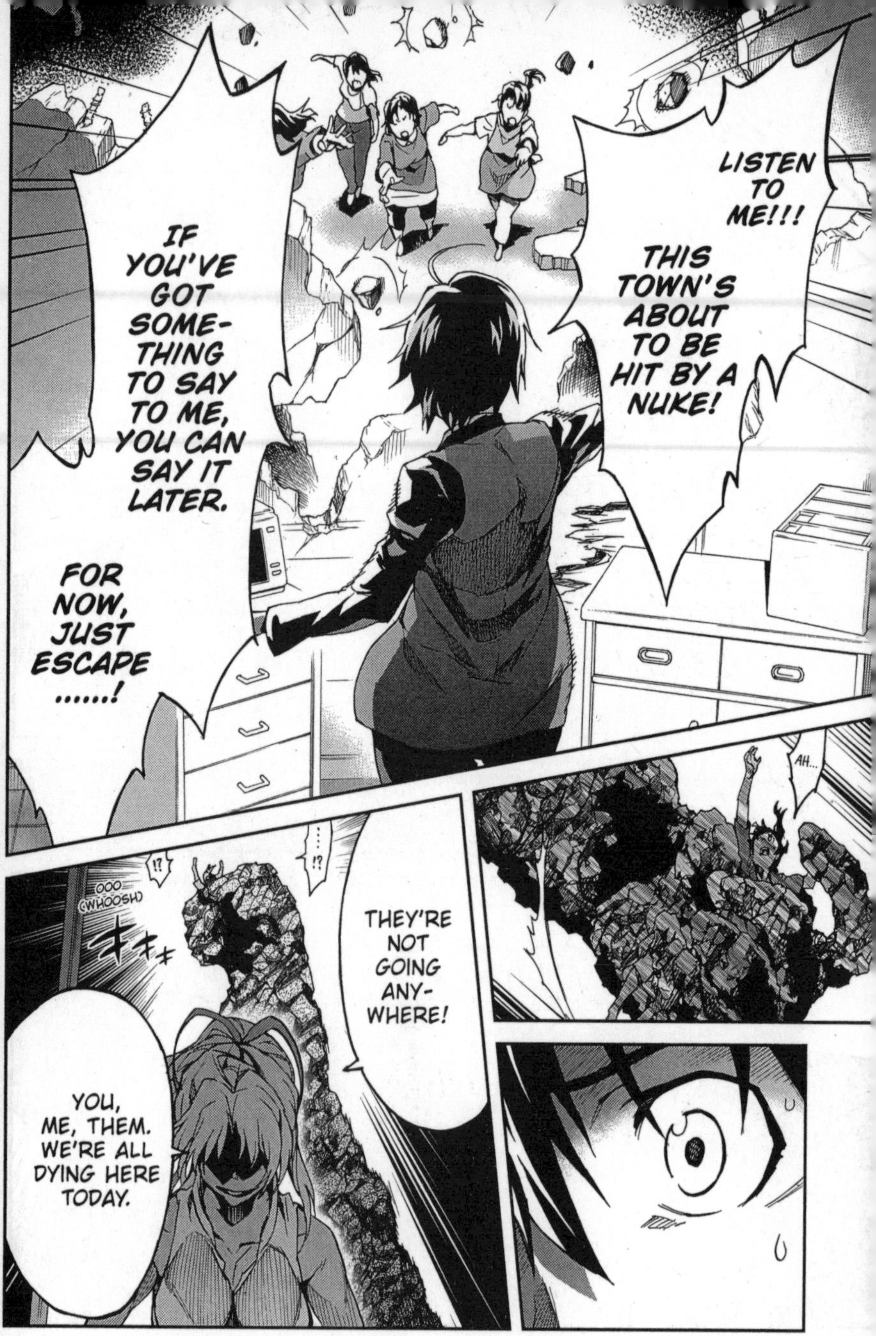
LISTEN TO ME!!!
THIS TOWN'S ABOUT TO BE HIT BY A NUKE!
IF YOU'VE GOT SOMETHING TO SAY TO ME, YOU CAN SAY IT LATER.
FOR NOW, JUST ESCAPE......!
AH...
......!?
THEY'RE NOT GOING ANYWHERE!
!?
OOO (WHOOSH)
YOU, ME, THEM. WE'RE ALL DYING HERE TODAY.

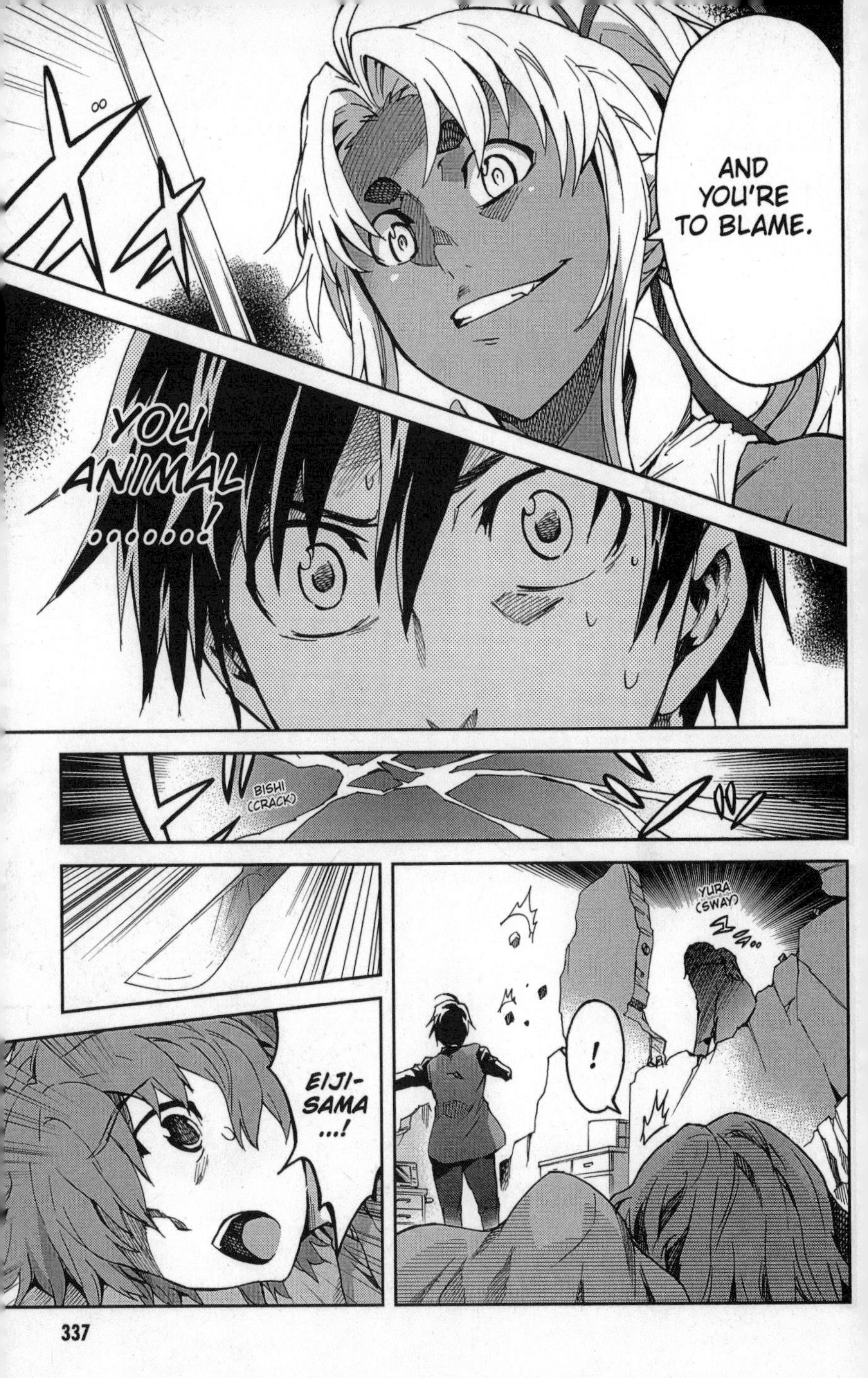
AND YOU'RE TO BLAME.
YOU ANIMAL .......!
BISHI (CRACK)
YURA (SWAY)
!
EIJI-SAMA ...!

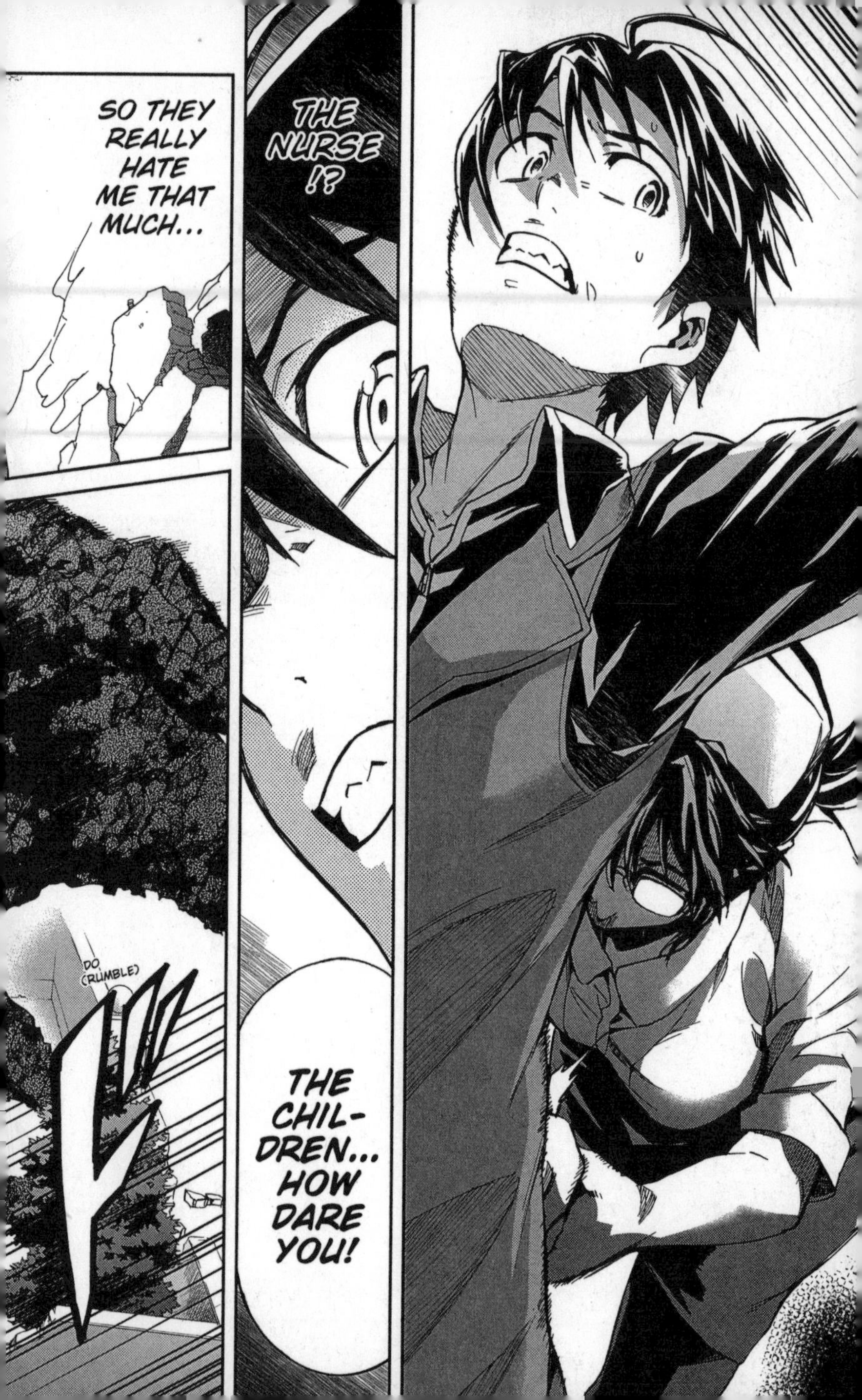
THE NURSE!?
THE CHIL-DREN... HOW DARE YOU!
SO THEY REALLY HATE ME THAT MUCH...
DO (RUMBLE)

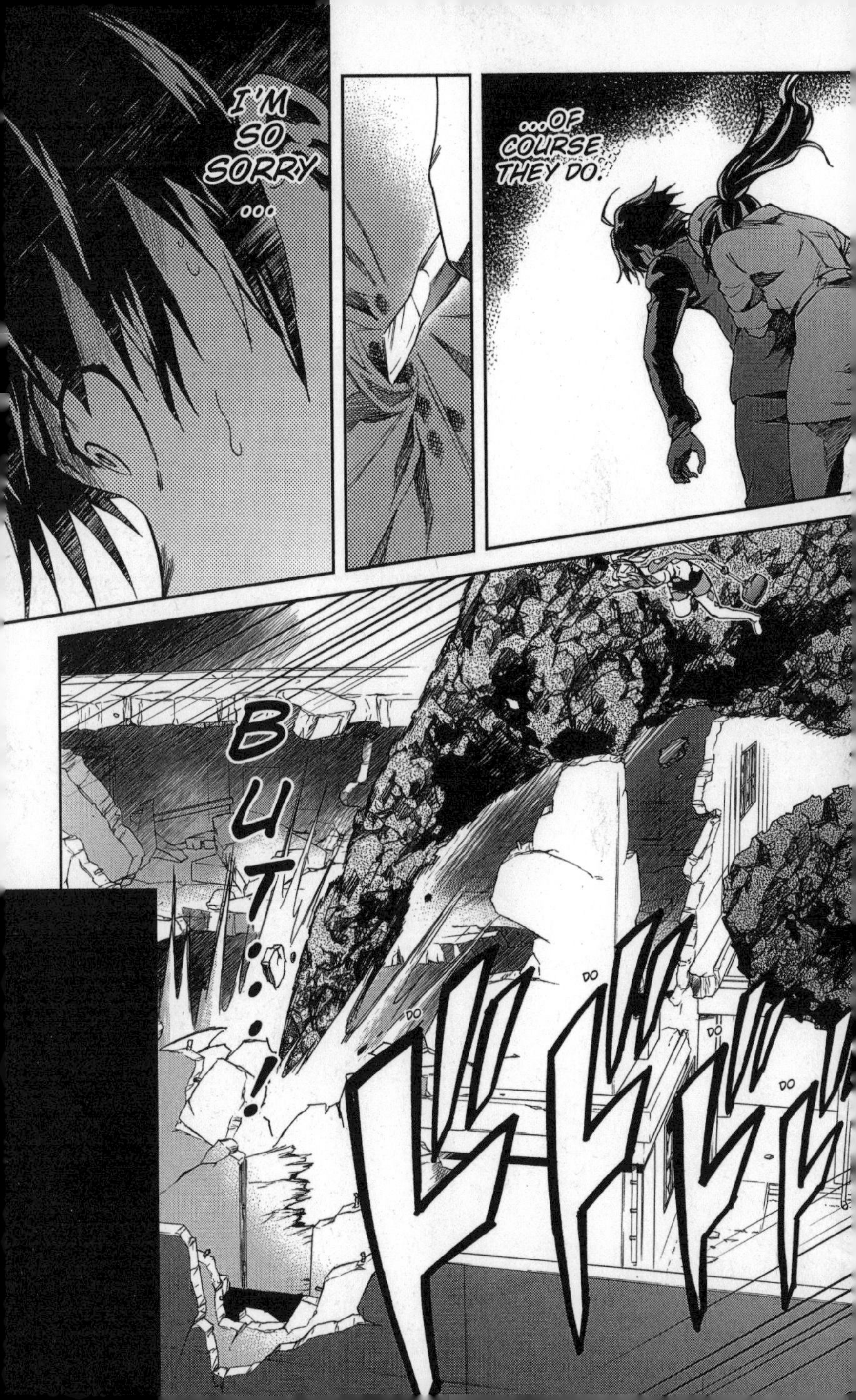
...OF COURSE THEY DO.
I'M SO SORRY...
BUT...!
DO
DO
DO
DO

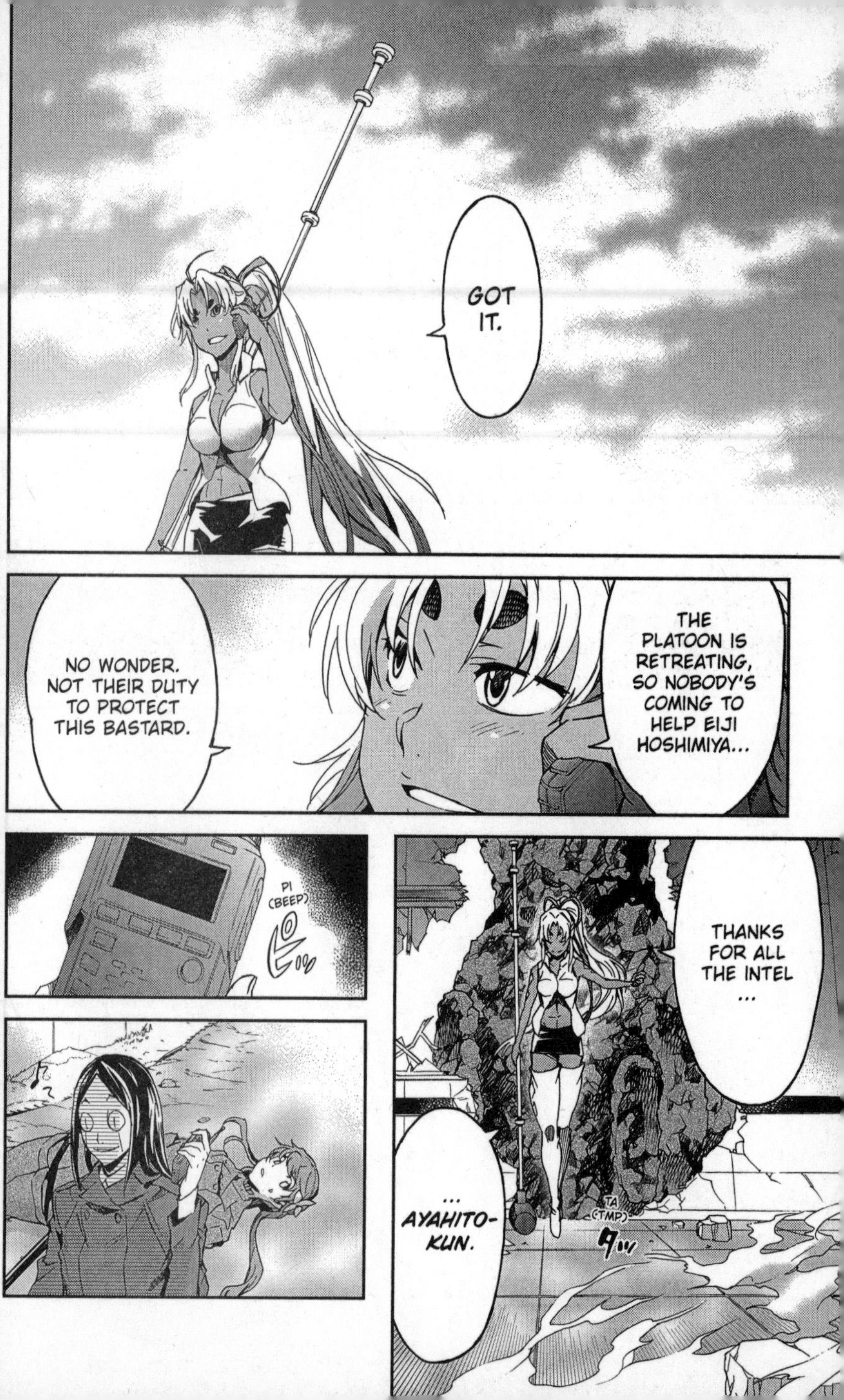
GOT IT.
THE PLATOON IS RETREATING, SO NOBODY'S COMING TO HELP EIJI HOSHIMIYA...
NO WONDER. NOT THEIR DUTY TO PROTECT THIS BASTARD.
THANKS FOR ALL THE INTEL ...
... AYAHITO-KUN.
TA (TMP)
PI (BEEP)

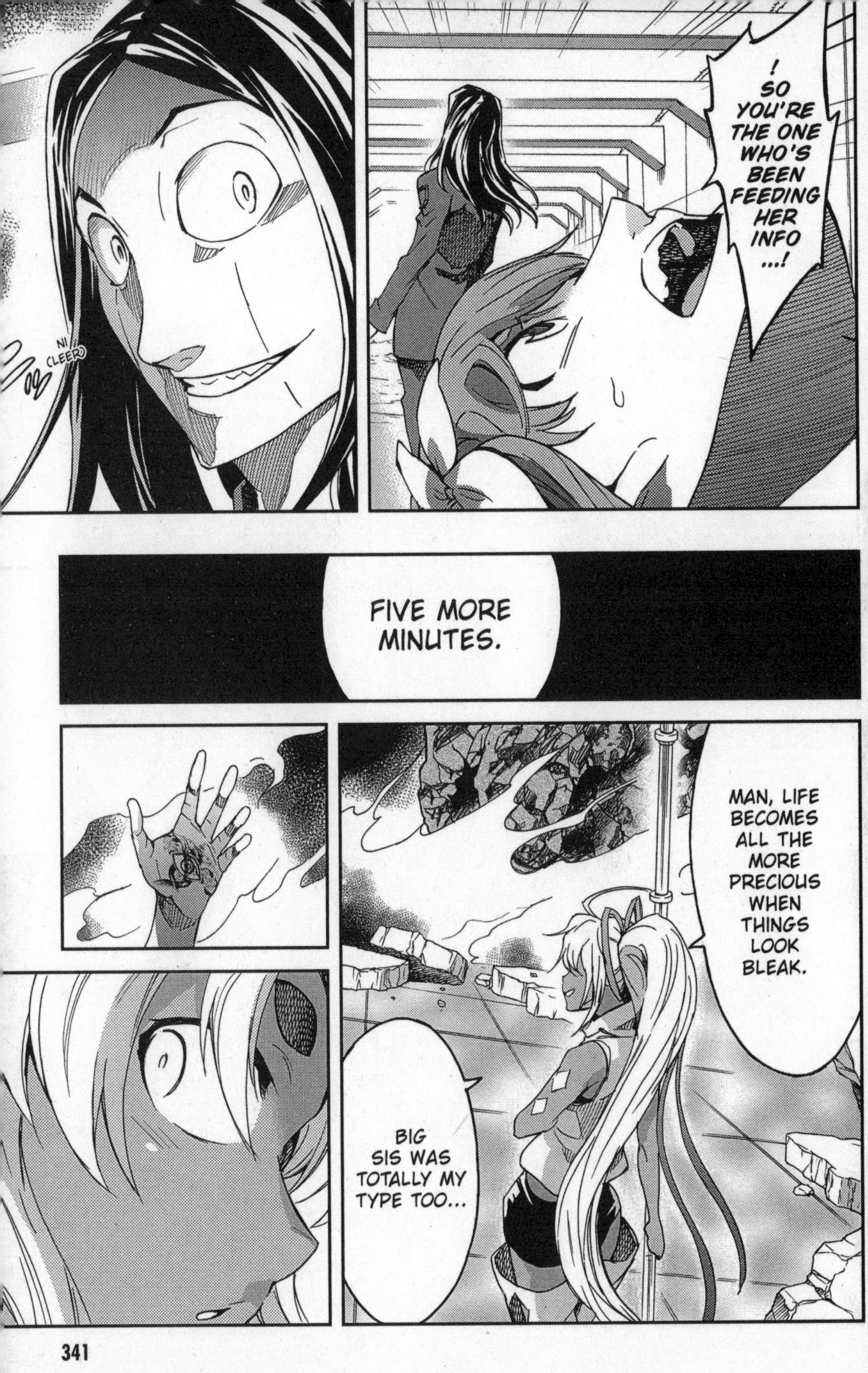
! SO YOU'RE THE ONE WHO'S BEEN FEEDING HER INFO ...!
NI (LEER)
FIVE MORE MINUTES.
MAN, LIFE BECOMES ALL THE MORE PRECIOUS WHEN THINGS LOOK BLEAK.
BIG SIS WAS TOTALLY MY TYPE TOO...

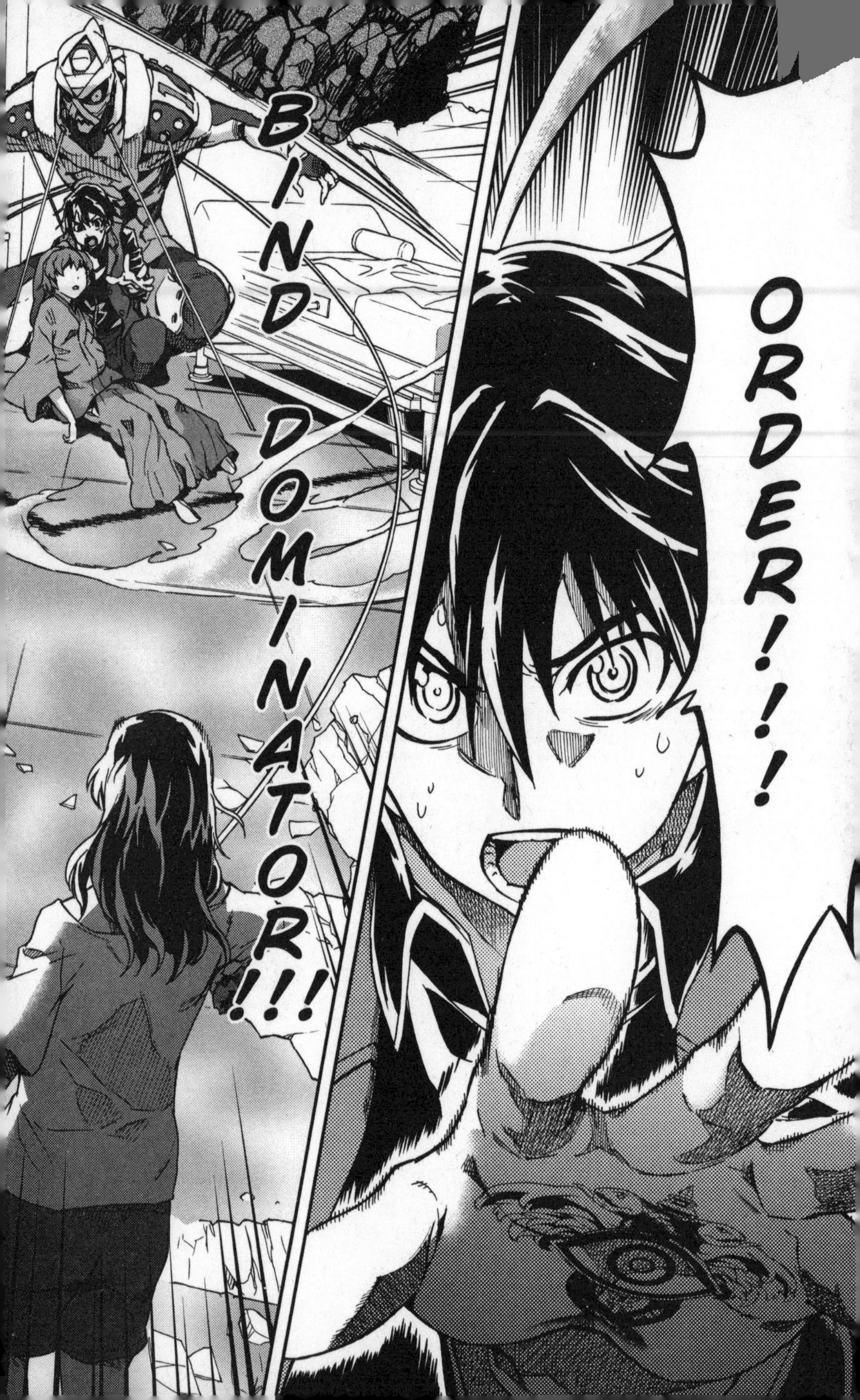
ORDER!!!
BIND DOMINATOR!!!

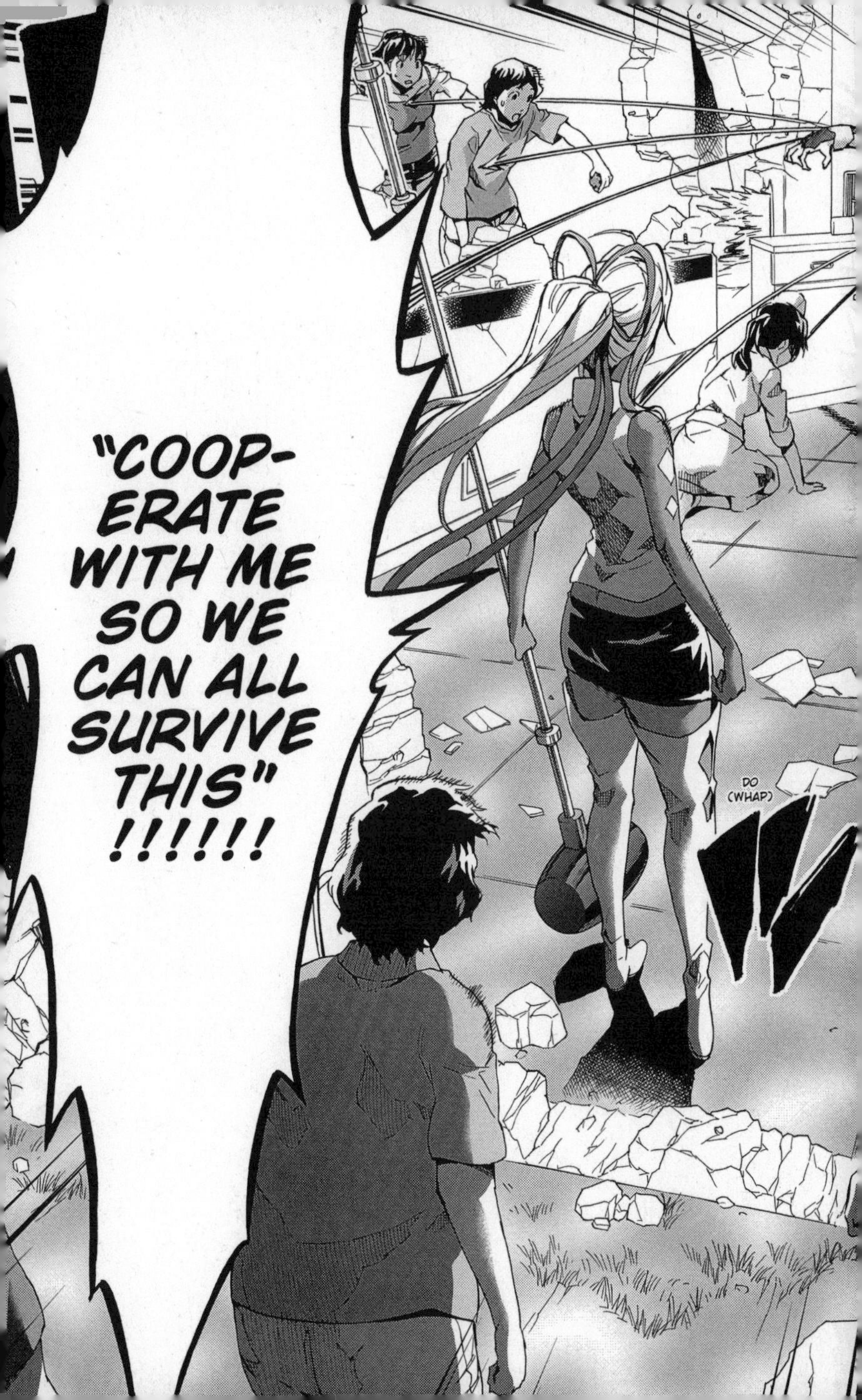
"COOP-
ERATE
WITH ME
SO WE
CAN ALL
SURVIVE
THIS"
!!!!!!
DO
(WHAP)

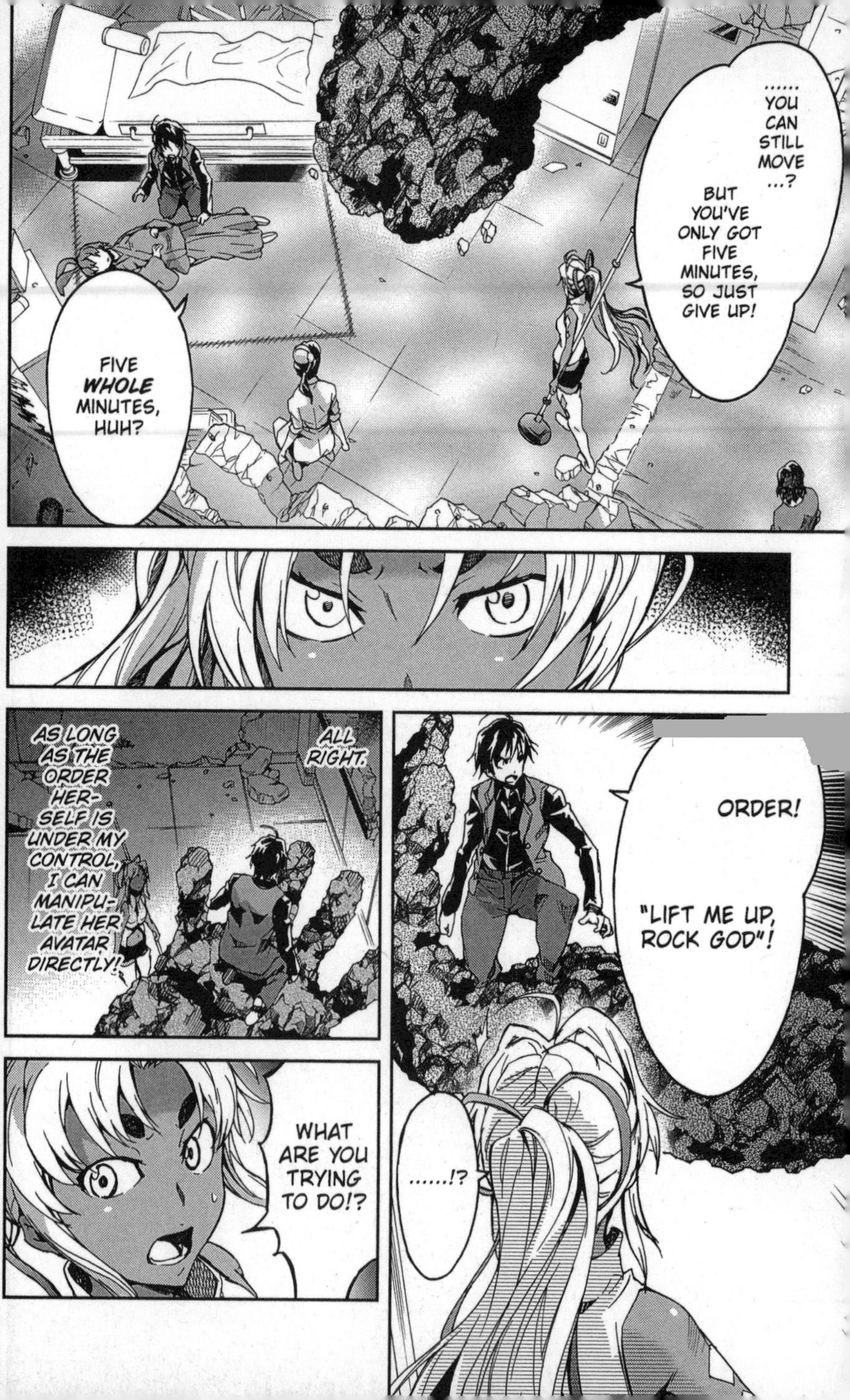
......YOU CAN STILL MOVE...?
BUT YOU'VE ONLY GOT FIVE MINUTES, SO JUST GIVE UP!
FIVE *WHOLE* MINUTES, HUH?
ORDER!
"LIFT ME UP, ROCK GOD"!
......!?
ALL RIGHT.
AS LONG AS THE ORDER HERSELF IS UNDER MY CONTROL, I CAN MANIPULATE HER AVATAR DIRECTLY!
WHAT ARE YOU TRYING TO DO!?

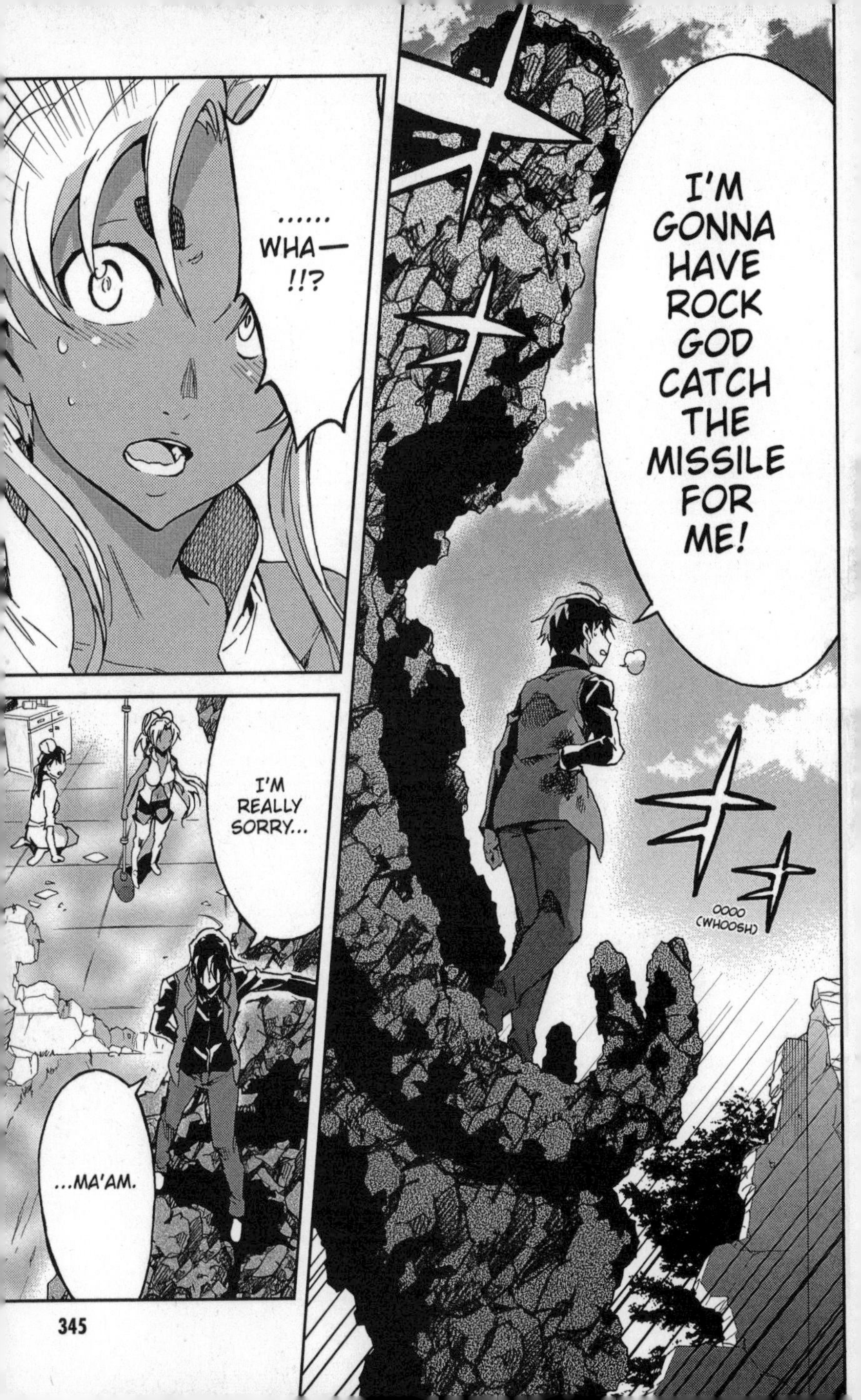
I'M GONNA HAVE ROCK GOD CATCH THE MISSILE FOR ME!
OOOO (WHOOSH)
...... WHA— !!?
I'M REALLY SORRY...
...MA'AM.

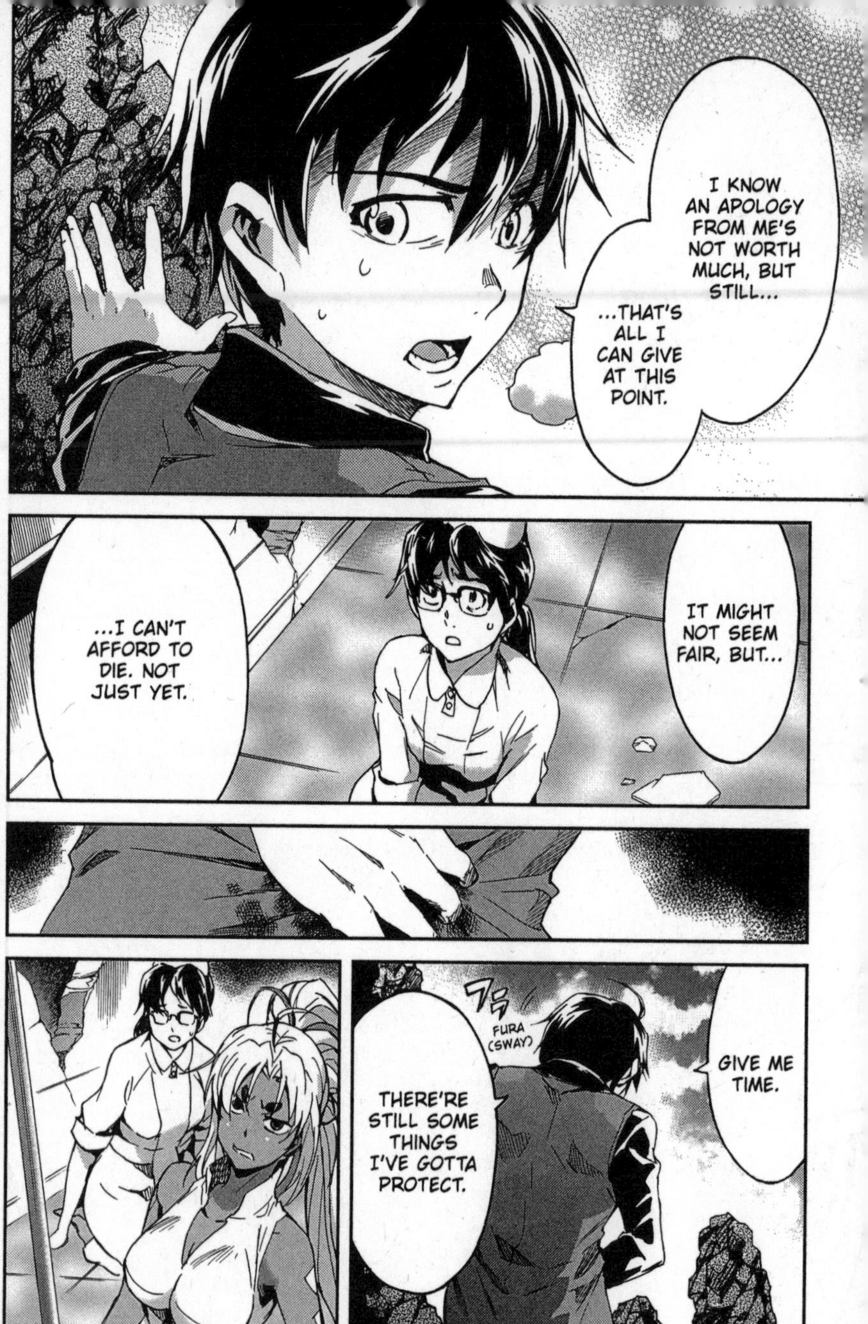
I KNOW AN APOLOGY FROM ME'S NOT WORTH MUCH, BUT STILL...
...THAT'S ALL I CAN GIVE AT THIS POINT.
IT MIGHT NOT SEEM FAIR, BUT...
...I CAN'T AFFORD TO DIE. NOT JUST YET.
GIVE ME TIME.
フラ
FURA (SWAY)
THERE'RE STILL SOME THINGS I'VE GOTTA PROTECT.

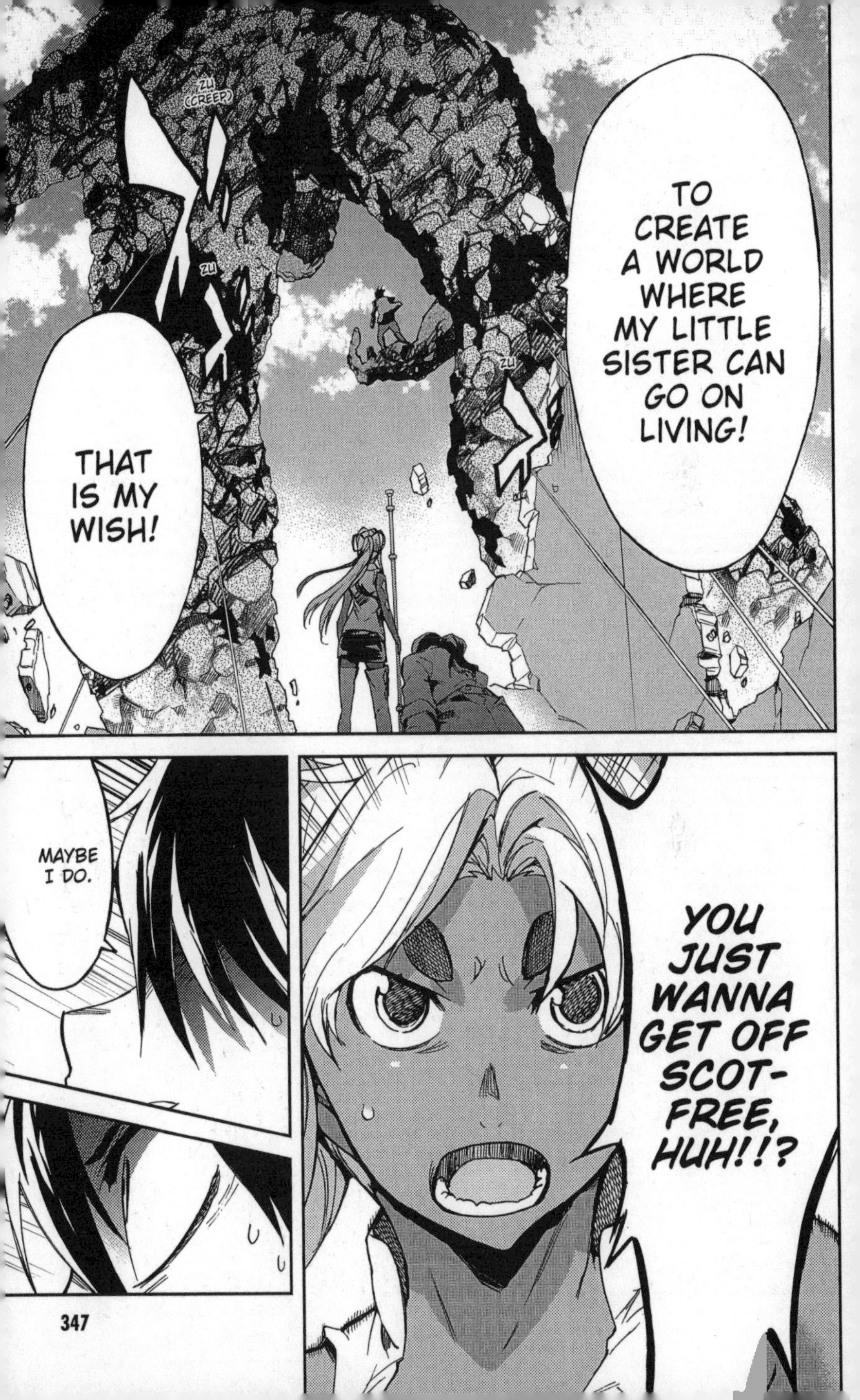
ZU (CREEP)
ZU
ZU
TO CREATE A WORLD WHERE MY LITTLE SISTER CAN GO ON LIVING!
THAT IS MY WISH!
YOU JUST WANNA GET OFF SCOT-FREE, HUH!!?
MAYBE I DO.

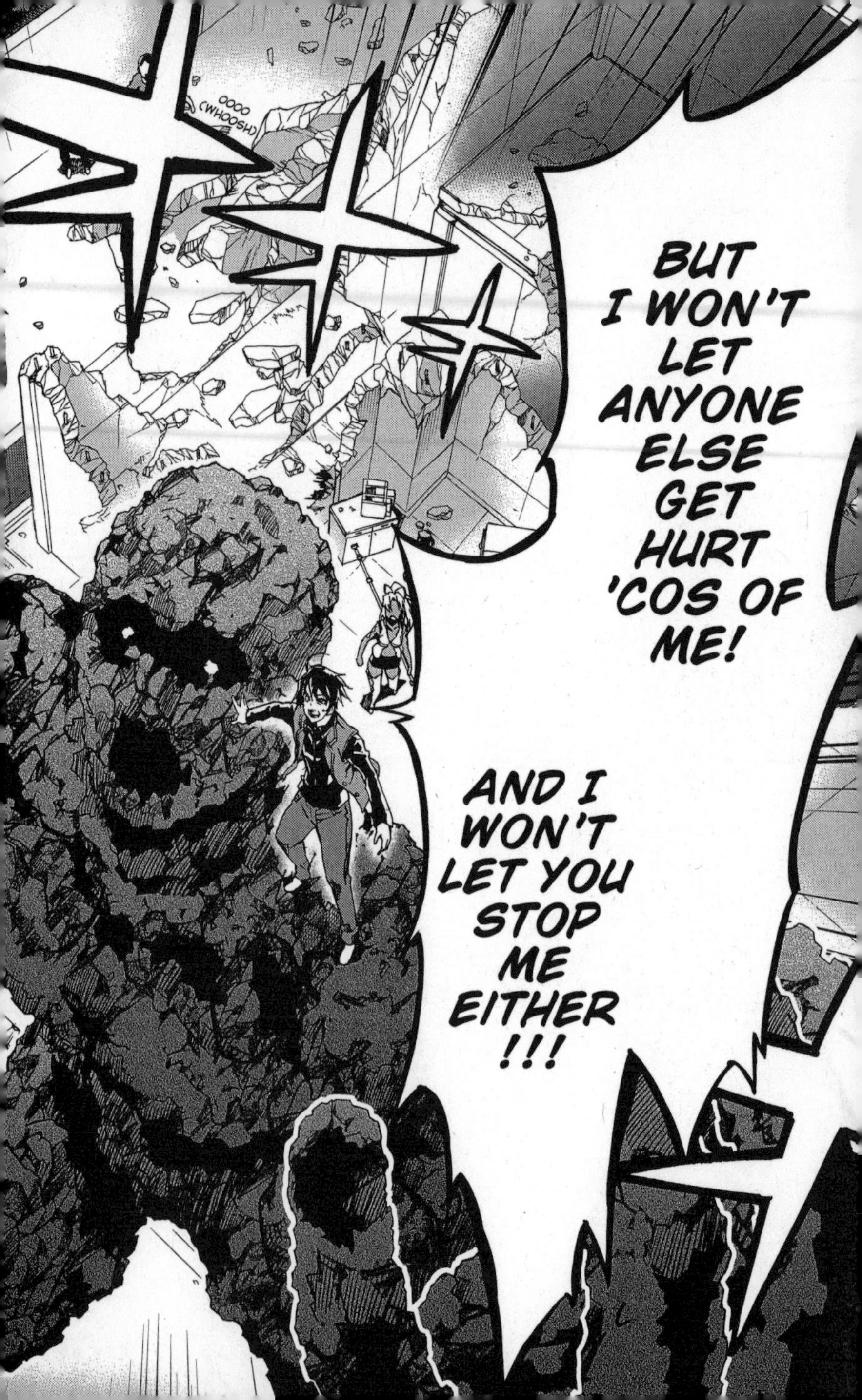
OOOO (WHOOSH)
BUT I WON'T LET ANYONE ELSE GET HURT 'COS OF ME!
AND I WON'T LET YOU STOP ME EITHER!!!

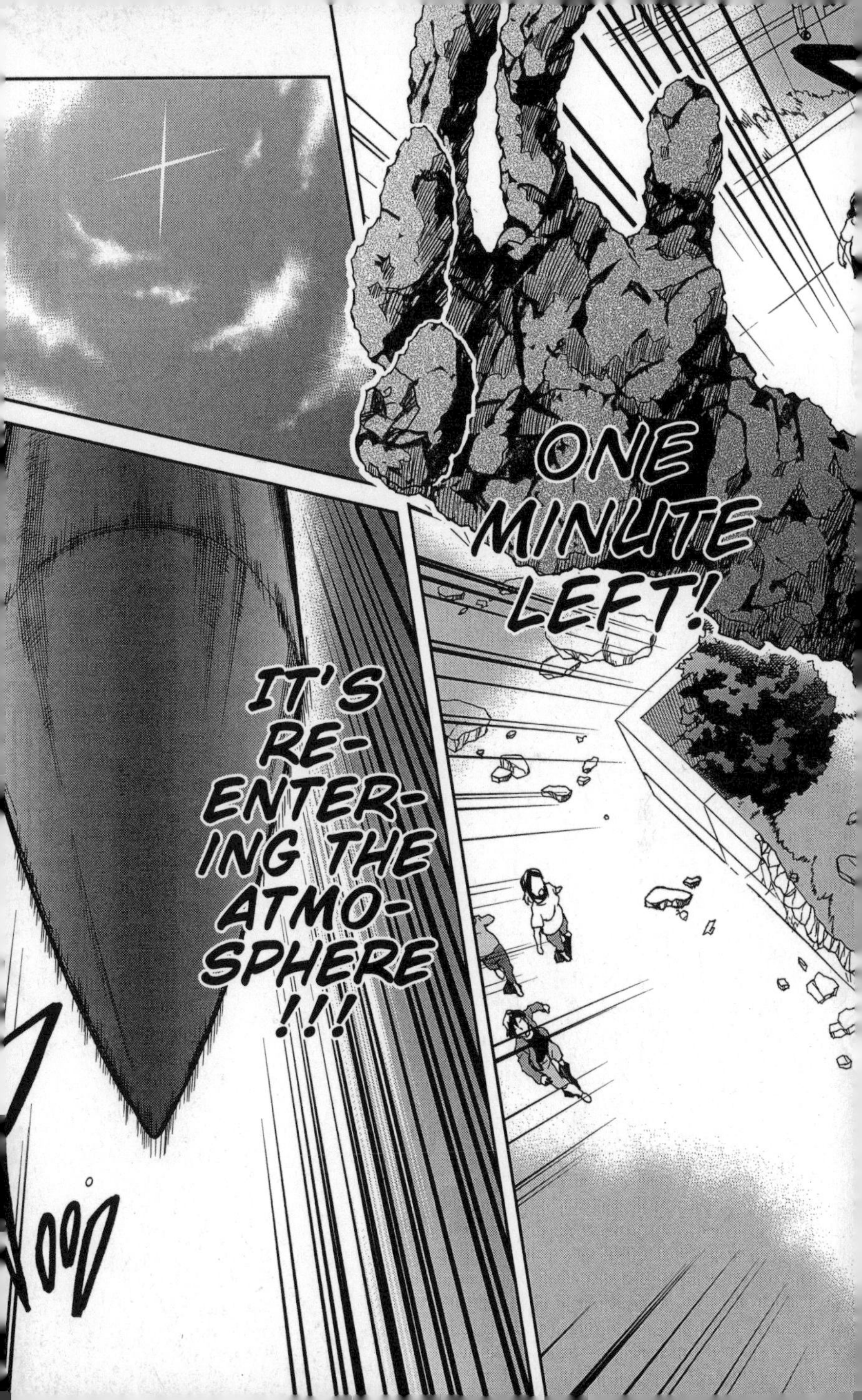
ONE MINUTE LEFT!
IT'S RE-ENTERING THE ATMOSPHERE!!!

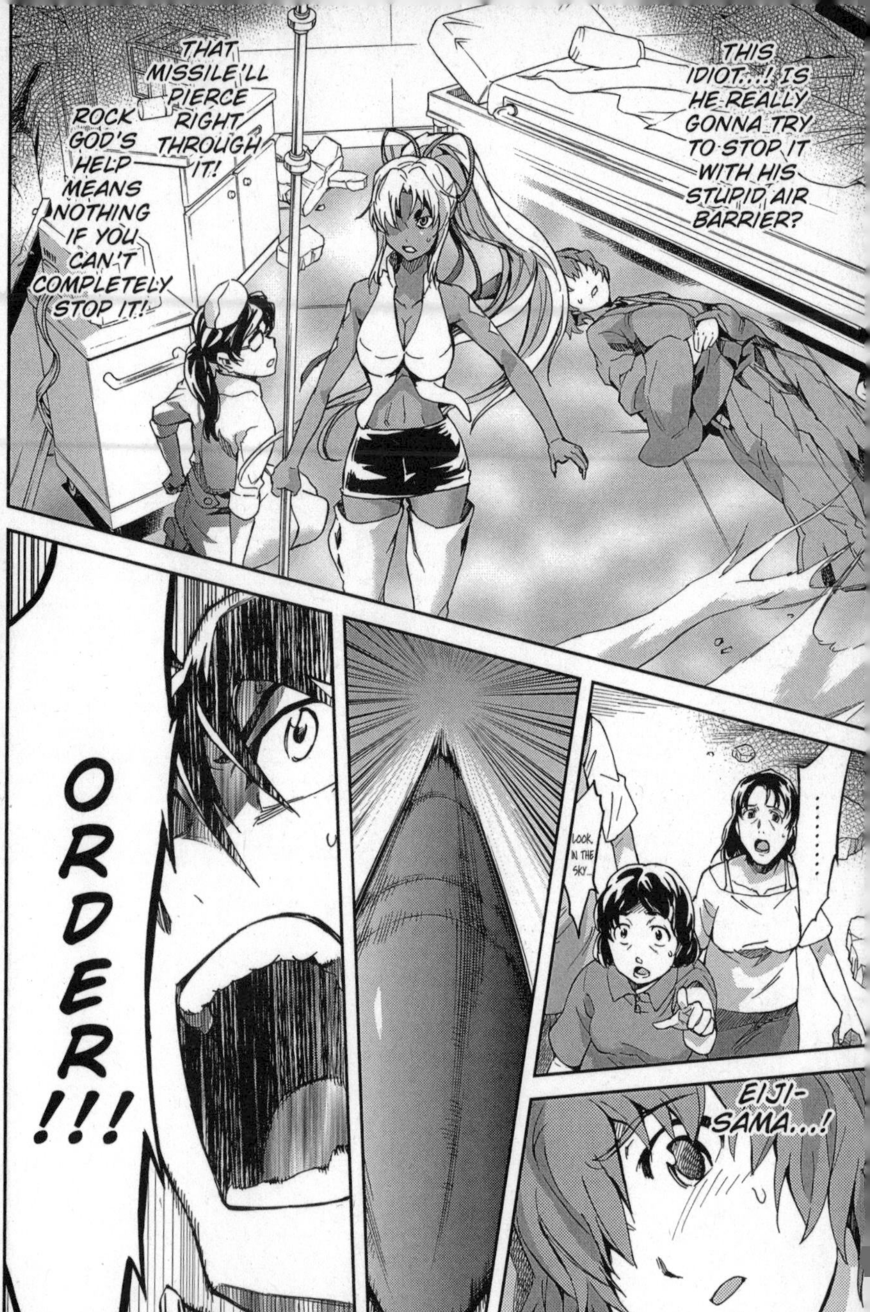
THIS IDIOT...! IS HE REALLY GONNA TRY TO STOP IT WITH HIS STUPID AIR BARRIER?
THAT MISSILE'LL PIERCE RIGHT THROUGH IT!
ROCK GOD'S HELP MEANS NOTHING IF YOU CAN'T COMPLETELY STOP IT!
......
LOOK, IN THE SKY...
EIJI-SAMA...!
ORDER!!!

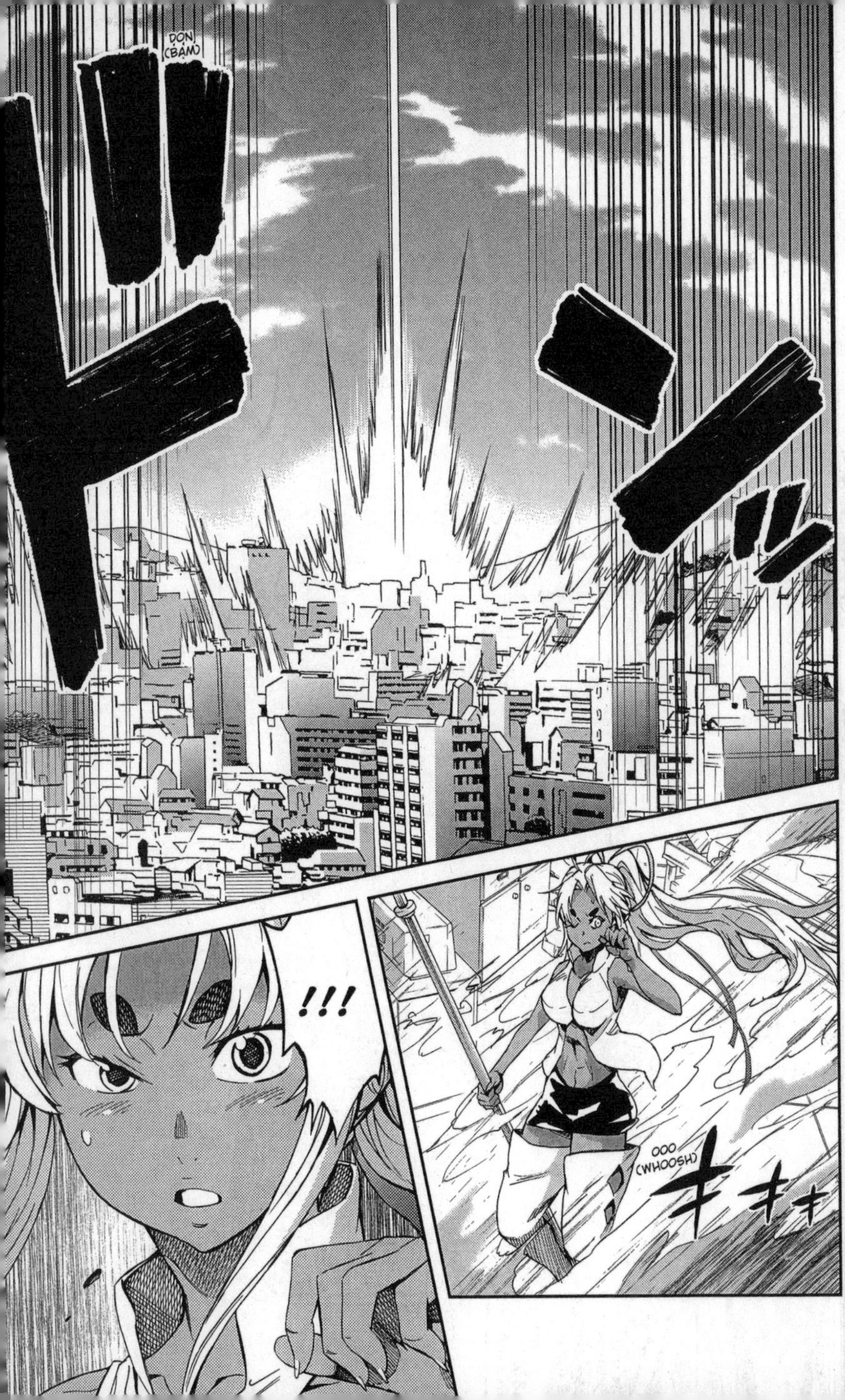
DON (BAM)
!!!
OOO (WHOOSH)

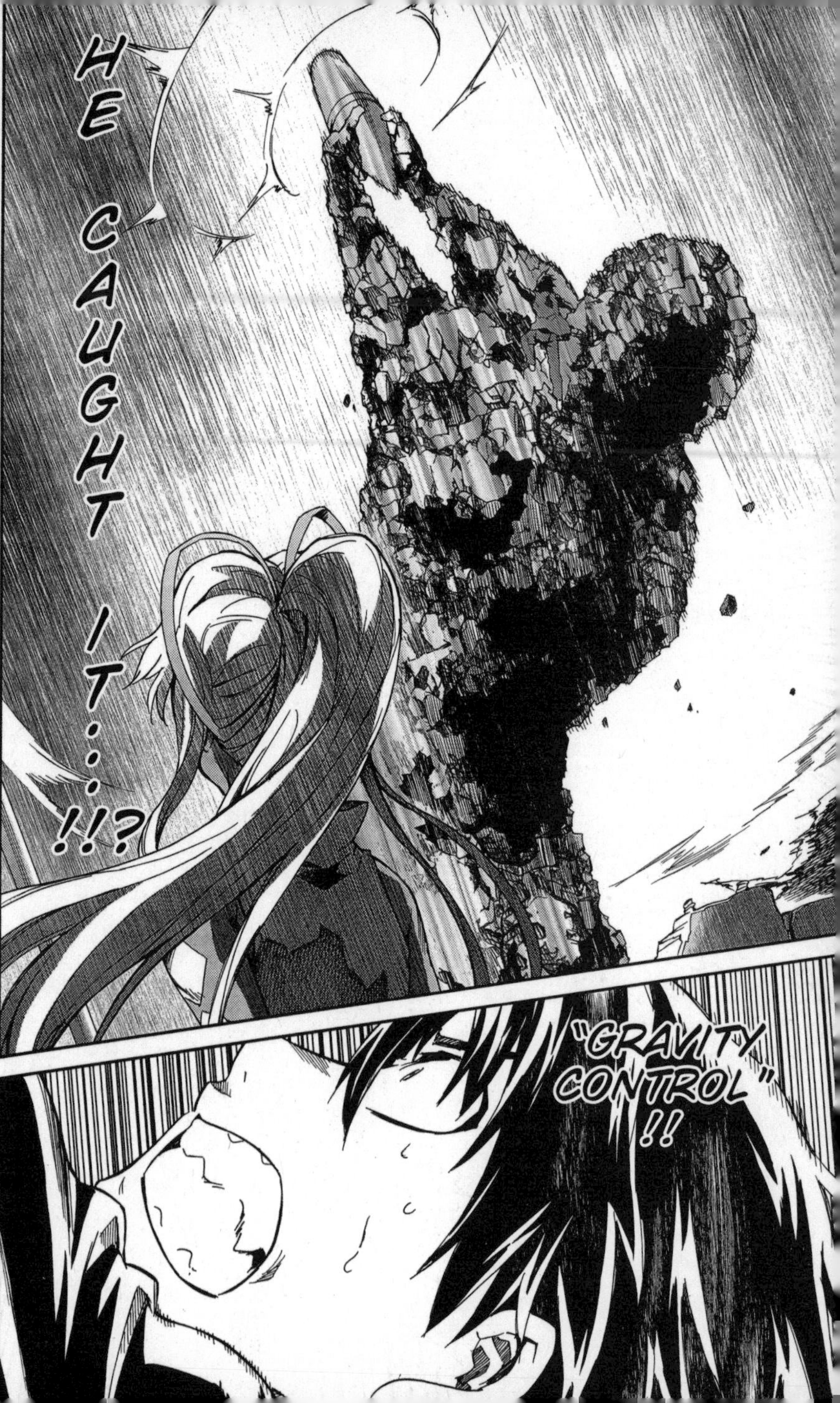
HE CAUGHT IT...!!?
"GRAVITY CONTROL"!!

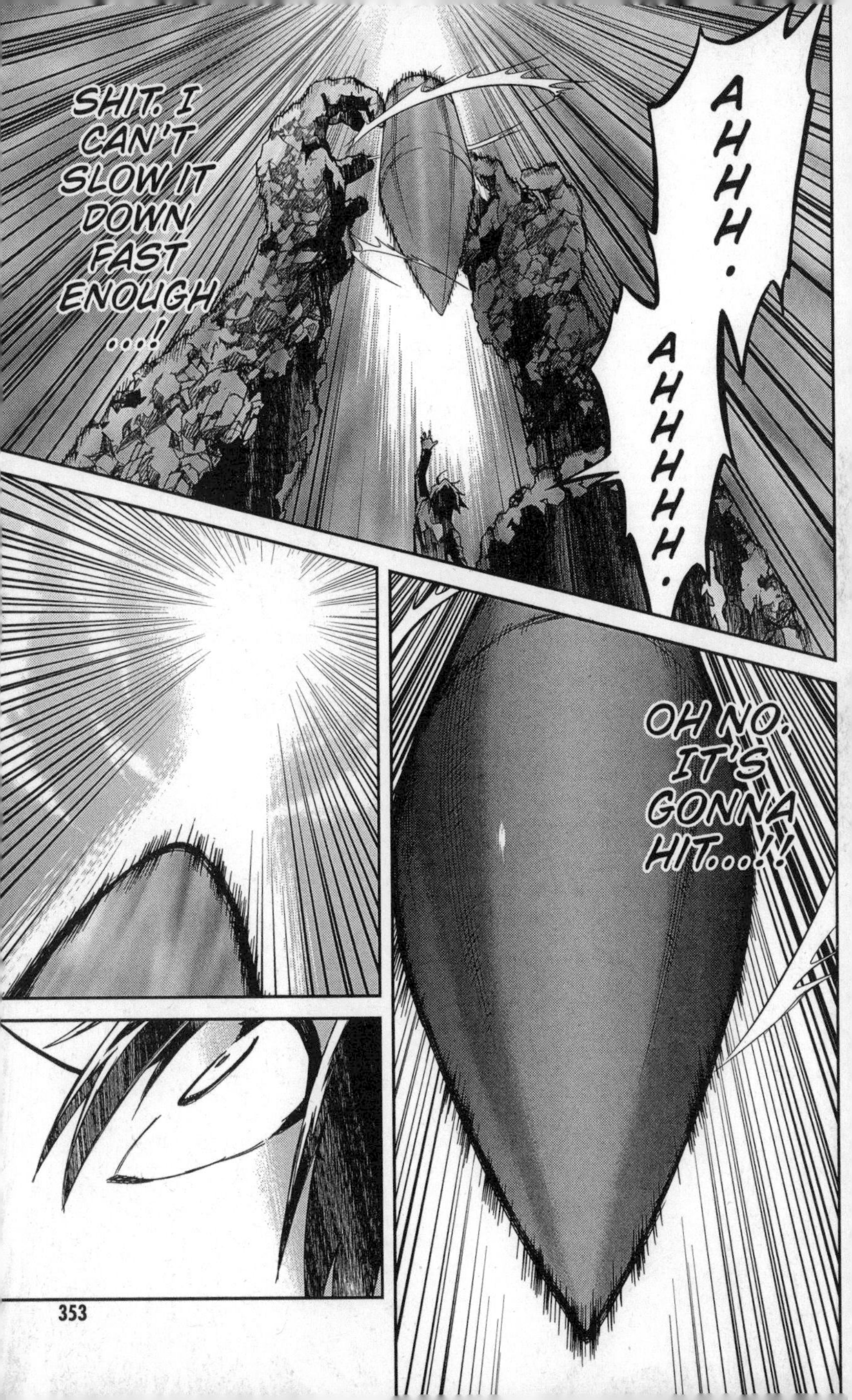
AHHH. AHHHHHH.
SHIT. I CAN'T SLOW IT DOWN FAST ENOUGH...!
OH NO. IT'S GONNA HIT...!!

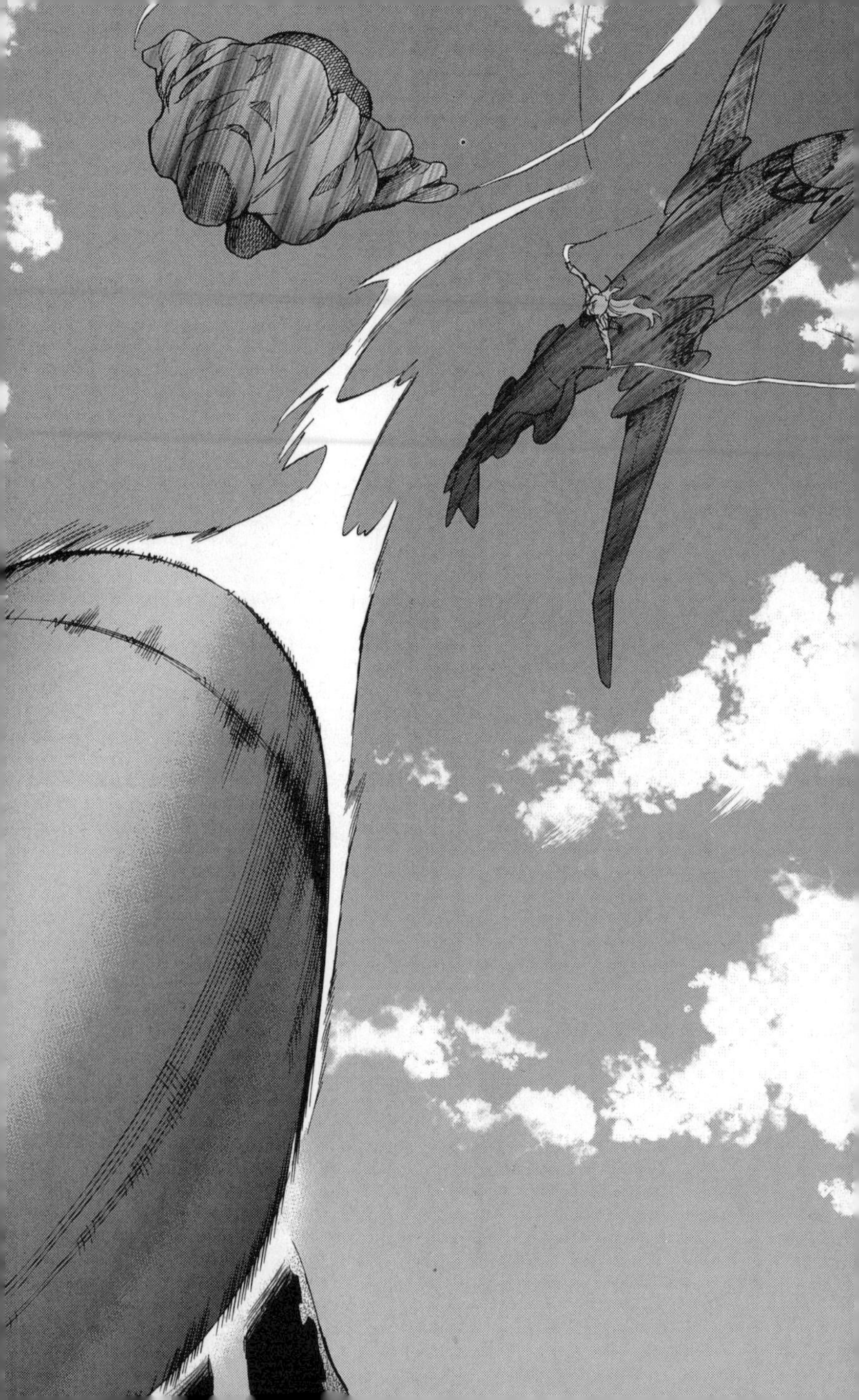

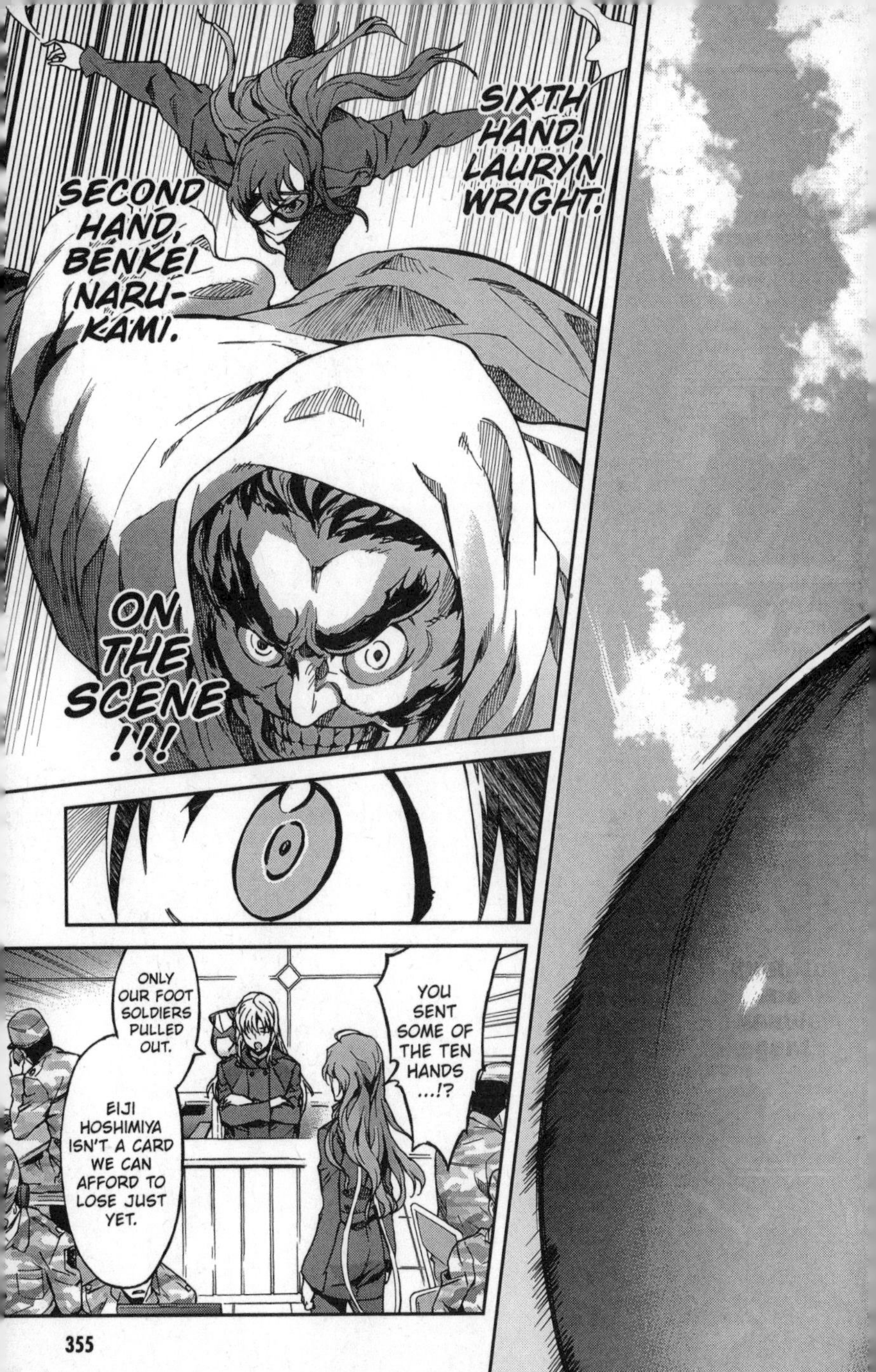
SIXTH HAND, LAURYN WRIGHT.
SECOND HAND, BENKEI NARU-KAMI.
ON THE SCENE!!!
YOU SENT SOME OF THE TEN HANDS ...!?
ONLY OUR FOOT SOLDIERS PULLED OUT.
EIJI HOSHIMIYA ISN'T A CARD WE CAN AFFORD TO LOSE JUST YET.

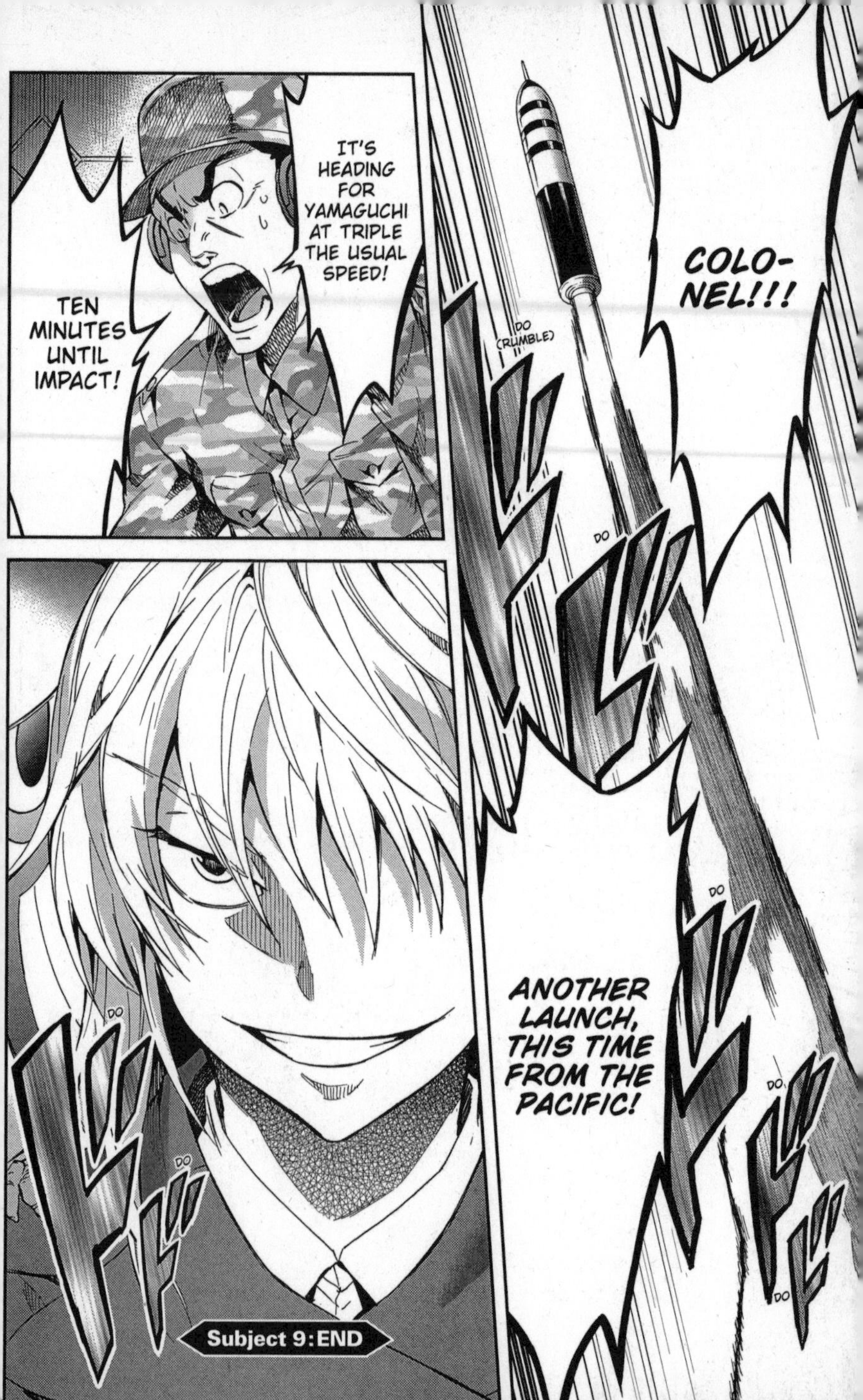
COLO-NEL!!!
DO (RUMBLE)
DO
DO
ANOTHER LAUNCH, THIS TIME FROM THE PACIFIC!
DO
DO
IT'S HEADING FOR YAMAGUCHI AT TRIPLE THE USUAL SPEED!
TEN MINUTES UNTIL IMPACT!
DO
DO
Subject 9: END

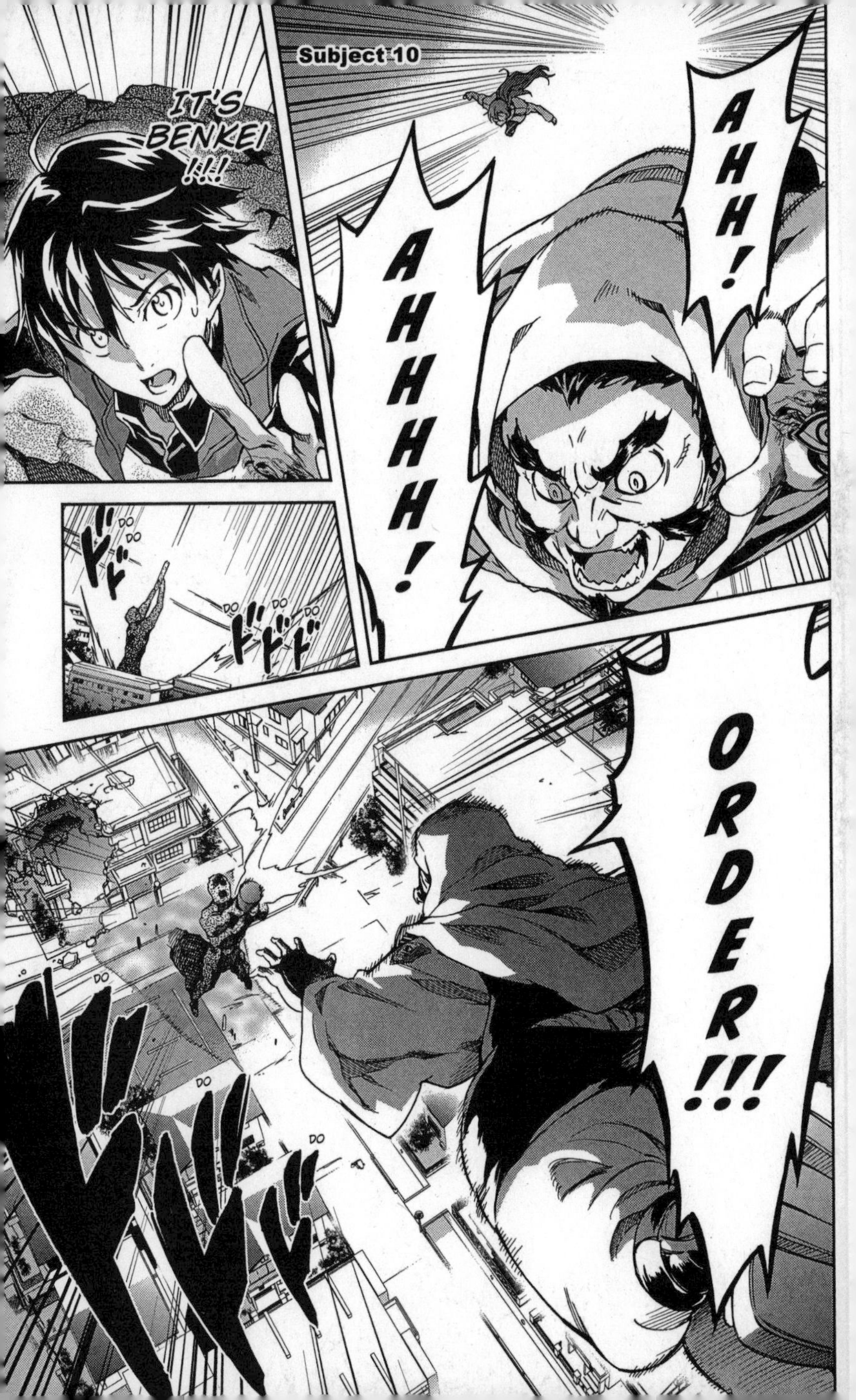
Subject 10
AHH!
AHHHHHH!
IT'S BENKEI!!!
DO DO
DO DO DO
ORDER!!!
DO
DO
DO

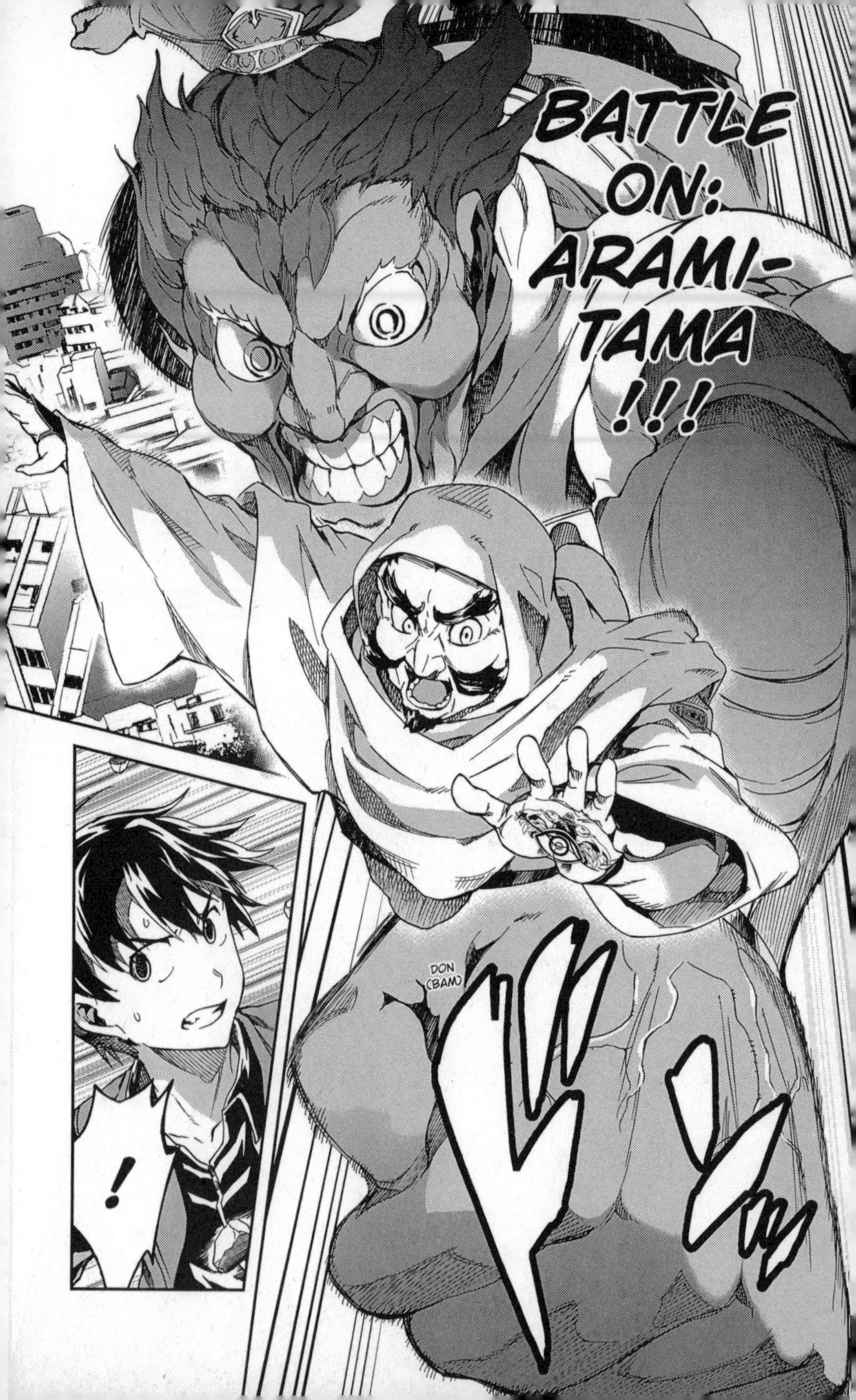
BATTLE ON: ARAMI-TAMA!!!
DON (BAM)
!

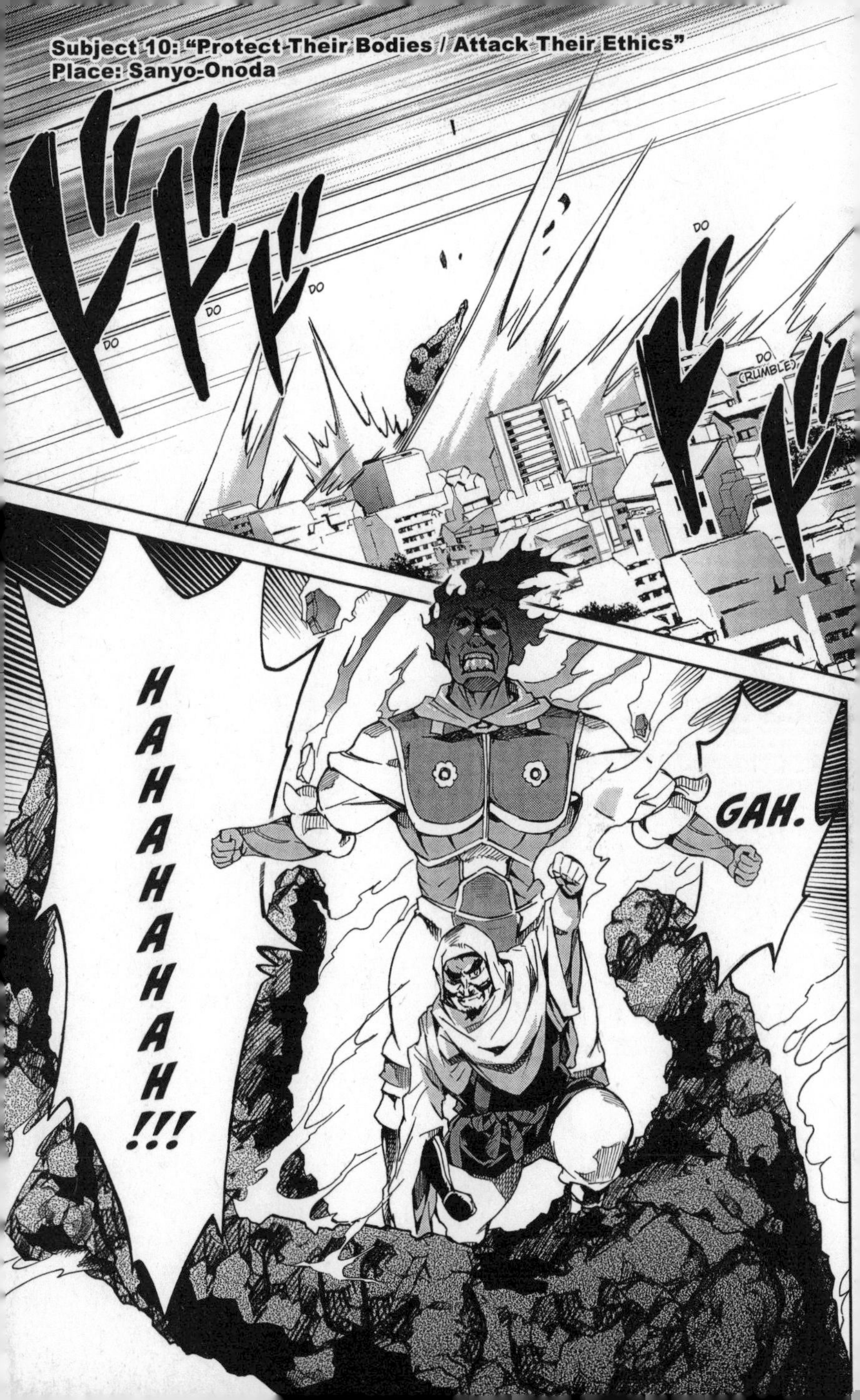
Subject 10: "Protect Their Bodies / Attack Their Ethics"
Place: Sanyo-Onoda
ドドド
DO
DO (RUMBLE)
ドドド
DO
DO
DO
GAH.
HAHAHAHAHAH!!!

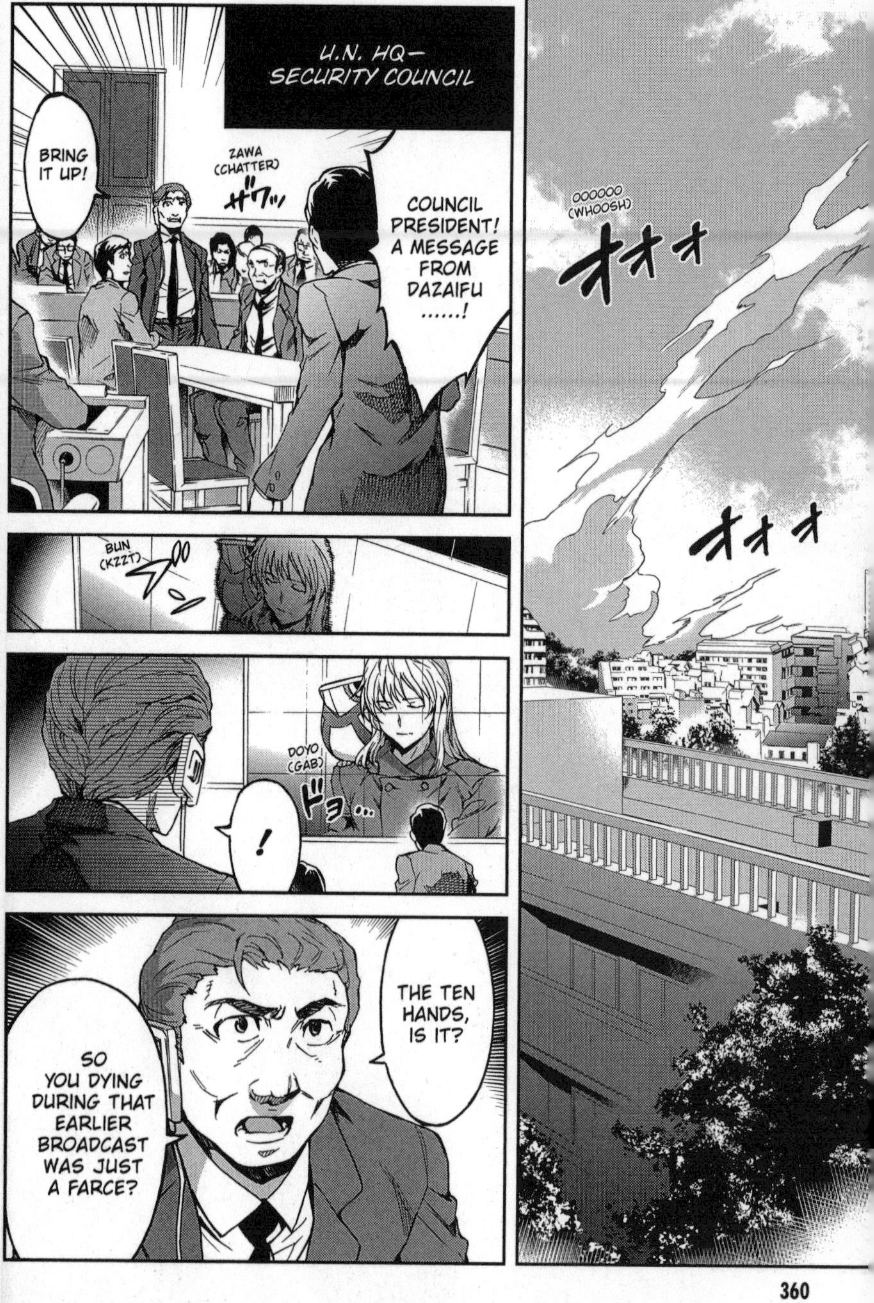
OOOOOO (WHOOSH)
オオオ
オオオ
U.N. HQ— SECURITY COUNCIL
COUNCIL PRESIDENT! A MESSAGE FROM DAZAIFU......!
ZAWA (CHATTER)
ザワッ
BRING IT UP!
BUN (KZZT)
DOYO (GAB)
ドョ...
!
THE TEN HANDS, IS IT?
SO YOU DYING DURING THAT EARLIER BROADCAST WAS JUST A FARCE?

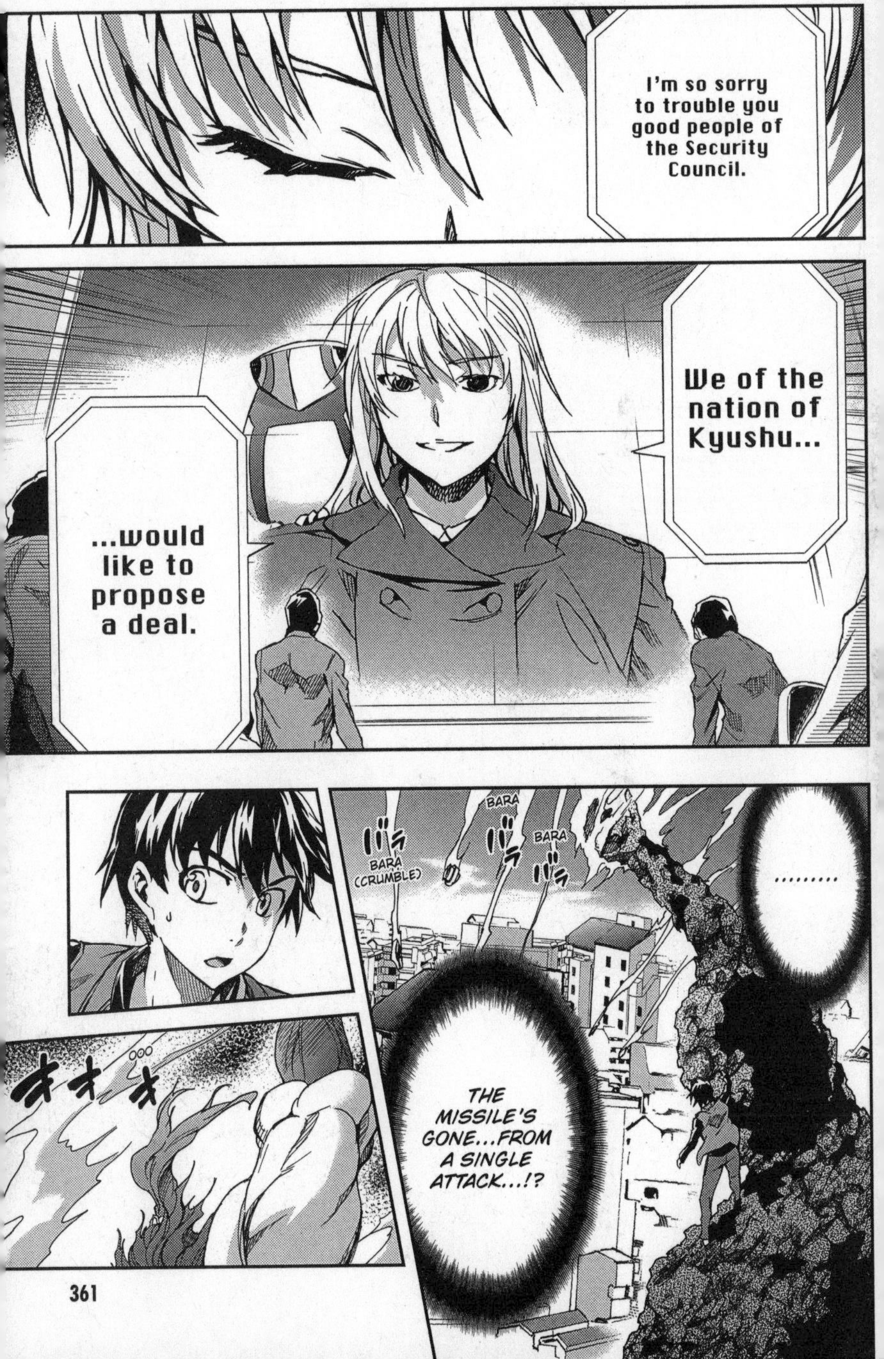
I'm so sorry to trouble you good people of the Security Council.
We of the nation of Kyushu...
...would like to propose a deal.
.........
バラ BARA
バラ BARA
バラ BARA (CRUMBLE)
THE MISSILE'S GONE...FROM A SINGLE ATTACK...!?
オオオ OOO

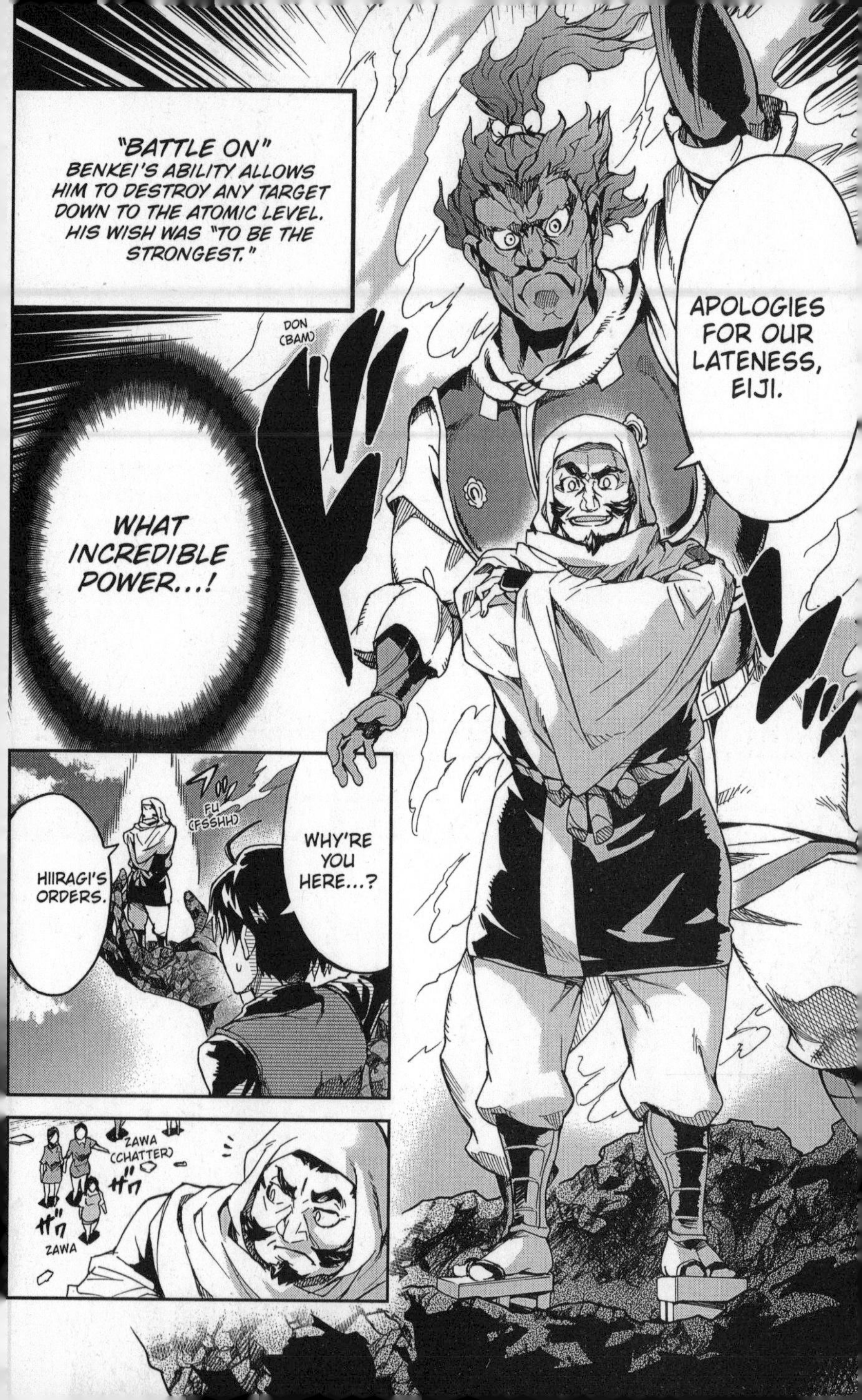
APOLOGIES FOR OUR LATENESS, EIJI.
DON (BAM)
"BATTLE ON" BENKEI'S ABILITY ALLOWS HIM TO DESTROY ANY TARGET DOWN TO THE ATOMIC LEVEL. HIS WISH WAS "TO BE THE STRONGEST."
WHAT INCREDIBLE POWER...!
WHY'RE YOU HERE...?
FU (FSSHH)
HIIRAGI'S ORDERS.
ZAWA (CHATTER)
ZAWA

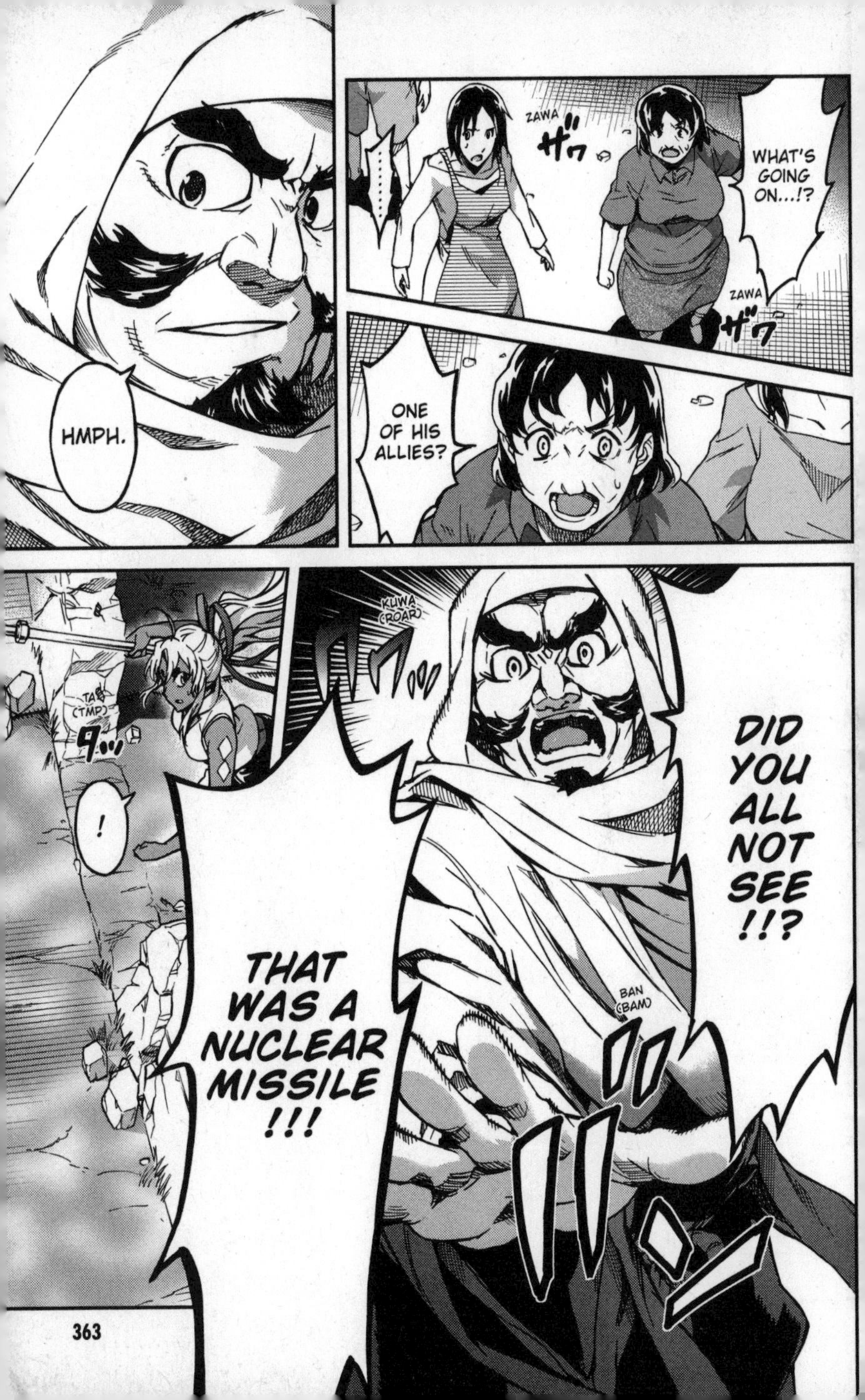

ZAWA
WHAT'S GOING ON...!?
ZAWA
ONE OF HIS ALLIES?
HMPH.
KUWA (ROAR)
DID YOU ALL NOT SEE!!?
BAN (BAM)
THAT WAS A NUCLEAR MISSILE!!!
TA (TMP)
!

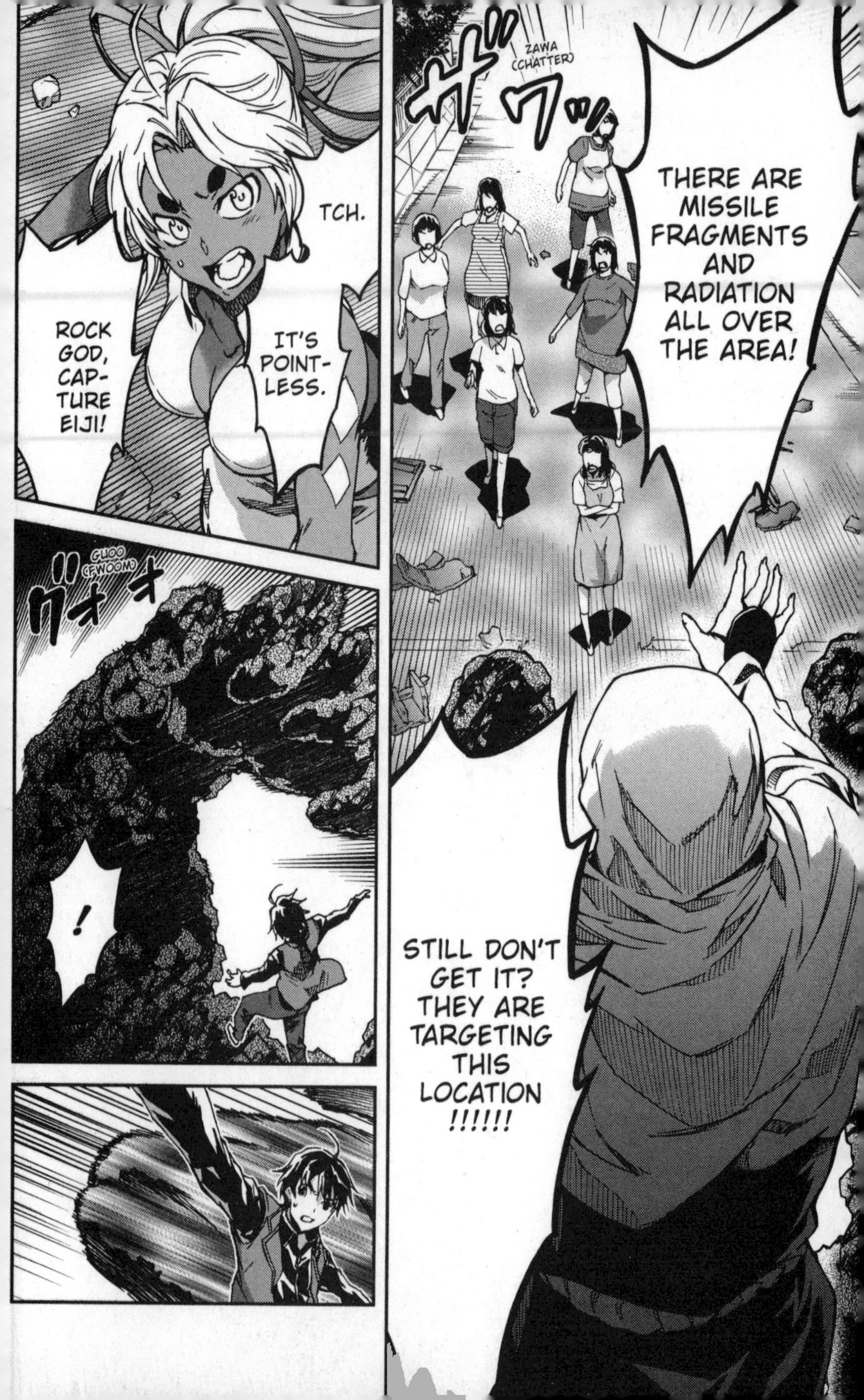
ZAWA (CHATTER)
THERE ARE MISSILE FRAGMENTS AND RADIATION ALL OVER THE AREA!
STILL DON'T GET IT? THEY ARE TARGETING THIS LOCATION !!!!!!
TCH.
IT'S POINTLESS.
ROCK GOD, CAPTURE EIJI!
GUOO (FWOOM)
!

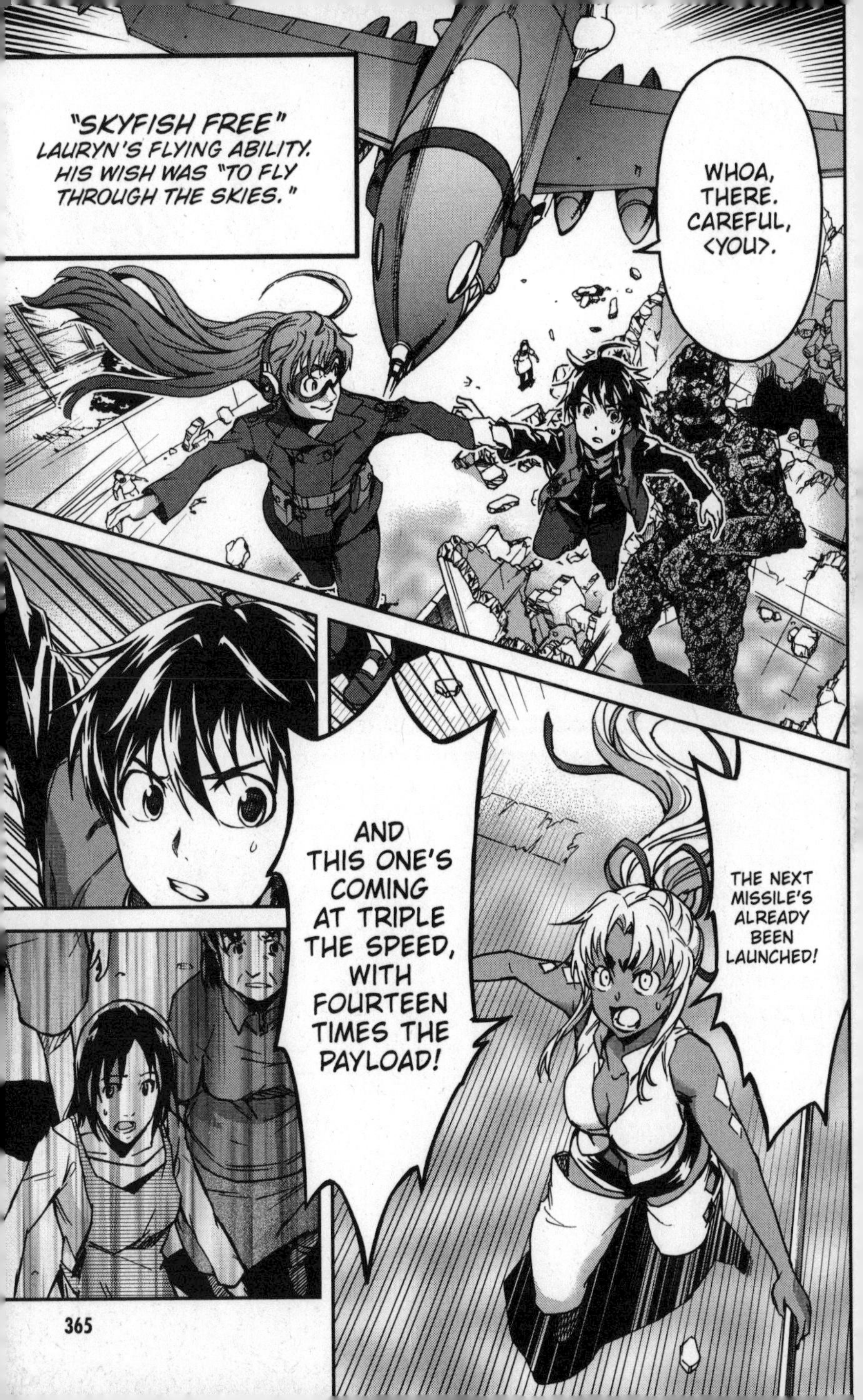
WHOA, THERE. CAREFUL, <YOU>.
"SKYFISH FREE" LAURYN'S FLYING ABILITY. HIS WISH WAS "TO FLY THROUGH THE SKIES."
THE NEXT MISSILE'S ALREADY BEEN LAUNCHED!
AND THIS ONE'S COMING AT TRIPLE THE SPEED, WITH FOURTEEN TIMES THE PAYLOAD!

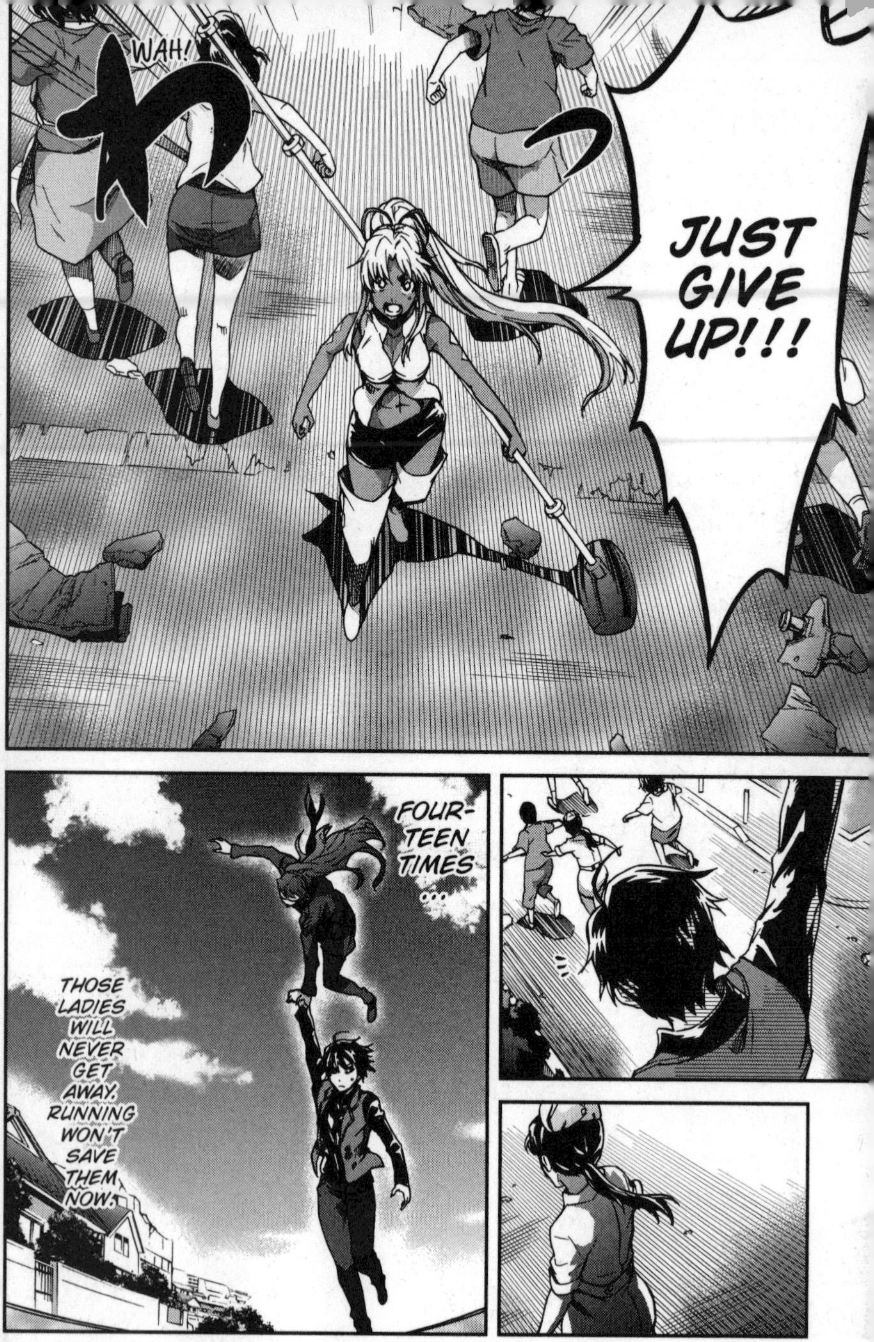
JUST GIVE UP!!!
WAH!
FOUR-TEEN TIMES...
THOSE LADIES WILL NEVER GET AWAY. RUNNING WON'T SAVE THEM NOW.

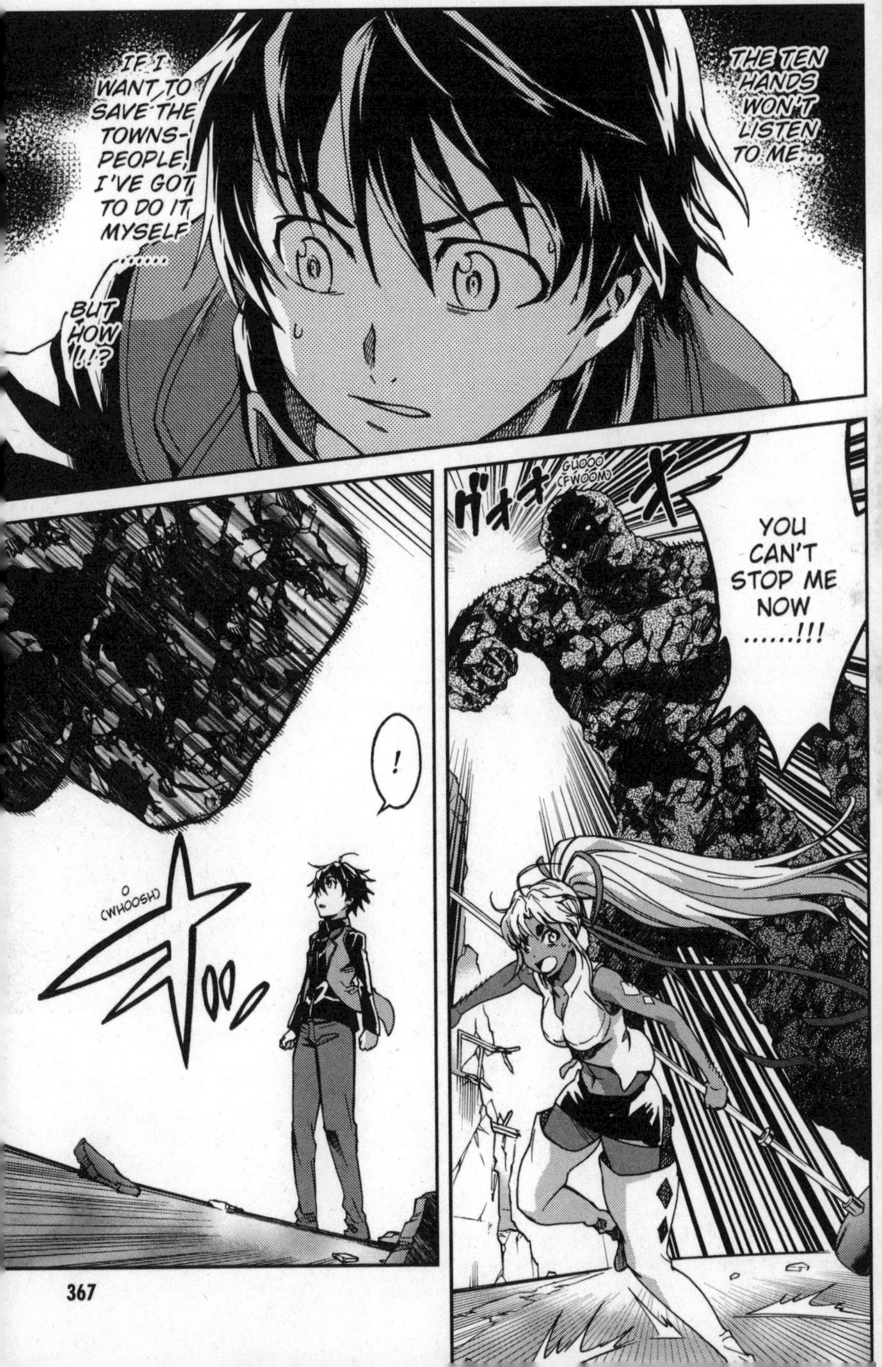
THE TEN HANDS WON'T LISTEN TO ME...
IF I WANT TO SAVE THE TOWNS-PEOPLE, I'VE GOT TO DO IT MYSELF......
BUT HOW!!?
GUOOO (FWOOM)
YOU CAN'T STOP ME NOW ......!!!
!
(WHOOSH)

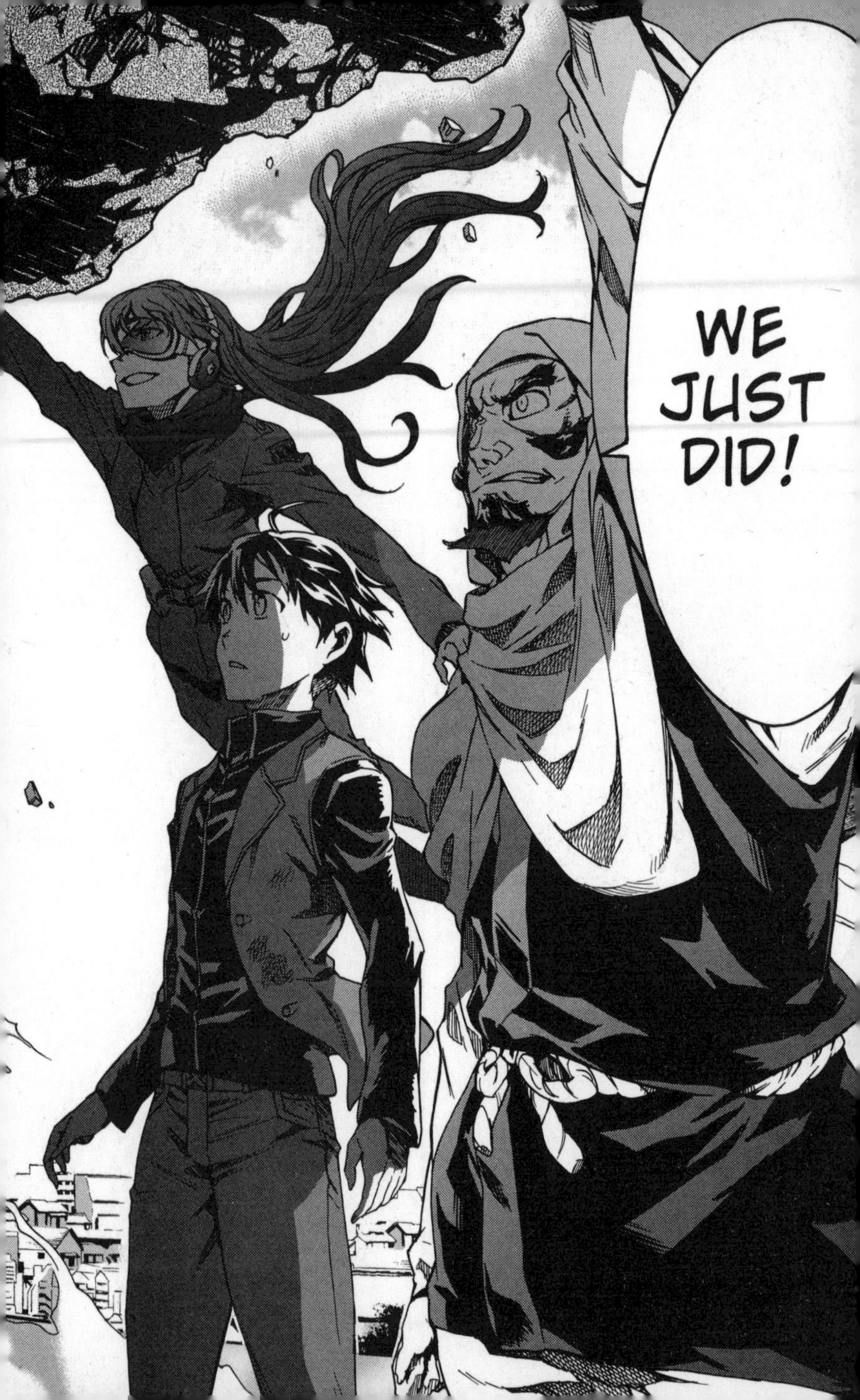
WE JUST DID!

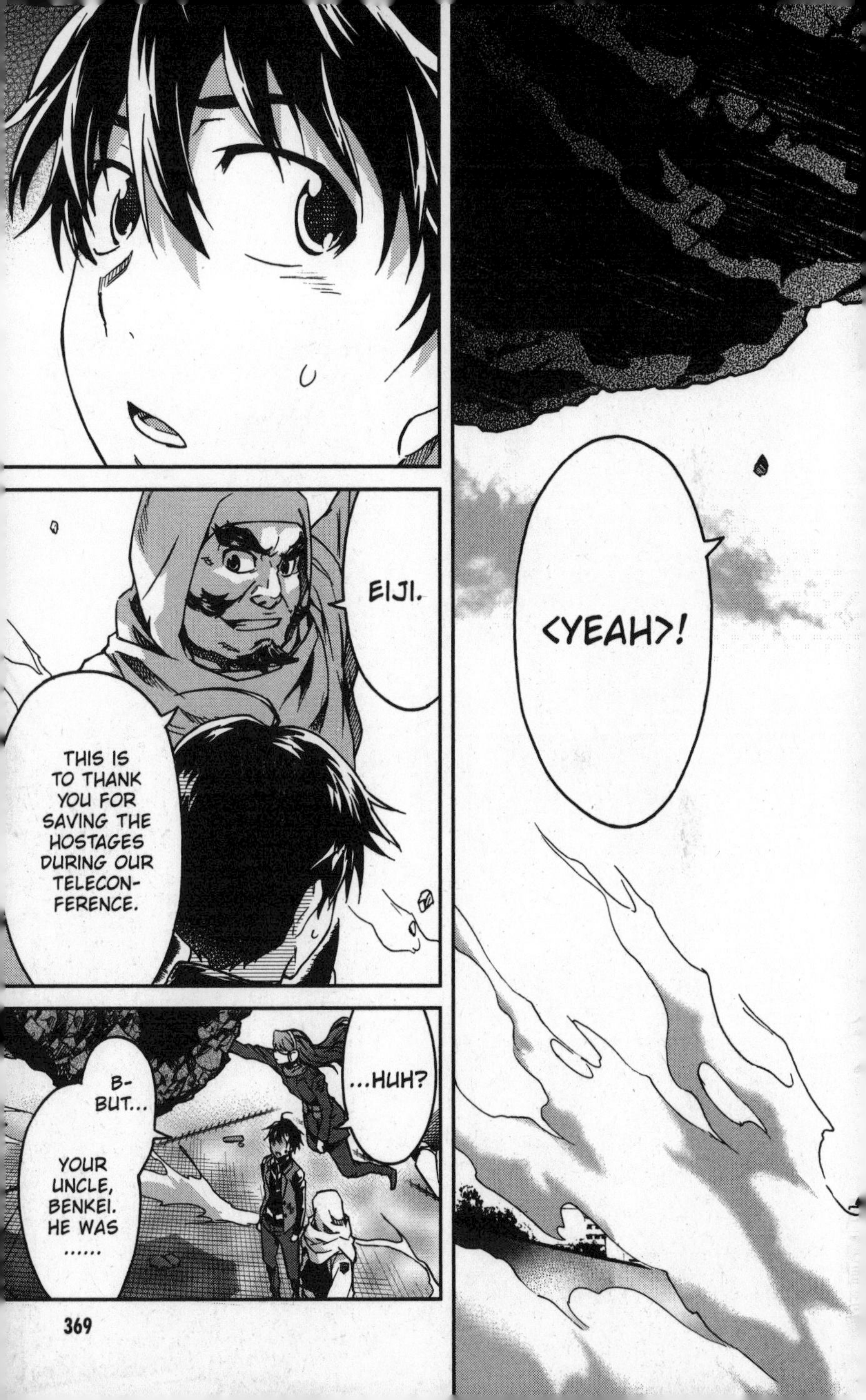
<YEAH>!
EIJI.
THIS IS TO THANK YOU FOR SAVING THE HOSTAGES DURING OUR TELECON-FERENCE.
...HUH?
B-BUT...
YOUR UNCLE, BENKEI. HE WAS ......

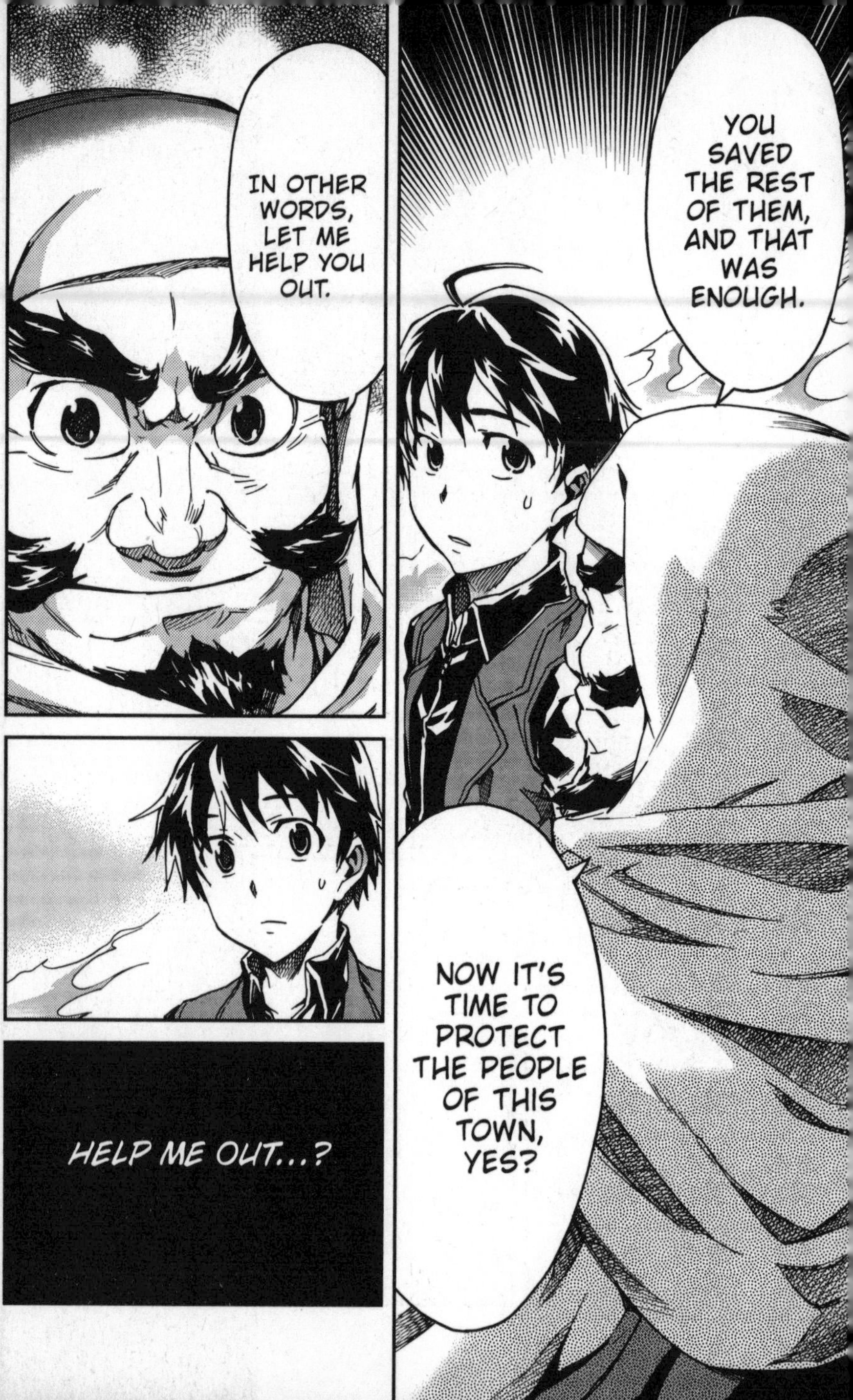
YOU SAVED THE REST OF THEM, AND THAT WAS ENOUGH.
NOW IT'S TIME TO PROTECT THE PEOPLE OF THIS TOWN, YES?
IN OTHER WORDS, LET ME HELP YOU OUT.
HELP ME OUT...?

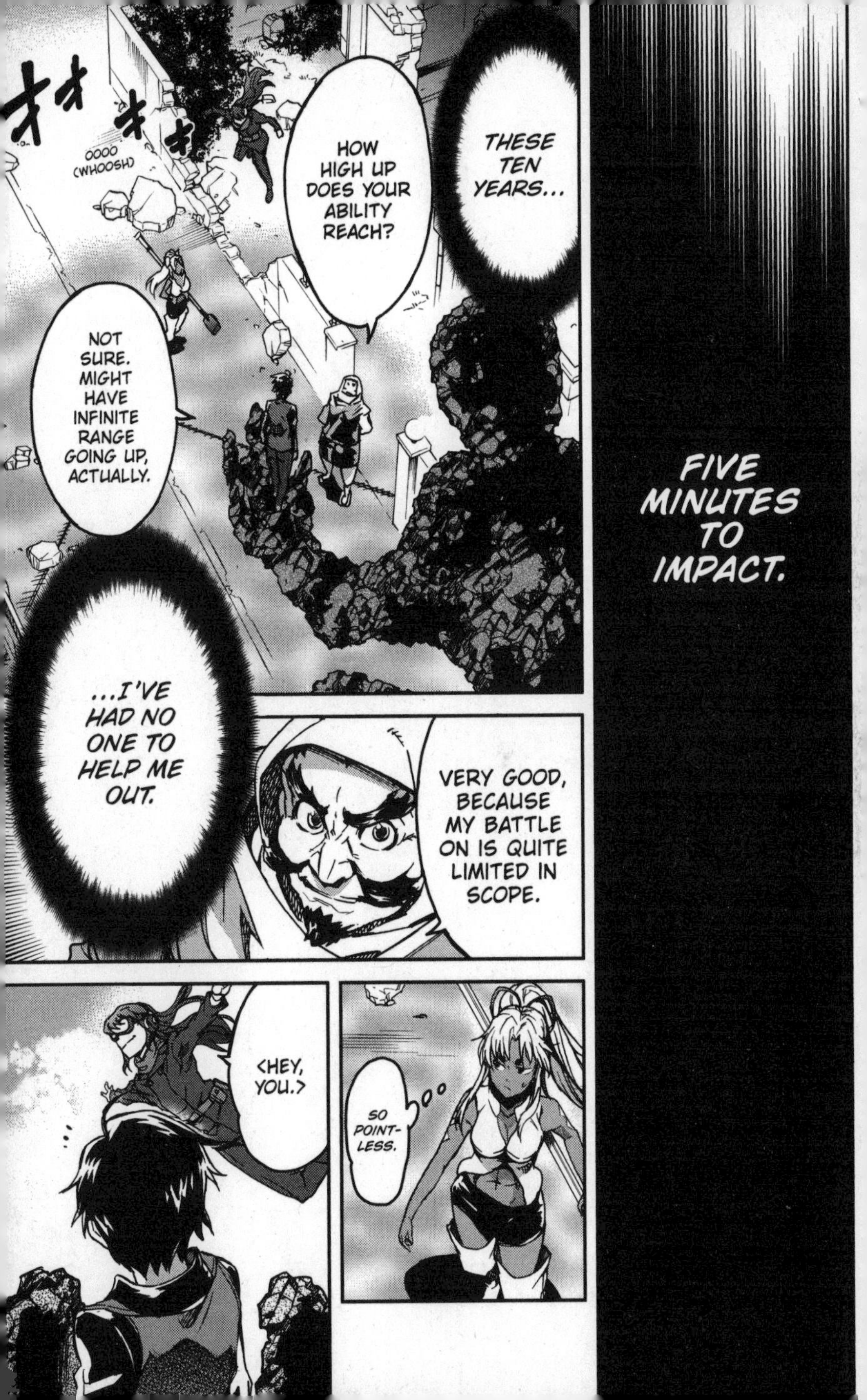
FIVE MINUTES TO IMPACT.
THESE TEN YEARS...
HOW HIGH UP DOES YOUR ABILITY REACH?
OOOO (WHOOSH)
NOT SURE. MIGHT HAVE INFINITE RANGE GOING UP, ACTUALLY.
...I'VE HAD NO ONE TO HELP ME OUT.
VERY GOOD, BECAUSE MY BATTLE ON IS QUITE LIMITED IN SCOPE.
SO POINTLESS.
<HEY, YOU.>

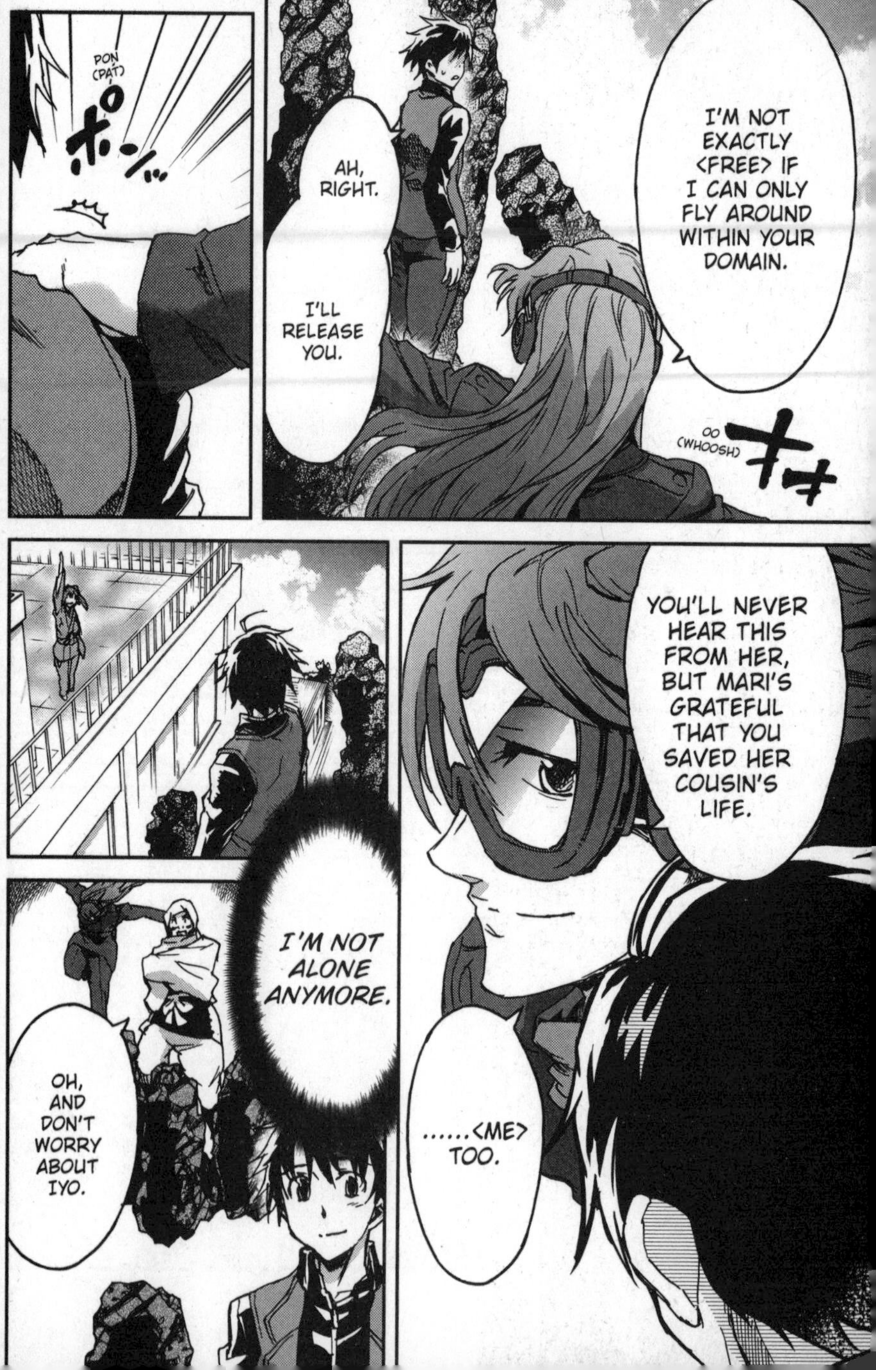
I'M NOT EXACTLY <FREE> IF I CAN ONLY FLY AROUND WITHIN YOUR DOMAIN.
AH, RIGHT.
I'LL RELEASE YOU.
OO (WHOOSH)
PON (PAT)
YOU'LL NEVER HEAR THIS FROM HER, BUT MARI'S GRATEFUL THAT YOU SAVED HER COUSIN'S LIFE.
......<ME> TOO.
I'M NOT ALONE ANYMORE.
OH, AND DON'T WORRY ABOUT IYO.

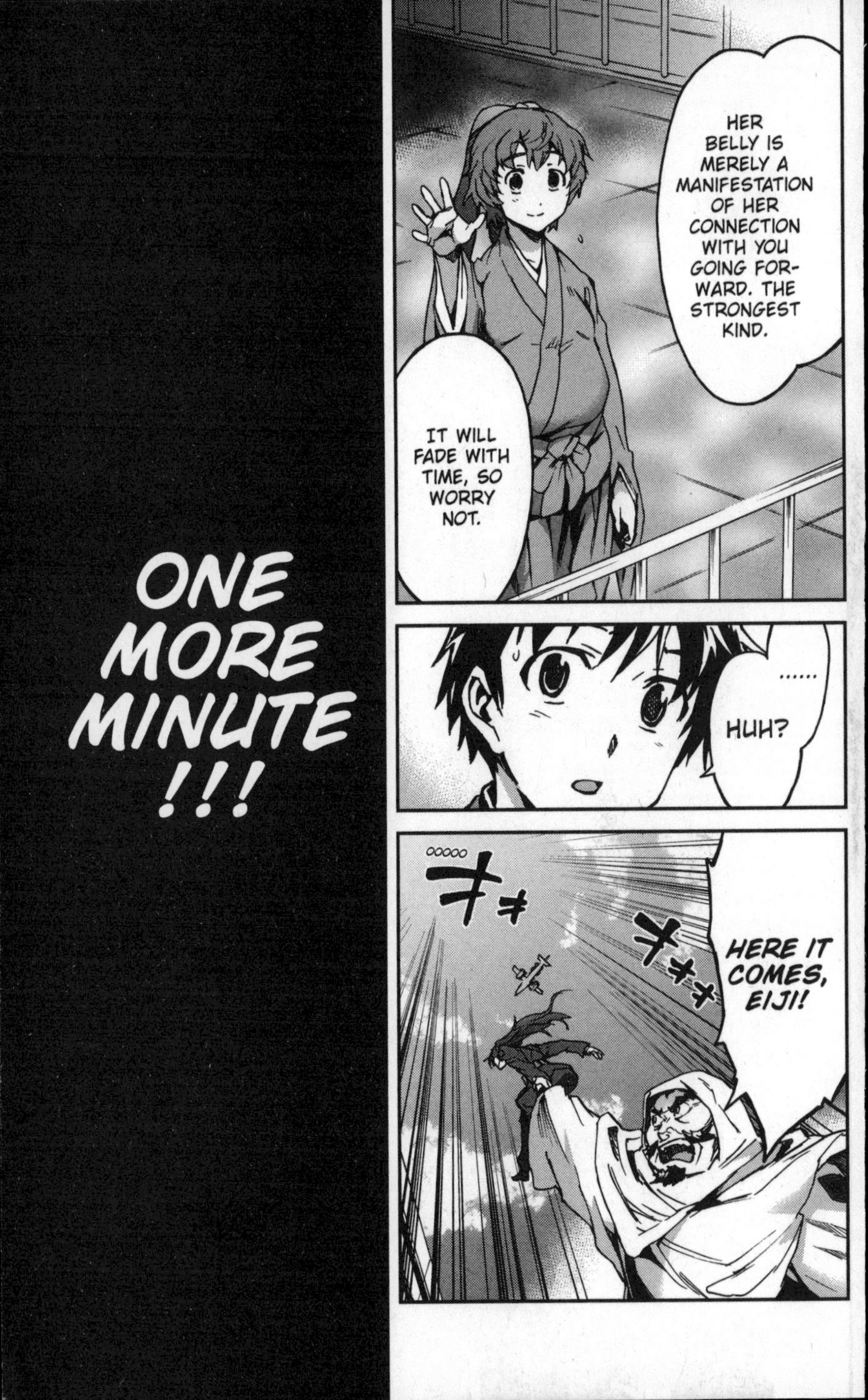
HER BELLY IS MERELY A MANIFESTATION OF HER CONNECTION WITH YOU GOING FOR-WARD. THE STRONGEST KIND.
IT WILL FADE WITH TIME, SO WORRY NOT.
......
HUH?
HERE IT COMES, EIJI!
OOOOO
ONE MORE MINUTE!!!

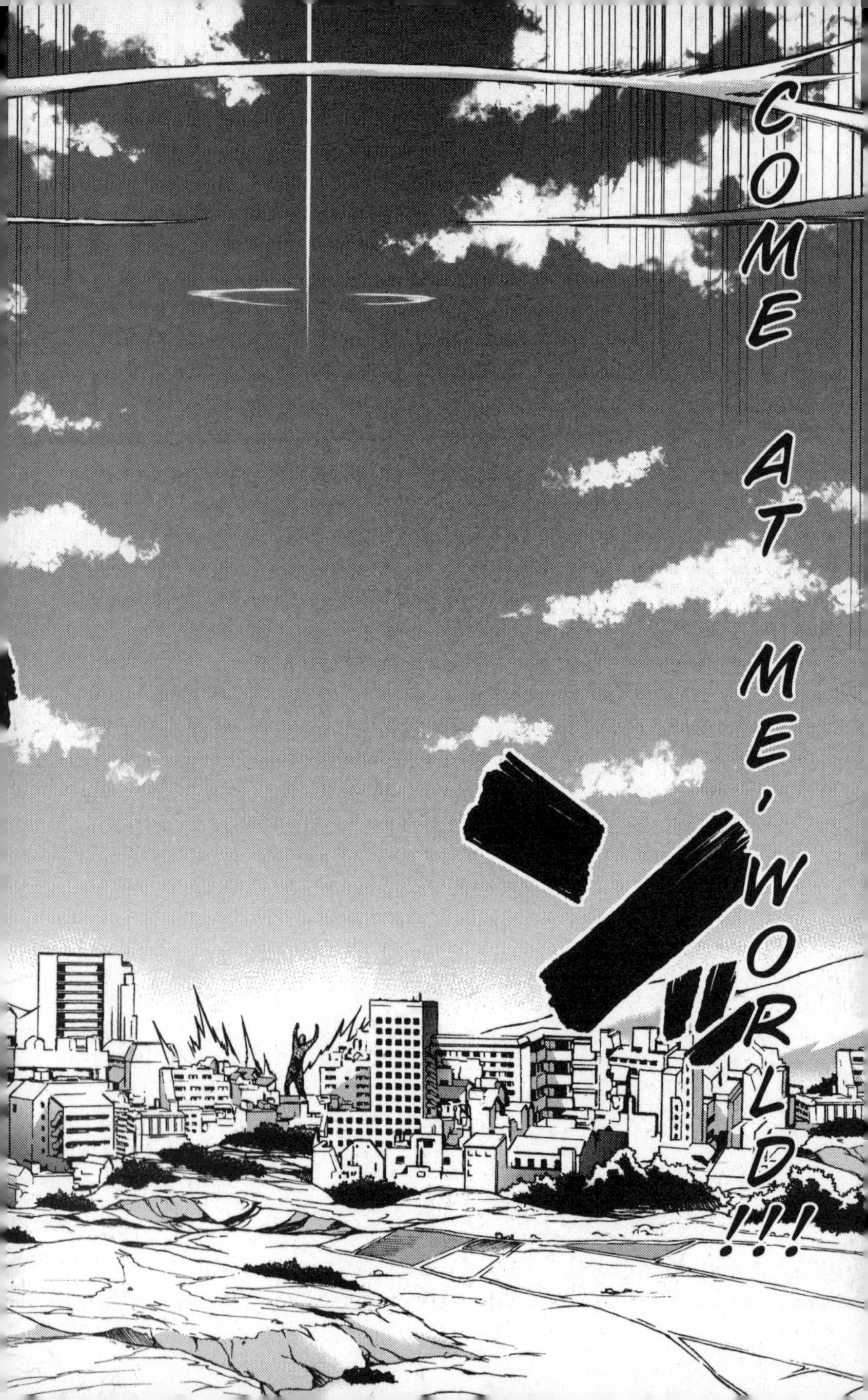
COME AT ME, WORLD!!!

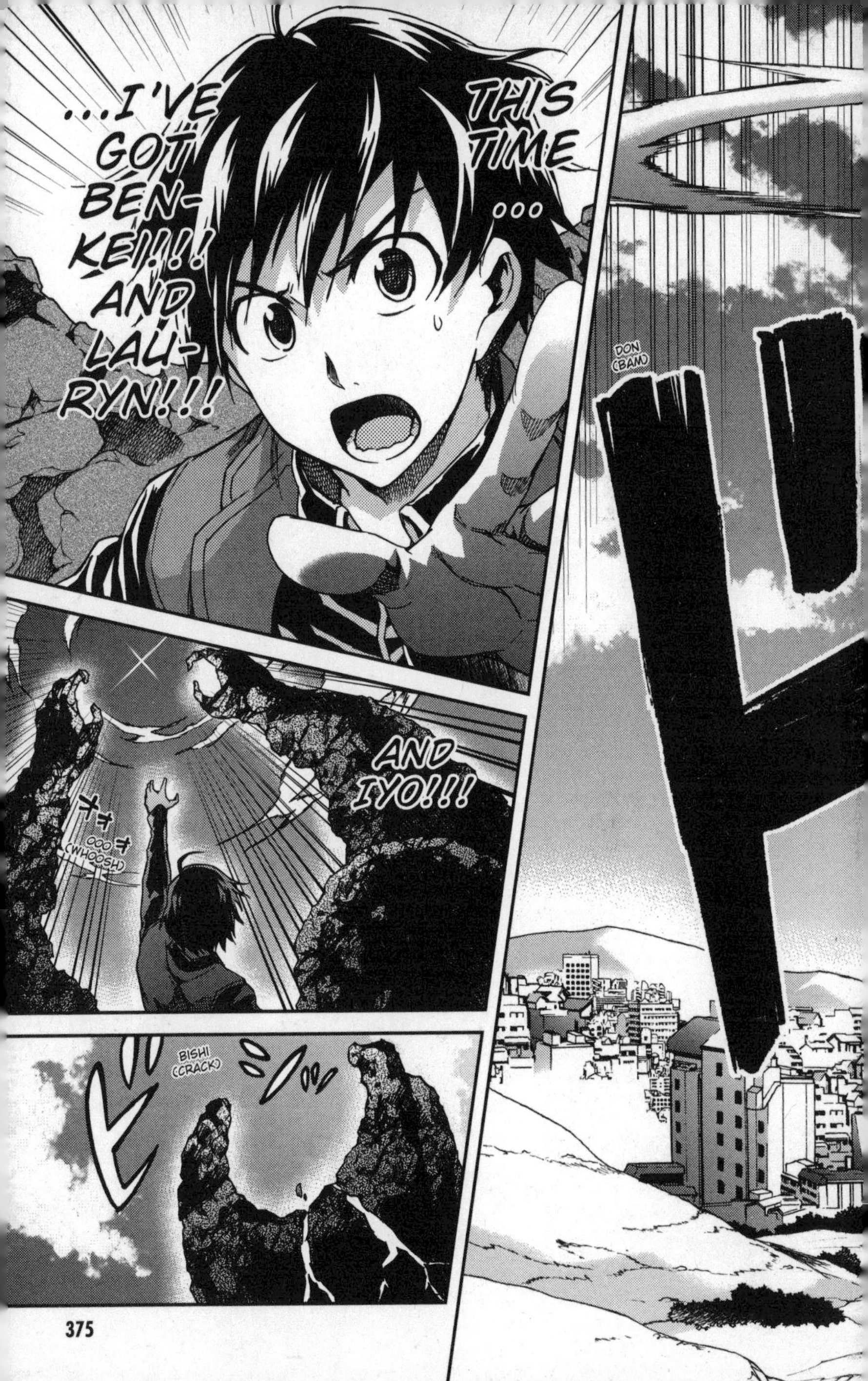
DON (BAM)
THIS TIME...
...I'VE GOT BEN-KEI!!! AND LAU-RYN!!!
AND IYO!!!
OOO (WHOOSH)
BISHI (CRACK)

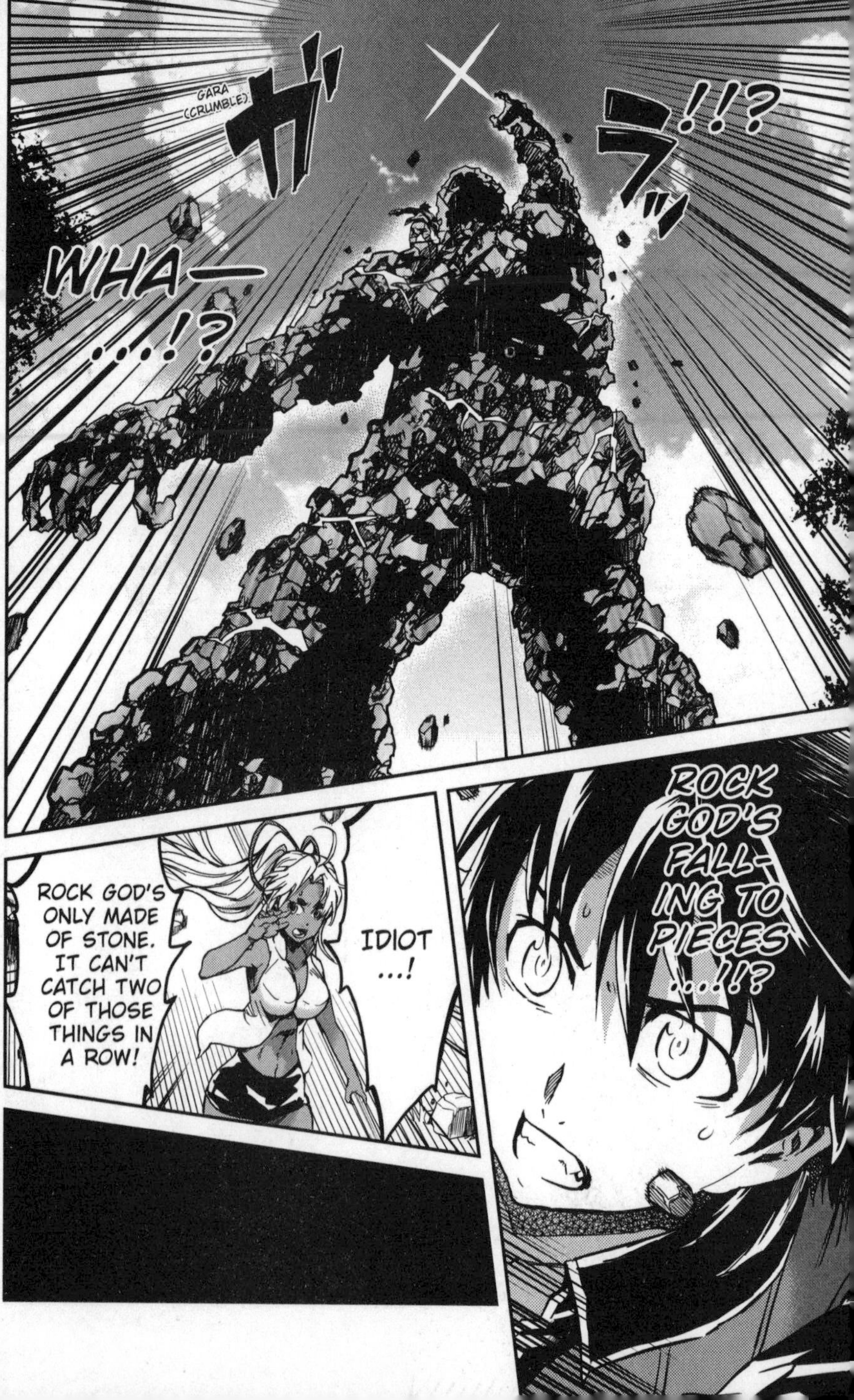
ガ
ラッ!!?
GARA (CRUMBLE)
WHA—...!?
ROCK GOD'S FALL-ING TO PIECES...!!?
IDIOT...!
ROCK GOD'S ONLY MADE OF STONE. IT CAN'T CATCH TWO OF THOSE THINGS IN A ROW!

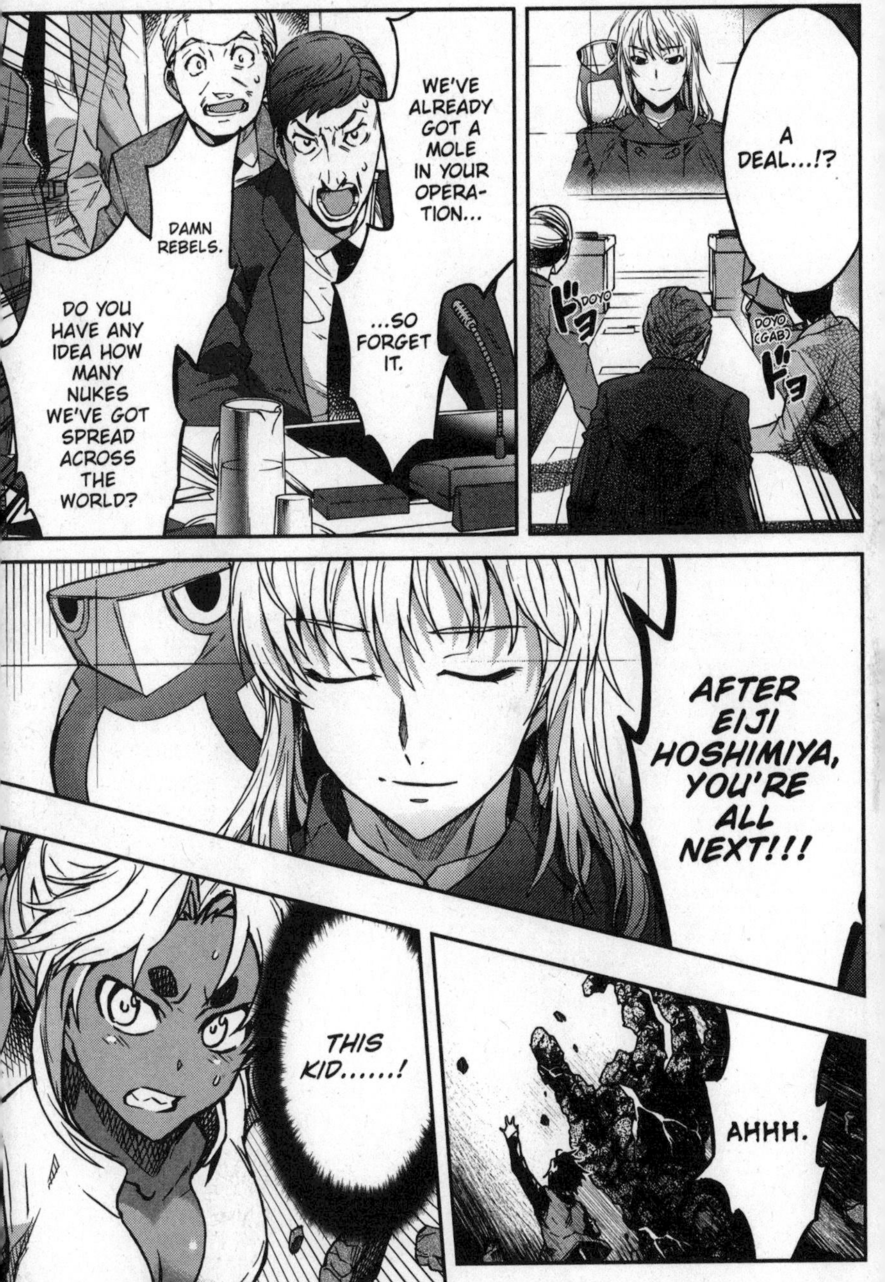
A DEAL...!?
ドヨ DOYO
DOYO (GAB) ドヨ
WE'VE ALREADY GOT A MOLE IN YOUR OPERATION...
...SO FORGET IT.
DAMN REBELS.
DO YOU HAVE ANY IDEA HOW MANY NUKES WE'VE GOT SPREAD ACROSS THE WORLD?
AFTER EIJI HOSHIMIYA, YOU'RE ALL NEXT!!!
AHHH.
THIS KID......!

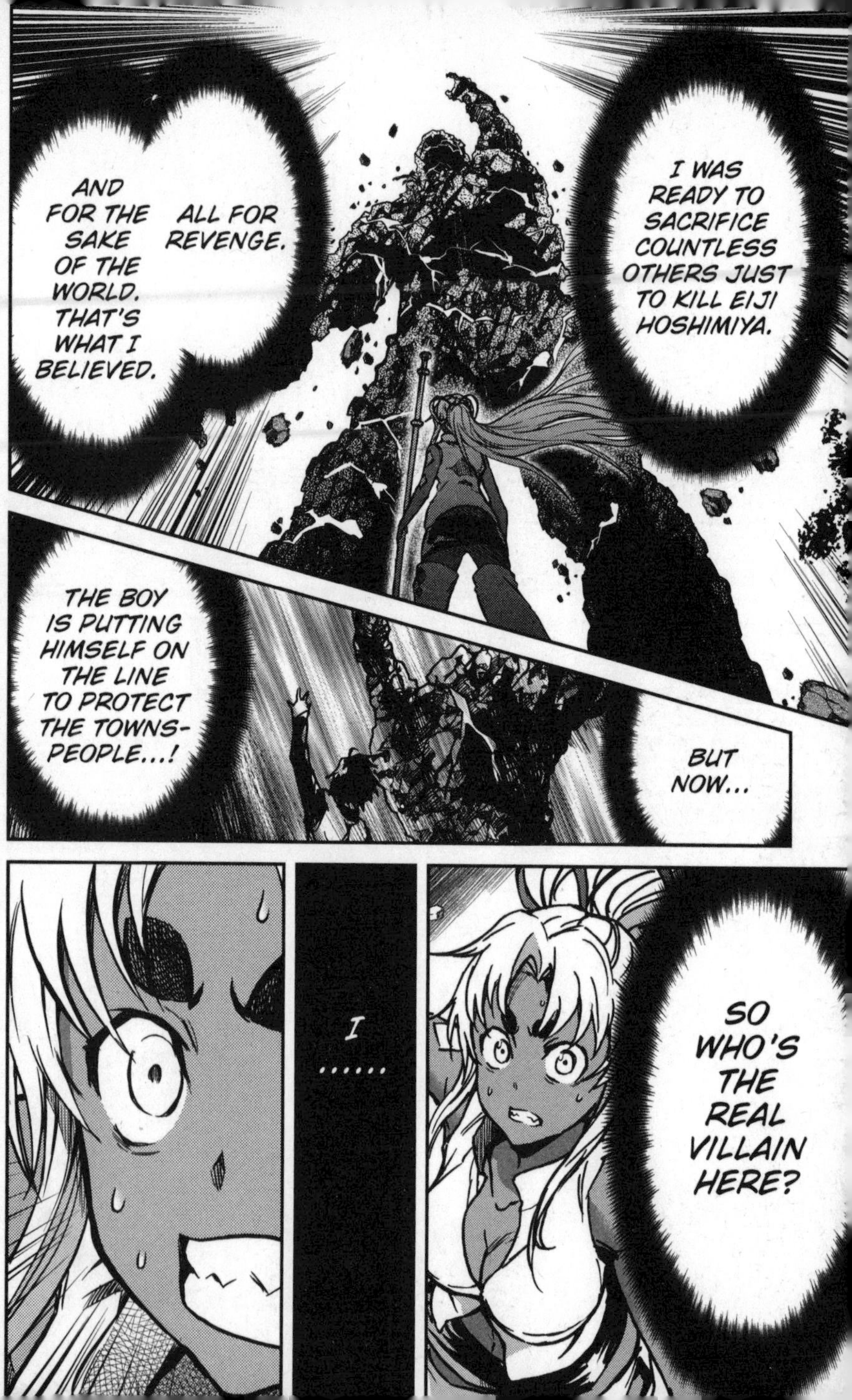
I WAS READY TO SACRIFICE COUNTLESS OTHERS JUST TO KILL EIJI HOSHIMIYA.
ALL FOR REVENGE.
AND FOR THE SAKE OF THE WORLD. THAT'S WHAT I BELIEVED.
BUT NOW...
THE BOY IS PUTTING HIMSELF ON THE LINE TO PROTECT THE TOWNS-PEOPLE...!
SO WHO'S THE REAL VILLAIN HERE?
I ......

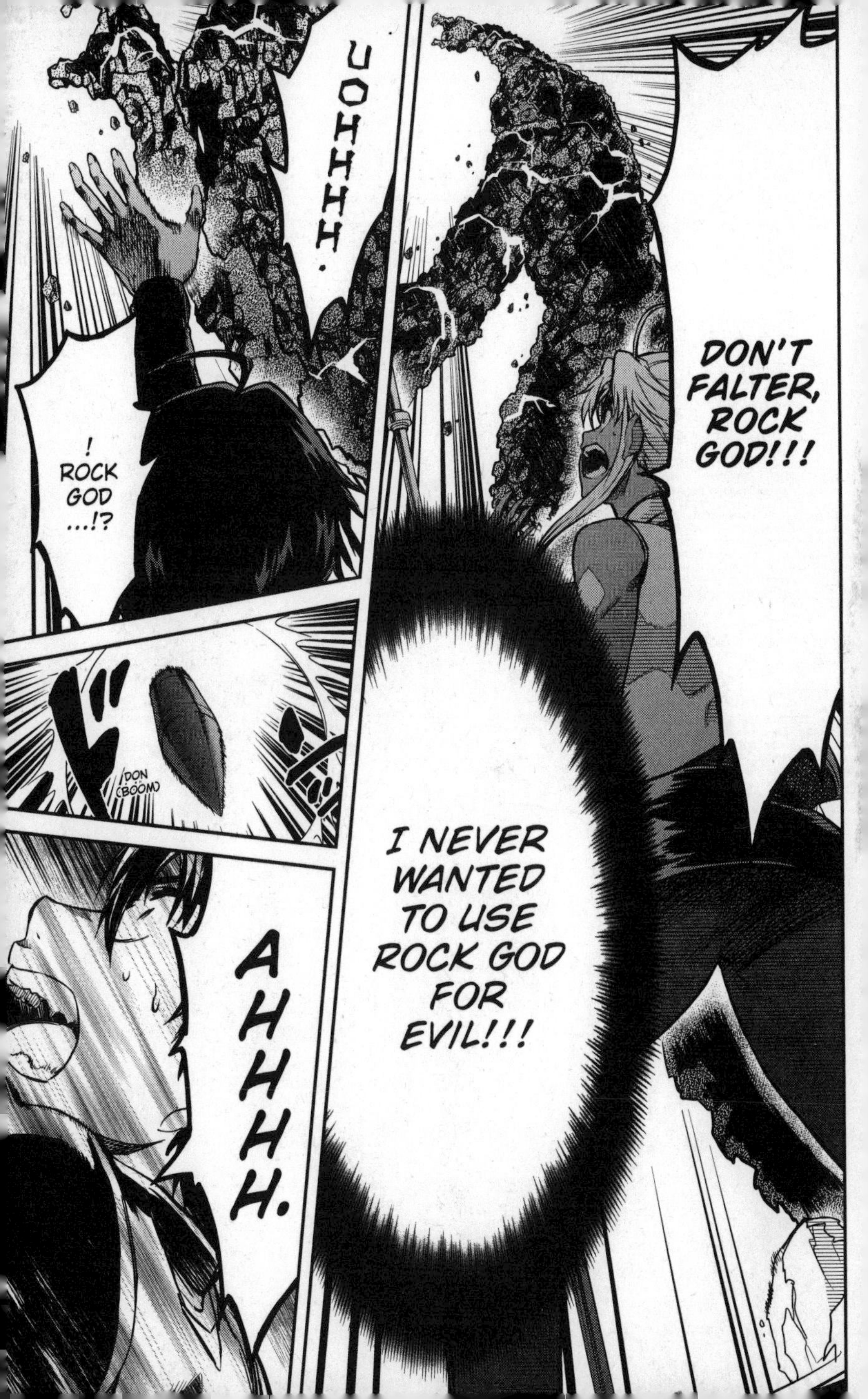
DON'T FALTER, ROCK GOD!!!
I NEVER WANTED TO USE ROCK GOD FOR EVIL!!!
UOHHHHH.
! ROCK GOD ...!?
DON (BOOM)
AHHHH.

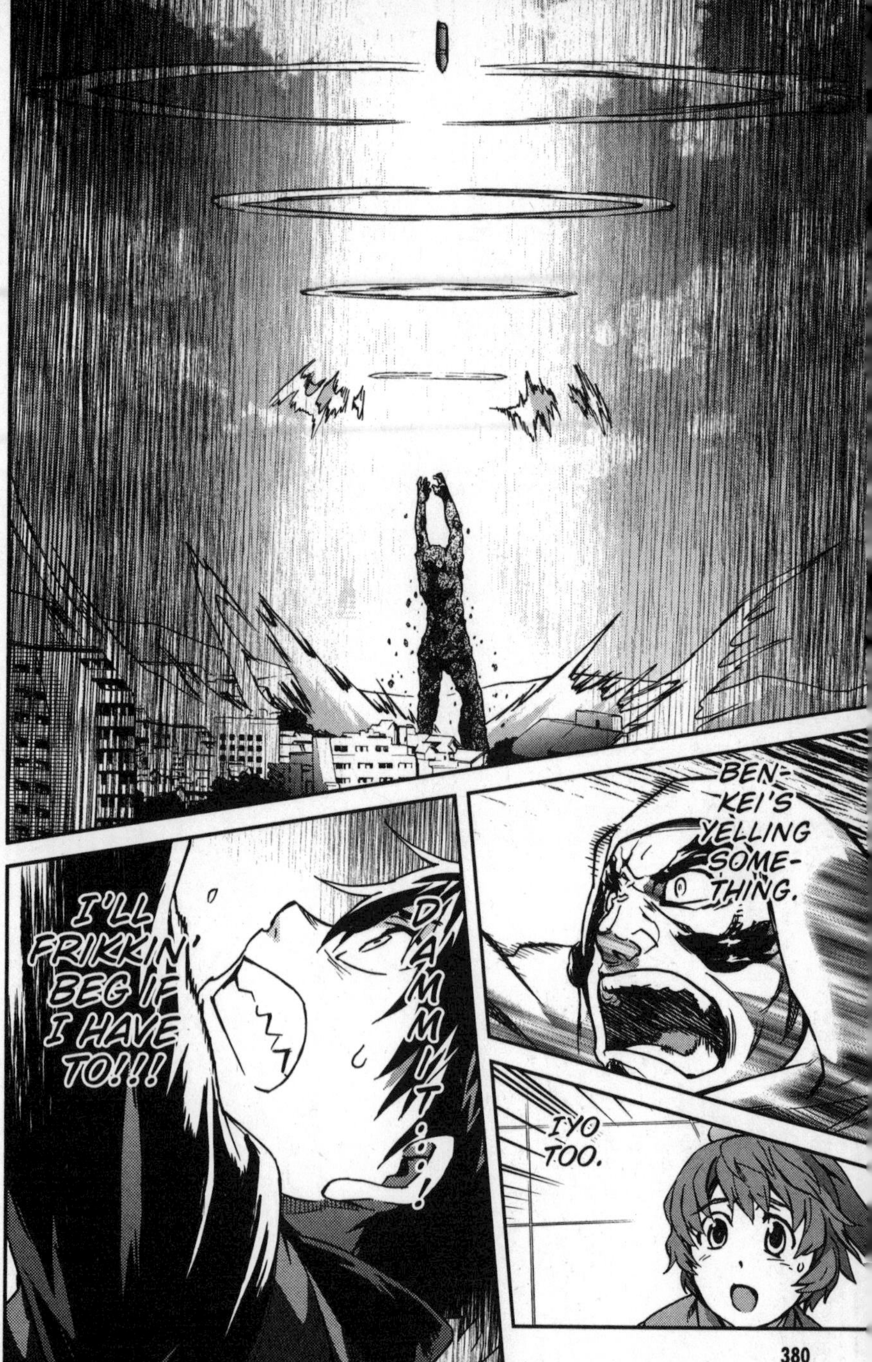
BEN-KEI'S YELLING SOME-THING.
IYO TOO.
DAMMIT...!
I'LL FRIKKIN' BEG IF I HAVE TO!!!

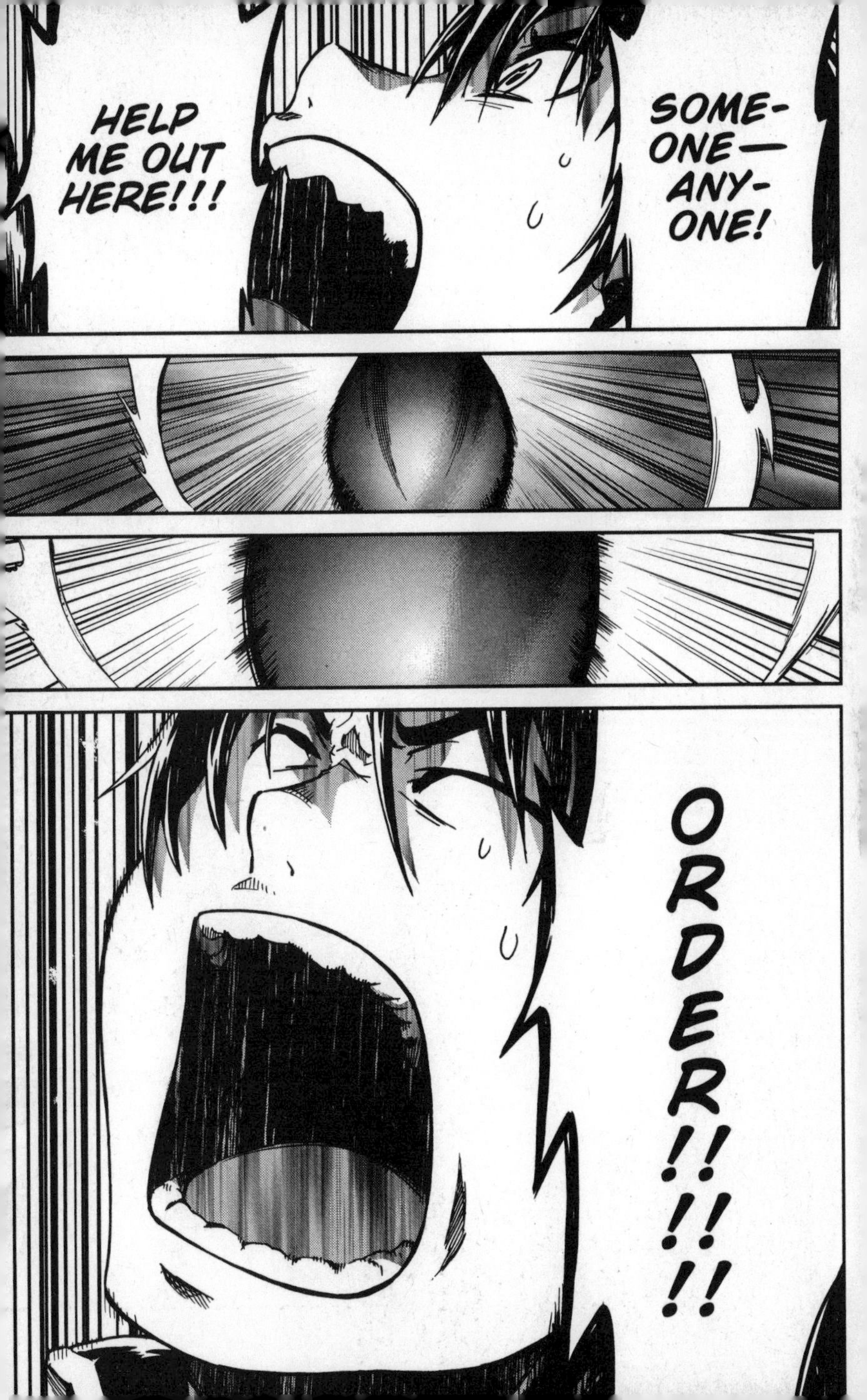
SOME-ONE—ANY-ONE!
HELP ME OUT HERE!!!
ORDER!!!!!!

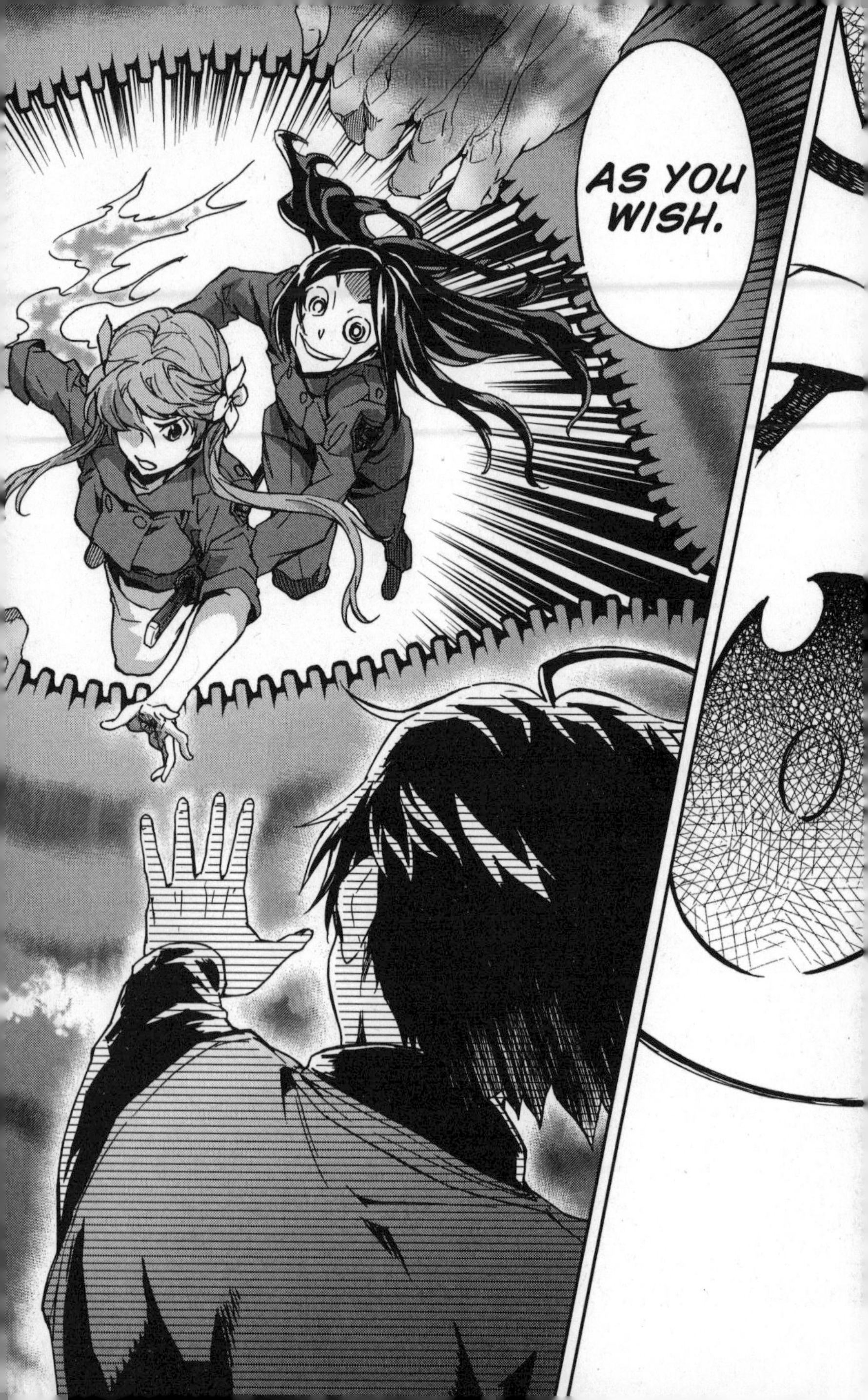
AS YOU WISH.

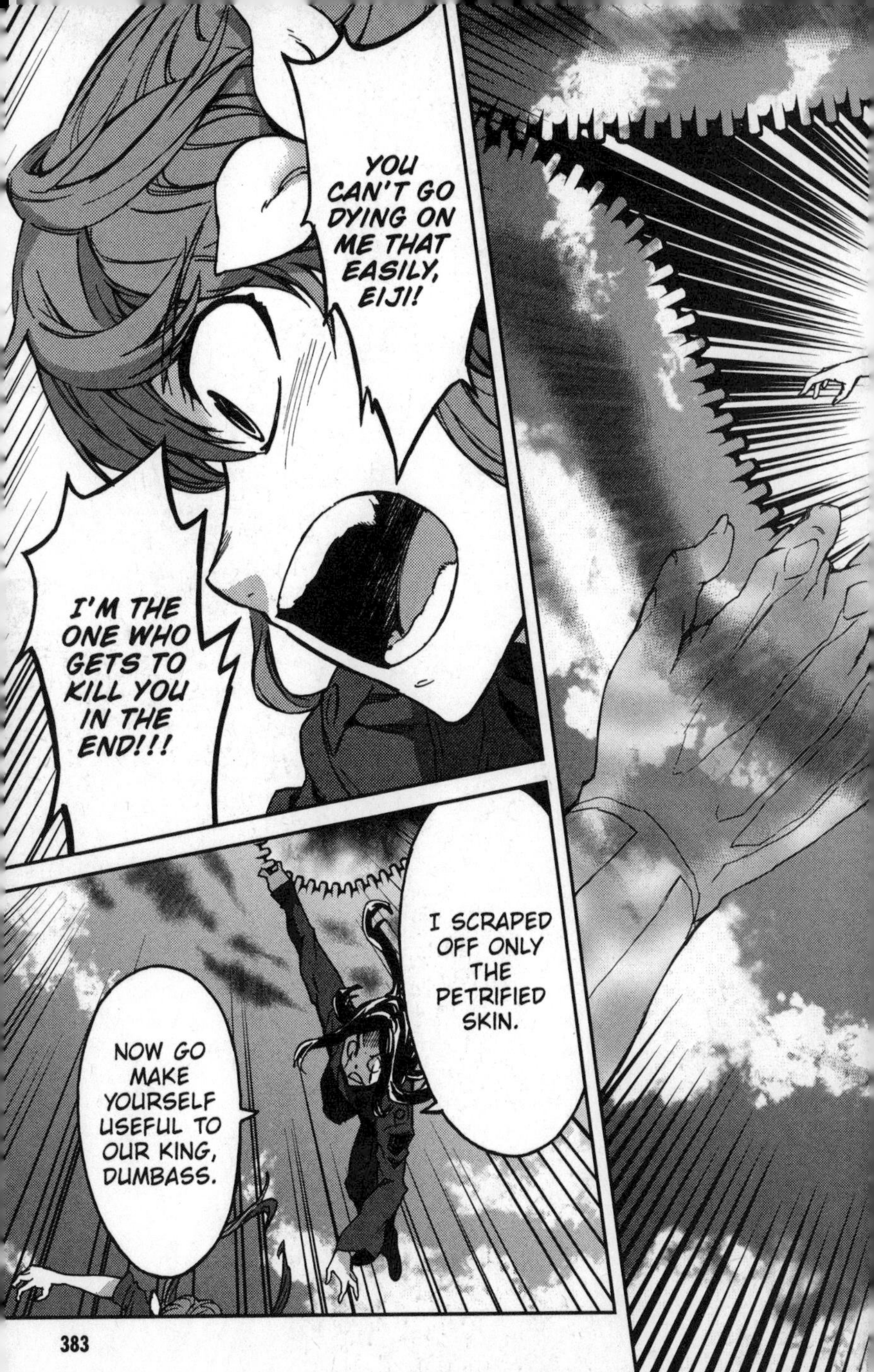
YOU CAN'T GO DYING ON ME THAT EASILY, EIJI!
I'M THE ONE WHO GETS TO KILL YOU IN THE END!!!
I SCRAPED OFF ONLY THE PETRIFIED SKIN.
NOW GO MAKE YOURSELF USEFUL TO OUR KING, DUMBASS.

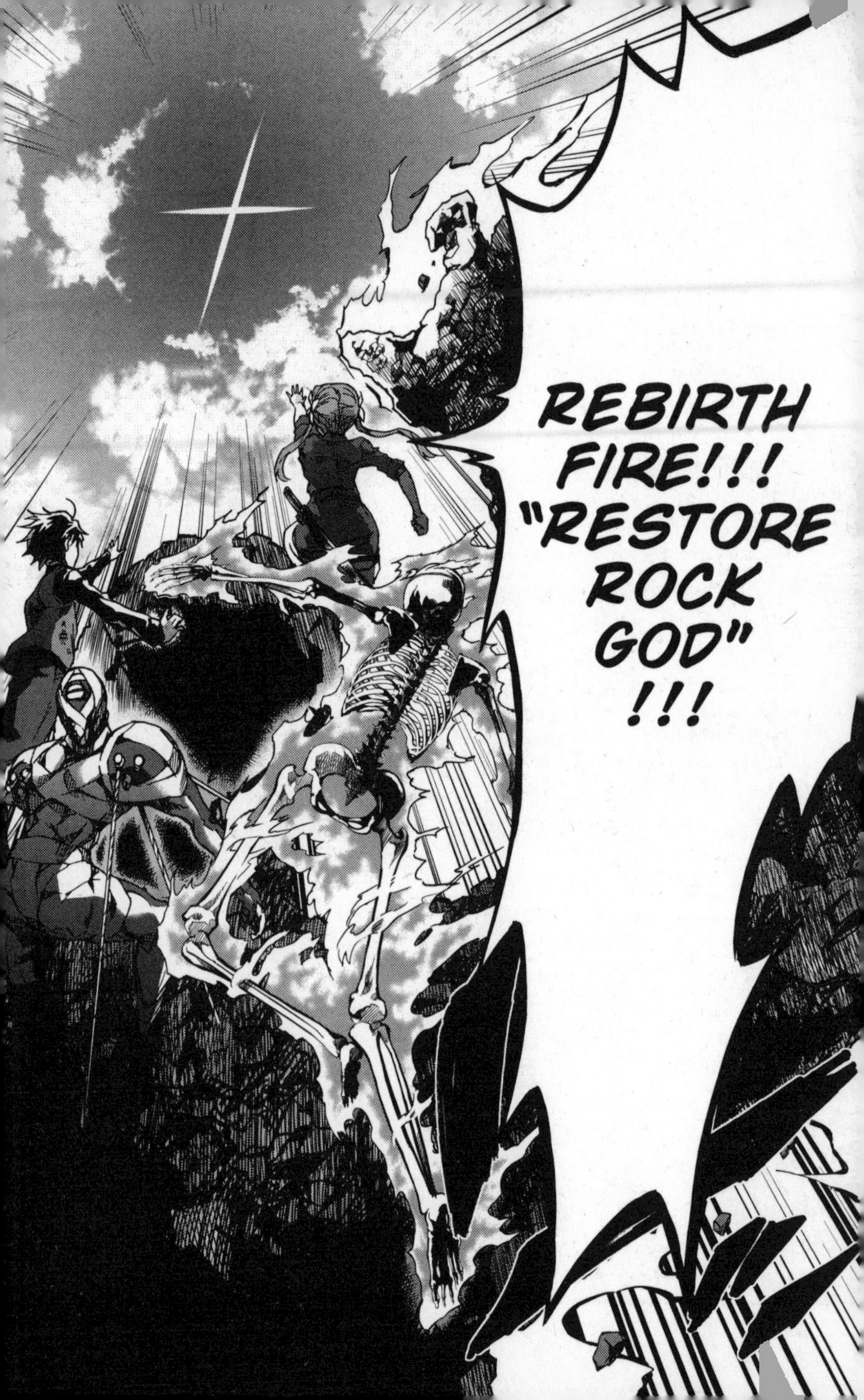
REBIRTH FIRE!!! "RESTORE ROCK GOD" !!!

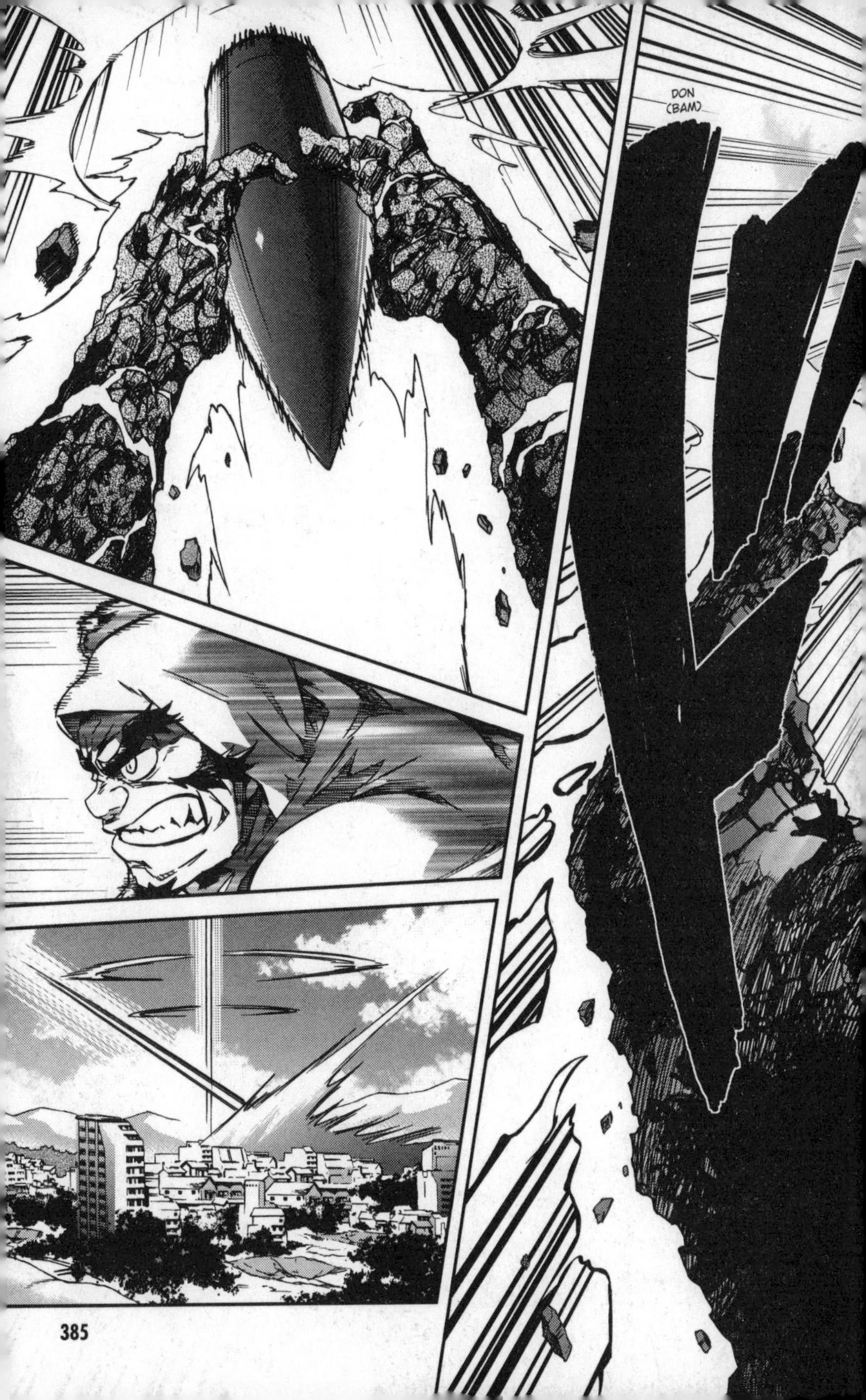
DON
(BAM)

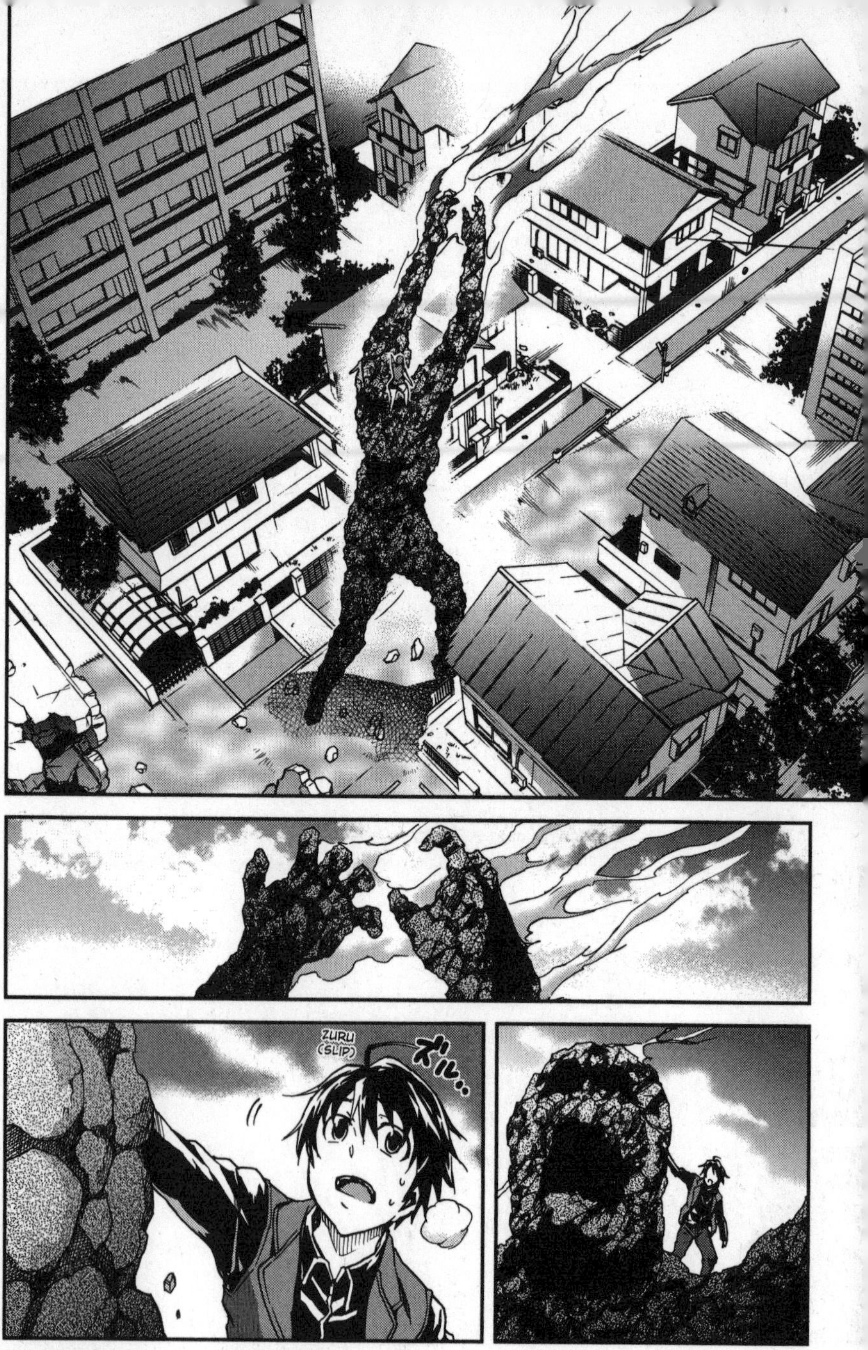
ズル..
ZURU
(SLIP)

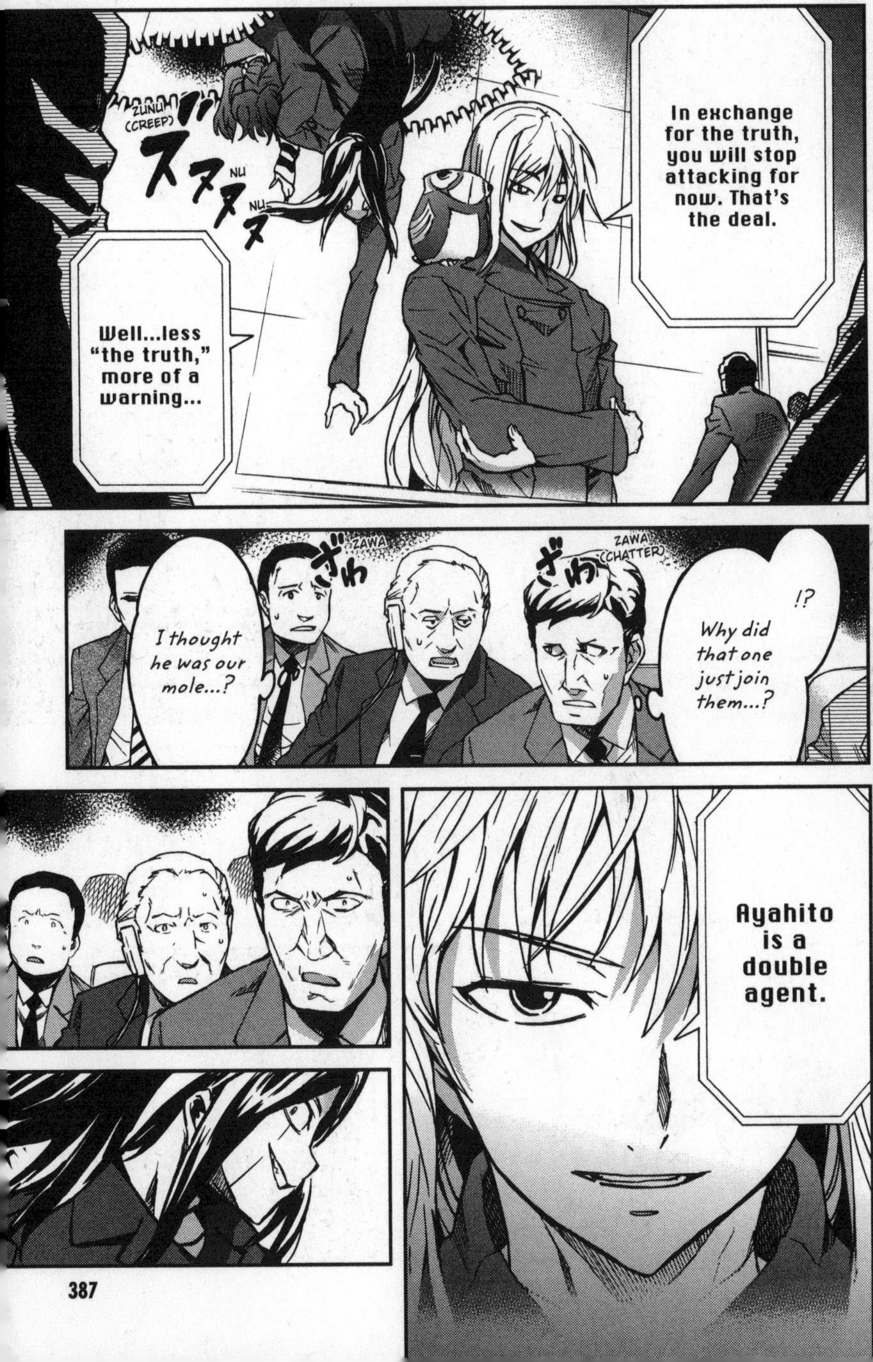
In exchange for the truth, you will stop attacking for now. That's the deal.
ZUNU (CREEP)
NU
NU
Well...less "the truth," more of a warning...
!?
Why did that one just join them...?
ZAWA (CHATTER)
ZAWA
I thought he was our mole...?
Ayahito is a double agent.

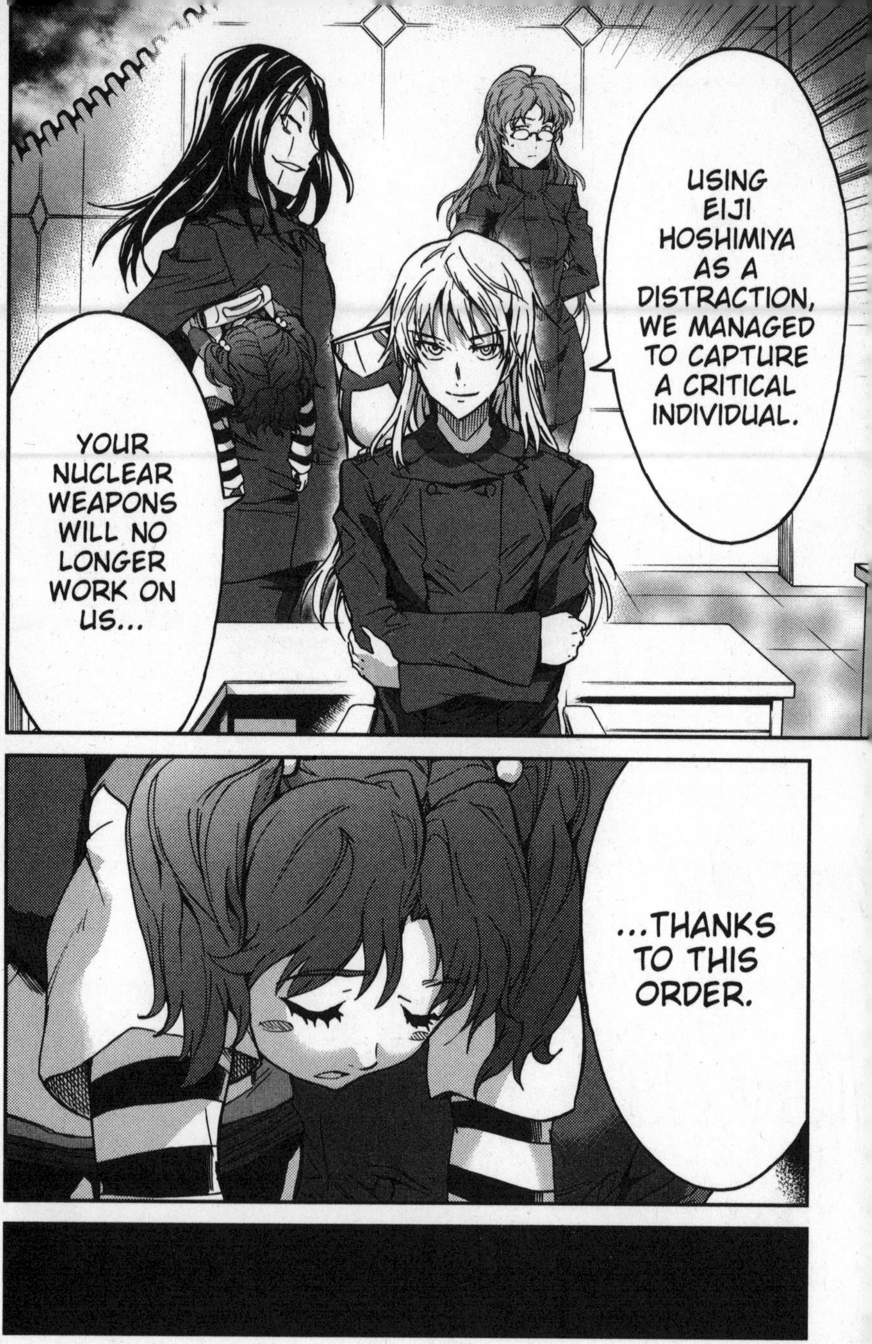
USING EIJI HOSHIMIYA AS A DISTRACTION, WE MANAGED TO CAPTURE A CRITICAL INDIVIDUAL.
YOUR NUCLEAR WEAPONS WILL NO LONGER WORK ON US...
...THANKS TO THIS ORDER.

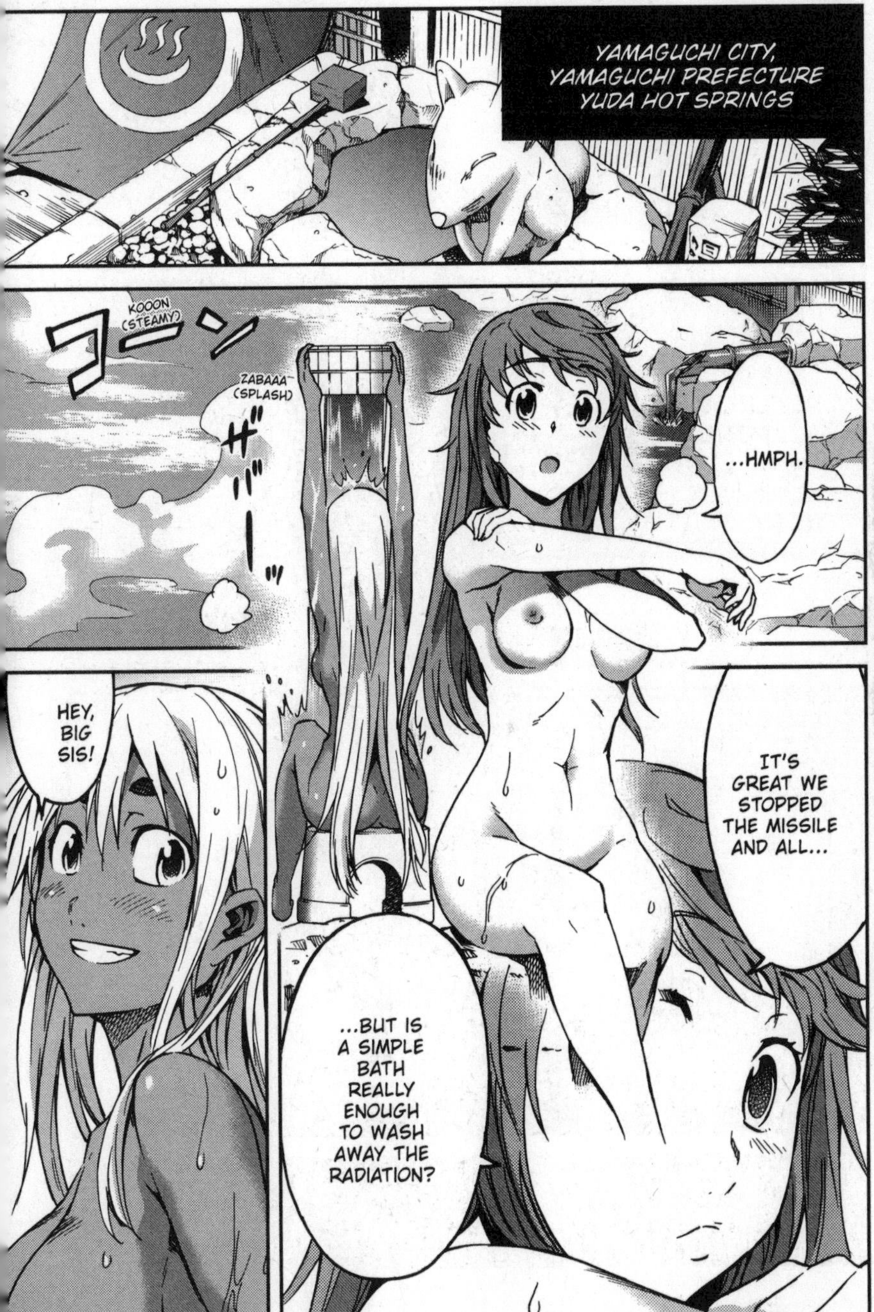
YAMAGUCHI CITY, YAMAGUCHI PREFECTURE YUDA HOT SPRINGS
...HMPH.
KOOON (STEAMY)
ZABAAA (SPLASH)
IT'S GREAT WE STOPPED THE MISSILE AND ALL...
...BUT IS A SIMPLE BATH REALLY ENOUGH TO WASH AWAY THE RADIATION?
HEY, BIG SIS!

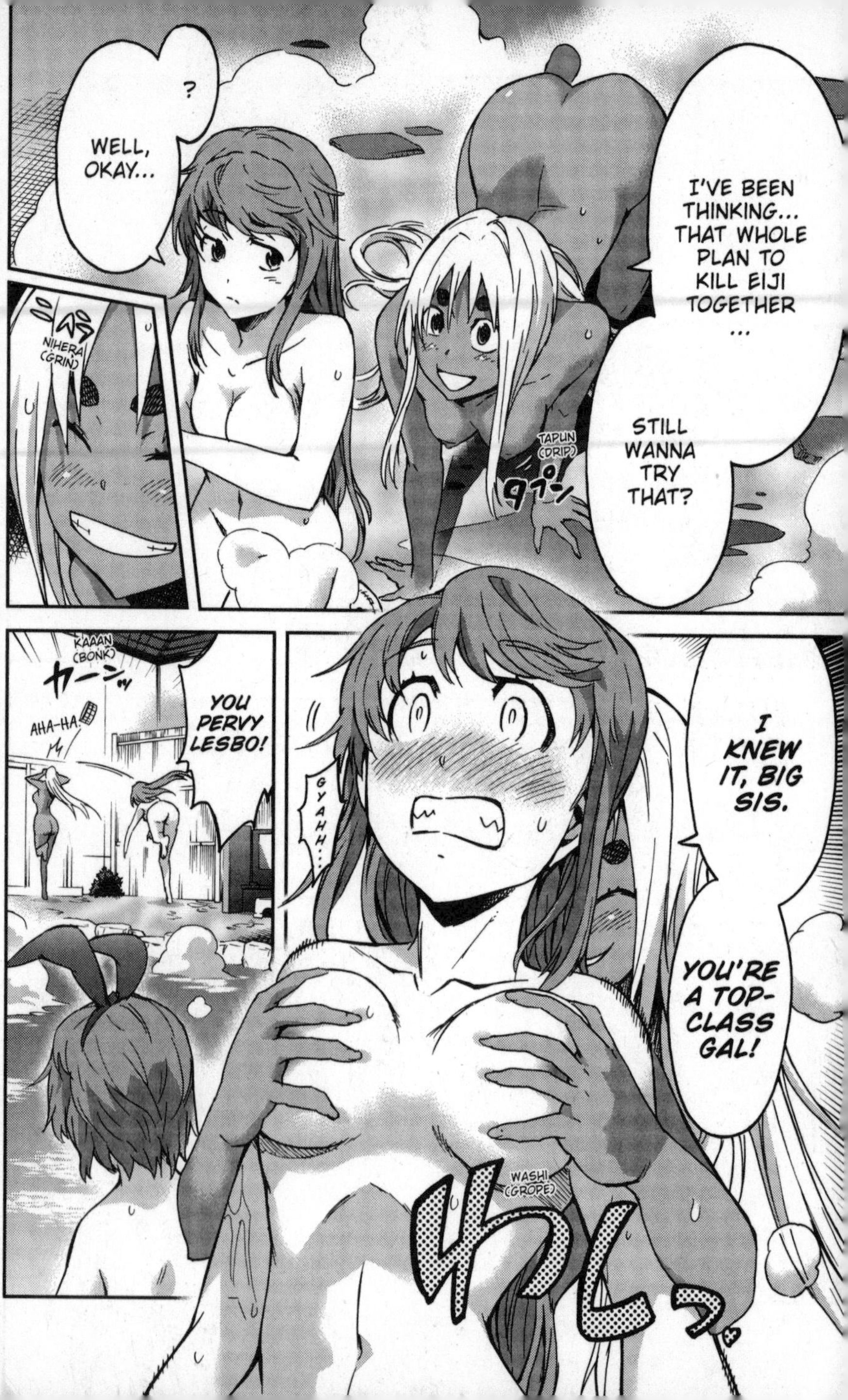
I'VE BEEN THINKING... THAT WHOLE PLAN TO KILL EIJI TOGETHER ...
STILL WANNA TRY THAT?
TAPUN (DRIP)
?
WELL, OKAY...
NIHERA (GRIN)
I KNEW IT, BIG SIS.
YOU'RE A TOP-CLASS GAL!
GYAHH...
WASHI (GROPE)
YOU PERVY LESBO!
KAAAN (BONK)
AHA-HA!

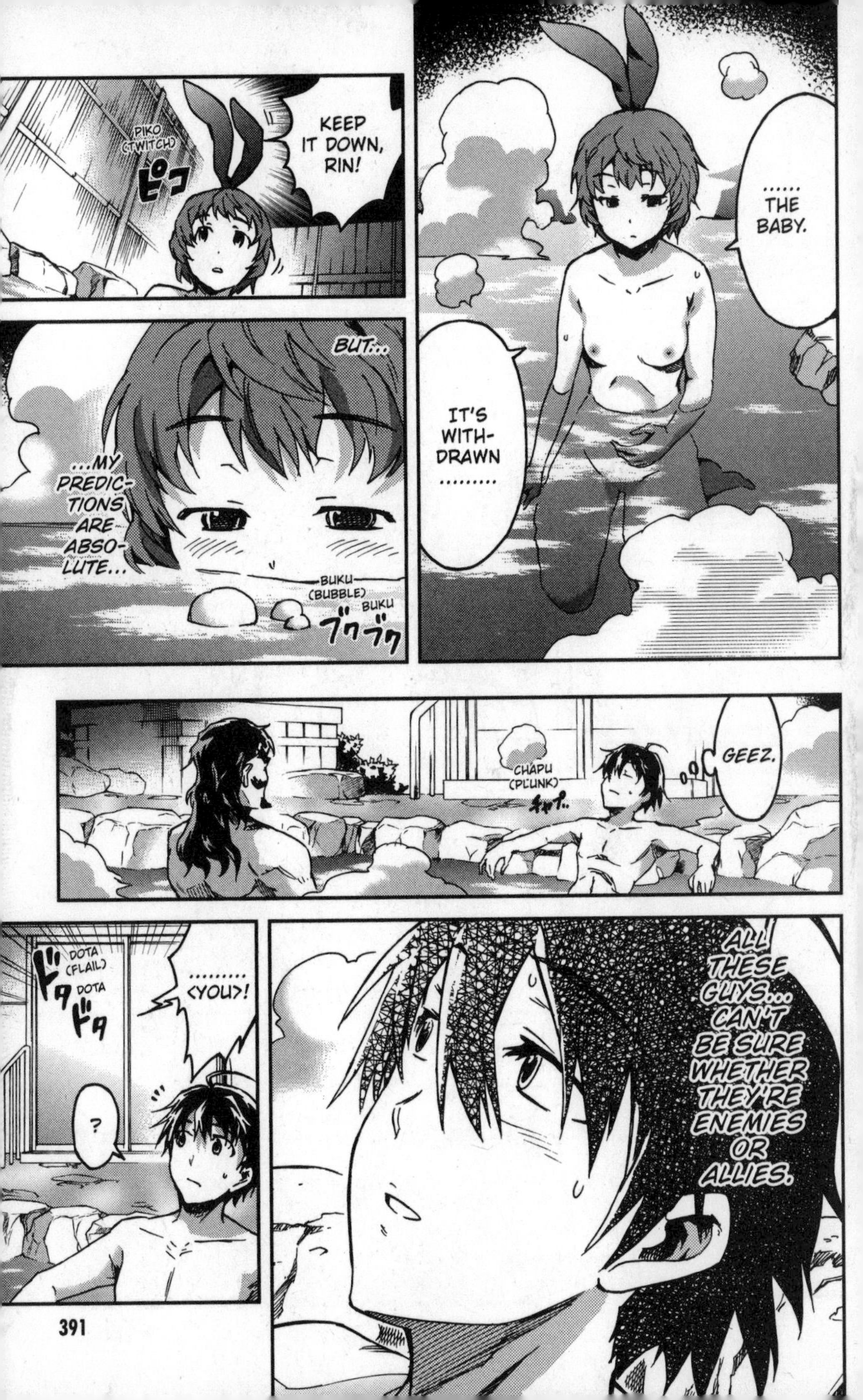

......THE BABY.
IT'S WITH-DRAWN ..........
KEEP IT DOWN, RIN!
PIKO (TWITCH) ピコ
BUT...
...MY PREDICTIONS ARE ABSOLUTE...
BUKU (BUBBLE) BUKU ブクブク
GEEZ.
CHAPU (PLUNK) チャプ..
ALL THESE GUYS... CAN'T BE SURE WHETHER THEY'RE ENEMIES OR ALLIES.
DOTA (FLAIL) DOTA ドタドタ
.........<YOU>!
?

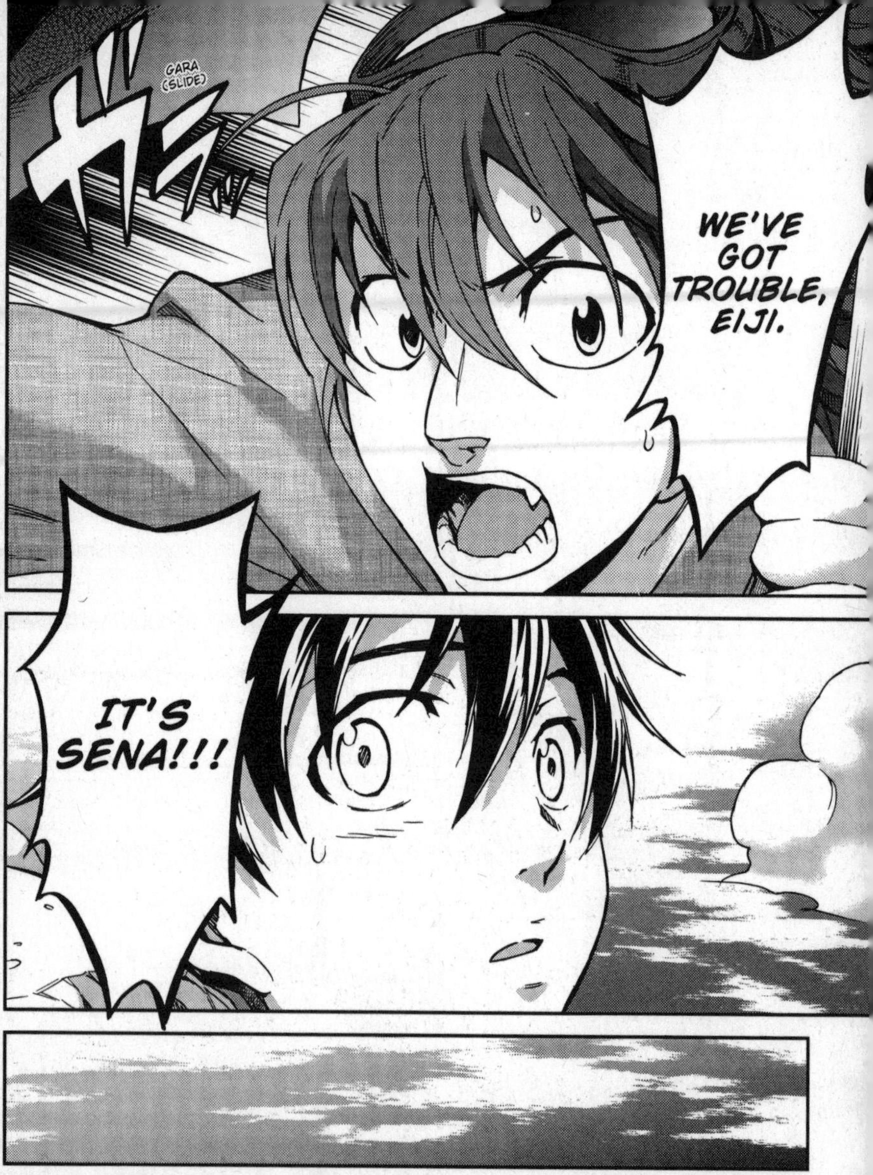
GARA (SLIDE)
WE'VE GOT TROUBLE, EIJI.
IT'S SENA!!!

Next Stop: **Hiroshima**

**Subject 10: END**

# Next time, it's the yakuza vs. ability users!!

**The setting?**
**The land of chivalry: Hiroshima!!**
**And what's going on with Eiji, Rin, and Iyo...!?**

# The earth-shattering "Hiroshima Arc," coming in Volume 2.

# BIG ORDER 01

Sakae Esuno

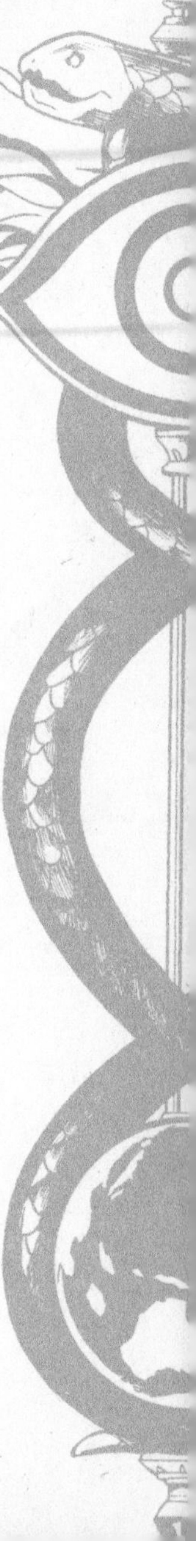

**Translation: Caleb Cook • Lettering: Phil Christie**

BIG ORDER Volume 1, 2
© Sakae ESUNO 2011, 2012

First published in Japan in 2011, 2012 by KADOKAWA CORPORATION, Tokyo.
English translation rights arranged with KADOKAWA CORPORATION, Tokyo
Tokyo through Tuttle-Mori Agency, Inc., Tokyo.

English translation © 2017 by Yen Press, LLC

Yen Press
1290 Avenue of the Americas
New York, NY 10104

Visit us at yenpress.com
facebook.com/yenpress
twitter.com/yenpress
yenpress.tumblr.com
instagram.com/yenpress

First Yen Press Edition: January 2017

Yen Press is an imprint of Yen Press, LLC.
The Yen Press name and logo are trademarks of Yen Press, LLC.

The publisher is not responsible for websites (or their content) that are not owned by the publisher.

Library of Congress Control Number: 2016958579

ISBN: 978-0-316-50462-1

10 9 8 7 6 5 4 3 2 1

BVG

Printed in the United States of America